PROFESSIONAL

PROFESSIONAL

WordPress®

PROFESSIONAL

WordPress®

DESIGN AND DEVELOPMENT

Third Edition

Brad Williams
David Damstra
Hal Stern

A Wiley Brand

Professional WordPress®: Design and Development, Third Edition

Published by
John Wiley & Sons, Inc.
10475 Crosspoint Boulevard
Indianapolis, IN 46256
www.wiley.com

Copyright © 2015 by John Wiley & Sons, Inc., Indianapolis, Indiana

Published simultaneously in Canada

ISBN: 978-1-118-98724-7
ISBN: 978-1-118-98718-6 (ebk)
ISBN: 978-1-118-98727-8 (ebk)

Manufactured in the United States of America

10 9 8 7 6 5 4 3 2

For general information on our other products and services please contact our Customer Care Department within the United States at (877) 762-2974, outside the United States at (317) 572-3993 or fax (317) 572-4002.

Wiley publishes in a variety of print and electronic formats and by print-on-demand. Some material included with standard print versions of this book may not be included in e-books or in print-on-demand. If this book refers to media such as a CD or DVD that is not included in the version you purchased, you may download this material at http://booksupport.wiley.com. For more information about Wiley products, visit www.wiley.com.

Library of Congress Control Number: 2014954687

In loving memory of my mother, Royce Jule Williams

—Brad

For my loving wife, Holly, and my children, Jack, Justin, and Jonah. Thanks for your love and support

—David

ABOUT THE AUTHORS

BRAD WILLIAMS Brad Williams is the co-founder of WebDevStudios.com and AppPresser.com, a co-host on the DradCast podcast, and the coauthor of *Professional WordPress* and *Professional WordPress Plugin Development*. Brad has been developing websites for nearly twenty years, including the last eight where he has focused on open-source technologies like WordPress. Brad has given presentations at various WordCamps across the globe and is a co-organizer for the Philadelphia WordPress Meetup and WordCamp Philly. You can follow Brad online on his personal blog at `http://strangework.com` and on Twitter `@williamsba`.

DAVID DAMSTRA is Vice President of Marketing Services and Creative Director for CU*Answers where his team of developers empowers clients with WordPress. David manages a team of developers to create websites and web applications for the financial industry. His team uses WordPress as the foundation for many web projects. David is also a Zend Certified Engineer for PHP5. You can find David online professionally at `http://ws.cuanswers.com`, where he focuses on web technology and best practices for web development, especially pertaining to the credit union industry, and personally at `http://mirmillo.com`.

HAL STERN is a technology leader for a healthcare company and contributed to the first two editions of this book. He has been using WordPress for over a decade to power his personal rants at `http://snowmanonfire.com` about New Jersey, sports, and food. Hal's interest in WordPress internals grew out of diagnosing a content search problem with his own website.

ABOUT THE TECHNICAL EDITOR

LISA SABIN-WILSON lives in Wisconsin and has been developing websites with the WordPress content management system since 2003. Lisa is a partner at WebDevStudios, a custom WordPress design and development agency specializing in WordPress builds for big enterprise brands. Lisa is also the co-founder of AppPresser, a plugin that enables you to create an iOS and/or Android app with WordPress. When she is not editing Brad Williams' Professional WordPress book, Lisa is the author of her own series of WordPress books for the For *Dummies* brand, including the best-selling *WordPress for Dummies*, currently in its Seventh Edition.

CREDITS

EXECUTIVE EDITOR
Carol Long

PROJECT EDITOR
Chris Haviland

TECHNICAL EDITOR
Lisa Sabin-Wilson

PRODUCTION EDITOR
Dassi Zeidel

COPY EDITOR
Nancy Rapoport

MANAGER OF CONTENT DEVELOPMENT AND ASSEMBLY
Mary Beth Wakefield

MARKETING DIRECTOR
David Mayhew

MARKETING MANAGER
Carrie Sherrill

PROFESSIONAL TECHNOLOGY AND STRATEGY DIRECTOR
Barry Pruett

BUSINESS MANAGER
Amy Knies

ASSOCIATE PUBLISHER
Jim Minatel

PROJECT COORDINATOR, COVER
Patrick Redmond

PROOFREADER
Josh Chase, Word One New York

INDEXER
Johnna vanHoose Dinse

COVER DESIGNER
Wiley

COVER IMAGE
© PhotoAlto Images/Footsearch

ACKNOWLEDGMENTS

THANK YOU to the love of my life, April, for your endless support and friendship, and for continuing to put up with my nerdy ways. Thank you to my Dad for inspiring me to become the man I am today; to my awesome nieces, Indiana Brooke and Austin Margaret; to the entire WordPress community for your support, friendships, motivation, and guidance; and to Michael, Jason, Freddy, and Hannibal for always lurking in the shadows. Last but not least, thank you to my ridiculous zoo: Lecter, Clarice, and Squeaks the Cat (aka Kitty Galore). Your smiling faces and wiggly butts always put a smile on my face.

—BRAD WILLIAMS

THANKS TO MY FAMILY—Holly, Jack, Justin, and Jonah—for their love and support while I was writing away. I'd also like to thank my parents, family, friends, and coworkers who have all helped in some way and encouraged me to write this book. Finally, I would like to thank the entire WordPress community for creating such a robust and powerful application.

—DAVID DAMSTRA

CONTENTS

INTRODUCTION

DEAR READER, thank you for picking up this book. WordPress is the most popular self-hosted website software in use today. It is available as an open source project, licensed under the GPL, and is built largely on top of the MySQL database and PHP programming language. Any server environment that supports that simple combination can run WordPress, making it remarkably portable as well as simple to install and operate. You don't need to be a systems administrator, developer, HTML expert, or design aesthete to use WordPress. On the other hand, because WordPress has been developed using a powerful set of Internet standard platforms, it can be extended and tailored for a wide variety of applications. WordPress is the publishing mechanism underneath millions of individual blog voices and the engine that powers high-volume, high-profile sites such as CNN's websites and blogs. It was designed for anyone comfortable navigating a browser, but is accessible to web designers and developers as well.

Given that range of applications and capabilities, it can prove hard to know where to start if you want to make use of the power of WordPress for your specific purposes. Should you first study the database models and relationships of content and metadata, or the presentation mechanics that generate the HTML output? This book was designed for readers to develop a knowledge of WordPress from the inside out, focusing on the internal structure and flow of the core code as well as the data model on which that code operates. Knowing how something works often makes you more adept at working with it, extending it, or fixing it when it breaks. Just as a race car driver benefits from a fundamental knowledge of combustion engines, aerodynamics, and the mechanics of automobile suspension, someone driving WordPress through its full dynamic range will be significantly more adept once acquainted with the underlying software physics.

WHO IS THIS BOOK FOR?

It was the dichotomy between the almost trivial effort required to create a WordPress-based website and publish a first post to the world and the much more detailed, broad understanding required to effect mass customization that led us to write this book. Many books on the market provide guidance to beginning bloggers by walking you through the typical functions of creating, configuring, and caring for your WordPress site. Our goal was to bridge the gap between an expert PHP developer who is comfortable reading the WordPress Codex in lieu of a manual and the casual WordPress user creating a public persona integrated with social networking sites and advertising services, with a tailored look and feel.

In short, we hope to appeal to a range of developers, from the person looking to fine-tune a WordPress theme to a more advanced developer with a plugin concept or who is using WordPress in a large enterprise integrated into a content management system. We do this by exploring WordPress from the inside out. Our goal for this book is to describe the basic operation of a function and then offer guidance and examples that highlight how to take it apart and reassemble that function to fit a number of needs. WordPress users who are not hardened PHP developers may want to skim through the developer-centric section, whereas coders looking for specific patterns to implement new WordPress functionality can start in the middle and work toward the end.

HOW THIS BOOK IS STRUCTURED

This book is divided into three major sections: Chapters 1 through 4 are an overview of the WordPress system, its major functional elements, and a top-level description of what happens when a WordPress-generated web page is displayed. Chapters 5 through 9 build on this foundation and dive into the core of WordPress, describing internal code flow and data structures. This middle section is strongly developer-oriented, and describes how to extend WordPress through plugins and customize it via themes. The last section, Chapters 10 through 15, combines a developer view of user experience and optimization with the deployer requirements for performance, security, and enterprise integration.

The following is a detailed chapter-by-chapter overview of what you can expect to find in this book.

Chapter 1, "First Post," contains a brief summary of the history of the WordPress software core, explores some popular hosting options and why community matters in a content-centric world, and concludes with the basics of do-it-yourself WordPress installation and debugging.

Chapter 2, "Code Overview," starts with the mechanics of downloading the WordPress distribution and describes its basic contents and file system layout. A top-to-bottom code flow walks you from an index or specific post URL, through the process of selecting posts, assembling content, and generating the displayed HTML. This chapter is a map for the more detailed code tours in the developer-focused section.

Chapter 3, "Working with WordPress Locally," covers the many benefits to working with WordPress on your local computer. This chapter also reviews the various setups for local development on a Microsoft Windows or Apple computer. Finally, you'll cover how to deploy your local changes to a remote server using various deployment methods.

Chapter 4, "Tour of the Core," examines the essential PHP functions within the basic WordPress engine. It serves as an introduction to the developer-focused middle section of the book and also lays the foundation for the deployment-, integration-, and experience-focused chapters in the last section. This chapter also covers using the core as a reference guide, and why it is best not to hack the core code to achieve desired customizations.

Chapter 5, "The Loop," is the basis for the developer-centric core of this book. The WordPress main loop drives the functions of creating and storing content in the MySQL database, as well as extracting appropriate chunks of it to be sorted, decorated, and nested under banners or next to sidebars, in both cases generating something a web browser consumes. This chapter disassembles those processes of creating, saving, and publishing a new post as well as displaying content that has been stored in the WordPress MySQL databases. The underlying database functions and the management of content metadata are covered in more detail to complete a thorough view of WordPress's internal operation.

Chapter 6, "Data Management," is the MySQL-based counterpart to Chapter 5. The core functions create, update, and manipulate entries in multiple MySQL database tables, and this chapter covers the database schema, data and metadata taxonomies used, and the basic relations that exist between WordPress elements. It also includes an overview of the basic query functions used to select and extract content from MySQL, forming a basis for extensions and custom code that needs to be able to examine the individual data underlying a blog.

Chapter 7, "Custom Post Types, Custom Taxonomies, and Metadata," explores the different types of content and associated data in WordPress. You'll cover how to register and work with custom post types for creating custom content in WordPress. Custom taxonomies are also dissected, and we'll dive into the various setups with examples. Finally you'll cover post metadata and the proper ways to store arbitrary data against posts in WordPress.

Chapter 8, "Plugin Development," starts with the basic plugin architecture and then explores the hook, action, and filter interfaces that integrate new functionality around the WordPress core. This chapter demonstrates the interposition of functions into the page composition or content management streams and how to save plugin data. Examples of building a plugin using a simple framework outline the necessary functionality of any plugin. This chapter also covers creation of widgets, simpler-to-use plugins that typically add decoration, additional images, or content to a blog sidebar; many plugins also have a widget for easier management. Publishing a plugin to the WordPress repository and pitfalls of plugin conflict round out the discussion of WordPress's functional extensions.

Chapter 9, "Theme Development," is the display and rendering counterpart to Chapter 8. Plugins add new features and functions to the core, whereas themes and CSS page templates change the way that content is displayed to readers. Starting with a basic theme, this chapter covers writing a theme, building custom page templates, menu management, widget areas, post formats, theme installation, and how thematic elements are used by the functions described in previous chapters. This chapter ends the deep developer-focused middle section of the book.

Chapter 10, "Multisite," explores the popular Multisite feature of WordPress. You'll learn the advantages of running your own Multisite network and how to properly install Multisite, work in a network, create sites and users, manage themes and plugins, and even conduct domain mapping. The last part of the chapter explores coding for Multisite and the various functions and methods available for use.

Chapter 11, "Migrating to WordPress," looks at the migration process when migrating existing data to a WordPress website. You'll learn about the migration process and data mapping guides, and how to work with a newer tool, WP-CLI, for larger migrations.

Chapter 12, "Crafting a User Experience," looks at a WordPress installation from the perspective of a regular or potential reader. Usability, testing, and the ease of finding information within a WordPress website form the basics, with added emphasis on web standards for metadata and search engine optimization so a page, or a specific post, can be found through an appropriate Google search. This chapter focuses on how to get your content to show up elsewhere on the web. Alternatives for adding search functionality, one of WordPress's weaknesses, are discussed, along with content accessibility and delivery to mobile devices.

Chapter 13, "Securing WordPress," deals with good and bad popularity. Keeping a WordPress installation safe from malicious attackers is a key part of configuration and management, and this chapter covers the general best practices and addresses them with some of the more popular security and anti-spam plugins and features.

Chapter 14, "Application Framework," goes beyond blogging to examples of WordPress as an application framework to be used as a base when creating web applications. You'll explore popular application framework features and how they relate in WordPress.

Chapter 15, "WordPress in the Real World," tackles issues of scale and integration. WordPress addresses deficiencies in "enterprise scale" content management tools, and building on the mechanisms covered in Chapter 12, this chapter shows how to use WordPress in real-world situations with confidence.

Chapter 16, "WordPress Developer Community," is an introduction to contributing to the WordPress ecosystem by working on the core, submitting plugins or themes, adding to the documentation canon, and assisting other developers. An overview of WordPress sister projects such as bbPress for forums is provided along with a brief summary of other developer resources and a glossary of WordPress context-sensitive terms.

WHAT YOU NEED TO USE THIS BOOK

You'll need at least a rudimentary understanding of HTML and some knowledge of cascading style sheets (CSS) to make use of the theme and user experience sections of the book. Experience in writing and debugging PHP code is a prerequisite for more advanced developer sections, although if you're just going to make changes based on the samples in this book, you can use the code as a template and learn on the fly. A basic knowledge of databases, especially the syntax and semantics of MySQL, is in order to make the most out of the chapter on data management as well as develop plugins that need to save data.

It's helpful to have an interactive development environment in which to view PHP code, or PHP code sprinkled through HTML pages. Choosing a set of developer tools often borders on religion and deep personal preference (and we know plenty of coders who believe that vi constitutes a development environment). Some of the more user-friendly tools will make walking through the WordPress code easier if you want to see how functions used in the examples appear in the core.

Most important, if you want to use the code samples and examples in this book, you'll need a WordPress website in which to install them. Chapter 1 covers some basic WordPress hosting options as well as the simple mechanics of downloading the components and installing WordPress on a desktop or test machine for debugging and closer inspection. Chapter 3 covers how to install and configure WordPress locally on your computer.

Finally, some people might argue that to really take advantage of WordPress you need to be able to write, but that ignores the basic beauty of the WordPress platform: It takes the power of the printing press to an individual level. This book isn't about what you say (or might say); it's about how you're going to get those ideas onto the web and how the world will see them and interact with your blog.

CONVENTIONS

To help you get the most from the text and keep track of what's happening, we've used a number of conventions throughout the book.

> **WARNING** *Warnings hold important, not-to-be forgotten information that is directly relevant to the surrounding text.*

> **NOTE** *Notes indicate tips, hints, tricks, or asides to the current discussion.*

As for styles in the text:

- ➤ We *italicize* new terms and important words when we introduce them.
- ➤ We show file names, URLs, and code within the text like so: `persistence.properties`.
- ➤ We present code in two different ways:

```
We use a monofont type with no highlighting for most code examples.
```

SOURCE CODE

As you work through the examples in this book, you may choose either to type in all the code manually, or to use the source code files that accompany the book. All of the source code used in this book is available for download at `www.wrox.com`. Specifically for this book, the code download is on the Download Code tab at:

`www.wrox.com/go/wordpress3e`

For this edition of the book, Chapters 8, 10, and 11 have companion code files that you can download. The code is in the specific chapter's download file and individually named according to the code filenames noted throughout the chapter.

Most of the code on `www.wrox.com` is compressed in a .ZIP, .RAR, or similar archive format appropriate to the platform. Once you download the code, just decompress it with an appropriate decompression tool.

> **NOTE** *Because many books have similar titles, you may find it easiest to search by ISBN; this book's ISBN is 978-1-118-98724-7.*

Once you download the code, just decompress it with your favorite compression tool. Alternately, you can go to the main Wrox code download page at www.wrox.com/dynamic/books/download .aspx to see the code available for this book and all other Wrox books.

ERRATA

We make every effort to ensure that there are no errors in the text or in the code. However, no one is perfect, and mistakes do occur. If you find an error in one of our books, such as a spelling mistake or faulty piece of code, we would be very grateful for your feedback. By sending in errata, you may save another reader hours of frustration, and at the same time, you will be helping us provide even higher quality information.

To find the errata page for this book, go to

    www.wrox.com/go/wordpress3e

and click the Errata link. On this page you can view all errata that has been submitted for this book and posted by Wrox editors.

If you don't spot "your" error on the Book Errata page, go to www.wrox.com/contact/ techsupport.shtml and complete the form there to send us the error you have found. We'll check the information and, if appropriate, post a message to the book's errata page and fix the problem in subsequent editions of the book.

P2P.WROX.COM

For author and peer discussion, join the P2P forums at http://p2p.wrox.com. The forums are a web-based system for you to post messages relating to Wrox books and related technologies and interact with other readers and technology users. The forums offer a subscription feature to e-mail you topics of interest of your choosing when new posts are made to the forums. Wrox authors, editors, other industry experts, and your fellow readers are present on these forums.

At http://p2p.wrox.com, you will find a number of different forums that will help you, not only as you read this book, but also as you develop your own applications. To join the forums, just follow these steps:

1. Go to http://p2p.wrox.com and click the Register link.

2. Read the terms of use and click Agree.

3. Complete the required information to join, as well as any optional information you wish to provide, and click Submit.

4. You will receive an e-mail with information describing how to verify your account and complete the joining process.

> **NOTE** *You can read messages in the forums without joining P2P, but in order to post your own messages, you must join.*

Once you join, you can post new messages and respond to messages other users post. You can read messages at any time on the web. If you would like to have new messages from a particular forum e-mailed to you, click the Subscribe to this Forum icon by the forum name in the forum listing.

For more information about how to use the Wrox P2P, be sure to read the P2P FAQs for answers to questions about how the forum software works, as well as many common questions specific to P2P and Wrox books. To read the FAQs, click the FAQ link on any P2P page.

1

First Post

- ➤ Appreciating the provenance of the WordPress platform
- ➤ Choosing a suitable platform for your WordPress installation
- ➤ Downloading, installing, and performing basic configuration of WordPress
- ➤ Diagnosing and resolving common installation problems

If displaying "Hello World" on an appropriate device defines minimum competence in a programming language, generating your first post is the equivalent in the online publishing world. This chapter provides a brief history of WordPress and then explores several options for hosting a WordPress installation. Common miscues and misperceptions along with their resolutions round out the chapter and put you on the edge of publishing your wit and wisdom.

Once you've installed, configured, and completed the barebones administration, you're ready to take advantage of the code walk-throughs and detailed component descriptions in later chapters. Of course, if you already have a functional WordPress website, you can skip this chapter, and dive in headfirst to explore the core code in Chapter 2, "Code Overview."

WHAT IS WORDPRESS?

WordPress is one of the most popular open source content management systems available, with global and vibrant user, developer, and support communities. While it can be compared to Drupal and Joomla as a user-generated content workhorse, WordPress distinguishes itself with a broad array of hosting options, functional extensions (plugins), and aesthetic designs and elements (themes).

With the rise of self-publishing, low-cost web hosting, and freely available core components such as the MySQL database, blogging software followed the same trend as most other digital technologies, moving from high-end, high-cost products to widely available, low-cost consumer or "hobbyist" systems. WordPress isn't simply about creating a blog so that you can have a digital diary attached to your vanity URL; it has evolved into a full-fledged content management system and burgeoning application development framework used by individuals and enterprises alike. This section takes a brief tour through the early history of WordPress and brings you up to speed on the current release and user community.

WordPress started similarly to many other popular open source software packages: Some talented developers saw a need to create a powerful, simple tool based on an existing project licensed under the GPL. Michel Valdrighi's b2/cafelog system provided the starting point, and WordPress was built as a fork of that code base by developers Matt Mullenweg and Mike Little. WordPress first appeared in 2003 and was also built on the MySQL open source database for persisting content with PHP as the development platform. Valdrighi remains a contributor to the project, which is thriving as it has a growing and interested community of users and developers.

As with other systems written in PHP, it is self-contained in the sense that installation, configuration, operation, and administration tasks are all contained in PHP modules. WordPress's popularity has been driven in part by its simplicity, with the phrase "five-minute installation" making appearances in nearly every description or book about WordPress. Beyond getting to a first post, WordPress was designed to be extended and adaptable to the different needs of different people.

WordPress today is supported by a handful of core developers and many key contributors. Mike Little runs the WordPress specialty shop `zed1.com` and he contributes the occasional patch to the code. Matt Mullenweg's company, Automattic, continues to operate the `wordpress.com` hosting service as well as fund development of related content and site management tools, including Akismet, multi-site WordPress, Gravatar, and most recently plugins such as JetPack. Akismet is a robust, Automattic-hosted spam detection and protection service with a statistically (and incredibly) low failure-to-detect rate. Previously known as WordPress MU, multi-site WordPress functions are at the heart of the `wordpress.com` hosting system and are now merged into the main WordPress source tree. Gravatar dynamically serves images tied to e-mail addresses, providing a hosted icon with a variety of display options. Think of it as a service to make hot-linking your profile picture technically and socially acceptable. JetPack is a multifunction plugin offering a vast array of common needs for the website owner. The JetPack plugin is covered further in Chapter 16.

As a content management system, the WordPress system definition does not stop at time-serialized posts with comments. BuddyPress is a set of themes and plugins that extends WordPress into a functional social networking platform, allowing registered users to message and interact with each other, again with all content managed within the WordPress framework. Similarly, bbPress is a PHP- and MySQL-based system designed for forums (bulletin boards) that is distinct from WordPress but is commonly integrated with it.

Chapter 16 covers some of the WordPress adjunct systems in more detail, but they are included here to provide a sense of how WordPress has expanded beyond a basic single-user–oriented tool. At the same time, we are not endorsing or making a commercial for Automattic, but delving into the guts of WordPress without a spin of the propeller hat toward Mullenweg and Little is somewhere between incorrigible and bad community behavior.

POPULARITY OF WORDPRESS

This book is based on the WordPress 4.1 major release, but really focuses on foundational WordPress tactics. Each successive release of WordPress has included improvements in the administration and control functions (Dashboard); backup, export, and import functions; and installation and upgrade features. Even if you start with a slightly down-rev version of WordPress, you will be able to bring it up to the current release and maintain the freshness of your install. Install and upgrade paths are touched on later in this chapter. But just how popular is WordPress?

Current State

Interest in WordPress and WordPress usage is booming. You're holding in your hands a testament to that. Just four years ago, very few WordPress books were available. Now this third edition has been published. "Popular" is always a subjective metric, but statistics add some weight to those perceptions. According to Automattic, as of 2014, tens of thousands of new WordPress sites are created every day (http://en.wordpress.com/stats/) not including standalone self-hosted WordPress sites. That includes sites using WordPress for content management, blogging, and personal rants, and has to be discounted by those of you who have multiple WordPress installations to their names, but even with that estimate of the order of magnitude, WordPress is immensely popular. Automattic no longer discloses how many sites they host on WordPress.com, but in 2012 they reported nearly 74 million WordPress websites globally with about half of them hosted at WordPress.com, and in 2010 that number was at only 5 million sites. In 2008, the official WordPress plugin repository hosted over 6,300 plugins, double the number from 2007. In 2012, the second edition of this book cited 19,000 plugins in the repository, and at the time of this writing, the number of plugins is nearing 32,000 (http://wordpress.org/plugins/). Since the last publication of this book, the community has contributed over 1,000 unique themes to the official WordPress theme repository, which now has more than 2,500 listed. This does not include all the commercial theme vendors and independent developers creating their own custom themes.

The combinations of plugins and themes require scientific notation to represent in complexity, but at the same time, they are all equally simple to locate, integrate, and use. That's the result of a solid architecture and an equally solid community using it. In short, the ecosystem surrounding WordPress is alive and thriving—even booming.

Today, WordPress powers many large media companies' websites or portions thereof, including CNN's blogs, the *Wall Street Journal*'s *All Things D*, Reuters, and Forbes. Fortune 500 companies such as GM, UPS, and Sony use WordPress. WordPress is a viable choice for a range of users, from international conglomerates to major recording artists to huge media publishing companies. Some need reassurance before choosing WordPress and focus on which big boys are using it; you can find a list online at the WordPress Notable Users showcase (http://en.wordpress.com/notable-users/).

But the simplicity, ease of use, and ultimately the power of the plugins and themes also makes WordPress suitable for your mom's family information website, your local elementary school teacher's classroom newsletter, and the hobbyist. These are truly some of the WordPress success stories of today and these widely accessible, more narrowly popular websites are what makes WordPress popular. WordPress is adaptable and will be as simple or complex as you need it to be. Empowering "lower tech" users to be web publishers and then spreading the word (pun intended) to their families and friends about how easy WordPress is to use have fueled this explosive growth and adoption.

Where do you get started? Wordpress.org is the home for the current released and in-development versions of the code. Click through to `wordpress.org` for a starting point in finding plugins, themes, and wish lists of ideas and features to be implemented.

Wordpress.com has both free and paid hosting services. Over at `www.wordpress.org/hosting` you will find a list of hosting providers that support WordPress and often include some additional first-time installation and configuration support in their packaging of the code for delivery as part of their hosting services. You will also find concentrated WordPress hosting providers that strictly host WordPress sites and offer additional specialization features and options.

Intersecting the Community

WordPress thrives and grows based on community contributions in addition to sheer usage. Like high school gym class, participation is the name of the game, and several semi-formal avenues along which to channel your efforts and energies are available.

WordCamp events are community-hosted and locally operated, and now happen in dozens of cities around the world. Official WordCamps are listed on wordcamp.org, but you will do just as well to search for a WordCamp event in a major city close to you. WordCamps occur nearly every weekend with bloggers, photographers, writers, editors, developers, and designers of all experience and skill levels counted among their attendees. WordCamps are a low-cost introduction to the local community and often a good opportunity to meet WordPress celebrities. Visit `www.wordcamp.org` to find the next WordCamp.

Less structured but more frequently convened than WordCamps are WordPress Meetups, comprising local users and developers in nearly 400 (up from the 200 mentioned in the second edition of this book, and 40 in the first) cities. You'll need a meetup.com account, but once you're registered, you can check on locations and timetables at `www.wordpress.meetup.com` to see when and where people are talking about content management.

A rich, multi-language documentation repository is hosted at `www.codex.wordpress.org`. The WordPress Codex, with all due respect to the term reserved for ancient handwritten manuscripts, represents the community-contributed tips and tricks for every facet of WordPress, from installation to debugging. If you feel the urge to contribute to the WordPress documentation, register and then write to your heart's content in the WordPress Codex. We hope that you will find this book a cross between a companion and a travel guide to the Codex.

Finally, mailing lists (and their archives) exist for various WordPress contributors and communities. A current roster is available online at `www.codex.wordpress.org/Mailing_Lists`; of particular interest may be the `wp-docs` list for Codex contributors and the `wp-hackers` list for those who work on the WordPress core and steer its future directions.

WordPress and the GPL

WordPress is licensed under the Gnu Public License (GPL) version 2, contained in the `license.txt` file that you'll find in the top-level code distribution. Most people do not read the license and simply understand that WordPress is an open source project; however, pockets of corporate legal departments still worry about the viral component of a GPL license and its implications for additional code or content that gets added to, used with, or layered on top of the original distribution. Much of this confusion stems from liberal use of the words "free" and "copyright" in contexts where they are inappropriately applied.

The authors of this book are not lawyers—nor do they play them on the Internet or on television—and if you really want to understand the nuances of copyright law and what constitutes a "conveyance" of code, pick up some of Lawrence Lessig's or Cory Doctorow's work in those areas. This section is included to minimize the concerns of IT departments who may be dissuaded from using WordPress as an enterprise content management system by overly zealous legal teams. Do not let this happen to you; again, if WordPress is acceptable to CNN and the *Wall Street Journal*, two companies that survive on the copyrights granted to their content, it probably fits within the legal strictures of most corporate users as well.

The core tenet of the GPL ensures that you can always get the source code for any distribution of GPL-licensed software. If a company modifies a GPL-licensed software package and then redistributes that newer version, it has to make the source code available as well. This is the "viral" nature of GPL at work; its goal is to make sure that access to the software and its derivatives is never reduced in scope. If you plan on modifying the WordPress core and then distributing that code, you will need to make sure your changes are covered by the GPL and that the code is available in source code form. Given that WordPress is written in PHP, an interpreted language, distributing the software and distributing the source code are effectively the same action.

Following are some common misperceptions and associated explanations about using WordPress in commercial situations.

➤ **"Free software" means you cannot commercialize its use.** You can charge people to use your installation of WordPress, or make money from advertisements running in your website, or use a WordPress content management platform as the foundation of an online store. That is how wordpress.com works; it also enables Google to charge advertisers for using their Linux-based services. You can find professional quality WordPress themes with non-trivial price tags, or you can pay a hosting provider hundreds or even thousands of dollars a year to run your MySQL, PHP, Apache, and WordPress software stack; both involve commercialization of WordPress.

➤ **If you customize the code to handle your own {content types, security policies, or obscure navigational requirements} you will have to publish those changes.** You are only required to make the source code available for software that you distribute. If you choose to make those changes inside your company, you do not have to redistribute them. On the other hand, if you've made some improvements to the WordPress core, the entire community would benefit from them. Getting more staid employers to understand the value of community contribution and relax copyright and employee contribution rules is sometimes a bit challenging, but the fact that you had a solid starting point is proof that other employers made precisely that set of choices on behalf of the greater WordPress community.

➤ **The GPL will "infect" content that you put into WordPress.** Content—including graphic elements of themes, posts, and pages managed by WordPress—is separated out from the WordPress core. It is managed by the software, but not a derivative of or part of the software. Themes, however, are a derivative of the WordPress code and therefore also fall under the GPL, requiring you to make the source code for the theme available. Note that you can still charge for the theme if you want to make it commercially available. Again, the key point here is that you make the source code available to anyone who uses the software. If you are going to charge for the use of a theme, you need to make the source code available under the GPL as well, but as pointed out previously, users installing the theme effectively get the source code.

More important than a WordPress history lesson and licensing examination are the issues of what you can do with WordPress and why you would want to enjoy its robustness. The next section looks at WordPress as a full-fledged content management system, rather than simply a blog editing tool.

CONTENT AND CONVERSATION

Multiple linear feet of shelves in bookstores are filled with volumes that will improve your writing voice, literary style, blogging techniques, and other aspects of your content creation abilities. One of the goals of this book is to define the visual, stylistic, and context management mechanisms you can build with WordPress to shape vibrant user communities around your content. That context stimulates conversation with your readers. Publishing is not just about the words in each post, or even if you are an interesting writer. How will people find you? How will you stand out in the crowd? How do you put your own imprint on your site, and personalize it for whatever purpose: personal, enterprise, community, or commercial?

WordPress as a Content Management System

Blogging systems have their roots in simple content management operations: Create a post, persist it in stable storage such as a filesystem or database, and display the formatted output based on some set of temporal or keyword criteria. As the richness and types of content presented in blog pages expanded, and the requirements for sorting, searching, selecting, and presenting content grew to include metadata and content taxonomies, the line between vanilla, single-user-targeted blogging software and enterprise-grade content management systems blurred.

Content management systems (CMS) handle the creation, storage, retrieval, description or annotation, and publication or display of a variety of content types. CMS also covers workflow tasks, typically from an editorial or publishing perspective, and includes actions such as approval and marking content for additional editing or review. The WordPress Dashboard provides those elements of workflow management and editorial control. WordPress is not the only open source content management system in widespread use today; the Drupal and Joomla projects are equally popular choices. Drupal and Joomla start from the perspective of managing content repositories; they handle a variety of content types, multiple authors in multiple roles, and delivering the content to a consumer that requests it. WordPress is at its heart a publishing system, and the end focus is on displaying content to a reader. Although areas of functional overlap exist, you can integrate WordPress with other content management systems, a process covered in detail in Chapter 15.

WordPress has established itself as a *bona fide* content management system through its design for extensibility and the separation of content persistence from content display. Taking some liberties with the Model-View-Controller design pattern, WordPress separates the MySQL persistence layer as a data model, the theme-driven user interface and display functions, and the plugin architecture that interposes functionality into the data to presentation flow. Most important, WordPress stores content in raw form, as input by the user or an application posting through the WordPress APIs. Content is not formatted, run through templates, or laid out until the page is rendered, yielding immense power to the functions that generate the actual HTML. At the same time, the data model used by WordPress uses a rich set of tables to manage categories (taxonomies), content tags (folksonomies), author information, comments, and other pieces of cross-reference value. The WordPress database schema that makes this possible is explored in Chapter 6.

Although that design gives WordPress incredible power and flexibility as a content management system, it also requires knowledge of how those data persistence and control flows are related. (It was a search for such a dissection of WordPress in functional terms that got us together to write this book.)

Creating Conversation

Conversation is king; content is just something to talk about.

— Cory Doctorow

A robust CMS is measured by the utility of its content. Even the richest content types and most well-managed processes are of low return if nobody actually consumes the outputs. It is not sufficient to install blogging software, write a few posts, and hope the world shows up on your virtual doorstep; you need to create what Tim O'Reilly calls an "architecture of participation." Social networking, advertising, feeds, and taking steps to ensure your site shows up in search engine results will drive readers to your site; the design, branding, and graphic elements coupled with the quality of your content will encourage them to take the steps toward active participation.

Look at the problem from the perspective of a reader: In a world of tens of millions of websites (many of which have a "first post" and not much else), how will you be found, heard, and echoed? Your Twitter followers should want to read your site, and your WordPress site can update your Twitter feed. Conversely, your Twitter updates may appear in your WordPress sidebar, marrying the ultra-short content timeline to the more thoughtful one. If you are active on Facebook, you can import entries into a public figure page and Facebook readership will drive traffic back to your website. If you cover specific, detailed, or arcane areas in your writing, Google searches for those terms should direct readers to you, where they will join the conversation. Chapter 12 looks at how your WordPress content can be more broadly distributed.

GETTING STARTED

Before any serious work on presentation, style, or content begins, you need a home for your website (despite the previous discussion about WordPress and content management systems, we will refer to your website and the actual WordPress installation that implements it interchangeably, mostly for convenience and brevity). Factors affecting your choice include:

➤ **Cost**—Free hosting services limit your options as a developer and frequently preclude you from generating money from advertising services. More expensive offerings may include better support, higher storage or bandwidth limits, or multiple database instances for additional applications.

➤ **Control**—What tools are provided for you to manage your MySQL database, files comprising the WordPress installation, and other content types? If you want to be able to muck around at the SQL level, or manage MySQL through a command-line interface, you should ensure your hosting provider supports those interfaces.

➤ **Complexity**—You can install the Apache or nginx web server with a PHP interpreter, MySQL, and the WordPress distribution yourself, but most hosting providers have wrapped up the installation process so that some of the rough edges are hidden from view. If you expect to need technical support on the underlying operating system platform, find a provider (including your own IT department) that provides that support in a reasonable time frame.

This section takes a quick look at some hosting options, walks you through the basics of a do-it-yourself installation, and concludes with an overview of the ways in which WordPress and MySQL choose to ignore each other when installation goes into the weeds.

Hosting Options

Three broad categories of WordPress hosting exist, each with trade-offs between administrative complexity and depth of control. The easiest and most popular is to use wordpress.com, a free hosting service run by Automattic using the multi-site version of WordPress (originally WordPress MU). You can install themes and plugins through the Dashboard but you can only enable or disable the choices that come preinstalled. Further, you will not have access to the underlying MySQL databases and core code, or be able to integrate WordPress with other systems. You can redirect one of your own URLs to wordpress.com, but if you want full control over everything from the code to the URLs used, you are probably looking at a paid option. The free route may be a reasonable first step for you, but for this book it is assumed that you are going to want to perform surgery on your installation.

You will find a starter list of for-fee hosting providers on www.wordpress.org, including the paid option on wordpress.com. Most have the latest, or close to latest, releases of the WordPress core available as a package to be installed in conjunction with MySQL and a web server. The third hosting option is to install everything on servers that you own and operate. If your servers live in a hosting facility but you enjoy root administrative access that is equivalent to a do-it-yourself installation. These are all options for putting your WordPress installation on the public Internet. If you are just looking to explore, Chapter 3 covers running WordPress locally for development.

WordPress requires a web server with PHP support, a URL rewriting facility, and an instance of MySQL. Apache is the most popular option for front-ending WordPress because it provides PHP interpretation through mod_php and URL rewriting in mod_rewrite. There is growing interest in lighttpd (Lighty) and nginx as replacements for Apache. Finally, you can use Microsoft's IIS 7.0 as a web server with its URL _ rewrite module. The emphasis on URL rewriting stems from WordPress's support for "pretty" permalinks to content entries, allowing you to create a URL tree organized by date, category, tag, or other metadata. Those mnemonic, or human-readable, URLs are converted into MySQL database queries to extract the right WordPress content based on titles or other keywords as part of the WordPress main loop, which is covered in detail in Chapter 5. Your web server decides whether the URL should be parsed by WordPress or if it refers to a specific HTML file based on what is in the .htaccess file, and the URL rewriting rules ensure that its contents are interpreted properly. Technically, URL rewriting is not required to install WordPress, but it is good to have because it gives you tremendous flexibility in the presentation and naming conventions used for your content's URLs. Permalink design and practices are covered in more detail in Chapter 2, but keep the requirement in mind as you select your WordPress substrate.

Up to this point, MySQL has been mentioned only in passing, but a brief review of MySQL requirements rounds out the hosting prerequisite list. It is worth establishing some terminology and distinguishing between the MySQL software, database instances, and WordPress instances using MySQL. When you install and configure MySQL, you have a full-fledged relational database system up and running. It does not have to be configured on the same machine as your web server, and some hosting providers will create horizontally scalable MySQL "farms" in parallel to their web server front ends. An *instance* of MySQL running on a server can support multiple *databases*, each with a unique name. When you install WordPress, you will need to know the *name* of the MySQL database reserved for your content, although this information may be auto-generated and configured for you if you are using a provider that supports WordPress and MySQL as an integrated package. WordPress creates a number of relational data *tables* in that named database for each website that you create.

Confusion can result from nomenclature and complexity. You (or your hosting provider) may run multiple MySQL instances on multiple servers, and you will need to know where your database is hosted. Because each instance of MySQL can run multiple databases, and each database contains groups of tables, it is possible, even common, to run multiple MySQL-based applications on the same hosting platform, using one MySQL instance or even one MySQL database.

If you want to have multiple WordPress sites on the same server, you can share a single MySQL database instance for all of them provided you configure WordPress to distinguish the MySQL database table names within the MySQL database. It is a simple configuration option that is covered in the next section, and it highlights the distinction between multiple sets of tables in a database and multiple databases for distinct applications.

Once you have secured the necessary foundation, it is time to get the code up and running. Even if you are using a hosting provider that installs MySQL and WordPress for you, it is worth knowing how the server-side components interact in case you need to track down a problem when you're deep in plugin development.

Do It Yourself Installation

The famous, fabled, fabulous five-minute WordPress installation is a reality when everything is configured and coordinated properly. This section walks you through the steps that are often hidden from view when you use a provider with packaged installs, and highlights some of the common misfires between WordPress and MySQL instances.

The installation process is quite simple (assuming that your web server and MySQL server are already running): Download the WordPress package and install it in your web server's directory tree, and then navigate to your top-level URL and complete the configuration. One (compound) sentence describes it completely.

It is possible and even advisable to install a fully functioning WordPress instance on your laptop or development machine, particularly if you are going to be working on the core, developing plugins, or otherwise making changes that would create embarrassing failures during testing on a public website. Mac OS X comes with an Apache web server (with PHP and URL rewriting); download MySQL from www.mysql.com, or use a prepackaged configuration such as MAMP (www.mamp.info, which includes the phpMyAdmin tool), and you will have a self-contained development and deployment lab. For other platforms, XAMPP (www.apachefriends.org) has a neatly integrated platform stack that runs on Windows, Mac OS, and Linux foundations. Furthermore, the use of virtual machines for your development environment has grown immensely, and now there are packaged VM solutions to get you started. Having everything under one hood is a powerful option for examining failure modes, as you will see in the next two sections. More information on working with WordPress locally is covered in Chapter 3.

Installing WordPress Files

If you download the WordPress code from wordpress.org, you will get a zip (or tarball) archive that expands into a directory called wordpress. The first part of a WordPress installation is to get the code into your web server's directory structure; ensuring you have it in the right place is a critical step. Gloss over this part and you will find your website ends up with a URL like http://example.com/wordpress and you will either have to start over or e-mail ugly URLs to your friends and family. If that is what you want—to distinguish your WordPress site from other content on your website or to isolate multiple sections—choosing the filesystem layout is equally important.

Pick the top-level directory where you want to install WordPress. Most commonly, this is the root directory for your web server, and if you are using a hosting provider it is probably the subdirectory called public_html in the file tree. If you are using a packaged install where there is a menu asking you for the target location, make sure you pick this top-level directory (and yes, you know that it already exists, that's the point!); if you are copying files from your local machine to the web server target using an FTP client, make sure you pick the right destination. The somewhat obvious move to copy the zip file to the server and then unpack it will put everything into a wordpress subdirectory, and if you want your WordPress site's URL to be http://example.com rather than http://example.com/wordpress, move the files up one directory level before proceeding. There is a configuration option to have your WordPress installation in a subdirectory to your top-level URL, so it is not fatal if you drop WordPress into a less-than-desirable filesystem geography. That is covered at the end of this section.

Once the WordPress files are installed, your filesystem browser should show you something like Figure 1-1, with an index.php and template wp-config-sample.php file. That's the entirety of the WordPress system, which runs effectively within the web server's PHP interpreter.

At this point, if you are doing a manual installation, you will want to create your own wp-config.php file by editing the provided sample file, wp-config-sample.php, and saving it in your top-level WordPress directory. As an alternative, you can navigate to your website's URL, and the WordPress code will notice there is no configuration file. After you select your installation language, WordPress presents you with dialog boxes like those in Figures 1-2 and 1-3 where you can fill in the details. You will need the MySQL database name, database username, and some idea of the WordPress database table prefix (other than the default wp _). These lower-level details are the guts of the next section on database configuration. If you are using a hosting provider with packaged installations, you probably will not see this step because the WordPress files will be extracted and the MySQL database information will be automatically inserted into a configuration file, no end user–serviceable parts inside.

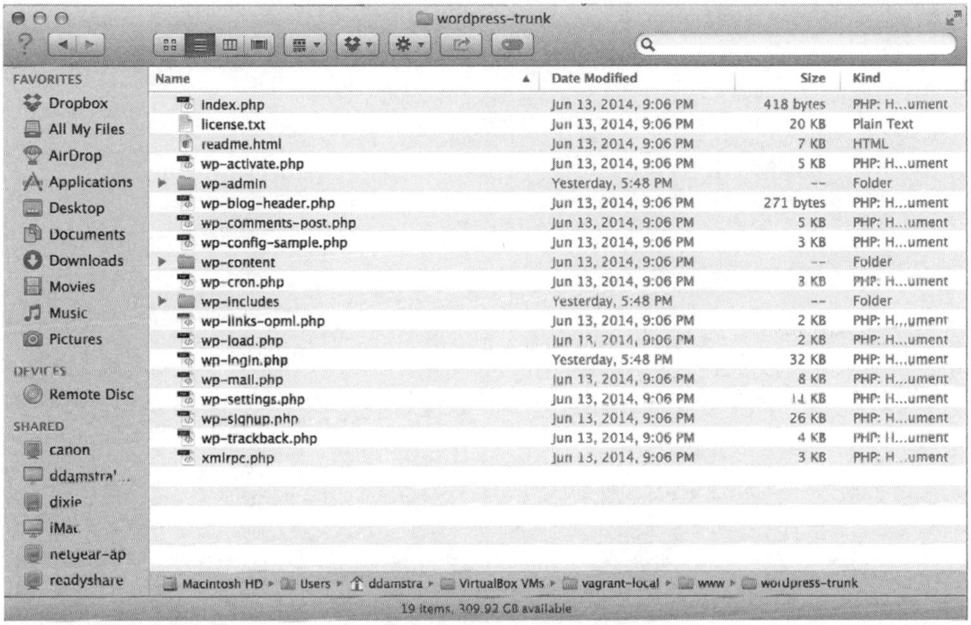

FIGURE 1-1: A clean but unconfigured WordPress installation

What do you do if you already have HTML or other content at your target URL and you want to add WordPress to an existing site? Disposition of existing files depends on your desired first user experience upon navigating to your URL. To use WordPress as a content management system as described here, your best choice is to save existing content and convert it into new posts or pages, effectively making your previous site color commentary and context for your WordPress-driven site. Alternatively, you can install WordPress in a subdirectory, keep your existing index.html file, and direct readers to your new content through a button or link on your extant home page. Do not leave this to chance; if you have an index.html file and then install WordPress, you will have an index.php and an index.html file side by side and users will see one or the other depending upon the Directory Index configuration of your site's web server. Actions on existing content should be informed by how much traffic that content is driving to your site: if your pages are responsible for search engine traffic, you probably do not want to disrupt the existing URLs that have been cached and should install WordPress in a subdirectory. If you feel strongly about making WordPress the wrapper around the user experience, move the content and include URL rewriting or redirection for pages that move into the WordPress world.

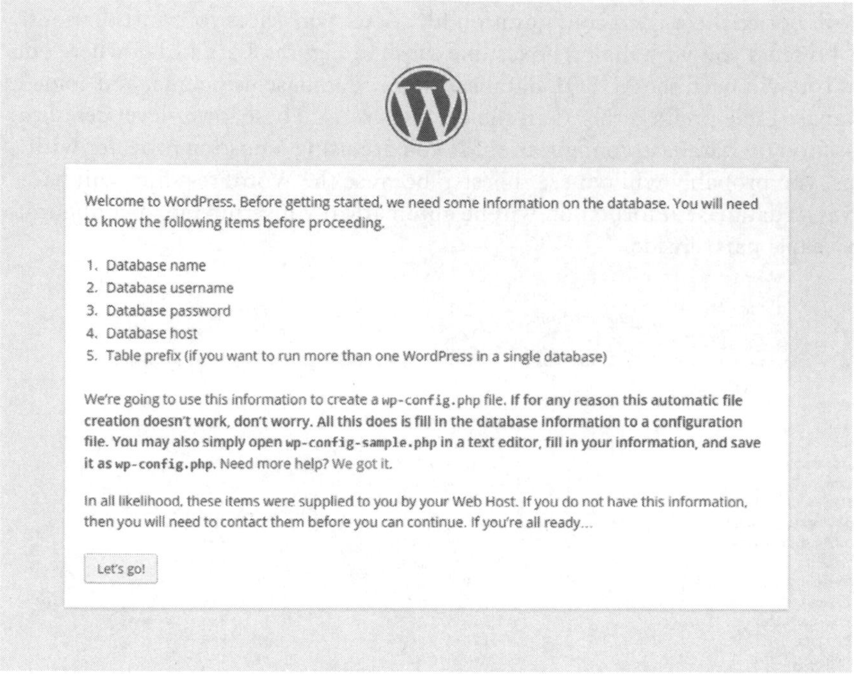

Welcome to WordPress. Before getting started, we need some information on the database. You will need to know the following items before proceeding.

1. Database name
2. Database username
3. Database password
4. Database host
5. Table prefix (if you want to run more than one WordPress in a single database)

We're going to use this information to create a `wp-config.php` file. If for any reason this automatic file creation doesn't work, don't worry. All this does is fill in the database information to a configuration file. You may also simply open `wp-config-sample.php` in a text editor, fill in your information, and save it as `wp-config.php`. Need more help? We got it.

In all likelihood, these items were supplied to you by your Web Host. If you do not have this information, then you will need to contact them before you can continue. If you're all ready…

Let's go!

FIGURE 1-2:   WordPress will create a new wp-config file if one does not exist.

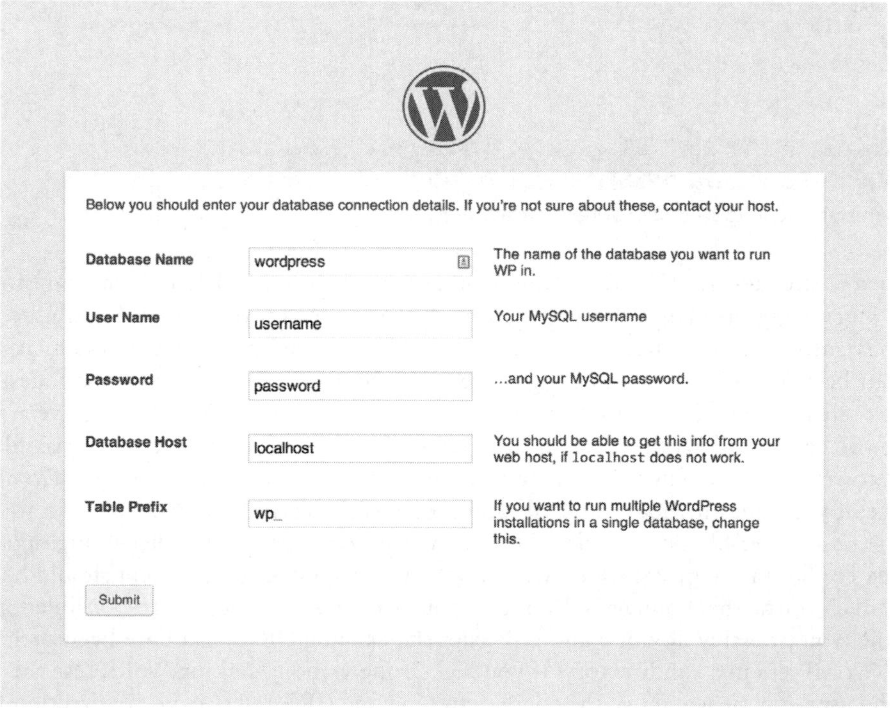

Below you should enter your database connection details. If you're not sure about these, contact your host.

Database Name	wordpress	The name of the database you want to run WP in.
User Name	username	Your MySQL username
Password	password	…and your MySQL password.
Database Host	localhost	You should be able to get this info from your web host, if `localhost` does not work.
Table Prefix	wp_	If you want to run multiple WordPress installations in a single database, change this.

Submit

FIGURE 1-3:   Database configuration dialog box

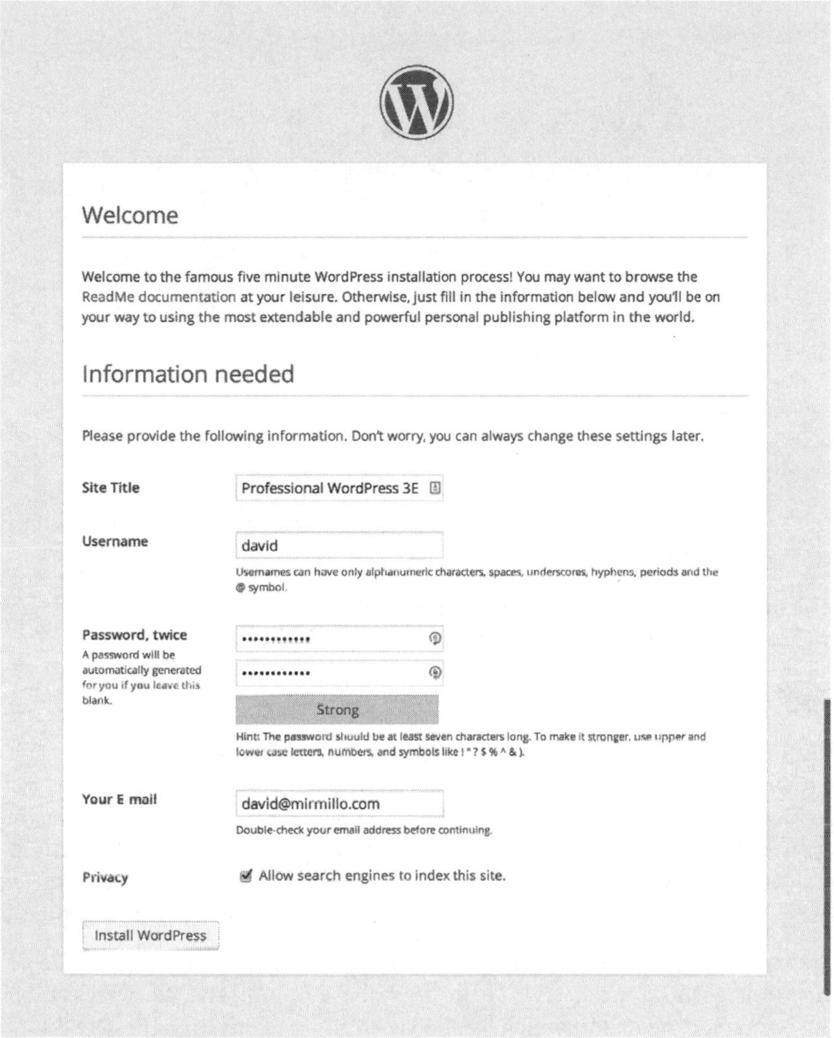

FIGURE 1-4: Complete website details and set up admin user.

If you used a hosting provider's packaged installation, or if you manually created a `wp-config.php` file and then navigated to your top-level URL, WordPress should have completed creating the database tables, created an administrative user for your WordPress, and set an initial password, as shown in Figure 1-4. Make sure you change the username to something different than admin.

Upon a successful installation, you should see a box like Figure 1-5 that indicates your five minutes of famed installation is done.

The next section covers the MySQL-WordPress configuration dance in more detail and is suitable reading even if thinking about SQL gives you hives. If you are up and running, you can skip the next section and go right to the section "Finishing Up."

FIGURE 1-5: Administrative information at the conclusion of a clean install

Database Configuration

If your hosting provider spun up a MySQL database and created a user for you, check your resultant wp-config.php file to gather this information. It is necessary for the MySQL probing covered in this section, and it is good to have in case you run into MySQL problems later on. There is a username and password combination included in that file, so treat it the way you would treat other login information. On the other hand, if you are going deep on the do-it-yourself route, this section gives you a sense of what is likely to create confusion or consternation as you pull the pieces together.

In theory, MySQL setup for WordPress is trivial: Make sure MySQL is up and running, create a WordPress user in MySQL, and then have that user create a database to hold the WordPress tables. You can use the MySQL command line or tools such as phpMyAdmin or Chive for these tasks, but bear in mind that MySQL has its own set of users and permissions granted to those users, distinct from those used by your (or your hosting provider's) operating system. Once MySQL is installed, it will create a default table of users and grants, adding a root user on Unix systems that is a MySQL superuser, unrelated to the Unix root user. However, if you are attempting to connect to your MySQL instance as the MySQL root user, those connections can only be made from localhost—the same machine on which MySQL is running. If you want to learn more about MySQL permissions, the table governing grants of those permissions to users, and how MySQL users are managed, refer to the "MySQL Reference Manual" (http://dev.mysql.com/doc/) and the sections on securing the initial MySQL accounts.

No set naming conventions exist for WordPress users or databases; hosting providers will typically append the name of the package or your account information to distinguish users that benefit from MySQL database co-tenancy. Again, it is possible to have multiple databases, owned by the same user or different MySQL users, running in a single MySQL database server instance. In the example shown in Figure 1-3, wp_ is used as a prefix for both usernames and database names, at least providing a hint to the database administrator that these belong to a WordPress installation. Security best practices recommend not using wp_ as your table prefix; this is covered more in Chapter 13.

What can go wrong between WordPress and MySQL? The following are the three primary root causes of installation failure. Note that all of these conditions need to be fulfilled at installation time; there has to be some basic database structure to contain the admin user before you can log in as that admin.

➤ **Web server cannot find MySQL.** Either you have the hostname for the MySQL server noted incorrectly in the wp-config.php file, or the web server is looking for a local MySQL instance and cannot open the socket connection to it. Here is a simple example: when you run WordPress locally on Mac OS, MySQL creates the socket /tmp/mysql.sock for local connections, but the WordPress PHP code is going to look for /var/mysql/mysql.sock through the PHP engine's MySQL module. Simply symbolically link one to the other:

```
# ln -s /tmp/mysql.sock /var/mysql/mysql.sock
```

The actual filesystem path to the local MySQL socket is a function of the database configuration; when it starts up, it creates the local socket. Where the PHP engine, and therefore any PHP-based applications, looks for this socket is PHP configuration dependent. If you want to figure out exactly where the mismatch is, a bit of heavy-handed printf() style debugging helps.

Edit wp-includes/wp-db.php, the set of functions that establish WordPress's database connection. If you are seeing the "Error establishing a database connection" message during installation, insert an echo(mysql_error()); statement where the error is detected to see the details displayed along with the generic message, as shown in Figure 1-6:

```
if (!$this->dbh) {
        echo(mysql_error());
    $this->bail(sprintf(/*WP_I18N_DB_CONN_ERROR*/"
    <h1>Error establishing a database connection</h1>
```

The mysql_error() function is a PHP library function that spits out the error generated by the last MySQL function called.

➤ **WordPress finds MySQL but cannot log in.** Most of the time, the MySQL username or password is wrong, particularly when you have to copy some arbitrary username generated by a hosting provider. Double-check your username data, and verify that it is reflected properly in your wp-config.php file. You may also run into a password authentication issue when using MySQL 4.1 or MySQL 5.0 with some web servers' PHP implementations; they only support the older MySQL 4.0 password hashing scheme. If this is the case, use MySQL's OLD_PASSWORD() function to hash your WordPress user's password in the backward-compatible format; use the magic SQL incantation (at the MySQL command-line prompt or within the SQL window of MAMP) to address the following:

```
SET PASSWORD FOR user@host = OLD_PASSWORD('password');
```

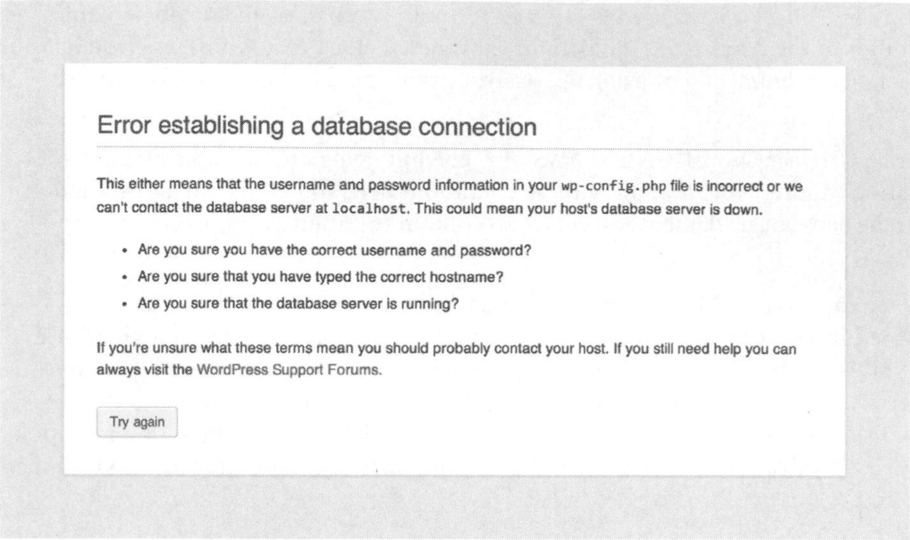

FIGURE 1-6: mysql_error( ) reporting a socket problem

In this instance, user@host is your WordPress database username and database hostname, and password is the (clear text) password you provided in the configuration file.

➤ **WordPress connects to MySQL but cannot select the database.** Just because the web server can log in to the database server with your WordPress database user information does not mean that there is necessarily a database available to that user. This is another scenario best diagnosed with mysql_error(), by inserting it in wp-db.php where the selection error is identified:

```
function select($db) {
    if (!@mysql_select_db($db, $this->dbh)) {
        $this->ready = false;
         echo(mysql_error());
        $this->bail(sprintf(/*WP_I18N_DB_SELECT_DB*/'
... <h1>Can&#8217;t select database</h1>
        ..
```

If, after inserting the mysql_error() statement as described earlier, your attempts to complete installation result in an error box like that shown in Figure 1-7, your MySQL database was not created under the appropriate database user, or the database user does not have privileges to use it. Double-check what MySQL believes using the following command line:

```
vagrant@vvv:~$ mysql -u root -p
Enter password:
Welcome to the MySQL monitor.  Commands end with ; or \g.
Your MySQL connection id is 98
Server version: 5.5.37-0ubuntu0.14.04.1 (Ubuntu)

Copyright (c) 2000, 2014, Oracle and/or its affiliates. All rights reserved.
```

```
Oracle is a registered trademark of Oracle Corporation and/or its
affiliates. Other names may be trademarks of their respective
owners.

Type 'help;' or '\h' for help. Type '\c' to clear the current input statement.

mysql> show databases;
+--------------------+
| Database           |
+--------------------+
| information_schema |
| mysql              |
| performance_schema |
| wordpress_default  |
| wordpress_develop  |
| wordpress_trunk    |
| wordpress_unit_tests |
+--------------------+
7 rows in set (0.00 sec)

mysql>
```

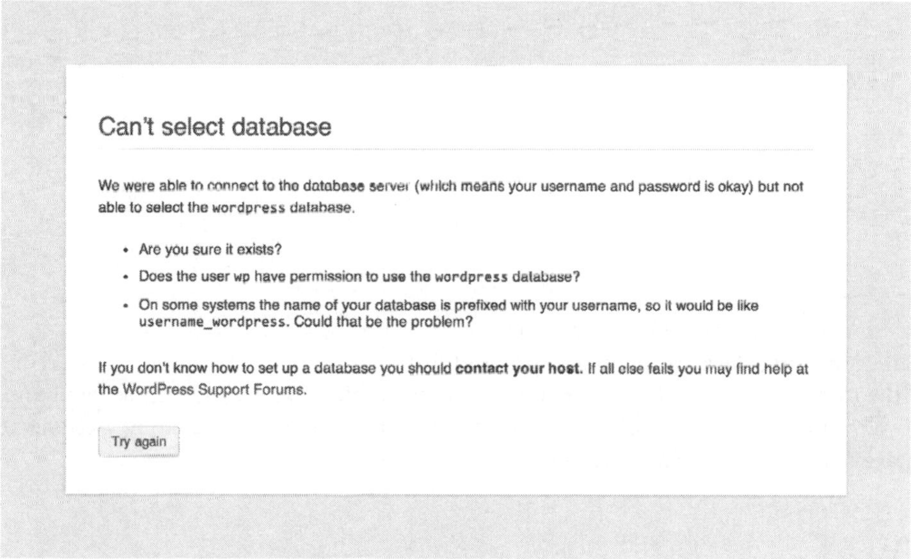

FIGURE 1-7: MySQL database selection error

Once you logged in as your designated MySQL database user, you did not see the MySQL database—in this case, it was probably created by the MySQL user root, and permissions to access or modify it were not granted to the WordPress installation's MySQL user. If you have MySQL root access, or sufficient MySQL user privileges to create new databases within the MySQL instance, it is easy enough to create a database once logged in on the command line:

```
mysql> create database wordpress_trunk;
Query OK, 1 row affected (0.00 sec)
```

Again, it is important to distinguish operating system users from MySQL users from WordPress users. MySQL users are defined in the database and granted privileges to create databases, muck with tables, and otherwise generate useful data. WordPress users exist within the WordPress database tables created during install; they only have privileges, context, and meaning once you are logged in to WordPress.

Once you have a clean WordPress installation, you should see a collection of tables named according to the table prefix you set in `wp-config.php`; again, this is easy enough to verify using the MySQL command line:

```
mysql> use wordpress_trunk; show tables;
Reading table information for completion of table and column names
You can turn off this feature to get a quicker startup with -A
Database changed
+---------------------------+
| Tables_in_wordpress_trunk |
+---------------------------+
| wp_commentmeta            |
| wp_comments               |
| wp_links                  |
| wp_options                |
| wp_postmeta               |
| wp_posts                  |
| wp_term_relationships     |
| wp_term_taxonomy          |
| wp_terms                  |
| wp_usermeta               |
| wp_users                  |
+---------------------------+
11 rows in set (0.00 sec)

mysql>
```

In this example, you set the database table prefix to wp _ ; if you later add another WordPress installation using the same database user and instance, you can simply set a different prefix and have the two sites co-mingled in the same database table. You dig into the schema and uses of the basic WordPress database tables in Chapter 6. For now, once you are happily connected to MySQL, you are ready for some final clean-up and first-time administration.

FINISHING UP

At this point, your MySQL database is up and running. There is a home for your content, and your web server is happily executing the WordPress core code. There are just a couple more things to discuss.

First-Time Administration

Once you have completed the installation, proceed to log in with the credentials you set up in Figure 1-4 and you'll see the basic WordPress Dashboard captured in Figure 1-8.

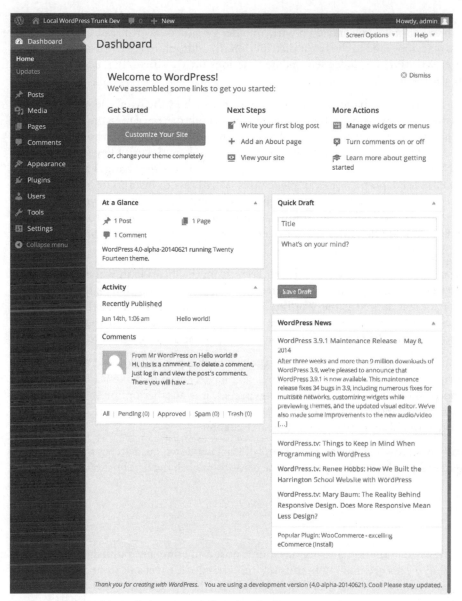

FIGURE 1-8: Dashboard view upon a first-time login

If you are not redirected to the Dashboard through the Log In button, or if you happen to visit your website's top-level URL first, either click the Log In link on your website or explicitly go to the `wp-admin` subdirectory (`example.com/wp-admin`) to be presented with a login dialog box. Logging in to your website takes you to the WordPress Dashboard, which is both amazingly simple in its power and rich in its complexity and exposed features.

What you do next with the Dashboard depends on how happy you are with the basic installation. If, as in the preceding example, you ended up with an older version of WordPress, click the Update button to do an in-place upgrade to the latest distribution. In addition to having a strong self-installation feature, WordPress includes self-update functions (in `wp-admin/includes/update.php` if you are looking for them).

You may decide to change some basic configuration options, such as the database name or the MySQL database user, although you will only change the default of `root@localhost` if you have full control over the web and database servers. The configuration file also has entries for "security keys" that are used to provide stronger security for browser cookies. Security keys are discussed in more detail in Chapter 13. Editing your `wp-config.php` file affects the changes right away. Changing the database table prefix, for example, causes WordPress to instantiate a new set of tables and create a clean-slate installation. Make those edits and then go back to your top-level URL and you will find yourself with new admin user information and logged in to a starter Dashboard, as in Figure 1-8. Old tables are not removed from MySQL, so you'll have to do manual cleanup.

At this point, if you want to set your URL to be different from the location in which you installed WordPress, you can choose Settings and General from the Dashboard and change the URLs for both your top-level address as well as the WordPress installation directory. If you dissociate your site's URL and the WordPress directory, make sure you move the `index.php` file to the desired top-level URL, and then edit the last line to include the proper subdirectory path to WordPress.

Before creating your first post, it is also a good idea to establish a permalink structure so that everything you write follows the naming conventions you have chosen to make it relatively easy for readers to find, share, and link to your content. As expected, it is another option in the Settings portion of the Dashboard; options for permalink naming and their impact on performance and database schema are covered in more detail in the next chapter.

Whether it has really been five minutes, or a few hours of tracking down mismatches in hostnames, usernames, and database configurations, you are now ready to publish the first post of your own writing.

First Post

A successful WordPress installation already has a first post and comment published, thus ensuring that all of the moving pieces are moving in unison, and giving your website some initial content. When you are ready to add your own first words, either use the right-hand QuickDraft panel in the Dashboard to post an entry (you may need to dismiss the new website help first), or go to Posts and click Add New to be taken to the built-in WordPress editor. Figure 1-9 shows an entry in progress in the QuickDraft panel, followed by the updated Dashboard after it has been successfully posted.

If your tastes run more old-school, you can always crank out content in your favorite text editor and then copy it into the editing pane. Be careful with WYSYIWIG word processors such as Microsoft Word or OpenOffice if you want to copy into the WordPress HTML composition window because the HTML will be riddled with additional tag and style information. Finally, a variety of standalone editors publish to WordPress using the Atom Publishing Protocol or XML-RPC. Options for

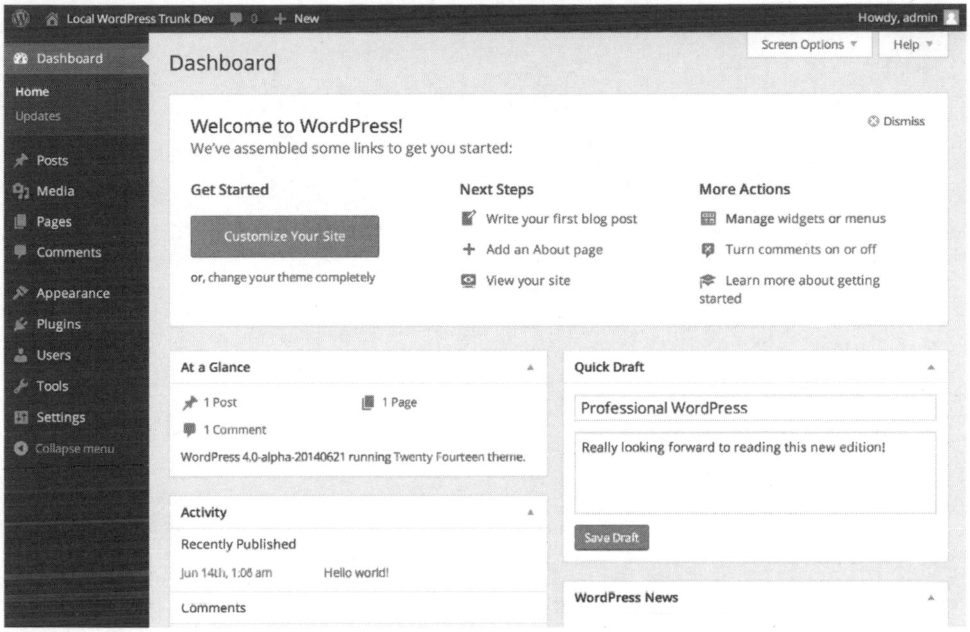

FIGURE 1-9: Publishing from the QuickDraft panel

enabling posts to be published remotely are, as you would expect, in the Dashboard's Settings section under Writing options.

Click Publish for your own "Hello World" moment. Multiple subsystems created that editing pane, saved the content in a database, generated and saved the referential metadata, and then emitted nice-looking HTML. Most of the user-visible pieces are governed through the Dashboard and certain functions will be covered in various chapters.

SUMMARY

This chapter covered how WordPress got to where it is today with a brief history lesson and also touched on its current popularity. Part of WordPress's rise in the web realm is attributed to the simplicity of the installation process. The next chapter dives into the core of WordPress so that you can take advantage of its extensibility, friendly design, and function.

2

Code Overview

WHAT'S IN THIS CHAPTER?

➤ Downloading WordPress

➤ Configuring wp-config.php and .htaccess

➤ Exploring the wp-content directories

➤ Enabling maintenance mode in WordPress

WordPress is a software package that comprises groups of source code files that perform specific tasks within the system. Understanding the code, including file and folder structure, is essential to understanding how WordPress works as a whole.

After reading this chapter, you will be familiar with downloading and exploring the WordPress filesystem. This chapter also discusses configuring key WordPress files, including the powerful wp-config.php and .htaccess files. It also covers some advanced configuration options available in WordPress.

DOWNLOADING

The first step to installing WordPress is to download the source files required for WordPress to run. This section digs deeper into the core of WordPress.

Download Locations

You can download the latest stable release of WordPress directly from WordPress.org by visiting the download page located at http://wordpress.org/download/.

You can also update WordPress directly from your current WordPress installation by visiting the Updates WordPress section under the Dashboard ➤ Updates screen. Click the Download button to download the latest version of WordPress to your computer.

WordPress also features Subversion (SVN) access. Subversion is a free, open source version control system. WordPress uses Subversion to manage files and directories and the changes made to them. You can download the latest WordPress source code by checking out `http://core.svn` `.wordpress.org/trunk/`.

The SVN trunk directory contains the *bleeding edge* version of WordPress that is actively being developed. Typically, this version of WordPress contains bugs and is generally used for testing purposes. Running a production website using the trunk version of WordPress is not recommended.

SVN is the mechanism developers use to actively develop on the WordPress core software. With SVN, you can create and submit patch files for inclusion into the WordPress core. Chapter 16 covers this in detail.

Git is another very popular source code management system. Many developers, and not just in the WordPress community, have switched from SVN to Git for version control because of the many benefits Git offers over SVN. The WordPress core team has set up a Git mirror for WordPress core development. To access the Git repository run the command `git clone git://develop.git` `.wordpress.org/`. For more information on working with Git and WordPress core development, visit `http://make.wordpress.org/core/2014/01/15/git-mirrors-for-wordpress/`.

The SVN and Git repositories are considered equals, so if you plan to work with the WordPress core you can use the version control system that you are most comfortable with.

Available Formats

The default format for the WordPress software download is in a compressed zip archive named `latest.zip`. You can also download WordPress in a compressed tar archive named `latest.tar.gz`. There is no difference between the files in the archive, only the compression method used.

You can download the zip and tar archives directly from these URLs:

➤ `http://wordpress.org/latest.zip`

➤ `http://wordpress.org/latest.tar.gz`

These download links never change. Each new version of WordPress is automatically compressed and saved at this location when the version is tagged. When you save the archive to your computer, you should rename the file to include the WordPress version number, such as `wordpress-4.1.zip`. This will help you remember what version of WordPress you saved to your computer.

Release Archive

WordPress.org features a release archive for WordPress. The Release Archive features a list of downloadable archives for every release of WordPress since version 0.71. The archive is located at `http://wordpress.org/download/release-archive/`.

Remember that only the most current version of WordPress is actively maintained so these downloads are more for reference than actual use. "Actively maintained" means that critical fixes for security, performance, or reliability problems are made to the active branch and not applied retroactively to previous releases. If you need the fix, you'll need to upgrade your installed version of WordPress.

Another great use for these older versions of WordPress is to roll a website back to a previous version. For example, if you update a very old version of WordPress to the latest stable version and run into problems, you could easily download the old version that the website was originally running to revert to. The Release Archive also features a download for every beta and release candidate version of WordPress as well. This is great to see the overall growth of WordPress as a software platform.

The release archives are also useful if you need to update an old version of WordPress that has hacks made to the core. Simply compare the website's WordPress source code with the same version of WordPress from the release archive and any differences, or core hacks, will be discovered.

DIRECTORY AND FILE STRUCTURE

The WordPress source code features many different PHP, JavaScript, and CSS code files. Each file serves a specific purpose in WordPress. The beauty of open source software is that all code is publicly available, which means you can easily explore the code to better understand how WordPress functions. The best resource for learning WordPress is the WordPress software itself.

After extracting the WordPress download, you will notice the set file structure for WordPress, as shown in Figure 2-1.

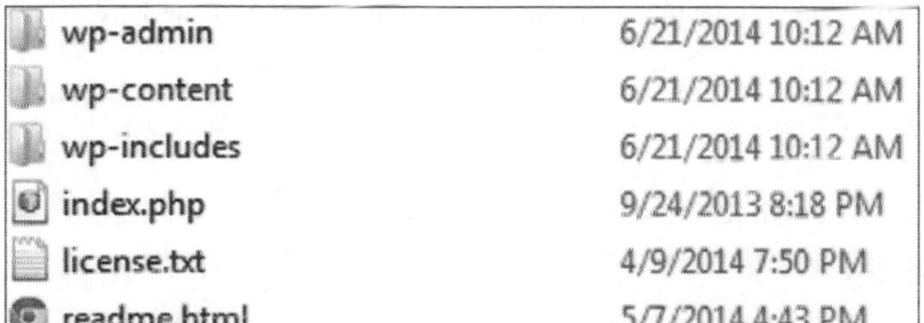

wp-admin	6/21/2014 10:12 AM
wp-content	6/21/2014 10:12 AM
wp-includes	6/21/2014 10:12 AM
index.php	9/24/2013 8:18 PM
license.txt	4/9/2014 7:50 PM
readme.html	5/7/2014 4:43 PM
wp-activate.php	12/24/2013 1:57 PM
wp-blog-header.php	1/8/2012 12:01 PM
wp-comments-post.php	2/18/2014 4:45 PM
wp-config-sample.php	10/24/2013 6:58 PM
wp-cron.php	9/24/2013 8:18 PM
wp-links-opml.php	10/24/2013 6:58 PM
wp-load.php	10/24/2013 6:58 PM
wp-login.php	4/13/2014 12:06 PM
wp-mail.php	11/13/2013 6:58 AM
wp-settings.php	4/7/2014 4:15 PM
wp-signup.php	11/12/2013 10:23 PM
wp-trackback.php	10/24/2013 6:58 PM
xmlrpc.php	2/9/2014 3:39 PM

FIGURE 2-1: Default WordPress file and folder structure

WordPress comes with three directories by default: `wp-admin`, `wp-content`, and `wp-includes`. *Core files* are all files in the `wp-admin` and `wp-includes` directories and the majority of the files in the root WordPress directory. The `wp-content` directory holds all of your custom files, including themes, plugins, and media. This directory contains the code that controls content manipulation and presentation in WordPress. WordPress HTML content, such as pages and posts, is stored in the MySQL database along with metadata such as tag and category structures, both of which are covered in detail in Chapter 6.

Modifying any of the core WordPress files can result in an unstable website. An innocuous but badly executed change to the Dashboard or login functions, for example, will leave you with a WordPress installation that can't be managed. Core changes also make it very difficult to update WordPress because all changes made are overwritten when the updated version of WordPress is installed. As discussed in the previous section, critical fixes to the WordPress core are only made in the current branch, so if you are forced to update WordPress to pick up a security fix, you're going to have to re-integrate any core changes you've made and hope they don't conflict with the changes you want. Maintaining the integrity and stability of your WordPress installation over time is much simpler when you're not changing files in the core.

In general, the `wp-admin`, `wp-includes`, and root directory core WordPress files should *never* be edited, but the next section covers some core root directory files that can be modified as part of advanced configuration. In general, however, follow this rule that is revisited in Chapter 4: Don't hack the core!

WORDPRESS CONFIGURATION

WordPress features specific files that can be edited for different purposes. These files can alter how WordPress functions. Always test changes in a development environment before publishing to a production server.

This section covers database connections, storing FTP info, enabling debugging tools, and more using `wp-config.php`. It also covers the power of the `.htaccess` file, including increasing PHP memory limits and max upload sizes, creating redirects, and setting access restrictions.

wp-config.php File

The most important file in any WordPress installation is the `wp-config.php` file. This file contains all database connection settings, including the database name, username, and password, to access your MySQL database. This file also stores additional database and other advanced WordPress settings. The `wp-config.php` file was originally named `wp-config-sample.php`. Renaming the file to `wp-config.php` is one of the first steps to installing WordPress.

The `wp-config.php` file is typically stored in the root directory of WordPress. Alternatively, you can move the `wp-config.php` file out of the WordPress root directory and into the parent directory. So if your WordPress directory is located here:

```
/public_html/my_website/wp-config.php
```

you can safely move the file to here:

```
/public_html/wp-config.php
```

WordPress looks for the wp-config.php file in the root directory first, and if it can't find that file it looks in the parent directory. This happens automatically so no settings need to be changed for this to work.

> **NOTE** *Moving the* wp-config.php *out of the root WordPress directory is a good security measure, making it nearly impossible to potentially access this file from a web browser.*

Some options in WordPress are stored as constants and these can be seen in the wp-config.php file. The constants all have the same format:

```
define('OPTION_NAME', 'value' );
```

OPTION _ NAME is the name of the option constant being set; value is the option value and can be updated to whatever setting you would like to save for that option. When adding new options to the wp-config.php file, it's important the options are added above the line that reads:

```
/* That's all, stop editing! Happy blogging. */
```

If your WordPress installation is having problems connecting to your database, this is the first place to start troubleshooting. If you receive the error message "Error establishing a database connection," the first thing to do is verify that the DB _ NAME, DB _ USER, and DB _ PASSWORD options are correctly set for your database server. Also verify that the DB _ HOST name is set to the correct host for your server. Typically, this is set to localhost, but some hosting companies configure WordPress packages with web servers and MySQL servers on different machines, necessitating a host company–specific configuration option to locate the MySQL database. Contact your hosting tech support or consult their online documentation for the correct host value to set here.

You can change the database character set (charset) by changing the DB _ CHARSET option value. By default, this is set to utf8 (Unicode UTF-8), which supports any language, and is almost always the best option.

Since WordPress 2.2, the DB _ COLLATE option has allowed designation of the database collation, that is, sort order of the character set. (A *character set* is a collection of symbols that represents words in a language. The collation determines the order to use when sorting the character set, usually alphabetical order.) This option, by default, is blank and should typically stay that way. If you would like to change the database collation, just add the appropriate value for your language. You should change this option before installing WordPress. Altering this value after installation could cause problems in WordPress.

WordPress security can be strengthened by setting secret keys in your wp-config.php file. A secret key is a hashing salt, which makes your site harder to hack by adding random elements (the salt) to the password you set. These keys aren't required for WordPress to function, but they add an extra layer of security on your website.

To have secret keys auto-generated for you, visit the link to WordPress.org for secret key generation in your wp-config.php file (https://api.wordpress.org/secret-key/1.1/salt/), shown in Figure 2-2. Alternatively you can just type a bunch of random characters in place of "put your unique phrase here." The goal is to use secret keys that are 100 percent random and unique.

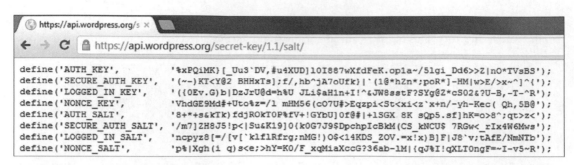

FIGURE 2-2: Randomly generated secret keys

You can add or change these keys at any time; the only thing that will happen is all current WordPress cookies will be invalidated and your users will be required to log in again.

Another security feature included in `wp-config.php` is the ability to define the database table prefix for WordPress. By default, this option value is set to `wp_`. You can change this value by setting the `$table_prefix` variable value to any prefix, like so:

```
$table_prefix  = 'lecter_';
```

If a hacker is able to exploit your website using a SQL injection attack, this will make it harder for them to guess your table names and quite possibly keep them from doing SQL injection at all. Setting the table prefix to a unique value also makes it possible to run multiple WordPress installations in a single database. If you want to change the table prefix after you have installed WordPress, you can use the Change DB Prefix plugin (`http://wordpress.org/plugins/db-prefix-change/`) to do so. Make sure you make a good backup before doing this, however.

The `wp-config.php` file also contains the option for localizing your installation of WordPress. WordPress has the built-in capability to be used in many different languages. Setting the `WPLANG` option value sets the default language for WordPress to use. A corresponding MO (machine object) file for the selected language must be installed to `wp-content/languages` for this option to work. MO files are compressed PO (portable object) files, which contain translations for WordPress messages and text strings in a specific language. The MO and PO files are components of the GNU "gettext" subsystem that underlies the WordPress multi-language capabilities. For a full list of available MO language files, visit the following resources:

➤ **WordPress in Your Language Codex page**—`http://codex.wordpress.org/WordPress_in_Your_Language`

➤ **WordPress Language File Repository**—`http://svn.automattic.com/wordpress-i18n/`

Debugging errors in WordPress can be made easier using the `WP_DEBUG` option. Enabling `WP_DEBUG` displays WordPress errors on the screen, rather than suppressing those errors with a white screen. To enable `WP_DEBUG`, just set the option value to `true`:

```
define( 'WP_DEBUG', true );
```

New installations of WordPress will have this option defined in wp-config.php as false. If this option is not defined, it defaults to false and error messages are not displayed. Remember to disable or remove this option when you are done debugging because error messages might help hackers find vulnerabilities in your website.

> **NOTE** *We recommend that you always keep* WP _ DEBUG *enabled when developing in WordPress to address any warnings or errors that might be displayed.*

Advanced wp-config.php Options

You can set additional advanced options in your wp-config.php file. These options are not in the wp-config.php file by default so you will need to manually add them to the file.

To set your WordPress address and blog address, use the following two options:

```
define( 'WP_SITEURL', 'http://example.com/wordpress' );
define( 'WP_HOME', 'http://example.com/wordpress' );
```

The WP _ SITEURL option allows you to temporarily change the WordPress site URL. This does not alter the database option value for siteurl, but instead temporarily changes the value. If this option is removed, WordPress reverts back to using the siteurl database setting. The WP _ HOME option works the exact same way, letting you temporarily change the home value for WordPress. Both values should include the full URL including http://.

> **NOTE** *This is a useful technique if you are building a WordPress website under a temporary development URL, such as* new.example.com. *You can simply remove these two options when you go live and WordPress will load using the production URL instead.*

WordPress version 3.7 introduced automatic background updates for WordPress. By default, only minor releases (for example, 4.1.*x*, 4.2.*x*, and so on) are updated automatically. There are currently four types of automatic background updates:

➤ Core updates

➤ Plugin updates

➤ Theme updates

➤ Translation file updates

To completely disable all automatic updates, which includes all four types just listed, you'll set the AUTOMATIC _ UPDATER _ DISABLED constant to true, as shown here:

```
define( 'AUTOMATIC_UPDATER_DISABLED', true );
```

Alternately, you can enable automatic updates for major releases and development purposes. Using the WP_AUTO_UPDATE_CORE constant, you can define auto updates in one of three ways:

➤ true—Major, minor, and development automatic updates are all *enabled*.

➤ false—Major, minor, and development automatic updates are all *disabled*.

➤ minor—Minor updates are *enabled*. Major and development updates are *disabled*.

As an example, let's look at the various ways you can configure the automatic update settings:

```
// Enables all core updates, including minor and major:
define( 'WP_AUTO_UPDATE_CORE', true );

// Disables all core updates:
define( 'WP_AUTO_UPDATE_CORE', false );

// Enables core updates for minor releases (default):
define( 'WP_AUTO_UPDATE_CORE', 'minor' );
```

For more information on configuring WordPress automatic updates, visit http://codex .wordpress.org/Configuring_Automatic_Background_Updates.

WordPress also features an option that allows you to move the wp-content directory. The two required options are:

```
define( 'WP_CONTENT_DIR', $_SERVER['DOCUMENT_ROOT'] .
         '/blog/wp-content' );
define( 'WP_CONTENT_URL', 'http://example.com/blog/wp-content');
```

The WP_CONTENT_DIR option value is the full local path to your wp-content directory. The WP_CONTENT_URL is the full URI of this directory. Optionally, you can set the path to your plugins directory like so:

```
define( 'WP_PLUGIN_DIR', $_SERVER['DOCUMENT_ROOT'] . '/blog/wp-content/plugins' );
define( 'WP_PLUGIN_URL', 'http://example/blog/wp-content/plugins');
```

WP_PLUGIN_DIR and WP_PLUGIN_URL are options used by developers to determine where your plugin folder resides. If a developer is not using these constants, there is a very good chance their code will break if you move your wp-content directory. Never move the wp-content directory on your production server without first testing in a development environment.

As with the wp-content and plugin directories, you can also move the uploads directory in WordPress. This directory is where WordPress stores all files uploaded through the WordPress dashboard. To set a custom location for the uploads directory, you'll use the UPLOADS constant shown here:

```
define( 'UPLOADS', 'blog/wp-content/my-filez' );
```

The uploads directory must exist within the directory containing your WordPress core files or a subdirectory within and cannot exist outside of the WordPress folder structure.

WordPress saves post revisions for each saved edit made to a post or page. Edits are saved by clicking either the Save or Publish button, and also by the built-in auto-save feature of WordPress.

Imagine if each post you create has 10 revisions. If you had 100 posts, that would be 1,000 records in your database. This can quickly increase the size of your database and may even slow down your website because table records can take longer to fetch in larger databases. Luckily, WordPress has a built-in post revisions option called WP_POST_REVISIONS. You can set this option to false to completely disable post revisions altogether, or you can specify a maximum number of revisions to keep for each post or page. Following are examples of both scenarios:

```
define( 'WP_POST_REVISIONS', false );
define( 'WP_POST_REVISIONS', 5 );
```

You can also configure the auto-save interval by setting the AUTOSAVE_INTERVAL option. WordPress uses AJAX when editing a post to auto-save revisions. By default, this interval is 60 seconds. You can set the interval in seconds for auto-save in wp-config.php. Set auto-save to 5 minutes by using this code:

```
define( 'AUTOSAVE_INTERVAL', 300 );
```

A great debugging option is SAVEQUERIES. Activating this option saves all database queries into a global array that can be displayed on your page. This can help you debug query issues, and also to see exactly what WordPress is executing on each page load. If you are working on a theme or plugin, and can't seem to get the right set of posts back, this debug option will show you exactly what WordPress is asking for out of the database. Enable this option by setting the value to true:

```
define( 'SAVEQUERIES', true );
```

To display the query array in your theme, add the following code to any theme template file to view:

```
if ( current_user_can( 'manage_options' ) ) {
   global $wpdb;
   print_r( $wpdb->queries );
}
```

The preceding code displays the saved query array only if the logged-in user has the ability to manage options, essentially locking it down so only site administrators will see the output. Themes and template files are covered in Chapter 9.

You can also enable logging directly from your wp-config.php file. To enable logging, first you need to create a php_error.log file and upload it to your root WordPress directory. Then simply turn on the log_errors PHP option and point to your logging file:

```
@ini_set( 'log_errors','On' );
@ini_set( 'display_errors','Off' );
@ini_set( 'error_log','/public_html/wordpress/php_error.log' );
```

All errors will now be logged to this file. This will also log any errors produced by enabling the WP_DEBUG option discussed earlier. In the preceding example display_errors is set to Off, which is perfect for a production website because you don't want error messages displayed. If you are debugging and want to view errors in real time, just set that option to On. Remember the error_log value is relative to the web server's document root, not the WordPress root.

You can also set the memory limit WordPress is allowed to use with the WP_MEMORY_LIMIT option. If your website hits the memory limit set for WordPress to run, you will see the error

"Allowed memory size of xxxxx bytes exhausted." Increasing the memory limit fixes this problem. The memory limit is set by defining the megabytes needed:

```
define( 'WP_MEMORY_LIMIT', '64M' );
```

Setting this option only works if your hosting company allows it. Some hosting companies will not allow you to dynamically change the memory limit and will have this value set very low. This problem is usually found on lower-cost hosting companies that maintain their price points by packing more web server instances onto a single physical host, creating contention for memory footprint.

This increases the memory only for WordPress and not other applications running on your server. To increase the memory limit across all of your websites, set the php_value memory_limit variable in your php.ini file. For example, when importing large amounts of content, say months or years worth of blog posts, it's likely you'll hit this memory limit.

One amazing feature of WordPress is the built-in localizer. WordPress displays in English by default, but can easily be set to display any language that has been translated. Setting the WPLANG option triggers WordPress to load the specified language files:

```
define ( 'WPLANG', 'en-GB' );
```

The option value shown previously comprises the ISO-639 language code followed by the ISO-3166 country code. So en-GB would be English-Great Britain. This setting will reference your .mo and .po files for language translation.

You can also define the LANGDIR option. This option defines what directory will hold your language .mo files. By default, WordPress looks in wp-content/languages for the .mo file. If you would like to move this folder, just set the LANGDIR option like so:

```
define( 'LANGDIR', '/wp-content/bury/my/languages' );
```

WordPress will now look in the new location for your .mo files.

CUSTOM_USER_TABLE and CUSTOM_USER_META_TABLE are also very powerful options. They are useful if you want to have two or more individual WordPress installs use the same user accounts. Remember to set this prior to installing WordPress.

```
define( 'CUSTOM_USER_TABLE', 'joined_users' );
define( 'CUSTOM_USER_META_TABLE', 'joined_usermeta' );
```

Setting these two options enables you to define the name of the default WordPress user and usermeta database tables. Doing this means both websites share user information including usernames, passwords, author bios, and so on. This is a great way to set up a new installation of WordPress but not lose sync with your current user accounts.

If you would like your users to have different roles on each WordPress install, but still share user accounts, don't set the CUSTOM_USER_META_TABLE option. Everything stored in the user tables will stay the same, but everything else will be blog-specific (that is, user level, first and last name, and so on).

You can set multiple cookie options such as COOKIE_DOMAIN, COOKIEPATH, and SITECOOKIEPATH. These options are typically used in a WordPress Multisite installation utilizing subdomains for websites. This allows you to set the primary domain so cookies can be created and validated on all subdomains in the network.

```
define( 'COOKIE_DOMAIN', '.domain.com' );
define( 'COOKIEPATH', '/' );
define( 'SITECOOKIEPATH', '/' );
```

Typically, you won't need to use or change this option, but if you run into issues with cookies, this is the first place to check.

Since the inclusion of the automatic installer functionality for plugins and themes, as well as the automatic update process, you can set FTP settings directly in your wp-config.php file. This is only needed if your host is not configured to support the automatic install process. This is easily detectable because each time you try to install a plugin or theme you are asked for your FTP information.

To save your FTP information in WordPress, add the following options in your wp-config.php file:

```
define( 'FTP_USER', 'username' );
define( 'FTP_PASS', 'password' );
define( 'FTP_HOST', 'ftp.example.com:21' );
```

Just enter your FTP username, password, and host with port and you're all set! WordPress will no longer ask for your FTP information when using the automatic installer.

You can set additional FTP/SSH options for various configurations:

```
// sets the filesystem method: "direct", "ssh", "ftpext", or "ftpsockets"
define( 'FS_METHOD', 'ftpext' );
// absolute path to root installation directory
define( 'FTP_BASE', '/public_html/wordpress/' );
// absolute path to wp-content directory
define( 'FTP_CONTENT_DIR', '/public_html/wordpress/wp-content/' );
// absolute path to wp-plugins directory
define( 'FTP_PLUGIN_DIR ', '/ public_html /wordpress/wp-content/plugins/' );
// absolute path to your SSH public key
define( 'FTP_PUBKEY', '/home/username/.ssh/id_rsa.pub' );
// absolute path to your SSH private key
define( 'FTP_PRIVKEY', '/home/username/.ssh/id_rsa' );
// secure FTP SSL-connection if supported by the hosting company
define( 'FTP_SSL', false );
```

You can also override default file permissions in WordPress using the FS_CHMOD_FILE and FS_CHMOD_DIR options:

```
define( 'FS_CHMOD_FILE', 0644 );
define( 'FS_CHMOD_DIR', 0755 );
```

The numeric single digit values represent the User, Group, and World permissions set for files and folders on your web server. To learn more about WordPress and file permissions visit http://codex.wordpress.org/Changing_File_Permissions.

These settings can help with certain hosting companies that use restrictive permissions for all user files. This will override the server settings and should allow WordPress updates and auto installations to work.

The WP_CACHE option is required for some caching plugins to work. Enabling this option will include the file wp-content/advanced-cache.php. To enable this option, use the following code:

```
define( 'WP_CACHE', true );
```

WordPress has numerous constant options that you can set. There is a PHP function to view all constants currently set on your installation:

```
print_r( @get_defined_constants() );
```

An advanced option is forcing SSL on login to your WordPress site. This requires users to log in via the HTTPS access link and encrypts all data being transferred to and from your website. To activate SSL on login, add the FORCE_SSL_LOGIN option like so:

```
define( 'FORCE_SSL_LOGIN', true );
```

You can also force all admin pages to use SSL. This is activated with the FORCE_SSL_ADMIN option, like so:

```
define( 'FORCE_SSL_ADMIN', true );
```

This forces all admin dashboard pages (/wp-admin) to be encrypted with SSL. Keep in mind that activating this setting slows down your admin page load times, but all data passed to and from WordPress will be encrypted using SSL. Also remember that your website must be configured to work with SSL. The quick way to test is to visit your site using https, as in https://example.com. If the page loads, SSL is set up on your server.

> **NOTE** *Forcing SSL on the admin side of WordPress is a great security enhancement. All data passed to and from WordPress will be encrypted, preventing someone from potentially stealing your WordPress login credentials.*

Since version 2.9, WordPress has featured a trash bin. This trash bin contains any posts, pages, attachments, and comments that have been deleted. This allows you to recover any content that you might have accidentally deleted in WordPress. By default, the trash bin is emptied every 30 days. Emptying the trash bin will permanently delete any items in the trash. You can modify this interval by setting the EMPTY_TRASH_DAYS option like so:

```
define( 'EMPTY_TRASH_DAYS', 7 );
```

The trash will now automatically be emptied every 7 days. You can also disable the trash completely by setting the option value to 0. The trash link will now be replaced with a Delete Permanently link. Keep in mind that WordPress will not ask for a confirmation when you click Delete Permanently.

There is also an option to disable WordPress cron. Cron is used to execute scheduled tasks in WordPress. Some common schedule tasks include posting a scheduled post and checking for new versions of WordPress, themes, and plugins. To disable WordPress cron, add this option to your wp-config.php file:

```
define( 'DISABLE_WP_CRON', true );
```

You can also define WordPress Multisite options in your `wp-config.php` file. To enable the Multisite feature of WordPress, simply add the `WP_ALLOW_MULTISITE` constant:

```
define( 'WP_ALLOW_MULTISITE', true );
```

Setting this option to `true` will expose a new submenu under Tools ➢ Network Setup. The Network Setup section of the dashboard allows you to enable and configure WordPress Multisite. You'll learn more about the Multisite feature of WordPress in Chapter 10.

This section covered a lot of common options for `wp-config.php`. There are many more, less common, options for `wp-config.php` available in WordPress. A great resource for learning about `wp-config.php` options is the Codex: `http://codex.wordpress.org/Editing_wp-config.php`.

.htaccess

The `.htaccess` file is used primarily for creating pretty permalinks and keyword injected URLs for your website. WordPress by default creates ugly query-string formed URLs, usually with an ID present, such as `http://example.com/?p=45`. These URLs are completely functional but aren't very friendly to search engines and site visitors. By enabling pretty permalinks, WordPress creates URLs based on site content, such as post and page titles, category and tag names, and dates for archives.

Enabling Permalinks

To enable permalinks, visit the Settings ➢ Permalinks screen on your WordPress Dashboard, as shown in Figure 2-3. Select any permalink structure other than Default and click the Save Changes link.

Upon saving your changes, WordPress tries to create your default `.htaccess` file. If your root WordPress directory is writable by the server, the file is created automatically. If WordPress is unable to create the `.htaccess` file, you will see instructions on how to manually create the file, as shown in Figure 2-4.

Setting a permalink structure using the month and year like this:

```
/%year%/%monthnum%/%postname%/
```

creates a permalink like this:

```
http://example.com/2015/10/happy-halloween/
```

Using permalinks offers many advantages, such as:

➢ **Search Engine Optimization (SEO)**—Keywords in your URL can give your website a big SEO boost. Search engines will use these keywords in their algorithm for positioning in their search results.

➢ **Forward compatibility**—Regardless of what platform your website uses (WordPress, Drupal, Joomla!), having a solid permalink structure can be easily replicated should you ever migrate.

➢ **Usability**—Visitor-unfriendly ID URLs make it equally unpleasant to share a link with a friend. It's difficult to differentiate the content between your ID-driven URLs.

➢ **Sharing**—In this Internet era of social networking, sharing is a natural extension of your online presence. Keywords in the URL would make finding your link extremely easy and convey an immediate context for the content.

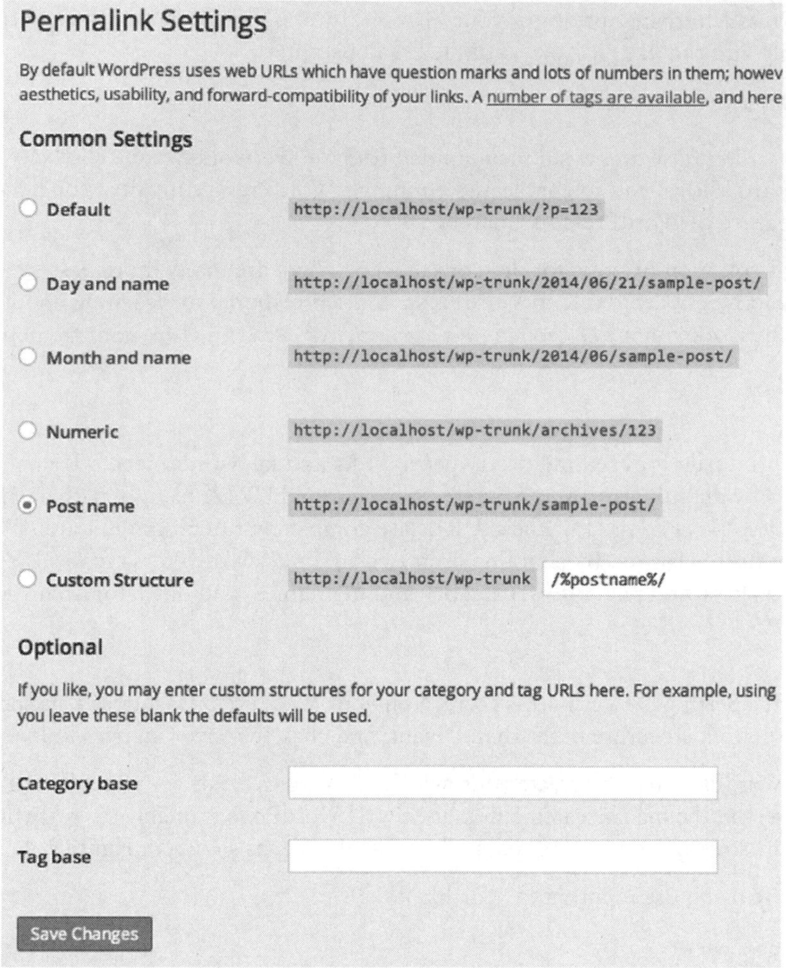

Permalink Settings

By default WordPress uses web URLs which have question marks and lots of numbers in them; howev aesthetics, usability, and forward-compatibility of your links. A number of tags are available, and here

Common Settings

○ **Default**   `http://localhost/wp-trunk/?p=123`

○ **Day and name**   `http://localhost/wp-trunk/2014/06/21/sample-post/`

○ **Month and name**   `http://localhost/wp-trunk/2014/06/sample-post/`

○ **Numeric**   `http://localhost/wp-trunk/archives/123`

◉ **Post name**   `http://localhost/wp-trunk/sample-post/`

○ **Custom Structure**   `http://localhost/wp-trunk` `/%postname%/`

Optional

If you like, you may enter custom structures for your category and tag URLs here. For example, using you leave these blank the defaults will be used.

Category base   [   ]

Tag base   [   ]

[Save Changes]

FIGURE 2-3:   Enabling permalinks in WordPress

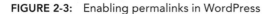

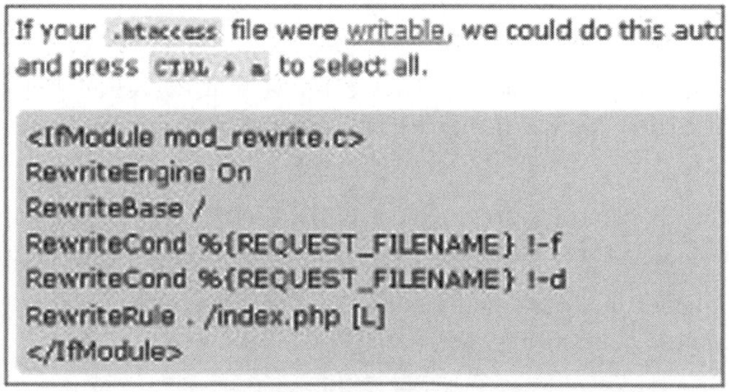

If your `.htaccess` file were writable, we could do this aut and press `CTRL + A` to select all.

```
<IfModule mod_rewrite.c>
RewriteEngine On
RewriteBase /
RewriteCond %{REQUEST_FILENAME} !-f
RewriteCond %{REQUEST_FILENAME} !-d
RewriteRule . /index.php [L]
</IfModule>
```

FIGURE 2-4:   Manual info for creating the .htaccess file

By default, pretty permalinks are controlled by the `mod_rewrite` Apache module. If your web server does not support `mod_rewrite`, or pretty permalinks, WordPress will use standard querystring based URLs like `http://example.com/?p=3416`.

.htaccess Rewriting Rules

Usually a web server takes a URL that references a file in the server's document filesystem, loads that file, and processes the content in it to generate HTML sent back to the user's browser. For WordPress files such as `wp-login.php`, that's exactly how the login screen is generated. When presented with a pretty permalink such as `example.com/2015/travel/haddonfield/`, the web server just needs to load the main loop of WordPress so that the core code can parse the URL and turn it into a database query that finds a post with the title Haddonfield in the category Travel. Unlike a static website where you would have created a file with that name, WordPress stores its content in a database—only a few files are loaded directly.

The "secret sauce" behind the WordPress permalink mechanism is summarized in three rewriting rules added to the `.htaccess` file when you enable permalinks:

```
RewriteCond %{REQUEST_FILENAME} !-f
RewriteCond %{REQUEST_FILENAME} !-d
RewriteRule . /index.php [ L]
```

Quite simply, these rules check the URL used to access your site to see if it refers to an existing file or directory in the filesystem hierarchy. The `!-f` and `!-d` notations are negations; `.htaccess` is ensuring that the URL does not refer to any valid file or directory pathname. If the URL does, in fact, match a valid file—for example, a WordPress administrative function such as `wp-login.php`—then no rewriting is done and the web server tries loading that file (to execute the PHP code contained within). If there's no file or directory at the path specified by the supplied URL, then the incoming URL is rewritten to `index.php`, invoking the core of the WordPress system. You'll dig into the steps used to convert a URL string into a MySQL query in a bit more detail as a preface to the discussion of the content display loop in Chapter 5.

> **NOTE** *The simple check for whether a file or directory exists can have unintended side effects if you put non-WordPress web server content in the same directory structure as the WordPress code. For example, consider a directory of images as a peer directory of* `wp-content`: `example.com/wp-content` *and* `example.com/images`. *You might choose to bypass the WordPress media library because those images are managed by their own set of ingest processes. What happens when a user forms a URL with a mistyped image name that points to a nonexistent file? The* `.htaccess` *rewriting rule will fire because there is no file with that name, and the WordPress core will be started. A user expecting to see an image will instead get the default WordPress site content when they should have received a 404 error for a nonexistent URL target. If you are going to add directories around your WordPress installation, either place WordPress in its own subdirectory (*`example.com/wordpress`*) or add a rewrite rule to* `.htaccess`

continues

continued

> *that recognizes your added peer directories and immediately hands those URLs off to the web server:*
>
> ```
> RewriteRule  ^images/(.*)  images/$1 [L]
> ```
>
> *This rule effectively says, "Take any URL that starts with the component* images, *and pass it off to the web server." The [L] directive means "stop processing after matching this rule," and the rewrite itself simply echoes back what it was passed. If you're going to have a few directories sitting in parallel with the WordPress installation, you'll need one rewrite rule for each.*

The .htaccess file can also manage URL redirects. If you change your About page from http://example.com/about to http://example.com/about-me, anyone who visits your original URL will hit a 404 page. A URL redirect will redirect from the old URL to the new URL so your visitors won't get lost. This also alerts search engines about the new URL so they can update their index.

Following is an example of a 301 permanent redirect to a static page:

```
redirect 301 /about http://example.com/about-me
```

WordPress does some additional rewriting and cleanup of URLs to improve search engine results, as you'll see in Chapter 5.

Configuration Control Through .htaccess

The .htaccess file is very powerful and can control more than just URL structure. For instance, you can control PHP configuration options using the .htaccess file. To increase the memory allotted to PHP use this command:

```
php_value memory_limit 64M
```

This increases the memory limit in PHP to 64MB. You can also increase the max file size upload and post size:

```
php_value upload_max_filesize 20M
php_value post_max_size 20M
```

Now the maximum file size you can post from a form and upload is set to 20MB. Most hosting companies set these values to around 2MB by default so these are settings that will be used often for larger file uploads. Not all hosting companies will allow these values to be set in your .htaccess file, and they could create an error on your website if that is the case.

The .htaccess file can also be used for security purposes. Using .htaccess allows you to restrict access to your website by IP address, essentially locking it down from anonymous visitors. To lock down your website by IP addresses, add the following code to your .htaccess file:

```
AuthUserFile /dev/null
AuthGroupFile /dev/null
AuthName "Access Control"
```

```
AuthType Basic
order deny,allow
deny from all
#IP address to whitelist
allow from xxx.xxx.xxx.xxx
```

Replace xxx.xxx.xxx.xxx with any IP address that you want to grant access to your website. You can have multiple allow from lines so add as many IP addresses as you need. This allows access to your website only if you are using an IP address defined here.

A more widely used option is to lock down your wp-admin directory. This means that only IP addresses you specify can access your admin dashboard URLs. This makes it much harder for anyone else to try to hack your WordPress back end. To accomplish this, create a separate .htaccess file in your wp-admin directory with the preceding code.

Remember that most ISPs assign client addresses dynamically so the IP address of the computer you are using will change on occasion. If you get locked out, just update your .htaccess file with your new IP address or delete the file altogether. This is not a good tip if you allow open registrations on your website because you need to allow your users access to the wp-admin directory.

You can also allow wildcard IP addresses. For example, 123.123.123.* would allow access to anyone who matches the first three IP address octets, with the final digit being a wildcard. You can also allow a range of IP addresses. For example 123.123.123.110-230 would allow anyone with an IP address between 123.123.123.110 and 123.123.123.230.

You can also enable error logging from the .htaccess file. The first step is to create a php-errors .log file in your WordPress root directory. Then add the following code to your .htaccess file to enable error logging:

```
php_flag display_startup_errors off
php_flag display_errors off
php_flag html_errors off
php_flag log_errors on
php_value error_log /public_html/php-errors.log
```

This enables error logging but suppresses any error messages from displaying. Again this is a perfect setup for a production environment because you don't want errors publicly displayed.

The .maintenance File

WordPress has a built-in maintenance mode that can be enabled by the .maintenance file. The .maintenance file is used by WordPress during the auto-update process. This prevents visitors from seeing any error messages as WordPress core files are updated. To test this feature, simply create a new .maintenance file and add the following line of code:

```
<?php $upgrading = time(); ?>
```

Add this file to your WordPress root directory and your website will instantly enter maintenance mode. This locks down your website for all visitors and displays a generic maintenance message "Briefly unavailable for scheduled maintenance. Check back in a minute." The time() function can be replaced with any UNIX-formatted timestamp.

You can set a custom maintenance page by creating a `maintenance.php` file and placing it in your `wp-content` directory. WordPress uses this file to display during any forced maintenance periods that you set. This allows you to create a custom maintenance notice to your website visitors.

This file is also used by the WordPress automatic update process. A `.maintenance` file is created right before WordPress installs the new core files during an update. This ensures there are never any error messages for your visitors during this process.

WP-CONTENT USER PLAYGROUND

The `wp-content` directory stores just about every file for customizing WordPress. This directory stores your plugins, themes, uploaded media, and additional files to extend WordPress in any way imaginable.

The `wp-content` directory has a single PHP file, `index.php`. The contents of this file are shown here:

```php
<?php
// Silence is golden.
```

So what's the point of this file? Actually this is a very important file. The `index.php` file blocks anyone from viewing a directory listing of your `wp-content` folder. If the `index.php` file didn't exist, and your web server allowed directory listings, visiting `http://example.com/wp-content/` would display all of the files and folders in that directory. This can help hackers gain access to key files that might help exploit your website; for example if a vulnerability were discovered in a plugin, being able to view the list of directories in the WordPress plugin directory would quickly and easily inform an attacker if your site was a viable target.

If you are manually updating WordPress, make sure you avoid overwriting your `wp-content` directory.

Plugins

Plugins are stored in the `wp-content/plugins` directory. A plugin can be a single file or multiple files inside of a folder. Any files inside the `/plugins` directory are scanned by WordPress to determine if the file is a properly formatted WordPress plugin. If the file is determined to be a plugin, it appears under the Plugins ➤ Installed Plugins screen on your admin dashboard ready to be activated.

> **NOTE** *Remember that to automatically deactivate a plugin, you can remove it from your `/plugins` folder. If an active plugin's files are missing, WordPress deactivates the plugin before trying to load the missing plugin code.*

Your `wp-content` directory might also include a `/mu-plugins` directory. Must-use (mu) plugins are plugins that are automatically enabled in WordPress. Any plugins that exist in this folder will be executed just like a standard activated plugin. The major difference is mu-plugins cannot exist in a subdirectory or they will be ignored. To learn more about mu-plugins visit http://codex.wordpress.org/Must_Use_Plugins.

You'll be revisiting plugins in Chapter 8.

Themes

Themes are stored in the wp-content/themes directory. Each theme must exist in its own subdirectory and must consist of the proper template files for WordPress to recognize it as a usable theme. At a minimum, an index.php and a style.css file must exist in the theme directory, along with proper tagging to display under the Appearance ➤ Themes screen on your admin dashboard.

WordPress can store as many themes in this directory as your server allows. You can easily view a preview of any theme, or activate a new theme, under the Appearance ➤ Themes screen. Chapter 9 covers themes in much more detail.

Uploads and Media Directory

WordPress stores uploaded media in the wp-content/uploads folder. This directory does not exist in a default installation of WordPress. The /uploads directory is created the first time you successfully upload a file to WordPress.

By default, WordPress stores uploads in month- and year-based folders. So your uploaded image would be stored like so:

```
/wp-content/uploads/2015/06/image.png
```

Before you can upload any images or files in WordPress, you need to set the /wp-content directory to be writable. When you upload your first image, WordPress auto-creates the /uploads directory and any needed subdirectories. After you have successfully uploaded your first image, reset the /wp-content permissions to not be writable, typically 755. Currently, there is no way to import images uploaded via FTP into the WordPress Media Library. If making the uploads directory writeable is not an option, there are plugins available (such as NextGen Gallery, described in detail in the Custom Directories section that follows) that include this functionality.

WordPress Multisite stores uploaded media in a different manner. Instead of one uploads directory, Multisite creates a sites directory inside the standard uploads directory. Inside this folder are multiple subdirectories named with a numerical ID. This ID is the blog ID the folder is attached to. Every site in a Multisite network has a unique blog ID. Chapter 10 covers this in more detail. For example, your second WordPress Multisite site upload directory would look like this:

```
/uploads/sites/2/files/
```

This helps keep individual site uploads separated and easier to maintain.

Upgrade Directory

The wp-content/upgrade directory is automatically created by WordPress when you use the automatic update process. This folder is used by WordPress to store the new version of WordPress that is downloaded from WordPress.org. The compressed WordPress download is extracted in this folder prior to the update. This folder should remain untouched for automatic updates to process successfully. If this directory is deleted, WordPress re-creates it the next time you run the auto-updater.

Custom Directories

Some plugins that require a lot of custom files will store those files in a directory in your wp-content folders.

The W3 Total Cache plugin (https://wordpress.org/plugins/w3-total-cache/) creates a /wp-content/cache directory to store all of the cached pages created for your website. A cached page is simply a fully generated page on your website saved as a static HTML file. Instead of generating the page each time a user clicks one of your links, the cache plugin serves up the static HTML file to the visitor. This dramatically decreases WordPress load times and increases performance because pages aren't generated on each view, but rather only when the cache is regenerated based on your settings.

The W3 Total Cache plugin also adds one file to your wp-content directory: advanced-cache.php. This file is required for W3 Total Cache to function correctly. When W3 Total Cache is activated, it tries to create this file. If it fails, a notice appears alerting you of this. The file exists in the W3 Total Cache plugin directory and can be manually moved to the wp-content directory.

The most popular image gallery plugin, NextGen Gallery (http://wordpress.org/extend/plugins/nextgen-gallery/), creates a /wp-content/gallery directory to store all of the images uploaded to your NextGen image galleries. Each gallery created is a subdirectory under /gallery. This helps keep your gallery image files very organized and easy to work with.

The WP-DB Backup plugin (http://wordpress.org/extend/plugins/wp-db-backup/) creates a /wp-content/backup-b158b folder (where b158b is a random string) to store local backups of your database. When you select the Save to Server option, all database backup files will be stored in this directory. It's important to not delete your backups unless you are sure they are not needed anymore.

SUMMARY

This chapter covered downloading WordPress. It also covered configuring key WordPress core files, wp-config.php and .htaccess, along with more advanced configurations for each. You also reviewed the wp-content directory and how WordPress interacts with custom directories.

With that structural and configuration view of WordPress, it's time to learn how to create a local development environment so that you can begin customization and development without impacting a public website.

3

Working with WordPress Locally

WHAT'S IN THIS CHAPTER?

➤ Developing locally

➤ Getting started with a local development environment

➤ Configuring a local development environment—tips and tricks

➤ Moving your local project to production

Now that you know how to obtain WordPress as well as what the basic lay of the land looks like, let's take a look at how to get started doing something with WordPress, something beyond simply using WordPress as a website engine. Any user can install WordPress and use it to power a website, as you saw in Chapter 1, which is one of the reasons why WordPress has been so successful.

As a developer, however, you need a full-featured but sandboxed place to experiment, try out new ideas, and figure out what has failed, without taking down a production or public site. As the first step in building something, to take WordPress to the next step in your own projects, let's look at the benefits of setting up a local development environment on your workstation or laptop. This chapter starts with a brief swing outside the realm of WordPress to talk about general software development.

BENEFITS OF WORKING LOCALLY

Developing locally is considered a best practice. In general, you do not want to be actively developing on a live production website because you could have visitors accessing the site at any time and development involves iterations of breaking code and making it work again. This is not the experience you want to provide to your visitors.

What is "developing locally?" In short, it means you have a full WordPress installation to which you can make changes, add new code, and fail with impunity. It is a sandbox, and it is the first element in a successful deployment cycle.

Typical Deployment Cycle

Before diving into the reasons to develop locally first, let's explain the different phases of deployment. Deployment involves taking your code from the base development versions that you feel are now ready for the world through staging and testing to a production website. In general, there are three levels. Some workflows will have more, but these three steps are the essentials: development, staging, and production. This is a basic software development workflow and applies to more than just WordPress development.

First is the development environment, where you do all of your day-to-day work. As you will see in this chapter, this is typically your local workstation or laptop, but in some scenarios it might be a development location on a remote server. While it is best practice to develop your solution on a platform that is the same type of system as the production environment, this is not always practical. For example, your production web servers are high-end server class hardware running Linux, but because your developers need access to corporate resources such as Microsoft Exchange, they run Windows workstations for development.

This is why the second tier is introduced, which is the staging or testing environment. After the developer has tested his solution on his development environment, he prepares to deploy it on a staging server. The intention of the staging server is to bridge the gap between the development environment and the target production environment without the risk of breaking the live website. As you will see later in this chapter, there are variances you have to consider when developing cross-platform code—that is, code that can run on Windows, Mac OS X, or Linux. This staging environment gives the developer an opportunity to make sure his code will run on a server that is similar to the production server. For WordPress development, this staging environment could be a secret test site on your production server.

Finally, if the solution behaves as expected on the staging server, it can then be deployed to the live production server. The production server or servers are the ones that serve the website to the Internet. Using this three-tier workflow, developers are able to capitalize on the benefits of local development.

As explained, this is a very traditional, tried-and-true approach. The recent adoption of virtual machines for desktop development has changed this approach for some development environments. We will take a look at how to use VMs as your development platform later in this chapter.

Why So Much Process?

Now that you have a basic understanding of the workflow, let's circle back to why a developer should take these extra steps on the path to code deployment. While multiple phases seem at odds with a "get code working quickly" mantra, the benefits outweigh the overhead.

First, as explained earlier, developing locally allows the developer to test and try things without breaking the live website. Truly, this can be one of the most important aspects of this system. Once your website has grown beyond the hobbyist audience, you want to minimize downtime. Developers should not be trying things on the live website.

The second benefit is privacy. Developing locally means your project is only available on your local workstation, or sometimes your local area network. You are in control of who is able to access it. If you are developing on a public web server, however, while there are ways to restrict access, your potential audience is global.

This privacy gives you the opportunity to try things and play around. Think of it as your own private WordPress sandbox with no one watching. For example, you might want to try the Ninja Warrior obstacle course or even the Wipeout obstacle course, but you do not want a global audience while you try to figure it out. There is no shame in attempting something and failing, but when working on a project, you probably do not want it to be globally accessible while still in the development phase. While in development, your project could have security issues that have not been addressed yet and putting those on a production server puts the server at risk.

Developing locally can save time and is often one of the biggest boosts to productivity. When working locally, you do not need a connection to the Internet to test your code. Your project is self-contained on your workstation. This also means you do not have to push your files to a remote server to test them. You simply need to save your edits and refresh your browser. The time waiting for FTP connections can add up.

If you are developing a new theme, you can test your theme using different sets of content. For example, you may be building a custom theme for a specific project with an initial set of content, but you want to ensure that, in the future, new content added to the site is properly styled. Or you want to release your theme to the WordPress repository. While developing your theme on your local workstation, you can use different content than what is on the live site to make sure every element is formatted how you expect. This is part of the privacy of developing locally. Just because the initial website will have a certain content set for launch does not mean your local version must have the exact same content. This concept is covered in greater detail later in this chapter.

Locally, you can run multiple instances of WordPress. Furthermore, each instance can be a different version of WordPress. This allows you to track changes to the core WordPress and make sure your code will continue to run on future revisions. For example, you can test your theme or plugin on one local site that is running the current stable version of WordPress, but you can also have a second WordPress site on your workstation that is running the beta version of the next release, or tracking the nightly development release. This helps you keep on top of changes to the WordPress core that might affect your project.

There are many benefits and reasons to develop locally. In addition, for individual developers, there may be other reasons in addition to the privacy, security, and flexibility benefits outlined here. Every developer will have to do his own cost benefit analysis for each reason and determine if the risk or extra steps are worth the effort. At the end of this chapter, we touch on some of the ongoing challenges with developing locally and moving your project through the development and deployment workflow.

It is remarkably easy to set up a local WordPress development environment, using freely available tools that manage the major underlying components of the WordPress system: the web server with a PHP interpreter and the MySQL database.

TOOLS FOR COMPONENT ADMINISTRATION

Think about the prerequisites for WordPress, and then make a shopping list of the components you need for WordPress. WordPress is a web application. That means you need a web server. WordPress runs on PHP, a programming language for the web. That means your web server must support PHP. Apache is a good (and very popular) general-purpose web server that supports PHP, although there are many others that will work as well, including Microsoft IIS or Nginx. With WordPress version 4.1, the minimum version of PHP that is required is version 5.2.4. Ideally, you would like a web server that supports URL rewriting to make your permalinks work. Apache has a module called mod _ rewrite to make this work.

WordPress also needs a database to store the content of the site. WordPress only supports MySQL for the database and, as of version 3.2, the MySQL version must be 5.0 or greater. In addition, your PHP must have the appropriate MySQL libraries to make the database connection. Finally, you will also want a client to manage your database.

Getting Your Development Stack

This sounds like a confusing and daunting list. But while many of us think of WordPress as the platform that you build your projects on, WordPress is, in turn, built on a platform. Commonly called the LAMP (Linux, Apache, MySQL, and PHP) stack, it has been the foundation for many Internet projects, including Facebook. And it is also the same foundation needed for WordPress. This means that the WordPress community is not the only one that has these requirements.

As previously mentioned, this foundation is commonly called LAMP where the L stands for Linux. If you are running Linux as your workstation operating system, you can install the LAMP stack using your Linux distribution's package management system. For example, if you are on a Debian or Debian derivative you could run apt-get install apache to install the Apache web server. A common trick is to install PHPMyAdmin as the MySQL client—that is, run apt-get install phpmyadmin. PHPMyAdmin is a web application that requires Apache, PHP, and MySQL, and because it is the MySQL client, it will install the appropriate libraries to connect PHP and MySQL.

More than likely, you are not running Linux as your desktop operating system. You can install each component individually and connect all the moving parts for it to work. That would be the hard way. Luckily for us, there are some industrious people who have put together several packages that make installing and configuring this LAMP foundation easy, and these packages exist for the various operating systems.

If you are running Mac OS X, you can use the MAMP installer. We hope you can put together that this stands for Macintosh, Apache, MySQL, and PHP. You can download MAMP from http://www.mamp.info.

Download MAMP, unpack it, and install it as you would any other Mac application. Once you drop it in your Applications folder, you can start MAMP and open your control panel. This is the control panel that controls the whole MAMP foundation, including your settings. One thing that we do not like about MAMP is that it does not use the default port for Apache. The standard for web servers to answer and respond is port 80, and browsers know this, which is why you never see an 80 in your browser's address bar. MAMP, however, defaults to port 8888. That means that when you try to access your local web server, you will have to browse to `http://localhost:8888` with your browser. Just keep that in mind as the examples in this book will be treated as though they are running on the standard port 80.

If you are running a Windows workstation, you have a couple of options. Notably, there are WAMP and XAMPP. WAMP is Windows-specific and available from `http://wampserver.com`. WAMP, obviously, stands for Windows, Apache, MySQL, and PHP. XAMPP runs on Windows but is also cross-platform and is available from `http://www.apachefriends.org`. The X in XAMPP stands for cross-platform and the extra P is included because XAMPP includes PERL, another programming language. They are both good options.

Download and install WAMP as you would any other Windows application. Once it is installed, you will have a new Windows system tray icon for WAMPSERVER that functions as your control panel.

Note that this foundation is actually several different applications working together in unison to provide you with a web development platform that happens to power WordPress. These WAMP and MAMP installers are purely automating the wiring of these packages together for a general-purpose use. Each individual application also has individual configuration files that you can adjust to meet your needs. Some common configuration changes are covered later in this chapter.

Adding WordPress to the Local Install

Now that you have a working foundation, you need to install WordPress. You will want to stop and consider how you intend on using this local development environment. Do you need only one installation of WordPress? If you want more than one, are you going to use subfolders or set up individual websites using virtual hosts? Are you going to use WordPress Multisite functionality for multiple sites? The next section discusses some of these options, but for now, take the simple route and set up one WordPress site.

To install WordPress, you can use the same source code control method using Git or Subversion, as shown in Chapter 2. Or you can use the traditional method of downloading the installation files from `http://wordpress.org`.

Either way, once you have the WordPress core files you will need to put them in your web server's document root. For MAMP, this is set up under the MAMP control panel ➤ Preferences ➤ Apache. You can accept the default or set this document root to wherever you would like. Commonly, Mac users put the document root in the Sites folder of their Mac.

The WAMP document root defaults to `c:\wamp\www`. You can quickly access this folder using the `www directory` option from the WAMPSERVER start tray option.

Copy your WordPress core files to the appropriate document root folder on your workstation.

Now open a web browser and browse to `http://localhost`. Do not forget that if your local web browser is not on the standard port, you may need to add that to the address bar. Also, if you copied WordPress into a subfolder of the document root, you may need to add that suffix to the URL—for example, `http://localhost/ddamstra/Documents/www`.

If your web and database servers are configured correctly, WordPress will create its databases and edit configuration files, and you should see the first page of the WordPress installation where you select your preferred language. Continuing on you will begin the WordPress installation as shown in Figure 3-1.

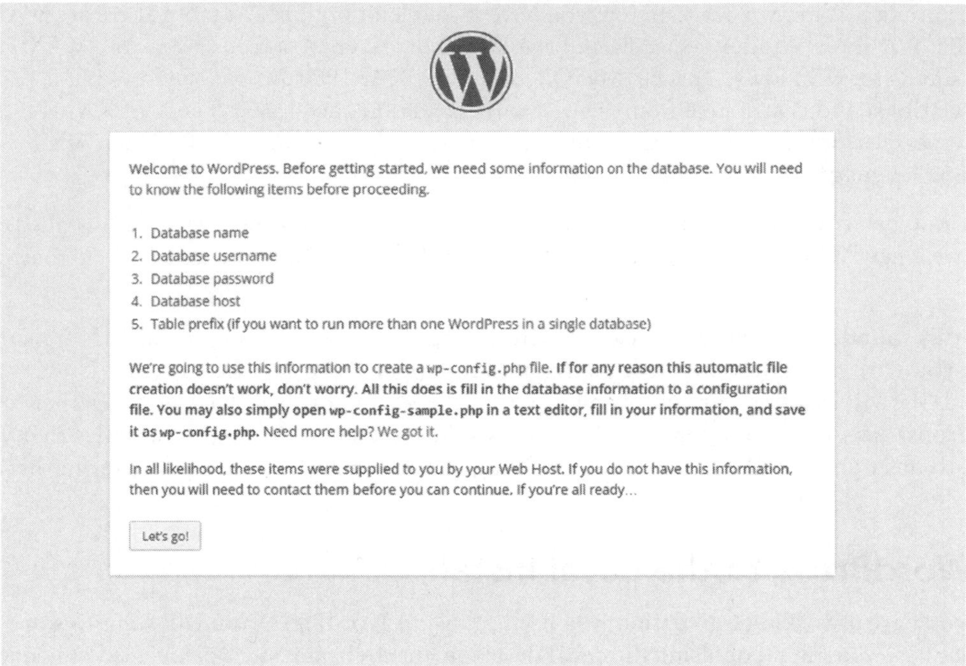

FIGURE 3-1: WordPress installation

As with any WordPress installation, you will need to have your database and database access credentials set up. Both WAMP and MAMP come with PHPMyAdmin to manage the MySQL. Use the WAMP or MAMP control panel to access PHPMyAdmin and set these up.

Finally, do the infamous five-minute WordPress install, as covered in Chapter 1.

If you have problems with getting your local development environment working, seek assistance through the appropriate support communities and documentation. While they are designed to be simple installations of the various components, every workstation is different and managing the configuration of these assorted moving parts is outside the scope of this book, and only tangentially WordPress-related.

CONFIGURATION DETAILS

The previous section walked you through how to set up a local development environment. While that section did not include an in-depth discussion, the basic idea is there. This section is about extending that environment and covers some tips to help you get the most out of working locally. Again, some of these pointers are about the LAMP foundation itself.

Here you will dig into configuration options in more detail. This section walks you through managing the filesystem tree seen by the web server, enabling debug data, and creating virtual server names.

Managing the Web Server Document Tree

In the previous section, you accepted the default document root for Apache. However, for various reasons, that may not be the best spot for your workflow or backup systems.

For example, in your development shop with multiple web developers, you may remap your Apache document root to c:\www. This way, everyone's document roots are all identical and it is a top-level folder that is easily accessible. Conversely, on your personal laptop, you may remap your document root to C:\Users\ddamstra\Documents\www because the Documents folder is backed up when connected to your home local area network.

Use caution when making changes to the configuration. As mentioned many times, there are multiple moving parts involved and throwing one part out of alignment can have significant consequences. MAMP allows you to change your document root through the control panel. With WAMP, you edit the configuration file for Apache. This file is called httpd.conf and can be found in your WAMPSERVER control panel under the Apache flyout.

Change the line that reads document root to indicate your chosen location, as shown in Figure 3-2.

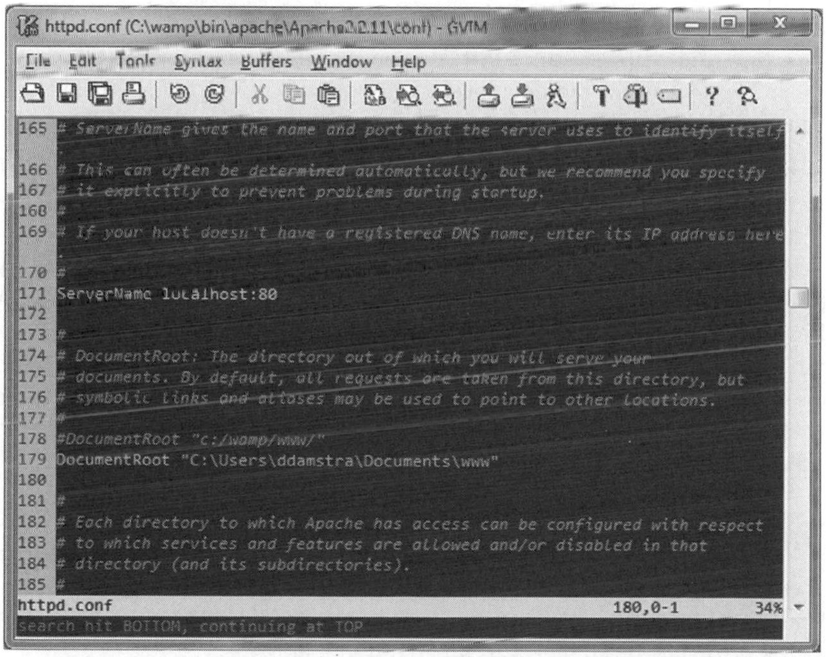

FIGURE 3-2: Apache document root

You will also need to change the Directory directive to match, as shown in Figure 3-3.

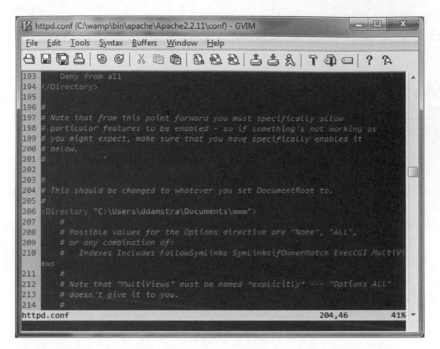

FIGURE 3-3: Apache Directory directive

Using the WAMP control panel, you will need to restart Apache (or all services) for this change to take effect. If you previously had files in the old document root, you will need to move them to the new document root for them to be accessible.

Take a moment to contemplate what you are publishing in your document root. You do not want to publish any private or confidential data. Consider which source code control system you are going to use. Is your source code control system also part of your deployment strategy? Make sure that if you are using a public repository such as GitHub that you do not push your `wp-config.php` file and expose your passwords. Likewise, if your development environment is accessible on your local area network, ensure you are not checking in configuration files with sensitive information. Some source code control systems, notably Subversion, store revisions in plain text in files in your project folder, potentially exposing credentials. This has happened to us on more than one internal penetration test exercise and the following is now part of our standard Apache configuration. You can configure your Apache to not serve these `.svn` directories by adding the lines shown in Figure 3-4 to your `httpd.conf` file.

Enabling Debug Information

When developing locally, you want to address as many potential errors and warnings as possible. At the very least, you need to be aware of them. For development, you should set your PHP error condition as high as possible to show these errors to you so that you can attend to them.

As discussed in Chapter 13, this is the exact opposite of what you want to do on your production server. On your production server, you want to hide all the errors from your visitors. On your local workstation, you are the only visitor, so you want to see them all since the errors are what you are working on.

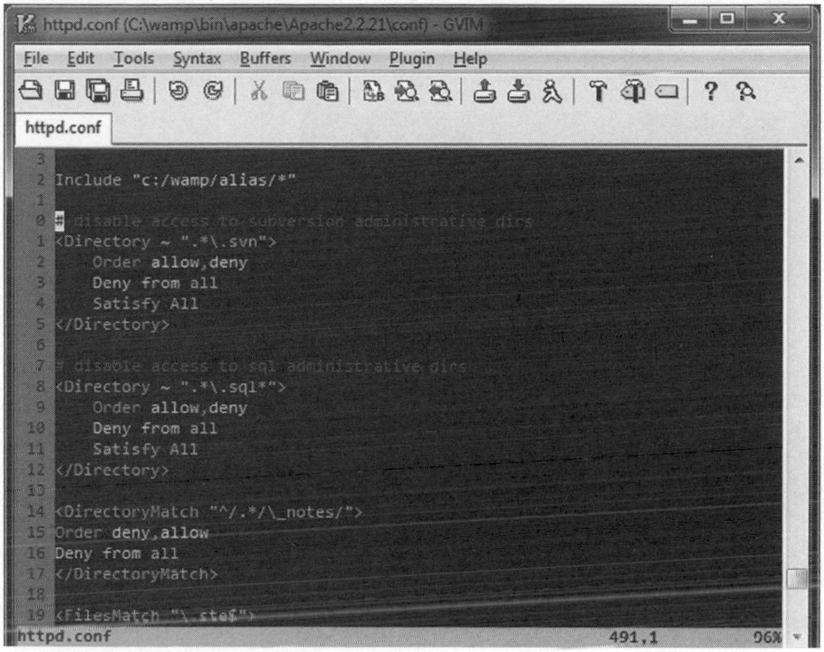

FIGURE 3-4: Apache block .svn files

You set your PHP error level in the `php.ini` file. With WAMP, you can access this file through the WAMP control panel, under the PHP flyout. Set your error reporting directive to be `E_ALL` and `E_STRICT`, as shown in Figure 3-5.

Until PHP version 5.4, the strict warnings and notices have not been included in the `E_ALL` level. By setting the error reporting directive as mentioned, you will ensure that you are seeing the most error reporting possible, and coding to reduce these notices will ensure that you are providing the most PHP interoperability. Again, you will need to restart Apache to make this setting take effect.

As previously mentioned, when developing on one operating system and deploying on another, you have to consider that not all systems have the same PHP API. For example, the `PHP $_SERVER[]` has values on Windows machines that are not on Linux machines. Windows is not case sensitive in the filesystem but Linux is. Developers have to remember that the target system may not be their development system. This is why you want the staging server to match the production server, so that discrepancies can be caught before being deployed.

When developing locally, enable WordPress debugging. Similar to the PHP error reporting, this allows the developer to see and address WordPress issues. Likewise, this should always be disabled on production websites.

Enable WordPress debugging by editing your `wp-config.php` file and setting `WP_DEBUG` to true, as shown in Figure 3-6. Unlike the previous Apache and PHP settings, which were global to all sites on your workstation, this setting is per WordPress installation.

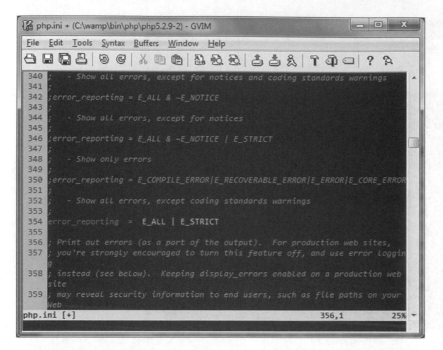

FIGURE 3-5: PHP error level

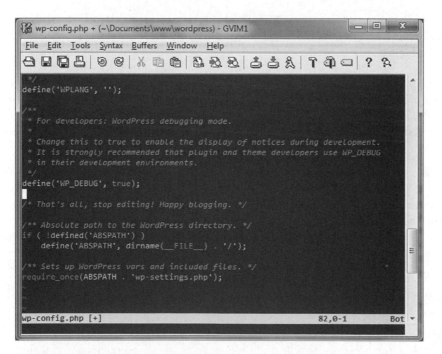

FIGURE 3-6: WordPress debug

Handling Local and Production Database

Out of the box, WordPress has configuration for one database. When working locally, you want your development site to connect to your local MySQL so you do not risk messing up the production database. Fundamentally, that is one of the reasons you are doing this.

A common method is to set the database host to be `localhost` and set your MySQL credentials and table name locally to the same as the production site. This is bad for security.

Mark Jaquith offers an alternative solution that allows for both a production and a local workstation set of database access credentials on his site at `http://markjaquith.wordpress .com/2011/06/24/wordpress-local-dev-tips/`. Essentially, he changes the `wp-config.php` file to look for an overriding set of credentials that exist on his development machine only. He then ignores this `wp-config-local.php` file in his source code control so that each developer can have his or her own controlled local credentials and so that this file never makes it to production.

Creating Virtual Local Server Names

Initially, you set up WordPress in the document root of your local Apache. If you wanted more than one local website, you could set each website in its own folder. This works and you could use it for many development sites. However, you can also set up each web server to respond to a local "fake" domain name. Sometimes, when moving to production, using this method makes the conversion from development to production easier. We address a migration method at greater length in Chapter 11.

Here is how it works using some networking magic. Everyone is familiar with the common top-level domain names, such as .com, .net, and .org, but there are, in fact, many more with even more on the horizon. These fully qualified domain names work through the DNS system where web browsers ask these Internet-accessible DNS servers for the IP address of the website domain you typed in.

However, your web browser uses the DNS resolver to check a local file first to see if there is predefined mapping. This file is called the *hosts file*. You can use this file and matching Apache configurations to make your workstation access local sites with fake fully qualified domain names.

There are a couple of approaches to this. Some developers set the domain name of the actual site they are working on to be their local workstation instead, pre-empting DNS requests. That means that until they revert these changes, they cannot access the live site, and all requests will go to the local site. For example, instead of having requests for `mirmillo.com` go to the server's publicly accessible IP address, these requests are intercepted and are redirected to the `localhost` IP address, which is always 127.0.0.1.

The other option is to set the development site with a fake name that is easy to replace in SQL during the deployment phase. In this case, we set the local development site to be `mirmillo.local`, which is an invalid top-level domain name (for now). This way, we can access `mirmillo.com` through traditional DNS and still work on our local development version by accessing `mirmillo.local` in our web browser. This is the example you are going to follow in this book.

First, you have to set up your Apache to support virtual hosts. The actual configuration here is going to vary depending on your Apache installation. Using WAMP, the first step was to set up a virtual host in Apache. This is done by editing the `httpd-vhosts.conf` file found in `C:\wamp\bin\apache\Apache2.2.11\conf\extra`. The default example comes with two sample virtual hosts. Change one of the existing examples to become your `localhost` virtual host. Then change the second example to match the settings you need for your local installation, such as `mirmillo.local`, as shown in Figure 3-7.

FIGURE 3-7: mirmillo.local virtual host

Next, you have to direct Apache to include this file. This is done by editing your `httpd.conf` file as you have done previously in this chapter. As shown in Figure 3-8, uncomment the line to include the virtual host configurations settings.

Next, edit your `hosts` file. On Mac OS X, this file is found in `/private/etc/hosts` and Linux has this file at `/etc/hosts`. On Windows, this file is `C:\Windows\System32\drivers\etc`. In short, this file is made up of IP address and domain name pairings. As shown in Figure 3-9, you can add a new mapping for `mirmillo.local`.

Finally, restart Apache and browse to `http://mirmillo.local` to complete the WordPress installation, as you did in Chapter 1.

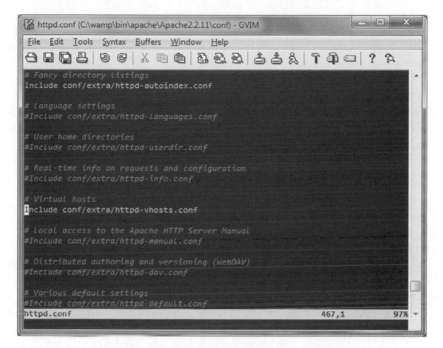

FIGURE 3-8: Apache includes virtual host config

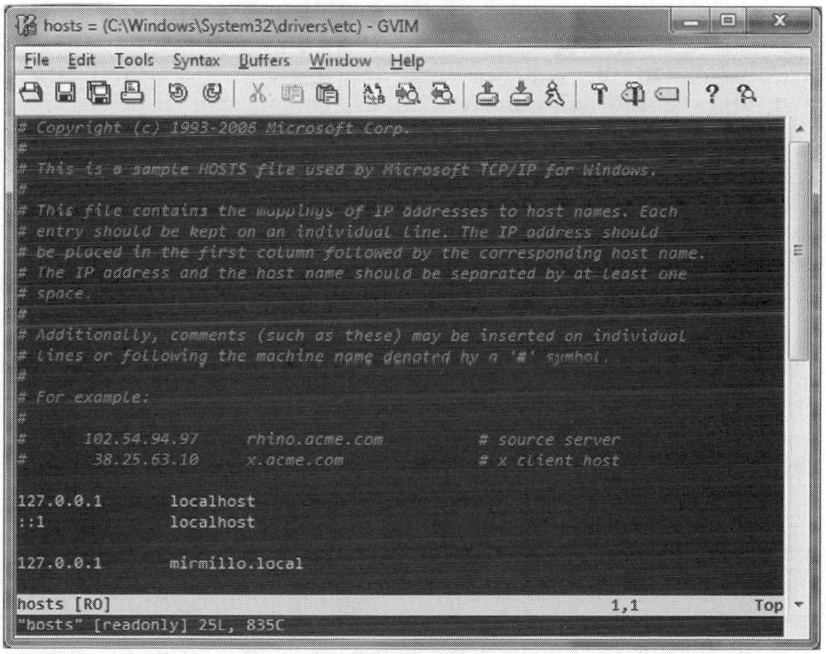

FIGURE 3-9: Hosts file mapping for virtual host

Local Theme and Plugin Development

If you are developing a theme, one of the benefits of developing locally is that you do not have to use the content that will be on the live site. In fact, if you are developing a theme that you plan to release to the population at large, you should use a content filler to make sure you style the vast spectrum of content. For example you can use the WordPress sample content available at `http://codex .wordpress.org/Theme_Unit_Test`. There are several alternative sample content import files such as the one provided by WPCandy at `http://wpcandy.com/made/the-sample-post-collection`, but the WordPress Theme reviewers will use theirs to approve your theme to be in the repository. You can review the entire Theme Repository checklist at `http://codex.wordpress.org/Theme_ Development_Checklist`. This is covered in greater detail in Chapter 9.

Say you are developing a theme and you want to test it with the sample content mentioned in the previous paragraph, but you also need to target specific content for the actual site you are developing the theme for. Here is a good use for WordPress Multisite. WordPress Multisite is covered in depth in Chapter 10, including how to set it up. But once you have it set up locally, WordPress Multisite allows you to leverage the same themes and plugins across multiple WordPress sites in a WordPress network. We set this up so that one of our WordPress sites has the sample content. Then we created a second site for the site-specific content. When you give this a try, you should network-enable the theme you are developing and activate it on both sites. This allows you to jump back and forth in your browser to two different WordPress content sets but only edit one set of theme files.

Likewise, if you are developing a new plugin, test it in WordPress Multisite to make sure it works. You can also set up several virtual hosts on your machine running different versions of WordPress, both a few revisions back and also development releases to make sure your plugin will continue to work with the next update. Although we all preach to users to keep WordPress current, the reality is that some sites lag behind, either because of hosting restrictions, ignorance, or laziness. It is important to make sure your plugin continues to work if you want people to use it.

> **NOTE** *See Chapter 8 for more information on using plugins.*

This local development method as explained is a tried and true environment used by developers around the world. As an essential skill for a WordPress developer, it is important to understand how the various components work together, and getting them set up yourself solidifies that knowledge. However, there are some new tools on the scene that are changing the way the developers work. The next section will briefly touch on this new methodology.

VIRTUAL MACHINES

Virtual machines have been used in the enterprise for many years; recently several tools have made them much more approachable for desktop development use. Using tools such as Oracle's VirtualBox and VMWare's Fusion, developers are able to run additional virtual machines on their desktop, which enables them to work in the different environments. Virtual machines are software-based emulations of an entirely different operating system, and therefore workstation or server, running locally.

As the use of virtual machines for desktop development has become more common, tools to manage these virtual machines have also been born. The challenge of managing the provisioning and configuration of virtual machines has prompted developers to create tools such as Vagrant, Puppet, and Chef to make their lives easier. These tools have focused on making the foundational server manageable; now developers are using these tools to generate entire development environments.

One such virtual machine development environment for WordPress is called Varying Vagrant Vagrants or VVV for short (`https://github.com/varying-vagrant-vagrants/vvv/`). VVV was developed by 10up for their internal development and workflow needs and recently released as a community project on GitHub. While using virtual machines for desktop development is a more advanced method, VVV's goal is to make WordPress development in this way much more approachable.

VVV used Oracle's VirtualBox and Vagrant to create a dedicated WordPress development platform. The VVV environment includes both the latest stable version of WordPress as well as the development branch so that developers can work either on their own projects or contribute to the WordPress core codebase. Additionally, several tools are included for debugging and profiling your code. VVV is extensible and can be used to create your own custom environments for your projects. While this is a more advanced method, VVV is well documented on the GitHub site.

Now that you have your new project working locally, either through a virtual machine or directly on your workstation, and you have removed all the errors and notices from WordPress and PHP, you are ready to push it to a live server. In the next section, you will look at some of the challenges and tactics for pushing code live.

DEPLOYING LOCAL CHANGES

First, distinguish between the different types of objects you are deploying. There is code, which could be plugin code, or theme and theme assets. There is content, which is the website subject matter from the posts and pages and is stored in the database. Finally, there is the configuration, which is also stored in the database.

Deploying the code is easy. Developers do this every day. One of the advantages of PHP and WordPress is that you can generally drop code into the document root and it runs at the next request. Deploying code is simple and you can use your FTP client to do it. But please use SFTP, if possible, because it is a secure protocol, whereas FTP is not. There are also more advanced methods for deploying code through continuous integration tools.

Deploying the content and the configuration is more difficult. WordPress uses fully qualified links in all the content. So every internal HREF and menu item has the full domain name embedded. Likewise, the configuration of the site is also tied to the domain name that WordPress was installed at. You cannot simply take a database dump and move it.

There is, however, an intermediate step to change the domain names in the database export before importing it into the production site. Use caution here that you are not going to steamroll any updated content on the live site with your content from the development site. How exactly you do this in your situation is dependent on your exact needs, but overall, this process is very similar to a situation in which you are moving your site from one domain to another. The process is extensively documented in various websites, the WordPress codex at `http://codex.wordpress.org/Moving_WordPress`, and many other tutorials. This is just one method.

In short, this is how the process works for us, assuming you want to move all content from your development database to the live site.

You are going to remove all the fully qualified links from the content on your development site. All future content you add to the production site, once the content is moved, will be fully qualified, but this is a method to make all the URLs root relative and then they will work on both your development site and the live site.

For this process you use the wp-DBManager plugin by Lester Chan available online at `https://wordpress.org/plugins/wp-dbmanager/`. This plugin allows you to make database backups and also perform SQL queries on the data. You could also use WordPress's built-in database export functionality and PHPMyAdmin to do the same.

Pretend you are moving from the local development site `mirmillo.local` to the live production site of `mirmillo.com`. This is where using the "fake" domain name virtual host option mentioned previously comes in handy.

Using the plugin, make a backup of your working test site. Download and save this backup file in case things go awry.

Next, in the SQL page of the plugin, you will run the queries shown in Figure 3-10 to update the URLs in your site's content. Essentially, you are removing the domain name from the URLs in the HTML code. Later, in Chapter 11, we introduce you to a new tool called WP-CLI that can help with this process, but as an introduction, it is important to see the fundamental steps.

Now export your content from your development site. Content export is found in your WordPress Dashboard under Tools ➤ Export. Download this file. This is your movable content with root relative links.

Import this content into your live site. The import functionality is found in your WordPress Dashboard under Tools ➤ Import. Again, be cautious that you do not overwrite newer content or content you want to keep.

Truly, it is not a difficult process; it is just one that requires some planning and coordination. There are some developers who are working on tools to make this process easier. In particular, we have been keeping an eye on RAMP by Alex King's Crowd Favorite, available online at `http://crowdfavorite.com/ramp/`. While we have not tried it yet, it looks promising. The challenge is always that, when using WordPress as a content management system, users can and will log in to the production site and make changes—that is the point. But in doing so, your development content gets out of sync. Ultimately, the goal will be to have a way to synchronize WordPress databases between live, staging, and development and be able to handle conflict resolution. There is no silver bullet here, but it seems to be a challenge that many developers are working on.

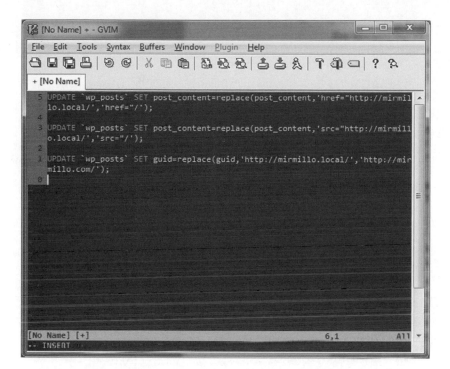

FIGURE 3-10: SQL queries to remove domain names

SUMMARY

This chapter reviewed some of the reasons and processes for a proper development workflow. In addition, it covered how to enable a local WordPress development environment in your own private sandbox. Finally, you examined a process to push a development site to a production server. The next chapter digs into the core files of WordPress and reviews how WordPress works.

4

Tour of the Core

WHAT'S IN THIS CHAPTER?

- ➤ Exploring the WordPress core files
- ➤ Searching through core files as reference
- ➤ Working with the WordPress Codex
- ➤ Navigating the WordPress Code Reference
- ➤ Understanding inline documentation

To understand how to extend WordPress properly, you must first learn how the core of WordPress functions. This will help you learn what tools are available in the WordPress core to make your life easier. WordPress handles most of the tedious coding and logic problems for you.

The WordPress core is the best resource for learning how WordPress works. The beauty of open source software is you have all of the code at your disposal. If you are ever unsure how a certain aspect of WordPress functions, just start digging into the code! The answers are all there; it's just a matter of finding and understanding them.

WHAT'S IN THE CORE?

The WordPress core is powered by a set of files that are part of the original WordPress software download. These are required "core" files that WordPress needs to function properly. The core files are expected to change only when you upgrade WordPress to a newer version.

The core does not include your custom files for plugins, themes, database settings, the .htaccess file, and so on. The core also does not include any media you have uploaded to WordPress. Basically, any files added to WordPress after installation are considered outside of the core.

The WordPress core files are primarily PHP files, but also contain CSS, JavaScript, HTML, and image files. These files control everything about WordPress including how content pages are generated to display, loading the configured theme and plugins, loading all options and settings, and much more. In short, the core contains several major function types:

➤ **Posts, pages, and custom content**—Creating, storing, retrieving, and interacting with the majority of your content in WordPress. The discussion of the loop that controls content display and ordering in Chapter 5 relies heavily on these functions.

➤ **Post types, taxonomies, and metadata**—Everything from custom post types, tags, and categories to user-created taxonomies. The data models used are explored in Chapter 7.

➤ **Themes**—Supporting functions for WordPress themes. Theme development and its relationship to these functions are discussed in Chapter 9.

➤ **Actions, filters, and plugins**—Framework for extending WordPress through plugins, covered in more detail in Chapter 8.

➤ **Users and authors**—Creating and managing access control to your site, and key to the security and enterprise use topics in Chapters 12 and 15.

➤ **Feeds, formatting, and comments**—These are discussed as needed throughout the book.

This chapter digs into these files as you explore the WordPress core files. Think of this chapter as your guidebook to the "how" of exploring the WordPress core; it is a field guide companion to the WordPress Codex documentation for user-contributed discussion and explanation. It's also imperative to be comfortable browsing and searching the core to complement the functional introduction provided here. An exhaustive list of every WordPress function is not included here, both because the list changes and evolves as the WordPress core undergoes continuous development, and because the goal here is to convey developer and deployer expertise and not to summarize the Codex.

WordPress comes packaged with two plugins: Akismet and Hello Dolly. These two plugins exist in your plugins directory inside `wp-content`. Even though these two plugins are a part of the WordPress core file package download, they are not considered core functionality because they must be activated to function and can easily be removed.

WordPress also comes packaged with three core themes: Twenty Twelve, Twenty Thirteen, and Twenty Fourteen. Twenty Fourteen is the default theme on a fresh installation of WordPress. As with the included plugins, these theme files are not considered core functionality because they can easily be replaced with any theme that you want to use on your website.

USING THE CORE AS A REFERENCE

Using the WordPress core as a reference is a quick and easy way to learn about various functionality in WordPress. Understanding how to navigate through the WordPress core files can help you find answers to your questions when developing for WordPress.

To use the WordPress core as a reference, you need to understand what to expect in the core files. Most WordPress core files contain documentation in the form of code comments. Typically, a code comment is displayed in the header of the file and gives an overall summary of the core file you are viewing.

To see this first-hand, open the `wp-login.php` file located in the root directory of WordPress. You'll notice the top of the file has a header comment describing the file's function:

```
/**
 * WordPress User Page
 *
 * Handles authentication, registering, resetting passwords, forgot password,
 * and other user handling.
 *
 * @package WordPress
 */
```

All core files, other than images, can be viewed using a text editor program. Depending on your default program settings, you may need to open up your text editor first and then open the file rather than just opening up the file directly. It's also helpful to use a text editor that has syntax highlighting, meaning PHP syntax would be highlighted to help you read the code easier.

There is a full list of compatible text editors on the WordPress.org Codex at `http://codex` `.wordpress.org/Glossary#Text_editor`.

Inline Documentation

Nearly all WordPress core files contain inline documentation in PHPDoc form. PHPDoc is a standardized method of describing a function's usage in PHP comment form. This means each function is explained in detail directly before the function in a comment block. The following is the defined template for documenting a WordPress function:

```
/**
 * Short Description
 *
 * Long Description
 *
 * @package WordPress
 * @since version
 *
 * @param    type    $varname    Description
 * @return   type                Description
 */
```

This is amazingly helpful in understanding how functions work. The comment includes a short and long description. It also includes the version of WordPress it was added in. This helps distinguish new functions added to WordPress when a new version is released.

Available parameters are also listed along with the parameter data type. A data type is the type of data that is required for the parameter. For example, an ID parameter would likely use the `int` (integer) data type. The final piece of information is the return value. The return value data type is also listed.

All new functions added to WordPress are documented using the preceding template. For more information on inline documentation in WordPress, see this Core Contributors Handbook article: `http://make.wordpress.org/core/handbook/inline-documentation-standards/` `php-documentation-standards/`.

Finding Functions

Looking up a function in the core is the quickest way to learn how a specific WordPress function works. You can see exactly what parameters are allowed to be sent to the function, as well as what the function actually does and what the return values are.

To start, make sure you have downloaded the latest version of WordPress locally to your computer. You will search these files as a reference for WordPress. Open up any text editor you have that can search files (TextPad for Windows and Sublime Text for Mac are recommended). When searching for a function, you want to eliminate calls to that function from your search. Do this by including the word "function" at the start of your search, as in function wp_head. Not everything in WordPress is a function, but this is a good place to start. If you don't find any matches, remove "function" from the beginning of your search. Also remember to set your text editor to search all files (*.*), not just .txt files.

Let's look at the is_super_admin() function. This function is used to check if a user is a super admin in WordPress Multisite. You need to know exactly what values the function expects before you can use it. Open your text editor and search all files in WordPress for function is_super_admin. The search should produce one result in wp-includes/capabilities.php:

```
function is_super_admin( $user_id = false ) {
```

Right away, you notice one parameter that can be sent to this function: $user_id. Notice the inline documentation listed directly above the function. In this case, the is_super_admin() documentation looks like this:

```
/**
 * Determine if user is a site admin.
 *
 * @since 3.0.0
 *
 * @param int $user_id (Optional) The ID of a user. Defaults to the current
user.
 * @return bool True if the user is a site admin.
 */
```

This is an extremely valuable block of content. The comment has a short description about what the function does, in this case, "Determine if user is a site admin." The comment also notes when the function was added (since version 3.0.0). There is also information about the single parameter, including the parameter type, what the parameter is responsible for, and the fact that the parameter is optional in this case. The comment also details what the expected return values will be. In this case, the function will return True if the user is a site admin and False if not.

This alone is enough information to understand how this function works, but let's dig into the code for a better understanding. The first few lines look like this:

```
if ( ! $user_id || $user_id == get_current_user_id() )
$user = wp_get_current_user();
else
$user = get_userdata( $user_id );
```

Based on the PHPDoc comment above the function, you know the $user _ id parameter is optional, so this code shows what happens if a $user _ id parameter is not passed to the function. The preceding if statement checks if the $user _ id variable contains a value. If it does not, or if the current user logged in matches the $user _ id, the wp _ get _ current _ user() function is called to get the user data for the currently logged in user. If the $user _ id variable contains a value, the get _ userdata() function is called to retrieve the user data based on the ID passed to the function.

Next, the function checks that the $user data actually exists before proceeding and, if not, will return false.

```
if ( ! $user || ! $user->exists() )
    return false;
```

Now that you know the $user data exists, you need to check if that user is actually a super admin:

```
if ( is_multisite() ) {
    $super_admins = get_super_admins();
    if ( is_array( $super_admins ) && in_array( $user->user_login,
$super_admins ) )
        return true;
} else {
    if ( $user->has_cap('delete_users') )
        return true;
}
```

Let's break down this if statement a bit:

```
if ( is_multisite() ) {
```

This if statement checks that Multisite is actually enabled in WordPress by calling the is _ multisite() function. Super admins will exist only if the Multisite feature of WordPress has been enabled.

Now that WordPress has determined Multisite is running, the function calls get _ super _ admins() to retrieve an array of all super admins in WordPress using the following code:

```
$super_admins = get_super_admins();
```

The $super _ admins variable is now an array of all super admin login usernames. The next line is the most important line in this function. This is the code that actually checks that a user is a super admin in WordPress:

```
$super_admins = get_super_admins();
if ( is_array( $super_admins ) && in_array( $user->user_login, $super_admins ) )
    return true;
```

Before working with an array, you always want to verify the variable is an actual array using the is _ array() PHP function. The second part of this line of code uses the in _ array() PHP function to check if the user's login exists in the super admin array. If it exists, the user is a super admin and the function returns true.

If the `is_multisite()` check covered earlier returns `false`, the function will execute the following `else` code:

```
} else {
    if ( $user->has_cap('delete_users') )
        return true;
}
```

The preceding code checks if the user has the `delete_users` capability. By default, this capability is assigned to regular administrator accounts in WordPress. If Multisite is disabled in WordPress, but you are an administrator, this code will return `true` when calling the `is_super_admin()` function.

The final line of code in the function is:

```
return false;
```

This code basically says that if any of the checks in the `is_super_admin()` function fail, return `false`. This is more of a safety measure to be certain a `true` or `false` value is always returned.

After viewing this example, it should be more apparent how useful the WordPress core code can be. You learned exactly how this function works by exploring the source code. All the answers to your questions exist within the core so it's essential to have a good understanding of how to utilize the core to your advantage.

Exploring the Core

The WordPress core has certain files that contain many of the more popular WordPress functions. These functions are used for all WordPress APIs and can be used in any custom plugin or theme. The following sections detail the WordPress core files that contain key pieces of code for working with WordPress. All of the files listed in the section that follows are located in the `/wp-includes` directory of WordPress.

Functions.php

The `functions.php` file contains the main WordPress API functions. These functions are used to easily interact with WordPress using a standardized method. Plugins, themes, and the WordPress core all use these functions:

➤ `current_time()`—Retrieves the current time based on specified type.

➤ `force_ssl_login()`—Requires SSL (https) login to WordPress.

➤ `wp_nonce_field()`—Adds a nonce hidden field for forms. A nonce field is used for verification purposes when submitting and processing data in WordPress. This is a critical step in securing your code.

➤ `absint()`—Converts value to nonnegative integer.

➤ `wp_die()`—Kills the WordPress execution and displays an HTML error message.

Option.php

The `option.php` file contains the main WordPress Options API functions. These functions are used for the following:

➤ `add_option()`, `update_option()`, `get_option()`—Functions to create, update, and display a saved option.

➤ `set_transient()`, `get_transient()`, `delete_transient()`—Functions to create, retrieve, and delete transients in WordPress. A *transient* is an option with an expiration time. When the expiration time is hit, the transient is automatically deleted in WordPress.

➤ `add_site_option()`, `update_site_option()`, `get_site_option()`—Functions to create, update, and display site options. If Multisite is enabled, function returns the network option; if not, the standard site option is returned.

Formatting.php

The `formatting.php` file contains the WordPress API formatting functions. These functions format the output in many different ways:

➤ `esc_attr()`—Used to escape a string for HTML attributes

➤ `esc_html()`—Used to escape a string for HTML

➤ `esc_url()`—Used to check and clean a URL

➤ `sanitize_text_field()`—Sanitizes a string from user input or from the database

➤ `is_email()`—Verifies that an e-mail is valid

➤ `capital_P_dangit()`—Famous filter that forces the P in WordPress to be capitalized when displaying in content

Pluggable.php

The pluggable functions file lets you override certain core functions of WordPress. WordPress loads these functions if they are still undefined after all plugins have been loaded. Some of the more commonly used functions include:

➤ `wp_mail()`—Sends e-mail from WordPress

➤ `get_userdata()`—Returns all user data from the specified user ID

➤ `wp_get_current_user()`—Returns user data for the currently logged-in user

➤ `wp_set_password()`—Updates a user's password with a new encrypted one

➤ `wp_rand()`—Generates a random number

➤ `wp_logout()`—Logs out a user, destroying the user session

➤ `wp_redirect()`—Redirects to another page

➤ `get_avatar()`—Returns the user's avatar

Plugin.php

The `plugin.php` file contains the WordPress Plugin API functions, including:

➤ `add_filter()`—Hooks that the WordPress core launches to filter content before displaying on the screen or saving in the database

➤ `add_action()`—Hooks that the WordPress core launches at specific points of execution

➤ `register_activation_hook()`—Hook called when a plugin is activated

➤ `register_deactivation_hook()`—Hook called when a plugin is deactivated

➤ `plugin_dir_url()`—Returns the filesystem directory path for the plugin

➤ `plugin_dir_path()`—Returns the URL for the plugin

➤ `doing_filter()` and `doing_action()`—Returns the name of the current filter or action being processed

User.php

The `user.php` file contains the WordPress User API functions, including:

➤ `get_users()`—Returns a list of users matching criteria provided

➤ `add_user_meta()`, `get_user_meta()`, `delete_user_meta()`—Used to create, retrieve, and delete user metadata

➤ `username_exists()`—Checks if a username exists

➤ `email_exists()`—Checks if an e-mail address exists

➤ `wp_insert_user()` and `wp_update_user()`—Create and update a user account

Post.php

The `post.php` file contains the functions used in the post process of WordPress, including:

➤ `wp_insert_post()`—Creates a new post

➤ `get_post()`—Retrieves a single post with all post data

➤ `get_posts()`—Retrieves a list of the latest posts' matching criteria

➤ `add_post_meta()`—Creates metadata (custom field data) on a post

➤ `get_post_meta()`—Retrieves metadata (custom field data) on a post

➤ `get_post_custom()`—Returns a multidimensional array with all metadata (custom field) entries for a post

➤ `set_post_thumbnail()`—Sets a featured image on a post

➤ `register_post_type()`—Registers a custom post type in WordPress

Taxonomy.php

The `taxonomy.php` file contains the functions used by the WordPress Taxonomy API. Taxonomies are used to manage the hierarchical relationships of metadata such as categories and tags (described in Chapter 6) and can also be extended, as you'll explore in Chapter 7. Functions in this file include:

➤ `register_taxonomy()`—Register a custom taxonomy in WordPress

➤ `get_taxonomies()`—Return a list of registered taxonomies

➤ `wp_insert_term()`, `wp_update_term()`—Insert or update a taxonomy term based on arguments provided

There are many more core functions that can be used when developing custom themes and plugins for WordPress. Take a few minutes and explore the core files inside `/wp-includes`. This directory contains most of the WordPress API core function files.

To learn more about any function listed here, open up the corresponding file and view the source code. Remember that each function will have inline documentation explaining how to utilize the function correctly. We cover the Plugin API functions in more detail in Chapter 8. The core functions used by themes are covered in Chapter 9.

Deprecated Functions

When a new version of WordPress is being developed, certain functions may become deprecated. A deprecated function means the function is not removed from WordPress, but it should not be used in your plugins and themes going forward. Typically in such a case, a new function has been created to replace the deprecated function. A function may be deprecated in WordPress for many different reasons, but the most common is that the function needs a complete rewrite to better handle the feature it adds to WordPress.

WordPress contains a file to store all functions that have been deprecated over the years. WordPress is known for having superior backwards compatibility. This means that when a new version of WordPress is released, a strong focus it put on backwards compatibility to verify new features and functions will not break existing sites running WordPress, even if the features in use are considered deprecated.

Let's look at the inline documentation for the `get_current_theme()` deprecated function:

```
/**
 * Retrieve current theme name.
 *
 * @since 1.5.0
 * @deprecated 3.4.0
 * @deprecated Use (string) wp_get_theme()
 * @see wp_get_theme()
 *
 * @return string
 */
```

You'll notice a few additional comment lines for deprecated functions. The first is the @deprecated line stating in what version of WordPress the function was deprecated, in this case v3.4. The second is @see which tells you what function should be used instead, in this case wp _ get _ theme().

The deprecated.php file is a very important file to check when a new version of WordPress is released. If a common function is deprecated, you should immediately stop using it and even consider updating your old code to use the replacement.

Generally speaking deprecated functions are usually not removed from the WordPress core, but there is no guarantee a deprecated function won't be removed in a future release.

WORDPRESS CODEX AND CODE REFERENCE

WordPress has many different online resources that are extremely useful when learning and working with WordPress. These resources should be bookmarked for quick reference and are used by beginners and experts alike.

In this section, we cover the two most popular online WordPress resources: WordPress Codex and the Code Reference.

What Is the Codex?

The WordPress Codex is an online wiki for WordPress documentation located on WordPress.org. WordPress.org describes the Codex as an "encyclopedia of WordPress knowledge." You can visit the WordPress Codex by going to http://codex.wordpress.org or by clicking the Support ➢ Documentation link in the header of WordPress.org.

The Codex is a wiki-based website, which means anyone can create, edit, and contribute to the articles within the Codex. The Codex is jam-packed with useful knowledge covering all aspects of WordPress. From "Getting Started with WordPress" to more advanced developer topics, the Codex is an essential resource for anyone looking to learn more about WordPress.

The Codex is available in many different languages. To find a Codex version translated into your language, visit the Multilingual Codex page at http://codex.wordpress.org/Multilingual_Codex. You can also contribute to the Codex and help expand on any language or create your own version of the Codex in any language if it is not listed.

Using the Codex

The Codex can be used in many different ways. The most common method is to search the Codex using the search box in the header, or you can visit http://wordpress.org/search/ to easily search through the Codex for appropriate articles matching your search criteria.

The WordPress.org search is powered by Google Custom Search, as shown in Figure 4-1. The search results returned are from all of WordPress.org, not just the Codex, so it's important to keep that in mind. There is a lesser known Codex-only search located at http://codex.wordpress.org/Special:Search.

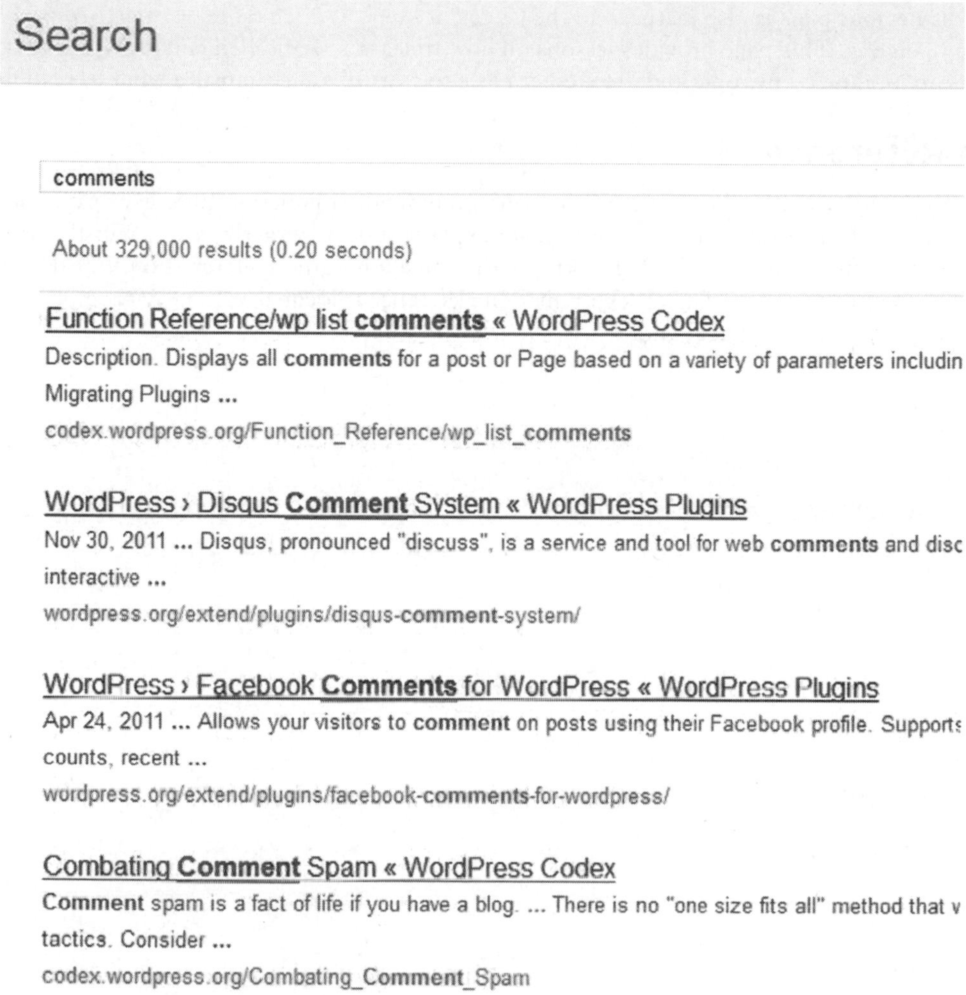

Search

comments

About 329,000 results (0.20 seconds)

Function Reference/wp list **comments** « WordPress Codex

Description. Displays all **comments** for a post or Page based on a variety of parameters includin
Migrating Plugins ...

codex.wordpress.org/Function_Reference/wp_list_**comments**

WordPress › Disqus **Comment** System « WordPress Plugins

Nov 30, 2011 ... Disqus, pronounced "discuss", is a service and tool for web **comments** and disc
interactive ...

wordpress.org/extend/plugins/disqus-**comment**-system/

WordPress › Facebook **Comments** for WordPress « WordPress Plugins

Apr 24, 2011 ... Allows your visitors to **comment** on posts using their Facebook profile. Supports
counts, recent ...

wordpress.org/extend/plugins/facebook-**comments**-for-wordpress/

Combating **Comment** Spam « WordPress Codex

Comment spam is a fact of life if you have a blog. ... There is no "one size fits all" method that v
tactics. Consider ...

codex.wordpress.org/Combating_**Comment**_Spam

FIGURE 4-1: WordPress.org search

You can also navigate through the index of articles on the Codex homepage. These articles are organized by topic and generally ordered by level of difficulty. There is also a topic toward the top for the latest version of WordPress. The articles here cover new features, compatibility tests for plugins and themes, installing, upgrading, and support for the new version.

An extensive glossary of terms is available for the Codex. This can help familiarize you with common words used throughout the Codex. You can view the official Codex Glossary at `http://codex.wordpress.org/Glossary`.

Another search method is to use the quick index. This index allows you to look up an article by the first letter of the article's title. You can find the quick index at `http://codex.wordpress.org/Codex:Quick_index`.

A WordPress Lessons page is also featured in the Codex at `http://codex.wordpress.org/` `WordPress_Lessons`. This page provides lessons on how to learn specific elements of WordPress. The lessons are organized by topic and are a great place to start if you are unsure what to read first.

Function Reference

WordPress functions are described in the Codex with an individual Function Reference page for each WordPress API function available. These pages explain in detail exactly how a WordPress function works, as shown in Figure 4-2. Bookmark this page for a quick reference on WordPress functions and their capabilities. The official Function Reference is located at `http://codex` `.wordpress.org/Function_Reference`.

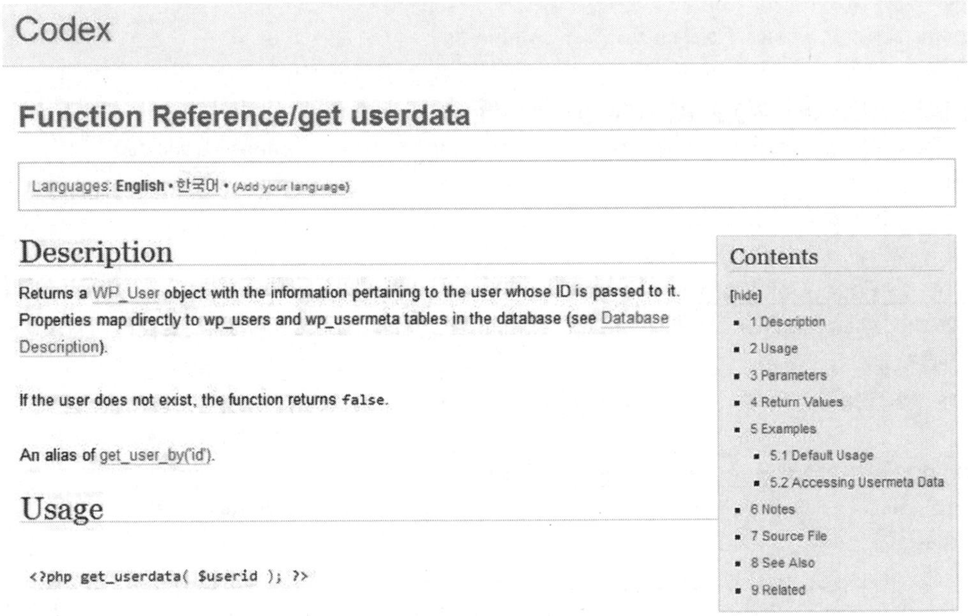

FIGURE 4-2: Function reference for get_userdata()

Think of the Function Reference as an online and expanded version of a function's inline documentation. The reference has a description explaining how the function works and how it is used. The individual parameters are listed along with data types and a description of each.

The most useful section of the Function Reference is the Examples section of the page. The examples make it very easy to see exactly how to use the function. The get_userdata() example is shown here:

```php
<?php $user_info = get_userdata(1);
    echo 'Username: ' . $user_info->user_login . "\n";
    echo 'User roles: ' . implode(', ', $user_info->roles) . "\n";
    echo 'User ID: ' . $user_info->ID . "\n";
?>
```

This example shows how to load specific user data for user ID 1. The example output is as follows:

```
Username: michael_myers
User Level: administrator
User ID: 1
```

This is a simple example, but this, along with the additional reference information, can help you easily learn a new function and how to use it properly in your code.

The Source File section of the Function Reference details where the function is located in the WordPress core. In our example, the `get_userdata()` function is located in `wp-includes/pluggable.php`. The location file is a link that points to the WordPress core file in Trac. This is a quick and handy way to view where the function is declared via your browser. We cover the Trac software in Chapter 16.

The final Function Reference topic lists Related functions. This can help you identify a similar function that may accomplish that task you are working on. For example, the `wp_insert_post()` function lists `wp_update_post()` and `wp_delete_post()` as related functions.

The majority of the WordPress API functions are well documented, but not all functions have a Function Reference page in the Codex. Any function displayed in red on the Function Reference homepage currently has no documentation. This is an ongoing community project so expect all functions to be fully documented in the Codex eventually.

> **NOTE** *Contributing to the Codex is a great way to get involved in WordPress. You don't need to be an advanced developer to contribute code examples, descriptions, and additional information about various features and functions in WordPress.*

WordPress APIs

WordPress features many different APIs that help interact with WordPress. Think of the APIs as gateways that let you add functionality or retrieve external content within WordPress without violating the "don't hack the core" maxim: Most APIs insert references to non-core code that will be added to the `wp-content` directory by registering its entry points with WordPress. Each API is documented in the Codex along with functions used in the API. An API is a set of predefined functions available for use in themes and plugins. The following is a list of the most common WordPress APIs:

➤ **Plugin API**—Used for custom plugin development. The Codex features an extensive Plugin API documentation page. There is an introduction to hooks, actions, and filters, the primary ways to interact with WordPress from a custom-built plugin. The Plugin API page links to the Function Reference pages for available API functions are located in `/wp-includes/plugins.php` at `http://codex.wordpress.org/Plugin_API`.

➤ **Widgets API**—Used to create and maintain widgets in your plugin. The widget will automatically appear under the Appearance ➢ Widgets screen and can be used on any defined sidebar on your theme. The widgets API is located at `http://codex.wordpress.org/Widgets_API`.

➤ **Shortcode API**—Used for adding shortcodes in your plugin. A *shortcode* is a macro code added to a post. This allows a plugin to grab that shortcode and execute specific commands and display elements in place of it in your post. Shortcodes can also accept parameters to alter the output.

An example core WordPress shortcode is [gallery]. Adding [gallery] to your post automatically displays all images uploaded to that post in a gallery style. When editing a post, you will see the [gallery] shortcode, but viewing it on the public side of your website displays the actual gallery of images. The shortcode API is found at http://codex.wordpress.org/Shortcode_API.

➤ **HTTP API**—Used for sending an HTTP request from WordPress. This API is a standardized method to grab the content of an external URL. Basically, it takes the provided URL and tests a series of PHP methods for sending the request. Depending on the hosting environment, WordPress uses the first method it deems to be configured correctly to make the HTTP request.

The current HTTP API PHP methods tested are cURL, Streams, and FSockopen. The methods are also checked exactly in that order. You can use the Core Control plugin (http://wordpress.org/extend/plugins/Core-control/) to specifically choose which method is used for all HTTP requests.

Using the HTTP API, you could easily interact with the Google Maps API to dynamically generate maps and plots. The HTTP API can also easily interact with the Twitter API, allowing you to post/read tweets directly from WordPress. The HTTP API is found at http://codex.wordpress.org/HTTP_API.

➤ **Settings API**—Used for creating a settings page. This API is used for creating and managing custom options for your plugins and themes. The main advantage of using the Settings API is security. The API sanitizes all of the setting data saved by the user. This means no more worrying about nonces, data validation, and cross-site scripting (XSS) attacks when saving setting data. This is much easier than the old method of data validation, which you had to use each time you needed to save settings in a plugin. The settings API is found at http://codex.wordpress.org/Settings_API.

➤ **Options API**—Used for storing option data in the WordPress database. The Options API provides an easy way to create, update, retrieve, and delete option values. The options API is found at the following URL: http://codex.wordpress.org/Options_API

➤ **Dashboard Widgets API**—Used for creating admin dashboard widgets. Widgets added from the API automatically contain all jQuery features that the core admin dashboard widgets have, including drag/drop, minimize, and hiding via screen options. The dashboard widgets API is found at http://codex.wordpress.org/Dashboard_Widgets_API.

➤ **Rewrite API**—Used for creating custom rewrite rules. This API allows you to create custom rewrite rules just as you would in your .htaccess file. You can also create custom permalink structure tags (that is, %postname%), add static endpoints (that is, /my-page/), and even add additional feed links. The Rewrite API functions are located in /wp-includes/rewrite.php at http://codex.wordpress.org/Rewrite_API.

Remember that all WordPress APIs can be used in custom plugin and theme development. This is the primary method of extending WordPress with additional features and functionality. Utilizing the preceding APIs creates an easy and standardized way of interacting with WordPress.

For more information on all WordPress APIs visit the Codex page at `http://codex.wordpress.org/WordPress_API's`.

Codex Controversy

As with any wiki, there will always be controversy over the accuracy of the articles in the Codex. One problem that has plagued the Codex is the freshness of the articles. WordPress is being developed at a decent pace and thus the Codex needs to keep up that pace in order to be accurate. Unfortunately, that doesn't always happen, and some material is outdated. The WordPress Codex is a community project, so you can easily create an account and start helping out! Contributing to WordPress is covered in Chapter 16.

Another problem that exists within the Codex is the organization of the content. Currently, there is so much information in the Codex that it can be hard and confusing to find the answers you are looking for. Again, one of the motivations for this introduction to the WordPress core is to provide you with a map to help narrow the scope of your searches and to introduce related functional topics.

Code Reference

The WordPress Code Reference is a newer online resource for WordPress. Launched in the spring of 2014, the Code Reference is an auto-generated online resource to help developers find more information on WordPress functions, classes, hooks, and more. You can visit the Code Reference by going to `http://developer.wordpress.org/reference/`.

The Code Reference content is generated using an open source project called WP Parser. This program parses through all WordPress core files and generates the reference entries from the WordPress core inline documentation. For more information on the WP Parser project, and to get involved, visit `https://github.com/rmccue/WP-Parser`.

Using the Code Reference

There are a few different ways you can use the Code Reference. As with all WordPress online documentation, a powerful search option is available. Searching the Code Reference can help you find a particular function you may be looking for if you don't know the name.

Alternately, you can browse various topics, including functions, hooks, classes, and methods. Filtering by topic will list all topics in alphabetical order and is a great way to learn about topics you may be less familiar with.

Another very valuable feature of the Code Reference is the ability to see all functions by WordPress version. For example, you can see all functions that were introduced in WordPress 4.0.0 by visiting `http://developer.wordpress.org/reference/since/4.0.0/`. To view older versions of WordPress, simply change the version in the URL to the version you'd like to see. If you need to see what functions were introduced in WordPress 2.5, visit `http://developer.wordpress.org/reference/since/2.5.0/`.

Code Reference Details

Every entry in the Code Reference has a detail page that lists all information about that entry. Let's look at the absint() WordPress function as an example, as shown in Figure 4-3.

Code Reference

Browse: Home / Reference / Functions / absint

```
absint ( mixed $maybeint = null )
```

Converts value to nonnegative integer.

Return: int An nonnegative integer

Since: WordPress 2.5.0

Source file: wp-includes/functions.php

View source

Parameters

$maybeint

(mixed) (Required) Data you wish to have converted to a nonnegative integer

Source

```
1  function absint( $maybeint ) {
2      return abs( intval( $maybeint ) );
3  }
```

View on Trac

FIGURE 4-3: WordPress Code Reference for absint()

The first section of the Code Reference includes the function with available parameters, a description about the function, the return value to expect, what version of WordPress the function was added to, and the source file where the function is declared. If you think this information looks familiar, you are absolutely right. The function details shown on the Code Reference page are pulled directly from the inline documentation for the absint() function in WordPress core.

The function parameters are detailed next. This section will list any and all parameters the function will accept. Each parameter is detailed along with the data type the function is expecting.

The final section is the actual source for the function declaration. This code is exactly what exists in the WordPress core for the function we are viewing. As you can see, the WordPress Code Reference is an online, prettier version of the actual WordPress core code.

Codex Versus Code Reference

The biggest benefit to the Code Reference over the Codex is accuracy. The Code Reference is automatically generated from the WordPress core files. This ensures all content in the Code Reference is completely accurate and always up to date with the latest version of WordPress. The WordPress Codex, on the other hand, is a wiki that is manually updated by contributors from all over the world.

The biggest benefit to the Codex over the Code Reference is the additional amount of content and examples provided. Because the Codex is a wiki, an unlimited amount of information, examples, and tutorials can exist for any given feature and function in WordPress. This can make understanding how to work with a specific function in WordPress much easier to grasp initially.

The Codex and the Code Reference have pros and cons, but ultimately they are two very good resources for learning to develop with WordPress and should be bookmarked for future reference.

DON'T HACK THE CORE!

Whereas exploring the WordPress core and using it as a reference is highly encouraged, hacking the core is not. Hacking the core means making any changes to the core files of WordPress. A change could be as simple as one line of code, but a hack is a hack and doing so could cause major problems down the road.

Why Not?

Hacking the WordPress core can make it very difficult to update to the latest version of WordPress. Keeping WordPress current is an important step in overall website security. If any security vulnerability is discovered, a patch is typically released very quickly. If you can't update because you have modified core files, you are opening up your website to these security vulnerabilities, and you increase the likelihood that your website will be hacked.

Hacking the core can also lead to an unstable website because many parts of WordPress rely on other parts to function as expected. If you make changes to those parts, it could break something completely unrelated to what you have changed.

Security is another reason why you shouldn't hack the core. WordPress core is viewed and scrutinized by security experts all over the world. By hacking the core, you are relying on your own expertise to make your hacks secure. If you don't understand the many different ways a hacker can exploit your code, you might end up creating a security vulnerability within the core of WordPress.

The final reason why you should never hack the core is compassion: that is, compassion toward the developer who comes after you to maintain the website. Most websites will change developers over the years so there is no guarantee you will be working on a particular website five years from now. Imagine the developer that follows you trying to determine what core files were hacked to make the website function. This can be a nightmare for any developer and it puts the website owner in a bad position because most developers will refuse to work on a hacked version of WordPress. If you hack the core, you are building dependencies that will either be misunderstood or hidden, and when the WordPress core is upgraded for this site, the hacked core will break in silent, evil, or loud ways.

Alternatives to Hacking the Core

Any feature or functionality that does not exist in WordPress can be added with a plugin. Sometimes a core hack may be the easy answer, but in the long run, it will make your life harder. (We have yet to come across a feature we needed that we couldn't incorporate with a plugin.) WordPress is extremely flexible, which is one of its major strengths, and therefore the core should never be hacked. Don't hack the core!

If you are fascinated by the WordPress core and its intricacies, you should join the WordPress Developer Community and get involved fixing bugs and contributing to the core build of WordPress. This is covered in detail in Chapter 16.

SUMMARY

In this chapter, you covered a tour of the WordPress core software. You explored what's in the core, how to use the core as a reference when developing for WordPress, and how to determine what functions are deprecated each release. You also learned about the WordPress Codex, the Code Reference, and the most commonly used APIs in WordPress.

Now that you understand the core of WordPress, it's time to learn how to utilize the WordPress Loop to customize the display of content.

5

The Loop

WHAT'S IN THIS CHAPTER?

➤ Understanding the flow of the Loop and where it can be used

➤ Determining content display using the Loop

➤ Customizing the Loop with different granularities of data access

➤ Using template tags

➤ Understanding global variables and their relationship to Loop processing

➤ Working outside of the Loop

The Loop refers to how WordPress determines what content (posts, pages, or custom content) to display on a page you are visiting. The Loop can display a single piece of content or a group of posts and pages that are selected and then displayed by looping through the content; thus, it's called the Loop.

This is how WordPress displays posts by default. The Loop selects posts from the MySQL database based on a set of parameters, and those parameters are typically determined by the URL used to access your WordPress website. For example, the homepage might show all blog posts in reverse chronological order by default. A category page, accessed via a URL such as http://example.com/category/halloween/, shows only blog posts assigned to that category, in this case posts put into the halloween category. An archive page shows only blog posts that are dated with that particular month and year. WordPress maps nearly every parameter about your posts into a selection variable, providing the basis for an equally wide number of different ways to alter the Loop's content selection algorithm. It is very easy to customize what content is displayed, and where, on your website with a thorough understanding of how the Loop translates a URL into what you see when you access that link.

This chapter discusses how the Loop works, where the Loop can be used, and the logical flow of the Loop. It also covers how to customize the Loop using the many different functions and data access methods available in WordPress. Global variables that maintain the current state are also discussed along with working outside of the Loop.

UNDERSTANDING THE LOOP

Understanding how the Loop functions will help you understand how you can control it. Controlling the Loop to display exactly the content you want will be one of your most used skills in developing WordPress-powered websites. Because the Loop is at the heart of every WordPress theme, being able to customize the display content opens up the doors to making WordPress look and act however you want.

To understand the Loop, it helps to break down the steps WordPress takes to generate a page's content:

1. The URL is matched against existing files and directories in the WordPress installation. If the file is there, it is loaded by the web server. WordPress doesn't actually get involved in this decision; it's up to your web server and the `.htaccess` file created by WordPress to decide if the URL is something handled by the web server or to be turned into a WordPress content query. This was covered in the discussion of permalinks in Chapter 2.

2. If the URL doesn't load a WordPress core file, it has to be parsed to determine what content to load. The web server starts by loading the WordPress core through `index.php` to begin the setup for the Loop. For example, when visiting a specific tag page such as `http://example.com/tag/bacon`, WordPress will determine that you are viewing a tag and load the appropriate template, select the posts saved with that tag, and generate the output for the tag page.

3. The translation of URL-to-content-selection magic happens inside of the `parse_query()` method within the `WP_Query` object that WordPress created early on in its processing. WordPress parses the URL first into a set of query parameters that are described in the next section. All query strings from the URL are passed into WordPress to determine what content to display, even if they look like nicely formatted pathnames. If your site is using pretty permalinks, the values between slashes in those permalinks are merely parameters for query strings. For example, `http://example.com/tag/bacon` is the same as `http://example.com?tag=bacon`, which conveys a query string of tag with a value of `bacon`.

4. WordPress then converts the query specification parameters into a MySQL database query to retrieve the content. The workhorse here is the `get_posts()` method within the `WP_Query` object that is described later in this chapter. The `get_posts()` method takes all of those query parameters and turns them into SQL statements, eventually invoking the SQL string on the MySQL database server and extracting the desired content. The content returned from the database is then saved in the `WP_Query` object to be used in the WordPress Loop and cached to speed up other references to the same posts made before another database query is executed.

5. Once the content is retrieved, WordPress sets all of the `is_` conditional tags such as `is_home()` and `is_page()`. These are set as part of executing the default query based on the URL parsing, and you'll consider cases where you may need to reset these tags.

6.   WordPress picks a template from your theme based on the type of query and the number of posts returned—for example, a single post or a category-only query—and the output of the query is passed to this default invocation of the Loop.

The Loop can be customized for different website purposes. For example, a news site might use the Loop to display the latest news headlines. A business directory could use the Loop to display local businesses alphabetically by name, or always put posts about sponsoring businesses at the top of every displayed page. An e-commerce site might use the Loop to display products loaded into the website. The possibilities are endless when customizing the Loop in WordPress because it gives you complete control over what content is selected and the order in which it is rendered for display.

From Query Parameters to SQL

Once the query parameters have been established, either by disassembling the URL provided by the reader or by having them explicitly set in a customized loop, the WP _ Query object's get _ posts() method translates those parameters into SQL for a database query. While you can exercise great control over the type, selection, and ordering of content through the query parameters, the WordPress core also exposes filters to allow you to change the generated SQL for even finer-grained control over content selection and grouping.

The basic format of a SQL query is: SELECT *fields* FROM *table* WHERE *conditions*. "Fields" are the columns of the database that you want returned; you usually don't need to modify this part of the query. The "conditions" specified in the WHERE clause change the ordering, grouping, and number of posts returned. If you dump out the generated SQL query by examining the request field of the WP _ Query object, you'll see that the WHERE portion of the SQL contains 1=1 as the first conditional. If there are no other content selection parameters, the 1=1 ensures that the generated SQL isn't syntactically malformed in the absence of other WHERE clauses; the SQL optimizer in MySQL knows enough to ignore the 1=1.

"Table" is not simply the "posts" table in the MySQL database that contains all post data; it may also refer to an SQL JOIN of two or more tables where you need to select posts based on hierarchical metadata. WordPress makes it easy to put multiple tags on a post, or to put a post in more than one category, but relational databases aren't adept at managing these hierarchical or networked relationships. As you see in Chapter 6, the WordPress data model uses multiple tables to manage these complex relationships, but that makes queries such as "find all posts tagged bacon" more difficult to execute. For example, to select the posts tagged bacon, an SQL JOIN is needed to first find bacon in the metadata taxonomy, build an intermediate, in-memory table of posts that have been tagged with bacon, and then select posts whose IDs appear both in the intermediate table and the main WordPress content table. Database aficionados call this a "Cartesian product" or inner join of two or more tables; the multiplicative description in both query complexity and memory consumption is accurate.

In Chapter 8, you will dig into plugins and how they attach to filter and action hook insertion points in the WordPress core. Within the SQL request generation, there are a number of filters that are invoked to give plugin authors late-binding and very explicit control over the SQL that gets executed. For example, consider a plugin that changes the post selection based on custom post metadata and context that the plugin maintains in a separate database table. Your plugin would use the posts _ join filter to rewrite the JOIN clause, adding another table and field match clause to further expand the selection set. If you want to explore the core for the gory details of SQL generation, most of the query-to-request parsing is done in wp-includes/query.php, and the bulk of the JOIN work is set up in wp-includes/taxonomy.php.

One final note on SQL generation: WordPress does a very good job of building canonical URLs, that is, one and only one way to reference a particular post. Search engines notoriously consider http://example.com/bacon and http://example.com/2012/bacon as distinct pages, even if they refer to the same piece of content (this is largely done to discourage more notorious practice of *link farming* where many distinct URLs are generated to feign the popularity of a single target). Part of the URL parsing function within the WordPress core attempts to clean up and redirect URLs to their canonical form; the same functions also make every effort to return some relevant content rather than a 404 page. As a result, if an attempt to load a page by name fails to return any content, WordPress will insert a LIKE modifier into the WHERE clause that contains the post name. For example, if a user supplies the URL http://example.com/2015/lecter, but you have no posts with the title "Lecter," the LIKE clause will match any posts that start with "Lecter," such as "Lecter Fish IPA Review." Canonical URLs and "like name" matching are part of the complex maze of URL rewriting and intent parsing that try to generate a pleasant user experience, rather than an annoying 404 error.

Understanding Content in WordPress

Before diving into the Loop in detail, it's important to understand the different types of content in WordPress. By default, WordPress defines two types of content: posts and pages. What you'll see in Chapter 6 is that all content types are stored in the same MySQL table, and are differentiated by their "post type." Since the release of WordPress 2.9, it's possible to define your own custom post types, which is basically custom content in WordPress. For example, you could have an Events custom post type to register events in WordPress.

Throughout this chapter, content is referred to as "posts," but it's important to remember that posts could really be any type of content in WordPress.

> **NOTE** *Custom post types are covered in Chapter 7.*

Putting the Loop in Context

The Loop is the heart of a theme, which is what controls how your content is displayed. It is the functional connection between the MySQL database data and the HTML that is rendered in the visitor's browser. Basically, anywhere a post or page is displayed, WordPress is going to use the Loop. This can be a single post or page, a loop of posts, or a sequence of loops with different display options.

Most WordPress themes feature a header, footer, and sidebar element. Figure 5-1 shows how the Loop is placed directly in the middle of these elements, creating your website content area. This section of your website is usually dynamic and will change as you navigate through it.

The Loop, by default, is used in your WordPress theme template files. Custom Loops can be created anywhere in your theme template files, as Figure 5-2 shows. Custom Loops are also used in plugins and widgets. Loops can be used anywhere inside of WordPress, but different methods exist for creating custom Loops depending on where they are used, and the potential side effects of each construction will differ.

Multiple Loops can be used throughout your theme template files. Custom Loops can be created in your header, sidebars, footer, and main content areas of your website. There is no limit to the number of Loops that can be displayed on your website. Keep in mind that a Loop is effectively a database query to select content and then an iteration over the selection to display it. The default Loop uses context from the visited URL to make that selection, but you can fine-tune and craft a query against the WordPress content database to implement any number of content management processes.

The following section looks at the basic flow control of the Loop and the WordPress template functions provided to customize the way content is displayed while being handled inside of a loop. Having armed you with the basics, you will now explore building custom Loops based on hand-tailoring those query parameters.

Flow of the Loop

The Loop uses some standard programming conditional statements to determine what and how to display. The first statement in the Loop is an `if` statement that checks whether any posts exist, because you might not have any posts with the specified category or tag. If content exists, the `while` statement is used to initiate the Loop and cycle through all posts

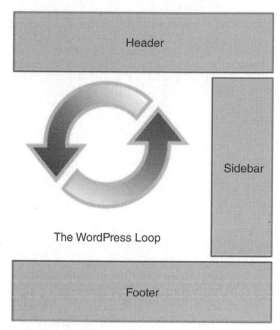

FIGURE 5-1: The WordPress Loop

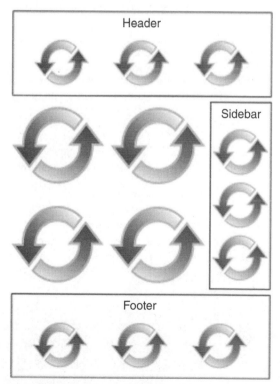

FIGURE 5-2: Using multiple Loops

or pages that need to be displayed. Finally, the_post() function is called to build the post data, making it accessible to other WordPress functions. Once the post data has been built, Loop content can be displayed in whatever format you like.

Following is a minimal Loop example. This example features the only required elements for the Loop to function properly:

```php
<?php
if ( have_posts() ) :
    while ( have_posts() ) :
        the_post();
        //loop content (template tags, html, etc)
    endwhile;
endif;
?>
```

Remember that this is PHP code, so it needs to be surrounded in <?php and ?> tags. This is the Loop in its simplest form. If you're wondering how the output from the database query got handed to this simple Loop when there are no variables passed as parameters, the answer lies in the global variable $wp_query, which is an instance of WP_Query that is referenced by the functions in the simple Loop. It is, in effect, the default query for the Loop. Note that by the time this default Loop is called, WordPress has already called the get_posts() method within the default query object to build the list of appropriate content for the URL being viewed, and the Loop in this case is charged with displaying that list of posts. Later on, you look at how to hand-structure queries to exercise fine-grain control over post selection, but for now it's safe to assume that the database heavy lifting has been done, and the results are stored in $wp_query, when the Loop is invoked.

Some very minimal requirements exist for the Loop to work in WordPress. Let's break down this example to look at the different parts of the Loop:

```php
if ( have_posts() ) :
```

This line checks if any posts or pages are going to be displayed on the current page you are viewing. If posts or pages exist, the next line will execute:

```php
while ( have_posts() ) :
```

The preceding while statement starts the Loop, essentially looping through all posts and pages to be displayed on the page until there are no more. The Loop will continue while content exists to be displayed. Once all content has been displayed, the while loop will end. The have_posts() function simply checks to see if the list of posts being processed is exhausted, or had no entries to begin with.

```php
the_post();
```

Next, the the_post() function is called to load all of the post data. This function must be called inside your loop for the post data to be set correctly. Calling the_post() in turn calls the setup_postdata() function to set up the per-post metadata such as the author and tags of the content you are displaying in the Loop, as well as the content of the post itself. This data is assigned to a global variable each time through the Loop iteration. Specifically calling the _ post() has the side effect of setting up the global $post variable used by most of the template tags described later on, and then advances to the next post in the list.

Setting up the post data also applies the appropriate filters to the raw content that comes out of the WordPress database. WordPress stores user-edited content exactly as entered, so if a user adds a shortcode, for example, to add a Google AdSense item at the end of a post, the shortcode is stored in the database content. When the post setup is done, the plugin that converts that shortcode to a chunk of JavaScript is called, along with other registered plugins that modify the raw post content. You'll look at the plugin mechanics in Chapter 8, but for now, it's important to note the distinction between the raw post data in the WordPress query object and the filtered content that is eventually rendered.

```
//loop content
```

This is where all Loop template tags are placed and any additional code you want displayed inside the Loop. This is covered in more detail later in this chapter.

```
endwhile;
endif;
```

The endwhile and endif calls end the Loop. Any code placed after these two lines will show at the bottom of your page, after all posts have been displayed. You could also place an else clause to display a message if there is no content to display in the Loop.

The Loop is usually surrounded by HTML tags in your theme template files. The following code shows how the Loop is structured in the core Twenty Fourteen theme that comes with WordPress:

```php
<div id="main-content" class="main-content">

<?php
    if ( is_front_page() && twentyfourteen_has_featured_posts() ) {
        // Include the featured content template.
        get_template_part( 'featured-content' );
    }
?>

    <div id="primary" class="content-area">
        <div id="content" class="site-content" role="main">

        <?php
            if ( have_posts() ) :
                // Start the Loop.
                while ( have_posts() ) : the_post();

                    /*
                     * Include the post format-specific template for the content.
                       If you want to
                     * use this in a child theme, then include a file
                       called called content-___.php
                     * (where ___ is the post format) and that will be used
                       instead.
```

```
                            */
                    get_template_part( 'content', get_post_format() );

                endwhile;
                // Previous/next post navigation.
                twentyfourteen_paging_nav();

            else :
                // If no content, include the "No posts found" template.
                get_template_part( 'content', 'none' );

            endif;
        ?>

        </div><!-- #content -->
    </div><!-- #primary -->
    <?php get_sidebar( 'content' ); ?>
</div><!-- #main-content -->
```

Notice how the minimal Loop elements exist but are surrounded by HTML tags. This is how a normal theme template file will be structured to utilize the Loop. The HTML elements can certainly change, but the Loop elements stay the same. Customizing the style in which content is displayed and choosing post metadata to include in the page composition is done through template tags.

TEMPLATE TAGS

PHP functions used in your WordPress theme templates to display Loop content are called *template tags*. These tags are used to display specific pieces of data about your website and content. This allows you to customize how and where content is displayed on your website.

For example, the `the_title()` template tag displays the title of your post or page inside the Loop. The major benefit of using template tags is that you don't need to know PHP code to use them.

Many different template tags are available in WordPress. Some template tags must be inside the Loop, whereas other tags can be used anywhere in your theme template files. Note that in this context, template tags refer to the WordPress functions used to extract post data for display; template files are the theme elements that control how content for a particular content type is displayed. Put another way, template files contain Loops comprising template tags. For an updated list of template tags available in WordPress, visit `http://codex.wordpress.org/Template_Tags`.

Commonly Used Template Tags

There is no shortage of template tags, but typically you will use only a handful of tags in your Loops. Following are the most commonly used template tags available in the Loop. These template tags will return and display the post data listed.

➤ `the_permalink()`—Displays the URL of your post.

➤ `the_title()`—Displays the title of the post.

- ➤ `the_ID()`—Displays the unique ID of your post.

- ➤ `the_content()`—Displays the full content of your post.

- ➤ `the_excerpt()`—Displays the excerpt of your post. If the `Excerpt` field is filled out on the Post edit screen, that will be used. If not, WordPress will auto-generate a short excerpt from your post content.

- ➤ `the_time()`—Displays the date/time your post was published.

- ➤ `the_author()`—Displays the author of the post.

- ➤ `the_tags()`—Displays the tags attached to the post.

- ➤ `the_category()`—Displays the categories assigned to the post.

- ➤ `edit_post_link()`—Displays an `edit` link that is shown only if you are logged in and allowed to edit the post.

- ➤ `comment_form()`—Displays a complete commenting form for your post.

To learn how template tags work, just place any template tag inside the Loop and view the results. The following example views the values of a couple different template tags:

```php
<?php
if ( have_posts() ) :
    while ( have_posts() ) :
        the_post();
        ?>
        <a href="<?php the_permalink(); ?>"><?php the_title(); ?></a>
        <br />
        <?php
        the_content();
    endwhile;
endif;
?>
```

As you can see, your post titles are displayed with links to the permalink for each post. The content of the post is displayed directly below the post title.

Tag Parameters

Most template tags have parameters that can be added to modify the value returned. For example, the the _ content() template tag has two parameters. The first parameter allows you to set the more link text like so:

```php
<?php the_content( 'Read more', false ); ?>
```

Your post content will be displayed as normal, but when the `<!--more-->` tag is found in your post, WordPress will automatically add the text Read more, which would link to the entire blog post. The second parameter determines whether to display the teaser paragraph again when viewing the full post. The default value is `false` so the teaser will be displayed in both places.

> **NOTE** *The* `more` *tag in WordPress allows you to display a defined teaser from the full post on your website. For example, you could display the first paragraph of a post on your homepage, and only show the full blog post when a visitor clicks the link to view the full post. To accomplish this, you can place* `<!--more-->` *in your content in HTML view where you want this break to happen. In the visual editor, there is a button to insert a* `More` *tag.*

You can also send multiple parameters to any template tag that supports it. For example, the template tag `the_title()` accepts three parameters: $before, $after, and $echo. The following code sets the `the_title()` tags $before and $after parameters to wrap the post title with h1 tags:

```php
<?php the_title( '<h1>', '</h1>' ); ?>
```

You can also view the actual function in the WordPress source code. The post template functions are located in `wp-includes/post-template.php`. Doing a quick search for `function the_title()` will lead you to the exact function for the `the_title()` tag. You can also use the Codex for a detailed description of the template tag you are working with, in this case `http://codex.wordpress.org/Template_Tags/the_title`.

CUSTOMIZING THE LOOP

The opening discussion of Loop flow of control mentioned that the main workhorse for data selection is the `get_posts()` method of the `WP_Query` object. In most cases, if you want to build a custom Loop, you'll build your own `WP_Query` object and reference it explicitly. Alternatively, you can use the lower-level `query_posts()` and `get_posts()` functions (not to be confused with the methods within the `WP_Query` object of the same name) to manipulate the output of the default query that was passed into your Loop. Both `query_posts()` and `get_posts()` use the `WP_Query` class to retrieve content. The final method you'll examine is the `pre_get_posts` hook. This hook is called after the query variable object is created but before the actual query is run. You'll look at the various approaches and discuss how and where you should—and shouldn't—use them, but let's start with a discussion of how you build a custom query object.

Using the WP_Query Object

Once WordPress is handed a URL to parse by the web server, it goes to work disassembling the tokens in that URL and converting them into parameters for a database query. Here's a bit more detail on what happens when manipulating your own `WP_Query`.

`WP_Query` is a class defined in WordPress that makes it easy to create your own custom Loops. Both `query_posts()` and `get_posts()` use the `WP_Query` class to retrieve the WordPress content. When you're using `query_posts()`, the global variable $wp_query is used as an instance of `WP_Query`, making $wp_query the default data store for several operations. Custom Loops can be used anywhere in your theme template files to display different types of content; they must build on separate instances of a `WP_Query` variable.

When you create a new WP_Query object, it's instantiated with some default functions for building queries, executing the query to get posts, and parsing parameters out of a URL. However, you can use these built-in object methods to construct your own parameter strings, creating custom loops that extract whatever particular content you need for that point in your Loop.

The following is an example of a custom Loop displaying the five most recent posts on your website:

```php
<?php
$myPosts = new WP_Query( 'posts_per_page=5' );while ( $myPosts-
>have_posts() )
: $myPosts->the_post();
?>
  <!-- do something -->
<?php endwhile; ?>
```

Rather than using the simpler have_posts() and the_post() calls that you saw in the basic Loop, this custom loop calls the methods of the newly created WP_Query object $myPosts. The explicit invocation shown here and the default have_posts() call are functionally equivalent; have_posts(), for example, is merely calling $wp_query->have_posts() using the global query variable for the default query—that is, the one generated from parsing the URL handed to WordPress by the web server.

Going into your default Loop from the URL used to invoke WordPress; there's an additional step that takes the URL and parses it into an appropriate query string using the parse_query() method of the query object. When you build your own custom Loop, you explicitly set the parameters you want to control the query. Here's a bit more detail on what happens inside the query function:

➤ Calling $myPosts->query() converts the parameters into an SQL statement via the function $myPosts->get_posts(), which then executes the query against the MySQL database and extracts the content you've requested.

➤ Equally important, the query call sets up the conditional tags such as is_home() and is_single() that are dependent upon the type of page displayed and the quantity of content for that page.

➤ The array of posts returned by the query is cached by WordPress so that future references to the same query won't generate additional database traffic.

The key to building a powerful custom Loop is to map your content selection criteria into the right set of query parameters.

Building a Custom Query

Parameters are used to define what content will be returned in your Loop, whether a custom Loop or altering the primary Loop. When creating Loops, it's essential to understand what parameters are available to help define what content will be displayed. You can use many different, sometimes confusing, parameters in creating your custom Loop to alter the output of your content.

Multiple parameters can also be set per query by separating the parameter name and values with an ampersand. For a detailed list of available parameters, visit http://codex.wordpress.org/ Class_Reference/WP_Query#Parameters.

The following sections cover some of the more commonly used parameters.

Post Parameters

The most obvious, and sometimes most used, parameters select the number and types of posts to be displayed:

➤   `p=2`—Loads an individual post by ID.

➤   `name=my-slug`—Loads posts based on post slug (permalink tail).

➤   `post_status=pending`—Loads posts by post status. For example, if you choose to see only drafts, use `post_status=draft`.

➤   `ignore_sticky_posts`—Excludes sticky posts from being returned first. A *sticky post* is one that always sorts to the top of the list of posts, independent of the other parameters set for the query. You can have multiple sticky posts, making them useful for calling attention to news announcements, highlighting changes, or otherwise grabbing the reader's attention, and this parameter lets you drop them from their priority slot at the top of the list.

➤   `post_type=post`—Loads posts based on type. If you only want to look at pages, not posts, `post_type=page` will retrieve them. This parameter enables special-purpose loops to select content based on custom post types, as you'll see in Chapter 7.

➤   `posts_per_page=5`—Number of posts to load per page. This is the default. To show all posts, set this parameter to –1.

➤   `offset=1`—Number of posts to skip before loading.

Page Parameters

Pages have parameters similar to those for posts to control their selection:

➤   `page_id=5`—Loads an individual page by ID. Like post IDs and user IDs, page IDs can be found in the dashboard by hovering over a page and looking at the URL displayed at the bottom on your browser.

➤   `pagename=Contact`—Loads a page by name, in this case the Contact page.

➤   `pagename=parent/child`—Loads a child page by slug, or hierarchy of slugs (that is, its path).

Category, Tag, and Author Parameters

Posts can also be sorted by the category into which they were placed, by tags applied to the post, or by author information:

➤   `cat=3,4,5`—Loads posts based on category ID.

➤   `category_name=About Us`—Loads posts based on category name. Note that if a post belongs to more than one category, it will show up in selections for each of those categories.

➤   `tag=writing`—Loads posts based on tag name.

➤   `tag_id=34`—Loads posts based on tag ID.

➤   `author=1`—Loads posts based on user ID.

➤ `author_name=brad`—Loads posts based on author's name.

➤ `author__in` & `author__not_in`—Loads posts based on user ID.

Date and Time Parameters

Parameters to select content based on their chronology are a key part of building an archive of posts, or providing a view into content through a calendar on your website's homepage.

➤ `monthnum=6`—Loads posts created in June.

➤ `day=9`—Loads posts created on the ninth day of the month.

➤ `year=2015`—Loads posts created in 2015.

Ordering and Custom Field Parameters

You can also change the sort parameter and the sort order. If you're building an online index, and want to show an alphabetical post listing, you'll set the parameters for querying posts by month and author, but order the results by title. Custom field parameters allow you to query posts based on post metadata.

➤ `orderby=title`—Field to order posts by.

➤ `order=ASC`—Defines ascending or descending order of `orderby`.

➤ `meta_key=color`—Loads posts by custom field name.

> **NOTE** *Refer to the custom taxonomy and data discussion in Chapter 7 to see how custom fields are added to posts.*

➤ `meta_value=blue`—Loads posts by custom field value. Must be used in conjunction with the `meta_key` parameter.

➤ `meta_query`—Used for more advanced custom field (metadata) queries.

Putting It Together

Now look at some examples using parameters. The following examples use the `$myPosts->query()` function from the `$myPosts` custom query object created in the example to select the content displayed in your custom Loop.

Display post based on post ID:

```
$myPosts = new WP_Query( 'p=1' );
```

Display the five latest posts, skipping the first post:

```
$myPosts = new WP_Query( 'posts_per_page=5&offset=1' );
```

Display all posts from today:

```
// display all posts from the current date
$today = getdate(); // get todays date
$myPosts = new WP_Query('year=' .$today["year"]
    .'&monthnum=' .$today["mon"] .'&day=' .$today["mday"] );
```

Display all posts from October 31, 2015:

```
$myPosts = new WP_Query( 'monthnum=10&day=31&year=2015' );
```

Display all posts from category ID 5 with the bacon tag:

```
$myPosts = new WP_Query( 'cat=5&tag=bacon' );
```

Display all posts with the bacon tag, excluding posts in category ID 5:

```
$myPosts = new WP_Query( 'cat=-5&tag=bacon' );
```

Display all posts with the tag writing or reading:

```
$myPosts = new WP_Query( 'tag=writing,reading' );
```

Display all posts with the tags writing and reading and tv:

```
$myPosts = new WP_Query( 'tag=writing+reading+tv' );
```

Display all posts with a custom field named color with a value of blue:

```
$myPosts = new WP_Query( 'meta_key=color&meta_value=blue' );
```

Adding Paging to a Loop

If your custom Loop requires paging (navigation links), you will need to take a few extra steps. Paging is currently designed to work only with the $wp_query global variable; that is, it works within the default Loop and requires some sleight of hand to make it work in custom Loops. You need to trick WordPress into thinking your custom query is actually $wp_query in order for paging to work.

```php
<?php
$temp = $wp_query;
$wp_query= null;
$paged = ( get_query_var( 'paged' ) ) ? get_query_var( 'paged' ) : 1;
$wp_query = new WP_Query( 'posts_per_page=5&paged='.$paged );
while ( $wp_query->have_posts() ) : $wp_query->the_post();
?>
    <h2>
    <a href="<?php the_permalink(); ?>"><?php the_title(); ?></a>
    </h2>
    <?php the_excerpt(); ?>
<?php endwhile; ?>
```

First, you have to store the original $wp_query variable into the temporary variable $temp. Next, you set $wp_query to null to completely flush it clean. This is one of the few times it's acceptable to overwrite a global variable value in WordPress. Now set your new WP_Query object into the $wp_query variable and execute it by calling the object's query() function to select posts for your custom Loop. Notice the $paged variable added to the end of the query. This stores the current page, using the get_query_var() function, so WordPress knows how to display the navigation links. Now display your navigation links for paging:

```
<div class="navigation">
  <div class="alignleft"><?php previous_posts_link( '&laquo; Previous' );
?></div>
  <div class="alignright"><?php next_posts_link( 'More &raquo;' ); ?></div>
</div>
```

Finally, you need to reset $wp_query back to its original value:

```
<?php
$wp_query = null;
$wp_query = $temp;
?>
```

Now your custom Loop will contain proper pagination based on the content returned.

Using the pre_get_posts Hook

The pre_get_posts hook allows you to modify any Loop query on your WordPress website. Generally, this hook is the preferred method for modifying the main WordPress Loop. The pre_get_posts hook accepts the global WordPress query by reference, which enables you to modify the query variables prior to having the query run. In short, this hook makes it very easy to modify a WordPress Loop prior to making a call to the database to retrieve the content.

When using the pre_get_posts hook, you'll generally place the code in your theme's functions.php file. Let's look at an example of pre_get_posts in action:

```
function prowp_exclude_category( $query ) {

    if ( $query->is_home() && $query->is_main_query() && ! is_admin() ) {
        $query->set( 'category_name', 'halloween' );
    }

}

add_action( 'pre_get_posts', 'prowp_exclude_category' );
```

> **NOTE** *Chapter 9 covers themes in detail.*

In the preceding example, you are modifying the main WordPress Loop to only show posts in the halloween category on the home page. As you can see, the example uses conditionals to verify that the query is only modified on the home page, is the main query, and is not the admin dashboard.

Using conditional functions allows you to modify the Loop only in specific areas of WordPress. A common example is modifying WordPress search results. By default, WordPress search includes posts and pages. Let's assume you want only posts returned in your search results:

```
function prowp_search_filter( $query ) {

    if ( ! is_admin() && $query->is_main_query() && $query->is_search() ) {

        $query->set( 'post_type', 'post' );

    }

}

add_action( 'pre_get_posts', 'prowp_search_filter' );
```

The pre_get_posts hook filters a WP_Query object, which means anything you can do with WP_Query you can also do with pre_get_posts using the set() function. This includes all of the Loop parameters you reviewed earlier in this chapter.

For more information on the pre_get_posts hook, visit the Codex page http://codex. wordpress.org/Plugin_API/Action_Reference/pre_get_posts.

Using query_posts( )

A tremendous amount of customization can be done by specifying the appropriate set of parameters for your Loop. While the WP_Query object is the most general-purpose mechanism for extracting content from the WordPress database, there are other lower-level methods that you'll encounter.

The query_posts() function is used to easily modify the content returned for the default WordPress Loop. Specifically, you can modify the content returned in $wp_query after the default database query has executed, fine-tune the query parameters, and re-execute the query using query_posts(). The downside to calling query_posts() in this fashion is that the previously cached results from the default query are discarded, so you're incurring a database performance hit to use this shortcut. The query_posts() function should be placed directly above the start of the Loop:

```
query_posts( 'posts_per_page=5&paged='.$paged );
if ( have_posts() ) :
    while ( have_posts() ) : the_post();
        //loop content (template tags, html, etc)
    endwhile;
endif;
```

This example tells WordPress to display only five posts.

Explicitly calling query_posts() overwrites the original post content extracted for the Loop. This means any content you were expecting to be returned before using query_posts() will not be returned. For example, if the URL passed to WordPress is for a category page at http://example .com/category/zombie/, none of the zombie category posts will be in the post list after query_posts() has been called unless one is in the five most recent posts. You explicitly overwrite the query parameters established by the URL parsing and default processing when you pass the query string to query _ posts().

To avoid losing your original Loop content, you can save the parsed query parameters by using the $query _ string global variable:

```
// initialize the global query_string variable
global $query_string;

// keep original Loop content and change the sort order
query_posts( $query_string . "&orderby=title&order=ASC" );
```

In the preceding example, you would still see all of your zombie category posts, but they would be ordered alphabetically by ascending title. This technique is used to modify the original Loop content without losing that original content.

You can also pack all of your query _ posts() parameters in an array, making it easier to manage. Following is an example of how to retrieve only the sticky post set in WordPress using an array called $args to store the parameter values:

```
$args = array(
    'posts_per_page' => 1,
    'post__in'  => get_option( 'sticky_posts' )
);
query_posts( $args );
```

If no sticky post is found, the latest post will be returned instead. The query _ posts() function is used to modify the main page Loop only. It is not intended to create additional custom Loops. If you want to make a slight change to the default query—for example, adding posts of a specific category or tag to every displayed page—then the query _ posts() approach is a shortcut. However, it's not without side effects or cautions:

➤ query_posts() modifies the global variable $wp_query and has other side effects. It should not be called more than once and shouldn't be used inside the Loop. The example shows the call to query_posts() before post processing has started, when the extra parameters are added to the query string but before the Loop has begun to step through the returned post list. Calling query_posts() more than once, or inside the Loop itself, can result in your main Loop being incorrect and displaying unintended content.

➤ query_posts() unsets the global $wp_query object, and in doing so, may invalidate the values of conditional tags such as is_page() or is_home(). Going through the entire WP_Query object instantiation sets all of the conditional tags appropriately. For example, you may find with the shortcut that you have added content to a selection that the default query found contained only one post, and therefore is_single() is no longer valid.

➤ Calling query_posts() executes another database query, invalidating all of the cached results from the first, default query. You at least double the number of database queries executed and are incurring a performance hit for each trip back to MySQL; on the other hand the default query has already been run by the time you get to the default Loop, so there's little chance to work around it if you're building an entirely custom main Loop.

Using get_posts( )

Like query _ posts(), there's an alternative, simpler access function called get _ posts() that retrieves raw post data. You'll see get _ posts() used in administration pages to generate a list of pages of a particular type, or it may be used within a plugin to grab all raw data for a set of posts and examine it for patterns such as common terms, tags, or external links, with the intent of discarding the content after a quick digestion. It's not intended for user-facing content display because it turns off much of query processing and filtering that is done within the more general WP _ Query approach.

What get _ posts() lacks, specifically, is the ability to set up all of the global data needed to make template tags reflect the current post data. One main issue is that not all template tags are available to get _ posts() by default. To fix this deficiency, you need to call the setup _ postdata() function to populate the template tags for use in your Loop. The following example shows how to retrieve a single random post using get _ posts():

```php
<?php
$randompost = get_posts( 'numberposts=1&orderby=rand' );
foreach( $randompost as $post ) :
    setup_postdata( $post );
?>
<h1><a href="<?php the_permalink(); ?>"><?php the_title(); ?></a></h1>
<?php the_content(); ?>
<?php endforeach; ?>
```

You'll notice another major difference using get _ posts()—the value returned is an array. The foreach loop code is used to cycle through the array values. This example returns only one post, but if more than one were returned, this would cycle through each. Then the setup _ postdata() function is called to populate the data for your template tags.

Remember that you can also set up your get _ posts() parameter using an array:

```php
<?php
$args = array(
    'numberposts' => 1,
    'orderby'  => rand
);
$randompost = get_posts( $args );
```

Although you may see older code using get _ posts() or query _ posts() constructions, WP _ Query is the preferred approach and should be the heart of custom loop syntax. However, there are times when you'll want the quick-and-dirty access provided by get _ posts() to generate additional context or data for further customization of your Loop or in a plugin.

When working with Loops in WordPress, it's important to understand what Loop method to use and when. The pre _ get _ posts hook should be used when altering the main query on the page. The WP _ Query object should be used for all secondary Loops in your theme templates and plugins.

Resetting a Query

When customizing the main Loop, or creating custom Loops, it's a good idea to reset the Loop data after you are done. WordPress features two different functions to handle this: wp _ reset _ postdata() and wp _ reset _ query().

The first method for resetting post data is wp _ reset _ data(). This function actually restores the global $post variable to the current post in the main query. This is the preferred method when using WP _ Query to create custom Loops.

For example, assume you have the following custom Loop in your theme's header.php file:

```php
<?php
$myPosts = new WP_Query( 'posts_per_page=1&orderby=rand' );
// The Loop
while ( $myPosts->have_posts() ) : $myPosts->the_post();
  ?><a href="<?php the_permalink(); ?>"><?php the_title(); ?></a><br
/><?php
endwhile;
?>
```

This will display a random post in the header of your theme. This code will also change the main query object for other Loops on the page. The original query data will not be available, which could produce unexpected results on the main posts' Loop for your theme.

To fix the problem, place a call to wp _ reset _ postdata() directly after your custom Loop like so:

```php
$myPosts = new WP_Query( 'posts_per_page=1&orderby=rand' );
// The Loop
while ( $myPosts->have_posts() ) : $myPosts->the_post();
  ?><a href="<?php the_permalink(); ?>"><?php the_title(); ?></a><br
/><?php
endwhile;
// Reset Post Data
wp_reset_postdata();
```

Calling this function will restore the $post variable to the current post in the query. This will eliminate any strangeness in the main query for the page you are viewing.

The second method available for resetting post data is the wp _ reset _ query() function. From time to time, you may run into problems with page-level conditional tags being used after a custom Loop has been created. Conditional tags allow you to run different code on different pages in WordPress— for example, using the conditional tag is _ home() to determine if you are viewing the main blog page. This problem is caused, as indicated in the "Using query_posts( )" section, by potentially changing the output of a database query after setting the conditional tags based on its original set of values. To fix this issue, you need to call wp _ reset _ query(). This function will properly restore the original query, including the conditional tags set up early in the URL parsing process.

Consider the following example:

```php
<?php query_posts( 'posts_per_page=5' ); ?>
<?php if ( have_posts() ) : while ( have_posts() ) : the_post(); ?>
    <a href="<?php the_permalink(); ?>"><?php the_title(); ?></a><br />
<?php endwhile; endif; ?>
<?php
if( is_home() && !is_paged() ):
    wp_list_bookmarks( 'title_li=&categorize=0' );
endif;
?>
```

Executing this code will return the latest five posts followed by the links saved in your WordPress link manager. The problem you will run into is that the is_home() conditional tag will not be interpreted correctly, meaning your links will show on every page, not just the homepage. To fix this issue, you need to include wp_reset_query() directly below your Loop:

```php
<?php query_posts( 'posts_per_page=5' ); ?>
<?php if ( have_posts() ) : while ( have_posts() ) : the_post(); ?>
    <a href="<?php the_permalink(); ?>"><?php the_title(); ?></a><br />
<?php endwhile; endif; ?>
<?php wp_reset_query(); ?>
<?php
if( is_home() && !is_paged() ):
    wp_list_bookmarks( 'title_li=&categorize=0' );
endif;
?>
```

Now that you have properly restored your Loop's instance of the WP_Query object, the conditional tag is_home() will be followed and your links will now display only on the homepage of your website. It's a good practice to add wp_reset_query() after using query_posts() in your Loop to ensure you do not run into problems down the road. The wp_reset_query() function actually calls wp_reset_postdata(), but it does one additional step. The function actually destroys the previous query before resetting it. In short, wp_reset_query() should always be used after a query_posts() Loop and wp_reset_postdata() should be used after a WP_Query or get_posts() custom Loop.

More Than One Loop

The Loop can be used multiple times throughout your theme and plugins. This makes it easy to display different types of content in multiple places throughout your WordPress website. Maybe you want to display your most recent blog posts below each page on your website. You can achieve this by creating more complex Loops that make multiple passes through the list of posts, or by generating multiple post arrays over which to loop.

Nested Loops

Nested Loops can be created inside your theme templates using a combination of the main Loop and separate WP_Query instances. For example, you can create a nested Loop to display related posts based on post tags. The following is an example of creating a nested Loop inside the main Loop to display related posts based on tags:

```php
<?php
if ( have_posts() ) :
    while ( have_posts() ) :
        the_post();
        //loop content (template tags, html, etc)
        ?>
        <h1><a href="<?php the_permalink(); ?>"><?php the_title();
?></a></h1>
        <?php
        the_content();
        $tags = wp_get_post_terms( get_the_ID() );
```

```php
        if ( $tags ) {
            echo 'Related Posts';
            $tagcount = count( $tags );
            for ( $i = 0; $i < $tagcount; $i++ ) {
                $tagIDs[$i] = $tags[$i]->term_id;
            }
            $args=array(
                'tag__in' => $tagIDs,
                'post__not_in' => array( $post->ID ),
                'posts_per_page' => 5,
                'ignore_sticky_posts' => 1
            );
            $relatedPosts = new WP_Query( $args );
            if( $relatedPosts->have_posts() ) {
                //loop through related posts based on the tag
                while ( $relatedPosts->have_posts() ) :
                    $relatedPosts->the_post(); ?>
                    <p><a href="<?php the_permalink(); ?>">
                        <?php the_title(); ?></a></p>
                    <?php
                endwhile;
            }
        }
    endwhile;
endif;
?>
```

This code will display all of your posts as normal. Inside the main Loop, you check if any other posts contain any of the same tags as your main post. If so, you display the latest five posts that match as related posts. If no posts match, the related posts section will not be displayed.

Multi-Pass Loops

The `rewind_posts()` function is used to reset the post query and loop counter, allowing you to do another Loop using the same content as the first Loop. Place this function call directly after you finish your first Loop. Here's an example that processes the main Loop content twice:

```php
<?php while ( have_posts() ) : the_post(); ?>
  <!-- content. -->
<?php endwhile; ?>
<?php rewind_posts(); ?>
<?php while ( have_posts() ) : the_post(); ?>
  <!-- content -->
<?php endwhile; ?>
```

Advanced Queries

You can also perform more advanced queries in your Loops. Let's construct a Loop that will compare a custom field value using the `meta_compare` parameter:

```php
$args = array(
    'posts_per_page' => '-1',
    'post_type'      => 'product',
```

```
                'meta_key'       => 'price',
                'meta_value'     => '13',
                'meta_compare'   => '<='
    );

    $myProducts = new WP_Query( $args );

    // The Loop
    while ( $myProducts->have_posts() ) : $myProducts->the_post();
        ?><a href="<?php the_permalink(); ?>"><?php the_title(); ?></a><br
    /><?php
    endwhile;

    // Reset Post Data
    wp_reset_postdata();
```

As you can see, the `meta_compare` parameter is used to display all products with a meta value for price that is less than or equal to (<=) 13. The `meta_compare` parameter can accept all sorts of comparison operators such as !=, >, >=, <, <=, and the default, which is =.

For more complex meta data queries, you'll use the `meta_query` parameter. Now you can expand upon the preceding example. Instead of just returning product entries that are less than or equal to a price of 13, you can also only return products that are the color blue:

```
    $args = array(
        'post_type'  => 'product',
        'meta_query' => array(
            array(
                'key' => 'color',
                'value' => 'blue',
                'compare' => '='
            ),
            array(
                'key' => 'price',
                'value' => '13',
                'type' => 'numeric',
                'compare' => '<='
            )
        )
    );
    $myProducts = new WP_Query( $args );
    // The Loop
    while ( $myProducts->have_posts() ) : $myProducts->the_post();
        ?><a href="<?php the_permalink(); ?>"><?php the_title(); ?></a><br
    /><?php
    endwhile;
    // Reset Post Data
    wp_reset_postdata();
```

Notice the `meta_query` parameter accepts an array of parameters. In this example, the first item in the array is an array to verify the products are blue. The second parameter is an array to verify the product price is less than or equal to 13.

Creating Loops using meta query parameters can be extremely powerful. This is an important tool for creating complex websites with various metadata options.

Complex date-based queries can be created using the date _ query parameter. Let's look at an example:

```
$args = array(
    'date_query' => array(
        array(
            'after' => array(
                'year'  => '2015',
                'month' => '6',
                'day'   => '1'
                ),
            'before' => array(
                'year'  => '2015',
                'month' => '8',
                'day'   => '31'
                ),
            'inclusive' => true
        ),
    )
);

$my_posts = new WP_Query( $args );

// The Loop
while ( $my_posts->have_posts() ) : $my_posts->the_post();
    ?><a href="<?php the_permalink(); ?>"><?php the_title(); ?></a><br
/><?php
endwhile;

// Reset Post Data
wp_reset_postdata();
```

The preceding code will display all posts published in the summer of 2015, between June 1 and August 31. Using the date _ query parameter, you set the after and before values based on the post published dates you want to display. The inclusive parameter is used when the after and before parameters are used, and sets whether the exact value should be matched or not. In this example, you want posts published on June 1 and August 31 to be included, so you set the value to true.

The before and after parameters also accept strtotime compatible strings, so you can simplify this query like so:

```
$args = array(
    'date_query' => array(
        array(
            'after'     => 'June 1st, 2015',
            'before'    => 'August 31st, 2015',
            'inclusive' => true
        )
    )
);

$my_posts = new WP_Query( $args );
```

The preceding code will return the exact same results as the first example, but it is much easier to read and understand.

The date _ query parameter can also be combined with regular Loop parameters. As an example, let's return the most commented posts in the last year:

```
$args = array(
    'date_query' => array(
        'after'     => '1 year ago',
        'before'    => 'today',
        'inclusive' => true,
    ),
    'orderby'        => 'comment_count',
    'order'          => 'DESC',
    'posts_per_page' => '5'
);

$my_posts = new WP_Query( $args );
```

In this example, you're using the date _ query parameter to return all posts published between 1 year ago and today. You are also setting the orderby value to comment _ count and order to DESC. This will return the posts with the highest comment counts first. The final parameter is posts _ per _ page, which tells the query to return only five posts.

It's easy to see how powerful the date _ query parameter can be in your Loops.

GLOBAL VARIABLES

A *global variable* is a variable that has a defined value that can be accessed anywhere within the WordPress execution environment. These variables store all types of information about the Loop content, author, and users, and specific information about the WordPress installation, such as how to connect to the MySQL database. Global variables should only be used to retrieve data, meaning you should never write data to these variables directly. Overwriting the global variable values could cause unexpected results in WordPress because significant parts of core and extended functionality depend on these values being set within one context and remaining consistent for the duration of a query, page load, or single-post handling. Assigning values to global variables almost always has unintended side effects, and they're almost always not what the user or blog author wanted. However, global variables are discussed here to shed more light on how post data can be manipulated, and you may see code snippets that utilize these functions for post processing outside of the Loop.

Post Data

You saw how the key first step in the Loop is calling the_post(). Once invoked, you will have access to all of the data in WordPress specific to the post being displayed. This data is stored in the global $post variable. The $post variable stores the post data of the last post displayed on the page. So if your Loop displays ten posts, the $post variable will store post data for the tenth post displayed.

The following example shows how you can reference the $post global variable and display all values in the array using the print _ r() PHP function.

```
<?php
global $post;
```

```
    print_r( $post );   //view all data stored in the $post array
    ?>
```

The preceding code will print the array values for the $post global variable. The default WordPress blog post would look like this:

```
WP_Post Object
(
    [ID] => 1
    [post_author] => 1
    [post_date] => 2015-06-09 19:05:19
    [post_date_gmt] => 2015-06-09 17:23:50
    [post_content] => Welcome to WordPress. This is your first post.
        Edit or delete it, then start blogging!
    [post_title] => Hello world!
    [post_excerpt] =>
    [post_status] => publish
    [comment_status] => open
    [ping_status] => open
    [post_password] =>
    [post_name] => hello-world
    [to_ping] =>
    [pinged] =>
    [post_modified] => 2015-06-09 19:04:12
    [post_modified_gmt] => 2015-06-09 19:04:12
    [post_content_filtered] =>
    [post_parent] -> 0
    [guid] => http://localhost/Brad/?p=1
    [menu_order] => 0
    [post_type] => post
    [post_mime_type] =>
    [comment_count] => 1
    [filter] => raw
)
```

As you can see, the $post global variable contains all sorts of data for the post. You can also display specific pieces of data from the array, such as the post title and content, like so:

```
<?php
global $post;
echo $post->post_title;   //display the post title
echo $post->post_content;   //display the post content
?>
```

Accessing the content through the global $post variable means that you are accessing the unfiltered content. This means any plugins that would normally alter the output of the content will not affect the global content value. For example, if you had the built-in [gallery] shortcode in your post to display all images uploaded on the post, retrieving the post content as shown would return [gallery] instead of the actual image gallery.

Remember that WordPress provides template tags that can be called anywhere to retrieve these values as well, and in most cases, template tags are going to be the preferred mechanism for getting at these bits. For example, if you need to get the permalink of your post, you can use the following method:

```php
<?php
global $post;
echo get_permalink( $post->ID );  //displays the posts permalink
?>
```

This is covered in more detail in the section "Working Outside the Loop," later in this chapter.

Author Data

$authordata is a global variable that stores information about the author of the post being displayed. You can use this global variable to display the author's name:

```php
<?php
global $authordata;
echo 'Author: ' .$authordata->display_name;
?>
```

The $authordata variable is created when setup_postdata() is called during the_post() function call in the Loop. This means the $authordata global variable will not be created until the Loop has run for the first time. Another problem with this method is that the global values do not get passed through hook filters, meaning that any plugin you install to override this functionality would not be run.

The preferred method for accessing the author metadata, like that for getting post data, is to use the available WordPress template tags. For example, to display the author's display name, you would use this code:

```php
<?php
echo 'Author: ' .get_the_author_meta( 'display_name' );
?>
```

The get_the_author_meta() and the_author_meta() functions are available for retrieving all metadata related to the author of the content. If this template tag is used inside the Loop, there is no need to pass the user ID parameter. If used outside of the Loop, the user ID is required to determine what author metadata to retrieve.

User Data

The $current_user global variable stores information on the currently logged-in user. This is the account that you are currently logged in to WordPress with. Following is an example showing how to display the logged-in user's display name:

```php
<?php
global $current_user;
echo $current_user->display_name;
?>
```

This is a useful technique if you want to display a welcome message to your users. Remember that the display name will default to the user's username. To display a welcome message to any user that is logged in, you could use this code:

```php
<?php
global $current_user;
if ( $current_user->display_name ) {
    echo 'Welcome ' .$current_user->display_name;
}
?>
```

Environmental Data

WordPress also has global variables created for browser detection. The following is an example showing how you can detect the user's browser version in WordPress using global variables:

```php
<?php
global $is_lynx, $is_gecko, $is_IE, $is_opera, $is_NS4,
$is_safari, $is_chrome, $is_iphone;
if ( $is_lynx ) {
    echo "You are using Lynx";
}elseif ( $is_gecko ) {
    echo "You are using Firefox";
}elseif ( $is_IE ) {
    echo "You are using Internet Explorer";
}elseif ( $is_opera ) {
    echo "You are using Opera";
}elseif ( $is_NS4 ) {
    echo "You are using Netscape";
}elseif ( $is_safari ) {
    echo "You are using Safari";
}elseif ( $is_chrome ) {
    echo "You are using Chrome";
}elseif ( $is_iphone ) {
    echo "You are using an iPhone";
}
?>
```

This is extremely useful when designing a website that needs to include browser-specific tasks or functionality. As always, it's best to stick with web standards and degrade gracefully for lesser browsers, but in some circumstances this can be very beneficial. For example, you can use the $is_iphone variable to load a custom style sheet for iPhone web users.

WordPress features another global variable to detect if the user is on a mobile device, which could be a smartphone or tablet. This global variable is called $is _ mobile. Rather than calling this global variable directly, there's a handy function available called wp _ is _ mobile(). This function detects if the user is on a mobile device. If you are browsing using a mobile device, the function returns true; if not, the function returns false, as shown here:

```php
if ( wp_is_mobile() ) {
    echo "You are viewing this website on a mobile device";
```

```
}else{
    echo "You are not on a mobile device";
}
```

WordPress also stores what type of web server the website is hosted on using the $is _ IIS and $is _ apache global variables. Here's an example:

```php
<?php
global $is_apache, $is_IIS;
if ( $is_apache ) {
    echo "web server is running Apache";
}elseif ( $is_IIS ) {
    echo "web server is running IIS";
}
?>
```

Depending on what web server a website is using, code can produce different results than expected. As a developer, you need to consider that your plugins and themes may be running on WordPress installations on different web servers; you might also need to check what the user is running in order to accomplish specific tasks.

Global Variables or Template Tags?

Generally speaking, template tags should be used whenever they can be. There will be certain instances where a template tag will not be available. In this case, global variables can be substituted to access the information you need. Also, global variables are great for retrieving unfiltered data, meaning the values will bypass any plugin, altering what would normally be used against the content and giving you the original value to work with. Once your code has accessed or processed the original value, you can still force the plugin filters to run using the following code:

```php
<?php apply_filters( 'the_content', $post->post_content );?>
```

While this is included in a discussion of working outside of the Loop, you can access these global variables inside the loop, but again remember to treat globals as read-only, as changing their values will have possibly negative side effects.

WORKING OUTSIDE THE LOOP

There are times when you'll want to access generic post information, or to manipulate some information about the currently displayed post outside of the Loop. WordPress provides some functions to operate on sets of posts for even finer-grain control over post display.

Along with access to global variables, there is a set of WordPress functions to return generic information that's not specific to a single post, or the post currently displayed. Following is a list of frequently used functions when working outside the Loop:

- ➤ `wp_list_pages()`—Displays a list of pages as links
- ➤ `wp_list_categories()`—Displays a list of categories as links
- ➤ `wp_tag_cloud()`—Displays a tag cloud from all tags
- ➤ `get_permalink()`—Returns the permalink of a post

➤ `next_posts_link()`—Link to display previous posts

➤ `previous_posts_link()`—Link to display next posts

You already saw how you could create navigational links using `next_posts_link()` and `previous_posts_link()` in the custom Loop example. Now explore some of these functions to get a real feel for how they work.

To display a list of pages in WordPress, you can use the `wp_list_pages()` function. This function will return your pages in a list format, so it's important to wrap the function call with `<ul>` tags, as shown here:

```
<ul>
    <?php wp_list_pages( 'title_li=' ); ?>
</ul>
```

The preceding code would generate a list of pages from WordPress with links. Notice that you set the parameter `title _ li` to nothing, which eliminates the default title displayed for your pages. The function would generate your menu list like so:

```
<ul>
    <li class="page_item page-item-1">
        <a href="http://example.com/about/" title="About">About</a>
    </li>
    <li class="page_item page-item-2">
        <a href="http://example.com/order/" title="Order">Order</a>
    </li>
    <li class="page_item page-item-3">
        <a href="http://example.com/contact/" title="Contact">Contact</a>
    </li>
</ul>
```

You can also use the `wp_page_menu()` function to generate a page menu. There are several advantages to this page listing function. The first is a new `show_home` parameter allowing a Home link to automatically be added to the list of pages. You also don't have to remove the title using `title_li`, as in the preceding code. This function also wraps a custom `<div>` around your menu, the class of which you can set. The following is an example of this function:

```
<?php wp_page_menu( 'show_home=1&menu_class=my-menu&sort_column=menu_order'
); ?>
```

Another common function for generating links is `wp _ list _ categories()`. This function lists your categories, and subcategories, in a list as well. Consider the following example:

```
<ul>
  <?php wp_list_categories(
'title_li=&depth=4&orderby=name&exclude=8,16,34' ); ?>
</ul>
```

This code will generate a list of categories with links. As before, you are setting your title to nothing, rather than the default Categories title. You are also setting the depth to 4. The depth parameter controls how many levels in the hierarchy of categories to be included in the list. The categories will be ordered by their name. You are also excluding three categories (8, 16, and 34) based on their IDs.

The functions `next_posts_link()` and `previous_posts_link()` are typically used directly after your Loop has completed. These two functions will generate the previous and next links for viewing more posts on your website. Notice that the `next_posts_link()` function actually returns your previous posts. The reason for this is that WordPress assumes your posts are displaying in reverse chronological order, meaning the next page of posts would actually be posts from earlier in the timeline.

Now imagine you'd like to load a single post outside of the Loop. To do this, you use the `get_post()` function to load your post data. The following example loads the post data for post ID 1031:

```php
<?php
$my_id = 1031;
$myPost = get_post( $my_id );
echo 'Post Title: ' .$myPost->post_title .'<br />';
echo 'Post Content: ' .$myPost->post_content .'<br />';
?>
```

The `get_post()` function has only one required parameter: the post ID you want to load. You must pass a variable containing an integer for the ID. Passing a literal integer (for example, 5) will cause a fatal error. The second optional parameter is how you would like the results returned: as an object, an associative array, or a numeric array. By default, an object is returned. To return an associative array you can run this code:

```php
<?php
$my_id = 1031;
$myPost = get_post( $my_id, ARRAY_A );
echo 'Post Title: ' .$myPost['post_title'] .'<br />';
echo 'Post Content: ' .$myPost['post_content'] .'<br />';
?>
```

No matter how you return the results, however, this invocation of `get_post()` returns the raw content from the WordPress database. Filters and processing normally done within the loop won't be applied to the returned content. The solution is to use the `setup_postdata()` function in conjunction with `get_post()` to set up your global post data and template tags for use with your post:

```php
<?php
$my_id = 1031;
$myPost=get_post( $my_id );
setup_postdata( $myPost );
the_title();
the_content();
?>
```

The `get_post()` function uses the internal WordPress object cache. This means that if the post you are loading is already in the cache, you will avoid running an unneeded database query. It's easy to see how useful this function can be to quickly and efficiently load a single post outside of the Loop.

Some functions that can be used inside the Loop can also be used outside of the Loop. For example, you can use the `the_author_meta()` function to retrieve specific author metadata:

```
The email address for user id 1 is <?php the_author_meta( 'user_email', 1
); ?>
```

Remember that when calling the the_author_meta() function outside of the Loop, you have to specify the author's ID that you want to load metadata for. If you call this function inside the Loop, you do not need to specify this ID because it will load the author data for the current post.

WordPress also features specific functions for retrieving individual data about a post outside of the Loop. For example, you can use the get_the_title() function to retrieve a post's title based on post ID like so:

```php
<?php
echo 'Title: ' .get_the_title( 1031 );
?>
```

You can also use a function to retrieve post metadata (custom fields) from an individual post. To do this, you use the get_post_meta() function, as shown here:

```php
<?php
echo 'Color: ' .get_post_meta( 1031, 'color', true );
?>
```

The get_post_meta() function accepts three parameters: post ID, key, and single. The post ID is the ID of the post you want to load metadata for. The key is the name of the meta value you want to load. The third optional value determines whether the results are returned as an array or whether the function will return a single result. By default, this is set to false so an array would be returned. As you can see, you can set this value to true so only a single color is returned.

SUMMARY

This chapter covered the basic mechanics of WordPress content selection and display and provided a guide to the WordPress core to help you locate the code used to implement these functions. The real power of WordPress is in its extensibility through plugins and themes. You are first going to look at the WordPress data model in more detail in Chapter 6, which shows you how the various data items saved for all content, users, and metadata relate to each other. Chapter 7 will cover custom post types, custom taxonomies, and metadata, and will show you the various types of content you can define and use in WordPress. You will then use that as the basis for a full-fledged plugin construction discussion in Chapter 8. Along with plugins, themes are the other primary avenue for extending and customizing WordPress, and you reapply some of the Loop constructs with a deeper look at templates and content presentation in Chapter 9.

6

Data Management

- ➤ Understanding the WordPress database
- ➤ Learning about database table relationships
- ➤ Working with the WordPress database class
- ➤ Debugging custom queries

Almost every website on the Internet today is connected to a database that stores information about that website. WordPress is no different and is powered by a MySQL database backend. This database stores all of the data for your website, including your content, users, links, metadata, settings, and more. This chapter covers how data is stored, what data is stored, and how to work with that data in WordPress to help you build amazing websites.

DATABASE SCHEMA

The default installation of WordPress contains 11 database tables. WordPress prides itself on being very lightweight and the database is the foundation for this. The database structure is designed to be very minimal yet allow for endless flexibility when developing and designing for WordPress. To understand the database schema, it helps to view a database diagram.

Figure 6-1 shows an overview of the WordPress database structure and the tables created during a standard WordPress installation. Keep in mind that plugins and themes have the ability to create custom tables. WordPress Multisite also creates additional tables so your WordPress database may contain more tables than just the default WordPress tables.

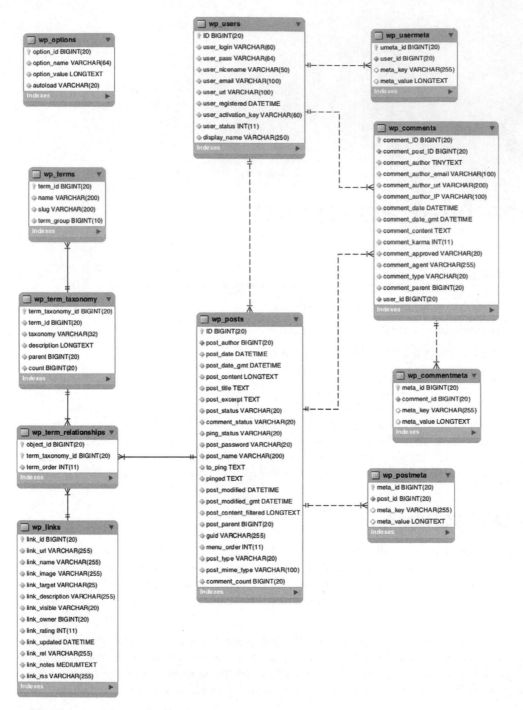

FIGURE 6-1: WordPress database diagram

When a new major release of WordPress is launched, a few database changes are usually made. These changes are usually very minor, such as changing a table field data type or removing a field that is no longer in use. Backward compatibility is a major focus for the WordPress development community so any changes made to the database are highly scrutinized and will rarely affect active plugins and themes. The Codex features a very thorough database changelog you can reference when a new version of WordPress is released: `http://codex.wordpress.org/ Database_Description#Changelog`.

The table structure in WordPress is very consistent. Each table in your database contains a unique ID field, which is the primary key of the table. Each table also contains one or more indexes on fields, which improves the speed of data retrieval when executing queries against the data. As you saw in Chapter 5, each trip through the Loop in a theme is going to generate at least one, and perhaps several, queries to extract posts, pages, and their related metadata or comments.

The most important field in every table is the unique ID field. This field is not always named ID but is an auto-incrementing field used to give each record in the table a unique identifier. For example, when you first install WordPress, a default post is created titled "Hello world!" Because this is the first post created in the `wp_posts` table, the ID for this post is 1. Each post is given a unique ID that can be used to load post-specific information and can also be used as the joining field against other tables in the database.

There is one caveat to this, which has to do with post revisions, attachments, and custom post types. Each one of these entries is saved as a new record in the `wp_posts` table so they each gets its own unique ID, which means your published post IDs may not be sequential. For example, your first post may have an ID of 1, whereas your second post may have an ID of 15. It all depends on how many additional entries have been created between each post.

TABLE DETAILS

Currently, 11 database tables have been created for WordPress. Following is a list of those tables and details on what data they store:

➤ `wp_commentmeta`—Contains all metadata for comments.

➤ `wp_comments`—Contains all comments within WordPress. Individual comments are linked back to posts through a post ID.

➤ `wp_links`—Contains all links added via the Link Manager section. The table still exists, but core functionality was deprecated in WordPress 3.5. For more information, visit `http:// codex.wordpress.org/Links_Manager`.

➤ `wp_options`—Stores all website options defined under the Settings Screen. Also stores plugin options, active plugins and themes, and more.

➤ `wp_postmeta`—Contains all post metadata (custom fields).

➤ `wp_posts`—Contains posts of all types (default and custom post types), pages, media records, and revisions. Under most circumstances, this is the largest table in the database.

➤ `wp_terms`—Contains all taxonomy terms defined for your website, mapping their text descriptions to term numbers that can be used as unique indexes into other tables.

- ➤ `wp_term_relationships`—Joins taxonomy terms with content, providing a membership table. It maps a term such as a tag or category name to the page or post that references it.

- ➤ `wp_term_taxonomy`—Defines the taxonomy to which each term is assigned. This table allows you to have categories and tags with the same name, placing them in different named taxonomies.

- ➤ `wp_users`—Contains all users created in your website (login, password, e-mail).

- ➤ `wp_usermeta`—Contains metadata for users (first/last name, nickname, user level, and so on).

Each database table has a specific purpose within WordPress. The next section breaks down some of the more common tables and looks at some examples of working with each.

WordPress Content Tables

To retrieve all of your website content, you'll be accessing the `wp_posts` table. This table stores all of your posts, pages, attachments, revisions, and more. Attachment records are stored in this table, but the actual attachments are not. They are physically stored on your hosting server as a standard file. The following SQL query is an example of how to extract all of your posts from the database, and is the short form of what happens in the default WordPress Loop:

```
SELECT * FROM wp_posts
WHERE post_type = 'post'
AND post_status = 'publish'
ORDER BY post_date DESC
```

This query selects all records from `wp_posts` with a `post_type` of `'post'`. The `post_type` field designates what type of content you are viewing. To return all pages, just change that value to `'page'`. In this example, you want published posts only, so make sure `post_status` is set to `'publish'`. You are also ordering your table records by `post_date` descending, so your posts will be displayed in reverse chronological order. Querying data and what tools are available to help you do so are discussed later in this chapter.

Let's explore some of the more useful fields in the `wp_posts` table. You already know your ID field contains your post's unique ID. The `post_author` field is the unique ID of the author of the post. You can use this to retrieve author-specific data from the `wp_users` table. The `post_date` is the date the post was created. The `post_content` field stores the main content of your post or page and `post_title` is the title of that content.

One very important field is the `post_status` field. Currently, eight different post statuses are defined in WordPress:

- ➤ `publish`—A published post or page.

- ➤ `inherit`—A post revision.

- ➤ `pending`—Post that is pending review by an administrator or editor.

- ➤ `private`—A private post.

- ➤ `future`—A post scheduled to publish at a future date and time.

- ➤ `draft`—A post still being created that has not been published.

➤ auto-draft—A post revision that WordPress saves automatically while you are editing.

➤ trash—Content is in the trash bin and can still be recovered.

Post status comes into play when contributor roles are used to limit a post creator's ability to post or edit existing content. As with almost everything in WordPress, custom post statuses can be created by plugins and themes.

> **NOTE** *The use of roles is discussed in Chapter 12, and their impact on content management workflow is discussed in Chapter 15.*

The post_type is also stored in the wp_posts table. This value is what distinguishes different types of content in WordPress: posts, pages, revisions, menus, and attachments. Since the release of WordPress 2.9, custom post types can be created, which opens the door to endless possibilities when defining custom content in WordPress.

The wp_users table contains data for your registered member accounts. Again, you see the ID field indicating the unique identifier for user records. The user_login is the username of the user. This is the value the user must enter when logging in to WordPress. The user_pass field contains the encrypted user password. The registered user's e-mail is stored in the user_email field. The user_url field contains the member's website and the user registration date is saved in user_registered.

Next you will explore the wp_comments table. This table stores all of the comments, pingbacks, and trackbacks for your website.

Viewing the comment records, you'll notice the ID field is named comment_ID. Even though this field is not named ID, it is still the unique identifier for this record in the table. The comment_post_ID is the unique ID of the post the comment was added to. Remember that by default you don't have to be logged in to make comments in WordPress. For this reason, you'll see similar fields as in your users table.

The comment_author field stores the name of the commenter. If the comment is a pingback or trackback, it will contain the name of the post that sent the ping. The comment_author_email contains the commenter's e-mail address, and his or her website is stored in comment_author_url. Another important field is the comment_date, which is the date the comment was created. This field is used to display your post comments in the correct order.

WordPress Taxonomy Tables

Terms, relationships, and taxonomies are broken into three distinct tables to allow many-to-one relationships between categories, tags, items in custom taxonomies, and posts. These relationships are hierarchical and multi-valued. While you could add an array of tag or category identifiers to each row in the wp_posts table, for example, that approach puts an explicit limit on the number of descriptive relationships for each post while also wasting space allocated for tags or categories that may not be assigned.

If you create a category called "scary stories," and put four posts in that category, all three taxonomy-related tables are updated:

➤ One row in the wp_terms table defines "scary stories" and its slug, or diminutive form, used in URLs. This relationship gets a unique identifier (key) useful for matching the term to other tables.

➤ One row in the `wp_term_taxonomy` table maps "scary stories" to the "category" taxonomy. This relationship also gets a unique key, representing the combination of "scary stories" in "category." If you also create a custom taxonomy and have a "scary stories" entry in it, there will be a different row in the `wp_term_taxonomy` table for that mapping, along with its unique key.

➤ Four rows in the `wp_term_relationships` table map the "scary stories in category" identifier to the post identifiers for each of the posts that are in the category.

The workhorse operator in working with taxonomy tables is the SQL JOIN, sometimes referred to as the "product" of two (or more) tables. A JOIN builds a temporary table with each row in one table mapped to every row in the second and successive tables; then the WHERE part of a JOIN operation selects those rows where specific fields in each row match. To find all of the posts in the "scary stories" category, WordPress first finds the identifier for this term and taxonomy pair, selects the appropriate rows from the `wp_term_relationships` table, and then does a JOIN on the `wp_posts` and the selected rows from the relationships table: That last JOIN is SQL-ese for "extract all of the posts with identifiers in this list" where the list is computed on-the-fly.

Figure 6-2 shows a graphical representation of the joins between the `wp_posts` table and taxonomy tables in WordPress.

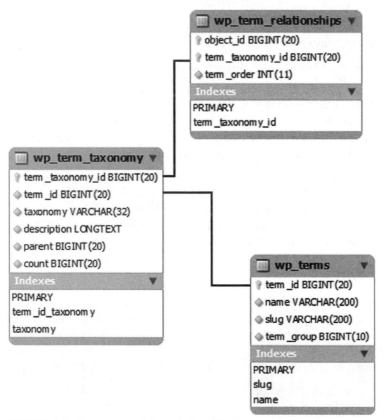

FIGURE 6-2: Taxonomy tables relationship

While this makes the SQL for selecting content associated with a particular tag or category more complex, requiring the use of a multi-table JOIN operations to implement the "name in a taxonomy in a relationship" matching, it is powerful in allowing content to be given rich and multi-valued descriptions, and for category, taxonomy, and tag names to have independent name spaces.

WORDPRESS DATABASE CLASS

WordPress features an object class with method functions for working with the database directly. This database class is called wpdb and is located in wp-includes/wp-db.php. Any time you are querying the WordPress database in PHP code, you should use the wpdb class. The main reason for using this class is to allow WordPress to execute your queries in the safest way possible.

Simple Database Queries

When using the wpdb class, you must first define $wpdb as a global variable before it will be available for use. To do so, just drop this line of code directly preceding any $wpdb function call:

```
global $wpdb;
```

One of the most important functions in the wpdb class is the prepare() function. This function is used for escaping variables passed to your SQL queries. This is a critical step in preventing SQL injection attacks on your website.

> **WARNING** *All queries should be passed through the* prepare() *function before being executed.*

The prepare() function accepts a minimum of two parameters:

```
$wpdb->prepare( $query, $value1 );
```

The $query parameter is the database query you want to run. The $value1 parameter is the first value you want to replace in the query. You can add additional value parameters as needed. Let's look at an example:

```php
<?php
global $wpdb;

$field_key = "address";
$field_value = "1428 Elm St";
$wpdb->query( $wpdb->prepare( "INSERT INTO $wpdb->my_custom_table
    ( id, field_key, field_value ) VALUES ( %d, %s, %s )", 1,
    $field_key, $field_value ) );
?>
```

This example adds data into a non-default, custom table in WordPress that you would have previously created. When using prepare(), make sure to replace any variables in your query with %s for strings, %d for integers, and %f for floats. Then list the variables as parameters for the prepare() function in the exact same order. In the preceding example, %d represents 1, %s represents $field_ key, and the second %s represents $field_value. Examples throughout this section all use the prepare() function, which highlights its importance when working with database queries.

Notice that this example uses $wpdb->my_custom_table to reference the table in WordPress. This translates to wp_my_custom_table if wp_ is the table prefix. This is the proper way to determine the correct table prefix when working with tables in the WordPress database.

> **NOTE** *When installing WordPress, you can set a custom database table prefix. By default, this is wp_, but many people choose to change this prefix for security purposes. Using $wpdb-> is the correct way to determine what this table prefix is for any WordPress installation.*

The wpdb query() method is used to execute a simple query. This function is primarily used for SELECT statements. Despite its name, it's not only for SQL SELECT queries, but will execute any SQL statement against the database. Here's a basic query function example:

```php
<?php
global $wpdb;

$wpdb->query( $wpdb->prepare( " DELETE FROM $wpdb->my_custom_table WHERE
id = %d AND field_key = %d ", 1, 'address' ) );
?>
```

As you can see, you execute your query using the wpdb class query() function to delete the field "address" with an ID of 1. Although the query() function allows you to execute any SQL query on the WordPress database, other database object class functions are more appropriate for SELECT queries. For instance, the get_var() function is used for retrieving a single variable from the database:

```php
<?php
global $wpdb;

$comment_count = $wpdb->get_var( $wpdb->prepare( "SELECT COUNT(*)
    FROM $wpdb->comments
    WHERE comment_approved = %d;", 1 ) );
echo '<p>Total comments: ' . $comment_count . '</p>';
?>
```

This example retrieves a count of all approved comments in WordPress and displays the total number. Although only one scalar variable is returned, the entire result set of the query is cached. It's best to try and limit the result set returned from your queries using a WHERE clause to only retrieve the records you actually need. In this example, all comment record rows are returned, even though you display the total count of comments. This would obviously be a big memory hit on larger websites.

Complex Database Operations

To retrieve an entire table row, you'll want to use the get_row() function. The get_row() function can return the row data as an object, an associative array, or a numerically indexed array. By default, the row is returned as an object, in this case an instance of the per-post data. Here's an example:

```php
<?php
global $wpdb;

$thepost = $wpdb->get_row( $wpdb->prepare( "SELECT *
    FROM $wpdb->posts WHERE ID = %d", 1 ) );
echo $thepost->post_title;
?>
```

This retrieves the entire row data for post ID 1 and displays the post title. The properties of $thepost object are the column names from the table you queried, which is wp_posts in this case. To retrieve the results as an array, you can send in an additional parameter to the get_row() function:

```php
<?php
global $wpdb;

$thepost = $wpdb->get_row( $wpdb->prepare( "SELECT
    * FROM $wpdb->posts WHERE ID = %d", 1 ), ARRAY_
print_r ( $thepost );
?>
```

By using the ARRAY_A parameter in get_row(), your post data is returned as an associative array. Alternatively, you could use the ARRAY_N parameter to return your post data in a numerically indexed array.

Standard SELECT queries should use the get_results() function for retrieving multiple rows of data from the database. The following function returns the SQL result data as an array:

```php
<?php
global $wpdb;

$liveposts = $wpdb->get_results( $wpdb->prepare( "SELECT ID, post_title
    FROM $wpdb->posts WHERE post_status = %d ", 'publish' ) );
foreach ( $liveposts as $livepost ) {
    echo '<p>' .$livepost->post_title. '</p>';
}
?>
```

The preceding example is querying all published posts in WordPress and displaying the post titles. The query results are returned and stored as an array in $liveposts, which you can then loop through to display your query values.

The WordPress database class also features specific functions for UPDATE, INSERT, and DELETE statements. These three functions eliminate the need for custom SQL queries because WordPress will create them for you based on the values passed into the function. Here is how the insert() function is structured:

```php
$wpdb->insert( $table, $data, $format );
```

The $table variable is the name of the table you want to insert a value into. The $data variable is an array of field names and data to be inserted into those field names. The final parameter is $format, which defines an array of formats to be mapped to each of the values in $data. So, for example, if you want to insert data into the post meta table, you would execute this:

```php
<?php
global $wpdb;

$wpdb->insert(
    $wpdb->postmeta,
    array(
        'post_id'    => '1',
        'meta_key'   => 'address',
        'meta_value' => '1428 Elm St.'
    ),
    array(
        '%d',
        '%s',
        '%s'
    )
);
?>
```

In this example you execute the insert() function, passing in three variables through an array. Notice how you set post _ id, meta _ key, and meta _ value as the three fields you are inserting. You can pass any field available in the table you are inserting with data to insert into that field. The final value is the formatting array, which works very much like the prepare() function formatting we discussed earlier in this chapter. The array contains a format for each of the three values being inserted into the database.

The update() function works very similarly to the insert() function, except you also need to set the $where clause and $where _ format variables so WordPress knows which records to update and how to format:

```php
$wpdb->update( $table, $data, $where, $format, $where_format );
```

The $where variable is an array of field names and data for the SQL WHERE clause. This is normally set to the unique ID of the field you are updating, but can also contain other field names from the table.

```php
<?php
global $wpdb;

$wpdb->update(
    $wpdb->postmeta,
    array(
        'meta_value' => '333 Wonderview Ave'
    ),
    array(
        'post_id'  => '1',
        'meta_key' => 'address'
    ),
    array(
```

```
            '%s'
        ),
        array(
            '%d',
            '%s'
        )
    );
?>
```

In the preceding example, you execute the update() function to update the post metadata inserted in the previous example. Notice that the third parameter you send is an array containing your WHERE clause values, in this case the post ID and meta key name. The preceding query updates the post meta address value for post ID 1. Remember that you can send multiple values through the WHERE parameter when updating a table record. The final two array parameters are used to format the values being updated.

The delete() function is used to delete data from a WordPress database table. This function is structured similarly to the previous two functions, shown here:

```
$wpdb->delete( $table, $where, $where_format );
```

The $where parameter sets the WHERE clause in your query, which determines what data to delete. The $where _ format parameter is used to set the format of the values you are passing to the function. As an example, let's delete the post address meta data you created in the previous examples:

```
$wpdb->delete(
    $wpdb->postmeta,
    array(
        'post_id'  => '1',
        'meta_key' => 'address'
    ),
    array(
        '%d',
        '%s'
    )
);
```

> **WARNING** *Any time you are deleting data, it is very important you test your code thoroughly on dummy data to verify it works as expected. Running untested code on a production website could have disastrous results.*

The insert(), update(), and delete() functions shown do not need to be wrapped with the prepare() function. These functions actually use the prepare() function after concatenating the query from the values passed to the functions. This is a much easier method than manually creating your INSERT, UPDATE, and DELETE queries in WordPress.

Dealing with Errors

Any time you are working with queries, it's nice to see error messages. By default, if a custom query fails, nothing is returned so it's hard to determine what is wrong with your query. The wpdb class provides functions for displaying MySQL errors to the page. Here's an example of using these functions:

```php
<?php
$wpdb->show_errors();
$liveposts = $wpdb->get_results( $wpdb->prepare("SELECT ID, post_title
    FROM $wpdb->posts_FAKE WHERE post_status = 'publish'") );
$wpdb->print_error();
?>
```

The `show_errors()` function must be called directly before you execute a query. The `print_error()` function must be called directly after you execute a query. If there are any errors in your SQL statement, the error messages are displayed. You can also call the `$wpdb->hide_errors()` function to hide all MySQL errors, or call the `$wpdb->flush()` function to delete the cached query results.

The database class contains additional variables that store information about WordPress queries. Following is a list of some of the more common variables:

```php
var_dump( $wpdb->num_queries ); // total number of queries ran
var_dump( $wpdb->num_rows ); // total number of rows returned by the last query
var_dump( $wpdb->last_result ); // most recent query results
var_dump( $wpdb->last_query ); // most recent query executed
var_dump( $wpdb->col_info ); // column information for the most recent query
```

Add the preceding code directly after you execute a query to see the results. This is very useful when determining why a database query isn't working as expected.

Another very powerful database variable is the `$queries` variable. This stores all of the queries run by WordPress. To enable this variable, you must first set the constant value SAVEQUERIES to `true` in your `wp-config.php` file. This tells WordPress to store all of the queries executed on each page load in the `$queries` variable. First drop this line of code in your `wp-config.php` file:

```php
define( 'SAVEQUERIES', true );
```

Now all queries will be stored in the `$queries` variable. You can display all of the query information like so:

```php
var_dump( $wpdb->queries ); // displays all queries executed during page load
```

This is especially handy when troubleshooting slow load times. If a plugin is executing an obscene number of queries, that can dramatically slow down load times in WordPress. Remember to disable the SAVEQUERIES constant option when you are finished viewing queries because storing all queries can also slow down load times.

The database query class is a major asset when working with the WordPress database directly, as you will see when developing a plugin or building a more complex Loop. All of the previously mentioned database class functions use specific escaping techniques to verify that your queries are executed in the safest manner possible. To borrow from Randall Munroe's "Little Bobby Tables" xkcd joke (xkcd #327), you don't want a user handcrafting an input item that contains DROP TABLES as a malicious SQL injection, resulting in the loss of your WordPress database tables. The query preparation and escaping functions ensure that inputs don't become SQL functions, no matter how craftily they're set up. It is essential that you follow these methods for querying data to ensure your website is the most efficient and uses the safest techniques possible.

DIRECT DATABASE MANIPULATION

There may be times when you want to work with the WordPress database data directly. This can include accessing custom database tables created by a plugin or theme. To do this, you'll need to use SQL to query the data from the MySQL database. Remember that the WordPress APIs provide access to all of the WordPress tables and only very occasionally will you need to access the tables directly. All example queries in this chapter use the wp_ prefix for tables, but your database tables may use a different prefix as defined in your wp-config.php file when installing WordPress.

One of the most common methods for working with a WordPress database directly is to use phpMyAdmin. As described in Chapter 3, phpMyAdmin is a free software tool provided by most hosting companies for administering MySQL databases through a web interface. Most of the examples in this section involve direct interaction with MySQL, and you'll need to use an SQL command line for their execution. Figure 6-3 shows the default database view using phpMyAdmin.

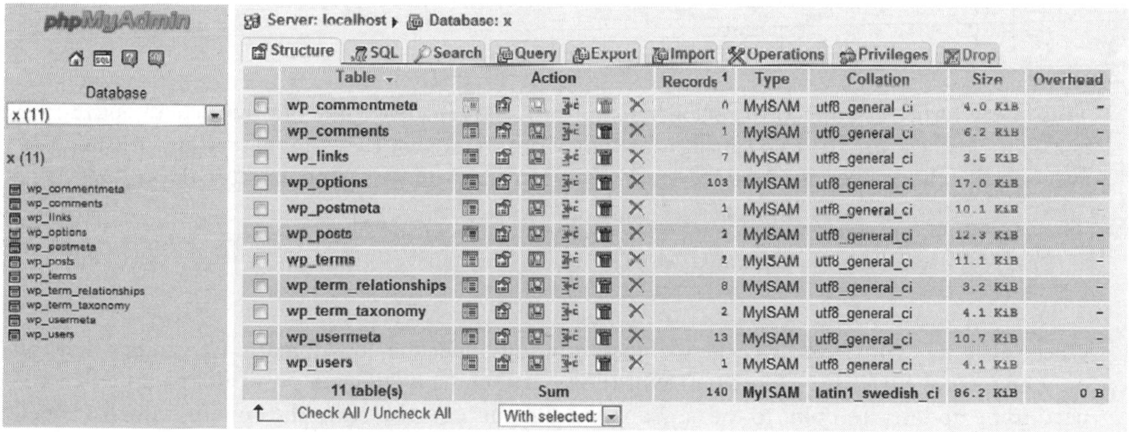

FIGURE 6-3: phpMyAdmin viewing a WordPress database

To run SQL statements in phpMyAdmin, simply click the SQL tab across the top. Here you can execute any queries against your WordPress database. We always recommend creating your query directly in phpMyAdmin first before moving it over to your PHP scripts. The reasoning behind this is that debugging SQL statements is much faster directly in phpMyAdmin than it is using PHP code in WordPress. Once you have perfected your query, you can use it in your PHP code and you can be confident the results will be as expected. In the examples that follow, you'll be using raw SQL queries. Remember that if you want to run these queries in a theme or plugin, you'll need to wrap the queries in the WordPress database class.

One of the most commonly accessed tables is the wp _ posts table. Remember that this table stores all posts, pages, custom post types, revisions, and even attachment records. The different types of content are defined by the post _ type field. WordPress 2.9 introduced the ability for developers to define custom post types, which is discussed in greater detail in Chapter 7. This means that additional post _ type values may exist in this field. To view all post revisions in your database, you can run this query:

```
SELECT * FROM wp_posts
WHERE post_type = 'revision'
```

This returns all records in wp _ posts that are of a revision post _ type. You can modify the preceding query to view all post attachments that have been uploaded to WordPress:

```
SELECT guid, wp_posts.* FROM wp_posts
WHERE post_type = 'attachment'
```

This example places the field guid as the first value to be returned in the query. The guid field contains the full URL of the attachment file on the server.

The wp _ options table contains all of the settings saved for your WordPress installation. Options saved in this table are saved with an option _ name and option _ value. Therefore, the actual field name you call will always be those two names, rather than a specific field based on the option value. Following are two extremely important records in this table:

```
SELECT * FROM wp_options
WHERE option_name IN ( 'siteurl','home' )
```

This query returns two records, one where option _ name is home and another where option _ name is siteurl. These are the two settings that tell WordPress what the domain of your website is. If you ever need to change your website's domain, you can run a query to update these two values like so:

```
UPDATE wp_options
SET option_value = 'http://yournewdomain.com'
WHERE option_name IN ('siteurl','home')
```

Once this query runs, your website will instantly run under the new domain. Remember that this only updates the website's domain in WordPress. Attachment URLs in posts and pages will also need to be updated to point to the new domain. Plugins can also store the domain information, so be sure to test in a development environment before updating a production website. If you access the old domain, you will be redirected to the new one. If you were logged in, your cookies and session will be invalidated and you will have to log in again. This is a great technique if you built a new website under a subdomain (for example, http://new.example.com) and are updating the URLs to push the website live.

The wp _ options table contains other very important fields. To view all active plugins on your website, you can view the active _ plugins option _ name like so:

```
SELECT *
FROM wp_options
WHERE option_name = 'active_plugins'
```

The options table also stores all options defined by plugins. Most plugins activated in WordPress will have some type of settings page. These settings are generally saved in wp _ options so the plugins can retrieve these settings as needed. For example, the Akismet plugin stores an option named akismet _ spam _ count that stores the total number of spam comments. You can view this option by running the following query:

```
SELECT * FROM wp_options
WHERE option_name = 'akismet_spam_count'
```

The wp _ users table contains all of the users you currently have set up in WordPress. If you allow open registration on your website, new users will be created in this table as they join your site. The wp _ users table stores very important user information including username, password, e-mail, website URL, and date registered. Say you want to export all of your users' e-mail addresses. You can easily do so by running the following query:

```
SELECT DISTINCT user_email
FROM wp_users
```

Now you can easily export all of the e-mail addresses loaded into WordPress! Another common query used in wp _ users is to reset a user's password. You can do this in a couple of different ways, but if you are absolutely locked out of WordPress, you can always reset the password directly in the database. To do so, you need to update the user _ pass field from the MySQL command line:

```
UPDATE wp_users
SET user_pass = MD5('Hall0w33n')
WHERE user_login ='admin'
LIMIT 1;
```

Running this query resets the admin password to Hall0w33n. Notice how you wrap the new password in MD5(). This converts the password to an MD5 hash. Since WordPress 2.5, passwords are now salted and hashed using the phpass encryption library rather than MD5. Not to worry, however, because WordPress is built to detect MD5 hash passwords and convert them to phpass encryption instead. So the preceding query will successfully reset your password in WordPress.

The wp _ comments table stores all comments submitted to your website. This table contains the comment, author, e-mail, website URL, IP address, and more. Here's an example query for displaying comments:

```
SELECT wc.* FROM wp_posts wp
INNER JOIN wp_comments wc ON wp.ID = wc.comment_post_ID
WHERE wp.ID = '1554'
```

This query returns all comments for post ID 1554. Another important field in wp _ comments is the user _ id field. If a user is logged in to your website and posts a comment, this field will contain his or her user ID. Consider the following code, which displays all comments left by the user admin:

```
SELECT wc.* FROM wp_comments wc
INNER JOIN wp_users wu ON wc.user_id = wu.ID
WHERE wu.user_login = 'admin'
```

In the database diagram in Figure 6-1, the arrows show the relationships between each table. This is incredibly useful when writing custom queries to retrieve data directly from the database. For example, to retrieve all comments for a particular post you could run this query:

```
SELECT * FROM wp_comments
INNER JOIN wp_posts ON wp_comments.comment_post_id = wp_posts.ID
WHERE wp_posts.ID = '1'
```

This query returns all comments for post ID 1. Notice how you join the wp _ comments.comment _ post _ ID field to the wp _ posts.ID field. The SQL JOIN is necessary because there is an N:1 relationship between comments and posts; each post may have many comments but comments apply to only one post. These two fields are shown in the diagram as the joining fields for these tables. Also consider the following example, which demonstrates how to join the wp _ users and wp _ usermeta tables together:

```
SELECT * FROM wp_users
INNER JOIN wp_usermeta ON wp_users.ID = wp_usermeta.user_id
WHERE wp_users.ID = '1'
```

As you can see in the database diagram, the wp _ users.ID field was joined to the wp _ usermeta .user _ id field. The preceding query retrieves all of the user information, including user metadata, for user ID 1, which is the default admin account. Again, the database diagram makes it extremely easy to determine how tables are joined by index value inside the WordPress database, and how logical INNER JOIN operations can build result sets of related table rows.

If you are interested in learning more about SQL, you can read some amazing tutorials at http:// www.w3schools.com/sql/.

SUMMARY

This chapter covered the WordPress database schema, database table relationships, the WordPress database class, and the proper way to debug database queries. Whether working with themes, plugins, or custom functions, understanding how to work with the WordPress database is very important. Understanding where and how WordPress stores data in the database can help as you develop more complex website features.

Next we'll cover custom content in WordPress using custom post types. We'll also cover custom taxonomies, custom metadata, and the power and importance of both when developing WordPress websites.

7

Custom Post Types, Custom Taxonomies, and Metadata

WHAT'S IN THIS CHAPTER?

➤ Understanding and creating custom post types

➤ Displaying and using custom post type content

➤ Creating and using custom taxonomies

➤ Understanding and using metadata

The most important part of any WordPress website is the content. WordPress, by default, has various types of content and taxonomies defined, but often, you will need to define your own types of content to build the exact website you want.

WordPress includes some very advanced, and easy-to-use, tools for working with all sorts of custom content. This has helped WordPress evolve into a full-fledged content management system capable of powering absolutely any type of website setup, regardless of the content.

In this chapter, you learn how to create custom post types and content in WordPress. You also learn how to work with custom taxonomies to group and classify your content. Finally, you learn how to attach and retrieve arbitrary pieces of metadata to your content.

UNDERSTANDING DATA IN WORDPRESS

When working with various types of data in WordPress, it's important to understand what that data is and how it can be customized. WordPress has five predefined post types in a default installation:

➤ **Post**—Posts or articles generally ordered by date

➤ **Page**—Hierarchical static pages of content

➤ **Attachment**—Media uploaded to WordPress and attached to post type entries, such as images and files

➤ **Revision**—A revision of a post type used as backup and can be restored if needed

➤ **Nav Menus**—Menu items added to a nav menu using WordPress's menu management feature

For a basic blog or smaller website, these default post types are all you might need. However, if you plan on building a more complex CMS-type website, you'll want to utilize the power of custom post types.

What Is a Custom Post Type?

A custom post type in WordPress is a custom defined piece of content. It really is that simple. Using custom post types, you can define any type of content in WordPress, and you are no longer forced to use just the default post types listed in the previous section. This opens the door to an endless number of possibilities.

Potential custom post type ideas include, but are not necessarily limited to, the following:

➤ Products

➤ Events

➤ Videos

➤ Rotator

➤ Testimonials

➤ Quotes

➤ Error Log

Remember that custom post types can be absolutely anything, not just public-facing pieces of content. For example, you can set up a custom post type as an error log to track errors in your application. When it comes to custom post types, the only limitation is your imagination.

Register Custom Post Types

To create a new custom post type, you'll use the `register_post_type()` function, as shown here:

```php
<?php register_post_type( $post_type, $args ); ?>
```

The `register_post_type()` function accepts two parameters:

➤ `$post_type`—The name of the post type. Should contain only lowercase letters, no spaces, and a max length of 20 characters.

➤ `$args`—An array of arguments that define the post type and various options in WordPress.

Now look at a basic example of registering a custom post type. You can register a post type in WordPress in two different places. The first is in your theme's `functions.php` file. The second is in a custom plugin.

> **NOTE** *When registering custom post types and taxonomies in WordPress, it's generally recommended to do so in a plugin. The primary reason for this is to avoid losing your custom post type and taxonomy registrations if you switch your WordPress theme in the future.*

You could add the following code to a custom plugin, but for this example, add the following code to your theme's `functions.php` file.

```php
<?php
add_action( 'init', 'prowp_register_my_post_types' );

function prowp_register_my_post_types() {

    register_post_type( 'products',
        array(
            'labels' => array( 'name' => 'Products' ),
            'public' => true,
        )
    );

}
?>
```

Now visit your WordPress admin dashboard. You'll notice that a new menu called Products has appeared just below Comments, as shown in Figure 7-1. That is the new custom post type you just registered with the preceding code.

As you can see, WordPress will automatically create the admin UI for your new custom post type. The new menu item allows you to create new post type product entries as well as edit existing entries, just like posts and pages in WordPress. This is a basic example, but you can already tell the ease with which you can define custom content in WordPress.

FIGURE 7-1: Products custom post type

> **NOTE** *You should always use the* `init` *action hook when registering your custom post types. This is the first hook available after WordPress is fully initialized and will verify that your custom post type is registered early enough in the process.*

There are many different arguments available when registering your custom post type. It's important to understand these arguments to know what's available.

public

The `public` argument sets whether a post type is publicly available on the admin dashboard or front-end of your website. By default, this is set to `false`, which will hide the post type from view.

The default settings for `show_ui, exclude_from_search, publicly_queryable`, and `show_in_nav_menus` are inherited from this setting.

show_ui

The `show_ui` argument determines whether or not to create a default UI in the WordPress admin dashboard for managing this post type. It defaults to the value defined by the `public` argument.

publicly_queryable

The `publicly_queryable` argument determines if the post type content can be publicly queried on the front end of your website. If it is set to `false`, all front end queries for entries under the custom post type will return a 404, since it is not allowed to be queried. It defaults to the value defined by the `public` argument.

exclude_from_search

The `exclude_from_search` argument allows you to exclude custom post type entries from the WordPress search results. It defaults to the value defined by the `public` argument.

show_in_nav_menus

The `show_in_nav_menus` argument determines if the post type is available for selection in the menu management feature of WordPress. It defaults to the value defined by the `public` argument.

supports

The `supports` argument allows you to define what meta boxes appear on the screen when creating or editing a new post type entry. This defaults to the `title` and `editor`. Several options are available:

- `title`—Sets the post title.
- `editor`—Displays the content editor on the post editing screen with a media uploader.
- `author`—Selects box to choose the author of the post.
- `thumbnail`—Featured image meta box for the post.
- `excerpt`—Displays an excerpt editor on the post type editing screen.
- `comments`—Sets whether comments will be enabled for posts of this type.
- `trackbacks`—Sets whether trackbacks and pingbacks will be enabled for posts of this type.
- `custom-fields`—Displays the custom field editing area meta box.
- `page-attributes`—Displays the attributes box for choosing the post order. The `hierarchical` argument must be set to `true` for this to work.
- `revisions`—Displays the post revisions meta box.
- `post-formats`—Displays the post formats meta box with registered post formats.

To disable the `title` and `editor` defaults, set the `supports` argument to `false`.

labels

The `labels` argument sets an array of labels that represents your post type in the admin dashboard. See the section "Setting Post Type Labels" later in this chapter for details on each label.

hierarchical

The `hierarchical` argument allows you to define if the post type is hierarchical, like pages in WordPress. A `hierarchical` post type allows you to have a tree-like structure for your post-type content. By default, this argument is set to `false`.

has_archive

The `has_archive` argument enables your post type to have an archive page. A post type archive page is like the WordPress posts page, which displays the site's latest blog entries. This allows you to display a list of your post type entries, with the order being defined in your theme's template file.

can_export

The `can_export` argument determines if the post type content is available for export using the built-in WordPress export feature under Tools ➤ Export. This argument is set to `true` by default.

taxonomies

The `taxonomies` argument names an array of registered taxonomies to attach to the custom post type. For example, you can pass in `category` and `post_tag` to attach the default Categories and Tags taxonomies to your post type. By default, there are no taxonomies attached to a custom post type.

menu_position

The `menu-position` argument enables you to set the position in which the custom post type menu shows in the admin menu. By default, new post types are displayed after the Comments menu.

menu_icon

The `menu_icon` argument sets a custom menu icon for your post type. By default, the posts icon is used.

WordPress 3.8 introduced Dashicon support. To view a full list of the Dashicons available in WordPress visit `http://melchoyce.github.io/dashicons/`. To set a specific Dashicon, simply click the icon and copy the icon name to the `menu_icon` value. For example, to use the Carrot icon, set `menu_icon => 'dashicons-carrot'`.

show_in_menu

The `show_in_menu` argument determines whether or not to display the admin menu for your post type. This argument accepts three values: `true`, `false`, or a string. The string can be either a top-level page, such as `tools.php` or `edit.php?post_type=page`. You can also set the string to the `menu_slug` parameter to add the custom post type as a submenu item to an existing custom menu. It defaults to the value defined by the `show_ui` argument.

show_in_admin_bar

The `show_in_admin_bar` argument sets whether or not to show your custom post type in the WordPress admin bar. It defaults to the value defined by the `show_in_menu` argument.

capability_type

The `capability_type` argument names a string or an array of the capabilities for this post type. By default, the value is set to `post`.

capabilities

The `capabilities` argument is an array of custom capabilities required for editing, deleting, viewing, and publishing posts of this post type.

query_var

The `query_var` argument sets the query variable for posts of this post type. The default value is `true` and is set to the `$post_type` value.

rewrite

The `rewrite` argument creates the unique permalinks for this post type. This allows you to customize the post type slug in your URL. This argument can be set to `true`, `false`, or an array of values. If passing an array, it accepts the following values:

➤ `slug`—Sets a custom permalink slug. Defaults to the `$post_type` value.

➤ `with_front`—Sets whether your post type should use the front base from your permalink settings. For example, if you prefixed your permalinks with `/blog`, and `with_front` is set to `true`, your post type permalinks would include `/blog` at the beginning.

➤ `pages`—Sets whether the permalink provides for pagination. Defaults to `true`.

➤ `feeds`—Sets whether a feed permalink will be built for this post type. Defaults to `has_archive` value.

By default, the `rewrite` argument is set to `true` and the `$post_type` is used as the slug.

This section has covered a lot of custom post type arguments. The following example puts some of the more common arguments to use.

```php
<?php
add_action( 'init', 'prowp_register_my_post_types' );

function prowp_register_my_post_types() {

  $args = array(
        'public'       => true,
        'has_archive'  => true,
        'labels'       => array( 'name' => 'Products' ),
        'taxonomies'   => array( 'category' ),
        'rewrite'      => array( 'slug' => 'product' ),
```

```
            'supports'    => array( 'title', 'editor', 'author',
                'thumbnail', 'comments' )
    );

    register_post_type( 'products', $args );

}
?>
```

In this example, you first set the post type to be public. You also enabled the post type to have an archive page by setting the `has_archive` argument to `true`. The `labels` argument sets the display name of your post type; in this example you set the name to Products. Using the `taxonomies` argument, you attached the default Category taxonomy to your product's custom post type.

In this example, you want to change the permalink slug for your post type. Instead of `http://example.com/products/zombie-bait`, using the default slug `products` from the post type name, you want to set your post type slug to the singular `product`. This will generate your permalink as `http://example.com/product/zombie-bait`. This is done using the `rewrite` argument and defining a custom slug for your post type. The final argument you set is `supports`. The code adds the title, editor, author, featured image, and comments meta box to your custom post type create and edit screens.

> **NOTE** *When registering a new custom post type, it's important to flush the rewrite rules in WordPress. You can do this by calling the function* `flush_rewrite_rules()` *in your plugin's activation hook or manually by going to Settings ➤ Permalinks and saving your permalink settings. This will eliminate 404 errors on your new post type permalinks.*

To learn more about the `register_post_type()` function, visit the official Codex page at `http://codex.wordpress.org/Function_Reference/register_post_type`.

Setting Post Type Labels

When creating a custom post type in WordPress, several text strings are shown throughout the WordPress admin dashboard for your post type. These text strings are typically a link, button, or extra information about the post type. By default, the term "post" is used for non-hierarchical post types and "page" for hierarchical post types.

For example, when you use the basic custom post type registration code earlier in this chapter, you'll notice the text "Add New Post" at the top of the page when you add a new Product. The reason for this is Product is a post of type Product. This isn't very accurate, as you aren't actually adding a post, but rather a new Product. Setting the `labels` argument when registering your custom post type will allow you to define exactly what is shown.

The available labels for your custom post types include:

> ➤ name—General name for the post type, which is usually plural. Used in the WordPress admin and by other plugins and themes.

➤ `singular_name`—The singular version of the name for the post type. It is also used in the WordPress admin and by other plugins and themes.

➤ `add_new`—The label for the Add New submenu item. The text defaults to "Add New."

➤ `add_new_item`—Used as the header text on the main post listing page to add a new post. By default, the text is "Add New Post/Page."

➤ `edit_item`—Used as the text for editing an individual post. Defaults to "Edit Post/Page."

➤ `new_item`—Text for creating a new post. By default, it is set to "New Post/Page."

➤ `view_item`—Text for viewing a single post entry. Defaults to "View Post/Page."

➤ `all_items`—Text used for the all items text in the menu. This is the text displayed directly below the top-level menu name. Defaults to the value of `name`.

➤ `menu_name`– Text used in the admin menu. Defaults to the value of `name`.

➤ `name_admin_bar`—Text used in the admin bar. Defaults to `singular_name` if it exists, otherwise the `name` value.

➤ `search_items`—Text displayed for searching the posts of this type. It defaults to "Search Posts/Pages."

➤ `not_found`—The text shown when no posts were found in a search. By default, it displays "No posts/pages found."

➤ `not_found_in_trash`—The text shown when no posts are in the trash. Defaults to "No posts/pages found in Trash."

➤ `parent_item_colon`—Text shown when displaying a post's parent. This text is only used with hierarchical post types and displays "Parent Page:" by default.

Setting each value makes for a much better user experience when administering a WordPress website. In the following code, the original custom post type registration code has been modified, and the labels for the Product post type have been set.:

```php
<?php
add_action( 'init', 'prowp_register_my_post_types' );

function prowp_register_my_post_types() {

    $labels = array(
        'name'               => 'Products',
        'singular_name'      => 'Product',
        'add_new'            => 'Add New Product',
        'add_new_item'       => 'Add New Product',
        'edit_item'          => 'Edit Product',
        'new_item'           => 'New Product',
        'all_items'          => 'All Products',
        'view_item'          => 'View Product',
        'search_items'       => 'Search Products',
        'not_found'          => 'No products found',
        'not_found_in_trash' => 'No products found in Trash',
        'menu_name'          => 'Products'
```

```
    );

    $args = array(
        'labels'    =>    $labels,
        'public'    =>    true
    );

    register_post_type( 'products', $args );

}
?>
```

Working with Custom Post Types

Now that you understand how to register a custom post type, let's explore how you use them in your WordPress website. Typically it's the job of your theme to display posts on the front end of your site. However, that may not always be the case as certain custom post types may not need to be publicly displayed—for example, an error log. It all depends on what the function of your post type is.

To display custom post type data, you can use the WP_Query custom Loop example from Chapter 5. Remember that WP_Query accepts a post_type parameter that determines what type of content to return. In the example that follows, you'll return all of your product entries in WordPress:

```
$args =  array(
    'posts_per_page' => '-1',
    'post_type'      => 'products',
);

$myProducts = new WP_Query( $args );

// The Loop
while ( $myProducts->have_posts() ) : $myProducts->the_post();
    ?><a href="<?php the_permalink(); ?>"><?php the_title(); ?></a><br /><?php
endwhile;

// Reset Post Data
wp_reset_postdata();
```

Notice the post_type parameter is set to products, which is the $post_type parameter value used when you registered the Products custom post type.

Now modify the custom Loop to return only products in the Specials category:

```
$args =  array(
    'posts_per_page' => '-1',
    'post_type'      => 'products',
    'tax_query'      => array(
            array(
                'taxonomy' => 'category',
                'field'    => 'slug',
                'terms'    => 'specials'
            )
    )
```

```
    );

    $myProducts = new WP_Query( $args );

    // The Loop
    while ( $myProducts->have_posts() ) : $myProducts->the_post();
        ?><a href="<?php the_permalink(); ?>"><?php the_title(); ?></a><br /><?php
    endwhile;

    // Reset Post Data
    wp_reset_postdata();
```

Using the `tax_query` parameter in `WP_Query`, the custom Loop will return only product post type entries assigned to the Specials category.

You can use all of the same methods for creating custom Loops with `WP_Query`, as covered in detail in Chapter 5, to display your custom post type content. It's easy to see the power custom post types bring to WordPress when developing more complex websites.

Custom Post Type Template Files

Earlier in the chapter, you learned about the `has_archive` argument when registering a custom post type. Enabling this argument will allow you to create an archive template file that will display all of your custom post type entries by default. The archive template for a custom post type must be named in the form of `archive-{post-type}.php`. For example, an archive template for your Products custom post type would be named `archive-products.php`. This archive template is a perfect place to display all of your products.

Just like the archive template, WordPress will also recognize a single template for your post type entries. This is the template that is loaded when you visit a single entry for your custom post type. The single template must be named in the form of `single-{posttype}.php`. So your products single template would be named `single-products.php`. When visiting a single product URL, such as `http://example.com/products/zombie-bait`, the `single-products.php` template would load if it exists.

Theme template files, including custom post types, are covered in more detail in Chapter 9.

Special Post Type Functions

WordPress features many different post type–specific functions to make working with custom post types that much easier. In this section, you will review some of the more common functions you might use when building your websites.

To return a list of all registered post types in WordPress, you'll use the `get_post_types()` function:

```
<?php get_post_types( $args, $output, $operator ); ?>
```

This function accepts three optional parameters:

➤ `$args`—An array of arguments to match against the post type.

➤ `$output`—The type of output to return, either `names` or `objects`. Defaults to `names`.

➤ `$operator`—Operator to use with multiple `$args`. Defaults to `and`.

Using the `get_post_types()` function, use the following to return a list of all custom post types registered in WordPress:

```
$args = array(
    'public'   => true,
    '_builtin' => false
);

$post_types = get_post_types( $args, 'names', 'and' );

foreach ( $post_types  as $post_type ) {
    echo '<p>'. $post_type. '</p>';
}
```

As shown in the preceding code, you'll set two arguments in the `$args` array: `public` and `_builtin`. The `public` argument will only return custom post types that are set to be publicly viewable. The `_builtin` argument is set to `false`, which will not return default post types like posts and pages. You also set the `$output` argument to return just the post type name, and the `$operator` argument to use "and" for the multiple `$args` you passed to the function.

To determine what post type a piece of content is, you'll use the `get_post_type()` function:

```
<?php get_post_type( $post ); ?>
```

This function accepts only one parameter—$post—which is a post object or a post ID. If the parameter is empty, the current post will be used.

You can display the post type of a post in a loop using the following code:

```
<?php echo 'The post type is: '.get_post_type( get_the_ID() ); ?>
```

There may be a time when you want to work with a custom post type that was created by a plugin or theme. The first thing you should always do is to verify that the custom post type you are looking for exists. To do so, you'll use the `post_type_exists()` function.

```
<?php post_type_exists( $post_type ); ?>
```

The function accepts a single required parameter—$post_type—which is the post type you want to verify has been registered.

If you wanted to verify the `products` custom post type exists, you use this code:

```
if( post_type_exists( 'products' ) ) {
  echo 'The Products post type exists';
}
```

Another useful function when working with other custom post types is `add_post_type_support()`. This function allows you to register support for certain features on a post type, such as the featured image meta box.

```
<?php add_post_type_support( $post_type, $supports ) ?>
```

This is a useful function if the existing post type doesn't have support for a feature that you need. The add_post_type_support() function accepts two parameters:

➤ $post_type—The post type name you are adding support to

➤ $supports—A string or array of features to add

As an example, assume the products post type does not support featured images or comments. To add support for both of these features, use the following code example:

```
add_post_type_support( 'products', array( 'thumbnail', 'comments' ) );
```

This function is very useful if you need to work with a custom post type that is defined in a separate plugin or theme. Rather than hacking the registration code in that plugin or theme, you can use the add_post_type_support() function to enable any feature needed for your code to work.

You can also remove post type feature support using the remove_post_type_support() function. This function works exactly like the preceding function, but will remove feature support for a given post type:

```
remove_post_type_support( 'products', array( 'thumbnail', 'comments' ) );
```

WordPress also features a function to change the post type of a post entry. You can do so by using the set_post_type() function:

```
<?php set_post_type( $post_id, $post_type ); ?>
```

The function accepts two parameters:

➤ $post_id—The ID of the post you want to update. This field is required.

➤ $post_type—The post type name to change the post to. This is an optional field and defaults to post.

WORDPRESS TAXONOMY

Taxonomy is defined as a way to group similar items together. This basically adds a relational dimension to your website's content. In the case of WordPress, you use categories and tags to group your posts. By grouping these posts, you are defining the taxonomy of those posts. Taxonomy can be hierarchical (that is, categories and subcategories), but it is not required. Tags are a perfect example of a taxonomy without a hierarchy.

Default Taxonomies

By default, WordPress comes loaded with two taxonomies:

➤ **Category**—A bucket for grouping similar posts together

➤ **Tag**—A label attached to a post

Categories are hierarchical and defined when creating a post. *Tags* do not use hierarchy and are also defined when creating a post. Both out-of-the-box taxonomies are available for use in a default installation of WordPress.

Each category or tag you create is a term of that taxonomy. For example, a category named Music is a term of the category taxonomy. A tag named Ketchup is a term of the tag taxonomy. Understanding taxonomy and terms will help you when defining your own custom taxonomies in WordPress.

Understanding how you can classify your content using a solid taxonomy structure will make structuring website content in WordPress much easier from the start. Developing a solid taxonomy framework enables easy and accurate information access throughout your website.

Taxonomy Table Structure

WordPress features three database tables that store all taxonomy information: wp _ terms, wp _ term _ relationships, and wp _ term _ taxonomy. This taxonomy schema, which was added in WordPress 2.3, makes the taxonomy functionality extremely flexible in WordPress. This means you can create and define any type of custom taxonomy to use on your website.

The wp _ terms table stores all of your taxonomy terms. This can be categories, tags, link categories, and any custom taxonomy terms you have defined. The wp _ term _ taxonomy table defines what taxonomy each term belongs to. For example, all of your tag IDs will be listed in this table with a taxonomy value of post _ tag. If you created a custom taxonomy, the taxonomy value would be the name of your custom taxonomy. The wp _ term _ relationships table is the cross-reference table that joins taxonomy terms with your content. For example, when you assign a tag to your post, a new record is created here joining your post ID and the term ID together.

Understanding Taxonomy Relationships

To really understand the relationship between the taxonomy tables, it's helpful to look at a database diagram of the taxonomy table structure, as shown in Figure 7-2.

As you can see, the three taxonomy tables are joined together by unique IDs. The following is a query to display all posts along with all taxonomy terms assigned to those posts:

```
SELECT wt.name, wp.post_title, wp.post_date FROM wp_terms wt
INNER JOIN wp_term_taxonomy wtt ON wt.term_id  = wtt.term_id
INNER JOIN wp_term_relationships wtr ON wtt.
   term_taxonomy_id = wtr.term_taxonomy_id
INNER JOIN wp_posts wp ON wtr.object_id = wp.ID
WHERE wp.post_type = 'post'
```

Notice how you are joining on the table fields, as depicted in Figure 7-2. The preceding example returns only three fields: the taxonomy term, post title, and the post date. This query example returns all posts in your WordPress database along with all taxonomy terms attached to those posts.

> **NOTE** *To learn more about taxonomy table relationships and why WordPress needs to decompose these multi-valued relationships into multiple tables, see the "WordPress Taxonomy Tables" section of Chapter 6.*

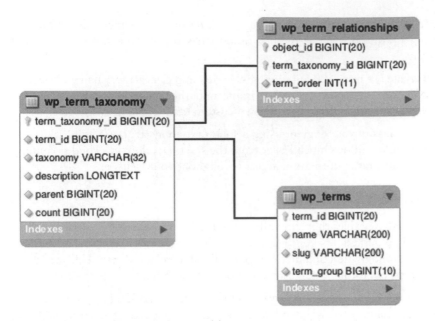

FIGURE 7-2: WordPress taxonomy table structure

BUILDING YOUR OWN TAXONOMIES

Creating your own custom taxonomies has many benefits. Imagine running a food blogging website. When creating new posts, you'll want to label a certain recipe as Asian, but you also may want to label the individual ingredients, heat factor, prep time, and so on. Building custom taxonomies allows you the freedom to define these different methods of categorizing your content and really expands WordPress from blogging software into a full-fledged content management system (CMS).

Custom Taxonomy Overview

With the revamp of the taxonomy schema in WordPress 2.3, you now have the capability to define custom taxonomies for your content. WordPress makes it easier than ever to create custom taxonomies, as well as integrate your new taxonomies into WordPress.

WordPress includes the ability to automatically display a meta box to the post type edit screen for adding taxonomy terms directly to your posts. WordPress will also create a menu item to access the new taxonomy admin panel for administering your taxonomy terms.

Creating Custom Taxonomies

Now it's time to build your first custom taxonomy! You are going to create a simple taxonomy for defining Types for your `products` custom post type registered earlier in this chapter. If you are selling Products online, you'll need a way to group specific Product types together. You are going to set up a custom taxonomy to define each type of Product in WordPress.

First, you are going to define your new taxonomy using the `register_taxonomy()` WordPress function. This function allows you to customize how your new taxonomy will work and look. The following code would work in a custom plugin, but for this example, you'll use the `functions.php` file in your theme folder. Open up `functions.php` in your theme and add the following code:

```php
<?php
add_action( 'init', 'prowp_define_product_type_taxonomy' );

function prowp_define_product_type_taxonomy() {

    register_taxonomy(
        'type',
        'products',
        array(
            'hierarchical' => true,
            'label'        => 'Type',
            'query_var'    => true,
            'rewrite'      => true
            )
        );

}
?>
```

The taxonomy definition starts by calling the `init` hook, which tells WordPress to execute your custom `prowp_define_product_type_taxonomy()` function during initialization. Your function then calls the WordPress function `register_taxonomy()`. This function is used to create your custom taxonomy based on what values you send.

You can now break down the parameters you are sending to the `register_taxonomy()` function. The first parameter is the taxonomy name, in this case `type`. This is the name that will define this taxonomy in the database. The second parameter is the object type. For this example, you will use `products`, which is the name of your custom post type. The third and final parameter is for arguments, meaning you actually send multiple values to this parameter.

In this example, you'll pass four arguments. The first is `hierarchical`, which defines whether or not your custom taxonomy can support nested taxonomies, forming a hierarchy. In the preceding example, you set this to `true`, so your taxonomy will function just like WordPress's built-in categories that may contain sub-categories. The next argument, `label`, is used to set the name of your taxonomy for use in admin pages within WordPress. If the `query_var` argument is set to `false`, then no queries can be made against the taxonomy; if `true`, then the taxonomy name (with dashes replacing spaces) is used as a query variable in URL strings. Specifying a string value for the `query_var` overrides the default. For example, `query_var => 'strength'` would permit URL strings of the form `example.com/?strength=weapons` to be used to select content from the custom taxonomy.

The final argument is for `rewrite`, which you set to `true`. This tells WordPress whether or not you want a pretty permalink when viewing your custom taxonomy. By setting this to `true`, you can access your custom taxonomy posts such as `example.com/type/weapons` rather than the ugly method of `example.com/?type=weapons`.

Now that you have created your custom taxonomy for `type`, take a look at what WordPress has done with your new taxonomy. The first thing you will notice on your admin dashboard is a new link under the Products menu for your taxonomy labeled Type, as shown in Figure 7-3.

Clicking this new menu item brings you to the custom taxonomy admin panel for types, shown in Figure 7-4. This admin panel works exactly as the post categories admin panel does. Here you can create new taxonomy terms, edit and delete existing terms, find how many products are assigned to each, and also search taxonomy terms.

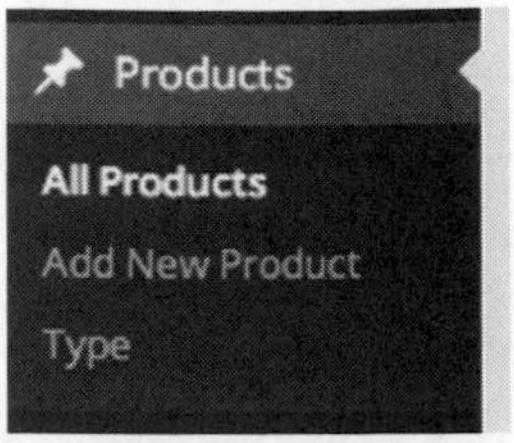

FIGURE 7-3: Custom taxonomy menu option

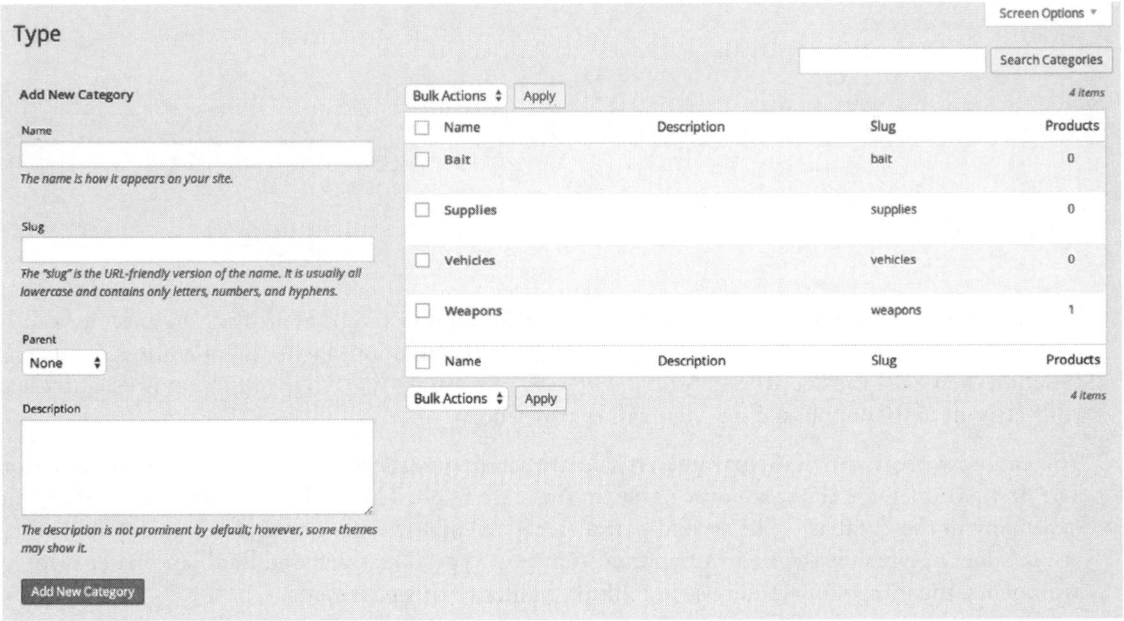

FIGURE 7-4: Custom taxonomy admin panel

The final new item added for your custom taxonomy is a meta box on the product edit screen, shown in Figure 7-5. To view this, click Add New Product. The meta box appears on the right side of your screen and looks very similar to the Category meta box. Here you can easily add and delete new types on your products.

As with custom post types, you can set a variety of different arguments when registering a custom taxonomy:

➤ `public`—Sets whether a custom taxonomy is publicly available on the admin dashboard or front-end of your website. By default, this is set to `true`. The default settings for `show_ui` and `show_in_nav_menus` are inherited from this setting.

➤ show_ui—Sets whether to create a default UI in the WordPress admin dashboard for managing this taxonomy. Defaults to the value defined by the public argument.

➤ show_in_nav_menus—Sets whether the post type is available for selection in the menu management feature of WordPress. Defaults to the value defined by the public argument.

➤ show_tagcloud—Sets whether to allow the built-in Tag Cloud widget to use this taxonomy. Defaults to the value defined by the show_ui argument.

➤ show_admin_column—Sets whether to display the taxonomy column on the post listing screen.

➤ hierarchical—Sets whether this custom taxonomy is hierarchical (like categories) or not hierarchical (like tags). By default, this argument is set to false.

➤ update_count_callback—Function name that will be called when a term in your taxonomy gets a count update. The default value is none.

➤ query_var—Enables the public query var for the taxonomy. Acceptable values are true, false, or a string to set a custom query var value.

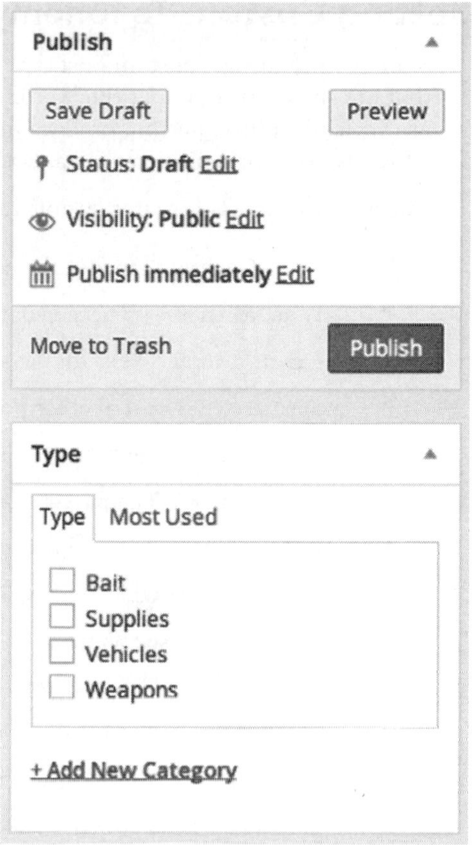

FIGURE 7-5: Custom taxonomy meta box

➤ rewrite—The rewrite argument sets the URL parsing rules for permalinks referring to this taxonomy. This allows you to customize the taxonomy slug in your URL. This argument can be set to true, false, or an array of values. If passing an array, it accepts the following values. By default this argument is set to true and the $taxonomy name is used as the slug.

➤ slug—Set a custom permalink slug. Defaults to the taxonomy name value.

➤ with_front—Sets whether your taxonomy should use the front base from your permalink settings. For example, if you prefixed your permalinks with /blog, and with_front is set to true, your taxonomy permalinks would include /blog at the beginning.

➤ hierarchical—Allow hierarchical URLs. Defaults to false.

To learn more about the register_taxonomy() function, visit the official Codex page at http://codex.wordpress.org/Function_Reference/register_taxonomy.

Setting Custom Taxonomy Labels

Similar to creating a custom post type in WordPress, custom taxonomies feature several text strings that are shown throughout the WordPress admin dashboard for your taxonomy. These text strings are typically a link, button, or extra information about the custom taxonomy. By default, the term "Tag" is used for non-hierarchical taxonomies and "Category" for hierarchical taxonomies.

The available labels for your custom taxonomy include the following:

➤ name—General name for the taxonomy, which is usually plural.

➤ singular_name—The singular version of the name for the taxonomy.

➤ search_items—Text for the search items button.

➤ popular_items—Label for popular items text.

➤ all_items—Label for all items text.

➤ parent_item—The parent item text. Not used on non-hierarchical taxonomies.

➤ parent_item_colon—Same as parent_item, but with a colon at the end.

➤ edit_item—Used as the text for editing an individual taxonomy term.

➤ view_item—Used as the view item text.

➤ update_item—Used as the text for updating an individual taxonomy term.

➤ add_new_item—Text for creating a new taxonomy term.

➤ new_item_name—The new item text name text.

➤ separate_items_with_commas—The separate items with commas text used in the taxonomy meta box. Not used on hierarchical taxonomies.

➤ add_or_remove_items—Text displayed in the taxonomy meta box when JavaScript is disabled. Not used on hierarchical taxonomies.

➤ choose_from_most_used—The "choose from most used" text used in the taxonomy meta box. Not used on hierarchical taxonomies.

➤ menu_name—The menu name text. Defaults to the value of name.

➤ not_found—The text displayed when you click "Choose from the most used tags" and no tags are available.

Setting these labels makes it much easier on users when administering custom taxonomy terms. Now modify the custom taxonomy registration code from earlier with custom labels:

```php
<?php
add_action( 'init', 'prowp_define_product_type_taxonomy' );

function prowp_define_product_type_taxonomy() {
    $labels = array(
        'name'                => 'Type',
        'singular_name'       => 'Types',
```

```
                'search_items'      => 'Search Types',
                'all_items'         => 'All Types',
                'parent_item'       => 'Parent Type',
                'parent_item_colon' => 'Parent Type:',
                'edit_item'         => 'Edit Type',
                'update_item'       => 'Update Type',
                'add_new_item'      => 'Add New Type',
                'new_item_name'     => 'New Type Name',
                'menu_name'         => 'Type',
                'view_item'         => 'View Types'
        );

        $args = array(
                'labels'       => $labels,
                'hierarchical' => true,
                'query_var'    => true,
                'rewrite'      => true
        );

        register_taxonomy( 'type', 'products', $args );
}
?>
```

Using Your Custom Taxonomy

Now that you've created your custom taxonomy, you need to know how to use it on your website. As always, WordPress features some very easy-to-use functions for working with your custom taxonomy. The following shows how you can display a tag cloud showing your custom taxonomy terms:

```
<?php wp_tag_cloud( array( 'taxonomy' => 'type', 'number' => 5 ) ); ?>
```

The wp_tag_cloud() function can accept many different arguments, but in this example, you're using only two: taxonomy and number. First, you set your taxonomy to type; this tells WordPress to return only taxonomy terms defined under the custom taxonomy you created for types. Next, you define the number of terms you want to display, which in this example is 5. Calling this function in your theme sidebar displays a nice tag cloud that shows the five taxonomy terms with the most products assigned to them.

You can also create a custom Loop using WP_Query to display products for a specific taxonomy term. Say you want to create a custom Loop to display only products that have the term weapons attached as the type custom taxonomy:

```
<?php
$args = array(
    'post_type' => 'products',
    'tax_query' => array(
    array(
        'taxonomy' => 'type',
        'field'    => 'slug',
        'terms'    => 'weapons'
        )
    )
);
```

```
$products = new WP_Query( $args );

while ( $products->have_posts() ) : $products->the_post();
    ?><a href="<?php the_permalink(); ?>"><?php the_title(); ?></a><br /><?php
endwhile;

wp_reset_postdata();
?>
```

That's it! The two `WP_Query` arguments you send are the `post_type`, `products` in this case, and the `tax_query`, which specifies which taxonomy term to use.

You can also easily display custom taxonomy terms assigned to each post. To do this, you'll be using the `get_the_term_list()` WordPress function. This function works very similarly to `get_the_tag_list()` but is for building a custom taxonomy term list instead.

```
<?php echo get_the_term_list( get_post_ID(), 'type', 'Product Type: ',
    ', ', '' ); ?>
```

The preceding code displays all custom taxonomy terms assigned to the post you are viewing. This code does need to be in the Loop in your theme template file to work correctly. To execute the function, you send in the post ID, custom taxonomy name, and the title you want displayed next to the terms. Remember that you can always visit the function reference to learn more about this function and what parameters are allowed: `http://codex.wordpress.org/Function_Reference/get_the_term_list`.

The `get_terms()` function can also be used to retrieve an array of your custom taxonomy values. In the following example, you retrieve all of the terms for your `type` taxonomy and loop through the values displaying the term name:

```
<?php
$terms = get_terms( 'type' );
foreach ( $terms as $term ) {
    echo '<p>' .$term->name. '</p>';
}
?>
```

Keep in mind that you need to make sure the taxonomy is defined before you start working with custom taxonomy values. If any of the preceding examples return blank, that means they were executed before your `register_taxonomy()` function was called to define your custom taxonomy.

Defining custom taxonomies in WordPress is a very powerful way to organize your website content. Using the preceding methods can help transform your website into a content management system using the power of WordPress.

METADATA

In this chapter, you've learned how to create custom post types to add to the basic content types managed by WordPress, and custom taxonomies to organize and collect those content types. This chapter wraps up with a look at extending the content management descriptors of a post with custom metadata.

What Is Metadata?

Metadata in WordPress refers to additional pieces of data attached to a post. For example, your `products` custom post type might need a price stored with each Product entered. The price could be stored as metadata and easily displayed on the Product detail page.

Post metadata is often referred to as Custom Fields in WordPress terminology. This is a more user-friendly term in the admin dashboard of WordPress. WordPress adds a Custom Fields meta box on the post-editing screen by default, as shown in Figure 7-6. If a custom post type has the `custom-fields` value defined for the `supports` argument, this meta box will also appear.

All post metadata is stored in the `wp_postmeta` table in your WordPress database.

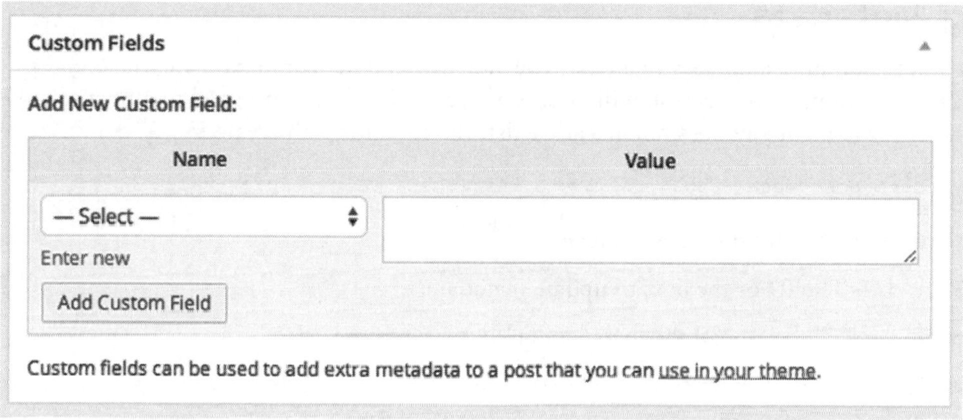

FIGURE 7-6: Custom Field meta box

Adding Metadata

WordPress features a simple function to add new post metadata called `add_post_meta()`. This function will attach a piece of metadata to the post specified as follows:

```php
<?php add_post_meta( $post_id, $meta_key, $meta_value, $unique ); ?>
```

This function accepts the following four parameters:

➤ `$post_id`—The ID of the post to add metadata.

➤ `$meta_key`—The name of the metadata field.

➤ `$meta_value`—The value of the metadata field.

➤ `$unique`—A value identifying whether or not the key should be unique. The default value is `false`.

Now that you understand the parameters for the `add_post_meta()` function, you can use it to add some metadata to your products.

```php
<?php add_post_meta( 420, 'prowp_price', '34.99', true ); ?>
```

This code example adds a metadata entry called `prowp_price` with a value of 34.99 to product ID 420. You also set the `$unique` value to `true`, which means there cannot be multiple entries for the `prowp_price` field on this product. Now if you edit the product in WordPress, you will see a `prowp_price` field and value in the custom fields meta box.

> **NOTE** *To prevent metadata keys from appearing in the Custom Fields meta box on the Post Edit screen, prefix the meta key with an underscore like _prowp_ price. This will hide the data from the user and is common practice when creating custom meta boxes.*

Updating Metadata

As easy as it is to add new metadata to a post, you can also update metadata using the `update_post_meta()` function. This function will update a piece of metadata attached to a post specified, as shown here. If the meta key does not already exist, the function will create it.

```php
<?php update_post_meta( $post_id, $meta_key, $meta_value, $prev_value ); ?>
```

This function accepts the following parameters:

➤ `$post_id`—The ID of the post to update metadata.

➤ `$meta_key`—The name of the metadata field.

➤ `$meta_value`—The value of the metadata field.

➤ `$prev_value`—The old value of the metadata field to update. This is to differentiate between several fields with the same key and is an optional field.

For example, you can update the price on your product from earlier as follows:

```php
<?php update_post_meta( 420, 'prowp_price', '6.99' ); ?>
```

The preceding code example updates the previously added metadata field `prowp_price` to 6.99 for product ID 420.

Deleting Metadata

Now that you understand how to add and update post metadata, you can learn how to delete that data. To delete post metadata, you'll use the `delete_post_meta()` function.

```php
<?php delete_post_meta( $post_id, $meta_key, $meta_value ); ?>
```

This function accepts the following parameters:

➤ `$post_id`—The ID of the post to delete metadata from.

➤ `$meta_key`—The name of the metadata field.

➤ `$meta_value`—The value of the metadata field. This is to differentiate between several fields with the same key and is an optional field.

Let's delete the post metadata you created earlier:

```php
<?php delete_post_meta( 420, 'prowp_price' ); ?>
```

The preceding code example will delete the prowp_price metadata from product ID 420. You did not define the $meta_value parameter, so all prowp_price entries will be deleted from product ID 420.

Retrieving Metadata

You've covered how to add, update, and delete metadata, so now you will review how to retrieve and display metadata. WordPress makes it easy to retrieve post metadata for display or use in other code. A good place to use this code is within a Loop to display custom metadata for a particular piece of content.

To retrieve metadata, you'll use the get_post_meta() function:

```php
<?php $meta_values = get_post_meta( $post_id, $key, $single ); ?>
```

The function accepts these parameters:

➤ $post_id—The ID of the post to retrieve metadata for.

➤ $meta_key—The name of the metadata field.

➤ $single—A value identifying whether to return a single meta value field (true) or return an array of values (false). By default, this parameter is set to false.

Let's retrieve and display the price for your product created earlier:

```php
<?php
$product_price = get_post_meta( 420, 'prowp_price', true );
echo 'Price $' .$product_price;
?>
```

The product price is retrieved and displayed for product ID 420. Now assume you want to store various colors for the product. Instead of creating a separate metadata entry for each color, you'll create an array of color entries in a single metadata field:

```php
<?php
add_post_meta( 420, 'prowp_colors', 'orange', false );
add_post_meta( 420, 'prowp_colors', 'black', false );

$product_colors = get_post_meta( 420, 'prowp_colors', false );

echo '<ul class="product-colors">';

foreach ( $product_colors as $color ) {
    echo '<li>' .$color .'</li>';
}

echo '</ul>';
?>
```

First you have to create the metadata entries for the product colors. This is done using the `add_post_meta()` function. Next, set the meta key name to the same and the `$unique` parameter to `false`, which will allow multiple entries under the same meta key.

Next, you'll use the `get_post_meta()` function to retrieve the product colors you just set. Notice the `$single` parameter is set to `false`, which allows you to return all entries for `prowp_colors` for product ID 420 as an array. Finally, you'll loop through the colors array and display each product color.

Another powerful function for retrieving post metadata is the `get_post_custom()` function. This function returns a multidimensional array of all metadata for a particular post.

```php
<?php get_post_custom( $post_id ); ?>
```

This function accepts a single required parameter—`$post_id`—the ID of the post whose custom fields will be retrieved.

Let's retrieve and display all metadata entries for your product:

```php
<?php
$product_metadata = get_post_custom( 420 );

foreach( $product_metadata as $name => $value ) {

    echo '<strong>' .$name .'</strong>  =>  ';

    foreach( $value as $nameAr => $valueAr ) {

        echo '<br />' .$nameAr." =>  ";
        echo var_dump( $valueAr );

    }

    echo '<br />';
}
?>
```

The preceding code example will retrieve all metadata for product ID 420. Because the value returned is a multidimensional array, you have to do multiple loops to display all of the data. This is the preferred method when retrieving multiple pieces of metadata for a post because it retrieves all metadata in a single database query instead of running separate queries for each piece of data requested. As you can tell, this is a more advanced method for retrieving post metadata.

COMMUNITY PROJECTS

Custom post types, taxonomies, and metadata are a big part of many WordPress projects. This has led to a large number of community projects to help make the process of registering these content types much easier. Below is a list of some of the more popular community projects focused on custom post types, taxonomies, and metadata:

➤ **CMB2**—Custom Metaboxes and Fields 2 is a tool that allows you to create custom metaboxes and forms with custom fields in WordPress. These fields can be attached to your posts, comments, and even users. You can get this tool at `https://github.com/WebDevStudios/CMB2`.

➤ **Custom Meta Boxes**—This is a framework that can be used to easily add custom fields to the WordPress post edit page. You can get it at `https://github.com/humanmade/Custom-Meta-Boxes`.

➤ **CPT_Core**—This is a helper class used for registering custom post types in WordPress. You can get it at `https://github.com/WebDevStudios/CPT_Core`.

➤ **Taxonomy_Core**—This is a Helper class used for registering custom taxonomies in WordPress. You can get it at `https://github.com/WebDevStudios/Taxonomy_Core`.

➤ **Custom Post Type UI**—This tool provides an easy-to-use admin interface to register custom post types and taxonomies in WordPress. You can get it at `https://wordpress.org/plugins/custom-post-type-ui/`.

SUMMARY

It's very easy to see how using a combination of custom post types, custom taxonomies, and metadata in WordPress opens the doors to endless possibilities. These features have morphed WordPress from a simple blogging platform into a full-fledged content management system capable of handling any type of data you can conceive.

In the next chapter you'll dive into creating custom plugins for WordPress. You'll learn the proper ways to integrate into various areas of WordPress, understanding data validation to develop secure code, and even how to publish your plugins to the WordPress.org Plugin Directory.

8

Plugin Development

WHAT'S IN THIS CHAPTER?

➤ Creating plugin files

➤ Data validation and plugin security

➤ Using WordPress filter and action hooks

➤ How to properly use the Settings API

➤ Creating a widget and dashboard widget

➤ Creating custom shortcodes

➤ Supporting language translation

➤ Publishing a plugin to the official Plugin Directory

➤ Plugin Directory header and icon assets

WROX.COM CODE DOWNLOADS FOR THIS CHAPTER

The wrox.com code downloads for this chapter are found at www.wrox.com/go/wordpress3e on the Download Code tab. The code is in the Chapter 8 download file and individually named according to the code filenames noted throughout the chapter.

One of the main reasons WordPress is such a popular software platform is the ease with which it can be extended. Plugins are the primary reason for this and allow endless possibilities in extending WordPress. This chapter discusses everything you need to know to create amazing plugins in WordPress.

You are going to look at plugins from both a functional and structural perspective. Starting with the packaging of plugin files, you'll dig into the API hooks that connect your custom plugin code to the WordPress core and show how to integrate a plugin into various parts of the WordPress editing, management, and display processes. Finally, you will see how to publish a plugin for others to use. At the end of this chapter, you build a WordPress plugin from the ground up. You'll utilize many of the features discussed in this chapter and learn the proper way to extend WordPress through a custom plugin.

PLUGIN PACKAGING

When developing plugins in WordPress, it's best to follow a standard plugin packaging template—that is, certain functional and descriptive components that will exist in all plugins you create for WordPress. This chapter discusses the requirements for a plugin, as well as recommended additions such as software license and internationalization. While the actual code implementation of the plugin is the exciting part of the process, consider the plugin packaging as you would elementary grammar rules for a new language: necessary for making yourself understood.

Creating a Plugin File

The first step in creating a WordPress plugin is to create a new PHP file for your plugin code. The plugin file name should be descriptive of your plugin so it's easy to identify your plugin in the `plugins` directory. It should also be unique because all WordPress plugins exist in the same folder. If your plugin file name is too generic, you run the risk of another plugin having the same file name, which would be an obvious problem.

A plugin can also exist in a folder containing all of the necessary files the plugin needs to run. A folder should always be used because it helps keep the user's plugin folder organized. It's also a good idea to maintain a clean folder structure, which refers to keeping all similar files together. For example, if your plugin includes images, you should create a `/images` folder inside your plugin folder to store any custom images your plugin might use.

Let's look at a standard folder structure for a plugin:

- `/unique-plugin-name` (no spaces or special characters)
    - `unique-plugin-name.php`—Primary plugin PHP file
    - `uninstall.php`—The uninstall file for your plugin
    - `/js`—Folder for JavaScript files
    - `/css`—Folder for style sheet files
    - `/includes`—Folder for additional PHP includes
    - `/images`—Folder for plugin images

Keeping your files organized using a clean folder structure can make it much easier to track the flow of your plugin over time.

Creating the Plugin Header

A requirement for all WordPress plugins is a valid plugin header. The plugin header must be defined at the very top of your main PHP file as a PHP comment. It does not need to exist in every file for your plugin, only the main PHP file. This header tells WordPress that your PHP file is in fact a legitimate WordPress plugin and should be processed as such. Following is an example of a standard plugin header:

```php
<?php
/*
Plugin Name: Halloween Plugin
Plugin URI: http://example.com/wordpress-plugins/halloween-plugin
Description: This is a brief description of my plugin
Version: 1.0
Author: Michael Myers
Author URI: http://example.com
Text Domain: prowp-plugin
License: GPLv2
*/
```

The only required line in the plugin header is the Plugin Name. The rest of the information is optional but highly recommended. The information listed in your plugin header is used on the Manage Plugins section of WordPress. You can see what the header looks like in WordPress in Figure 8-1.

☐ **Halloween Plugin**   This is a brief description of my plugin
   Activate | Edit | Delete   **Version 1.0 | By** Michael Myers | Visit plugin site

FIGURE 8-1: Example plugin listing

You can see how important the plugin header information is, including all optional data. The information should be accurate and provide good links to your website and the plugin URI for additional information and support regarding your plugin.

Plugin License

When developing a plugin you plan on releasing to the public, it's customary to include the software license that the plugin is released under just below your plugin header. This is not a requirement for the plugin to function, but is a good idea to clearly state what software license your plugin uses. A license comment block will also state that there is no warranty, which protects you from liability should someone decide your plugin destroyed his or her site. Following is a standard GPL license, under which most WordPress plugins are released:

```php
<?php
/*  Copyright YEAR  PLUGIN_AUTHOR_NAME  (email : PLUGIN AUTHOR EMAIL)
    This program is free software; you can redistribute it and/or modify
    it under the terms of the GNU General Public License as published by
    the Free Software Foundation; either version 2 of the License, or
    (at your option) any later version.
    This program is distributed in the hope that it will be useful,
    but WITHOUT ANY WARRANTY; without even the implied warranty of
    MERCHANTABILITY or FITNESS FOR A PARTICULAR PURPOSE.  See the
    GNU General Public License for more details.
    You should have received a copy of the GNU General Public License
```

```
        along with this program; if not, write to the Free Software
        Foundation, Inc., 51 Franklin St, Fifth Floor, Boston, MA  02110-1301  USA
*/
?>
```

To use this license in your plugin, fill in the year, plugin author name, and plugin author e-mail in the preceding comment. By doing so, your plugin will be licensed under the GPL.

WordPress is licensed under the GPLv2 software license. This is a very common software license for open source projects. Since plugins are dependent on WordPress to function, they should also be released under a GPL, or compatible, software license. For more information on GPL licensing visit http://www.gnu.org/licenses/licenses.html.

Activating and Deactivating Functions

You'll want to utilize some important functions when creating plugins. The first of these is called the register_activation_hook() function. This function is executed when your plugin is activated in the WordPress Plugins screen. The function accepts two parameters: the path to the main plugin file and the function to execute when the plugin is activated.

In most of the code examples in this chapter, you're going to use prowp as a function and variable prefix, as well as a descriptive name for your plugin. It's just a unique short name prefix, but one that you're going to see in a lot of code. The following example executes the function prowp_install() when the plugin is activated:

```php
<?php
register_activation_hook( __FILE__, 'prowp_install' );

function prowp_install() {
    //do something
}
?>
```

This is an extremely useful function if you need to execute any actions when your plugin is activated. For example, you may want to check the current WordPress version to verify that your plugin is compatible. You may also want to create some default option settings.

One important check you should always do when your plugin is activated is to verify that the version of WordPress the user is running is compatible with your plugin. This ensures any functions, hooks, and so on that your plugin requires are available in WordPress.

```php
register_activation_hook( __FILE__, 'prowp_install' );

function prowp_install() {
    global $wp_version;

    if ( version_compare( $wp_version, '4.1', '<' ) ) {

        wp_die( 'This plugin requires WordPress version 4.1 or higher.' );

    }
}
```

The preceding function uses the global variable $wp _ version, which stores the currently running version of WordPress and verifies that it is not running a version lower than 4.1. You do the version comparison using the version _ compare() PHP function. If the WordPress version is lower than 4.1, you display an error message to the users that they need to update. The register _ activation _ hook is only triggered when the user activates the plugin and not when an automatic plugin update occurs.

There is also a function that executes when a plugin is deactivated called register _ deactivation _ hook(). This function is executed when your plugin is deactivated in the WordPress Plugins screen. This function accepts the same two arguments as the register _ activation _ hook function. Following is an example using the deactivation function:

```php
<?php
register_deactivation_hook( __FILE__, 'prowp_deactivate()' );

function prowp_deactivate() {
    //do something
}
?>
```

> **NOTE** *It's important to remember that deactivating is not uninstalling. You should never include uninstall functionality in your deactivation function. Imagine that a user accidentally deactivates your plugin and all of their settings are deleted. That would not be a good user experience and should be avoided.*

Internationalization

Internationalization, sometimes shortened to "i18n" in the WordPress Codex, is the process of making your plugin or theme ready for translation, or localized. In WordPress, this means marking strings that should be translated. Localization is the process of translating the text displayed by the theme or plugin into different languages. This isn't a requirement, but internationalization should be used on any plugin you plan on distributing. This opens up your plugin to the widest possible audience.

WordPress features many different functions to make a string translatable. The first function is __ (). That isn't a typo; the function is two underscores, as shown here:

```php
<?php $howdy = __( 'Howdy Neighbor!', 'prowp-plugin' ); ?>
```

The first parameter you pass is the string that you want to be translated. This string is what will be displayed to the browser if the text is not translated into a different language. The second parameter is the text domain. In the case of themes and plugins, the domain should be a unique identifier, which is used to distinguish between all loaded translations.

If your code should echo the translatable string to the browser, you'll want to use the _e() function, as shown here:

```php
<?php _e( 'Howdy Neighbor!', 'prowp-plugin' ); ?>
```

This function works exactly the same as __(); the only difference is that the value is echoed to the browser.

Placeholders need special consideration when internationalizing your plugins and themes. As an example, look at an error message you want to make translatable:

```
Error Code 6980: Email is a required field
```

The obvious, but incorrect, way to attempt to split a string into translatable parts is to separate the field name, error number, and descriptive string:

```php
<?php
$error_number = 6980;
$error_field = "Email";
$error = __( 'Error Code ', 'prowp-plugin' ) .$error_number. ': '
.$error_field .__( ' is a required field', 'prowp-plugin' );
echo $error;
?>
```

This is actually the wrong way to include dynamic values in your translatable string because your translatable string is cut into two parts. These two parts may not work independently in another language. This could also seriously confuse the translator viewing a bunch of cryptic phrases that mean nothing when separated. The proper way is shown here:

```php
<?php
$error_number = 6980;
$error_field = "Email";
printf( __( 'Error Code %1$d: %2$s is a required field', 'prowp-plugin' ),
$error_number, $error_field );
?>
```

As you can see, this uses the PHP printf() function, which outputs the formatted string. Your two variables are passed to printf() and inserted into the string in the designated spots. In this example, a developer translating your plugin messages into another language would see the line as Error Code %1$d: %2$s is a required field and know it's possible to move around the error number and field values to make sense in the target language. Splitting the strings leads to split translations and possibly unintentionally funny translated grammar. Alternatively, you could use the PHP sprintf() function if you want to store the error message value in a variable prior to displaying it.

Plurals also need special consideration when defining your translatable strings. Say you need to translate a string like this:

```php
<?php
$count = 1;
printf( __( 'You have %d new message', 'prowp-plugin' ), $count );
?>
```

This works great if you have one new message, but what if you have more than one new message? Fortunately, WordPress contains a function you can use to handle this problem called _n(). The following code shows it in action:

```php
<?php
$count = 34;
printf( _n( 'You have %d new message', 'You have %d new messages',
$count, 'prowp-plugin'), $count );
?>
```

This function accepts four parameters: the singular version, the plural version, the actual number, and the domain text for your plugin. The _n() function uses the number parameter ($count in the example) to determine whether the singular or plural string should be returned.

WordPress also features a translation function you can use to add comments to your translatable strings. This is helpful if you have a string set up for translation that might have multiple meanings. To do this, you use the _x() function, as shown in the following code:

```php
<?php
echo _x( 'Editor', 'user role', 'prowp-plugin' );
echo _x( 'Editor', 'rich-text editor', 'prowp-plugin' );
?>
```

As you can see, there are three parameters for this function. The first is the text string to translate. The second, and most important, is the context information for the translators. This allows you to add custom comment messages that the translator can read to explain the context of your text to be translated. The final parameter is the text domain.

Now that you've prepared your plugin for translation, you must load the localization file to do the translation. To do so, you execute the load_plugin_textdomain() function as shown here:

```php
<?php
add_action( 'init', 'prowp_init' );
function prowp_init() {
    load_plugin_textdomain( 'prowp-plugin', false,
    plugin_basename( dirname( __FILE__ ) .'/localization' ) );
}
?>
```

The first parameter you pass is the domain text name that you've used to identify all of your translatable strings. The second parameter is the path relative to the ABSPATH variable; however, this parameter is now deprecated in favor of the third parameter. The final parameter is the path to your translation files from the /plugins directory. To store these files, you should create a folder inside your plugin directory called /localization. You use the plugin_basename() and dirname() functions to retrieve the path to your localization folder.

You can learn more about the process of creating translation files in the WordPress Codex at http://codex.wordpress.org/I18n_for_WordPress_Developers.

Determining Paths

When creating WordPress plugins, you will often need to reference files and folders throughout the WordPress installation and your plugins. Installing a fresh copy of WordPress, you have the ability to move this directory anywhere you want. Because of this, you should never use hard-coded paths in a plugin. WordPress has a set of functions to determine the path to the wp-content and plugins directories, as well as directories within your plugins. You can use these functions in your plugins to verify that any paths you are referencing are correct regardless of where the actual directory might exist on the server.

Local Paths

To determine the local server path to your plugin, you'll use the plugin_dir_path() function. This function extracts the physical location relative to the plugins directory from its file name.

```php
<?php echo plugin_dir_path( __FILE__ ); ?>
```

You can see that you pass the __FILE__ PHP constant to the plugin_dir_path() function. This returns the full local server path to your plugin directory:

```
/public_html/wp-content/plugins/halloween-plugin/
```

Now let's assume you need to reference the local path to a file in a subdirectory in your plugin. You can use the plugin_dir_path() function along with the subdirectory and files you want to reference, as shown here:

```php
<?php echo plugin_dir_path( __FILE__ ) .'js/script.js'; ?>
```

The preceding example would produce the following result:

```
/public_html/wp-content/plugins/halloween-plugin/js/script.js
```

URL Paths

To determine the full URL to any file in your plugin directory, you'll use the plugins_url() function as shown here:

```php
<?php echo '<img src="' .plugins_url( 'images/icon.png', __FILE__ ). '">'; ?>
```

You can see the plugins_url() function accepts two parameters. The first parameter is the path relative to the plugins URL. The second parameter is the plugin file that you want to be relative to. In this case, you'll use the __FILE__ PHP constant. The preceding example will return a full URL to your plugin's icon.png file located in the images directory, as shown here:

```html
<img src="http://example.com/wp-content/plugins/halloween-plugin/images/icon.png">
```

The following is a list of the many advantages of using the plugins_url() function to determine plugin file URLs:

➤ Supports the /mu-plugins plugin directory.

➤ Auto-detects SSL. If SSL is enabled, the returned URL would contain https://.

➤ Can detect the location of the plugin even if the user has moved his /wp-content directory to a custom location.

➤ Supports Multisite.

WordPress also features various functions to determine URLs in WordPress. The following is a list of the functions available:

➤ admin_url()—Admin URL (http://example.com/wp-admin/)

➤ site_url()—Site URL for the current site (http://example.com)

➤ home_url()—Home URL for the current site (http://example.com)

➤ includes_url()—Includes directory URL (http://example.com/wp-includes/)

➤ content_url()—Content directory URL (http://example.com/wp-content/)

➤ wp_upload_dir()—Returns an array with location information on the configured uploads directory

Understanding the proper way to access files in your plugins is essential to ensure maximum compatibility with all WordPress installations, regardless of how customized they are.

PLUGIN SECURITY

One of the most important steps in creating a plugin is making sure it is secure from hacks and exploits. If a plugin contains security holes, it opens up the entire WordPress website for malicious hackers to wreak havoc. WordPress features some built-in security tools that you should always utilize to make sure your plugins and themes are as secure as can be.

Remember that all data external to your plugin code is suspect until proven valid. Always validate your data before displaying to the browser or inserting into the database to help keep your plugins secure from hacks and exploits. You'll be using the mentioned escape and sanitize functions discussed in this section throughout the chapter.

> **NOTE** *Even though this chapter is specific to plugin development, the development security tools described in this section should be used for all WordPress development, including themes.*

Nonces

Nonces, which stands for "number used once," are used in requests (saving options, form posts, Ajax requests, actions, and so on) to stop unauthorized access by generating a secret key. This secret key is generated prior to generating a request (that is, form post). The key is then passed in the request to your script and verified to be the same key before anything else is processed. Now let's look at how you can manually create and check nonces. The following example uses a nonce in a form:

```
<form method="post">
    <?php wp_nonce_field( 'prowp_settings_form_save', 'prowp_nonce_field' ); ?>
    Enter your name: <input type="text" name="text" /><br />
    <input type="submit" name="submit" value="Save Options" />
</form>
```

When creating a form nonce, the function wp_nonce_field() must be called inside of your <form> tags. There are actually no required parameters for this function to work, but for increased security there are two parameters you should set. The first parameter is $action, which should be a unique string that is descriptive of the action being performed. The second parameter is a unique name for the field, $name. By default, the field name will be _wpnonce, but you can define a custom unique name in this parameter. When the wp_nonce_field() function is called, it will generate a unique secret key that will be added as a hidden form field and passed with your form data. Viewing the source of the form would look something like this:

```
<form method="post">
    <input type="hidden" id="prowp_nonce_field"
        name="prowp_nonce_field" value="1cfd4c0539" />
    <input type="hidden" name="_wp_http_referer"
        value="/wp-trunk/contact/" />
    Enter your name: <input type="text" name="text" /><br />
    <input type="submit" name="submit" value="Save Options" />
</form>
```

After your form is posted, the first thing you need to do is check your nonce secret key using the wp_verify_nonce() function like so:

```
if ( isset( $_POST['submit'] ) ) {
    //check nonce for security
            wp_verify_nonce( 'prowp_settings_form_save', 'prowp_nonce_field' );
            //nonce passed, now do stuff
}
```

Verifying that the nonce is valid is as simple as calling the wp_verify_nonce() function and passing it your unique nonce action and name that you defined earlier. If the nonce secret key does not match the secret key created on your form, WordPress will stop processing the page and issue an error message. This primarily protects it from cross-site request forgery, or CSRF.

Nonces can also be used on links that perform actions. To create a URL nonce, you use the wp_nonce_url() function. This can be used in conjunction with multiple query strings in your URL like so:

```
<?php
$link = 'my-url.php?action=delete&ID=15';
?>
<a href="<?php echo wp_nonce_url( $link, 'prowp_delete_action',
    'prowp_nonce_url_check' ); ?>">Delete</a>
```

The wp_nonce_url() function accepts three parameters: the URL to add the nonce to, the action being performed, and the unique nonce name you are creating. The preceding code would generate a link that looks like this:

```
http://example.com/wp-admin/my-url.php?
    action=delete&ID=15& prowp_nonce_url_check=e9d6673015
```

Notice how the prowp_nonce_url_check query string is appended to the link. This is the secret key value that was generated for your URL nonce. If your URL has no query strings, the wp_nonce_url() function will add the nonce value as the only query string being passed. If your URL contains query strings, that nonce value will be added to the end of the URL. You can verify that the nonce is correct just as you did with your form—by using the wp_verify_nonce() function:

```
if ( isset( $_GET['action'] ) ) {
    //check nonce for security
    wp_verify_nonce( 'prowp_delete_action', 'prowp_nonce_url_check' );
    //do stuff
}
```

This function verifies that your action query string is set before checking your nonce value. Once the nonce has been validated, the script will continue. Remember that if the nonce is not validated, the page execution will stop, preventing any type of hack attempt.

Data Validation and Sanitization

Any data that comes from somewhere external to your code (such as user input) needs to be scrubbed to verify that it's free from illegal characters and potentially unsafe data. Data validation is essential to proper plugin security. Improperly validated data can lead to SQL injection hacks, exploits, errors, and much more.

WordPress features a set of escaping functions that you can use to verify that your data is escaped properly when being displayed to the screen. These escaping functions follow a set naming standard (see the following list), which makes it easy to identify what they are escaping. Figure 8-2 shows the escaping function naming template.

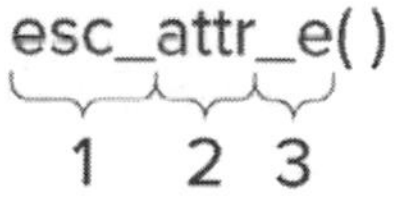

esc_attr_e( )

1 2 3

FIGURE 8-2: Escaping API breakdown

➤ esc_: The prefix for the escaping functions.

➤ attr: The escaping context (attr, html, textarea, js, sql, url, and url_raw).

➤ _e: The optional translation suffix. Available suffixes are __ and _e.

The esc_html() function is used for escaping data that contains HTML. This function encodes special characters into the equivalent HTML entities. These characters include &, <, >, ", and ' as follows:

```
<?php esc_html( $text ); ?>
```

The esc_attr() function is used for escaping HTML attributes. This function should be used whenever you need to display data inside an HTML element:

```
<input type="text" name="first_name" value="<?php echo esc_attr( $text ); ?>">
```

The esc_textrea() function is used for escaping HTML <textarea> values. This function should be used to encode text for use in a <textarea> form element as follows:

```
<textarea name="description"><?php echo esc_textarea( $text ); ?></textarea>
```

WordPress also features a function for validating URLs called esc_url(). This function should be used to scrub the URL for illegal characters. Even though the href is technically an HTML attribute, you should use the esc_url() function like so:

```
<a href="<?php echo esc_url( $url ); ?>">
```

The esc_js() function escapes text strings in JavaScript:

```
<script>
    var bwar='<?php echo esc_js( $text ); ?>';
</script>
```

The esc_sql() function escapes data for use in a MySQL query. This function is really just a shortcut for $wpdb->escape() as follows:

```
<?php esc_sql( $sql ); ?>
```

The optional translation suffix (__ or _e) is used for translating the escaped data. The _e suffix will echo the escaped translated text, whereas __ only returns the escaped translated value.

```
<?php
//escapes, translates, and displays the text
esc_html_e( $text, 'prowp-plugin' );
//escapes, translates, but does NOT display
$text = esc_html__( $text, 'prowp-plugin' );
?>
```

If the data you are validating is supposed to be an integer, use the intval() PHP function to verify that. The intval() function will return the integer value of a variable. If the variable is a string, and therefore not an integer, it will return 0.

```
$variable = 12345;
$variable = intval( $variable );
```

Another useful function for working with integers is the absint() WordPress function. This function ensures that the result is a non-negative integer:

```
$variable = 12345;
$variable = absint( $variable );
```

WordPress also features some very useful sanitizing functions. These functions should be used to sanitize any data prior to saving it in the database. One of those functions is sanitize_text_field(). This function will remove all invalid UTF-8 characters, convert single < into HTML entities, and remove all HTML tags, line breaks, and extra white space.

```
<?php sanitize_text_field( $text ); ?>
```

The `sanitize_text_field()` function is the perfect function to use when verifying that user-submitted data is safe, especially when storing in the database.

You can also sanitize an e-mail address using `sanitize_email()`. This function will strip out all characters that are not allowable in an e-mail address. Consider the following code:

```php
<?php
$sanitized_email = sanitize_email( '        éric@loremipsum.com!' );
echo $sanitized_email; //will output: ric@loremipsum.com
?>
```

You can see that the `sanitize_email()` function removes the extra spaces and illegal characters from the e-mail address submitted.

A very powerful function for processing and sanitizing untrusted HTML is `wp_kses()`. This function is used in WordPress to verify that only allowed HTML tags and attributes can be submitted by users. By defining allowed HTML tags, you can avoid cross-site scripting (XSS) attacks through your code. Consider the following example:

```php
$allowed_tags = array(
    'strong'    =>    array(),
    'a'         =>    array(
        'href'       =>    array(),
        'title'      =>    array()
    )
);
$html = '<a href="#" class="external">link</a>.
    This is <b>bold</b> and <strong>strong</strong>';
echo wp_kses( $html, $allowed_tags );
```

The first step is to define an array of all HTML tags and attributes. In this example, you are allowing the <strong> and <a> tags. The <a> tag is allowed to include the `href` and `title` attributes. Next, you build an `$html` variable to test out the function. The final step is to pass the `$html` string and `$allowed_tags` arguments to the `wp_kses()` function.

The preceding example would display the following code:

```
<a href="#">link</a>.  This is bold and <strong>strong</strong>
```

Notice the <b></b> tags have been completely removed. The function also removed the `class` attribute from the <a> tag because you didn't specify that as an allowed attribute. This basic example really shows the power of this function. Any time you need to allow users to input HTML code, you should always use the `wp_kses()` function to verify that only acceptable HTML tags and attributes are allowed.

For more information on data validation in WordPress, check out the following Codex article: `http://codex.wordpress.org/Data_Validation`.

> **NOTE** *Throughout this chapter, you'll be using various data validation techniques in the code examples. The goal of this is to stress the importance of keeping security in the front of your mind when developing plugins for WordPress.*

KNOW YOUR HOOKS: ACTIONS AND FILTERS

One of the most important features for extending WordPress is called a *hook*. Hooks are simply a standardized way of "hooking" into WordPress. Using hooks, you can execute functions at specific times in the WordPress process, allowing you to alter how WordPress functions and the expected output. Hooks are the primary way plugins interact with your content in WordPress. Up to this point, you've focused on the structure and format of plugins, but now you're actually going to make a plugin do something!

A hook is simply a PHP function call with various parameters that can be sent. Following is an example showing a properly formatted Action hook call:

```php
<?php add_action( $tag, $function_to_add, $priority, $accepted_args ); ?>
```

Actions and Filters

Two types of hooks can be used: actions and filters. Action hooks are triggered by events in WordPress. For example, an Action hook is triggered when a new post is published. Filter hooks are used to modify WordPress content before saving it to the database or displaying it to the screen. For example, a Filter hook is available for the content of the post or page. This means you can alter that content after it is retrieved from the database but before it is displayed in your browser.

Look at an example of a Filter hook in action. Remember that Filter hooks modify content, so this example modifies the post content:

```php
<?php add_filter( 'the_content', 'prowp_function' ); ?>
```

The `add_filter()` function is used to execute a Filter action. You are using the filter called `the_content`, which is the filter for your post content. This tells WordPress that every time the content is displayed, it needs to pass through your custom function called `prowp_function()`. The `add_filter()` function can accept four parameters:

➤ `filter_action (string)`—The filter to use.

➤ `custom_filter_function (string)`—The custom function to pass the filter through.

➤ `priority (integer)`—The priority in which this filter should run. When multiple callback functions are attached to the same hook, the `priority` parameter determines the execution order.

➤ `accepted_args (integer)`—The number of arguments the function accepts.

Here's an example of `the_content` filter in action:

```php
<?php
add_filter( 'the_content', 'prowp_profanity_filter' );

function prowp_profanity_filter( $content ) {

    $profanities = array( 'sissy', 'dummy' );
```

```
    $content = str_ireplace( $profanities, '[censored]', $content );
    return $content;

}
?>
```

The `prowp_profanity_filter()` function will replace the words "sissy" and "dummy" with [censored] automatically on all posts and pages on your website. You are using the `str_ireplace()` PHP function to handle the replacement. This function will replace some characters in a string with other characters in a string. The `str_ireplace()` function is also case-insensitive. Because you are using a Filter hook, the content isn't actually modified in the database; instead, it's modified during processing of the `_post()`, before being displayed, when this filter is invoked. The content in the database is not affected so the words "sissy" and "dummy" will still exist in your content, and if you ever disable or change the plugin, those words will appear in the displayed text. Filter hooks always receive data; in this case, the `$content` variable is passed to your function and contains your post content. Also notice the last line of your function returns the `$content` variable. Remember that you must always return the content you are modifying or else it returns empty and therefore displays nothing.

Now that you've seen the Filter hook in action, take a look at the Action hook and what it can do. The Action hook is triggered by events in WordPress. WordPress doesn't require any return values from your Action hook function; the WordPress Core just notifies your code that a specific event has taken place. The Action hook is structured exactly like a Filter hook, as you can see in the following code:

```
<?php add_action( 'hook_name', 'prowp_function' ); ?>
```

The `add_action()` function accepts four parameters just like the `add_filter()` function. Here you can set the hook name you want to hook into, the custom function name you are going to execute when the event is triggered, and the priority and the number of accepted args. Here's a real example using an Action hook:

```
<?php
add_action( 'comment_post', 'prowp_email_new_comment' );

function prowp_email_new_comment() {

    wp_mail( 'me@example.com', 'New blog comment',
    'There is a new comment on your website: http://example.com' );

}
?>
```

Notice that you are using the `comment_post` Action hook. This action is triggered whenever a new comment is posted in WordPress. As you can see, the `prowp_email_new_comment()` function will send an e-mail any time a new comment is created. Also notice that you are not sending in any variables to your function or returning any values out of your function. Action hooks don't require this, but if needed, you can pass values into your function.

Popular Filter Hooks

More than 2,000 different hooks are available in WordPress, which is a bit overwhelming at first. Fortunately, a handful of them are used much more often than the rest. This section explores some of the more commonly used hooks in WordPress.

Some of the more common Filter hooks are:

➤ `the_content`—Applied to the content of the post, page, or custom post type before displaying

➤ `the_content_rss`—Applied to the content of the post, page, or custom post type for RSS inclusion

➤ `the_title`—Applied to the post, page, or custom post type title before displaying

➤ `comment_text`—Applied to the comment text before displaying

➤ `wp_title`—Applied to the page `<title>` header tag before displaying

➤ `the_permalink`—Applied to the permalink URL

Let's look at some of the more popular Filter hooks in WordPress, starting with a more practical example than your profanity filter, which uses the `_content` Filter hook. This hook allows you to alter the content for posts, pages, and custom post types prior to it being displayed in the browser. By using this hook, you can add your custom content either before, in the middle, or after the content:

```php
<?php
add_filter ( 'the_content', 'prowp_subscriber_footer' );

function prowp_subscriber_footer( $content ) {

    if( is_single() ) {
        $content.= '<h3>Enjoyed this article?</h3>';
        $content.= '<p>Subscribe to my
            <a href="http://example.com/feed">RSS feed</a>!</p>';
    }

    return $content;

}
?>
```

In this example, you are adding your subscribe text to the bottom of the content of your posts. Notice that you are also using the `is_single()` conditional tag to verify that your subscribe text is added only on a single post page. If you did not use this conditional tag, the subscribe text would show up below all content on your website, including pages and custom post types. The `$content` variable stores all of the post content, so by appending your subscribe text you are adding it to the bottom of your post content. This is the ideal way to add content to the bottom of all posts because you aren't actually modifying the post. In the future, if you decide to change this message you can change it in one place, rather than updating every post in your website.

Another powerful Filter hook is `the _ title`. This hook is used for changing the post or page title prior to being displayed. Here's an example that uses this filter:

```php
<?php
add_filter( 'the_title', 'prowp_custom_title' );

function prowp_custom_title( $title ) {

    $title .= ' - By Example.com';
    return $title;

}
?>
```

This example adds "By Example.com" to all of your post and page titles. Remember that this doesn't actually modify the title in the database but instead modifies the display of the title generated for the end user.

The `default _ content` Filter hook is useful for setting the default content when creating a new post or page. This is helpful if you have a set format for all of your posts as it can save you valuable writing time:

```php
<?php
add_filter( 'default_content', 'prowp_default_content' );

function prowp_default_content( $content ) {

    $content = 'For more great content please subscribe to my RSS feed';
    return $content;

}
?>
```

Filter hooks are exceptionally powerful for inserting your own processing into a variety of points in the Loop processing of each post. Realizing the full power of the WordPress plugin system means also using action hooks to fire your own code in response to events within the WordPress core.

Popular Action Hooks

Some of the more common Action hooks are:

- ➤ `publish_post`—Triggered when a new post is published.

- ➤ `create_category`—Triggered when a new category is created.

- ➤ `switch_theme`—Triggered when you switch themes.

- ➤ `admin_head`—Triggered in the `<head>` section of the admin dashboard.

- ➤ `wp_head`—Triggered in the `<head>` section of your theme.

- ➤ `wp_footer`—Triggered in the footer section of your theme usually directly before the `</body>` tag.

➤ init—Triggered after WordPress has finished loading, but before any headers are sent. Good place to intercept $_GET and $_POST HTML requests.

➤ admin_init—Same as init but only runs on admin dashboard pages.

➤ user_register—Triggered when a new user is created.

➤ comment_post—Triggered when a new comment is created.

One of the most commonly used Action hooks is the wp_head hook. Using the wp_head hook, you can insert any custom code into the <head> section of the WordPress theme. Consider the following example:

```php
<?php
add_action( 'wp_head', 'prowp_custom_css' );

function prowp_custom_css() {
 ?>
    <style type="text/css">
    a {
        font-size: 14px;
        color: #000000;
        text-decoration: none;
    }
    a:hover {
        font-size: 14px
        color: #FF0000;
        text-decoration: underline;
    }
    </style>
<?php
}
?>
```

This code will drop anything inside your prowp_custom_css() function into the header of the WordPress theme, in this case your custom CSS script.

The wp_footer hook is also a very commonly used Action hook. Using this hook you can insert any custom code in the footer of the WordPress theme. This is a great method for adding analytic tracking code to your website:

```php
<?php
add_action( 'wp_footer', 'prowp_site_analytics' );

function prowp_site_analytics()  {
?>
    <script type="text/javascript">
    var gaJsHost = (("https:" == document.location.protocol) ?
      "https://ssl." : "http://www.");
    document.write(unescape("%3Cscript src='" + gaJsHost +
      'google-analytics.com/ga.js' type='text/javascript'%3E%3C/script%3E"));
    </script>
    <script type="text/javascript">
    var pageTracker = _gat._getTracker("UA-XXXXXX-XX");
```

```
        pageTracker._trackPageview();
        </script>
<?php
}
?>
```

In the preceding example, you can see how you can easily insert your Google Analytics tracking code to the footer of every page on your website.

The `admin_head` Action hook is very similar to the `wp_head` hook, but rather than hooking into the theme header, it hooks into the admin dashboard header. This is useful if your plugin requires custom CSS on the admin dashboard, or any other custom header code.

The `user_register` Action hook is executed when a new user is created in WordPress. This user can be created by an admin or by the new user. This is a useful hook if you want to set some default values for a new user or to e-mail your new members thanking them for joining your website.

Hooks are probably one of the most under-documented features in WordPress. It can be a real challenge finding the correct hooks to use for the job. The first resource to use is always the Codex. Here you can find the Filter Reference (`http://codex.wordpress.org/Plugin_API/ Filter_Reference`) and Action Reference (`http://codex.wordpress.org/Plugin_API/Action_ Reference`) sections helpful in tracking down appropriate hooks.

Another highly recommended reference is the Plugin Directory (`https://wordpress.org/ plugins/`) on WordPress.org. Sometimes the best way to figure something out is to see how other developers accomplished a similar task. Find a plugin in the directory that is similar in functionality to what you want to build. Most likely, the plugin author will have already dug up the correct hooks for WordPress that you will be using. It never hurts to learn by example, and published plugins are the perfect examples in this case!

PLUGIN SETTINGS

Most plugins feature a settings page. This helps users configure the plugin to act in different ways without actually modifying the code behind the plugin by saving various option settings. The first step in this process is saving and retrieving options in WordPress.

Saving Plugin Options

Chances are that, when building a plugin, you will need to save some options for your plugin. WordPress features some very easy-to-use functions to save, update, and delete options. Two functions are available for creating options: `add_option()` and `update_option()`. Both functions create options, but `update_option()` also updates the option if it already exists. Here's an example of adding a new option:

```
<?php add_option( 'prowp_display_mode', 'Spooky' ); ?>
```

The first parameter you send to the `add_option()` function is the name of your option. This is a required field and must be unique from all other options saved in WordPress, including from other plugins. The second parameter is the option value. This is also a required field and can be a string, an array, an object, or a serialized value. You can also use `update_option()` to create new options. This function checks whether the option exists first, and if not creates it. If, however, the option already exists, it updates the value with the new option value you are sending in. You call the `update_option()` function exactly as you did when adding an option like so:

```php
<?php update_option( 'prowp_display_mode', 'Scary' ); ?>
```

Generally, the `update_option()` function is used for both adding and updating options in plugins. It's much easier to stay consistent with one function call for both rather than calls to different functions for adding and updating your plugin options.

Retrieving an option value is just as easy. To retrieve any option, use the `get_option()` function, as shown here:

```php
<?php echo get_option( 'prowp_display_mode' ); ?>
```

The only required field for `get_option()` is the name of the option you want to retrieve. If the option exists, it is returned to display or it is stored in a variable. If the option doesn't exist, the function returns FALSE.

Options can be deleted as easily as they are created. To delete an option, use the `delete_option()` function. The only parameter is the option name that you want to delete:

```php
<?php delete_option( 'prowp_display_mode' ); ?>
```

A good rule of thumb is to start all of your option names with the same prefix, like `prowp_` in the preceding examples. This is useful for a couple of reasons: uniqueness and readability. Using a prefix will help validate the uniqueness of your option names. If you have a number of options, it is a smart idea to store them in an array (see the next section). This also makes it much easier to follow your code logic when there is a set naming convention used on variables, functions, and so on.

Options in WordPress are not reserved for just plugins. Themes can also create options to store specific theme data. Many of the themes available today offer a settings page, enabling you to customize the theme through settings rather than code.

Array of Options

Every option you create in WordPress adds a new record to the `wp_options` database table. Because of this, it's a smart idea to store your options in an array, thus creating fewer records in the database and fewer `update_option()` calls you need to make.

```php
<?php
$prowp_options_arr = array(
    'prowp_display_mode'    => 'Spooky',
    'prowp_default_movie'   => 'Halloween',
    'prowp_default_book'    => 'Professional WordPress'
    );

update_option( 'prowp_plugin_options', $prowp_options_arr );
?>
```

In this code, you are creating an array to store your plugin option values. So rather than call `update_option()` three times, and save three records in the database, you need to call it only once and save your array to the option named `prowp_plugin_options`. This is a small example but imagine a collection of plugins that store 50 options to the database's `options` table. That would really start to clutter up your options table and would most likely slow down your website load speeds due to the repeated database queries to fetch or set those options individually.

To retrieve the array of options, you use the same `get_option()` function as before:

```php
<?php
$prowp_options_arr   = get_option( 'prowp_plugin_options' );
$prowp_display_mode  = $prowp_options_arr['prowp_display_mode'];
$prowp_default_movie = $prowp_options_arr['prowp_default_movie'];
$prowp_default_book  = $prowp_options_arr['prowp_default_book'];
?>
```

The next section discusses how to create a menu for your plugin settings page.

Creating a Menu and Submenus

WordPress features two different ways to create a custom menu for your plugin. The first thing you'll want to decide is where to locate your options page. The options page link can be located in its own top-level menu (My Plugin Settings), or as a submenu item of an existing menu (Settings ➤ My Plugin Settings). This section explores both methods and how to configure each.

Creating a Top-Level Menu

The first method you'll explore is creating a new top-level menu. Using a top-level menu is useful if your plugin has multiple settings pages that need to be separate. To create your own top-level menu, you'll use the `add_menu_page()` function, as shown here:

```php
<?php add_menu_page( page_title, menu_title, capability,
menu_slug, function, icon_url, position ); ?>
```

Here's a breakdown of the parameters allowed:

➤ `page_title`—Text used for the HTML title (between `<title>` tags).

➤ `menu_title`—Text used for the menu name in the Dashboard.

➤ `capability`—Minimum user capability required to see menu.

➤ `menu_slug`—Unique slug name for your menu.

➤ `function`—Displays page content for the menu settings page.

➤ `icon_url`—Path to custom icon for menu (default: `images/generic.png`).

➤ `position`—The position in the menu order the menu should appear. By default, the menu will appear at the bottom of the menu structure.

You can also create submenu items for your new menu. You use the `add_submenu_page()` function to create additional submenu items:

```php
add_submenu_page( parent, page_title, menu_title, capability,
menu_slug, [function] );
```

Create a custom menu for a plugin with multiple submenu items, as shown in Figure 8-3.

```php
<?php
// create custom plugin settings menu
add_action( 'admin_menu', 'prowp_create_menu' );

function prowp_create_menu() {

    //create new top-level menu
    add_menu_page( 'Halloween Plugin Page', 'Halloween Plugin',
        'manage_options', 'prowp_main_menu', 'prowp_main_plugin_page',
        plugins_url( '/images/wordpress.png', __FILE__ ) );

    //create two sub-menus: settings and support
    add_submenu_page( 'prowp_main_menu', 'Halloween Settings Page',
        'Settings', 'manage_options', 'halloween_settings',
'prowp_settings_page' );
    add_submenu_page( 'prowp_main_menu', 'Halloween Support Page',
        'Support', 'manage_options', 'halloween_support', 'prowp_support_page' );

}
?>
```

First you call the `admin_menu` Action hook. This hook is triggered after the basic admin panel menu structure is in place and is the only hook you should use when registering a custom menu. Once triggered, you call your custom function `prowp_create_menu()` to build your menu.

To create your menu, you call the `add_menu_page()` function. The first two parameters set your page title and menu title. You also set the capability level to `manage_options` so only an admin will see this new menu. Next, you set the menu slug to `propwp_main_menu`, which is the unique slug for your menu. Your custom menu function name is next, in this case `prowp_main_plugin_page`.

FIGURE 8-3: Custom top-level menu

Remember that you haven't created this function yet so when viewing the settings page, you will get a PHP warning. Finally, you set the custom icon location to display the WordPress logo.

Notice your top-level menu sits just below the Settings menu. That's because you didn't set the `$position` parameter when registering your custom menu. To define where you menu is located, simply set the integrator position. The following is a list of the integer positions for each core WordPress menu:

➤ Dashboard—2

➤ Posts—5

➤ Media—10

➤ Pages—20

➤ Comments—25

➤ Appearance—60

➤ Plugins—65

➤ Users—70

➤ Tools—75

➤ Settings—80

For example, if you wanted your menu to appear between the Dashboard and Posts menus, set your `$position` parameter to 3.

Now that you've created your top-level menu, you need to create your submenu items. In this example, you are creating two submenu items: Settings and Support. To do this, you use the `add _ submenu _ page()` function.

The first parameter you send is the menu slug of the top-level menu you want this to fall under. Remember that you set this to `prowp _ main _ menu`, which is a unique slug for your plugin menu. Next, you set the page title and menu title just like before. You also set the access level for viewing to `manage _ options`. You also have to create a unique menu slug for your submenu items; in this example, you'll use a custom named value, `halloween _ settings` and `halloween _ support`. The final value is the custom function to build the settings page for each submenu.

Adding to an Existing Menu

Next, you'll explore how to add a submenu item to an existing menu in WordPress. Most plugins have only one options page and therefore do not require an entirely separate top level menu. To accomplish this, you can add a plugin option page to any existing menu in WordPress. Add a submenu to the Setting menu:

```php
<?php
add_action( 'admin_menu', 'prowp_create_settings_submenu' );

function prowp_create_settings_submenu() {

    add_options_page( 'Halloween Settings Page', 'Halloween Settings',
    'manage_options', 'halloween_settings_menu', 'prowp_settings_page' );

}
?>
```

WordPress features multiple functions to make adding submenus extremely easy. To add your Halloween Settings submenu you use the `add _ options _ page()` function. The first parameter is the page title followed by the submenu display name. Like your other menus, you set the capability to `manage _ options`, so the menu is viewable only by administrators. Next, you set the unique menu handle to `halloween _ settings _ menu`. Finally, you call your custom `prowp _ settings _ page()` function to build your options page. The preceding example adds your custom submenu item Halloween Settings at the bottom of the settings menu.

Following is a list of the available submenu functions in WordPress. Each function can be used exactly as the preceding example; just swap out the function name called with one of the functions listed here:

➤ `add_dashboard_page()`—Adds submenu items to the Dashboard menu

➤ `add_posts_page()`—Adds submenu items to the Posts menu

➤ `add_media_page()`—Adds a submenu item to the Media menu

➤ `add_pages_page()`—Adds a submenu item to the Pages menu

➤ `add_comments_page()`—Adds a submenu item to the Comments menu

➤ `add_plugins_page()`—Adds a submenu item to the Plugins menu

➤ `add_theme_page()`—Adds a submenu item to the Appearance menu

➤ `add_users_page()`—Adds a submenu item to the Users page (or Profile based on role)

➤ `add_management_page()`—Adds a submenu item to the Tools menu

➤ `add_options_page()`—Adds a submenu item to the Settings menu

Now that you've created your menu and submenu items, you need to create an options page to display your plugin configuration.

Creating an Options Page

WordPress includes a Settings API that you will be using for all of the option methods you use in this section. The Settings API is a powerful set of functions to help make saving options in WordPress easy and secure. One of the major benefits of the Settings API is that WordPress handles the security checks, meaning you don't need to include a nonce in your form.

The first option page method you'll explore is to create a unique option page for your top-level menu. Remember that when using the `add_menu_page()` and `add_submenu_page()` functions, you defined your menu item function name to display your options page. To create an options page, you need to create this function to display your options. First set up your plugin menu:

```php
<?php
// create custom plugin settings menu
add_action( 'admin_menu', 'prowp_create_menu' );

function prowp_create_menu() {

    //create new top-level menu
    add_menu_page( 'Halloween Plugin Page', 'Halloween Plugin',
        'manage_options', 'prowp_main_menu', 'prowp_settings_page' );

    //call register settings function
    add_action( 'admin_init', 'prowp_register_settings' );

}
?>
```

Notice that you've added a new Action hook for `admin _ init` to execute your `prowp _ register _ settings()` function, as shown in the following code:

```php
<?php

function prowp_register_settings() {

    //register our settings
    register_setting( 'prowp-settings-group', 'prowp_options',
        'prowp_sanitize_options' );

}
?>
```

Using the Setting API's `register _ setting()` function, you define the option you are going to offer on your plugin options page. Your settings page will have three options, but you are going to store those three options in a single options array, so you only need to register a single setting here. The first parameter is the options group name. This required field needs to be a group name to identify all options in this set. The second parameter is the actual option name and must be unique. The third parameter is a callback function to sanitize the option values. Now that you've registered your options, you need to build your options page. To do so, you'll create the `prowp _ settings _ page()` function as called from your menu:

```php
<?php
function prowp_settings_page() {
?>
    <div class="wrap">
    <h2>Halloween Plugin Options</h2>

    <form method="post" action="options.php">
        <?php settings_fields( 'prowp-settings-group' ); ?>
        <?php $prowp_options = get_option( 'prowp_options' ); ?>
        <table class="form-table">
            <tr valign="top">
            <th scope="row">Name</th>
            <td><input type="text" name="prowp_options[option_name]"
                value="<?php echo esc_attr( $prowp_options['option_name']
); ?>" /></td>
            </tr>

            <tr valign="top">
            <th scope="row">Email</th>
            <td><input type="text" name="prowp_options[option_email]"
                value="<?php echo esc_attr( $prowp_options['option_email']
); ?>" /></td>
            </tr>

            <tr valign="top">
            <th scope="row">URL</th>
            <td><input type="text" name="prowp_options[option_url]"
                value="<?php echo esc_url( $prowp_options['option_url'] );
?>" /></td>
            </tr>
```

```
    </table>

            <p class="submit">
                <input type="submit" class="button-primary" value="Save Changes" />
            </p>

        </form>
        </div>
<?php
}
?>
```

As you can see, this looks like a standard form with a couple of noticeable differences. The `<form>` tag must be set to post to `options.php`. Inside your form, you need to define your settings group, which you set to `prowp-settings-group` when you registered your settings. This establishes the link between your options and their values. You do so with this line of code:

```
<?php settings_fields( 'prowp-settings-group' ); ?>
```

Next, you'll load the existing options array, if there are any, to the `$prowp _ options` variable using the `get _ option()` function. You'll use this variable to display the existing options that are set in your form.

Then you build the table to display your form options. Notice the name of the form field needs to be in the format of `option _ name[field _ name]`. This is because you are storing all option values in a single array.

```
<input type="text" name="prowp_options[option_email]"
    value="<?php echo esc_attr( $prowp_options['option_email'] ); ?>" />
```

After you have displayed all of your form fields, you need to display a Submit button to post the form and save your options. The final step is to create the `prowp _ sanitize _ options()` function. This function will be used to sanitize all data submitted in your plugin settings prior to saving in the database. This is an extremely important step because unsanitized data could potentially open up a security vulnerability in your plugin.

```
<?php
function prowp_sanitize_options( $input ) {

    $input['option_name']  = sanitize_text_field( $input['option_name'] );
    $input['option_email'] = sanitize_email( $input['option_email'] );
    $input['option_url']   = esc_url( $input['option_url'] );

    return $input;

}
?>
```

Notice how each option value is being sanitized with a specific function. The name option uses the WordPress function `sanitize _ text _ field()` to strip any HTML, XML, and PHP tags from the submitted value. You use the `sanitize _ email()` WordPress function to sanitize the e-mail value and `esc _ url()` to sanitize the URL value.

That's it! You have just created a very basic plugin options page using the Settings API in WordPress. Listing 8-1 shows the entire code to build an options page.

LISTING 8-1: Building the Options Page (filename: `prowp3-settings-api-plugin.zip`)

```php
<?php
/*
Plugin Name: ProWP3 Settings Example
Plugin URI: http://strangework.com/wordpress-plugins
Description: This is a plugin demonstrating the WordPress Settings API
Version: 1.0
Author: Brad Williams
Author URI: http://strangework.com
License: GPLv2
*/

// create custom plugin settings menu
add_action( 'admin_menu', 'prowp_create_menu' );

function prowp_create_menu() {

    //create new top-level menu
    add_menu_page( 'Halloween Plugin Page', 'Halloween Plugin',
        'manage_options', 'prowp_main_menu',
        'prowp_settings_page' );

    //call register settings function
    add_action( 'admin_init', 'prowp_register_settings' );

}

function prowp_register_settings() {

    //register our settings
    register_setting( 'prowp-settings-group',
        'prowp_options', 'prowp_sanitize_options' );

}

function prowp_sanitize_options( $input ) {

    $input['option_name']  =
        sanitize_text_field( $input['option_name'] );
    $input['option_email'] =
        sanitize_email( $input['option_email'] );
    $input['option_url']   =
        esc_url( $input['option_url'] );

    return $input;

}

function prowp_settings_page() {
```

continues

LISTING 8-1: *(continued)*

```
?>
    <div class="wrap">
    <h2>Halloween Plugin Options</h2>

    <form method="post" action="options.php">
        <?php settings_fields( 'prowp-settings-group' ); ?>
        <?php $prowp_options = get_option( 'prowp_options' ); ?>
        <table class="form-table">
            <tr valign="top">
            <th scope="row">Name</th>
            <td><input type="text"
                name="prowp_options[option_name]"
                value="<?php echo esc_attr(
                    $prowp_options['option_name'] ); ?>" /></td>
            </tr>

            <tr valign="top">
            <th scope="row">Email</th>
            <td><input type="text"
                name="prowp_options[option_email]"
                value="<?php echo esc_attr(
                    $prowp_options['option_email'] ); ?>" /></td>
            </tr>

            <tr valign="top">
            <th scope="row">URL</th>
            <td><input type="text"
                name="prowp_options[option_url]"
                value="<?php echo esc_url(
                    $prowp_options['option_url'] ); ?>" /></td>
            </tr>

        </table>

        <p class="submit">
            <input type="submit" class="button-primary"
                value="Save Changes" />
        </p>

    </form>
    </div>
<?php
}
```

The second option page method is to add your plugin settings to an existing Settings page in WordPress, as shown in Figure 8-4. You will also be using the WordPress Settings API functions to hook into these pages and add your plugin settings.

Now look over at the code to create your custom settings section. In the following example, you are going to add a new settings section at the bottom of the Settings ➢ Reading Settings page. This section will contain options for your plugin.

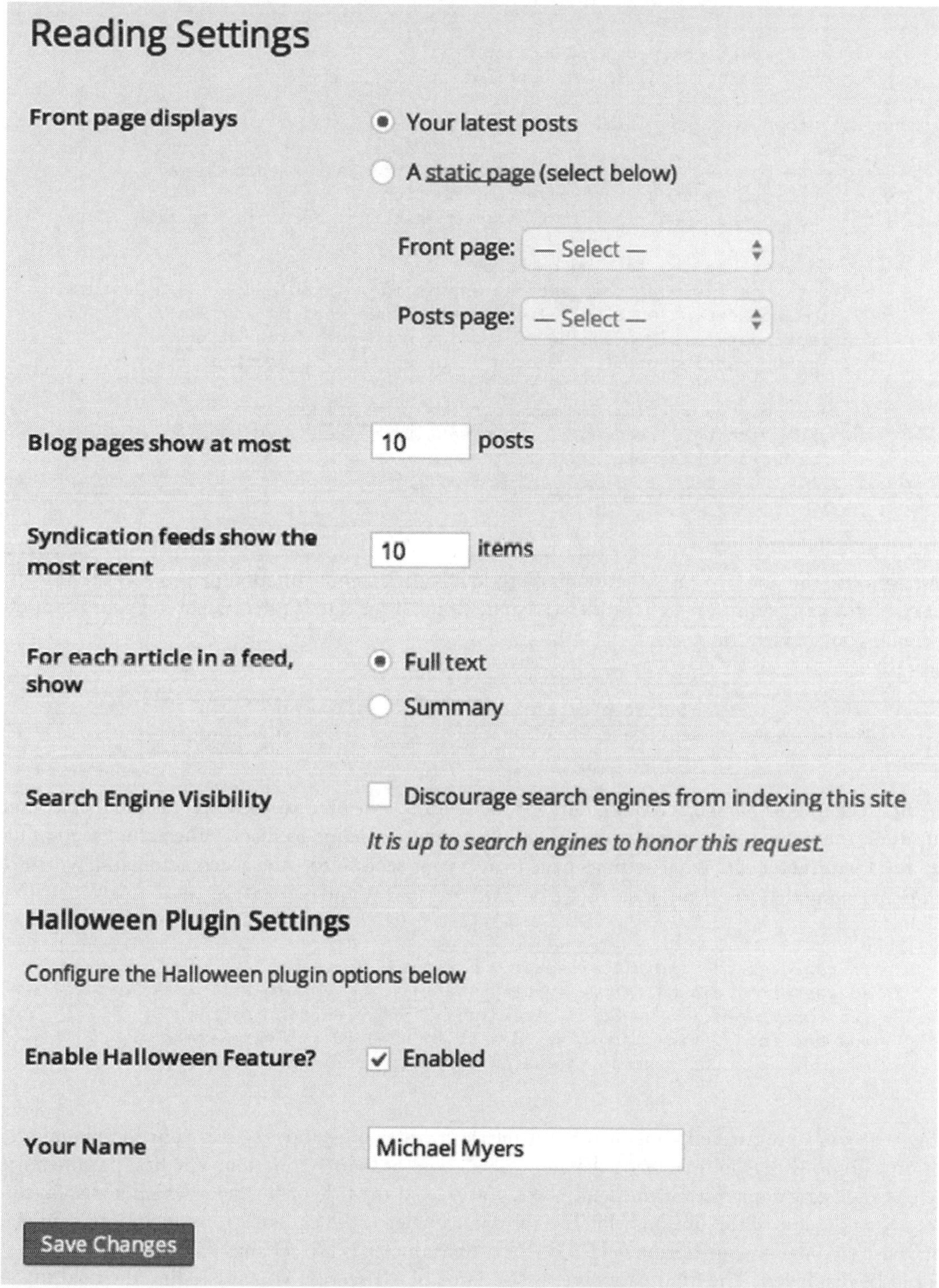

Reading Settings

Front page displays

- ● Your latest posts
- ○ A <u>static page</u> (select below)

  Front page: — Select — ▲▼

  Posts page: — Select — ▲▼

Blog pages show at most `10` posts

Syndication feeds show the most recent `10` items

For each article in a feed, show

- ● Full text
- ○ Summary

Search Engine Visibility ☐ Discourage search engines from indexing this site

It is up to search engines to honor this request.

Halloween Plugin Settings

Configure the Halloween plugin options below

Enable Halloween Feature? ☑ Enabled

Your Name `Michael Myers`

`Save Changes`

FIGURE 8-4: Custom settings section

```php
<?php
//execute our settings section function
add_action( 'admin_init', 'prowp_settings_init' );

function prowp_settings_init() {

    //create the new setting section on the Settings > Reading page
    add_settings_section( 'prowp_setting_section',
        'Halloween Plugin Settings', 'prowp_setting_section', 'reading' );

    // register the two setting options
    add_settings_field( 'prowp_setting_enable_id', 'Enable Halloween Feature?',
        'prowp_setting_enabled', 'reading', 'prowp_setting_section' );
    add_settings_field( 'prowp_saved_setting_name_id', 'Your Name',
        'prowp_setting_name', 'reading', 'prowp_setting_section' );

    // register the setting to store our array of values
    register_setting( 'reading', 'prowp_setting_values',
        'prowp_sanitize_settings' );

}
?>
```

First, you use the `admin_init` Action hook to load your custom function `prowp_settings_init()` before any admin page is rendered. Next, you call the `add_settings_section()` function to create your new section:

```php
<?php
add_settings_section( 'prowp_setting_section', 'Halloween Plugin Settings',
    'prowp_setting_section', 'reading' );
?>
```

The first parameter passed is a unique ID for the section. The second parameter is the display name output on the page. Next, you pass in the callback function name to display the actual section itself. The final parameter sets what settings page to add your section to. The accepted default WordPress values are `general`, `writing`, `reading`, `discussion`, `media`, and `permalink`.

```php
<?php
    // register the individual setting options
    add_settings_field( 'prowp_setting_enable_id', 'Enable Halloween Feature?',
        'prowp_setting_enabled', 'reading', 'prowp_setting_section' );
    add_settings_field( 'prowp_saved_setting_name_id', 'Your Name',
        'prowp_setting_name', 'reading', 'prowp_setting_section' );
?>
```

Now that you've registered your custom settings section, you need to register your individual setting options. To do this, you'll be using the `add_settings_field()` function. The first parameter you are passing is a unique ID for the field. Next, you pass in the title of the field, which is displayed directly to the left of the option field. The third parameter is the callback function name, which you'll use to display your option field. The fourth parameter is the settings page where the field should be displayed. The final parameter is the name of the section you are adding the field to, which in this example is the prowp _ setting _ section you created with the add _ setting _ section() function call.

```php
<?php
register_setting( 'reading', 'prowp_setting_values', 'prowp_sanitize_settings' );
?>
```

Next, you need to register your setting field. In this example, you are going to register two different settings: one for an enable/disable check box and one for the user's name. Even though you have two setting fields, you are going to store both values in an array, so you only need to register one setting called prowp _ setting _ values. The first parameter you pass is the option group. In this example, you are saving your options in the reading group with the rest of the reading options. The second parameter is the option name. The option name should be unique and is used to retrieve the value of the option. A third optional parameter can be set for a custom function used to sanitize the option values. In this example, you'll create a function called prowp _ sanitize _ settings() to sanitize the option values entered by the user.

```php
<?php
function prowp_sanitize_settings( $input ) {

    $input['enabled'] = ( $input['enabled'] == 'on' ) ? 'on' : '';
    $input['name'] = sanitize_text_field( $input['name'] );
    return $input;

}
?>
```

As always, you'll want to sanitize all option values that are entered by the user. The enabled option is a check box, and therefore can only be one of two values: either checked or not. The preceding example uses a PHP ternary operator to determine the value of Enabled. If the check box equals "on," you know the value is enabled and should save the option value as "on." If not, the option will save the value as empty, which means the check box is not checked. Now that you've registered your setting section, you need to create your custom functions to display it. The first function you'll create is the prowp _ setting _ section() that you called in when you created your setting section:

```php
<?php
function prowp_setting_section() {
    echo '<p>Configure the Halloween plugin options below</p>';
}
?>
```

This is where you can set the subheading for your settings section. This section is great for plugin instructions, configuration information, and more. Next, you need to create the function to display your first settings field, Enabled:

```php
<?php
function prowp_setting_enabled() {

    //load plugin options
    $prowp_options = get_option( 'prowp_setting_values' );
```

```
        //display the checkbox form field
        echo '<input '.checked( $prowp_options['enabled'], 'on', false ).'
            name="prowp_setting_values[enabled]" type="checkbox" /> Enabled';

    }
    ?>
```

This is the callback function you defined when you used the add_settings_field() function. The first step is to load the options array if it exists. Because this option is a check box, you know that if it is set, the check box should be checked. In this example, you'll use the checked() WordPress function. This function has three parameters. The first and second parameters are two values to compare. If the two values are the same, the function will echo checked="checked" thus checking the form element. The third parameter determines whether to echo the value or just return it. In this case, you just want to return it so you set that value to False.

Next, you display the actual setting field that will be used in the setting section. Your field input name needs to be the same setting name you registered previously. Because you are saving your options as an array, you need to define the array name value; in this example, it's prowp_setting_values[enabled]. This is how the Settings API knows what option to save and where. Your Enabled check box field will display at the bottom of the Settings ➤ Reading page. Now you need to create the function for your second setting field:

```
<?php
function prowp_setting_name() {

    //load the option value
    $prowp_options = get_option( 'prowp_setting_values' );

    //display the text form field
    echo '<input type="text" name="prowp_setting_values[name]"
        value="'.esc_attr( $prowp_options['name'] ).'" />';

}
?>
```

As with your check box option, the first thing to do is load the current option value. Then you display your input text field with the same name as defined previously in the register_setting() function. As always, be sure to escape the value before displaying in the form field.

That's it! You have successfully created your custom settings section and added it to the Settings ➤ Reading screen. Listing 8-2 shows the full code.

LISTING 8-2: Custom Settings Section (filename: prowp3-reading-settings-plugin.zip)

```
<?php
//execute our settings section function
add_action( 'admin_init', 'prowp_settings_init' );

function prowp_settings_init() {

    //create the new setting section on the Settings > Reading page
```

```
        add_settings_section(
            'prowp_setting_section',
            'Halloween Plugin Settings',
            'prowp_setting_section',
            'reading'
        );

        // register the two setting options
        add_settings_field(
            'prowp_setting_enable_id',
            'Enable Halloween Feature?',
            'prowp_setting_enabled',
            'reading',
            'prowp_setting_section'
        );
        add_settings_field(
            'prowp_saved_setting_name_id',
            'Your Name',
            'prowp_setting_name',
            'reading',
            'prowp_setting_section'
        );

        // register the setting to store our array of values
        register_setting(
            'reading',
            'prowp_setting_values',
            'prowp_sanitize_settings'
        );

}

function prowp_sanitize_settings( $input ) {

    $input['enabled'] = ( $input['enabled'] == 'on' ) ? 'on' : '';
    $input['name'] = sanitize_text_field( $input['name'] );

    return $input;

}

// settings section
function prowp_setting_section() {
    echo '<p>Configure the Halloween plugin options below</p>';
}

// create the enabled checkbox option to
// save the checkbox value
function prowp_setting_enabled() {

    //load plugin options
    $prowp_options = get_option( 'prowp_setting_values' );

    //display the checkbox form field
```

continues

LISTING 8-2: *(continued)*

```php
        echo '<input '.checked( $prowp_options['enabled'], 'on',
            false ).' name="prowp_setting_values[enabled]"
            type="checkbox" /> Enabled';

}

// create the text field setting to save the name
function prowp_setting_name() {

    //load the option value
    $prowp_options = get_option( 'prowp_setting_values' );

    //display the text form field
    echo '<input type="text" name="prowp_setting_values[name]"
        value="'.esc_attr( $prowp_options['name'] ).'" />';

}
```

WORDPRESS INTEGRATION

Integrating your plugin into WordPress is an essential step for users to interact with your plugin in the admin dashboard. WordPress features many different areas where your plugin can be integrated, including a meta box, sidebar and dashboard widgets, and custom shortcodes.

Creating a Meta Box

WordPress features multiple meta boxes on the Add New Post and Page screens. These meta boxes are used for adding additional information to your posts, pages, and content. For example, when creating a new post, you will see a Category meta box, which allows you to select what categories your post will be in.

Meta boxes can be created in a plugin using the add_meta_box() function in WordPress. This function accepts seven parameters, as shown here:

```php
<?php add_meta_box( $id, $title, $callback, $page,
    $context, $priority, $callback_args ); ?>
```

Each parameter helps define where and how your meta box is displayed.

➤ $id—The HTML ID attribute for the meta box

➤ $title—The title displayed in the header of the meta box

➤ $callback—The custom function name to display your meta box information

➤ $page—The page you want your meta box to display on ('post', 'page', or custom post type name)

➤ $context—The part of the page where the meta box should be displayed ('normal', 'advanced', or 'side')

➤ `$priority`—The priority within the context where the meta box should display (`'high'`, `'core'`, `'default'`, or `'low'`)

➤ `$callback_args`—Arguments to pass into your callback function

Now that you understand the add _ meta _ box() function, you can build your first custom meta box in WordPress:

```php
<?php
add_action( 'add_meta_boxes', 'prowp_meta_box_init' );

// meta box functions for adding the meta box and saving the data
function prowp_meta_box_init() {

    // create our custom meta box
    add_meta_box( 'prowp-meta', 'Product Information',
        'prowp_meta_box', 'post', 'side', 'default' );

}
?>
```

The first step to adding your own meta box is to use the add _ meta _ boxes Action hook to execute your custom function prowp _ meta _ box _ init(). In this function, you will call the add _ meta _ box() function to create your custom meta box for Product Information.

You set the HTML ID attribute to prowp-meta for your meta box. The second parameter is the title, which you set to Product Information. The next parameter is your custom function prowp _ meta _ box(), which will display the HTML for your meta box. Next you define your meta box to display on the post page and in the sidebar. Finally, you set the priority to default. Now create your custom prowp _ meta _ box() function to display your meta box fields:

```php
<?php
function prowp_meta_box( $post, $box ) {

    // retrieve the custom meta box values
    $prowp_featured = get_post_meta( $post->ID, '_prowp_type', true );
    $prowp_price = get_post_meta( $post->ID, '_prowp_price', true );

    //nonce for security
    wp_nonce_field( plugin_basename( __FILE__ ), 'prowp_save_meta_box' );

    // custom meta box form elements
    echo '<p>Price: <input type="text" name="prowp_price"
        value="'.esc_attr( $prowp_price ).'" size="5" /></p>';
    echo '<p>Type:
        <select name="prowp_product_type" id="prowp_product_type">
            <option value="normal" '
                .selected( $prowp_featured, 'normal', false ). '>Normal
            </option>
            <option value="special" '
                .selected( $prowp_featured, 'special', false ). '>Special
            </option>
            <option value="featured" '
                .selected( $prowp_featured, 'featured', false ). '>Featured
```

```
            </option>
            <option value="clearance" '
                .selected( $prowp_featured, 'clearance', false ). '>Clearance
            </option>
        </select></p>';

    }
    ?>
```

The first step in your custom function is to retrieve the saved values for your meta box. If you are creating a new post, there won't be any saved values yet. Next you display the form elements in your meta box. Notice that you don't need any <form> tags or a submit button. Also notice that you are using the wp _ nonce _ field() function to create a custom nonce field in your form.

The custom function you just created will generate your custom meta box, as shown in Figure 8-5.

Now that you have your meta box and form elements, you need to save that data when your post is saved. To do so, you'll create a custom function, prowp _ save _ meta _ box(), which is triggered by the save _ post Action hook:

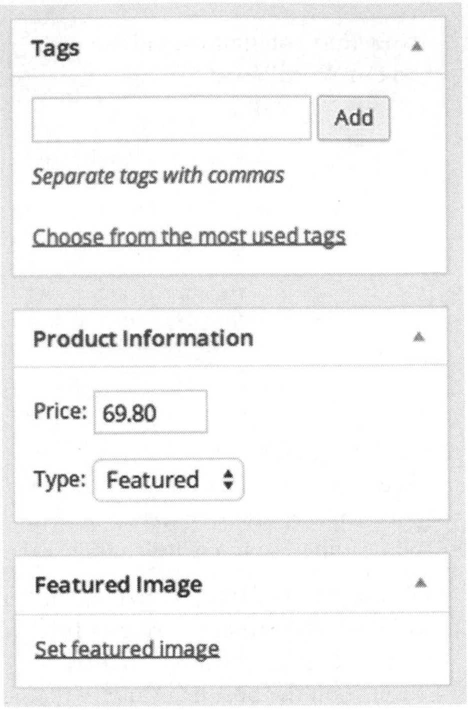

Tags

Separate tags with commas

Choose from the most used tags

Product Information

Price: 69.80

Type: Featured ⇕

Featured Image

Set featured image

FIGURE 8-5: Custom meta box

```php
<?php
// hook to save our meta box data when the post is saved
add_action( 'save_post', 'prowp_save_meta_box' );

function prowp_save_meta_box( $post_id ) {

    // process form data if $_POST is set
    if( isset( $_POST['prowp_product_type'] ) ) {

        // if auto saving skip saving our meta box data
        if ( defined( 'DOING_AUTOSAVE' ) && DOING_AUTOSAVE )
            return;

        //check nonce for security
        wp_verify_nonce( plugin_basename( __FILE__ ), 'prowp_save_meta_box' );

        // save the meta box data as post meta using the post ID as a unique prefix
        update_post_meta( $post_id, '_prowp_type',
            sanitize_text_field( $_POST['prowp_product_type'] ) );
        update_post_meta( $post_id, '_prowp_price',
            sanitize_text_field( $_POST['prowp_price'] ) );

    }
```

```
}
?>
```

The `save _ post` Action hook runs whenever a post is saved in WordPress. Because you only want to work with the custom metadata in the meta box, the first thing you'll do is verify that the `$ _ POST['prowp _ product _ type']` value is set. Next, you need to verify that the post being saved is an active post and not an auto save. To do so, you check that the post is not auto-saving and, if so, you exit the function. The next step is to verify that the nonce value is the expected value. If the post is active and your form elements have been set, you save the form data. Once all checks have passed, you use `update _ post _ meta()` to save your meta box data as metadata against your post.

As you can see, you send in the post ID as the first parameter to `update _ post _ meta()`. This tells WordPress what post the meta data will be attached to. Next, you pass in the name of the meta key you are updating. Notice the meta key name is prefixed with an underscore. This prevents these values from being listed in the custom fields meta box on the post edit screen. Because you've provided a UI to edit these values, you don't need them in the custom fields box. The final parameter you send is the new value for the meta key, which is being sanitized using the `sanitize _ text _ field()` WordPress function.

You now have a fully functional custom meta box that saves individual data against each post. Listing 8-3 shows the full custom meta box code.

> **LISTING 8-3: Custom Meta Box (filename: prowp3-custom-meta-box.zip)**

```php
<?php
/*
Plugin Name: ProWP3 Custom Meta Box Plugin
Plugin URI: http://strangework.com/wordpress-plugins
Description: This is a plugin demonstrating meta boxes in WordPress
Version: 1.0
Author: Brad Williams
Author URI: http://strangework.com
License: GPLv2
*/

add_action( 'add_meta_boxes', 'prowp_meta_box_init' );

// meta box functions for adding the meta box and saving the data
function prowp_meta_box_init() {

    // create our custom meta box
    add_meta_box( 'prowp-meta', 'Product Information',
        'prowp_meta_box', 'post', 'side', 'default' );

}

function prowp_meta_box( $post, $box ) {

    // retrieve the custom meta box values
```

continues

LISTING 8-3: *(continued)*

```php
    $prowp_featured = get_post_meta( $post->ID, '_prowp_type',
        true );
    $prowp_price = get_post_meta( $post->ID, '_prowp_price',
        true );

    //nonce for security
    wp_nonce_field( plugin_basename( __FILE__ ),
        'prowp_save_meta_box' );

    // custom meta box form elements
    echo '<p>Price: <input type="text" name="prowp_price"
        value="'.esc_attr( $prowp_price ).'" size="5" /></p>';
    echo '<p>Type:
        <select name="prowp_product_type" id="prowp_product_type">
            <option value="normal" '
                .selected( $prowp_featured, 'normal', false )
                . '>Normal</option>
            <option value="special" '
                .selected( $prowp_featured, 'special', false )
                . '>Special</option>
            <option value="featured" '
                .selected( $prowp_featured, 'featured', false )
                . '>Featured</option>
            <option value="clearance" '
                .selected( $prowp_featured, 'clearance', false )
                . '>Clearance</option>
        </select></p>';

}

// hook to save our meta box data when the post is saved
add_action( 'save_post', 'prowp_save_meta_box' );

function prowp_save_meta_box( $post_id ) {

    // process form data if $_POST is set
    if( isset( $_POST['prowp_product_type'] ) ) {

        // if auto saving skip saving our meta box data
        if ( defined( 'DOING_AUTOSAVE' ) && DOING_AUTOSAVE )
            return;

        //check nonce for security
        wp_verify_nonce( plugin_basename( __FILE__ ),
            'prowp_save_meta_box' );

        // save the meta box data as post meta using the post ID as a unique prefix
        update_post_meta( $post_id, '_prowp_type',
            sanitize_text_field( $_POST['prowp_product_type'] ) );
        update_post_meta( $post_id, '_prowp_price',
            sanitize_text_field( $_POST['prowp_price'] ) );

    }

}
```

Now that you've saved your meta box data, you'll probably want to display it somewhere. You can easily display your saved meta box data in your theme using the get _ post _ meta function inside the Loop like so:

```php
<?php
    $prowp_type = get_post_meta( $post->ID, '_prowp_type', true );
    $prowp_price = get_post_meta( $post->ID, '_prowp_price', true );
    echo '<p>Price: ' .esc_html( $prowp_price ). '</p>';
    echo '<p>Type: ' .esc_html( $prowp_type ). '</p>';
?>
```

Adding a custom meta box is a great way to extend the data on posts and pages and is very intuitive for users as well.

Shortcodes

WordPress features a Shortcode API that can be used to easily create shortcode functionality in your plugins. Shortcodes are basically text macro codes that can be inserted into a post, page, or custom post type. When being displayed, these shortcodes are replaced by some other type of content. Consider a simple example using the Shortcode API:

```php
<?php
add_shortcode( 'mytwitter', 'prowp_twitter' );

function prowp_twitter() {
    return '<a href="http://twitter.com/williamsba">@williamsba</a>';
}
?>
```

Now any time you use the [mytwitter] shortcode in your content, it will be replaced with an HTML link to my Twitter account when displayed in the browser. As you can see, this is a very powerful feature in WordPress, which many plugins out there currently take advantage of, often inserting small pieces of JavaScript to place a button or advertisement in the specific spot in a post.

Shortcodes can also be configured to accept attributes. This is very useful for passing arguments to your custom functions, thereby altering the output of the shortcode based on those arguments. Modify your shortcode function to accept a site parameter:

```php
<?php
add_shortcode( 'mytwitter', 'prowp_twitter' );

function prowp_twitter( $atts, $content = null ) {
    extract( shortcode_atts( array(
        'person' => 'brad' // set attribute default
    ), $atts ) );

    if ( $person == 'brad' ) {
        return '<a href="http://twitter.com/williamsba">@williamsba</a>';
    }elseif ( $person == 'david' ) {
        return '<a href="http://twitter.com/mirmillo">@mirmillo</a>';
```

```
        }elseif ( $person == 'lisa' ) {
            return '<a href="http://twitter.com/lisasabinwilson">@lisasabinwilson</a>';
        }
    }
    ?>
```

This code creates the same shortcode as before, but now you are defining an attribute called person. With this attribute, you can specify which person you want to display a Twitter link for. To display the Twitter URL for David, you would use the shortcode [mytwitter person="david"]. Alternatively, you can also easily display the Twitter URL for Lisa like so: [mytwitter person="lisa"]. Shortcodes can also accept multiple attributes from the array set in your shortcode function.

Creating a Widget

Widgets are a common feature included in many WordPress plugins. By creating a widget with your plugin, you can easily give users a way to add your plugin information to their sidebar or other widgetized areas.

To understand how widgets work, it's helpful to view an overview of the WP _ Widget class in WordPress. The widget class features built-in functions for building a widget, each with a specific purpose, as shown in the following code:

```
<?php
class My_Widget extends WP_Widget {
    function My_Widget() {
        // process the widget
    }
    function form($instance) {
        // widget form in admin dashboard
    }
    function update($new_instance, $old_instance) {
        // save widget options
    }
    function widget($args, $instance) {
        // display the widget
    }
}
?>
```

For the purposes of this lesson, you'll create a basic bio widget. This widget will allow you to set a person's name and custom bio to display in a widgetized sidebar in WordPress.

The first step in creating your own widget is to use the appropriate hook to initialize your widget. This hook is called widgets _ init and is triggered right after the default WordPress widgets have been registered:

```
add_action( 'widgets_init', 'prowp_register_widgets' );
function prowp_register_widgets() {
    register_widget( 'prowp_widget' );
}
```

Calling the Action hook `widgets_init` executes the function `prowp_register_widgets()`, as shown in the preceding code. Here you register your widget called `pro_widget`. You could also register multiple widgets in this function if needed.

The Widget API makes creating a widget in WordPress fairly straightforward. To begin, you have to extend the preexisting `WP_Widget` class by creating a new class with a unique name, as shown here:

```php
class prowp_widget extends WP_Widget {
```

Next, you'll add your first function. This is referred to as the *constructor:*

```php
function __construct() {

    $widget_ops = array(
        'classname'   => 'prowp_widget_class',
        'description' => 'Example widget that displays a user\'s bio.' );
    parent::__construct( 'prowp_widget', 'Bio Widget', $widget_ops );

}
```

In your `prowp_widget()` function, you define your classname for your widget. The classname is the class name that will be added to the HTML tag wrapping the widget when it's displayed. Depending on the theme the class may be in a `<div>`, `<aside>`, `<li>`, or other HTML tag. You also set the description for your widget. This is displayed on the widget dashboard below the widget name. These options are then passed to `WP_Widget`. You also pass the HTML ID name (`prowp_widget_class`) and the widget name (Bio Widget).

Next, you need to create the function to build your widget settings form. Widget settings are located on the widget admin page upon expanding any widget listed on a sidebar. The widget class makes this process very easy, as shown in the following code:

```php
function form( $instance ) {
    $defaults = array(
        'title' => 'My Bio',
        'name'  => 'Michael Myers',
        'bio'   => '' );
    $instance = wp_parse_args( (array) $instance, $defaults );
    $title = $instance['title'];
    $name = $instance['name'];
    $bio = $instance['bio'];
    ?>
        <p>Title:
            <input class="widefat"
                name="<?php echo $this->get_field_name( 'title' ); ?>"
                type="text" value="<?php echo esc_attr( $title ); ?>" /></p>
        <p>Name:
            <input class="widefat"
                name="<?php echo $this->get_field_name( 'name' ); ?>"
                type="text" value="<?php echo esc_attr( $name ); ?>" /></p>
        <p>Bio:
            <textarea class="widefat"
                name="<?php echo $this->get_field_name( 'bio' ); ?>" >
                <?php echo esc_textarea( $bio ); ?></textarea></p>
    <?php
}
```

The first thing you do is define your default widget values. If the user doesn't fill in the settings, you can default these values to whatever you like. In this case, you're setting the default title to My Bio and default name to Michael Myers. Next, you pull in the instance values, which are your widget settings. If the widget was just added to a sidebar, there are no settings saved so these values will be empty. Finally, you display the three form fields for your widget settings: title, name, and bio. The first two values are using text input boxes and the bio value is using a text area box. Notice that you don't need <form> tags or a submit button; the widget class will handle this for you. Remember to use the appropriate escaping functions when displaying your data, in this case esc _ attr() for the two text fields and esc _ textarea() for the text area field. Next, you need to save your widget settings using the update() widget class function:

```
function update( $new_instance, $old_instance ) {

    $instance = $old_instance;
    $instance['title'] = sanitize_text_field( $new_instance['title'] );
    $instance['name']  = sanitize_text_field( $new_instance['name'] );
    $instance['bio']   = sanitize_text_field( $new_instance['bio'] );

    return $instance;

}
```

This function is pretty straightforward. You'll notice you don't need to save the settings yourself, the widget class does it for you. You pass in the $new _ instance values for each of your setting fields. You're also using sanitize _ text _ field() to strip out any HTML that might be entered. If you want to accept HTML values, you'd use wp _ kses() instead, which was covered in the section "Data Validation and Sanitization," earlier in this chapter.

The final function in your prowp _ widget class displays your widget:

```
function widget( $args, $instance ) {
    extract( $args );
    echo $before_widget;
    $title = apply_filters( 'widget_title', $instance['title'] );
    $name = ( empty( $instance['name'] ) ) ? ' ' : $instance['name'];
    $bio = ( empty( $instance['bio'] ) ) ? ' ' : $instance['bio'];
    if ( !empty( $title ) ) { echo $before_title . esc_html( $title )
        . $after_title; };
    echo '<p>Name: ' . esc_html( $name ) . '</p>';
    echo '<p>Bio: ' . esc_html( $bio ) . '</p>';
    echo $after_widget;
}
```

The first thing you do is extract the $args parameter. This variable stores some global theme values such as $before _ widget and $after _ widget. These variables can be used by theme developers to customize what code will wrap your widget—for example, a custom <div> tag. After extracting the $args parameter, you display the $before _ widget variable. The $before _ title and $after _ title are also set in this variable. This is useful for passing custom HTML tags to wrap the widget title in.

Next, you display your widget values. The title is displayed first and wrapped by $before _ title and $after _ title. Next, you echo out the name and bio values. Remember to escape the widget values for security reasons. Finally, you display the $after _ widget value.

That's it! You've just created a custom widget for your plugin using the widget class in WordPress. Remember that by using the new widget class, you can add multiple copies of the same widget to the sidebar or additional sidebars. Listing 8-4 shows the completed widget code.

LISTING 8-4: Custom Widget (filename: `prowp3-custom-widget.zip`)

```php
<?php
/*
Plugin Name: ProWP3 Custom Widget Plugin
Plugin URI: http://strangework.com/wordpress-plugins
Description: This is a plugin demonstrating how to create a widget
Version: 1.0
Author: Brad Williams
Author URI: http://strangework.com
License: GPLv2
*/

// use widgets_init Action hook to execute custom function
add_action( 'widgets_init', 'prowp_register_widgets' );

 //register our widget
function prowp_register_widgets() {

    register_widget( 'prowp_widget' );

}

//prowpwidget class
class prowp_widget extends WP_Widget {

    //process our new widget
    function __construct() {

        $widget_ops = array(
            'classname'   => 'prowp_widget_class',
            'description' => 'Example widget that displays
                a user\'s bio.' );
        parent::__construct( 'prowp_widget', 'Bio Widget',
            $widget_ops );

    }

     //build our widget settings form
    function form( $instance ) {
        $defaults = array(
            'title' => 'My Bio',
            'name'  => 'Michael Myers',
            'bio'   => '' );
        $instance = wp_parse_args( (array) $instance, $defaults );
        $title = $instance['title'];
        $name = $instance['name'];
        $bio = $instance['bio'];
        ?>
```

continues

LISTING 8-4: *(continued)*

```php
            <p>Title:
                <input class="widefat" name="<?php
                    echo $this->get_field_name( 'title' ); ?>"
                    type="text" value="<?php
                    echo esc_attr( $title ); ?>" /></p>
            <p>Name:
                <input class="widefat" name="<?php
                    echo $this->get_field_name( 'name' ); ?>"
                    type="text" value="<?php
                    echo esc_attr( $name ); ?>" /></p>
            <p>Bio:
                <textarea class="widefat" name="<?php
                    echo $this->get_field_name( 'bio' ); ?>">
                    <?php echo esc_textarea( $bio ); ?>
                </textarea></p>
        <?php
    }

    //save our widget settings
    function update( $new_instance, $old_instance ) {

        $instance = $old_instance;
        $instance['title'] =
            sanitize_text_field( $new_instance['title'] );
        $instance['name']  =
            sanitize_text_field( $new_instance['name'] );
        $instance['bio']   =
            sanitize_text_fiel( $new_instance['bio'] );

        return $instance;

    }

    //display our widget
    function widget( $args, $instance ) {
        extract( $args );

        echo $before_widget;

        $title = apply_filters( 'widget_title', $instance['title'] );
        $name = ( empty( $instance['name'] ) )
            ? ' ' : $instance['name'];
        $bio = ( empty( $instance['bio'] ) )
            ? 'nbsp;' : $instance['bio'];

        if ( !empty( $title ) ) { echo $before_title
            . esc_html( $title ) . $after_title; };
        echo '<p>Name: ' . esc_html( $name ) . '</p>';
        echo '<p>Bio: ' . esc_html( $bio ) . '</p>';

        echo $after_widget;

    }
}
```

Creating a Dashboard Widget

Dashboard Widgets are the widgets displayed on the main Dashboard of your WordPress installation. Along with these widgets comes the Dashboard Widgets API, which allows you to create any custom Dashboard Widget that you would like.

To create a custom Dashboard Widget, you'll use the wp_add_dashboard_widget() function, as shown here:

```php
<?php
add_action( 'wp_dashboard_setup', 'prowp_add_dashboard_widget' );

// call function to create our dashboard widget
function prowp_add_dashboard_widget() {

    wp_add_dashboard_widget(
        'prowp_dashboard_widget',
        'Pro WP Dashboard Widget',
        'prowp_create_dashboard_widget'
    );

}

// function to display our dashboard widget content
function prowp_create_dashboard_widget() {

    echo '<p>Hello World! This is my Dashboard Widget</p>';

}
?>
```

First you call the wp_dashboard_setup Action hook to execute the function to build your custom Dashboard Widget. This hook is triggered after all of the default Dashboard Widgets have been built. Next you execute the wp_add_dashboard_widget() function to create your Dashboard Widget. The first parameter is the widget ID slug. This is used for the class name and the key in the array of widgets. The next parameter is the display name for your Dashboard Widget. The final parameter you send is your custom function name to display your widget contents. An optional fourth parameter can be sent for a control callback function. This function would be used to process any form elements that might exist in your Dashboard Widget.

After executing the wp_add_dashboard_widget() function, your custom function is called to display your widget contents. In this example, you display a simple string. The result is a custom Dashboard Widget, as shown in Figure 8-6.

Creating Custom Tables

WordPress contains a variety of tables in which to store your plugin data. However, you might find that your plugin needs a custom table or two to store plugin data. This can be useful for more complex plugins such as an e-commerce plugin, which stores order history, product and inventory data, and other data that is accessed using database SQL semantics rather than the simple key and value pairing of the options table.

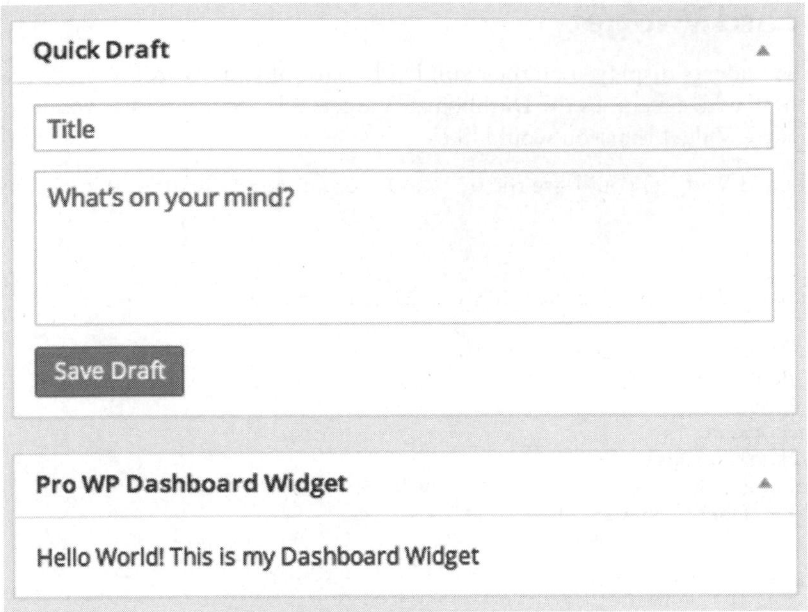

FIGURE 8-6: Example dashboard widget

The first step in creating a custom database table is to create an installation function. You will execute this function when the plugin is activated to create your new table.

```php
<?php
register_activation_hook( __FILE__, 'prowp_install' );

function prowp_install() {
}
?>
```

Now that you have an installation function, you need to define your custom table name. Remember that the table prefix can be custom defined by the user in `wp-config.php`, and as discussed in Chapter 10, WordPress Multisite can insert additional prefix data into the table names so you need to incorporate these table prefixes for your custom table name. To get the table prefix, you use the global `$wpdb->prefix` value like so:

```php
global $wpdb;
//define the custom table name
$table_name = $wpdb->prefix .'prowp_data';
```

This code stores your table named `wp _ prowp _ data` in the `$table _ name` variable, assuming your WordPress table prefix is set to `wp _ `.

Now it's time to build your SQL query for creating your new table. You'll create your query in a variable called `$sql` before executing it. You also need to include the `upgrade.php` file prior to executing your query like so:

```php
$sql = "CREATE TABLE " .$table_name ." (
    id mediumint(9) NOT NULL AUTO_INCREMENT,
```

```
        time bigint(11) DEFAULT '0' NOT NULL,
        name tinytext NOT NULL,
        text text NOT NULL,
        url VARCHAR(55) NOT NULL,
        UNIQUE KEY id (id)
    );";
    require_once( ABSPATH . 'wp-admin/includes/upgrade.php' );
    //execute the query creating our table
    dbDelta( $sql );
```

After this executes, your new table has been created in the database. The dbDelta() function will verify first that the table you are creating doesn't exist so you don't have to worry about checking if a table exists before creating it. It's also a good idea to save the version number for your database table structure. This can help down the road if you upgrade your plugin and need to change the table structure. You can check what table version the users have installed for your plugin and determine if they need to upgrade:

```
$prowp_db_version = '1.0';
add_option( 'prowp_db_version', $prowp_db_version );
```

Look at the full function in action:

```
register_activation_hook( __FILE__, 'prowp_install' );

function prowp_install() {
    global $wpdb;

    //define the custom table name
    $table_name = $wpdb->prefix .'prowp_data';

    //build the query to create our new table
    $sql = "CREATE TABLE " .$table_name ." (
            id mediumint(9) NOT NULL AUTO_INCREMENT,
            time bigint(11) DEFAULT '0' NOT NULL,
            name tinytext NOT NULL,
            text text NOT NULL,
            url VARCHAR(55) NOT NULL,
            UNIQUE KEY id (id)
        );";

    require_once( ABSPATH . 'wp-admin/includes/upgrade.php' );

    //execute the query to create our table
    dbDelta( $sql );

    //set the table structure version
    $prowp_db_version = '1.0';

    //save the table structure version number
    add_option( 'prowp_db_version', $prowp_db_version );

}
```

If you want to upgrade your table structure for a new version of your plugin, you can just compare the table structure version numbers:

```
$installed_ver = get_option( 'gmp_db_version' );
if( $installed_ver != $prowp_db_version ) {
    //update database table here
    //update table version
    update_option( 'gmp_db_version', $prowp_db_version );
}
```

Before creating a custom table for your plugin, you should consider whether this is the best method. It's generally a good idea to avoid creating custom tables unless there is no alternative. Remember that you can easily store options in WordPress using the options API. You can also utilize the wp_*meta tables for storing extended data about posts, pages, comments, and users. Custom post types are also a great place to store data.

To work with a custom table once you've created it, you'll need to use the WordPress database class, as shown in Chapter 6.

Uninstalling Your Plugin

A nice feature to include with your plugin is an uninstall feature. WordPress features two ways to register the uninstaller for your plugin: the uninstall.php method and the uninstall hook. Both methods are executed when a deactivated plugin is deleted in the WordPress admin dashboard.

The first method you'll look at is the uninstall.php uninstaller method. This is the preferred method for uninstalling a plugin. The first step to using this method is to create an uninstall .php file. This file must exist in the root directory of your plugin, and if it does, it will execute in preference to the uninstall hook.

```
<?php
// If uninstall/delete not called from WordPress then exit
if( !defined( 'ABSPATH' ) && !defined( 'WP_UNINSTALL_PLUGIN' ) )
    exit();
// Delete option from options table
delete_option( 'prowp_options_arr' );
// Delete any other options, custom tables/data, files
?>
```

The first thing your uninstall.php file should check is that ABSPATH and WP_UNINSTALL_PLUGIN constants have been defined, meaning they were actually called from WordPress. This is a security measure to ensure this file is not executed except during the uninstall process of your plugin. The next step is to remove any options and custom tables your plugin created. In a perfect uninstall scenario there would be no trace of your plugin left over in the database once it had been uninstalled. The preceding example uses delete_option() to delete the option array. Remember that once this function runs, all custom plugin data saved will be destroyed.

The second method for uninstalling a plugin is to use the Uninstall hook. When a plugin is deleted, and uninstall.php does not exist but the Uninstall hook does exist, the plugin will be run one last time to execute the Uninstall hook. After the hook has been called, your plugin will be deleted. Here's the Uninstall hook in action:

```php
<?php
register_uninstall_hook( __FILE__, 'prowp_uninstall_hook' );
function prowp_uninstall_hook() {
    delete_option( 'prowp_options_arr' );
    //remove any additional options and custom tables
}
?>
```

First you call your custom uninstall function to properly uninstall your plugin options. If you do include uninstall functionality in your plugin, such as removing custom tables and options, make sure to warn the users that all plugin data will be deleted if they delete the plugin.

The difference between this method and the `register_deactivation_hook` is that the `register_uninstall_hook` is executed when a deactivated plugin is deleted. The `register_deactivation_hook` is executed when the plugin is deactivated, which means the user may want to activate the plugin again eventually. You wouldn't want to delete all of the plugin settings if the user is planning on using your plugin again.

CREATING A PLUGIN EXAMPLE

Now that you've seen the many different options WordPress provides for use in your plugins, you can put that knowledge to work! In this example, you will utilize many of the features covered in this chapter. At the end of this section, the entire plugin source code will be available.

The example plugin you are going to build is a basic Halloween Store. The goal of this plugin is to create an easy way to add products to WordPress and display the products in your Halloween Store. This plugin will include the following features:

➤ Settings page using the Settings API

➤ Widget for displaying newest products using the `Widget` class

➤ Post meta box for adding product metadata

➤ Shortcode support to easily display product data in a post

➤ Internationalization support using translation functions

The first step in creating your plugin is to create your plugin files. For this plugin, you'll have two files: `halloween-store.php` and `uninstall.php`. Because your plugin contains two files, you'll need to save these files in a separate folder for your plugin named `halloween-store`. Next, you need to set up your plugin header and license.

To start, you'll be working in `halloween-store.php`. First you want to define your plugin header, as shown here:

```php
<?php
/*
Plugin Name: Halloween Store
```

```
Plugin URI: https://github.com/williamsba/HalloweenStore
Description: Create a Halloween Store to display product information
Version: 3.0
Author: Brad Williams
Author URI: http://webdevstudios.com
License: GPLv2
*/

/*  Copyright 2015  Brad Williams  (email : brad@webdevstudios.com)

    This program is free software; you can redistribute it and/or modify
    it under the terms of the GNU General Public License as published by
    the Free Software Foundation; either version 2 of the License, or
    (at your option) any later version.

    This program is distributed in the hope that it will be useful,
    but WITHOUT ANY WARRANTY; without even the implied warranty of
    MERCHANTABILITY or FITNESS FOR A PARTICULAR PURPOSE.  See the
    GNU General Public License for more details.

    You should have received a copy of the GNU General Public License
    along with this program; if not, write to the Free Software
    Foundation, Inc., 51 Franklin St, Fifth Floor, Boston, MA  02110-1301  USA
*/
```

As you can see, you created the appropriate plugin header for your new plugin. Because you will be releasing this plugin, you'll want to include the GPL software license below your plugin header.

Next you are going to call the `register_activation_hook()` function to set up your default plugin settings. Remember that this function is triggered when a user activates your plugin in WordPress.

```
// Call function when plugin is activated
register_activation_hook( __FILE__, 'halloween_store_install' );

function halloween_store_install() {

    //setup default option values
    $hween_options_arr = array(
        'currency_sign' => '$'
    );

    //save our default option values
    update_option( 'halloween_options', $hween_options_arr );

}
```

As you can see, this plugin will store an array of settings in a single option called `halloween_options`. When the plugin is activated, you set the default `currency_sign` value to $.

Next, you call the `init` hook to register the custom post type for Products. This is how you will add and manage your Halloween Store products.

```
// Action hook to initialize the plugin
add_action( 'init', 'halloween_store_init' );
```

```
//Initialize the Halloween Store
function halloween_store_init() {

    //register the products custom post type
    $labels = array(
        'name'                  => __( 'Products', 'halloween-plugin' ),
        'singular_name'         => __( 'Product', 'halloween-plugin' ),
        'add_new'               => __( 'Add New', 'halloween-plugin' ),
        'add_new_item'          => __( 'Add New Product', 'halloween-plugin' ),
        'edit_item'             => __( 'Edit Product', 'halloween-plugin' ),
        'new_item'              => __( 'New Product', 'halloween-plugin' ),
        'all_items'             => __( 'All Products', 'halloween-plugin' ),
        'view_item'             => __( 'View Product', 'halloween-plugin' ),
        'search_items'          => __( 'Search Products', 'halloween-plugin' ),
        'not_found'             => __( 'No products found', 'halloween-plugin' ),
        'not_found_in_trash'    => __( 'No products found in Trash',
            'halloween-plugin' ),
        'menu_name'             => __( 'Products', 'halloween-plugin' )
    );

    $args = array(
        'labels'                => $labels,
        'public'                => true,
        'publicly_queryable'    => true,
        'show_ui'               => true,
        'show_in_menu'          => true,
        'query_var'             => true,
        'rewrite'               => true,
        'capability_type'       => 'post',
        'has_archive'           => true,
        'hierarchical'          => false,
        'menu_position'         => null,
        'supports'              => array( 'title', 'editor', 'thumbnail', 'excerpt' )
    );

    register_post_type( 'halloween-products', $args );
}
```

Notice that you are wrapping each translatable term in the _ _ () translation function. This allows users to translate the terms into any language they want. You'll see these translation functions used throughout this plugin example.

Now you'll create the Halloween Store settings page. The first step is to add a Settings submenu item for your settings page using the add _ options _ page() function:

```
// Action hook to add the post products menu item
add_action( 'admin_menu', 'halloween_store_menu' );

//create the Halloween Masks sub-menu
function halloween_store_menu() {

    add_options_page( __( 'Halloween Store Settings Page',
        'halloween-plugin' ), __( 'Halloween Store Settings',
```

```
                    'halloween-plugin' ), 'manage_options', 'halloween-store-settings',
                    'halloween_store_settings_page' );

    }
```

As you can see, this function is used to create your submenu item. Your Halloween Store Settings submenu item will be located at the bottom of the Settings menu in your Dashboard. You also set this menu item to be viewable by an administrator only.

Now you need to build the actual settings page. As shown in the preceding code, the Halloween Store Settings page triggers your custom `halloween _ store _ settings _ page()` function.

```
//build the plugin settings page
function halloween_store_settings_page() {

    //load the plugin options array
    $hween_options_arr = get_option( 'halloween_options' );

    //set the option array values to variables
    $hs_inventory = ( ! empty( $hween_options_arr['show_inventory'] ) ) ?
        $hween_options_arr['show_inventory'] : '';
    $hs_currency_sign = $hween_options_arr['currency_sign'];
    ?>
    <div class="wrap">
    <h2><?php _e( 'Halloween Store Options', 'halloween-plugin' ) ?></h2>
    <form method="post" action="options.php">
        <?php settings_fields( 'halloween-settings-group' ); ?>
        <table class="form-table">
            <tr valign="top">
            <th scope="row"><?php _e( 'Show Product Inventory',
                'halloween-plugin' ) ?></th>
            <td><input type="checkbox" name="halloween_options[show_inventory]"
                <?php echo checked( $hs_inventory, 'on' ); ?> /></td>
            </tr>
            <tr valign="top">
            <th scope="row"><?php _e( 'Currency Sign', 'halloween-plugin' ) ?></th>
            <td><input type="text" name="halloween_options[currency_sign]"
                value="<?php echo esc_attr( $hs_currency_sign ); ?>"
                size="1" maxlength="1" /></td>
            </tr>
        </table>
        <p class="submit">
        <input type="submit" class="button-primary"
            value="<?php _e( 'Save Changes', 'halloween-plugin' ); ?>" />
        </p>
    </form>
    </div>
    <?php
}
```

Your Halloween Store plugin has two options: whether to show product inventory and the currency sign to use. First you load your plugin options array value. Next, set the two option values to variables. You use a PHP ternary operator to set the default value for Inventory. You also load in the current currency value into a variable for display. Next, you display your settings page form with both option form fields listed. Notice that you are using the settings _ fields() function to link your settings form to your registered setting that you will define in the code that follows. The settings _ fields() function will also include a form nonce for security. This is the proper way to save your setting options in an array using the Settings API.

When the form is submitted, WordPress will use the Settings API to sanitize the form values and save them in the database. To make this work, you need to register your settings field and sanitization functions:

```
// Action hook to register the plugin option settings
add_action( 'admin_init', 'halloween_store_register_settings' );
function halloween_store_register_settings() {
    //register the array of settings
    register_setting( 'halloween-settings-group',
        'halloween_options', 'halloween_sanitize_options' );
}
function halloween_sanitize_options( $options ) {
    $options['show_inventory'] = ( ! empty( $options['show_inventory'] ) ) ?
        sanitize_text_field( $options['show_inventory'] ) : '';
    $options['currency_sign'] = ( ! empty( $options['currency_sign'] ) ) ?
        sanitize_text_field( $options['currency_sign'] ) : '';
    return $options;
}
```

Using the register _ setting() function, you register the settings group, halloween settings-group, and the option name, halloween-options, to be used in your settings form. The halloween _ sanitize _ options() function is used to sanitize the user input for each setting prior to saving in WordPress. This is a very important security step to verify that the data being submitted is properly sanitized before being saved in the database.

Now that your plugin settings are saved, it's time to register the Meta Box for saving Product metadata:

```
//Action hook to register the Products meta box
add_action( 'add_meta_boxes', 'halloween_store_register_meta_box' );

function halloween_store_register_meta_box() {
    // create our custom meta box
    add_meta_box( 'halloween-product-meta',
        __( 'Product Information','halloween-plugin' ),
        'halloween_meta_box', 'halloween-products', 'side', 'default' );
}
```

Using the add _ meta _ boxes action hook, you'll call your custom function for registering the Products meta box. The add _ meta _ box() function is used to do the actual registering. Now that the meta box is registered, you need to build the meta box form:

```
//build product meta box
function halloween_meta_box( $post ) {

    // retrieve our custom meta box values
    $hs_meta = get_post_meta( $post->ID, '_halloween_product_data', true );

    $hween_sku = ( ! empty( $hs_meta['sku'] ) ) ? $hs_meta['sku'] : '';
```

```php
$hween_price = ( ! empty( $hs_meta['price'] ) ) ? $hs_meta['price'] : '';
$hween_weight = ( ! empty( $hs_meta['weight'] ) ) ? $hs_meta['weight'] : '';
$hween_color = ( ! empty( $hs_meta['color'] ) ) ? $hs_meta['color'] : '';
$hween_inventory = ( ! empty( $hs_meta['inventory'] ) ) ?
    $hs_meta['inventory'] : '';

//nonce field for security
wp_nonce_field( 'meta-box-save', 'halloween-plugin' );
// display meta box form
echo '<table>';
echo '<tr>';
echo '<td>' .__('Sku', 'halloween-plugin').':</td>
    <td><input type="text" name="halloween_product[sku]"
    value="'.esc_attr( $hween_sku ).'" size="10"></td>';
echo '</tr><tr>';
echo '<td>' .__('Price', 'halloween-plugin').':</td>
    <td><input type="text" name="halloween_product[price]"
    value="'.esc_attr( $hween_price ).'" size="5"></td>';
echo '</tr><tr>';
echo '<td>' .__('Weight', 'halloween-plugin').':</td>
    <td><input type="text" name="halloween_product[weight]"
    value="'.esc_attr( $hween_weight ).'" size="5"></td>';
echo '</tr><tr>';
echo '<td>' .__('Color', 'halloween-plugin').':</td>
    <td><input type="text" name="halloween_product[color]"
    value="'.esc_attr( $hween_color ).'" size="5"></td>';
echo '</tr><tr>';
echo '<td>Inventory:</td><td><select
    name="halloween_product[inventory]" id="halloween_product[inventory]">
        <option value="In Stock"'
            .selected( $hween_inventory, 'In Stock', false ). '>'
            .__( 'In Stock', 'halloween-plugin' ). '</option>
        <option value="Backordered"'
            .selected( $hween_inventory, 'Backordered', false ). '>'
            .__( 'Backordered', 'halloween-plugin' ). '</option>
        <option value="Out of Stock"'
            .selected( $hween_inventory, 'Out of Stock', false ). '>'
            .__( 'Out of Stock', 'halloween-plugin' ). '</option>
        <option value="Discontinued"'
            .selected( $hween_inventory, 'Discontinued', false ). '>'
            .__( 'Discontinued', 'halloween-plugin' ). '</option>
    </select></td>';
echo '</tr>';

//display the meta box shortcode legend section
echo '<tr><td colspan="2"><hr></td></tr>';
echo '<tr><td colspan="2"><strong>'
    .__( 'Shortcode Legend', 'halloween-plugin' ).'</strong></td></tr>';
echo '<tr><td>' .__( 'Sku', 'halloween-plugin' )
    .':</td><td>[hs show=sku]</td></tr>';
echo '<tr><td>' .__( 'Price', 'halloween-plugin' )
    .':</td><td>[hs show=price]</td></tr>';
echo '<tr><td>' .__( 'Weight', 'halloween-plugin' )
    .':</td><td>[hs show=weight]</td></tr>';
echo '<tr><td>' .__( 'Color', 'halloween-plugin' )
```

```
        .':</td><td>[hs show=color]</td></tr>';
    echo '<tr><td>' .__( 'Inventory', 'halloween-plugin' )
        .':</td><td>[hs show=inventory]</td></tr>';
    echo '</table>';
}
```

Your Halloween Store plugin saves five different product values on every product: SKU, price, weight, color, and inventory. For efficiency reasons, you are storing all five product values as a single options array. As you can see, the first step is to load these five custom field values. Next, you display the meta box form and fill in the current values if any exist. Below the meta box form, you display a simple shortcode legend to show the user what shortcode options are available for displaying the product metadata. Once completed, your custom meta box will look like Figure 8-7.

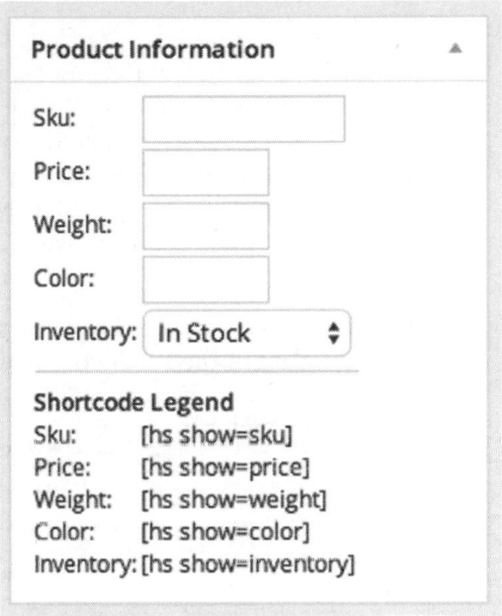

Now that you've created your custom meta box, you need to save the data entered in the form, as shown in the following code:

Product Information ▲

Sku:

Price:

Weight:

Color:

Inventory: In Stock ⬍

Shortcode Legend

Sku: [hs show=sku]
Price: [hs show=price]
Weight: [hs show=weight]
Color: [hs show=color]
Inventory: [hs show=inventory]

FIGURE 8-7: Post product meta box

```
// Action hook to save the meta box data when the post is saved
add_action( 'save_post','halloween_store_save_meta_box' );

//save meta box data
function halloween_store_save_meta_box( $post_id ) {

    //verify the post type is for Halloween Products and metadata has been posted
    if ( get_post_type( $post_id ) == 'halloween-products'
        && isset( $_POST['halloween_product'] ) ) {

        //if autosave skip saving data
        if ( defined( 'DOING_AUTOSAVE' ) && DOING_AUTOSAVE )
            return;

        //check nonce for security
        wp_verify_nonce( 'meta-box-save', 'halloween-plugin' );

        //store option values in a variable
        $halloween_product_data = $_POST['halloween_product'];

        //use array map function to sanitize option values
        $halloween_product_data =
            array_map( 'sanitize_text_field', $halloween_product_data );

        // save the meta box data as post metadata
```

```
        update_post_meta( $post_id, '_halloween_product_data',
            $halloween_product_data );

    }

}
```

First you need to verify that the post being saved is a `halloween-products` custom post type entry. You also verify that the `$_POST['halloween_product']` value is set before proceeding. After you have verified that an SKU exists, you need to verify that the post is not an autosave. You also need to verify the nonce for security using `wp_verify_nonce()`. After all checks have passed, you save your custom product fields as product metadata for the product you are creating or updating. Notice how the PHP `array_map()` function is used to pass each value of the product data array through the `sanitize_text_field()` function. This will sanitize each value in the array prior to saving the meta data.

Next, you're going to set up the plugin shortcode. This will allow you to easily display any or all Product metadata in the Product content.

```php
// Action hook to create the products shortcode
add_shortcode( 'hs', 'halloween_store_shortcode' );

//create shortcode
function halloween_store_shortcode( $atts, $content = null ) {
    global $post;

    extract( shortcode_atts( array(
        "show" => ''
    ), $atts ) );

    //load options array
    $hween_options_arr = get_option( 'halloween_options' );

    //load product data
    $hween_product_data = get_post_meta( $post->ID,
        '_halloween_product_data', true );

    if ( $show == 'sku') {

        $hs_show = ( ! empty( $hween_product_data['sku'] ) )
            ? $hween_product_data['sku'] : '';

    }elseif ( $show == 'price' ) {

        $hs_show = $hween_options_arr['currency_sign'];
        $hs_show = ( ! empty( $hween_product_data['price'] ) )
            ? $hs_show . $hween_product_data['price'] : '';

    }elseif ( $show == 'weight' ) {

        $hs_show = ( ! empty( $hween_product_data['weight'] ) )
            ? $hween_product_data['weight'] : '';

    }elseif ( $show == 'color' ) {
```

```
            $hs_show = ( ! empty( $hween_product_data['color'] ) )
                ? $hween_product_data['color'] : '';

    }elseif ( $show == 'inventory' ) {

            $hs_show = ( ! empty( $hween_product_data['inventory'] ) )
                ? $hween_product_data['inventory'] : '';

    }

    //return the shortcode value to display
    return $hs_show;
}
```

The first thing you do is initialize the global variable $post. This will bring in the $post->ID
value for the post in which you are using the shortcode. Next, you extract the shortcode attributes
that you've defined, in this case show. Finally, you check what attribute value is being sent to the
shortcode to determine what value to show. Using the shortcode like [hs show=price] would
display the price of the product. If the price metadata is being displayed, you'll need to retrieve the
currency sign option value that was set by the user.

Next up, you are going to create your products widget:

```
// Action hook to create plugin widget
add_action( 'widgets_init', 'halloween_store_register_widgets' );
//register the widget
function halloween_store_register_widgets() {
    register_widget( 'hs_widget' );
}
//hs_widget class
class hs_widget extends WP_Widget {
```

First you have to register your widget as hs _ widget using the register _ widget() function.
Next, you extend the Widget class as hs _ widget. Now you need to create the four widget
functions needed to build your widget:

```
//process our new widget
function __construct() {

    $widget_ops = array(
        'classname'   => 'hs-widget-class',
        'description' => __( 'Display Halloween Products',
            'halloween-plugin' ) );
    parent::__construct( 'hs_widget', __( 'Products Widget','halloween-plugin')
        , $widget_ops );

}
```

The first function you create is the _ _ construct() function, also known as the *constructor*. Here,
you set the widget title, description, and class name for your custom widget:

```
//build our widget settings form
function form( $instance ) {
```

```php
        $defaults = array(
            'title'           => __( 'Products', 'halloween-plugin' ),
            'number_products' => '3' );

        $instance = wp_parse_args( (array) $instance, $defaults );
        $title = $instance['title'];
        $number_products = $instance['number_products'];
        ?>
            <p><?php _e('Title', 'halloween-plugin') ?>:
                <input class="widefat"
                    name="<?php echo $this->get_field_name( 'title' ); ?>"
                    type="text" value="<?php echo esc_attr( $title ); ?>" /></p>
            <p><?php _e( 'Number of Products', 'halloween-plugin' ) ?>:
                <input name="
                    <?php echo $this->get_field_name( 'number_products' ); ?>"
                    type="text" value="<?php
                        echo absint( $number_products ); ?>"
                    size="2" maxlength="2" />
            </p>
        <?php
    }
```

The second function you define is the form() function. This builds the form for saving your widget settings. You are saving two settings in your widget: the widget title and the number of products to display. First, you define the setting defaults if no settings have been saved. Next, you load in the saved values for your two settings. Finally, you display both setting form fields with the setting values if they exist.

```php
    //save our widget settings
    function update( $new_instance, $old_instance ) {

        $instance = $old_instance;
        $instance['title'] = sanitize_text_field( $new_instance['title'] );
        $instance['number_products'] = absint( $new_instance['number_products'] );

        return $instance;

    }
```

The next function you create is the update() function. This function saves your widget settings. Notice how you utilize the sanitize_text_field() function to sanitize your widget title. You also use the PHP absint() function to verify that the value for the number of products is a non-negative integer.

```php
    //display our widget
    function widget( $args, $instance ) {
        global $post;

        extract( $args );

        echo $before_widget;
        $title = apply_filters( 'widget_title', $instance['title'] );
        $number_products = $instance['number_products'];
```

```php
        if ( ! empty( $title ) ) { echo $before_title
            . esc_html( $title ) . $after_title; };

        //custom query to retrieve products
        $args = array(
            'post_type'      => 'halloween-products',
            'posts_per_page' => absint( $number_products )
        );

        $dispProducts = new WP_Query();
        $dispProducts->query( $args );

        while ( $dispProducts->have_posts() ) : $dispProducts->the_post();

            //load options array
            $hween_options_arr = get_option( 'halloween_options' );

            //load custom meta values
            $hween_product_data =
                get_post_meta( $post->ID, '_halloween_product_data', true );

            $hs_price = ( ! empty( $hween_product_data['price'] ) )
                ? $hween_product_data['price'] : '';
            $hs_inventory = ( ! empty( $hween_product_data['inventory'] ) )
                ? $hween_product_data['inventory'] : '';
            ?>
            <p>
                <a href="<?php the_permalink(); ?>" rel="bookmark"
                    title="<?php the_title_attribute(); ?> Product Information">
                    <?php the_title(); ?>
                </a>
            </p>
            <?php
            echo '<p>' . __( 'Price', 'halloween-plugin' )
                . ': '.$hween_options_arr['currency_sign'] .$hs_price .'</p>';

            //check if Show Inventory option is enabled
            if ( $hween_options_arr['show_inventory'] ) {

                //display the inventory metadata for this product
                echo '<p>' . __( 'Stock', 'halloween-plugin' ). ': '
                    .$hs_inventory .'</p>';

            }
            echo '<hr>';

        endwhile;

        wp_reset_postdata();

        echo $after_widget;

    }
}
```

The final function defined is the `widget()` function. This function displays your widget on the public side of your website. First you initialize the global `$post` variable and extract the `$args` for the widget. Then you display the `$before_widget` variable. This variable can be set by theme and plugin developers to display specified content before and after the plugin. Next, you retrieve your two setting values. If the `$title` value is not empty, you use it, but if it is, you'll use the default title you defined earlier.

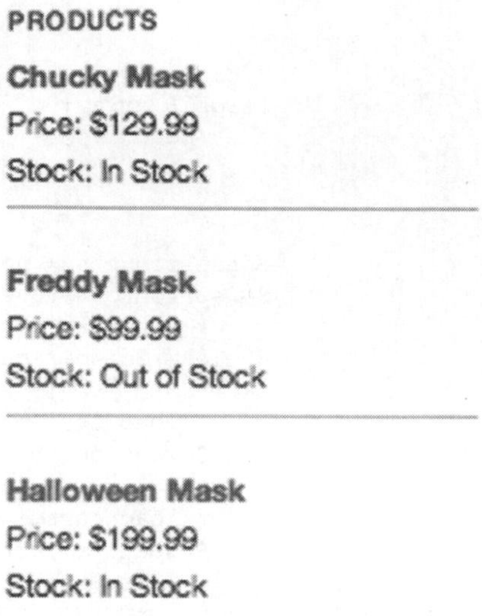

To display the products in your widget, you are creating a custom Loop using `WP_Query`, as discussed in Chapter 5. Remember that because this is not your main Loop, you'll want to use `WP_Query` to create your custom Loop. To define your custom Loop, you pass in two parameters: one for the post type and one for number of products to display. The first value (`post_type=halloween-products`) tells your custom Loop to only return Halloween product entries. The second value, `posts_per_page`, determines how many products to display. This number is pulled from the widget options value set by the user.

PRODUCTS

Chucky Mask
Price: $129.99
Stock: In Stock

Freddy Mask
Price: $99.99
Stock: Out of Stock

Halloween Mask
Price: $199.99
Stock: In Stock

FIGURE 8-8: Products widget

Next, you load your option values and the custom metadata values you will be displaying in your widget. Finally, you display your product values in the widget. If the option Show Inventory is enabled, the inventory value will be displayed. After successfully creating the Products widget, it should look like Figure 8-8.

The final step for your Halloween Store plugin is to create your `uninstall.php` file:

```php
<?php
//if uninstall/delete not called from WordPress exit
if( ! defined( 'ABSPATH' ) && ! defined( 'WP_UNINSTALL_PLUGIN' ) )
    exit ();
// Delete options array from options table
delete_option( 'halloween_options' );
?>
```

The first thing you check is that `ABSPATH` and `WP_UNINSTALL_PLUGIN` constants exist. This means they were called from WordPress and add a layer of security on the uninstaller. After you have verified that the request is valid, you delete your single option value from the database. You could also define other uninstall functionality here, if needed, such as removing every product metadata value you saved in the database.

That's it! You just successfully built an entire plugin that includes many of the features covered in this chapter. This is a fairly basic plugin but should give you the examples and tools needed to expand upon. Listing 8-5 shows the plugin source code in its entirety. To access this code online, visit `https://github.com/williamsba/HalloweenStore`.

LISTING 8-5: Complete Plugin Source Code (filename: `halloween-store.zip`)

```php
<?php
/*
Plugin Name: Halloween Store
Plugin URI: https://github.com/williamsba/HalloweenStore
Description: Create a Halloween Store to display product information
Version: 3.0
Author: Brad Williams
Author URI: http://webdevstudios.com
License: GPLv2
*/

/*  Copyright 2015  Brad Williams  (email : brad@webdevstudios.com)

    This program is free software; you can redistribute it and/or modify
    it under the terms of the GNU General Public License as published by
    the Free Software Foundation; either version 2 of the License, or
    (at your option) any later version.

    This program is distributed in the hope that it will be useful,
    but WITHOUT ANY WARRANTY; without even the implied warranty of
    MERCHANTABILITY or FITNESS FOR A PARTICULAR PURPOSE.  See the
    GNU General Public License for more details.

    You should have received a copy of the GNU General Public License
    along with this program; if not, write to the Free Software
    Foundation, Inc., 51 Franklin St, Fifth Floor, Boston, MA  02110-1301  USA
*/

// Call function when plugin is activated
register_activation_hook( __FILE__, 'halloween_store_install' );

function halloween_store_install() {

    //setup default option values
    $hween_options_arr = array(
        'currency_sign' => '$'
    );

    //save our default option values
    update_option( 'halloween_options', $hween_options_arr );

}


// Action hook to initialize the plugin
add_action( 'init', 'halloween_store_init' );

//Initialize the Halloween Store
function halloween_store_init() {

    //register the products custom post type
```

continues

LISTING 8-5: *(continued)*

```php
    $labels = array(
        'name'              => __( 'Products',
            'halloween-plugin' ),
        'singular_name'     => __( 'Product',
            'halloween-plugin' ),
        'add_new'           => __( 'Add New',
            'halloween-plugin' ),
        'add_new_item'      => __( 'Add New Product',
            'halloween-plugin' ),
        'edit_item'         => __( 'Edit Product',
            'halloween-plugin' ),
        'new_item'          => __( 'New Product',
            'halloween-plugin' ),
        'all_items'         => __( 'All Products',
            'halloween-plugin' ),
        'view_item'         => __( 'View Product',
            'halloween-plugin' ),
        'search_items'      => __( 'Search Products',
            'halloween-plugin' ),
        'not_found'         => __( 'No products found',
            'halloween-plugin' ),
        'not_found_in_trash' => __( 'No products found in Trash',
            'halloween-plugin' ),
        'menu_name'         => __( 'Products', 'halloween-plugin' )
    );

    $args = array(
        'labels'            => $labels,
        'public'            => true,
        'publicly_queryable' => true,
        'show_ui'           => true,
        'show_in_menu'      => true,
        'query_var'         => true,
        'rewrite'           => true,
        'capability_type'   => 'post',
        'has_archive'       => true,
        'hierarchical'      => false,
        'menu_position'     => null,
        'supports'          => array( 'title', 'editor',
            'thumbnail', 'excerpt' )
    );

    register_post_type( 'halloween-products', $args );

}

// Action hook to add the post products menu item
add_action( 'admin_menu', 'halloween_store_menu' );

//create the Halloween Masks sub-menu
function halloween_store_menu() {
```

```php
    add_options_page(
        __( 'Halloween Store Settings Page', 'halloween-plugin' ),
        __( 'Halloween Store Settings', 'halloween-plugin' ),
        'manage_options',
        'halloween-store-settings',
        'halloween_store_settings_page'
    );

}

//build the plugin settings page
function halloween_store_settings_page() {

    //load the plugin options array
    $hween_options_arr = get_option( 'halloween_options' );

    //set the option array values to variables
    $hs_inventory = (
        ! empty( $hween_options_arr['show_inventory'] ) )
        ? $hween_options_arr['show_inventory'] : '';
    $hs_currency_sign = $hween_options_arr['currency_sign'];
    ?>
    <div class="wrap">
    <h2><?php _e( 'Halloween Store Options',
        'halloween-plugin' ) ?></h2>

    <form method="post" action="options.php">
        <?php settings_fields( 'halloween-settings-group' ); ?>
        <table class="form-table">
            <tr valign="top">
            <th scope="row"><?php _e( 'Show Product Inventory',
                'halloween-plugin' ) ?></th>
            <td><input type="checkbox"
                name="halloween_options[show_inventory]" <?php
                echo checked( $hs_inventory, 'on' ); ?> /></td>
            </tr>

            <tr valign="top">
            <th scope="row"><?php _e( 'Currency Sign',
                'halloween-plugin' ) ?></th>
            <td><input type="text"
                name="halloween_options[currency_sign]"
                value="<?php echo esc_attr( $hs_currency_sign ); ?>"
                size="1" maxlength="1" /></td>
            </tr>
        </table>

        <p class="submit">
        <input type="submit" class="button-primary"
            value="<?php _e( 'Save Changes',
                'halloween-plugin' ); ?>" />
        </p>

    </form>
    </div>
```

continues

LISTING 8-5: (*continued*)

```php
<?php
}

// Action hook to register the plugin option settings
add_action( 'admin_init', 'halloween_store_register_settings' );

function halloween_store_register_settings() {

    //register the array of settings
    register_setting( 'halloween-settings-group',
        'halloween_options', 'halloween_sanitize_options' );

}

function halloween_sanitize_options( $options ) {

    $options['show_inventory'] = (
        ! empty( $options['show_inventory'] ) )
        ? sanitize_text_field( $options['show_inventory'] ) : '';
    $options['currency_sign'] = (
        ! empty( $options['currency_sign'] ) )
        ? sanitize_text_field( $options['currency_sign'] ) : '';

    return $options;

}

//Action hook to register the Products meta box
add_action( 'add_meta_boxes',
    'halloween_store_register_meta_box' );

function halloween_store_register_meta_box() {

    // create our custom meta box
    add_meta_box( 'halloween-product-meta',
        __( 'Product Information','halloween-plugin' ),
        'halloween_meta_box', 'halloween-products',
        'side', 'default' );

}

//build product meta box
function halloween_meta_box( $post ) {

    // retrieve our custom meta box values
    $hs_meta = get_post_meta( $post->ID,
        '_halloween_product_data', true );

    $hween_sku = ( ! empty( $hs_meta['sku'] ) )
        ? $hs_meta['sku'] : '';
    $hween_price = ( ! empty( $hs_meta['price'] ) )
        ? $hs_meta['price'] : '';
    $hween_weight = ( ! empty( $hs_meta['weight'] ) )
```

```php
        ? $hs_meta['weight'] : '';
$hween_color = ( ! empty( $hs_meta['color'] ) )
    ? $hs_meta['color'] : '';
$hween_inventory = ( ! empty( $hs_meta['inventory'] ) )
    ? $hs_meta['inventory'] : '';

//nonce field for security
wp_nonce_field( 'meta-box-save', 'halloween-plugin' );

// display meta box form
echo '<table>';
echo '<tr>';
echo '<td>' . __('Sku', 'halloween-plugin').':</td>
    <td><input type="text" name="halloween_product[sku]"
    value="'.esc_attr( $hween_sku ).'" size="10"></td>';
echo '</tr><tr>';
echo '<td>' . __('Price', 'halloween-plugin').':</td>
    <td><input type="text" name="halloween_product[price]"
    value="'.esc_attr( $hween_price ).'" size="5"></td>';
echo '</tr><tr>';
echo '<td>' . __('Weight', 'halloween-plugin').':</td>
    <td><input type="text" name="halloween_product[weight]"
    value="'.esc_attr( $hween_weight ).'" size="5"></td>';
echo '</tr><tr>';
echo '<td>' . __('Color', 'halloween-plugin').':</td>
    <td><input type="text" name="halloween_product[color]"
    value="'.esc_attr( $hween_color ).'" size="5"></td>';
echo '</tr><tr>';
echo '<td>Inventory:</td>
    <td>
    <select name="halloween_product[inventory]"
        id="halloween_product[inventory]">
    <option value="In Stock"'
        .selected( $hween_inventory, 'In Stock', false )
        . '>' .__( 'In Stock', 'halloween-plugin' ). '</option>
    <option value="Backordered"'
        .selected( $hween_inventory, 'Backordered', false )
        . '>' .__( 'Backordered', 'halloween-plugin' )
        . '</option>
    <option value="Out of Stock"'
        .selected( $hween_inventory, 'Out of Stock', false )
        . '>' .__( 'Out of Stock', 'halloween-plugin' )
        . '</option>
    <option value="Discontinued"'
        .selected( $hween_inventory, 'Discontinued', false )
        . '>' .__( 'Discontinued', 'halloween-plugin' )
        . '</option>
    </select></td>';
echo '</tr>';

//display the meta box shortcode legend section
echo '<tr><td colspan="2"><hr></td></tr>';
echo '<tr><td colspan="2"><strong>'
    .__( 'Shortcode Legend',
    'halloween-plugin' ).'</strong></td></tr>';
```

continues

LISTING 8-5: *(continued)*

```php
    echo '<tr><td>'
        .__( 'Sku', 'halloween-plugin' ) .':</td>
        <td>[hs show=sku]</td></tr>';
    echo '<tr><td>'
        .__( 'Price', 'halloween-plugin' ).':</td>
        <td>[hs show=price]</td></tr>';
    echo '<tr><td>'
        .__( 'Weight', 'halloween-plugin' ).':</td>
        <td>[hs show=weight]</td></tr>';
    echo '<tr><td>'
        .__( 'Color', 'halloween-plugin' ).':</td>
        <td>[hs show=color]</td></tr>';
    echo '<tr><td>'
        .__( 'Inventory', 'halloween-plugin' ).':</td>
        <td>[hs show=inventory]</td></tr>';
    echo '</table>';
}

// Action hook to save the meta box data when the post is saved
add_action( 'save_post','halloween_store_save_meta_box' );

//save meta box data
function halloween_store_save_meta_box( $post_id ) {

    //verify the post type is for Halloween Products
    // and metadata has been posted
    if ( get_post_type( $post_id ) == 'halloween-products'
        && isset( $_POST['halloween_product'] ) ) {

        //if autosave skip saving data
        if ( defined( 'DOING_AUTOSAVE' ) && DOING_AUTOSAVE )
            return;

        //check nonce for security
        wp_verify_nonce( 'meta-box-save', 'halloween-plugin' );

        //store option values in a variable
        $halloween_product_data = $_POST['halloween_product'];

        //use array map function to sanitize option values
        $halloween_product_data =
            array_map( 'sanitize_text_field',
                $halloween_product_data );

        // save the meta box data as post metadata
        update_post_meta( $post_id, '_halloween_product_data',
            $halloween_product_data );

    }

}

// Action hook to create the products shortcode
```

```php
add_shortcode( 'hs', 'halloween_store_shortcode' );

//create shortcode
function halloween_store_shortcode( $atts, $content = null ) {
    global $post;

    extract( shortcode_atts( array(
        "show" => ''
    ), $atts ) );

    //load options array
    $hween_options_arr = get_option( 'halloween_options' );

    //load product data
    $hween_product_data = get_post_meta( $post->ID,
        '_halloween_product_data', true );

    if ( $show == 'sku') {

        $hs_show = ( ! empty( $hween_product_data['sku'] ) )
            ? $hween_product_data['sku'] : '';

    }elseif ( $show == 'price' ) {

        $hs_show = $hween_options_arr['currency_sign'];
        $hs_show = ( ! empty( $hween_product_data['price'] ) )
            ? $hs_show . $hween_product_data['price'] : '';

    }elseif ( $show == 'weight' ) {

        $hs_show = ( ! empty( $hween_product_data['weight'] ) )
            ? $hween_product_data['weight'] : '';

    }elseif ( $show == 'color' ) {

        $hs_show = ( ! empty( $hween_product_data['color'] ) )
            ? $hween_product_data['color'] : '';

    }elseif ( $show == 'inventory' ) {

        $hs_show = ( ! empty( $hween_product_data['inventory'] ) )
            ? $hween_product_data['inventory'] : '';

    }

    //return the shortcode value to display
    return $hs_show;
}

// Action hook to create plugin widget
add_action( 'widgets_init', 'halloween_store_register_widgets' );

//register the widget
function halloween_store_register_widgets() {
```

continues

LISTING 8-5: *(continued)*

```php
    register_widget( 'hs_widget' );

}

//hs_widget class
class hs_widget extends WP_Widget {

    //process our new widget
    function __construct() {

        $widget_ops = array(
            'classname'   => 'hs-widget-class',
            'description' => __( 'Display Halloween Products',
                'halloween-plugin' ) );
        parent::__construct( 'hs_widget', __( 'Products Widget',
            'halloween-plugin'), $widget_ops );

    }

    //build our widget settings form
    function form( $instance ) {

        $defaults = array(
            'title'            =>
                __( 'Products', 'halloween-plugin' ),
            'number_products' => '3' );

        $instance = wp_parse_args( (array) $instance, $defaults );
        $title = $instance['title'];
        $number_products = $instance['number_products'];
        ?>
            <p><?php _e('Title', 'halloween-plugin') ?>:
                <input class="widefat" name="<?php
                echo $this->get_field_name( 'title' ); ?>"
                type="text" value="<?php
                echo esc_attr( $title ); ?>" /></p>
            <p><?php _e( 'Number of Products',
                'halloween-plugin' ) ?>:
                <input name="<?php
                echo $this->get_field_name( 'number_products' ); ?>"
                type="text" value="<?php
                echo absint( $number_products ); ?>"
                size="2" maxlength="2" />
            </p>
        <?php
    }

    //save our widget settings
    function update( $new_instance, $old_instance ) {

        $instance = $old_instance;
        $instance['title'] =
            sanitize_text_field( $new_instance['title'] );
```

```php
    $instance['number_products'] =
        absint( $new_instance['number_products'] );

    return $instance;

}

//display our widget
function widget( $args, $instance ) {
    global $post;

    extract( $args );

    echo $before_widget;
    $title = apply_filters( 'widget_title',
        $instance['title'] );
    $number_products = $instance['number_products'];

    if ( ! empty( $title ) ) {
        echo $before_title . esc_html( $title ) . $after_title;
    };

    //custom query to retrieve products
    $args = array(
        'post_type'      => 'halloween-products',
        'posts_per_page' => absint( $number_products )
    );

    $dispProducts = new WP_Query();
    $dispProducts->query( $args );

    while ( $dispProducts->have_posts() ) :
        $dispProducts->the_post();

        //load options array
        $hween_options_arr = get_option( 'halloween_options' );

        //load custom meta values
        $hween_product_data =
        get_post_meta( $post->ID,
            '_halloween_product_data', true );

        $hs_price = ( ! empty( $hween_product_data['price'] ) )
            ? $hween_product_data['price'] : '';
        $hs_inventory = (
            ! empty( $hween_product_data['inventory'] ) )
            ? $hween_product_data['inventory'] : '';
        ?>
        <p>
            <a href="<?php the_permalink(); ?>"
            rel="bookmark"
            title="<?php the_title_attribute(); ?>
            Product Information">
                <?php the_title(); ?>
            </a>
```

continues

LISTING 8-5: *(continued)*

```php
            </p>
            <?php
            echo '<p>' . __( 'Price', 'halloween-plugin' )
            . ': '.$hween_options_arr['currency_sign']
            .$hs_price .'</p>';

            //check if Show Inventory option is enabled
            if ( $hween_options_arr['show_inventory'] ) {

                //display the inventory metadata for this product
                echo '<p>' . __( 'Stock', 'halloween-plugin' )
                . ': ' .$hs_inventory .'</p>';

            }
            echo '<hr>';

        endwhile;

        wp_reset_postdata();

        echo $after_widget;

    }

}
```

PUBLISHING TO THE PLUGIN DIRECTORY

Now it's time to release your plugin to the world! Releasing your plugin on WordPress.org is not a requirement, but it is the best way to get your plugin publicized and have other WordPress users download and install it. Remember that the Plugin Directory on WordPress.org is directly hooked to every installation of WordPress, so if your plugin exists in the directory then anyone running WordPress can easily download and install it.

Restrictions

A few restrictions exist to submitting your plugin to the Plugin Directory:

➤ Plugin must be compatible with GPLv2 or any later version.

➤ Plugin must not do anything illegal or morally offensive.

➤ Must use the Subversion (SVN) repository to host your plugin.

➤ Plugin must not embed external links on the user's site (such as a "powered by" link) without asking the plugin user's permission.

Make sure to follow these guidelines or your plugin will be removed from the Plugin Directory.

Submitting Your Plugin

The first step is to create an account on WordPress.org if you don't already have one. To register a new account, visit the registration page at `http://wordpress.org/support/register.php`. This WordPress.org account is used in the Plugin Directory as well as the support forums.

After you have registered your account and signed in, it's time to submit your plugin for inclusion in the Plugin Directory on WordPress.org. To submit your plugin, visit the Add Your Plugin page at `https://wordpress.org/plugins/add/`.

The first required field is the Plugin Name. The plugin name should be the exact name you want to use for your plugin. Keep in mind that the plugin name will be used as the URL in the directory. For example, if you submit a plugin named WP Brad, the URL to your plugin in the Plugin Directory will be `https://wordpress.org/ plugins/wp-brad/`. As you can see, the name you insert here is very important and cannot be changed.

The second required field is the Plugin Description. This field should contain a detailed description about your plugin. Remember that the description is really the only information used to decide whether or not to allow your plugin in the directory. Clearly state the plugin functionality, the purpose of the plugin, and installation instructions for the plugin.

The final field is the Plugin URL. This is not a required field, but it's highly recommended that you include a download link to your plugin. This enables the reviewer of your plugin to download and look at your plugin if needed. Again this is not a required field but you are strongly encouraged to fill it in.

After you have filled out all of the information, click the Send Post button to submit your plugin request. The Plugin Directory states, "Within some vaguely defined amount of time, someone will approve your request." This doesn't really tell you much, but most plugins are approved within a day or so. The fact that your plugin has been approved does not mean you are done. The next step is to upload your plugin to the Subversion Repository that has been created for it.

Creating a readme.txt File

One file that is required to submit your plugin to the Plugin Directory is `readme.txt`. This file is used to fill in all of the plugin information on the Plugin detail page in the Directory. WordPress has developed the readme file standard, which details exactly how your `readme.txt` file should be defined. Here's an example `readme.txt` file:

```
=== Plugin Name ===
Contributors: williamsba1, jtsternberg, coreymcollins
Donate link: http://example.com/donate
Tags: admin, post, images, page, widget
Requires at least: 3.8
Tested up to: 4.2
Stable tag: 1.1.0.0
License: GPLv2
Short description of the plugin with 150 chars max.  No markup here.
== Description ==
This is the long description.  No limit, and you can use Markdown
```

```
Additional plugin features
*    Feature 1
*    Feature 2
*    Feature 3
For support visit the [Support Forum](http://example.com/forum/ " Support Forum")
== Installation ==
1. Upload 'plugin-directory' to the '/wp-content/plugins/' directory
2. Activate the plugin through the 'Plugins' screen in WordPress
3. Place '<?php prowp_custom_function(); ?>' in your theme templates
== Frequently Asked Questions ==
= A question that someone might have =
An answer to that question.
= Does this plugin work with WordPress Multisite? =
Absolutely!  This plugin has been tested and
verified to work on the most current version of WordPress Multisite
== Screenshots ==
1. Screenshot of plugin settings page
2. Screenshot of plugin in action
== Changelog ==
= 1.1 =
* New feature details
* Bug fix details
= 1.0 =
* First official release
== Upgrade Notice ==
= 1.1 =
* Security bug fixed
```

For an online readme.txt example, visit the Readme Standard at https://wordpress.org/plugins/about/readme.txt.

WordPress.org also features a readme.txt validator so you can verify you have a properly formatted readme.txt file before submitting to the Subversion directory. You can access the validator at https://wordpress.org/plugins/about/validator/. Let's break down the individual readme.txt sections:

```
=== Plugin Name ===
Contributors: williamsba1, jtsternberg, coreymcollins
Donate link: http://example.com/donate
Tags: admin, post, images, page, widget
Requires at least: 3.8
Tested up to: 4.2
Stable tag: 1.1.0.0
License: GPLv2
Short description of the plugin with 150 chars max.  No markup here.
```

The Plugin Name section is one of the most important parts of your readme.txt file. The first line lists the contributors to the plugin. This is a comma-separated list of WordPress.org usernames that helped contribute to the plugin. The donate link should be a URL to either a donate link or a web page that explains how users can donate to the plugin author. This is a great place for a PayPal donation link. Tags are a comma-separated list of tags describing your plugin.

The "Requires at least" field is the minimal version of WordPress required to run the plugin. If your plugin won't run on anything prior to 3.8, then 3.8 would be the "Requires at least" value.

Likewise, "Tested up to" is the latest version the plugin has been tested on. This will typically be the latest stable version of WordPress. The Stable tag is also a very important field and should be the current version of the plugin. This value should always match the version number listed in the plugin header. Last is a short description of the plugin, which should be no more than 150 characters and cannot contain any markup.

```
== Description ==
This is the long description.  No limit, and you can use Markdown
Additional plugin features
*    Feature 1
*    Feature 2
*    Feature 3
For support visit the [Support Forum](http://example.com/forum/ " Support Forum")
```

The Description section features a detailed description of your plugin. This is the default information displayed on the plugin detail page in the Plugin Directory. There is no limit to the length of the description. You can also use unordered lists, shown in the preceding example, and ordered lists in your description. Links can also be inserted.

```
== Installation ==
1. Upload 'plugin-directory' to the '/wp-content/plugins/' directory
2. Activate the plugin through the 'Plugins' screen in WordPress
3. Place '<?php prowp_custom_function(); ?>' in your theme templates
```

The Installation section details the steps involved to install a plugin. If your plugin has very specific installation requirements, make sure they are listed here in detail. It's also a good idea to list the function name and shortcode that can be used with the plugin.

```
== Frequently Asked Questions ==
= A question that someone might have =
An answer to that question.
= Does this plugin work with WordPress Multisite? =
Absolutely!  This plugin has been tested and
verified to work on the most current version of WordPress Multisite
```

The FAQ section is the perfect place to list frequently asked questions, of course! This helps answer commonly asked questions and can eliminate many support requests. You can list multiple questions with answers, as this example shows:

```
== Screenshots ==
1. Screenshot of plugin settings page
2. Screenshot of plugin in action
```

The Screenshots section is used to add individual screenshots of your plugin to the plugin detail page. This is actually a two-step process. The first step is to list out each screenshot description in an ordered list. The next step is to place image files in your trunk directory (which is discussed in more detail next). These image file names must match the listing number. For instance, the screenshot of your settings page should be named screenshot-1.png. The screenshot of your plugin in action should be named screenshot-2.png. The file types accepted are .png, .jpg, .jpeg, and .gif.

```
== Changelog ==
= 1.1 =
* New feature details
* Bug fix details
= 1.0 =
* First official release
```

The next section is the Changelog. This section is important for listing out what each plugin version release has added or fixed. This is a very helpful section for anyone looking to upgrade to the latest version. It's always nice to know exactly what is being added and fixed to determine how critical the plugin update is. A new item should be added for each version you release to the Plugin Directory, regardless of how minor that update may be.

```
== Upgrade Notice ==
= 1.1 =
* Security bug fixed
```

The final section is the Upgrade Notice section. This section allows you to send specific upgrade notice messages to the WordPress user. These messages are shown on the Dashboard ➤ Updates screen when a new version of your plugin is released.

The readme.txt file can also accept arbitrary sections in the same format as the rest. This is useful for more complicated plugins that need to provide additional information. Arbitrary sections will be displayed below the built-in sections described previously.

Setting Up SVN

The Plugin Directory uses Subversion (SVN) for handling plugins. To publish your plugin to the directory, you'll need to set up and configure an SVN client. If you are familiar with command-line SVN, that would also be an option. In this example, you are going to use TortoiseSVN for Windows. TortoiseSVN is a free GUI client interface for SVN. For a list of additional SVN clients for different platforms, visit http://subversion.apache.org/.

First you'll need to download the appropriate installer at http://tortoisesvn.net/downloads .html. After installing TortoiseSVN, you'll need to reboot your computer. The next step is to create a new directory on your computer to store your plugin files. It is recommended that you make a folder to store all of your plugins in, such as c:\projects\wordpress-plugins. This makes it much easier going forward if you create and release multiple plugins to WordPress.org.

Next, navigate to your new wordpress-plugins directory and create a new directory for your plugin. Right-click this new folder to pull up a context menu. You'll notice the new TortoiseSVN options listed: SVN Checkout and TortoiseSVN. Select SVN Checkout and a dialog box appears, as shown in Figure 8-9.

The URL of the repository was provided to you in the e-mail you received when your plugin was approved. This URL should be the same as the plugin URL so in this example the URL would be http://plugins.svn.wordpress.org/wp-brad. The Checkout directory is the local folder in which to store your plugin. In this case, you will use the new folder you created at c:\projects\ wordpress-plugins\wp-brad. Make sure Checkout Depth is set to Fully Recursive. Also verify that the Revision is set to HEAD Revision. Finally, click OK. TortoiseSVN will connect to the SVN Repository for your plugin and, if all goes well, will create three new directories in your folder called branches, tags, and trunk. These three folders each serve a specific purpose for SVN:

➤ **Branches**—Every time a new major version is released, it gets a branch. This allows for bug fixes without releasing new functionality from trunk.

➤ **Tags**—Every time a new version is released, you'll make a new tag for it.

➤ **Trunk**—Main development area. The next major release of code lives here.

FIGURE 8-9: SVN Checkout dialog box

Now that you've connected to your plugin's SVN Repository, you need to move your plugin files to the trunk directory. Remember to also place your readme.txt file and any screenshots, includes, and so on in the trunk directory for your plugin. Remember that you're just staging the plugin files to publish to the plugin directory. Publishing the files to WordPress.org is covered in the next section.

Once you've verified all of the plugin files are in trunk, you are ready to publish your plugin to the Plugin Directory!

Publishing to the Plugin Directory

Publishing your plugin to the Plugin Directory is a two-step process. First you need to SVN Commit the `trunk` folder to your SVN Repository. Second, you need to tag your plugin release. Once both steps have been completed, your new plugin will appear in the Plugin Directory within about 15 minutes.

To commit your plugin trunk, simply right-click the `trunk` folder and select SVN Commit. You'll be presented with a dialog box to enter a log message and to select which files to commit to the trunk. Fill in a brief log message, such as "Adding WP-Brad 1.1," and select all of the files you want to commit. TortoiseSVN will automatically select all files that have changed so you probably won't need to change this. Next, click OK and you will be prompted to enter a username and password. This is the username and password you created on WordPress.org.

Next, you need to tag your plugin version. To tag your plugin version, simply right-click the trunk directory and select TortoiseSVN ➢ Branch/tag from the context menu. In the dialog box that appears, fill in the path to your tag directory. Using this example, the URL would be `http://plugins.svn.wordpress.org/wp-brad/tags/1.1.0.0/`. This tag version should match the stable tag in your plugin's `readme.txt` file—in your case, version 1.1.0.0. Also type in a log message, such as "tagging version 1.1.0.0" and verify that "HEAD revision in the repository" is selected for the Create Copy option. Click OK and your plugin will create a new directory in your `tags` folder for version 1.1.0.0 with the appropriate plugin files.

That's it! If everything worked successfully, your plugin should appear in the Plugin Directory within about 15 minutes. Once your plugin is successfully published, you'll want to verify that all of the information is correct. One way to verify that your plugin was published successfully is to visit the Subversion URL, which for this example would be `http://plugins.svn.wordpress.org/wp-brad/`. Here you can ensure the `trunk` and `tag` directories were uploaded successfully. After 15 minutes, you can also verify your plugin by visiting the official Plugin Directory page at `https://www.wordpress.org/plugins/wp-brad`.

If you need to make any changes to your `readme.txt` file, simply edit it locally in your `trunk` folder, right-click the file, and click SVN Commit.

Releasing a New Version

A great feature of WordPress plugins is that you can easily release updates for your plugins in the Plugin Directory. When a new plugin version is released, a notice is displayed on any WordPress site that currently has that plugin uploaded to its server, whether or not it is activated. The user can use the automatic upgrade process to easily upgrade the plugin to the latest version. This is especially important if there are security patches in your plugin to help keep WordPress secure.

To release a new plugin version, make sure you copy the updated plugin files to the `/trunk` directory you set up earlier. This folder should contain all files for the updated plugin version. Once you have verified that all of the updates plugin files exist, simply right-click the `trunk` directory and select SVN Commit. Remember to type in a brief message such as "Committing version 1.2." TortoiseSVN should have already selected all of the files that have changed, but if not, select all of the files you want to publish and click OK.

The final step is to tag your new version. To tag your new release, right-click the `trunk` directory and select TortoiseSVN ➤ Branch/tag. For this example, the URL would be `http://plugins.svn. wordpress.org/wp-brad/tags/1.2.0.0/`. Remember to write a brief log entry such as "Tagging version 1.2" and click OK. That's it! Your new plugin version will be published in the Plugin Directory within 15 minutes. After the new version has been released, your plugin will appear at the top of the Recently Updated Plugins list on WordPress.org.

The WordPress Plugin Directory is a great source for inspiration and reference when building custom plugins. Don't be scared to look at another plugin source code for reference. Find a plugin that functions similarly to what you want and see how the plugin author structured the code or used hooks to interpose his or her plugin ideas in the WordPress core processing.

Plugin Assets

When publishing plugins to the WordPress.org Plugin Directory, there are certain assets you can include to make your plugins really pop! The first asset is a Plugin Header image. This image appears on your plugin detail page, as shown in Figure 8-10.

FIGURE 8-10: Plugin header image

It's easy to see how a plugin header image can really make your WordPress plugin stand out. Including a header image is very easy. First create an `assets` directory in the root of your plugin's SVN directory. The `assets` directory should sit alongside your `trunk`, `branches`, and `tags` directories. This directory will contain all plugin assets, such as the header image. Next, add a 772 × 250 pixel `.jpg` or `.png` file. This image file will be used as the header image on your plugin's detail page. The image name must be formatted like `assets/banner-772x250.(png|jpg)`.

The plugin header image can also support high-DPI displays, also known as retina displays. To include a retina-friendly header image, simply include a 1544 × 500 `.jpg` or `.png` file to your assets directory in the same format as before: `assets/banner-1544x500.(png|jpg)`.

A newer plugin asset, introduced with WordPress 4.0, is the plugin icon. The plugin icon is used in the plugin installer in WordPress, shown in Figure 8-11, and on the plugin listing screens in the WordPress.org Plugin Directory.

FIGURE 8-11: Plugin icon example

Plugin icons support standard resolutions as well as retina displays. To include a plugin icon, simply add a 128 × 128 `.jpeg` or `.png` file to your `assets` directory for standard display and a 256 × 256 icon for retina displays. The format for both icons would be `assets/icon-128x128.(png|jpg)` and `assets/icon-256x256.(png|jpg)`.

Including high-quality plugin assets helps give your plugin a polished look and really stand out from the pack.

SUMMARY

In this chapter, you learned WordPress plugin packaging with the required plugin header, including a WordPress compatible software license with your plugin, and activating and deactivating functions. You also covered very important data validation and sanitization for plugin security. The chapter also covered powerful hooks, plugin setting options, and multiple ways to integrate your plugins into WordPress.

Plugins are only half of the WordPress extensibility story; they give you the power to add custom functions and event-driven processing to your site. If you want to change the look and feel of your site, change the way in which WordPress displays posts, or provide slots for those widgets you created, you'll want to extend WordPress through theme development, which is the focus of Chapter 9.

9

Theme Development

WHAT'S IN THIS CHAPTER?

➤ Understanding the various files and templates that constitute a theme

➤ Modifying an existing theme to meet your own needs

➤ Identifying the different reasons to use a project theme or a child theme

Content is king, right? That is certainly true. Nothing is going to drive visitors to your site, and keep them coming back, except for your content. Even if you have the best content on the Internet for your topic, you have to present it to the reader, the browser, and to the search engines so that your content can be consumed.

That is what themes are for. Themes control the presentation layer of your site, including both the user experience and how it is offered to the consumer. Themes also control the logic that determines which type of page and, therefore, which type of loop is to be used.

This chapter reviews how to install a theme on your website and then takes you through the various aspects of a theme and how they apply to the presentation of your content. You will also review different strategies for creating your theme, whether specifically for a project, or as an adaptation of a theme framework. By the end of this chapter, you will have an understanding of theme functionality and a solid foundation on which to build your own custom project or child themes from scratch for use in your own projects.

WHY USE A THEME?

Your website theme is essentially the face of your website. It is what makes the first impression on your visitor. Even though surely none of us is shallow enough to judge a book simply by its cover, if your website has valuable content but your theme makes the content hard to read, hard to find, or generally inaccessible in any way, or your site is slow to load, not to mention downright ugly, you have probably lost that visitor. You may never have had that visitor to lose.

The theme accomplishes many things for your website. Generally, people think of the theme as the appearance of your site. It is the look and feel that gives your website that certain style or flair. It is the x-factor that gives your site a personality and makes your site stand out from the crowd. Your theme is all that; a picture really is worth a thousand words.

But this is simply the graphical aspect of your site; your theme is so much more than the cohesive marketing and branding façade. Your theme encompasses the entire user experience and more. It controls what content gets rendered, including any error conditions. Your theme converts your content and look and feel into the raw HTML that is delivered to the browser through its various templates.

In general, that is what this chapter is about: using your theme to structure and control the content delivery and the overall personality of your website. Your theme also has other functions, including user experience and search engine optimization, which are addressed in later chapters.

INSTALLING A THEME

Starting back in 2010, WordPress began shipping a new default theme each year. The Twenty Ten theme, released in—you guessed it, 2010—was the first to replace the venerable Kubrick theme that had been around since 2005. The Twenty Eleven and Twenty Twelve themes—both general purpose themes—came next. Automattic began specializing themes with the Twenty Thirteen theme. Twenty Thirteen was designed to focus on blogging and includes special formatting for all the different post formats. Twenty Fourteen is what is called a *magazine theme* and includes sliders and gratuitous use of featured images. At the time of this writing, planning for the Twenty Fifteen theme is currently underway. These default themes are all pretty solid themes to use for your site, but they are the defaults. That means you see them on many sites across the web. Being unique, or custom, may or may not be important to you or your goals, but for the sake of this chapter, pretend it is and you do not want to use a stock, out-of-the box theme.

How do you make WordPress use a new theme? First, you either have to find one you like or make one. Countless WordPress theme resources are available, and they all vary in quality. It is best to try some out and see how they work with your content and if they match the personality and branding you want your site to convey.

You have two simple ways to activate a new theme on your website. There is the traditional FTP installation and, as of WordPress 2.8, there is a new integrated theme browser and installer. The Theme Browser is limited in that it allows you to install themes only from the sanctioned WordPress Theme Directory on WordPress.org. This is not inherently bad because plenty of solid, good-looking themes are in the Theme Directory and they are all GPL licensed and free (two of the requirements for being listed in the Directory). However, the Directory is a limited market; heaps of other sites offer valuable WordPress themes, still of varying quality, both for free and for premiums. In order to install these non-Directory themes, you will have to use the FTP method.

FTP Installation

File Transfer Protocol, or FTP, is the old standby for transferring files from your local workstation to the server. If your host supports it, you should use a secure form of transfer, such as SFTP or SCP, to move the files, but the concepts here are similar.

Download a theme package from `http://wordpress.org/themes` that you would like to try to your local computer and unzip it to a local directory. If you have shell access on your server, you can unzip on the server to save in transfer time. Using your FTP client, connect to your web server. FTP or copy the files into your themes directory of your site. Your themes folder is located in `/example .com/wp-content/themes/`.

Once your theme files are on the server, log in to your site's WordPress Dashboard. Under Appearance, select Themes, then select your theme to preview it, and then activate it. Your website is now using the new theme. This is an instantaneous change for your visitors.

Theme Installer

The Themes menu reveals which themes are currently available to your WordPress installation. WordPress 2.8 introduced a new Theme Installer. Currently, the theme installer is offered as a new button on your Themes screen.

The Add New button allows the site administrator (or anyone else with proper permissions) to search and filter the online WordPress Theme Directory for existing published themes. All themes in the Directory are subject to certain conditions in order to be listed; most notably, they must be licensed to be GPL-compatible.

This new Theme Installer is pretty slick. You simply peruse the pre-selected menus or work the filters and search terms to browse the Directory. Browse the thumbnail screenshots until you find one you like. Then you can either click Install Now to make it available to your current WordPress installation or you can preview the theme in a larger format with a variety of HTML elements displayed for you to examine the CSS styling. Finally, you can read the theme details and user star ratings in the sidebar. Notice also that the sidebar includes Previous and Next buttons to actually browse the themes in the directory.

On a development system running Microsoft Windows 7 and WAMP, this just works, which is a little disconcerting. It is a permissions issue in your Webroot. Although this raises some concerns about what else could so easily be installed on the site, in this case, it is just a development machine, and the convenience of being able to test drive new themes outweighs the concerns.

Trying the Theme Installer on a production server for a WordPress site running on Ubuntu Linux may yield different results. After selecting an appropriate obnoxious theme to try out, the Theme Installer asks for FTP credentials to put the files on the server, in this case because the file security permissions on the production server are properly set for production and to not allow this sort of thing. Again, there is some concern about the actual security implications of giving out FTP credentials that are required to proceed. This is similar to how the WordPress core updates and plugin updates work.

> **NOTE** *See Chapter 13 on securing your WordPress installation for information about directory permissions.*

In short, the Theme Installer is really slick and convenient for development to test out new themes, but because of possible security implications, carefully consider its use in a production environment. The balance of convenience and security is often a difficult choice.

WHAT IS A THEME?

What actually makes up a theme? You have an idea of what themes do, but how do they do it and what is really involved? As previously mentioned, a theme does several things, including structuring your content and providing the personality of your website. This is done through a combination of files and file types. You will notice a mix of PHP files, CSS files, and JavaScript files in the theme. A good WordPress theme keeps the style, which is CSS, separate from the structure and logic, which make up the PHP files. Although there are always reasons for breaking the rules, striving to keep these separate will improve the maintainability and efficiency of your theme. Each theme has variations on these files and each theme's files are different.

Template Files

Template files are the meat of your theme. Template files are PHP code files that control what content is shown to your visitor. These files also generate the HTML for the browser to control how your content is shown. WordPress actually decides which template file to use based on the content requested. Certain template files are used for different tasks. At first glance, the quantity of template files in a theme can be daunting. Although each theme is different, some have only a couple of files, while others can be very complex. After you learn the different files involved in a theme, you will review the template hierarchy, which is the mechanism WordPress uses to determine which templates to use when.

This template hierarchy, covered later in this chapter, and the numerous types of template files available can be overwhelming when you are starting out on theme design, but you will develop an appreciation for the power of this setup. This flexibility allows for a huge amount of control over your site and what is delivered to the browser, which is the beauty of WordPress and definitely one of its strongest traits.

CSS

WordPress themes truly strive to separate content from style. A theme developer can ignore these guidelines and create a poorly divided theme, but a good theme developer does this well.

A theme must have at least one cascading style sheet. The primary style sheet for the theme must be named `style.css`. In addition, the first few lines of this style sheet file must adhere to certain guidelines. These specific requirements are covered later in this chapter in the "Style.css" section. WordPress uses this information to determine which themes are available to the WordPress site and to make them show up in the Themes screen. If the style sheet header is not coded to the standard expectation of WordPress, it will not show up in the Administration screen.

The style sheet is just what it sounds like. It is where you put all your CSS styles. How you structure it, or what you do with it, is entirely up to the theme developer. CSS development is both an art and a science and a whole topic worthy of its own discussion. This book does not cover the intricacies of CSS, but Wrox has a number of excellent CSS titles that can assist you on this topic.

Images and Assets

The theme probably includes some image files and other creative assets or JavaScript files such as jQuery plugins. These assets are used in your theme to give your website a special look and feel—the look *you* want. How these files are structured in your theme is up to you; generally, they are placed in a subfolder of the theme's main directory, such as img/, images/, assets/, or js/ depending on the file type. One of the nice things about themes being compartmentalized and packaged as they are is that the images can be referenced with relative paths from your CSS file.

In addition, these creative assets can be referenced from your template files using built-in WordPress functions such as bloginfo('stylesheet_directory'). This keeps the theme very portable, if done properly.

Plugins

As covered in Chapter 8, plugins contribute advanced functionality to a website. Some themes require specific plugins because the functionality is part of the theme's personality, or they are needed to achieve a certain purpose in the theme. These plugins may be packaged with the theme or may require separate downloads. All plugins reside in the plugin folder. So while plugins are not directly part of the theme, they may be required to make the theme behave as the theme creator intended.

CREATING YOUR OWN THEME

Now you know how to install and activate a theme on your site as well as what the different aspects of the theme are. It is time to take the next step and make your own theme. You can start a theme from scratch, but why not stand on the shoulders of giants and start with a theme that is similar to the look you want? Or, if you cannot find one, start with a theme framework where most of the heavy lifting is already done for you. There is no sense in reinventing the wheel, especially when you can use the power of open source software and start from working code.

Project Themes vs. Child Themes

Before diving in, let's talk about theme development strategies. Essentially, there are two classes of themes used in daily development. Which kind you choose to create depends on the amount of customization and the specific project you are producing. The goal of this section is not to show that one is better than the other; you, as the developer, will have to determine what meets your needs and goals.

Let's first discuss project themes. These are one-off themes, often a modification of an existing theme to meet the specific needs and design goals of a single project. These could be greenfield project themes built entirely from scratch or they could be a fork of an existing theme that you modify for the purpose of your project. In addition, there are starter themes that are designed to be the foundation for a project theme. Sometimes these themes are called *bare-bones* or *naked* themes. They intentionally have minimal styling and function as a blank slate with just enough to get you started. The reason to choose a project theme for your project is you have full flexibility to edit the PHP and template files. However, in doing so, you lose the ability to update the starter theme without steamrolling your customizations. Automattic's Underscores (_s) theme is an example of a starter theme available at `http://underscores.me/`.

A second option is what is called a *child theme*. A child theme inherits from a parent theme. That means you get all the functionality and styling of the parent theme and then override certain aspects with your child theme. A child theme can take two different approaches. If you have found a theme that mostly fits your project's needs and you can make cosmetic changes or minor functionality adjustments, then this is the way to go. The Genesis themes from StudioPress are examples of child themes. Check out StudioPress's themes at `http://www.studiopress.com/features`.

Another approach is to use a theme framework. Theme frameworks are much like starter themes for project themes, except they are designed to be parent themes to your child theme. Theme frameworks create the groundwork for your theme. You create a child theme of that theme framework with all your modifications. By using a child theme and a theme framework, you can make modifications to your child theme and retain the ability to update the framework as new revisions come out. Again, StudioPress's Genesis Theme is a prime example.

You may have put it together already that technically there is a third approach. You can develop your own theme framework or parent theme to use in your own projects first, and then use that to make your child theme for your specific project.

The strategy you take really depends on your project's goals and needs. To reiterate, every project is different and every developer is different. You will ultimately have to decide which method works for you and your project, and balance future maintainability with functionality requirements. In general, if you are modifying a theme, a child theme is the proper approach. However, in the real world (including but not limited to deadlines and budgets), project themes can offer the flexibility you need.

For the sake of going in-depth, you are going to explore a project theme in this chapter. With the basics of a project theme under your belt, you will be able to apply these principles to child themes as well. You will come back to child themes and theme frameworks at the end of this chapter for some more discussion.

What to Look for in a Starter Theme

Sometimes it is easiest to find a theme close to what you have in mind, use this as your starter theme, and modify it. At the minimum, you can add your own logo. Of course you have to pay special attention to the licensing on the theme. Conveniently, themes in the WordPress.org Theme Directory are all GPL themes, so you can modify and use them however you desire. Exploring a working theme is also an excellent learning method. Open Source Software, being part of the maker culture, encourages the breaking and fixing of things to learn how they work.

Things to consider when starting from a working theme include:

- ➤ Licensing on the original theme
- ➤ Code quality
- ➤ How much modification will be required
- ➤ Source artwork for the creative assets

You will want to make sure that you are permitted to change the source theme you are starting with. You will also want to review the code quality of the theme because you will be the one making the modifications going forward. Does the theme accomplish the same presentation goals as your site, template-wise; does it convey your data the way you want it conveyed? There is no point in starting with a theme that you have to completely retool; if this is the case, you would be better off starting with a theme framework and making a child theme. Does the theme have enough CSS hooks for you to style? Was search engine optimization (SEO) a consideration when the theme was developed? How much modification will be needed to meet your requirements and will you be happy with the end result? Finally, does the theme come with source art, like the original Photoshop document, for you to modify? If not, do you need it, or will you be able to re-create any assets you must have?

There are many considerations when developing a new project theme or modified child theme for either yourself or a client. The convenience of modifying a pre-built theme is quite a temptation when you need to get a site up and running and out the door quickly. In practice, many sites have been built this way, where a client could select a stock template with a few minor modifications needed to quickly launch a new site. The catch is when a site goes beyond these simple modifications and you are stuck with modifying a poorly built theme. For that reason, even if a client likes a particular theme preview, you may find it easier in the long run to rebuild a similar theme from scratch with a starter theme as the launching point.

CREATING YOUR OWN THEME: GETTING STARTED

Creating your own theme can be as simple or as complicated as you want it to be. Sometimes, you merely want to change a logo or a color and it is a basic process. Often, you are creating a theme from scratch to meet a certain need or condition, or solely to obtain a specific design look and feel. Whatever your motivations are, this section discusses the basics for getting a new theme and site design up quickly using the Twenty Fourteen theme as a foundation. This example uses Twenty Fourteen because it ships with WordPress, not because it is endorsed as the best choice for a starter theme. In practice, however, it has been used both as a starter theme and a parent theme for client projects. The Twenty Fourteen theme is a magazine theme, so it fills a certain niche for certain projects. While it is not widely considered a general purpose theme, the code quality is excellent and makes for a decent starting point.

In the next several sections, you will tour the Twenty Fourteen theme as an example of the elements of a working theme. You will also take this opportunity to modify the theme into your own version with your own customizations allowing you to leave the existing Twenty Fourteen theme intact. It should also be mentioned that the Twenty Fourteen theme uses HTML5 elements and an HTML5 shim. HTML5 is covered in more detail in Chapter 12, but just be forewarned that while using HTML5 is becoming more and more commonplace every day, it is still on the newer edge of web technology and all browsers may not support it. It all depends on which browser you choose, or are forced, to support.

Essential File: Style.css

The `style.css` file is what WordPress uses to reference your theme, and this file is required for your theme to work. You could create a new theme with only a style sheet and `index.php` template file, although the index file can be empty. Using the power of WordPress's theme hierarchy, WordPress automatically substitutes missing templates if your new theme does not have them. More on that later, but understand that a customized style sheet is what allows you to get started creating your own theme.

> **NOTE** *In practice, a* `style.css` *file is all you need to create a new theme. See the section "Theme Hierarchy and Child Themes" later in the chapter.*

When creating your own `styles.css` for your new theme, the first few lines are absolutely critical. These lines provide information to WordPress to use in the Theme screens and further reference your theme in the core. Your first few lines should read as follows (substitute your information, of course):

```
/*
Theme Name: My Theme
Theme URI: http://mirmillo.com/mytheme
Author: The Professional WordPress team
Author URI: http://mirmillo.com/
Description: Theme for my new site.  Based on Twenty Fourteen
Version: 1.0
License: GNU General Public License v2 or later
License URI: http://www.gnu.org/licenses/gpl-2.0.html
Tags: black, green, white, light, dark, two-columns, three-columns,
 left-sidebar, right-sidebar, fixed-layout, responsive-layout,
 custom-background, custom-header, custom-menu, editor-style,
 featured-images, flexible-header, full-width-template, microformats,
 post-formats, rtl-language-support, sticky-post, theme-options,
 translation-ready, accessibility-ready
Text Domain: twentyfourteen
*/
```

The information here is pretty self-explanatory. There is an additional optional field for theme hierarchy, covered later in the chapter. Make sure your theme name is unique to your installation. If you intend to release your theme for public use, either for free or for a premium, you should try to come up with a unique name to reduce naming collisions in the directory and other installations. In addition, if you are deriving your theme from another theme, license permitting of course, you should uphold the license and copyright information from the original theme. Once you have addressed this required information for WordPress, the remainder of the file is traditional CSS and subject to the rules and structure imposed as such.

To reiterate, in this example, you are making a copy of the Twenty Fourteen theme and making it your own. This is not a child theme process. Child theme functionality will be covered later. In some cases, the workflow fits better if a new theme is created by copying and renaming the starter theme to a new folder and revising the `style.css` to reflect the new project. This technique has pros and cons, but it works well for some teams because the foundation theme does not change often enough to warrant more complex methodologies. Plus, when you have a theme in production, you do not want a change to the parent theme to cause a cascading rendering issue in your successfully deployed site. Creating a copy and making a working theme in this new directory removes the dependency on future browser rendering testing, which is a time- and human-intensive procedure—that is, no one has automated this procedure yet. In the event that there is a substantial change to the parent theme, changes can be ported to the derivative themes on a case-by-case basis and tested as needed. Making a copy of the starter theme also enables you to create a handcrafted CSS file by modifying the actual theme files rather than overriding the styles and carrying that additional byte baggage.

Moving forward, CSS rules are written out in the `style.css` file to turn your minimal layout into the professionally designed theme you are creating. Because you are working on your own copy of Twenty Fourteen, a fork of it, so to speak, you can edit your own theme's style sheet directly. CSS coding is outside the scope of this book and if done well, is an art and skill. Again, Wrox has several great books on working with CSS.

Showing Your Content: Index.php

When creating your theme, you often have a chicken-and-egg problem. Maybe you are lucky and you know exactly what content is going to be published on your WordPress site, and exactly how it is going to be structured. Maybe you even know exactly how the final theme is going to look, or you have had a professional designer create some mock-ups for you. But odds are, your site is going to grow organically, and to see how the design, and therefore the style sheet, is going to play out, you need to have some content to display.

> **NOTE** *You can use various stock content files to import into your site and work through all the styles, or you can start building your site. Theme Unit Tests and stock content files are covered in Chapter 3.*

The `index.php` file is the default template of your site. WordPress has a built-in decision engine that decides which type of information your visitor is requesting and then determines if there is a template file available for that information type. This hierarchy is covered later in the chapter, but the `index.php` template is the default, or template of last resort. If WordPress does not determine that there is a more specific template to use, `index.php` is it.

Usually, the `index.php` file contains your standard loop. This is a traditional blog format where the posts are displayed in reverse chronological order. For example, the following is some of the code from Twenty Fourteen's index file:

```php
<?php
  if ( have_posts() ) :
    // Start the Loop.
    while ( have_posts() ) : the_post();
```

```
        /*
         * Include the post format-specific template for the content.
         * If you want to use this in a child theme, then include a file called
         * called content-___.php (where ___ is the post format) and that will be
         * used instead.
         */
        get_template_part( 'content', get_post_format() );

    endwhile;
    // Previous/next post navigation.
    twentyfourteen_paging_nav();

else :
    // If no content, include the "No posts found" template.
    get_template_part( 'content', 'none' );
endif;
?>
```

As covered in Chapter 5, the loop is really the heart of WordPress. It is the most important concept to grasp because this is how your content is selected and ordered for publishing. You may look at the preceding code snippet and notice that the loop is really a small part of the code and that the content of the posts is not even being rendered in HTML.

And you would be correct. The preceding snippet uses the `get_template_part()` function, which was introduced in WordPress 3.0. This is a WordPress function that is very similar to PHP's `include()` and `require()` functions, but it is more powerful because it is WordPress-specific. The `get_template_part()` function allows the theme developer to pull out specific code components for reuse, or for replacing in child themes.

In the preceding example, WordPress is looking for a specific PHP file to include as the rendering of the posts in the HTML. This is actually a fairly complex example because it uses the `get_post_format()` function to fill in the second parameter of the include. This function will do exactly what it says and return the format of the post. Post formats are covered a little later in this chapter. For the sake of this example, just know that if the post were marked as an image, this function would return `image`, or if it were published as a traditional post or marked as standard in the Post screen, it would return "false."

The `get_template_part()` function will look for the template file in the current theme directory, first as the specific version using the second parameter and then for the generic version ignoring the second parameter. That is, if you use the following code in your theme:

```
<?php get_template_part( 'content', 'link' ); ?>
```

WordPress will first look for a file named `content-link.php` in your theme folder and, if it cannot find that file, will settle for `content.php`. If you are creating a child theme and neither of the preceding files is found, WordPress will continue the search in the parent theme folder.

In the Twenty Fourteen example, the `get_post_format()` function is performing as a switch to pull in the desired content template for the appropriate post format. You will notice in the Twenty Fourteen theme that there are many content templates—one for each post format type. This allows the theme developer to control how the different post formats are rendered in the browser.

Another advantage of this tactic is breaking your code into smaller, manageable portions. You will find this compartmentalization makes it easier to debug should you develop any problems with future changes, or need to add new functionality.

Showing Your Content in Different Ways: Index.php

The `index.php` file is really the most important template file in your theme. Although you cannot have an active theme in WordPress without `styles.css`—because that is how WordPress knows you have the theme available—`index.php` does the heavy lifting.

In the early days of WordPress, the index template was the only template. The whole theme was just this one file, and it was really just the loop. That worked fine for WordPress when you used it as a traditional blog and this bloggy look is probably why WordPress is occasionally still derided as a blog engine.

Hopefully you are reading this book because you know WordPress can be so much more, or if you did not know, you are realizing it now. Your index template is very important; this cannot be stressed enough. It is the template of last resort that WordPress will use when it cannot find a more specific one to use (see the section, "Template Hierarchy," later in the chapter.)

Nevertheless, your index file does not have to be a single loop showing your most recent posts. That is very traditional, and may work well for your site, but you can branch out. Your index file can be structured in so many different ways that it is truly limitless. It could contain multiple different loops from different tags or categories, or it could contain no loops at all. The index template could function as your error page, where you have more specific templates for every other piece of content in your site.

CREATING YOUR OWN THEME: DRY

As just discussed, these are the basics; WordPress requires a `style.css` file with properly formatted header information, and a theme must have an `index.php` template. Now you want to expand your theme to use more template files and capitalize on the robust theme engine found in WordPress.

A good developer knows that you do not want to repeat code in multiple places; it is a bad design and gives your code one of those nasty smells. (You knew that right?) The code smell is called Don't Repeat Yourself (DRY) and is, in fact, one of the easiest smells to get a whiff of and avoid. When you find yourself tempted to cut and paste a code block from one template to another, that should be your first whiff. Here is your opportunity to break out your templates into reusable parts. There are three obvious places where you can do this because you will reuse these components on nearly all pages on your site to give it that cohesive look and feel and structure. The header, the footer, and the sidebar information is essentially the same on all pages. You will also learn how to tweak these included files with additional logic to handle design exceptions.

Header.php

You may think this file is a misnamed, but it is the standard name of this file that WordPress looks for. The `header.php` file includes everything at the top of your rendered page, up to the content area. This can be confusing because a properly formatted HTML document includes its own <head> information, which has its own special requirements. This header.php template file includes the HTML head, but it also includes the start of the HTML document and usually includes the site logo and navigation, assuming you are using an across-the-top horizontal navigation scheme. It can also include any additional elements at the top of your page, such as secondary navigation or a search area.

Because this file includes so much more than the HTML header, the tendency is to take the printing term and call this area the *nameplate*, as in the nameplate of a newspaper or magazine. However, stick with tradition and leave the file name header.php in order to remain compatible with the built-in functionality of WordPress.

When creating your header template file, a very important WordPress function must be included: wp_head(). This is a hook for WordPress to be able to attach certain functionality into your site header and is also used by plugins.

The wp_head() function is dropped in your HTML <head> node and is critical to the long-term compatibility and functionality of your theme so make sure this is included.

Now that you have broken out the nameplate section of your pages into the separate header.php template, if you were building a theme complete from scratch you would need to adjust your index .php file to include it. You could use the traditional PHP include or require family of functions, but the WordPress core functionality has a handy function to get around the theme paths. This is similar to the get_template_part() function discussed earlier, but there is a specific function for the header template. At the top of your index.php (and subsequent template files discussed later) simply add the following code:

```php
<?php
    get_header();
?>
```

This function automatically includes the filename header.php from the current theme's directory into the current file for rendering. This function does not have any additional functionality over a PHP include besides determining the correct include path for you, but it is much more readable when working on a theme.

Optionally, you could split out additional components from your header.php file and include them back in with PHP includes. Occasionally, if a site has a particularly long or complex global navigation, it is broken out for inclusion. In practice, working on smaller files is easier for editing because each template file has a specific function and reduces the complexity of debugging.

> **NOTE** *In a past life, one of the authors of this book was called in to work on a web application where the entire application was created in a single file and the functionality was handled by triggering specific functions. Although the functions were nicely broken out, any time the application had to be debugged, the error messages were nearly meaningless. Although the line number would change (and skyrocket into the multiple thousands) they all occurred in* index.php *and inevitably the whole application had to be traced to determine what happened.*

> *Imagine how much easier it would be to troubleshoot a problem on the application if the error message indicated that the error took place in a 100-line navigation file, rather than a 10,000-line complete application file.*
>
> *Everyone writes bad code in his or her career, and certainly we (the authors) are no exception, although none of us wrote this atrocity. What we are saying is this: Do yourself a favor and break code into smaller, manageable files whenever possible.*

Footer.php

In the same vein as the `header.php` file, everything below your content area should be separated out into a footer file. The nature of footer files has changed in recent years. Historically, footers have been reserved for the copyright and contact information, but the current web trend is to use this real estate to include additional navigation options and information relevant to your site. Most modern themes, including Twenty Fourteen, include widget areas in the footer for customizable content. Widget areas are discussed later in this chapter. What you put in your footer is up to you, but because it remains by and large the same on every page, it is a prime candidate for breaking out into a separate include.

Again, make sure you incorporate the `wp_foot()` function into your footer template. This function allows WordPress to inject any necessary information from your active plugins. Make sure this function is invoked before your `</body></html>` closing tags.

Similar to the way your header template is included, WordPress offers the same functionality for your footer information with its own special include function. At the bottom of your template files, add the following code:

```php
<?php
    get_footer();
?>
```

Sidebar.php

Another candidate for breaking out is the sidebar, which is everything to the right or left of your content. Your sidebar could include the navigation of your site, if you have elected a vertical navigation scheme, or perhaps less important supporting information for your site content.

The Twenty Fourteen theme includes both a right or left sidebar using the `sidebar.php`, `sidebar-content.php` and `sidebar-footer.php` files. The Twenty Eleven theme allows for both a right and left sidebar using the same `sidebar.php` template and places it with CSS. However, you could have multiple sidebar files for each column or specific sidebars for different pages, depending on your design.

You need to consider a number of different issues when working with sidebars. You have to decide first how many sidebars you are going to have. Second, you have to decide if they are going to be static sidebars, widgetized sidebars, or a hybrid. Finally, you have to determine how the HTML is structured so that you can make the CSS put the sidebars in the correct spots. Then you have to test in your target browsers and in all likelihood start over. Such is the life of the web developer.

As mentioned, the Twenty Eleven theme's stock sidebars are both the same file, whether on the right or left, and are fully widgetized. Twenty Fourteen also has two sidebars, but using separate template files. These sidebars are also widgetized. Widgetized sidebars enable you to sketch up a site with relative ease and use the WordPress Administration screen to place widgets as needed.

In your template files, place the following code to include the `sidebar.php` file:

```php
<?php get_sidebar(); ?>
```

Sometimes having both sidebars in the same file does not pan out in the design, or more likely, the CSS. Or, you have broken out the sidebars into individual files for each sidebar location, in the Twenty Fourteen theme. For whatever reason, you can create two sidebar files for the traditional left and right places. For example,

```php
<?php
    get_sidebar('right');
?>
```

gets the file named `sidebar-right.php`, as indicated in the parameter of the function call, and includes it in the appropriate place. Again, this is similar to the `get_template_part()` function but is specifically designed for sidebars and is much more readable in the code. In the Twenty Fourteen theme, you see this as

```php
<?php
    get_sidebar('content');
?>
```

to include the right-hand content sidebar.

More advanced theme frameworks have multiple sidebars that deviate from the common notion that a sidebar is only vertical space on the left and right of your content. Some of these theme frameworks have what are essentially sidebars above, below, and even in the middle of the post loops. Having multiple widgetized areas like this transfers some power to the site administrator who can now place WordPress widgets all over the layout of the page. Twenty Fourteen does this with footer area sidebars, which is now pretty common among theme developers.

An important consideration when working with sidebars is keeping the balance between what portions are widgetized—meaning they can be controlled and managed by the content creator in the Administration screens—and what portions are hard-coded in PHP into the template file. Widgets can be very powerful, especially with many of the plugins that are available. But there are also cases where PHP code in the template file will get the job done and the content does not need to be updated by the administrator or is using built-in WordPress functionality to keep itself updated. Keeping this balance right is a developer decision.

Deviations from the Norm: Conditional Tags

You have been a good developer and broken out all your repeating code snippets into their own templates or inclusion files. Good job, but the marketing director just called, and even though the site is almost done, and he signed off on the design, he forgot to tell you that all the pages and posts in the Ponies category are supposed to have a pretty rainbow in the nameplate next to the site's logo. Personal taste aside, this sucks, because you just made all the `header.php` files the same, and now only a handful of them need some special consideration.

As with all things open source, there are many ways to handle this situation. You could probably handle such a simple example with some well-crafted CSS and the theme's body class alone. Alternatively, you could create a whole category template file (discussed later) to style just this category. But because you are dealing with only a tiny element, it seems like overkill to create a whole new template file.

But wait—all is not lost. WordPress developers have had to deal with marketing directors before and knew this type of situation would come up eventually, which is why they included conditional tags. WordPress has many conditional tags built in, and covering each one is outside the scope of this book, not to mention particularly boring. But rest assured—these conditional tags exist and can address specific needs such as what type of page is being viewed, or the meta information about the content on the page.

To appease the marketing director, you might include something like this in the `header.php` file:

```
<header id="masthead" class="site-header" role="banner">
  <div class="header-main">
    <h1 class="site-title">
      <a href="<?php echo esc_url( home_url( '/' ) ); ?>"
      rel="home"><?php bloginfo( 'name' ); ?>
      </a>
    </h1>
     if (is_category('Ponies')) { ?>
        // overlay a pretty rainbow on the logo for the ponies category
        <img id="rainbow"
          src="<?php bloginfo('template_directory');?>/img/rainbow.png"
          alt="OMG! Ponies! " />
      <?php } ?>
  ...
</header>
```

Now, any time the category of the content of the current page is in the Ponies category, your header also includes the `rainbow.png`. With PNG's alpha transparency, it actually turns out nicely. This example only works for the category pages and not for the individual single-post pages in the Ponies category.

CREATING YOUR OWN THEME: CONTENT DISPLAY

A good theme enhances the content on your site. Not only is it visually appealing, suitable for the nature of the site, and brand appropriate, but the theme should also structure the content properly. WordPress has a variety of different templates and functionality to meet the needs of every site type. The challenge here is to uncover the best combination of template files to include in order to achieve the optimal organization of your content. Not all themes need to have every template file type, and most do not; it is best to mix and match templates to meet your needs.

Customizing Your Homepage: Front-Page.php

Homepage—who uses that term anymore? It sounds so 1990s, but what else should you call it? This section covers the first page on your site when a visitor goes to your root URL. Apache users know that the index page of your site, the homepage if you will, is called "index." It is usually called "default" on a Microsoft IIS server. The WordPress Dashboard refers to this as the front page; you can run with it for consistency's sake.

A theme should always have an `index.php` template file because after all else, `index.php` is the template of last resort. What if want your front page to have a special layout, perhaps one that features something about your site—product pages, for example? You do not want to mess with your `index.php` layout because you do not want to reinvent your entire theme just to accommodate this one special layout.

Plugins and other tricks are available to handle this scenario; in fact, you can even use the WordPress Administration screen to set a static front page that is one of your existing published pages. But in this case, you are talking about a custom layout or HTML rendering, not a traditional page. The easiest way is to use the built-in template hierarchy and set a special front page by using a `front-page.php` template.

There are actually two template files that can function as your front page: `front-page.php` or `home.php`. In some older themes and even in the first edition of this book, `home.php` was the only option. With WordPress 3.0, `front-page.php` became the preferred template file name for the front page. There is a little more involved here, depending on how you set your reading preferences in the Dashboard. Later in this chapter, you will see the template hierarchy and how these two templates actually rank.

Creating a special layout, and therefore template file, for your front page is useful when your front page is unique. By and large, creating a unique front page is a marketing tool. Some reasons for creating a unique front page include:

➤ Featuring or showcasing a product or service

➤ Featuring or showcasing other portions of your website

➤ Driving traffic to a certain portion of your site

➤ Explanatory steps of the processes involved with your product

➤ Delineating tiered levels of service that you provide

Take a look at the basic example of how this looks using the Twenty Fourteen theme in Figure 9-1, where the front page is showcasing products or services that the website is marketing. These products would have their own supporting pages or posts in your site. Your front page has a nice image showcase front and center with links to the individual pages. Twenty Fourteen uses jQuery to enhance this showcase and rotate through the images. Alternatively, you could use a different JavaScript toolkit or Adobe Flash, but jQuery is already included with WordPress and, frankly, it rocks, so why not use that. The bottom portion of the layout will include a recent news section.

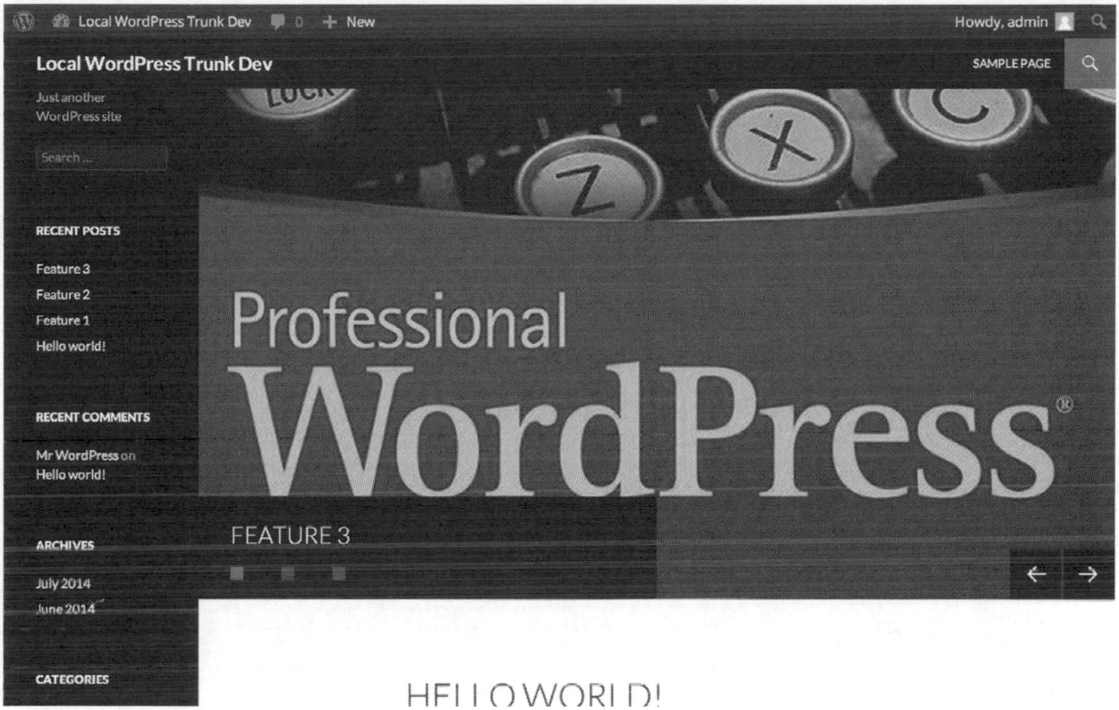

FIGURE 9-1: An index page slider can make your front page look unique.

While we accomplished this look with the Twenty Fourteen theme, interestingly enough none of the default themes from Automattic actually use this template file. Instead, they all utilize conditional tags as discussed in the previous section. If you look at the index.php template from Twenty Fourteen you will see:

```php
<?php
  if ( is_front_page() && twentyfourteen_has_featured_posts() ) {
    // Include the featured content template.
    get_template_part( 'featured-content' );
  }
?>
```

which accomplishes the slideshow functionality. This works, but because this section is about the front-page.php template file, let's look at how you accomplish something similar using a standalone file.

For this example, you will add a front-page.php template to the Twenty Eleven theme. Having two sets of content, the showcase slides and the news, is going to involve multiple loops. You will use the first loop to create the content for the showcase. This loop will pull posts from a specific category or a custom post type. That way, the site admin can add and remove content from the showcase as needed, without visiting the code at all. Of course there will be certain design restrictions, such as image size and format and possibly certain conventions that must be followed in the post, but the capability to change this information in the WordPress Dashboard screens is a very powerful tool.

The *showcase loop*, sometimes called *slideshows*, could look something like this:

```php
<div id="showcase">
  <?php
  global $post;
  $args = array(
    'post_type' =>'slides',
    'numberposts' => -1,
    'orderby' => 'rand'
    );
  $slider_posts = get_posts($args);
  // show showcase only if slides exist
  if($slider_posts) {
    foreach($slider_posts as $post) : setup_postdata($post);
      // get image
      $thumbnail = wp_get_attachment_image_src(get_post_thumbnail_id(),
        'home-slide');
      if ($thumbnail[1] == "600" && $thumbnail[2] == "160") {
      //checking thumbnail dimensions in css ?>
        <div id="feature-<?php echo $post->ID; ?>" class="slide">
          <a href="<?php the_permalink(); ?>" title="<?php the_title(); ?>">
          <img src="<?php echo $thumbnail[0]; ?>" title="<?php the_title(); ?>" />
          </a>
        </div>
      <?php } ?>
    <?php endforeach; ?>
    <?php wp_reset_postdata(); ?>
  <?php } ?>
</div>
```

> **NOTE** *In this example, you are using custom post types, which are covered in Chapter 7.*

This creates an HTML rendering, as shown in Figure 9-2, using the Twenty Eleven theme.

Take a look at what is happening here. The whole showcase loop is wrapped in a `<div>` with an ID of showcase. This is for the jQuery to hook onto later. In the PHP code, you are creating a custom query for the loop. The query is looking for custom post types called slides, which you would have previously established in the themes functions.php file and also set up in the WordPress Dashboard. This query is pulling all the slides from the custom post type and returning them in random order. The loop then proceeds to create `<div>` elements, each with a unique ID, again for jQuery and CSS hooks. The custom post type is set up to use the WordPress featured image as the slide content. This allows the site maintainer to upload the slide image that, in turn, links to a special landing page with more information in the post body. The preceding code snippet will only display the slide graphic if it is set to the specific dimensions, 600px wide by 160px tall in this case. Finally, countless jQuery plugins are available that can turn this now unwieldy block of content on your page into a very elegant slideshow. The bottom section could be a traditional loop similar to the index.php template stock loop.

FIGURE 9-2: An index page slider using the front-page.php template

Also, this is still not the only way to get this functionality. As of WordPress 2.1, you can control what is shown on your front page and set it to any static page you have created and then create a special page template to accomplish the previously described design decisions. You can also build multiple loops—one using posts in a category for the slides, the other loop excluding the category for the news. This is how you used to do it. Again, how you choose to skin this cat is one of those choices you have to make as a developer as you balance the needs of your client with the ease of maintenance for your developers.

Show Your Older Posts by Date: Archive.php

Eventually, if you are diligent, your site will have older content. And if you are really industrious you will be able to do those fun "One year ago on my site I told you about X" posts. Eventually, you may have copious amounts of content, so much that it is not feasible or appealing to show it all on the front page. That is, if content is being generated on a regular schedule, there will come a point in time when you will want to refer to something that is no longer on the front page or in the Recent Posts lists; this is the time when you need to delve into the vault of past content.

This is where the `archive.php` template steps in. You have many ways to present your older content. Harkening back to WordPress's blogging origins, the most obvious method is to continue in reverse chronological order of your posts.

If you do not have an archive template, WordPress simply uses your index template to show the older posts. The Twenty Fourteen theme has an interesting take on the `archive.php` template that dates back to some of the original starter themes such as the Sandbox theme. This approach is very flexible and creates date-based format visuals for the archives. Consider this code from the Twenty Fourteen `archive.php` template:

```php
<h1 class="page-title">
<?php
if ( is_day() ) :
  printf( __( 'Daily Archives: %s', 'twentyfourteen' ), get_the_date() );
elseif ( is_month() ) :
  printf( __( 'Monthly Archives: %s', 'twentyfourteen' ), get_the_date(
    _x( 'F Y', 'monthly archives date format',
    'twentyfourteen' ) ) );
elseif ( is_year() ) :
  printf( __( 'Yearly Archives: %s', 'twentyfourteen' ), get_the_date(
    _x( 'Y', 'yearly archives date format',
    'twentyfourteen' ) ) );
else :
  _e( 'Archives', 'twentyfourteen' );
endif;
?>
</h1>
```

This code block shows how the theme's archive template displays a unique header depending on whether the visitor is looking at the archived posts for a day, a month, or a whole year, or traversing by conventional pagination.

Except for the fact that WordPress is inherently date-based, the specific archive template is not all that important. Although having the date information is useful when determining how recent certain information is, in reality, do you ever go back and look for posts published in May of 2007? More likely, you are looking for posts on a certain topic or filed in a particular category or topic.

Showing Only One Category: Category.php

Enter the category template. The `category.php` template creates a loop of posts from only a specific category. The category template is invoked when a visitor hits a specific URL with the category name in it. This could be something like `http://example.com/category/zombies`. In the `category.php` template, WordPress has already determined that your visitor is looking for posts in the particular category request, so the default loop automatically makes this query for you, no special interaction required.

When you use this template, you can generically display category posts and information; this is exactly how the Twenty Fourteen theme is set up. For example, the Twenty Fourteen theme places a header and optional category explanation information pulled from the category description, if it is available:

```
<header class="archive-header">
  <h1 class="archive-title">
    <?php printf( __( 'Category Archives: %s', 'twentyfourteen' ),
     single_cat_title( '', false ) ); ?>
  </h1>

<?php
  // Show an optional term description.
  $term_description = term_description();
  if ( ! empty( $term_description ) ) :
    printf( '<div class="taxonomy-description">%s</div>', $term_description );
  endif;
?>
</header>
```

This covers the default category case, which is a nice default fallback template to have. But what if you want to make each category template have a unique look—for example, a color scheme or an icon?

Assume your pony-and-rainbow–fascinated marketing director now wants a Zombie category. Instead of using conditional tags, you can make a specific category template. Following the template hierarchy, WordPress will look to see if there exists a category template that is specific to the category requested in the URL. If you have not noticed yet, WordPress works from most specific to least specific until it finds the proper template. WordPress will select the most specific template for the type of information requested and work toward the more generic templates until it defaults to the index.php template. This is a critical aspect to learn when deciding on your theme templates, and it is something you will review again.

For the marketing director, you can make a category-3.php template, for example, because the Zombies category has an ID of 3.

The easiest way to find a category ID number is to hover over the category name in the Edit Category screen and look in the status bar at the bottom of the browser window, as shown in Figure 9-3.

There is a little bit of a chicken-and-egg problem when you want to create a category template for a specific category. In order to name the template file correctly, you must create the category first to get the category ID.

Lucky for you, there is also another way. Since WordPress 2.9, users have been able to make category templates that use the slug. And the slug template file is preferred by WordPress over the ID-based one. So to avoid the chicken-and-egg problem, you can create the category first and assign it a slug, in this case zombies. If you have this planned out ahead of time, you can make a category template file called category-zombies.php and be off to the races.

These specific category templates work exactly the same as the generic category templates and pull the posts for that category automatically. Technically, it works the other way around: WordPress already knows which posts it is going to show you; it is just determining how to show them to you. What you are gaining with using a specific category template is the flexibility to style each category individually.

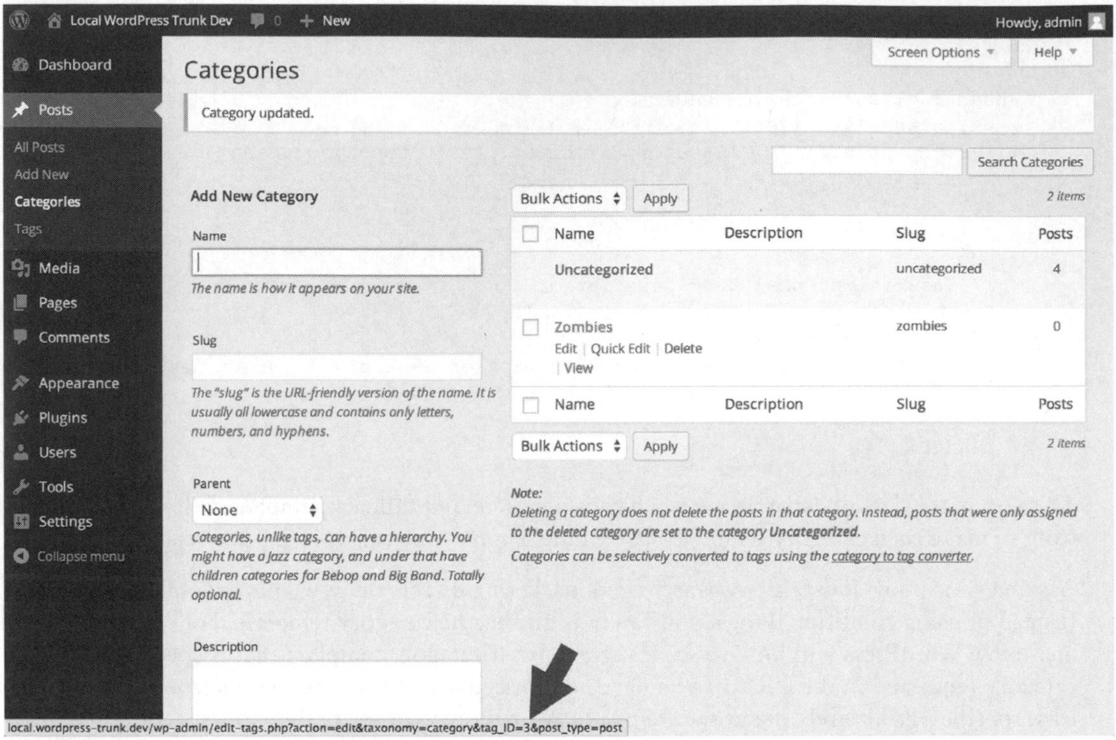

FIGURE 9-3: Hover over the category name in the Category Screen to see the category ID in the status bar.

You have probably noticed by now that with WordPress there is always more than one way to do something. In the simple example of the marketing director, you can solve his problem with conditional tags or category-specific templates, or most likely, you can meet his requirements by using CSS because most themes have rich CSS hooks. But the extensibility of this feature is the killer aspect. Just knowing that WordPress has the feature built in will save you one day.

Show Posts of a Specific Tag: Tag.php

The tag.php template functions nearly identically to the category.php template. It is invoked when a visitor requests a specific tag. This template is only beneficial if you are actively tagging the content on your site. Most likely, you are assigning categories to content because that is a natural human organization structure, but tagging is not as clear-cut and often feels like an additional step.

Nevertheless, if you are diligent in tagging content, a tag template is a nice addition to your layouts and can be beneficial to cross-pollinate posts with related content; in the Twenty Fourteen slideshow, tagging is what allocates specific posts for the slideshow. When this template is called, the loop automatically fills with posts of a particular tag for rendering.

> **NOTE** *See Chapter 5 for a more in-depth look at how the loop actually works.*

Likewise, you can create a template for a specific tag. As with categories, you can use either the tag's ID or slug to make the template file. If you want a special template for the Zombies tag, you use the slug of the tag to create a new template titled `tag-zombies.php`. You need to verify the tag's slug on the Tags screen in the Dashboard.

Using the category and tag templates may not be the way you envisioned your content being viewed, especially if you are using WordPress more as a content management system. However, simply including these templates delivers free functionality and customizability from the WordPress core. These templates enable your visitors to explore your content in different ways and perhaps add a little stickiness to your site because your content is viewed in new and interesting ways. Categories and tags group related content and using these templates create an organic presentation for discovery of your site.

Do not brush these templates off as simply reverse chronological listings of related content, such as an archives page. Envision creative ways to present your data; because you have visitors who are interested in at least some of your content, why not expose them to related items?

Other Archival Templates

With that in mind, WordPress's archival templates really bloomed recently. In addition to the templates discussed previously, you can also create special archive templates for custom taxonomies or custom post types. Although these templates fall in the archival template hierarchy, you can really think of any of these views as just groupings on a certain aspect of the content.

If you have custom post types set up in your theme or content, as you did with the slides in the showcase example previously in this chapter, you can have custom archive page templates for those, too. This template file has a slightly different naming convention than the rest. For the slides, you would create a template file called `archive-slides.php` where *slides* is the custom post type's name.

Likewise, if you are employing custom taxonomies in your theme, you can make custom archive templates for both the taxonomy and the specific term. WordPress will choose the most specific template file it can, so the term templates will be chosen before the general taxonomy templates.

> **NOTE** *Custom post types and custom taxonomies were covered in depth in Chapter 7.*

How to Show a Single Post: Single.php

You have set the bait with a great post headline, something witty and engaging. After the nibble, you set the hook with your excerpt of the post, and now you caught the visitor. He has clicked through to read the rest of the article.

The `single.php` template view is most likely the landing page on your site when a visitor arrives via a search engine. Assuming you have great content, the search engine will rank the explanatory page of your site higher than the index page, which usually only lists the excerpt. Therefore, it is best to invest some time in this template because it is very commonly viewed, perhaps the second most used template after your index page template. Enhancing this template with related posts and other teaser content only increases the possibility of enticing a visitor to further explore your site, bookmark it, subscribe to your feeds, or best of all, link back to you. All of these events increase your search engine respectability.

You can display the full content of a single post with the `single.php` template file. WordPress has decided that the visitor has requested the full content of a single post; thus this template does not need to contain a loop, but simply a call to the `the_post()` function to get the data from the database. If you look at the Twenty Fourteen theme, you will notice that the `single.php` template does, in fact, use a loop and the `get_content_part()` function to maintain consistency with the other templates, but because only one post is being shown, this is superfluous.

If you have a very long post, you can break it up among several pages by using the built-in WordPress functionality or special plugins. Internet users have very mixed feelings on this. Although general guidelines and studies have shown certain line lengths and content lengths improve readability, some vocal visitors detest the load time wait when paginating. This is a design choice based on your content type and site design.

Adding links that are related to this post is a great way to entice visitors to explore your site more. Several plugins add related content to the bottom of a single post page or scan your content for keywords and links. In practice, you will have to try these out and see how they work with your site.

Alternatively, the poor man's solution is to add a simple category or tag loop to grab some related-topic posts to the bottom of the page. It could be something as simple as this:

```
<h2>Other posts in this category</h2>
<ul id="related">
  <?php
  $category = get_the_category();
  $my_query = new WP_Query("category_name=".$category[0]->name."
      &showposts=5&orderby=rand");
  while ($my_query->have_posts()) : $my_query->the_post();
    echo '<li><a href="'. $post->permalink.'">"' . $post->post_title .'"</a>
          </li>';
  endwhile;
  ?>
</ul>
```

Here you are taking five random posts from the first category of the current post. It is not the most sophisticated method, but it is a simple way to show some related content links on the single post view. Another option is to show additional posts by the same author:

```
<h2>Other posts by this author</h2>
<ul id="related">
  <?php
  $author = get_the_author_meta('id');
  $my_query = new WP_Query("author=".$author&posts_per_page=5&orderby=rand");
```

```
    while ($my_query->have_posts()) : $my_query->the_post();
      echo '<li><a href="'. $post->permalink.'">"' . $post->post_title .'"</a>
          </li>';
    endwhile;
    ?>
</ul>
```

While having a single `single.php` template will suffice for most sites, WordPress does offer some more customizability for handling the individual custom post types. Using the slideshow showcase example from before, instead of rendering the clicked through landing page using `single.php`, you could create a special `single-slide.php` template. This template might leverage the featured image or other custom fields to make it more enticing or actionable.

Display a Page: Page.php

When you are using WordPress as a content management system, you have to make some decisions such as whether to use pages or posts. This is like cats or dogs—people have strong feelings about each. For the most part, this chapter has been talking about posts and custom post types.

When working with a client, you generally create hybrid designs that use both pages and posts. Posts are used for temporal-based items, such as news and promotions, whereas pages are used for static information that does not change very often, such as products or services. Product pages are then augmented with related posts. This gives the client the benefit of using the posts facets of the website to drive traffic to the static product pages. This is a very common website strategy.

The `page.php` template works essentially the same as the single post template. There is no loop—unless you have created a special page template, but technically that is a different template file—only the call to `the_post()`. Yes, this is the same function as in `single.php`. WordPress considers the posts and pages to be fundamentally the same type of content and `the_post()` gathers the content from the database.

As with previous examples, you can also have specific page templates for specific pages based on the ID of the page or the page's slug. These follow the same pattern as before. In addition, you can also have custom page templates that you can assign to any page on your site, but you will cover this in more depth later in this chapter.

Display Post Attachments: Attachment.php

To be honest, we (the authors) do not think we have ever used these template files in a production website intentionally. First introduced with WordPress 2.5, `image.php` was a special template just for showing—you guessed it—images from your gallery. Since then, this branch of the template hierarchy has grown and generalized to show any of the attachments you might add to a post based on MIME type. Many themes do not even have this set of templates; the Twenty Fourteen theme includes an `image.php` but not an `attachment.php` template. In essence, this template works very similarly to `single.php`, so much so that `single.php` is the next default if this template does not exist in your theme.

The most common use for this type is to create an `image.php` template. This template provides a special display strictly for viewing your media gallery. A gallery can contain many different types of media; that is, it is not limited to images. This template will be called for any media item, unless there is a more specific match, and usually includes a description of the media and comment functionality. A great use of this template file would be for a portfolio site, such as a photography studio or another artistic collection. Again, this template functions nearly identically to the single post template, with slight variation to render an image rather than a paragraph.

Similarly, template types can be used with media types other than images. You could create templates for video, audio, or applications; however, these would probably be very specific use cases, and in the wild you would rarely see or need these templates unless you were creating a specific niche website.

Display Custom Post Types

We touched on this briefly during the `single.php` template section, but if your site is leveraging Custom Post Types for specific content needs, you probably want a specific method to render them.

Custom Post Types, as discussed in Chapter 7, can be used to force a structure to the content being created. You might have specific fields or entries that the site admin will continually use to make these content pieces consistent.

Once you have set up your Custom Post Type, you can create a template file that renders that content very similarly to the `single.php` template. However, because you have structured data in the Custom Post Type, this template file will usually have that structure reflected in the HTML.

> **NOTE** *See Chapter 7 for information on using Custom Post Type content in your template files.*

Template Hierarchy

With all these template files to choose from, how does WordPress decide which one to use? The WordPress core is pretty smart in this regard. Based on the URL, WordPress determines what type of content is being requested and can make a starting determination. Then WordPress works out the specificity of the template to be used, using the most specific template that matches the criteria first, and falling back to more general templates until it finds a match. This system works well in that it is fault tolerant by always cascading back to `index.php` but extremely powerful because, as the developer, you can make custom templates for very specific situations if needed.

This is best illustrated with the flowchart in Figure 9-4 adapted from the WordPress Codex. There is a more complete version online.

As you can see, there is a nice decision tree happening here, and the flexibility is very powerful. Not all themes have or need all template files. But certain more customized or special use case themes can capitalize on this hierarchy and create a unique application of WordPress.

It is also worth mentioning that the search template hierarchy is defined in `template-loader.php`, where a hook is defined before the search tree is started—`template_redirect`—which lets you change the template selection process. This is used mostly for handling URL redirections, such as a "shortlink" defined for a page, which might hide some of the URL information normally used to decipher what templates WordPress applies.

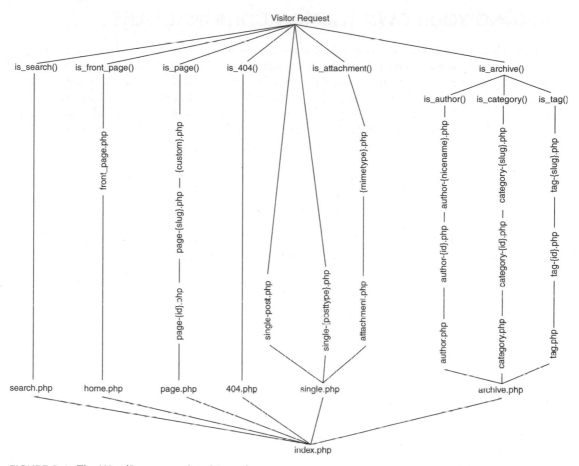

FIGURE 9-4: The WordPress template hierarchy

WARNING *On some sites we have built, there have been occasions where categories, tags, pages, and even authors have had the same or similar taxonomies. For example, on a corporate news site, you may have a page about a department and a department category for news about that department, and some information may be tagged by the department name. In cases like these, the WordPress template decision tree can get confused and make unintended choices. You can work around this in several ways: either by carefully crafting your taxonomy, by ensuring each slug is sufficiently unique to avoid collisions, or by enforcing your desired behavior via the* .htaccess *file. The crux of the issue here is how WordPress handles permalinks, which boils down to pattern matching on the slug metadata.*

CREATING YOUR OWN THEME: ADDITIONAL FILES

It is tough to sort out the various template files into which ones are critical, which are essential, and which are just nice to have. Each theme's template file collection will be different and tailored to match the content or design goals of the author. The truly critical and essential templates have already been covered. In some circles, many of the following templates would fall into the categories already discussed, so you will have to make your own decisions here. Do not think that because these templates are being covered later, they are any less important than any other template. Consider each template type a tool, and how you use the tools is what truly matters.

Handling 404 Errors: 404.php

A 404 page is a fact of life. Eventually, your visitors will find something that went stale. In contrast to a traditional website, WordPress really helps you avoid them because typically all the navigation items are dynamically created by content that actually exists. But it is still possible that your visitor will find a link that is no longer around, so your 404 page comes up.

The Twenty Fourteen theme provides a really good practice with the stock 404 template by including a search box. This way, visitors who stumble across this page have an opportunity to search for what they are looking for.

Other good practices include showing a list of possibly related content, in the form of "I couldn't find what you asked for, but maybe one of these posts would interest you." You do not want a 404 page to be a dead end; always offer something else to view and a way out.

At our shop, we trigger a developer e-mail or Twitter warning to let you know someone asked for a lost URL. Especially if there is a referrer in the HTTP headers, you can track down where the broken link originated. At the least you know something went wrong and can do some research.

Also, your 404 page should be funny. Humor is good medicine and it is nice to disarm visitors who might be upset that what they were looking for is not there. It is good practice to expose errors to your developers but show something useful and meaningful to your site visitor. Think back to the days of the Twitter fail whale. As Twitter was growing, it often had scalability issues and the fail whale was seen more often than not. But by keeping the error message lighthearted, the Twitter fail whale quickly emerged as an Internet icon and garnered its own cult following.

Although not strictly a template file, another error to hide from your visitors is a database connection error. The default database connection error is ugly and exposes a little too much information to your visitor, who hopefully is a good guy and not going to use that information against your website.

WordPress introduced a new function in version 2.5 and later back-ported it to previous versions where, if the database connection fails, WordPress looks for a `db-error.php` file in your `wp-content` directory.

> **NOTE** *This file resides outside of your theme directory. Because there is no database connection, WordPress does not know what theme to display.*

You can put whatever code and CSS in the db-error.php template you want, except dynamic data or WordPress functions, because they will not work without the database. This is another situation where we place a stock db-error.php in all of our WordPress sites, with a generic but friendly error message, and then notify the development team that an error has occurred.

The following is a sample db-error.php file:

```php
<?php
//error_reporting('E_ERROR');
mail('developers@example.com','WP SQL Connection Issue on '.$_SERVER['HTTP_HOST'],
'This is an automated message from the wordpress custom db error message file.');
?>
<html>
<head>
<title>Temporarily Unavailable</title>
<style>
body { background-color: #000; }
#wrapper
{
    width: 600px;
    height: 300px;
    margin: 2em auto 0;
    border: 4px solid #666;
    background-color: #fff;
    padding: 0 2em;
}
p { font-size: larger; }
</style>
</head>
<body>
<div id="wrapper">
    <center>
    <!-- /* This is the generic database error page that will be shown when a fatal
 db connection issue arises */ -->
        <h1><?php echo $_SERVER['HTTP_HOST']; ?> is Temporarily Unavailable</h1>
        <p>The webmaster has been alerted. Please try again later.</p>
    </center>
</div>
</body>
</html>
```

In the rare occurrence that WordPress cannot connect to the MySQL database, rather than showing an ugly database error, site visitors get a friendlier error message and the developers receive an e-mail. This also informs the visitors that no further action is required on their part, besides checking back later, because the error occurred on the web-hosting server and not on their side. This acknowledgment removes confusion or uncertainty on the visitor's side. The caveat to this is that when things go really wrong, beyond just a hiccup, the developers can get flooded with e-mails.

Author.php

Earlier, you were grouping historical content by category or tag; you can similarly use the author.php template to group all of an author's content into one view. In addition, you can create specific author templates either by the author's ID or by the author's nicename, which is the author's username. As before, the human readable nicename template is preferred by WordPress over the ID-based one.

Sometimes your site has multiple authors, such as your development team site at work. In such cases, a visitor may want to find additional articles posted by the same individual. The author.php template file shows only posts written by a specific author.

The author template behaves just like a category or tag loop. One nice feature of the Twenty Fourteen theme is that this template also includes any author information that the author chose to submit in the Administration screen.

```php
<?php if ( get_the_author_meta( 'description' ) ) : ?>
  <div class="author-description"><?php the_author_meta( 'description' ); ?></div>
<?php endif; ?>
```

If the author submitted some biographical data, that information is published here. This functionality could be enhanced if the profile page had a rich text editor for the biographical information, and possibly some expanded custom fields.

In production sites, these fields have been used to create a multi-business partner site where each author was, in effect, a company. You can also create a Rolodex-type site using this method.

Comments.php

The comments template used to be one of the more complex templates. This template file handles both the comment loop, including trackbacks and pings, and the input form for a visitor to submit the comment in both logged-in and logged-out cases. Although these tasks are functionally related, sorting through this template file, you used to see a lot of "if . . . else" conditionals that make it difficult to theme. Your theme may not even include comments, especially if you are using WordPress as a CMS, but if it does, you can include the comments functionality templates in your other templates with the following code:

```php
<?php comments_template(); ?>
```

Countless variations on the comments theme exist for the look and feel—way too many to discuss the merits of any in particular. One thing to consider when working on this template file is the threaded comments functionality introduced in WordPress 2.7. See the WordPress Codex for more information about using wp_list_comments().

It should also be noted that in WordPress 2.7, the comments loop was simplified to look more like a traditional post loop in the code. In addition, many new functions have been introduced to make the comment templates much more straightforward, and the Twenty Fourteen theme does a great job of utilizing these functions. The Twenty Fourteen comment template is a good place to start if you are looking at overhauling the comment section of your site.

One particular improvement is the comment_form() function. This function now handles the rendering of the actual comment form in the comment template. Prior to this function, all of the form and form logic was handled in the template itself, which added extensively to the complexity. This function was introduced in WordPress 3.0 and is pretty extensible if you need to customize your comment form.

Adding Functionality to Your Templates: Functions.php

The functions.php template is not a display template, so it is not like the other templates you have covered, but it is a very important file even though it does not directly display content on your website. Chiefly, the functions.php file is where the special sauce that makes your theme sizzle goes. It is the place where you can put what has traditionally been called "library code." If, in your templates, you find repeating code or need some special functionality, this is where it can go. WordPress automatically includes this file during execution so the functions are available in all of your template files.

Often, when you are adding functionality you have to decide if the code belongs in functions.php or in a plugin. A general rule of thumb is that if you are adding something that is configurable, as in the user may want to disable it without affecting the look and feel of the site, it belongs in a plugin. If you are including something that is essential, truly essential, to the theme and is always on, it belongs in functions.php. This template includes the setup features for your theme, such as menus and sidebars and also any helper functions for your templates.

The stock functions.php theme is very well commented. Each function and logic block of a function has a one-line comment explaining what it does. This makes functions.php easy to modify and extend. However, the majority of these functions will not need to be modified in your production site, unless you have very specific needs. Most of them simply add to the template files to create a hook-rich HTML template for your CSS styling skills.

One thing that is important to consider when adding on to your theme's functions.php file is whether the functionality you are adding really belongs compartmentalized by theme or whether it is standalone functionality that belongs in a plugin. This is about determining if the code you are adding is directly applicable to the theme or if it is portable and can be used no matter what theme the site is running—for example, if the functionality you are adding will be used on multiple sites with different themes. This can often be a difficult choice, especially when you realize that you use the same hooks and filters discussed in Chapter 8. In essence, the functions file is a library of plugins all nestled into one file, or occasionally structured as PHP includes of multiple files for more complex themes.

One of the main purposes of the functions.php file is to enable or disable certain WordPress features for your theme. In the Twenty Fourteen theme, this is all done during the twentyfourteen_setup() function. You will notice it enables support for various features including HTML5 elements, post-formats, custom background, featured content, and a few others. These are all features of WordPress that the Twenty Fourteen theme uses; therefore, they must be enabled. Think of this as feature flags. How each feature is enabled and configured is dependent on the specific feature. For example, enabling post-thumbnails or featured images is as simple as this:

```
// Enable support for Post Thumbnails, and declare two sizes.
add_theme_support( 'post-thumbnails' );
set_post_thumbnail_size( 672, 372, true );
add_image_size( 'twentyfourteen-full-width', 1038, 576, true );
```

Some feature flags can take, or may require, configuration information, such as the following:

```
/*
 * Enable support for Post Formats.
 * See http://codex.wordpress.org/Post_Formats
 */
```

```
add_theme_support( 'post-formats', array(
  'aside', 'image', 'video', 'audio', 'quote', 'link', 'gallery',
) );
```

However, each feature is different and will need to be enabled and configured based on your theme's needs.

In addition, the functions file establishes and identifies your navigation menus. In your functions file, you introduce how many menus your theme will have and assign them names. Later in this chapter, you will learn how to place menu locations in your template files and assign menus to these locations in the WordPress Administration screens.

Similar to menus, you also identify and create widget areas in your functions.php file. Generally, widget areas take more configuration than menus do. Like menus, you register widget areas, or sidebars, in the functions file and later in this chapter you will learn how to place these locations in your template files.

This file is for creating your own behavior and functionality for your theme. You could be introducing new presentation logic or new features that are specific to your needs and goals. But also, you can override or augment existing WordPress features—for example, in the Twenty Fourteen theme:

```
function twentyfourteen_body_classes( $classes ) {
  if ( is_multi_author() ) {
    $classes[] = 'group-blog';
  }

  if ( get_header_image() ) {
    $classes[] = 'header-image';
  } else {
    $classes[] = 'masthead-fixed';
  }

  if ( is_archive() || is_search() || is_home() ) {
    $classes[] = 'list-view';
  }

  if ( ( ! is_active_sidebar( 'sidebar-2' ) )
    || is_page_template( 'page-templates/full-width.php' )
    || is_page_template( 'page-templates/contributors.php' )
    || is_attachment() ) {
    $classes[] = 'full-width';
  }

  if ( is_active_sidebar( 'sidebar-3' ) ) {
    $classes[] = 'footer-widgets';
  }

  if ( is_singular() && ! is_front_page() ) {
    $classes[] = 'singular';
  }

  if ( is_front_page() && 'slider' == get_theme_mod(
```

```
        'featured_content_layout' ) ) {
        $classes[] = 'slider';
    } elseif ( is_front_page() ) {
        $classes[] = 'grid';
    }

    return $classes;
}
add_filter( 'body_class', 'twentyfourteen_body_classes' );
```

This function adds more parameters to the `body_class()` function that assigns CSS classes to the body HTML node. The default `body_class()` function returns many useful classes that you can hook into with your CSS styling, but sometimes you need something special. In the case of the Twenty Fourteen theme, the preceding function appends classes to the array that is returned based on certain criteria.

When modifying the starter theme functions, you have to make a choice. Sometimes, if you are making minimal changes to the file, you can just modify the file directly, accepting that this will break any upgradeability of the theme. Alternatively, you can include your own `custom_functions.php` from the `functions.php` file and make all your own custom changes here. The caveat is that if you overwrite the `functions.php` file, either through a theme update or other user error, you have to remember to put the `include` back in that file before your head gets too bloody from beating it against the wall wondering why your custom functions are not running. In practice, both of these scenarios have been used successfully.

The amount of power and control available to you in the functions file can be staggering and this power can quickly grow your file size out of control. For example, some of the more advanced themes and the premium theme frameworks include their own control panels to modify theme settings. These other theme frameworks are covered later in this chapter. Theme control panel code resides in the `functions.php` file.

For example, consider the popular Thematic theme framework which is available online at `http://themeshaper.com/thematic/`. To keep things manageable and distinct, the Thematic `functions.php` is simply a list of includes of other function files. This logically breaks up and separates the different facets of the theme framework and keeps the files from becoming unwieldy. This theme also includes a basic control panel to control some of the theme settings.

To create your own theme control panel, you have to register your theme control panel functions with WordPress. In addition, you have to create the HTML form for your control panel within your `functions.php` file. This is one of the reasons we like the way Thematic has broken up the files into separate areas of concern; the mixing of PHP and HTML code never turns out pretty or readable. It is best to keep this information separate and in maintainable file sizes.

Creating your own theme control panel is outside the scope of this book, but it is definitely a great feature to have and most of the premium theme frameworks include this functionality. Having a theme control panel helps your WordPress theme bridge that gap from blogging engine to full-fledged content management platform for the average user. However, the new Theme Customizer, released in WordPress 3.4 and covered later in this chapter, may work for many sites as a simpler theme control panel. For a coder, WordPress is easily extendable through the code and the vast WordPress functionality, but for the average user, who is probably your client, avoiding code is crucial, which makes these control panels and theme customizers ideal for your end user.

Search.php

The search template file is really a misnomer. This template is actually the search engine result page (SERP). The search form itself is called `searchform.php` and is covered in the next section. The concept of a search engine result page is pretty self-explanatory. It is going to show the results of what the visitor looked for, by default in reverse chronological order.

> **NOTE** *Chapter 12 covers some of the weaknesses with the built-in search functionality of WordPress and addresses some alternatives to enhance the user experience.*

This is all that the basic Twenty Fourteen search template does. If there are results, this template presents them to the browser, but if not, it shows a new search form.

You can do a couple of things to your search engine result page to improve on the default. First, you do not want your results page to be a dead end if there are not any search results. Plugins are available to offer related searches or spelling variation searches based on what was initially entered. This will make the search itself behave more like a traditional search engine.

Still, if you do not have any search results, offer up some alternative content that the visitor might be interested in. This might be a good place for a tag cloud or a list of your most popular content. Plugins are available for showcasing your most popular content or you could create a custom query, but you would have to decide what your metrics are.

For some sites, the top content was essentially a known issue—that is, we decided what the top content would be. In this case, we created a special post category and made a new loop to show only this category in the SERP page.

If you do have results, some people like to see the search terms highlighted in the search engine results page. The Twenty Fourteen theme uses `the_excerpt()` to display the content excerpt in the results. This is where you will make some changes to highlight the search terms. The downside of having your theme split up into many template files is that you have to chase the `include()` and the `get_template_part()` functions to find the correct file to edit. In the case of Twenty Fourteen, the `get_template_part()` is looking for the content template for the proper file type. For the sake of brevity, you can chase this back to `content.php` for general post content. In the `content.php` template, there is an "if" statement around line 47, checking if the content is being displayed on a search engine results page or not. This is where the theme decides whether it is showing all of the content or just an excerpt, so you can modify the way excerpts are displayed.

Replace this line:

```
<?php the_excerpt(); ?>
```

with the following:

```php
<?php
  $excerpt = get_the_excerpt();
  $keys = explode(" ",$s);
  $excerpt = preg_replace('/('.implode('|', $keys) .')/iu',
    '<span class="searchTerm">\0 </span>',$excerpt);
  echo $excerpt;
?>
```

Because the_excerpt() echoes the content directly to the rendering, you have to use the plugin API function get_the_excerpt(), which returns a string instead. Run this string through the PHP regular expression replace function to put span elements around all the search terms and then echo this out to the rendering. In your CSS, you can add a nice rule to highlight these span elements to match your theme.

Finally, if your visitors did not find what they were looking for after reviewing the search results, rather than forcing them to scroll back up to the top, you can provide a second search form at the bottom to refine their search. After the results loop, add something like the following:

```
<h2>Not seeing what you're looking for?  Try again</h2>
<?php get_search_form(); ?>
```

The Twenty Fourteen theme has the search form already enabled for you.

> **NOTE** *Chapter 12 discusses improving the way search works through plugins and some alternatives.*

SearchForm.php

The generic search form is pulled from the WordPress core template files and is pretty basic looking. In cases where your theme needs a customized search input field, create a new template named searchform.php. This form can then be styled to match the rest of your theme. The search widget automatically uses this template to include this form in your regular templates with the following code:

```php
<?php get_search_form(); ?>
```

The basic Twenty Fourteen search form looks like this (note that it is using HTML5 elements because Twenty Fourteen has the HTML5 flag set):

```html
<form role="search" method="get" class="search-form"
  action="<?php echo home_url( '/' ); ?>">
  <label>
    <span class="screen-reader-text">Search for:</span>
    <input type="search" class="search-field" placeholder="Search …"
      value="" name="s" title="Search for:" />
  </label>
  <input type="submit" class="search-submit" value="Search" />
</form>
```

Because this same form could be used in the unordered lists of the sidebar as well as wherever else you may include it, the HTML markup may need to be adjusted to be generic.

Another option is for special-case search forms, often seen in the nameplates of sites, to create a traditional PHP `include` for the search form. Make sure the filename is not one of the reserved filenames for the template engine, and then include it in the appropriate place in your other template:

```php
<?php include($bloginfo['template_directory'].'includeThis.php'); ?>
```

Remember to use the `bloginfo[]` array to keep the theme portable. You can also use this method to comply with the DRY principle when there are consistent elements across multiple pages but outside of the header and footer templates. WordPress itself does an excellent job of enforcing DRY through the variety of page templates, assuming you, as a developer, stick to the rules. But there are always more ways to skin a cat and traditional PHP operations can help out here. This functionality is often used to keep the template sizes manageable.

Other Files

Here are some other files that polish off your theme. For the Themes Administration screen, you will want to include a screenshot for easy visual recognition of your theme. Create an image file to represent your theme that is 880px wide by 660px tall and save it as a PNG. GIF and JPG are also accepted and preferred in that order. This is a large graphic size that will be scaled down for viewing in the Dashboard. Traditionally, this image is an actual screenshot of your site using your theme. The remainder of the information for each theme on the Manage Themes screen comes from your `style.css` header information.

Many themes include several language files and are ready out of the box for localization. If you intend to launch your site in multiple languages, pay attention to the special considerations involved. Localization and internationalization are well outside the scope of this book. Just bear in mind that WordPress supports this functionality when you need it.

CUSTOM PAGE TEMPLATES

Occasionally, you will have a specific page that requires a unique layout, relative to the rest of your website. This could be a contact page, or it could be that each product on a brochure website has its own specific page. It could be that you are making a custom-landing page for a marketing campaign or a QR code. Maybe using a general `page.php` template is not going to meet the needs of your site because each page has its own distinctive qualities. Possibly, you have widgets you would like to display on certain pages and not others, although you could probably accomplish this with a plugin like Widget Logic. Or perhaps you are integrating a third-party web application into your WordPress site. This is where page templates step in.

You can assign page templates to a page using the Page screen in the Administration Dashboard. WordPress will assign which page template to use when displaying your content following the already established specificity pattern. For example, if your page is assigned a page template, that will be selected because a page template is the most specific option. If the default page template is set, the traditional `page.php` template discussed earlier will be used to render your content. Finally, if neither of those templates is available, WordPress will use your `index.php` template.

In Figure 9-5, you can see several page templates to choose from, including the default page template; Twenty Fourteen's templates for a contributor page and full width (no-sidebar) page, discussed later; and the two added as examples, Boring and Fancy.

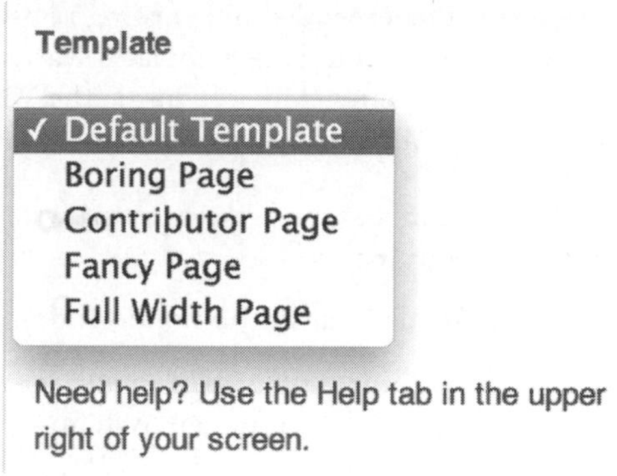

Template

√ Default Template
Boring Page
Contributor Page
Fancy Page
Full Width Page

Need help? Use the Help tab in the upper right of your screen.

FIGURE 9-5: Selecting the page template

When to Use Custom Page Templates

Many reasons exist for having custom page templates in your site. Custom page templates are very powerful tools to add to your arsenal, and when used effectively they can extend the breadth of your site immensely. Custom page templates are yet another way to assign templates to specific pages. Unlike previous examples, which relied on an inherent attribute of a page, such as the page slug or ID, category, or tag, custom page templates can be assigned arbitrarily through the Page screen to any page in your site.

A simple example is to create page templates for unique product pages, where the sidebar of each product page has unique data and links specific to that product. As with everything in WordPress, there are many ways to achieve this functionality, but sometimes all that is needed when creating custom page templates is a simple, straightforward method. And often, simplest is best.

Another simple example is to create a custom page template that uses an iFrame HTML element to include a third-party web application. Depending on the exact needs and aspirations of the site (not to mention budget), this can be a quick and dirty way to integrate two sites into one. The caveats to this method are the same as those you would usually find when using iFrames, that is, bookmarking does not work as expected and you introduce a competing look and feel from another website. But admittedly, this method has been used before because sometimes the quick and dirty method is all that you need.

More complex examples include integrating different web applications into your WordPress site. For example, a page template could be used to create a custom order page that posts directly back into your e-commerce package. This would be a nightmare to set up and maintain inside the WordPress Dashboard, but when using custom page templates, it is all in the code, and you still get the gooey goodness of WordPress to wrap it all in.

In real life, custom page templates are used for event calendaring and registration. On one occasion, an expansive education class was built offering web applications for searching and displaying courses as well as registering for attendance either in person or via the web. This system had been in place for several years and was heavily used. The simplest way to integrate this education registration system into WordPress client sites was to create custom page templates.

In essence, this extended the existing registration system with some REST web service commands. Then a set of custom page templates was created that communicated with the web services but displayed the contents locally inside the WordPress site wrapper, using the local style sheet. Although setting up the page templates was daunting at first, the benefits in the end were enormous:

➤ Continued use of the existing system that corporate staff was already knowledgeable about and trained to use.

➤ Extended registration options to multiple sites, therefore increasing the potential audience.

➤ Even though the registrations were spread across multiple web properties, they were still centralized into the one system.

➤ The education system matched the look and feel of the local website because it utilized the local theme of the WordPress site.

How to Use Custom Page Templates

Creating the custom page templates themselves is really easy. The goal of the templates and making the templates achieve the goals is what really complicates the matter.

To create a page template, copy an existing template that is similar to the new template you are going to make; usually this is the page.php template. Name this new template file whatever you want and keep it in your theme directory. However, in our development shops, we tend to follow a convention that page templates are named t_templatename.php. That is, they are prefixed with the t_ so it is easy to distinguish between traditional template files and individual page templates, although the name of this file really does not matter as long as you avoid the reserved filenames in the hierarchy.

Since WordPress 3.4, you can also save your page template files inside a subfolder of your theme. This makes organizing your theme significantly cleaner and you will notice the Twenty Fourteen theme uses a page-templates folder for this purpose.

To make your new template a page template, you must include a special comment section at the top of the file:

```php
<?php
/*
Template Name: Fancy Page Template
*/
?>
```

This must be in the first couple of lines of your file for WordPress to scan and register as a page template. In practice, the only thing above this stanza is the source code control comment.

The name of your template can be anything you want. It should be meaningful, but not too long, because WordPress will use this PHP comment to populate the drop-down box in the Dashboard screen. Your page template is now registered with WordPress.

The remainder of your page template can be whatever you need to accomplish your page template goals. You can, and most likely should, use the built-in WordPress functions such as get_header()

and `get_footer()` as well as the content gatherers. Basically you can do whatever you need to do here; just remember you will have to sleep in the bed that you make.

For example, if you remove the dynamic WordPress sidebar generation and replace it with static HTML, you have also removed all the functionality from the Dashboard to manage widgets on this page template. It would be a better practice to register a new widget area on this page template and continue to use the Widget screen to manage this content.

Keep in mind that page templates are not restricted to displaying page information. You could create a page template that displays a traditional post loop or do something that is completely unrelated to the WordPress content. Then just leave the page text editor blank, or use it to write instruction notes to yourself.

Stock Twenty Fourteen Page Templates

The Twenty Fourteen theme comes standard with two page templates for use on your site. Twenty Fourteen has a special folder for the page templates files unsurprisingly titled `page-templates`. You will look at those briefly here, since you have them available.

The first page template that comes with the Twenty Fourteen theme is `full-width.php`. This template is pretty simple and straightforward. Basically, it is a page without any sidebar content, hence full width. Pretty self-explanatory.

The second custom page template is not really more complicated. It is called `contributor.php`. The contributor page template is designed to be a fancier index page for your WordPress site authors or contributors. This page template uses a function found in the `functions.php` template to list all the authors who have published content on the site and includes their avatar image and biographical data from the user profile. Finally, the function displays links to the actual content.

Custom page templates are very powerful tools. Truly, if you cannot fit your content into the predefined template types, you always have this last trick up your sleeve to make a custom page template and override everything. This is also a great way to add special non-WordPress functionality to your website.

OTHER THEME ENHANCEMENTS

These are some additional enhancements that you can make to your theme. Most of the following ends up in your functions file and not as individual files. These are enhancements to your theme that enrich the site administrator's content management capabilities.

Menu Management

As mentioned before, most WordPress sites that are being used in a CMS capacity have a mixed bag of pages and posts. The most difficult part of the hybrid pages and posts layout is creating a meaningful navigation. Your site's global navigation is a very important aspect of your site if you intend to have any stickiness with your visitors. Visitors should be able to explore your content organically and experimentally through related posts and pages, but there should also be a strategy to your content organization and this is the function of your global navigation. On occasion, we have lucked out on the structure of a site and have been able to create two tiers of navigation, one for the page content and one for the post content. Before WordPress 3.0, the two content types essentially needed to be intertwined and the navigation had to be hand-coded using the `wp_list_pages()` functions with many different parameters to get the menus you wanted. This was all coded in the templates and not very flexible for the site administrator.

However, those days are gone. With WordPress 3.0, a new menu management system has been introduced. This menu management gives all the control to the site administrator. As a theme developer, you just have to set it up for your theme presentation.

The first step is to register the menus for your theme. Basically this means assigning named locations for each menu to earmark the HTML real estate for the menu. You will use the `register_nav_menu()` function for this. This function takes two parameters. The first one is a nickname or handle that you will use in the template files. The second parameter is a friendly human-readable name that is used in the WordPress Dashboard. For example, the following will create a single global navigation menu for use in your theme:

```
register_nav_menu('primary', 'Global navigation menu');
```

You can actually have as many menu locations in your theme as you want or need. Just feed the `register_nav_menus()` function an array of locations, as seen in Twenty Fourteen:

```
// This theme uses wp_nav_menu() in two locations.
register_nav_menus( array(
    'primary'   => __( 'Top primary menu', 'twentyfourteen' ),
    'secondary' => __( 'Secondary menu in left sidebar', 'twentyfourteen' ),
) );
```

This will notify WordPress that you have menu locations available and identified, but you also need to assign their position in the template files. Usually, because of the way websites are designed, this occurs in your `header.php` template. To place the desired menu in your template file, use the `wp_nav_menu()` function like so:

```
wp_nav_menu( array( 'theme_location' => 'primary', 'menu_class' => 'nav-menu' ) );
```

This function can take many parameters, passed in as an array, to control the HTML styling, but the important parameter is to identify which menu you want placed at this location. In the preceding example, the real estate is allocated for the menu nicknamed `primary`.

Finally, to glue this all together, your site administrator can use the Menus screen to manage the menu. Notice that you are identifying a menu location and then assigning that location to an actual position in the HTML hierarchy. This is all at the code level. In turn, the site administrator assigns content to these named locations through the Dashboard. So while they all must be set up together so that they work together, they are actually disconnected. Assigning meaningful names to the menu locations is important for the Dashboard aspect of menu management, but how the site administrator uses that menu may be different than you intend.

What is meant by "disconnected"? Let's go back in time to how WordPress used to build menus before the new menu system. This process involved using the `wp_list_pages()` function with many parameters to hand-craft the exact menu you needed. In fact, the first edition of this book devoted many pages to reviewing this topic. Creating the menus programmatically in the template file worked because it was directly tied to actual content of the site and the hierarchy of pages.

However, it was not perfect. You had to use tricks such as building a blank page to show up in the automated navigation menu, and then use the Page Links To plugin by Mark Jaquith to redirect that page to category or archive templates. In addition, the PageMash plugin was recommended to manage the page hierarchy and page order for the `wp_list_pages()` function. This tried and true method is frequently employed for many sites. It works because it is programmatic, meaning it is predictable. It works because it is directly tied to content. It sometimes does not work when the content gets a major change.

Sometimes, a change in the content means the `wp_list_pages()` parameters need to be adjusted. With this method, the changes have to be made at the code level, and the power is taken away from the site administrator. Whether this is good or bad is a choice you have to make based on the convenience and needs of your site.

The predictability of the new menu management system is another problem. With the menu system, your site navigation is arbitrary. It is not directly tied to your content. You can automatically add top-level pages to a menu, but you cannot automatically add the child pages. In addition, the page hierarchy is not reflected in the menu system. You have to manually manage the menu above and beyond the management of content. One possible trap is that when you delete a page from your site, the menu item remains. With the new menu system, you cannot programmatically plan for sub-tree menus to use as subsection navigation; you have to actually manage an additional menu structure.

This disconnect can be both a pro and a con. On the one hand, the site administrator really has complete control over the menu content. He can hand-craft the menu to meet his needs. However, it is important for your site administrator to understand that he has to manage the content and the menu. There can be confusion when some aspects of the site navigation are programmatically created in the theme templates, but the menu is handmade.

For example, imagine you have built a new theme for a client that has multiple product pages. These are special pages to highlight individual products with their specific information and details. To further enhance the user experience, and perhaps cross-sell some product, you have built a custom page template for the products pages that has a built-in related products section at the bottom. This related products section is generated by code in the imaginary t `product_page.php` custom page template. The challenge is that when a site administrator adds a new product page, it will show up automatically in this related product page code on some other sites, but will not show up automatically in the menu. The site administrator will have to manually edit the menu to add this page.

This is not a devastating issue; it is just disconnected and an extra step. The challenge is in empowering the site administrator and asking him or her to manually configure things, as opposed to simply adding code to have things happen automatically.

Widget Areas

Widget areas work very much the same way as menus. In your `functions.php` file, you identify and name different areas for different parts of the site. These are often thought of as sidebars but can be so much more. Do not restrict yourself to thinking widget areas only belong in the sidebars of your site. Many themes, including Twenty Fourteen, are expanding the number and location of widget areas to include the masthead or header area, the footer, and even the middle of the loop. We have even seen themes that have hundreds of widget areas.

The nice thing about widget areas is their flexibility. The number of widgets that can be placed into a widget area is immense. Having multiple widget areas empowers the site administrator to control subject matter in areas of the site that are really outside the primary content areas of the site.

As previously mentioned, setting up widget areas is very similar to setting up menus. In your `functions.php` file, you must identify and name your locations. Because widget areas have more flexible and varied content than menus, which are pretty much unordered lists, you generally pass some HTML wrapper information for use when rendering the widgets. Also, because widget areas have evolved from the traditional sidebar use, the function to register them is still named `register_sidebar()`, but again, do not let this pigeonhole them. Here is a widget area code snippet from Twenty Fourteen:

```php
register_sidebar( array(
    'name'          => __( 'Primary Sidebar', 'twentyfourteen' ),
    'id'            => 'sidebar-1',
    'description'   => __( 'Main sidebar that appears on the left.',
        'twentyfourteen' ),
    'before_widget' => '<aside id="%1$s" class="widget %2$s">',
    'after_widget'  => '</aside>',
    'before_title'  => '<h1 class="widget-title">',
    'after_title'   => '</h1>',
) );
```

Similar to menus, you pass the function a friendly name for use in the Dashboards and an identifier for use in the theme templates. Beyond that, the additional parameters are for styling the widget consistently. In this example, Twenty Fourteen is using HTML5 `aside` elements to wrap each widget and widget titles in `h1` tags. This code notifies WordPress that there is a widget area available for content.

The next step is to assign the HTML real estate position to this widget area. For this example, you will look at `sidebar.php` in Twenty Fourteen, but again, widget areas can be anywhere in your template. Here's the code:

```php
<?php if ( is_active_sidebar( 'sidebar-1' ) ) : ?>
  <div id="primary-sidebar" class="primary-sidebar widget-area"
    role="complementary">
    <?php dynamic_sidebar( 'sidebar-1' ); ?>
  </div><!-- #primary-sidebar -->
<?php endif; ?>
```

A couple of things are going on in this code snippet. First and foremost, the first line is looking to see if the widget area named `sidebar-1` has content assigned in the Dashboard, and if it does, it will display it. This is one of the big benefits of widget areas: If they do not have content, they do not display.

Post Formats

This is simply a feature flag that you can turn on or off in your `functions.php` file. If your theme intends to use the built-in post formats, or a subset of them, you can enable them.

Post formats are essentially a way to customize the display of certain types of posts. This is most commonly seen when you are using WordPress for blogging or archiving a journal. The different post formats can be used to pull different loop HTML rendering as you saw earlier in this chapter. This allows you to present quotes or links differently than full posts.

WordPress currently supports ten post formats for varying content. You can enable any or all of these formats depending on the goals of your theme. The standard format is for traditional posts and is enabled automatically. This is the format used in WordPress forever; it just now has a name assigned to it.

In addition, there are nine new formats as of WordPress 3.1. Here they are, with the recommended styling, although using the flexibility of WordPress, you can style these to fit your needs:

➤ **Aside**—This is similar to a quick note. It is usually presented without the post title.

➤ **Audio**—Obviously, this format is for an audio file, perhaps a podcast or a band releasing a single.

➤ **Chat**—This format is usually a chat transcript. This is usually styled using the pre HTML element to keep the line breaks.

➤ **Gallery**—This is a gallery of image media attachments. The actual post content will typically contain a gallery shortcode. This format is for styling the gallery.

➤ **Image**—This post format is for a single image. The single image can be embedded in the post content, or a URL in the post content will pull that image to your site.

➤ **Link**—This format is for a link to another URL. Generally, these are presented as simply the link, without the title. This format is often used for creating your own bookmark site or reminders about URLs that interested you.

➤ **Quote**—Another self-explanatory one—this format is for quotes. This format is used to archive quotes that have some special meaning to you. You can present this format without the title or flip it around and use the title information as the attribution to the quote.

➤ **Status**—Think of this format as Twitter or Facebook updates. Typically presented without a title. You can use this format to make your own Twitter clone.

➤ **Video**—Similar to image and audio, this format is for presenting a single video to your visitors. The video can be embedded in the content or as an external URL.

To enable post formats for your theme, simply select which formats you intend to use and pass them as a parameter array. For example, the Twenty Fourteen theme is supporting a subset of the previous formats:

```
/*
 * Enable support for Post Formats.
 * See http://codex.wordpress.org/Post_Formats
 */
add_theme_support( 'post-formats', array(
  'aside', 'image', 'video', 'audio', 'quote', 'link', 'gallery',
) );
```

Remember that the standard post format for traditional post content is always enabled. Post formats can tailor your theme to specific niche uses or broaden your theme to present different content types in unique and customized ways.

Theme Settings

Many of the theme frameworks offer a special Theme Settings screen for customizing the theme framework. This is a coded solution that comes from the theme developer but creates a new Administration screen with whatever settings the theme developer has opted to include. This is yet another feature that is a balance of empowering the site administrator as opposed to handling aspects in the theme template code.

Creating your own Theme Settings screen is a very complex endeavor that is outside the scope of this book. Each theme is different, and it is the developer's goals that determine which features or aspects of your theme are configurable.

To create a Theme Settings Administration screen you first have to build the control panel code and forms and register them with WordPress. You then have to take the configurable options and use them in your template files. The control you give to your site administrator can be very powerful, but it does make developing your templates a little trickier.

For more information about creating your own Theme Settings screen, check out the WordPress Codex and other theme frameworks; there are also many good tutorials online.

Theme Customizer

Some of the functionality of the Theme screen has been moved into the new Theme Customizer, which was introduced in WordPress 3.4.

This is a new screen for customizing the theme. The really neat thing is that it can show the site administrator a live preview of the site while he is customizing it. This is truly the biggest benefit of this component. This real-time live preview allows the site administrator to experiment with the site and see how it would look without affecting the live production site until he is done. In the past, this process involved making a change in a Theme screen, discussed previously, in the code, or in other customizable places, and publishing those changes to the live site. Then the site administrator had to browse to the live site to see the outcome. At the same time, any visitors browsing the site saw the in-process design changes. The change may or may not have been what the site administrator intended, or worse, may have broken some display aspect. The live preview presents this whole process while allowing great control.

Basically, the Theme Customizer screen uses the WordPress settings API to store configurable design information. Then using specially crafted functions in the functions.php file, WordPress applies the changes to the HTML.

In the Twenty Fourteen function for changing the header color, the functions.php file injects a new CSS stanza into the HTML head that overrides the style sheet. In practice, this is not really optimal code for a high-traffic site; however, this is yet another example of trading optimization for site administrator configurability.

THEME HIERARCHY AND CHILD THEMES

So far in this chapter, you have looked through the template files that make up a complete theme, focusing on the stock Twenty Fourteen theme. You even considered renaming it and making your custom theme in that new directory using the Twenty Fourteen theme as a starter theme. This is a good way to get started with theme creation as it helps you dive into the internals of how a theme works. And, in the real world, this is how many development teams work today. This method works well because you know exactly where your template files and CSS files are that need to be edited. The whole theme is self-contained, which minimizes workflow and deployment efforts—not that it's perfect, but it is very solid.

However, with the release of WordPress 2.7, child themes became a functional reality. While you could implement child themes prior to WordPress 2.7, it was not until template file inheritance was included that child themes became a viable development option. Child themes let you take an existing theme or theme framework and use the best parts of it, and then extend and modify it, license permitting, to meet your own theme's needs while maintaining future updates to the parent theme. After you have the basics of theme development down, it is highly recommend that you pick a theme framework you are comfortable with (a few are mentioned in the next section) and create child themes. Child themes are the future of theme development for WordPress.

This concept is pretty revolutionary for several reasons. First, it certainly opened the door for theme frameworks. Starting with a solid foundation, you can now make countless variations on the theme simply through inheritance. Theme frameworks tend to be very plain, and intentionally so, but by using child themes, you can inherit all the CSS semantic hooks and microformat gooey centers and build your own candy shell around it, basically taking the best parts and making a new creation.

Second, updates to the parent theme or theme framework will not overwrite your customizations. Previously, when you made modifications to your copy of the theme, you had to keep track of the changes you made so that you could reapply them when the theme was upgraded. This can be somewhat automated via a source code management solution, but it is arduous at best, when it works. And there is always the day when you forget to make a modification to the updated files.

Third, child themes led the way for auto-updating themes in the Theme screen Dashboard. Occasionally theme templates are vulnerable to security exploits such as cross-site scripting. Using a properly inherited child theme means the parent theme can auto-update to address security issues while not affecting your child theme. This creates a more secure implementation for your site.

There are a couple of caveats here. The functionality that keeps your child theme customizations unaffected works both ways. If you override a particular template file with your own customizations, any enhancements to the parent template file of the same name will not cascade to your unique file. In practice, this could create a false sense of security, where you may have copied a poorly coded template file to modify, and then changes were made to the parent version but your file is unaffected and still vulnerable. That is, because you are carrying forward the vulnerability in your extended code, you continue to override any repaired code. This would not only apply to security amendments but would also apply to any feature enhancements. That is, child themes do not totally remove you from the code management process.

In addition, there is a little bit of CSS overhead here. Generally, a child theme builds upon the CSS of the parent theme. And, in truth, that is exactly how CSS is designed to work, hence the word *cascading* in the name. So, for this to work in child themes, the child theme has to include the CSS from the parent theme, even the rules that get overridden in the child theme. That means that the byte weight of the CSS in your child theme may be quite a bit larger than what you actually use in the browser, but you have to transfer it all anyway. This is exactly the opposite thinking of the current "mobile first" design principles.

That said, child themes are a fantastic feature of WordPress, and we recommend using this methodology when the situation warrants it. Certainly, maintaining a pristine theme framework and then extending that theme to individual sites adds to the benefits of a common theme vernacular of CSS and functions, as well as the other benefits mentioned previously. Again, using child themes is the future for WordPress theme development and is a best practices recommendation.

Take a look at how child themes actually operate and what is required in making your first child theme. The first thing you need to do is find the theme you are using as the parent. Your parent theme does not have to be labeled a theme framework. You can extend any theme as long as it meets the following conditions:

➤ The licensing permits you to extend or modify the theme.

➤ The parent theme is not a child theme itself.

In this example, you will continue to build on the stock Twenty Fourteen theme, but you could use any theme or theme framework as the parent. As alluded to earlier in the chapter, to make your custom theme a child theme of another theme, you must add a line to the header information of your `style` `.css` file. This line informs WordPress of the location of the parent theme. Therefore, the variable in the comment should be the folder name of the theme. Although it depends on the server, it is best to be case-sensitive when naming your theme. In this instance, you are adding the following line:

```
Template: twentyfourteen
```

To illustrate this, the entire header comment block from the sample child theme reads as follows:

```
/*
Theme Name: A Twenty Fourteen Child Theme
Theme URI: mirmillo.com
Description: A sample child theme
Author: David Damstra
Author URI: mirmillo.com
Template: twentyfourteen
Version: 1.0
*/
```

As discussed previously, having the `style.css` file with the properly formatted header information in your uniquely named folder registers your theme with WordPress.

To retain backward compatibility with older themes that do not import their stylesheets, the next step is to import the CSS from the parent theme so that your custom theme has base rules to work with:

```
/* import the base styles */
@import url('../twentyfourteen/style.css');
```

This CSS import is not required in your child theme if your parent theme includes its stylesheets the correct WordPress way using the `wp_enqueue_style()` function.

At this point, you can activate your theme in the WordPress Theme screen. You have a fully functional child theme of the Twenty Fourteen theme. It will look exactly like the Twenty Fourteen theme because it is, in essence, an exact copy of the parent theme. The remainder of your style sheet operates like traditional CSS where you can override previous rules through the CSS rules of specificity and precedence, including the order in which they are listed—because your custom styles appear later, they will take precedence.

Again, working with CSS is outside the scope of this book, so let's, go ahead and extend the child theme a little bit. Although you can make these same changes with the Theme Customizer presented earlier, for the sake of this example make the changes in CSS. Update the child theme with a nice pink background and change the base font. Here's what the complete `style.css` file might look like:

```
/*
Theme Name: A Twenty Fourteen Child Theme
Theme URI: mirmillo.com
Description: A sample child theme
Author: David Damstra
Author URI: mirmillo.com
Template: twentyfourteen
Version: 1.0
*/
/* import the base styles */
@import url('../twentyfourteen/style.css');

body {
    background: #E0A3BD;
    color: #333;
    font: 100%/1.5 calibri, arial, verdana, sans-serif;
}
```

From here on out, your browser developer tool is your best friend. Use the inspector to see the current style rules applied to various elements and make the appropriate changes in your child theme's CSS file. Again, remember to follow the precedence and specificity rules of CSS.

Your child theme can be as simple or complex as you make it. You can create a completely unique theme by simply editing the style sheet, as you have done previously. Or your child theme can turn into a completely new theme with all new templates, although this most likely defeats the purpose of using a child at all.

Here is how it works. When WordPress makes a decision on which template file to use, first it scans your child theme directory for that file. If that file does not exist, the parent theme directory is scanned. WordPress will prefer your template files over those of the parent theme, which means you can override the functionality of specific templates while maintaining the core of the parent theme. Or, your child theme could introduce custom page templates, but the foundation templates are pulled from the parent. There is a wide scope of opportunities here, although keep in mind the previously mentioned limitations.

The easiest way to accomplish this is to copy the template file you want to modify from the parent theme directory into your child theme directory and then modify as needed.

For example, the author template in the Twenty Fourteen theme is perfectly functional, but suppose you want to add an author image from Gravatar to this template. Again, this is an intentionally simple example and there are many ways to copy this.

First, copy the `author.php` template from the Twenty Fourteen theme into your child theme directory. Second, edit your child copy to include the avatar image. You could add it around line 33 of the code, where the author's biographical content is displayed. It might read something like this:

```php
<?php if ( get_the_author_meta( 'description' ) ) : ?>
  <div class="author-description"><?php the_author_meta( 'description' ); ?>
  <?php echo get_avatar( get_the_author_meta( 'user_email' )); ?>
</div>
?>
```

In this example, you only show the author's avatar if the author has included biographical content in his user profile. You can see an example of what this looks like in Figure 9-6.

FIGURE 9-6: Child themes make it easy to apply styles and content to specific pages.

You can further extend the child theme with your own `functions.php` file. WordPress automatically includes the parent theme's functions, but in addition, it also includes your child theme functions. You do have to be conscientious about function naming. Be very careful not to create functions in your own theme that have the same name as a parent theme function. If you need to override functionality, our advice is to make a new function in your own theme with a new name to avoid name resolution conflicts and adjust the template files as necessary to call your function instead.

In addition, theme frameworks have advanced significantly and many include multitudes of custom hook locations and filters for you to capitalize on. Using these custom hooks and filters, you can actually use your child theme's `functions.php` to inject and modify the parent theme's HTML without making a second copy of the template files. This is a process that builds on the topics covered in Chapter 8. This is a much more complex way to build child themes but provides you the most safety because you are able to update the parent theme in the future as your child theme uses the hooks of the parent to amend and change the theme to make it your own.

As you can see, child themes are yet another powerful tool in the WordPress theme arsenal. You can quickly get a theme up and running using an established theme as a base, and then modify and extend only what is required to create your own theme, all the while future proofing the upgradeability of your foundation theme.

This really is a game changing feature once you grasp it. It is not a simple concept, especially when you use a framework with custom hooks and filters. Even if your design team hand-codes each theme from scratch, having a foundation to start from offers a number of benefits, including increasing efficiencies because commonly implemented features are already being implemented consistently, and they also have the familiar CSS and markup vocabulary that your team is intimately familiar with. Regardless of whether your parent theme is one of the popular theme frameworks or something you have developed in-house, the benefits are quite tangible.

PREMIUM THEMES AND OTHER THEME FRAMEWORKS

Thus far in this chapter, you have explored the Twenty Fourteen theme and used it in most of the examples. But certainly, it is not the only theme or theme framework out there and may not be the best match for you or your development team.

Many of these other themes you will look at briefly include another layer of abstraction in them or a flurry of functions in the `functions.php` file. Generally, this abstraction brings the ability to modify the theme into the WordPress Dashboard. This may be ideal for certain clients who are not PHP-savvy and want that control delegated to the site administrator rather than the developers.

The best way to make a choice here is to try each theme out and kick the tires. Find a theme or theme framework that fits your coding style and needs and then run with it. Remember that you can make child themes or modify themes to meet your needs (license permitting, of course) from basically any theme out there, but with the new child theme functionality from back in WordPress 2.7, there has been a growth spurt in theme frameworks. You take a cursory look at some of the more popular theme frameworks (at the time of this writing) here. Many are out there, so be sure to look around.

Please keep in mind that various terms are thrown about with regard to themes. *Magazine themes* and *premium themes* mean different things to different people. Sometimes "premium" means the theme costs money; other times it means it includes an administration screen. Some themes that are available for a fee are called *commercial* themes. A theme framework is typically developed to be built upon. Although they may stand by themselves, they are intentionally written for extension. *Starter* themes are meant to be forked and edited in place. Your needs may vary with every project, and certainly you need to find a theme that speaks to you.

The following is just a sampling of some more popular themes that we have used in the past. There are many more to choose from and we are not endorsing any one over another.

Underscores (_s) Theme

Underscores (_s) is Automattic's version of a starter theme. Available online at `http://underscores.me`, this very minimal theme is the starting point for most of Automattic's home grown themes on WordPress.com. Automattic does not recommend using _s as a parent theme, but rather this theme was designed to be explored and used as a starter for your next great masterpiece. This theme uses many cutting edge WordPress features and design patterns, so check it out.

Bones Theme

Bones is a starter theme by Eddie Machado. The Bones theme is built on top of HTML5 boilerplate as a foundation, meaning that it is pretty forward thinking. We like Eddie's philosophy that child themes and theme frameworks are great, but sometimes they make things more complicated than they need to be. The simplicity of taking a starter theme and making a one-off project theme for a site appeals to many seasoned developers and this is the goal of the Bones theme.

In addition to HTML5, the Bones theme is a responsive base using media queries and a mobile-first mentality. Responsive web design is covered a little more in Chapter 12, but know that if you are making sites that you expect to be viewed on smartphones, having responsive views from the get-go helps. Bones recently dropped LESS support but continues to support Sass CSS pre-processor functionality for advanced developers. Check out the Bones theme at `http://themble.com/bones`.

Carrington Core Theme

Carrington Core is a theme framework by Alex King's Crowd Favorite. Carrington is designed for child themes and is built to be very modular, meaning you add in what functionality you need. Carrington does this by abstracting code into small components. This allows code reusability and keeps things organized. At first glance, Carrington can seem complicated, but once you digest the processes involved, it makes sense.

Crowd Favorite also has some other interesting WordPress projects, including RAMP, which was mentioned in Chapter 3, and the Carrington Build theme, which is a drag-and-drop pay layout generator. Learn more about the Carrington theme at `http://crowdfavorite.com/carrington-core/`.

Genesis Theme

The Genesis theme framework by Brian Gardner's StudioPress is one of the most, if not *the* most, popular theme frameworks around. The Genesis theme framework is designed exclusively for child themes, and StudioPress even sells many variations. To this end, the Genesis framework has many additional hooks and filters for customizing your child theme to make it unique.

The Genesis theme framework is an evolution of the Revolution theme. The Revolution theme was a pioneer in WordPress themes and really raised the bar to change theme development standards. Revolution was one of the first themes to embrace the magazine theme style that helped WordPress transcend the blog stereotype and become a viable CMS solution. Magazine-style themes made WordPress look less bloggy and more like a traditional website. In addition, the Revolution theme was one of the early commercial themes. The Revolution theme has since been retired and is no longer available. However StudioPress has taken its experience and created Genesis and many child themes.

You can find the Genesis Theme online at `http://studiopress.com`.

Hybrid Core Theme

The Hybrid theme by Justin Tadlock is free; a club membership fee is charged for access to the theme documentation, tutorials, and support forums. This theme includes a nice control panel to toggle various features and CSS hooks on and off. The Hybrid theme has several ready-made child themes available.

This theme has rich CSS hooks throughout the posts and body tags. It also includes numerous widget-ready areas and many custom page templates in the stock installation. These custom page templates cover a variety of use cases and really add to the theme, if you know how to use them. The Hybrid Core theme is modular with many features and extensions that can be enabled if you need them.

You can find more information about the Hybrid Core theme at `http://themehybrid.com/`.

Other Themes

The themes mentioned are some of the venerable tried and true themes that have made the WordPress theme ecosystem what it is today. That is not to say that they are the greatest, the most current, or the best choices for the foundation of your new projects. New theme frameworks and starter themes appear all the time and finding the best one for the underpinning of your project is a task unto itself. You would be remiss if you did not do your own searching and exploration of the current crop of themes, many of which are adopting new development processes such as grunt and bower JavaScript tasks and Sass and LESS CSS preprocessors, to name a few.

SUMMARY

In this chapter, you covered how to use themes to organize, structure, and present your content. Your theme is the face of your site, and no matter how good your content is, this presentation is what really seals the deal on the user experience. A theme that looks amateurish can hurt the credibility of your site, whereas a sharp, professional theme can enhance the whole experience.

In the next chapter, you will look at taking external content sources and incorporating them into your WordPress site to further develop the quality of your content and the user experience.

10

Multisite

WHAT'S IN THIS CHAPTER?

➤ Understanding WordPress Multisite

➤ Differences between Multisite and standard WordPress

➤ Installing and configuring a Multisite network

➤ Coding for Multisite

➤ Multisite database schema

WROX.COM CODE DOWNLOADS FOR THIS CHAPTER

The wrox.com code downloads for this chapter are found at www.wrox.com/go/wordpress3e on the Download Code tab. The code is in the Chapter 10 download file and individually named according to the code file names throughout the chapter.

WordPress Multisite is a powerful core feature in WordPress. When enabled, Multisite allows you to create multiple websites with a single install of WordPress. This makes it easy to rapidly launch new WordPress websites. A Multisite network can even allow open user and site registration, enabling anyone to create a new site in your network. The largest WordPress Multisite network is WordPress.com, which is a great example of what Multisite can be.

WHAT IS MULTISITE?

Prior to WordPress 3.0, Multisite was called WordPress MU (or multi-user) and was a separate software package that needed to be downloaded and installed. WordPress 3.0 merged MU into the core of WordPress, and WordPress Multisite was born.

Multisite is not enabled by default, so it's important to understand the differences before enabling Multisite in your WordPress installation.

Multisite Terminology

It's important to understand the terminology used throughout this chapter when working with WordPress Multisite. Two important terms in Multisite are *network* and *site*. A network is the entire Multisite installation, or the network. A site is a single site inside the network. Therefore, WordPress Multisite is a network of sites.

Another important term is *Blog ID*. The Blog ID is a unique ID assigned to every new site created in Multisite. Many of the functions and code examples will reference the Blog ID. Sometimes this is also referred to as the *site ID*. Remember that WordPress was originally built as a blogging platform but has evolved over the years into a full-fledged content management system. Therefore, many of the functions and code in WordPress still reference items as "blogs" when really they are sites.

> **NOTE** *Don't let the term "blog" confuse you. A blog in WordPress Multisite is actually a site in the network. A Blog ID, as referred to by many functions and code examples, is the unique ID of the site in the network.*

Differences

When you install standard WordPress, you are installing a single website to run on WordPress. WordPress Multisite enables you to run an unlimited number of websites with a single install of WordPress. When enabling Multisite, you need to determine how sites will be viewed in WordPress, either using subdomains or subdirectories. The following is an example of both:

Subdirectory Example

➤ `http://example.com/site1`

➤ `http://example.com/site2`

Subdomain Example

➤ `http://site1.example.com/`

➤ `http://site2.example.com/`

As you can see, this is a pretty big decision and one that should be carefully considered. With a plugin, there are ways to map top-level domains to any site in your network (i.e., `http://mywebsite.com`), which is covered later on in this chapter.

Themes and plugins are also treated differently in Multisite. Individual site administrators can enable themes and plugins on their site, but they can't install them.

WordPress Multisite also introduces a new user role: Super Admin. Super Admin users have access to the Network Admin section of Multisite. This section is where all Multisite configuration occurs. Super Admins also have full access to every site in the Multisite network, whereas normal Administrators only have access to the site they are an administrator of.

Advantages of Multisite

WordPress Multisite has a number of advantages over standard WordPress. The biggest advantage of Multisite is that you have a single install of WordPress to administer. This makes updates for WordPress core, themes, and plugins much easier. If you have a WordPress Multisite network of 50 sites, and a plugin update is released, you need to update that plugin only once and it will affect all sites in your network. If each of the 50 sites were a separate install of WordPress, you would have to update that plugin 50 separate times.

Aggregating content is also another big advantage. It is very easy to share content between your sites in a Multisite network. For example, if you have 50 sites in your network, you could easily aggregate posts from every site to your main blog to showcase your network of sites and content.

The biggest advantage to using Multisite is the speed in which you can launch new sites. With just a few clicks you can create new sites in your network. These sites can share themes, plugins, and even users.

Enabling Multisite

Enabling the Multisite feature of WordPress is a pretty straightforward process. The first step is to add the following line of code to your wp-config.php file:

```
define( 'WP_ALLOW_MULTISITE', true );
```

This line of code should be added just above the comment that reads:

```
/* That's all, stop editing! Happy blogging. */.
```

Save your wp-config.php file and upload to your server. Now log in to the admin dashboard of WordPress and you'll notice a new submenu item for Tools ➤ Network Setup, as shown in Figure 10-1.

The Network Setup screen will vary depending on your current WordPress setup. If your setup allows it, you will choose either Subdomains or Subdirectories for your Multisite setup. You also need to verify that the Server Address, Network Title, and Admin E-mail Address values are correct. These are filled in automatically by WordPress, but you can modify the values if needed. After you have confirmed that the settings are what you want, click the Install button to install Multisite in WordPress.

FIGURE 10-1: Network Setup submenu

The final step to enabling Multisite will be presented on the screen; it's a series of manual changes you need to make to WordPress.

The first step is to add some code to your wp-config.php file. This code defines the base settings for Multisite and will vary depending on your setup. The following is a code example for a Subdirectory install of Multisite under the example.com domain.

```
define('MULTISITE', true);
define('SUBDOMAIN_INSTALL', false);
define('DOMAIN_CURRENT_SITE', 'example.com');
define('PATH_CURRENT_SITE', '/');
```

```
define('SITE_ID_CURRENT_SITE', 1);
define('BLOG_ID_CURRENT_SITE', 1);
```

The final step is to replace your .htaccess file rules with the new rules provided:

```
RewriteEngine On
RewriteBase /
RewriteRule ^index\.php$ - [L]

# add a trailing slash to /wp-admin
RewriteRule ^([_0-9a-zA-Z-]+/)?wp-admin$ $1wp-admin/ [R=301,L]

RewriteCond %{REQUEST_FILENAME} -f [OR]
RewriteCond %{REQUEST_FILENAME} -d
RewriteRule ^ - [L]
RewriteRule ^([_0-9a-zA-Z-]+/)?(wp-(content|admin|includes).*) $2 [L]
RewriteRule ^([_0-9a-zA-Z-]+/)?(.*\.php)$ $2 [L]
RewriteRule . index.php [L]
```

These rules may differ depending on your Multisite setup, so make sure you copy the code provided in the Network Setup screen when enabling Multisite in WordPress.

After making the required changes, you will be required to log back in to WordPress. The easiest way to tell when Multisite is enabled is through the WordPress admin bar. You'll notice a new menu item named My Sites. When hovering over this menu, the first Submenu link is Network Admin, which is the main admin dashboard for Multisite. The My Sites menu will also list all sites you are a member of in your network, as shown in Figure 10-2. WordPress Multisite is now enabled and ready to use!

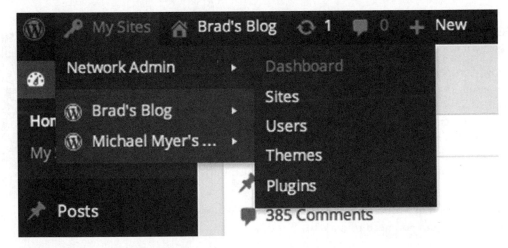

FIGURE 10-2: Multisite Network menu

WORKING IN A NETWORK

Now that you know how to enable Multisite in WordPress, it's important to understand how to manage your network. This section covers the Multisite Network Admin section of WordPress and how to manage a network.

Network Admin

The WordPress Multisite Network Admin is the central hub for all Multisite management of your network. You can access the Network Admin under the My Sites menu in the WordPress admin bar or by visiting `http://example.com/wp-admin/network/`.

The Network Admin should look very familiar because its layout and style are very similar to the standard WordPress admin dashboard.

Creating and Managing Sites

To view a list of all sites in your Multisite Network, visit the Sites menu. Here you will see every site registered in Multisite, regardless of the status of the site. The list screen gives you some important information, such as the site name, last updated date, registered date, and all users that are members of that site. To edit any site's settings, click on the site name to bring up the Edit Site screen.

The Edit Site section allows you to edit all settings of a specific site in your network. You'll notice tabs for each settings section, as shown in Figure 10-3.

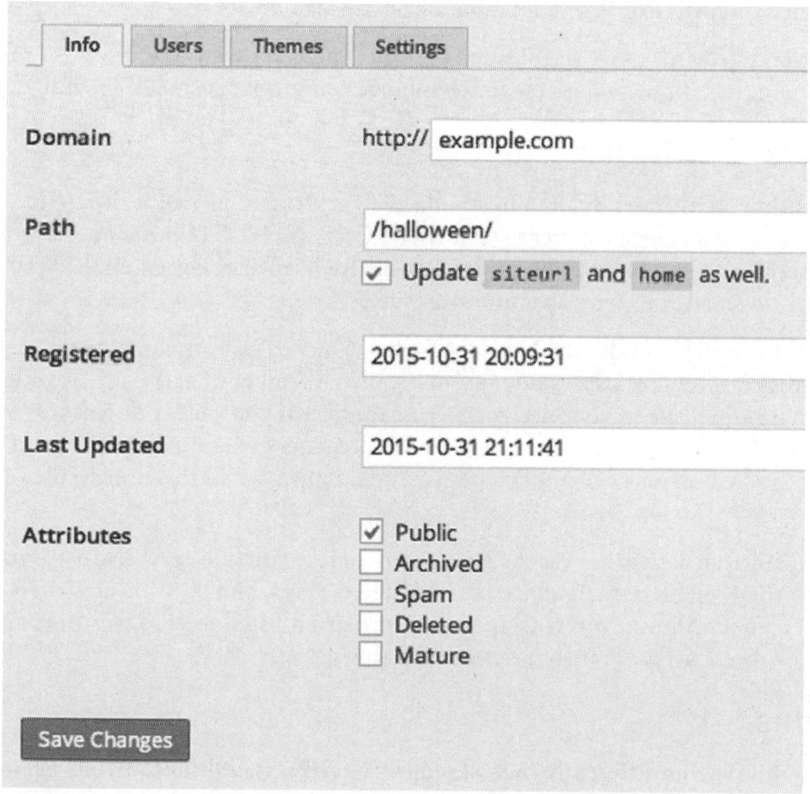

FIGURE 10-3: Edit Site section

The Info tab allows you to edit the domain and path of the site. These two settings are not configurable for the main site in your network. You can also change the Registered and Last updated date and timestamps. The final editable item is the Attributes, or site status, setting. Every site in your network can have one of the following five site statuses:

➤ Public—Site is public if privacy is set to enable search engines.

➤ Archived—Site has been archived and is not available to the public.

➤ Spam—Site is considered spam and is not available to the public.

➤ Deleted—Site is flagged for deletion and is not available to the public.

➤ Mature—Site is flagged as mature.

The only two statuses that don't remove the site from public viewing are Public and Mature.

The Users tab allows you to administer what users have access to this site. This section will list all users of the site with their role. You can also add new users to the site. The next section covers users in Multisite in more detail.

The Themes tab allows you to enable or disable themes for the site. Enabling a theme on this screen does not actually activate the theme for the site you are editing, but rather, makes that theme an available option for the site administrator to enable should he choose to do so.

The Settings tab enables you to edit all other settings for the site. There are a lot of options on this screen. As a good rule, if you don't know what you are changing, you probably shouldn't change it.

Working with Users and Roles

Users in a Multisite network work differently than in standard WordPress. The major difference is that each site in the network can have a different set of users. Users can also be a member of multiple sites in your network and even have a different user role for each site. For example, you could be an Administrator on site A, but only an Author on site X.

If Allow New Registrations is enabled under the Network Settings menu, visitors can register new user accounts in WordPress. A New User is not automatically a member of every site in your network, but rather the main (first) site in your network. For example, if your network features two sites, a Halloween site and a Christmas site, any visitor who registers would be a member of the Halloween site but not the Christmas site. Of course, you could always add this user to the Christmas site later.

To view all users in your Multisite network, visit the Users menu. Here you will see a list of all users in the network along with their names, e-mail addresses, registered dates, and a list of sites they are members of. If the user is a Super Admin, you will see that information listed next to her username. You can easily add, edit, or delete users from your network in this section.

Themes and Plugins

Multisite handles themes and plugins differently than standard WordPress. All sites in your network can run the same plugins and themes, or they can run a completely different set of plugins and themes. The flexibility of this really showcases the power of Multisite in WordPress.

Themes

To view all themes installed in WordPress, visit the Themes menu. The Network Admin Themes section lists all themes in a list similar to the standard WordPress Plugins section. The major difference is that rather than an `Activate` link for each theme, you'll notice a `Network Enable` link instead. Network Enabling any theme listed will make that theme an available option for all sites in your network. This doesn't actually activate the theme, but rather makes the theme available to site administrators under the Appearance ➢ Themes menu in WordPress. This allows you to control what themes are available for your site administrators to choose from.

Plugins

Plugins work differently from themes in Multisite. Plugins can be Network Activated, which means the plugin will run on every site in your network. If a plugin is not Network Activated, it can still be activated at the site level. This means that you can run plugins on any, or all, sites in your network.

To view all plugins available for use, visit the Plugins menu. Here you'll see a list of plugins that have been downloaded to WordPress. Clicking the Network Activate link will activate the plugin across every site in your network. If a plugin is not Network Activated, it will be available to activate at the site level under the standard Plugins menu.

> **NOTE** *It's important to verify that a plugin is Multisite-compatible prior to network-enabling the plugin. If the plugin hasn't been tested on Multisite, or coded properly, there is a chance it could break your network when activated network wide.*

Settings

The Settings menu lets you set network-wide settings in Multisite. Here you can enable user account registration and even site creation for your users. Enabling both of these features would allow visitors to register user accounts and even create new sites in your network.

You can also set what file types are allowed for upload, total site upload space, and the max upload file size. If you plan on launching a very large Multisite network, limiting site upload space and max upload size could save you a massive amount of disk space.

By default, the Plugins menu is hidden from site administrators. This allows only Super Admins to activate and deactivate plugins at the site level. If you want to enable the Plugins menu for regular administrators, you can do so under the Menu Settings section.

Domain Mapping

One very common feature for Multisite users is domain mapping. Earlier, you considered the two default site configurations for Multisite: Subdirectory or Subdomain. But what if you want each site in your network to have a unique domain name? There's a plugin for that! The WordPress MU Domain Mapping plugin (`https://wordpress.org/plugins/wordpress-mu-domain-mapping/`) allows you to do just that. This plugin makes it very easy to attach a top-level domain to any site in your network. The plugin also works with both Subdirectory and Subdomain setups. For example, instead of two sites like `http://example.com/brad` and `http://example.com/myers`, you could have `http://brad.com` and `http://myers.com`. All URLs will be served up using the top-level domain you have assigned to your sites.

There have been discussions around rolling domain-mapping functionality into the Core of WordPress, but for now you'll have to use a plugin to accomplish it.

CODING FOR MULTISITE

When Multisite is enabled in WordPress, you can take advantage of an entirely new set of Multisite-specific functions and APIs in your themes and plugins. Understanding these new features can help you make your themes and plugins Multisite-compatible.

Blog ID

Every site in your Multisite network has a unique ID associated with it. This unique ID is called the Blog ID. Almost every function you work with when writing Multisite-specific code will use this Blog ID. This is how WordPress determines what site you want to work with.

The Blog ID is also used in the database table prefix with each new site you create in your network. When you create new sites in Multisite, WordPress creates additional database tables to store that site's content and settings. For example, if you create a second site in your network, WordPress will create new tables prefixed like `wp_2_posts`, where `wp_` is the table prefix you defined when installing WordPress, and `2_` is the Blog ID of the new site.

The Blog ID is stored in the global variable `$blog_id`, as shown here:

```php
<?php
global $blog_id;
echo 'Current Blog ID: ' .$blog_id;
?>
```

In Multisite, the `$blog_id` will always be the ID of the current site you are viewing. In standard WordPress, the `$blog_id` global variable will always be 1.

Common Functions

Some common functions are available when working with Multisite. The most important function when working with Multisite is the `is_multisite()` function, as shown here:

```php
<?php
if ( is_multisite() ) {
    echo 'Multisite is enabled';
}
?>
```

This function determines whether Multisite is enabled and, if so, returns `true`. Anytime you plan on using Multisite-specific functions in WordPress, it's extremely important that you verify that

Multisite is actually enabled before doing so. If Multisite is not enabled, and you call a Multisite function, you will receive an error message and the site will break.

Another useful function for retrieving site-specific information is the `get_blog_details()` function.

```php
<?php get_blog_details( $fields, $getall ); ?>
```

The function accepts two parameters:

➤ `$fields`—Blog ID, a blog name, or an array of fields to query against

➤ `$getall`—Whether to retrieve all details

Using this function, you can retrieve general site information for any site specified.

```php
<?php print_r( get_blog_details( 1 ) ); ?>
```

Running the preceding code example displays the following results:

```
stdClass Object
(
    [blog_id] => 1
    [site_id] => 1
    [domain] => example.com
    [path] => /
    [registered] => 2012-10-31 19:01:47
    [last_updated] => 2012-10-31 19:01:49
    [public] => 1
    [archived] => 0
    [mature] => 0
    [spam] => 0
    [deleted] => 0
    [lang_id] => 0
    [blogname] => Halloween Site
    [siteurl] => http://example.com
    [post_count] => 420
)
```

When working in a Multisite network, you may need to retrieve a list of all sites in the network. To do this, you'll use the `wp_get_sites()` function. This function will return an array of sites in your network.

```php
<?php
$all_sites = wp_get_sites();

print_r( $all_sites );
```

The preceding code will return an array of all sites in the network with site-specific information including domain, date registered, and the site status:

```
Array(
    [0] => Array(
        [blog_id] => 1
```

```
                [site_id] => 1
                [domain] => example.com
                [path] => /
                [registered] => 2015-03-31 17:56:46
                [last_updated] => 2015-03-31 18:57:19
                [public] => 1
                [archived] => 0
                [mature] => 0
                [spam] => 0
                [deleted] => 0
                [lang_id] => 0
        )

    [1] => Array(
                [blog_id] => 2
                [site_id] => 1
                [domain] => example.com
                [path] => /halloweensite/
                [registered] => 2015-03-31 18:07:22
                [last_updated] => 2013-03-31 18:13:40
                [public] => 1
                [archived] => 0
                [mature] => 0
                [spam] => 0
                [deleted] => 0
                [lang_id] => 0
        )
    )
```

It's important to note that if you use this function on a large network, which by default is defined as a network with over 10,000 users or sites, this function will return an empty array. Querying for a list of all sites in a network with tens of thousands of sites would be a huge resource hog. You'll cover detecting large networks later on in this chapter.

Switching and Restoring Sites

One of the main advantages to using WordPress Multisite is how easy it is to aggregate content, and other data, between different sites in your Multisite network.

There are two primary functions you can use to retrieve data from other sites in your network. The first of these is the switch_to_blog() function. This function enables you to switch to any site in your network:

```php
<?php switch_to_blog( $blog_id, $validate ); ?>
```

The function accepts two parameters:

➤ $blog_id—The ID of the site you want to switch to.

➤ $validate—Whether to check if the site exists before proceeding. The default is false.

The second function is restore_current_blog(). This function does exactly what it sounds like: It restores the previous site after a switch_to_blog() function is called. There are no parameters for this function; simply call it after you are done gathering content and data from the site.

Consider the following example that uses these two functions. In this example, you'll create a custom shortcode to retrieve the latest five posts from a site in your network:

```
add_shortcode( 'show_network_posts', 'prowp_get_network_posts' );
```

First, register a new shortcode called show _ network _ posts using the add _ shortcode() function. The new shortcode will accept one parameter, which is the Blog ID you want to display the latest posts from. Next, you'll create the function to return the latest posts from a site in your network.

```
function prowp_get_network_posts( $atts ) {
    extract( shortcode_atts( array(
        'blog_id' => '1'
    ), $atts ) );

    //verify Multisite is enabled
    if ( is_multisite() ) {

        //switch to blog based on ID
        switch_to_blog( absint( $blog_id ) );

        //create a custom loop
        $recent_posts = new WP_Query();
        $recent_posts->query( 'posts_per_page=5' );

        $site_posts = '';

        //start the custom loop
        while ( $recent_posts->have_posts() ) :
            $recent_posts->the_post();

            //store the recent posts in a variable
            $site_posts .= '<p><a href="' . get_permalink() . '">'
                . get_the_title() . '</a></p>';

        endwhile;

        //restore the current site
        restore_current_blog();

    }

    //return the posts
    return $site_posts;

}
```

As always, you need to verify that Multisite is enabled using the is _ multisite() function check. Next, use the switch _ to _ blog() function to switch to the Blog ID passed in through the shortcode. If the user does not set the Blog ID in the shortcode, it will default to Blog ID 1. Now that you've switched to the site, you'll create a custom loop using WP _ Query to pull the latest posts from the site. Next, loop through the WP _ Query results, storing each post in a variable called $site _ posts.

After the loop has completed, you need to run `restore_current_blog()` to switch back to the previous site you were viewing. If you do not run this function, WordPress stays on Blog ID 10, so any subsequent loops or custom code will assume you are still on Blog ID 10, when in fact you are not. The final step is to return the variable `$site_posts`, which contain the latest five posts from Blog ID 10.

That's it! Now you can easily display the most recent blog posts from any site in your network using the shortcode: `[show_network_posts blog_id="10"]`. Listing 10-1 shows the entire code packaged up in a plugin.

LISTING 10-1: Multisite shortcode example (code file: `prowp3-multisite-shortcode.zip`)

```php
<?php
/*
Plugin Name: ProWP3 Multsite Shortcode Example
Plugin URI: http://strangework.com/wordpress-plugins
Description: A shortcode to display posts from any site in your network
Version: 1.0
Author: Brad Williams
Author URI: http://strangework.com
License: GPLv2
*/

add_shortcode( 'show_network_posts', 'prowp_get_network_posts' );

function prowp_get_network_posts( $atts ) {
    extract( shortcode_atts( array(
        'blog_id' => '1'
    ), $atts ) );

    //verify Multisite is enabled
    if ( is_multisite() ) {

        //switch to blog based on ID
        switch_to_blog( absint( $blog_id ) );

        //create a custom loop
        $recent_posts = new WP_Query();
        $recent_posts->query( 'posts_per_page=5' );

        $site_posts = '';

        //start the custom loop
        while ( $recent_posts->have_posts() ) :
            $recent_posts->the_post();

            //store the recent posts in a variable
            $site_posts .= '<p><a href="' . get_permalink() . '">'
                . get_the_title() . '</a></p>';

        endwhile;

        //restore the current site
        restore_current_blog();
```

```
        }

        //return the posts
        return $site_posts;

    }
```

When switching between sites in a network, you may need to determine if a switch is actually in effect. To do so, you'll use the ms _ is _ switched() function. This function returns True if switched and False otherwise.

```
<?php
if ( ms_is_switched() ) {

    //you are in a switched state

}
?>
```

The switch _ to _ blog() function is not just limited to site content, but can also retrieve other WordPress data including menus, widgets, sidebars, and more. Basically, any data stored in the content database tables (wp _ blogid _ tablename) is available when using switch _ to _ blog().

Consider a different example. This time you'll retrieve a specific menu from a site in your Multisite network.

```
<?php
switch_to_blog( 10 );
wp_nav_menu( 'Main Menu' );
restore_current_blog();
?>
```

First run switch _ to _ blog() to switch to Blog ID 10. Next, use the wp _ nav _ menu() WordPress function to display a menu named Main Menu from the site. Finally, run restore _ current _ blog() to reset back to the current site you are viewing. The preceding code will display the Main Menu nav menu from Site ID 10 anywhere you run this code.

It's important to note that the switch _ to _ blog() function has the potential to generate very large SQL queries, which could cause performance issues with WordPress. It's best to cache any data retrieved using this function in a transient, which enables data to be temporarily stored as a cached version. WordPress transients are covered in detail in Chapter 8.

Another important note is that switch _ to _ blog() only changes the database context; it does not inherit the entire site configuration. This means that a site's plugins are not included in a switch. If you switch to a site and try to execute a function specific to a plugin that is not enabled, you will receive an error message.

Creating a New Site

You've learned how to create new sites in the Network Admin of Multisite, so now you will see how to create new sites via code. To do so, you'll use the wpmu _ create _ blog() function.

```
<?php wpmu_create_blog($domain, $path, $title, $user_id, $meta, $site_id); ?>
```

This function accepts six parameters:

➤ `$domain`—The domain of the new site

➤ `$path`—The path of the new site

➤ `$title`—The title of the new site

➤ `$user_id`—The user ID of the user who will be the site admin

➤ `$meta`—Additional meta information

➤ `$site_id`—The site ID of the site to be created

Only the first four parameters are required; the last two are optional. The `$site_id` parameter is only used if you plan to run multiple WordPress Networks inside a single installation of WordPress. If the new site is created successfully, the function will return the newly created Blog ID of the site.

For example, you can build a plugin that uses the `wpmu_create_blog()` function to create new sites in your Multisite network, as follows:

```
add_action( 'admin_menu', 'prowp_multisite_create_menu' );

function prowp_multisite_create_menu() {
    //create custom top-level menu
    add_menu_page( 'Multisite Create Site Page', 'Multisite Create Site',
        'manage_options', 'prowp-network-create', 'prowp_multisite_create_sites' );
}
```

First, you'll create a new top-level menu called Multisite Create Site. This menu will link to a custom function called `prowp_multisite_create_sites()`, which will allow you to create sites in the network. Go ahead and create that function as follows:

```
function prowp_multisite_create_sites() {
    //check if multisite is enabled
    if ( is_multisite() ) {
```

Remember to always verify that Multisite is enabled using the `is_multisite()` function. Next, you'll add the code to retrieve the submitted form field values and create a new site in Multisite:

```
//if the form was submitted lets process it
if ( isset( $_POST['create_site'] ) ) {

    //check nonce for security
    check_admin_referer( 'create-network-site', 'prowp-network-plugin' );

    //populate the variables based on form values
    $domain = sanitize_text_field( $_POST['domain'] );
    $path = sanitize_text_field( $_POST['path'] );
    $title = sanitize_text_field( $_POST['title'] );
    $user_id = absint( $_POST['user_id'] );

    //verify the required values are set
```

```
if ( $domain && $path && $title && $user_id ) {

    //create the new site in WordPress
    $new_site = wpmu_create_blog( $domain, $path, $title, $user_id );

    //if successful display a message
    if ( $new_site ) {

        echo '<div class="updated">New site ' .$new_site
            . ' created successfully!</div>';
    }

//if required values are not set display an error
} else {

    echo '<div class="error">New site could not be created.
        Required fields are missing</div>';
}
}
```

First check if $ _ POST['create _ site'] is set. This field will be set only if the form has been submitted. As with any form, you'll include a nonce security check. Next you'll populate the variable values with the data submitted via the form. Notice that you're using the proper sanitizing functions to verify that the values submitted do not contain HTML and PHP code. You also verify the user _ id value is a positive integer using the WordPress absint() function.

Now that the variables are set, you want to verify they each have a value. If you are missing data for any of the four required parameters an error message is displayed. After you've verified that the values exist, it's time to execute the wpmu _ create _ blog() function to create the new site. If the new site is created successfully, the variable $new _ site will contain the new Blog ID of the site.

Now you will build the form for the new site fields using the following:

```
<div class="wrap">
    <h2>Create New Site</h2>
    <form method="post">
    <?php
    //create nonce hidden field for security
    wp_nonce_field( 'create-network-site', 'prowp-network-plugin' );
    ?>
    <table class="form-table">
    <tr valign="top">
        <th scope="row"><label for="fname">Domain</label></th>
        <td><input maxlength="45" size="25" name="domain"
            value="<?php echo esc_attr( DOMAIN_CURRENT_SITE ); ?>" /></td>
    </tr>
    <tr valign="top">
        <th scope="row"><label for="fname">Path</label></th>
        <td><input maxlength="45" size="10" name="path" /></td>
    </tr>
    <tr valign="top">
        <th scope="row"><label for="fname">Title</label></th>
        <td><input maxlength="45" size="25" name="title" /></td>
    </tr>
    <tr valign="top">
        <th scope="row"><label for="fname">User ID</label></th>
```

```
        <td><input maxlength="45" size="3" name="user_id" /></td>
    </tr>
    <tr valign="top">
        <td>
        <input type="submit" name="create_site"
            value="Create Site" class="button-primary" />
        <input type="submit" name="reset" value="Reset" class="button-secondary" />
        </td>
    </tr>
    </table>
    </form>
</div>
```

This is standard HTML to collect the required field data for creating the new site in Multisite. You can now easily create new sites in your network using the full plugin shown in Listing 10-2.

LISTING 10-2: Create sites in Multisite example (code file: prowp3-multisite-create-site.zip)

```php
<?php
/*
Plugin Name: ProWP3 Create Site Example Plugin
Plugin URI: http://strangework.com/wordpress-plugins
Description: A plugin to demonstrate creating sites in Multisite
Version: 1.0
Author: Brad Williams
Author URI: http://strangework.com
License: GPLv2
*/

add_action( 'admin_menu', 'prowp_multisite_create_menu' );

function prowp_multisite_create_menu() {

    //create custom top-level menu
    add_menu_page( 'Multisite Create Site Page',
        'Multisite Create Site', 'manage_options',
        'prowp-network-create', 'prowp_multisite_create_sites' );

}

function prowp_multisite_create_sites() {

    //check if multisite is enabled
    if ( is_multisite() ) {

        //if the form was submitted lets process it
        if ( isset( $_POST['create_site'] ) ) {

            //check nonce for security
            check_admin_referer( 'create-network-site',
                'prowp-network-plugin' );

            //populate the variables based on form values
```

```php
$domain = sanitize_text_field( $_POST['domain'] );
$path = sanitize_text_field( $_POST['path'] );
$title = sanitize_text_field( $_POST['title'] );
$user_id = absint( $_POST['user_id'] );

//verify the required values are set
if ( $domain && $path && $title && $user_id ) {

    //create the new site in WordPress
    $new_site = wpmu_create_blog( $domain, $path,
        $title, $user_id );

    //if successfully display a message
    if ( $new_site ) {

        echo '<div class="updated">New site ' . $new_site
            . ' created successfully!</div>';

    }

//if required values are not set display an error
} else {

    echo '<div class="error">New site could not be created.
        Required fields are missing</div>';

}

}
?>
<div class="wrap">
    <h2>Create New Site</h2>
    <form method="post">
        <?php
        //create nonce hidden field for security
        wp_nonce_field( 'create-network-site',
            'prowp-network-plugin' );
        ?>
    <table class="form-table">
    <tr valign="top">
        <th scope="row"><label for="fname">Domain</label></th>
        <td><input maxlength="45" size="25" name="domain"
            value="<?php echo esc_attr( DOMAIN_CURRENT_SITE ); ?>" /></td>
    </tr>
    <tr valign="top">
        <th scope="row"><label for="fname">Path</label></th>
        <td><input maxlength="45" size="10" name="path" /></td>
    </tr>
    <tr valign="top">
        <th scope="row"><label for="fname">Title</label></th>
        <td><input maxlength="45" size="25" name="title" /></td>
    </tr>
    <tr valign="top">
```

continues

LISTING 10-2: (Continued)

```
                 <th scope="row"><label for="fname">User ID</label></th>
                 <td><input maxlength="45" size="3" name="user_id" /></td>
             </tr>
             <tr valign="top">
                 <td>
                 <input type="submit" name="create_site"
                     value="Create Site" class="button-primary" />
                 <input type="submit" name="reset" value="Reset"
                     class="button-secondary" />
                 </td>
             </tr>
             </table>
             </form>
         </div>
         <?php
     } else {

         echo '<p>Multisite is not enabled</p>';

     }

 }
```

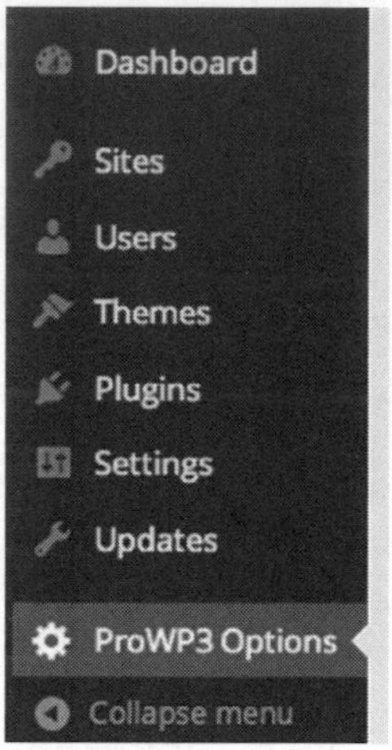

FIGURE 10-4: Network
Admin top-level menu

Network Admin Menus

Earlier in this chapter, we covered the Multisite Network Admin
section of WordPress. This Dashboard is where all network settings are
configured. As in standard WordPress, you can add menus and submenus
to the Network Admin screen. To do this, you'll use the network _
admin _ menu action hook, as shown here:

```
add_action( 'network_admin_menu', 'prowp_add_network_settings_menu' );
```

The network _ admin _ menu action hook is triggered after the default network admin menu
structure is in place. The second parameter is the custom function prowp _ add _ network _
settings _ menu(), which will register your new menu.

```
function prowp_add_network_settings_menu() {
    //add settings menu
    add_menu_page( 'ProWP3 Options Page', 'ProWP3 Options',
        'manage_options', 'prowp-network-settings', 'prowp_network_settings' );
}
```

As you can see, registering the new menu is exactly the same as registering a standard WordPress
menu. In this example, you use the add _ menu _ page() function to create a new top-level menu in
the Network Admin, as shown in Figure 10-4.

Just as easily as you can add a new top-level menu to the Network Admin, you can add submenu items to existing menus. To do this, you'll use the add_submenu_page() function, as shown here:

```
add_action( 'network_admin_menu', 'prowp_add_network_settings_menu' );

function prowp_add_network_settings_menu() {

    //add settings menu
    add_menu_page( 'ProWP3 Options Page', 'ProWP3 Options',
        'manage_options', 'prowp-network-settings', 'prowp_network_settings' );

    add_submenu_page( 'prowp-network-settings', 'ProWP3 Help Page',
        'ProWP3 Help', 'manage_options', 'prowp-network-help',
            'prowp_network_help' );

}
```

This function works exactly as in standard WordPress. The first parameter, settings.php in this case, is the most important. That value tells the function what top-level menu to add your submenu to. In this example, you added a submenu item called ProWP3 Options to the Settings menu in the Network Admin.

The following is a list of file names that you can add submenus to:

➤ index.php—Add submenu to the Dashboard menu.

➤ sites.php—Add submenu to the Sites menu

➤ users.php—Add submenu to the Users menu.

➤ themes.php—Add submenu to the Themes menu.

➤ plugins.php—Add submenu to the Plugins menu.

➤ settings.php—Add submenu to the Settings menu.

➤ update-core.php—Add submenu to the Updates menu.

As a general rule, it's best to add your network settings as a submenu of the Settings menu in the Network Admin. This is where most users will look for plugin settings, just like in standard WordPress.

Multisite Options

When storing options in Multisite, it's important to use the proper functions to store the options in the proper place. The question you should ask yourself is who should control the settings value. If the setting is specific to each site in the network, and can vary between sites, then you should store your options as site options. If the setting should be a network-wide setting that shouldn't vary between sites, then you should store your options as network options.

Site Options

To store site-specific options in Multisite, you can utilize the * _ blog _ option() functions. The following is a list of each function:

- ➤ add_blog_option()—Creates a new option
- ➤ update_blog_option()—Updates an option and creates it if it doesn't exist
- ➤ get_blog_option()—Loads a site option
- ➤ delete_blog_option()—Deletes a site option

These functions work almost identically to the standard WordPress option functions; the major difference is that the functions require a $blog _ id parameter to be defined, as shown here:

```php
<?php add_blog_option( $blog_id, $key, $value ); ?>
```

The $key parameter is the option name you want to set and the $value parameter is the value to set for the option.

Retrieving a site option is just as easy. The following example shows you how to use get _ blog _ option() to retrieve site-specific options for Blog ID 10:

```php
<?php
$blog_id = 10;
echo '<p>Site ID: ' .$blog_id .'</p>';
echo '<p>Site Name: ' .get_blog_option( $blog_id, 'blogname' ) .'</p>';
echo '<p>Site URL: ' .get_blog_option( $blog_id, 'siteurl' ) .'</p>';
?>
```

Network Options

To store network-wide options in Multisite, you can utilize the * _ site _ option() functions. The follow list describes each function:

- ➤ add_site_option()—Creates a new network option
- ➤ update_site_option()—Updates a network option and creates it if it doesn't exist
- ➤ get_site_option()—Loads a network option
- ➤ delete_site_option()—Deletes a network option

These functions work almost identically to standard WordPress option functions, but the option values are stored in the wp _ sitemeta Multisite database table. You can use these functions to store global Multisite settings that should be the same for all sites in your network.

```php
<?php add_site_option( $key, $value ); ?>
```

Notice that you do not need to define the Blog ID when adding a network option. Because you are storing a network option, it doesn't matter what Blog ID the code is being executed from.

If Multisite is not enabled, and your code calls one of the * _ site _ option() functions, WordPress will fall back to using standard * _ option() functions such as add _ option().

Network Options Example

Now that you understand how to create and retrieve network options, let's build a simple network options plugin for Multisite. In this example, you are going to build a plugin to store network wide options. The plugin will degrade gracefully, so if the user is not running Multisite, the options will be stored as standard WordPress options.

The first step in your plugin will be to add the network settings menu.

```
add_action( 'init', 'prowp_network_settings_menu' );
function prowp_network_settings_menu() {

    if ( is_multisite() ) {

        //Multisite is enabled so add menu to Network Admin
        add_action( 'network_admin_menu', 'prowp_add_network_settings_menu' );
    } else {

        //Multisite is NOT enabled so add menu to WordPress Admin
        add_action( 'admin_menu', 'prowp_add_network_settings_menu' );
    }

}
```

The init action hook is used to call your custom function to register the network options menu. Notice how the is_multisite() function is used in the preceding example. If the user has Multisite enabled, the new menu will be added to the Network Admin of Multisite. If the user does not have Multisite enabled, the menu will be added as a standard WordPress menu. This code is important to preserve compatibility regardless of whether Multisite is enabled or not.

Now that you've registered the proper menu action hook, you need to create the custom function to register the new menu.

```
function prowp_add_network_settings_menu() {
    //add settings menu
    add_menu_page( 'Network Options Page', 'Network Options',
        'manage_options', 'prowp-network-settings', 'prowp_network_settings' );
}
```

The preceding code uses the add_menu_page() function to create a new top-level menu labeled Network Options. Now that the menu has been created, you need to create the actual settings form.

```
//generate the settings page
function prowp_network_settings() {
    ?>
    <div class="wrap" >
        <div id="icon-options-general" class="icon32"></div>
        <h2>Network Settings</h2>
        <form method="post">
            <?php
            //load option values
            $network_settings = get_site_option( 'prowp_network_settings' );
            $api_key = $network_settings['api_key'];
            $holiday = $network_settings['holiday'];
```

```php
        $rage_mode = ( ! empty( $network_settings['rage_mode'] ) )
            ? $network_settings['rage_mode'] : '';

        //create nonce hidden field for security
        wp_nonce_field( 'save-network-settings', 'prowp-network-plugin' );
        ?>
        <table class="form-table">
            <tr valign="top"><th scope="row">API Key:</th>
                <td><input type="text" name="network_settings[api_key]"
                    value="<?php echo esc_attr( $api_key ); ?>" /></td>
            </tr>
            <tr valign="top"><th scope="row">Network Holiday</th>
                <td>
                    <select name="network_settings[holiday]">
                        <option value="halloween"
                            <?php selected( $holiday, 'halloween' ); ?> >
                                Halloween
                        </option>
                        <option value="christmas"
                            <?php selected( $holiday, 'christmas' ); ?> >
                                Christmas
                        </option>
                        <option value="april_fools"
                            <?php selected( $holiday, 'april_fools' ); ?> >
                                April Fools
                        </option>
                    </select>
                </td>
            </tr>
            <tr valign="top"><th scope="row">Rage Mode:</th>
                <td><input type="checkbox" name="network_settings[rage_mode]"
                    <?php checked( $rage_mode, 'on' ); ?> /> Enabled
                </td>
            </tr>
        </table>
        <p class="submit">
            <input type="submit" class="button-primary"
                name="network_settings_save" value="Save Settings" />
        </p>
    </form>
    </div>
    <?php
}
```

You'll use a standard HTML form to manage the network settings. The options will be stored as an array in a single option, as described in the Plugin Settings section of Chapter 8. The first step is to load any existing setting values. Using the get _ site _ option() function, you'll load the prowp _ network _ settings value, which is your options array, if any exists. Next, set each option value into individual variables. Before you actually create your form, use the wp _ nonce _ field() function to create a hidden form field nonce for security.

Now it's time to build the form. The first form field is an API Key, which is a standard text field. The second form field is a select field. Notice how you use the selected() function to determine which option should be selected. The final setting is a check box for Rage Mode. This option uses the checked() function to determine if the option is checked or not. Because you are using a standard HTML form, you'll need to add a submit button to submit the form values.

Now that your network settings form is set up, you'll need to create the function to process and save the form data.

```
add_action( 'admin_init', 'prowp_save_network_settings' );
//save the option values
function prowp_save_network_settings() {

    //if network settings are being saved, process it
    if ( isset( $_POST['network_settings'] ) ) {

        //check nonce for security
        check_admin_referer( 'save-network-settings', 'prowp-network-plugin' );

        //store option values in a variable
        $network_settings = $_POST['network_settings'];

        //use array map function to sanitize option values
        $network_settings = array_map( 'sanitize_text_field', $network_settings );

        //save option values
        update_site_option( 'prowp_network_settings', $network_settings );

    }

}
```

You'll use the admin_init hook for your custom function for saving the form data. The first step is to verify that form values have been posted. If the form wasn't submitted, there's nothing for you to process. You'll do this by verifying that $_POST['network_settings'] is actually set by using the isset() PHP function. Once you've verified that there is form data to process, you need to check your nonce using the check_admin_referer() function.

Once the nonce check passes, you'll store the post data in the $network_settings variable. Because the data that you are processing is user-provided, it's important to sanitize that data before storing it in the database. In this example, you'll use the array_map() PHP function, which will send each individual value of the array to any function specified, in this case the sanitize_text_field() WordPress function. Now that your data is properly sanitized, you'll save the option using the update_site_option() function.

That's it! You have just built a fully functional network settings section that is fully compatible with standard WordPress. If the user is running Multisite, the menu will show in the Network Admin and the option values will be stored in the wp_sitemeta table. If the user is not running Multisite, the menu will show in the standard WordPress Admin Dashboard and the option values will be stored in the wp_options table.

Listing 10-3 shows the finalized plugin.

LISTING 10-3: Multisite network settings (code file: `prowp3-multisite-network-settings.zip`)

```php
<?php
/*
Plugin Name: ProWP3 Network Settings Example
Plugin URI: http://strangework.com/wordpress-plugins
Description: This is a plugin demonstrating the Multisite Network WordPress
  Settings
Version: 1.0
Author: Brad Williams
Author URI: http://strangework.com
License: GPLv2
*/

add_action( 'init', 'prowp_network_settings_menu' );

function prowp_network_settings_menu() {

    if ( is_multisite() ) {

        //Multisite is enabled so add menu to Network Admin
        add_action( 'network_admin_menu', 'prowp_add_network_settings_menu' );

    } else {

        //Multisite is NOT enabled so add menu to WordPress Admin
        add_action( 'admin_menu', 'prowp_add_network_settings_menu' );

    }

}

function prowp_add_network_settings_menu() {

    //add settings menu
    add_menu_page( 'Network Options Page', 'Network Options',
        'manage_options', 'prowp-network-settings',
        'prowp_network_settings' );

}

//generate the settings page
function prowp_network_settings() {
    ?>
    <div class="wrap" >
        <div id="icon-options-general" class="icon32"></div>
        <h2>Network Settings</h2>
        <form method="post">
            <?php
            //load option values
            $network_settings =
                get_site_option( 'prowp_network_settings' );
            $api_key = $network_settings['api_key'];
            $holiday = $network_settings['holiday'];
            $rage_mode = ( ! empty( $network_settings['rage_mode'] ) )
                ? $network_settings['rage_mode'] : '';

            //create nonce hidden field for security
            wp_nonce_field( 'save-network-settings',
```

```php
                        'prowp-network-plugin' );
                ?>
            <table class="form-table">
                <tr valign="top"><th scope="row">API Key:</th>
                    <td><input type="text"
                        name="network_settings[api_key]"
                        value="<?php echo esc_attr( $api_key ); ?>" /></td>
                </tr>
                <tr valign="top"><th scope="row">Network Holiday</th>
                    <td>
                        <select name="network_settings[holiday]">
                            <option value="halloween" <?php selected( $holiday,
                                'halloween' ); ?> >Halloween</option>
                            <option value="christmas" <?php selected( $holiday,
                                'christmas' ); ?> >Christmas</option>
                            <option value="april_fools" <?php selected( $holiday,
                                'april_fools' ); ?> >April Fools</option>
                        </select>
                    </td>
                </tr>
                <tr valign="top"><th scope="row">Rage Mode:</th>
                    <td><input type="checkbox"
                        name="network_settings[rage_mode]"
                        <?php checked( $rage_mode, 'on' ); ?> /> Enabled</td>
                </tr>
            </table>
            <p class="submit">
                <input type="submit" class="button-primary"
                    name="network_settings_save" value="Save Settings" />
            </p>
        </form>
    </div>
    <?php
}

add_action( 'admin_init', 'prowp_save_network_settings' );

//save the option values
function prowp_save_network_settings() {

    //if network settings are being saved, process it
    if ( isset( $_POST['network_settings'] ) ) {

        //check nonce for security
        check_admin_referer( 'save-network-settings', 'prowp-network-plugin' );

        //store option values in a variable
        $network_settings = $_POST['network_settings'];

        //use array map function to sanitize option values
        $network_settings = array_map( 'sanitize_text_field', $network_settings );

        //save option values
        update_site_option( 'prowp_network_settings', $network_settings );

    }

}
```

Users in a Network

When working with users in a Multisite network, you should always verify that a user is a member of a specific site. To do this, you'll use the is_user_member_of_blog() function:

```php
<?php is_user_member_of_blog( $user_id, $blog_id ); ?>
```

The function accepts two optional parameters. The first parameter is the user ID of the user you want to check. If not set, the function will check the current user. The second parameter is the Blog ID. If this parameter isn't set, the function defaults to the current site you are on:

```php
<?php
if ( is_user_member_of_blog() ) {
    //current user is a member of this site
}
?>
```

The preceding code example will verify that the user is a member of the current site they are viewing.

Now that you understand how to verify that a user is a member of a site, you can add users to a site with the add_user_to_blog() function:

```php
<?php add_user_to_blog( $blog_id, $user_id, $role ); ?>
```

The function accepts three parameters:

➤ $blog_id—The ID of the site you want to add the user to

➤ $user_id—The ID of the user to add

➤ $role—The role the user will have on the site

Now build a plugin that automatically adds a logged-in user to any site that the user visits in your Multisite network, as follows:

```php
add_action( 'init', 'prowp_multisite_add_user_to_site' );
```

First, you'll use the init action hook to execute your custom function to add users to the site.

```php
function prowp_multisite_add_user_to_site() {
    //verify user is logged in before proceeding
    if( ! is_user_logged_in() )
        return false;

    //load current blog ID and user data
    global $current_user, $blog_id;
    //verify user is not a member of this site
    if( ! is_user_member_of_blog() ) {

        //add user to this site as a subscriber
        add_user_to_blog( $blog_id, $current_user->ID, 'subscriber' );

    }

}
```

The first step is to verify the user is logged in, and if not, exit the function by returning `false`. Next you'll call the global `$current _ user` and `$blog _ id` variables. These variables store the data of the current logged-in user and the Blog ID the user is currently viewing. Next, confirm that the user is not a member of the current site using the `is _ user _ member _ of _ blog()` function. The final step is to add the user to the site using the `add _ user _ to _ blog()` function. In this example you set the role of the user to subscriber, but you could easily change this to any role you'd like.

That's it! For this plugin to work across your entire network you'll either need to Network Activate the plugin or upload to the `/mu-plugins` directory. Either option will force the plugin to run across all sites in your network.

The finalized plugin is shown in Listing 10-4.

LISTING 10-4: Automatically add users to sites in Multisite (code file: `prowp3-multisite-add-users.zip`)

```php
<?php
/*
Plugin Name: ProWP3 Multisite Auto-Add User to Site
Plugin URI: http://strangework.com/wordpress-plugins
Description: Plugin automatically adds the user to any site they visit
Version: 1.0
Author: Brad Williams
Author URI: http://strangework.com
License: GPLv2
*/

add_action( 'init', 'prowp_multisite_add_user_to_site' );

function prowp_multisite_add_user_to_site() {

    //verify user is logged in before proceeding
    if( ! is_user_logged_in() )
        return false;

    //load current blog ID and user data
    global $current_user, $blog_id;

    //verify user is not a member of this site
    if( ! is_user_member_of_blog() ) {

        //add user to this site as a subscriber
        add_user_to_blog( $blog_id, $current_user->ID, 'subscriber' );

    }

}
```

Now that you understand how to add users to a site, you can remove users from a site. To remove users, you'll use the `remove _ user _ from _ blog()` function:

```php
<?php remove_user_from_blog( $user_id, $blog_id, $reassign ); ?>
```

This function accepts three parameters:

➤   `$user_id`—ID of the user you want to remove

➤   `$blog_id`—ID of the blog to remove the user from

➤   `$reassign`—ID of a user to reassign posts to

The `$user _ id` and `$blog _ id` parameters are required. The `$reassign` parameter is optional. This parameter should be the ID of the user you want to reassign posts to when removing a user.

> **NOTE** *Remember that adding and removing users from a site in Multisite is not actually creating or deleting the user in WordPress, but instead adding or removing them as a member of a specific site.*

To retrieve a list of all sites a user belongs to you'll use the `get _ blogs _ of _ user()` function. This function returns an array of objects containing the details of each site the user has access to. Here's an example:

```php
<?php
$user_id = 1;
$user_blogs = get_blogs_of_user( $user_id );
echo 'User '.$user_id.'\'s blogs:<ul>';
foreach ( $user_blogs AS $user_blog ) {
    echo '<li>' .$user_blog->blogname .'</li>';
}
echo '</ul>';
?>
```

The preceding code retrieves the site data for all sites that user ID 1 is a member of. You then loop through the returned array, displaying the `blogname` value for each site.

Super Admins

Earlier in this chapter, we covered the new user role introduced in Multisite, the Super Admin role. Any user set to the Super Admin role has full control over every site in your Multisite network. Users set to the Super Admin role also have full control over what themes and plugins are available, all users, and network-wide settings.

To retrieve a list of all Super Admins in Multisite you'll use the `get _ super _ admins()` function. This function accepts no parameters and returns an array of all Super Admin usernames in your network. Here's an example:

```php
<?php
$all_admins = get_super_admins();
print_r( $all_admins );
?>
```

The preceding code example would return the following array of Super Admins:

```
Array
(
    [0] => admin
    [1] => michael_myers
)
```

You can also check a specific user ID to determine if this user is a Super Admin in your network. To do so, use the is_super_admin() function, as shown here:

```
<?php
$user_id = 1;
if ( is_super_admin( $user_id ) ) {
    echo 'User is a Super Admin';
}
?>
```

The preceding code example checks if User ID 1 is a Super Admin. The function accepts a $user_id as an optional parameter. If the user ID isn't passed to the function, it defaults to the current user.

Now that you understand how to check for Super Admins, you can make a user a Super Admin. You can easily assign an existing user to the Super Admin role by using the grant_super_admin() function. This function accepts a single required parameter, which is the user ID you want to add to the Super Admin role.

```
<?php
$user_id = 34;
grant_super_admin( $user_id );
?>
```

You can also easily remove a user from the Super Admin role with the revoke_super_admin() function. As in the preceding code, this function accepts a single parameter, which is the user ID you want to remove from the Super Admin role:

```
<?php
$user_id = 34;
revoke_super_admin( $user_id );
?>
```

Both of these functions are located in wp-admin/includes/ms.php. This means that these functions are not available on the public side of your website and can only be used on the admin side.

Network Stats

Multisite features various functions to generate stats about your network. The get_blog_count() function returns the total number of sites in your network. To return the total number of users in your network, use the get_user_count() function:

```
<?php
$site_count = get_blog_count();
$user_count = get_user_count();
```

```
echo '<p>Total sites: ' .$site_count .'</p>';
echo '<p>Total users: ' .$user_count .'</p>';
?>
```

You can also use the `get_sitestats()` function to retrieve both values at once in an array:

```
<?php
$network_stats = get_sitestats();
echo '<p>Total sites: ' .$network_stats['blogs'] .'</p>';
echo '<p>Total users: ' .$network_stats['users'] .'</p>';
?>
```

Large Networks

WordPress Multisite networks can vary in size from a small network of just a few sites, to a very large network with thousands of sites. When working with Multisite, it's important to always keep this in mind. Writing code that affects all sites in the network may not work as well if the network is substantial in size. WordPress has a function to help determine if a Multisite network is considered to be a large network. The `wp_is_large_network()` function will check if your Multisite network has more than 10,000 users or more than 10,000 sites, and if so will return `True`. Let's look at an example:

```
<?php
if ( wp_is_large_network() ) {

    echo 'Your network is very large!';

}
?>
```

As you can see, this function is very important and should be used any time you plan on running resource-intensive code. This certainly doesn't mean you can't run intensive code on a large network, but you would need to consider caching and optimization techniques to ensure your code runs successfully.

MULTISITE DATABASE SCHEMA

WordPress Multisite features a different database schema from standard WordPress. When enabling Multisite, WordPress creates the necessary tables in your database to support Multisite functionality.

Multisite-Specific Tables

WordPress stores global Multisite settings in centralized tables. These tables are created only when Multisite is enabled and installed, excluding the `wp_users` and `wp_usermeta` tables, which exist in standard WordPress.

➤ `wp_blogs`—Contains each site created in Multisite.

➤ `wp_blog_versions`—Contains the current database version of each site in the network.

➤ wp_registration_log—A log of all users registered and activated in WordPress.

➤ wp_signups—Contains users and sites registered using the WordPress registration process.

➤ wp_site—Contains the primary site's address information.

➤ wp_sitecategories—Contains global terms. Only exists if global terms have been enabled in WordPress.

➤ wp_sitemeta—Contains option data for the network, including Super Admin accounts.

➤ wp_users—Contains all users registered in WordPress.

➤ wp_usermeta—Contains all metadata for user accounts in WordPress.

As you have probably noticed, some important WordPress tables are missing. The rest of the tables created for Multisite are site-specific.

Site-Specific Tables

Every site in your network features its own set of site-specific database tables. These tables contain the content and settings specific to that individual site. Remember that these tables are prefixed with the $table_prefix value defined in wp-config.php, followed by the $blog_id and then the table name.

➤ wp_2_commentmeta

➤ wp_2_comments

➤ wp_2_links

➤ wp_2_options

➤ wp_2_postmeta

➤ wp_2_posts

➤ wp_2_terms

➤ wp_2_term_relationships

➤ wp_2_term_taxonomy

Every time you create a new site in your Multisite network, WordPress will create the preceding nine tables in your database for the new site. As you can see, these tables can make your database quickly grow in size. That's why the only limitation to WordPress Multisite is the server resources available for your network of sites. If your network contains 1,000 sites, your database would have more than 9,000 tables. Obviously a network of this size would not work well on a small, shared hosting account.

In Chapter 6, we covered the importance of using the WordPress database class when querying the database directly. This is especially important in Multisite because the table prefix contains the Blog ID of the site you are viewing. When writing a custom query, you should always prefix the table reference with $wpdb->, which will include the site ID if you are running Multisite. For example, $wpdb->posts would query the wp_2_posts table, assuming you are working on Blog ID 2 in your network.

SUMMARY

WordPress Multisite is an amazing feature of WordPress with limitless possibilities. Now that Multisite is a core WordPress feature, many users are converting their standard WordPress website to a Multisite network to take advantage of the rapid site deployment features and network capabilities. As more and more users are becoming familiar with the power of Multisite, its use is growing at a very rapid pace. When developing for WordPress, it's very important to think about Multisite and how your code can utilize these powerful Multisite features covered in this chapter. As a WordPress user, it's also very important to verify the themes and plugins you are using are Multisite compatible.

The next chapter covers WordPress migrations. You'll learn to understand the content migration process, review various data mapping tools including WP-CLI, and walk through a data migration example.

11

Migrating to WordPress

WHAT'S IN THIS CHAPTER?

➤ Planning to move an existing site or content pages to WordPress

➤ Choosing among the different import options available

➤ Listing of potential cleanup or manual fine-tuning steps needed to complete a migration

➤ Using WP-CLI to simplify the process

WROX.COM CODE DOWNLOADS FOR THIS CHAPTER

The wrox.com code downloads for this chapter are found at www.wrox.com/go/wordpress3e on the Download Code tab. The code is in the Chapter 11 download file and individually named according to the filenames noted throughout the chapter.

The bulk of this book extols the virtues of WordPress and we hope it has made you more of a WordPress fan, evangelist, and expert. If you are ready, willing, and able to help WordPress conquer the world, but you are not starting with a clean slate, you will need to migrate existing content into WordPress. Alternatively, if you are adding "Family WordPress expert" to the title of "Family SysAdmin," you are likely to have a line of friends and family asking you to help them get started. Finally this chapter will also touch on taking a local test site to launch using a special WordPress command line tool.

A variety of reasons exist to move existing content into WordPress:

➤ You want to move from static, time-invariant content to a narrative style. Rather than publishing "brochureware," you want to tell a story, and the timeline element of a WordPress site is the best approach.

➤ You expect comments, and discussion around your content and organizing by post (topic) corrals the discussion better than an unstructured bulletin board.

➤ There is sufficient traffic coming to your site that online advertising or sponsorships are economically viable, and you need full control over the platform.

➤ You want to customize the user experience, style, and presentation of your site, or you are in a position to take an existing site, perhaps hosted by your employer, to a self-hosted environment.

The first part of this chapter looks at various ways to move static pages and existing sites to WordPress, with the assumption that you already have content that you need to import. Although WordPress makes it easy to publish content or delegate the writing to other users, gaining a critical mass of pages and posts is essential for generating readership and establishing context for online advertising engines. There is no easier way to get there than by moving your content into a fresh WordPress installation. This content migration will form the foundation for any move of any WordPress site, whether it is into WordPress from another source, or from WordPress to WordPress, such as when moving hosts. This groundwork helps you understand the process when we show you simpler but powerful command line tools at the end of the chapter.

UNDERSTANDING THE PROCESS

The first step in migrating a site to WordPress is to make a plan. It is equally important—and unexciting—to have a plan. Without a map of all of the components and targets, you will either lose content or end up repeating steps until your content is imported in some usable fashion. Spending a little time up front to plan will save time in the long run, and definitely reduce future frustrations.

Content Sources

When planning a migration you must decide what data sources you will want to move. Certainly, you will want to move the actual content and the related media; otherwise this whole exercise is silly. "Actual content" has many different interpretations, however: Are you moving posts from an existing site, documents in a word processing system, static HTML from your current site, or some combination of all of these options? We discuss migrating static content briefly in the next section; however, most of this chapter focuses on the bulk import of posts from other blogging systems and building custom import scripts.

When you decide to migrate to WordPress, you have an opportunity to revisit the pages-versus-posts dilemma covered in Chapter 9. If you are moving a static brochureware website to WordPress, you can probably get away with mapping existing pages to WordPress pages. By thinking outside the box, you may choose to have content on your existing site translate into posts in WordPress. Using a category template page, you can replicate the presentation feel of your old site in WordPress and add functionality available through the post structure. Finally, mapping static pages to posts also allows you to add a chronological background to shed light on how an idea or topic developed.

It is possible to migrate from bulletin boards such as phpBB to WordPress, but the conversion from a threaded discussion structure to posts, pages, and comments requires that you carefully plan the disposition of each topic. One common approach is to make each topic a new category and then organize stories (discussions) into posts in those categories, but you are probably going to end up hand-editing the import script to get the desired result. The custom import script described in this chapter, along with the migration checklist, should help you build a toolset to extract threaded content in a useful form.

Finally, make sure you have the rights to re-use whatever content you are looking to appropriate for your new site. If all of the content is your own, this issue is trivial, but if you have been posting on your employer's corporate site or sharing a site with coauthors, ensure you have appropriate rights to the content, including copyright, rights to redistribute, and rights for commercial use.

Migration Checklist

Migration is never a clean and simple process. Tools will help you automate the vast majority of the work, but the purpose of planning is to be sure you have accounted for all of the content, metadata, and supporting features to capture the desired intent of your migration to WordPress.

Here is a migration checklist:

➤ **Content identification**—Build a site map, as described in the section "Building a Custom Import Script," to be sure you do not orphan any pages in the process. If you are importing from word processor files, build a file inventory of what you want to capture.

➤ **Media**—Prepare any actual media assets that are in your content, even though they are not the theme and presentation graphics. Do you have any images, graphs, PowerPoint presentations or other linked documents that need to be moved over? Plan ahead of time where you are going to house these assets in the WordPress site. Are you going to follow WordPress convention or keep them in their current directory structure?

➤ **Metadata**—Is there any metadata that describes the content that you also need to move over and reapply, such as tag or category information, or will you let WordPress do the minimum import so you can fine-tune the categories and tags in post-import processing?

➤ **Authors and users**—Are you moving a single-author or non-attributed website, or do you need to keep content and author associations? This is a further complicating factor for discussing group migration: Are all registered users of the forum also authors?

➤ **Theme and presentation**—Rarely will an existing site's CSS and presentation HTML translate directly into a WordPress theme. Should you create a new theme for your target WordPress site that attempts to preserve the look and feel of the existing site, or are you going to break away and re-launch your new site with a whole new look and feel? You can review Chapter 9, which covers creating a new theme for your site. Also consider whether there is any special or unique content on your site that will require distinctive design concerns prompting custom page templates (again, Chapter 9) or custom post types (covered in Chapter 7).

➤ **Unique functionality**—Working with financial institution websites, we often run into financial calculators and various applications (like the paper kind you fill out) that will not immediately convert to the new site, or will require individual attention. This could be nearly anything; it could be something that was custom-coded for the website such as a poll, or a map for directions or CRM integration. Often you can find WordPress plugins that will provide similar functionality for your new site. Or, as we have often said, a strength of WordPress is that you can always write your own plugin, as covered in Chapter 8. Other times you can use the custom page templates to wrap your custom integration code inside of the WordPress framework. This topic is covered more a little later in this chapter.

➤ **Cleanup**—You will need to tweak and fine-tune your content, especially URLs. You will have to visually inspect a fair sampling of your new WordPress site for anomalies. You will want to map old URLs to new URLs so visitors can still find you and search engine results continue to work.

➤ **Launch**—Bite the bullet and launch your new site. No website is ever complete or perfect, but at some point it has to be good enough to let it loose on the web. Remember, shipping is a feature.

Recognize up front that any migration is not going to be perfect. You are moving core website content from where it was happily living (or perhaps not happily, and that is why you are migrating) to a whole new shell. There is going to be some work involved. We just want to set some expectations—we will look over each step in a little more depth.

Site Preparation

One quick thought before you get into the actual migration. You need a way to work on your new site while still serving up your content on your old site. How you go about this depends on what resources you have available to you. Setting up your development site, or import playground, also affects your URL structure and may require the manual editing changes discussed in the section "Cleaning Up," later in this chapter.

If you are adding content to an existing site, our recommended method is to set up a whole new WordPress instantiation on a new subdomain. For example, if your current site is `http://example.com`, make a new DNS entry and website host for a subdomain like `http://new.example.com` or `http://test.example.com`. This will make it so that you can work on the development site without interrupting your existing site. It will also permit you to use root relative links and make certain steps easier in the long run. On the other hand, if you are establishing a new WordPress site, use the basic installation as your starting point for importing content.

Although you can set up your test environment in other ways, this method can simplify some steps because you are working on what will eventually become your production site. Local development is a good method if you are the only developer working on the site. If you are developing your new site locally, you can use your hosts file to skip all the URL transitions discussed later. However, as you will see at the end of this chapter, handling URL changes in WordPress has been greatly simplified.

CONTENT IDENTIFICATION

All content migration follows a similar pattern: Extract bits from the existing repository, automate preparation for the new system as much as possible, and import the content, typically repeating that loop as you find steps that require manual editing or fine-tuning. This section identifies and prepares the content that we want to move to WordPress and walks you through the three major approaches to WordPress import functions, starting with the fully manual migration of text documents and then exploring the WordPress built-in administrative functions to convert popular formats. It concludes with an in-depth development of a custom extraction and import script.

Migrating Text Documents

We define "text documents" as content primarily associated with a word processor for manipulation, and many text documents will end up as pages in your WordPress site. The content is not static in the sense that it is fixed, but it is not part of the temporal narrative. These tend to be the product pages of your brochureware site.

Brute-force is often the simplest approach here. Copy and paste your text, or export a document as HTML and glue that into a WordPress page. Be warned, however, that most word processing applications insert a huge array of embedded HTML tags, local formatting, and other style elements that make the output page render the way it would as seen from the word processor, but not the way you would want it to within your WordPress theme structure. If you do not want to strip out all but the most elemental paragraph, table, and link information, consider exporting the file as raw text and then hand-editing it to match the style of your other pages. It is ugly, but so is removing half of the document in the form of HTML directives. Even something as simple as the Mac OS TextEdit application uses custom HTML tags for paragraphs if you use Save As for an HTML document. Save your text, without any formatting.

A variation on this theme is merging wiki entries into a site. Most wikis have their own somewhat arcane syntax, different enough from HTML to make copy and paste time-consuming but not worth automated editing unless you are moving a large wiki. If the wiki is really a collection of topics, it makes sense to migrate the wiki pages to WordPress posts, creating categories for each topic or set of topics and relying on tags to even more finely identify the content. The upside to migrating out of a wiki is that you gain use of the WordPress metadata functions and can parse comments and discussion into comment threads rather than endless edits to the wiki document; the downside is that you lose the edit history contained in platforms such as MediaWiki. If you are running a wiki with a MySQL database as the repository, you can use the custom extract and import script discussed later in this chapter to build a migration tool.

Built-In WordPress Import Tools

For most users looking to transport content from one home to another, WordPress offers a variety of built-in import facilities. This section covers the basic conversion process and the use of WordPress eXtended RSS (WXR) files for more flexible or powerful data conversion.

Site Conversion

WordPress offers basic importers for commonly used blogging platforms. You can find these built-in importers on the Import Screen in WordPress, and you will be prompted to install the selected plugin. These conversion tools fall into two main migration categories: They read a file exported by your current platform, or they use the source platform's API set to pull content and re-post it in WordPress. For example, LiveJournal and Tumblr are migrated using their APIs, whereas Movable Type and TypePad are handled by exporting the contents from those platforms into a file that is uploaded and executed by WordPress.

Using WordPress eXtended RSS Files

What if the simple site-to-site conversion does not work, or does not capture enough of the metadata, author information, or other content that you want to migrate? In the most basic case, what you are going to do is export your existing content into an XML import file in the WordPress eXtended RSS (WXR) format, which is, as it is named, an extension of the RSS format.

The process for creating a WXR file depends on the starting point for your source content. Some applications have a built-in WXR exporter function, which will create this file for you. For example, the WordPress Export dashboard will create this file, but this is only useful when moving content from an existing WordPress site to a new one. If your source content does not have this functionality, you can create the WXR file by hand in a text editor. The easiest way to start your WXR file, if you have to create it by hand, is to use the sitemap process.

To create a WXR file using a site map, first you need a site map of your source site. Start with a site map created for search engines, or use a whole site link checker such as Xenu (`http://home. snafu.de/tilman/xenulink.html`—the site is scary, but the tool works) to create one. Xenu is only available for Windows, but there are similar tools for Mac OS. This site map will list all the pages that need to be migrated.

We do so many migrations from static HTML or other random CMS systems that rather than working a migration plan for each site, we built a special PHP application that spiders a website and builds the WXR for us. Assuming each page is somewhat consistent, this works very well. Using a combination of PHP, curl, and jQuery, we can feed the page list in from the site map, parse the HTML, and gather the content, and then write it out in WXR format.

Once you have a WXR import file, you can then edit it to make any necessary changes to the file prior to importing. You probably will want to read this whole chapter ahead of time so you are aware of the pitfalls that can affect your import and you can benefit from some search and replace on the import file rather than hand-editing or fixing each occurrence later.

Because this WXR import file is straight up XML, you can edit it in your favorite text editor. This allows you to make some bulk changes to URLs, paths, authors, and anything ahead of doing the import. This can save you a lot of time in the long run, but do not go overboard. WordPress is set up to do an import and can automatically create a lot of information for you based on the import.

When editing the WXR import file, you can see how the import content will play out. The nice thing about this format is that it really is extended RSS, so the format is simple. Unfortunately, there is not much documentation about it on WordPress.org (`http://codex.wordpress.org/ Importing_Content#Importing_from_an_RSS_feed`). There is also some example WXR formatting to use as a model in the Google Blog Converter Google Code website at `http:// code.google.com/p/google-blog-converters-appengine/source/browse/trunk/samples/ wordpress-sample.wxr`.

This import file is an easy way to move content from your existing site. As discussed later in this chapter, other ways exist to move sites from other content management systems, but we often find it easier to use the WXR import file method.

Outside of the WordPress built-in migration functions, WXR files represent the fastest path to get your content moved into WordPress. In many cases, automating only the "easy" parts is sufficient to get your new site up and running. Assuming your current site has an Export to WXR, a live RSS feed, or some other export mechanism that you can then hand-edit into a WXR format, this can be your simplest approach.

Building a Custom Import Script

More advanced than a simple WXR migration is to extract entries from an existing content management system that is database (ideally MySQL) based, and attempt a direct data manipulation to migrate the content. In this case, you need to have your old and new database tables in the same MySQL database. Then you can run a set of SQL scripts that will read from the old database, transform the data appropriately, and import the content into the WordPress tables. This method can get tricky because you are juggling several SQL scripts to export, convert, and then import the content; however, it is also the most flexible and powerful approach that operates at the data management level.

Listing 11-1 explores an example script to import data directly into the WordPress database. Take a look at the full source before we break it down.

LISTING 11-1: MySQL import script

```php
<?php
//set database connection info for database to import
$hostname = "localhost";
$username = "USERNAME";
$password = "PASSWORD";
$sourcedb = "DATABASE"; // database to import from
$sourcetable = "storico"; // table that stores posts to import
$sourcecomments = "comment"; // table that stores comments to import

//set database connection info for WordPress database
$destdb = "WORDPRESS-DATABASE"; // WordPress database
$wp_prefix = "wp_"; // WordPress table prefix

//database connection
$db_connect = @mysql_connect($hostname, $username, $password)
  or die("Fatal Error: ".mysql_error());

mysql_select_db($sourcedb, $db_connect);

$srcresult = mysql_query("select * from $sourcetable", $db_connect)
  or die("Fatal Error: ".mysql_error());

// used to generate the dashed titles in the URLs
function sanitize($title) {
  $title = strtolower($title);
  $title = preg_replace('/&.+?;/', '', $title); // kill entities
  $title = preg_replace('/[^a-z0-9 -]/', '', $title);
  $title = preg_replace('/\s+/', ' ', $title);
  $title = str_replace(' ', '-', $title);
  $title = preg_replace('|-+|', '-', $title);
  $title = trim($title, '-');

  return $title;
}

while ($myrow = mysql_fetch_array($srcresult))
{

  //generate post title
```

continues

LISTING 11-1: (Continued)

```
$my_title = mysql_escape_string($myrow['title']);

//generate post content
$my_content = mysql_escape_string($myrow['content']);

//generate post permalink
$myname = mysql_escape_string(sanitize($my_title));
//generate SQL to insert data into WordPress
$sql = "INSERT INTO '" . $wp_prefix . "posts'
(

    'ID' ,

    'post_author' ,
    'post_date' ,
    'post_date_gmt' ,
    'post_content' ,
    'post_title' ,
    'post_name' ,
    'post_category' ,
    'post_excerpt' ,
    'post_status' ,
    'comment_status' ,
    'ping_status' ,
    'post_password' ,
    'to_ping' ,
    'pinged' ,
    'post_modified' ,
    'post_modified_gmt' ,
    'post_content_filtered' ,
    'post_parent',
    'post_type' )
    VALUES

(

    '$myrow[sid]',
        '1',
    '$myrow[time]',
    '0000-00-00 00:00:00',
    '$my_content',
    '$my_title',
    '$myname',
    '$myrow[category]',
    '',
    'publish',
    'open',
    'open',
    '',
    '',
    '',
    '$myrow[time]',
    '0000-00-00 00:00:00',
    '',
    '0',
```

```
'post' );";

mysql_select_db($destdb, $db_connect);
//execute query
mysql_query($sql, $db_connect);

// load the ID of the post we just inserted
$sql = "select MAX(ID) from " . $wp_prefix . "posts";
$getID = mysql_query($sql, $db_connect);
$currentID = mysql_fetch_array($getID);
$currentID = $currentID['MAX(ID)'];

// retrieve all associated post comments
$mysid = $myrow["pn_sid"];
mysql_select_db($sourcedb, $db_connect);
$comments = mysql_query("select * from "
    .$sourcecomments. " where pn_sid = $mysid", $db_connect);
//import post comments in WordPress
while ($comrow = mysql_fetch_array($comments))
{

  $myname - mysql_escape_string($comrow['pn_name']);
  $myemail = mysql_escape_string($comrow['pn_email']);
  $myurl = mysql_escape_string($comrow['pn_url']);
  $myIP = mysql_escape_string($comrow['pn_host_name']);
  $mycomment = mysql_escape_string($comrow['pn_comment']);
  $sql - "INSERT INTO '" . $wp_prefix . "comments'
  (
    'comment_ID' ,
    'comment_post_ID' ,
    'comment_author' ,
    'comment_author_url' ,

    'comment_author_IP' ,
    'comment_date' ,
    'comment_date_gmt' ,
    'comment_content' ,
    'comment_karma' ,
    'comment_approved' ,
    'user_id' )
    VALUES
    (
      '',
      '$currentID',
      '$myname',
      '$myemail',
      '$myurl',
      '$myIP',
      '$comrow[date]',
      '0000-00-00 00:00:00',
      '$mycomment',
      '0',
      '1',
      '0'
    );";
  if ($submit)
```

continues

LISTING 11-1: (Continued)

```
      {
        mysql_select_db($destdb, $db_connect);
        mysql_query($sql, $db_connect)
          or die("Fatal Error: ".mysql_error());
      }
    }


  }

  //Update comment count
  mysql_select_db($destdb, $db_connect);
  $tidyresult = mysql_query("select * from $wp_prefix" . "posts", $db_connect)
    or die("Fatal Error: ".mysql_error());

  while ($myrow = mysql_fetch_array($tidyresult))
  {
    $mypostid=$myrow['ID'];
    $countsql="select COUNT(*) from $wp_prefix" . "comments"
      . " WHERE 'comment_post_ID' = " . $mypostid;
    $countresult=mysql_query($countsql) or die("Fatal Error: ".mysql_error());
    $commentcount=mysql_result($countresult,0,0);
    $countsql="UPDATE '" . $wp_prefix . "posts'
      SET 'comment_count' = '" . $commentcount .
      "' WHERE 'ID' = " . $mypostid . " LIMIT 1";

    $countresult=mysql_query($countsql) or die("Fatal Error: ".mysql_error());

  }
```

At first glance this looks a little complicated, so let's break it down and discuss each section of the import script:

```
//set database connection info for database to import
$hostname = "localhost";
$username = "USERNAME";
$password = "PASSWORD";
$sourcedb = "DATABASE"; // database to import from
$sourcetable = "stories"; // table that stores posts to import
$sourcecomments = "comment"; // table that stores comments to import

//set database connection info for WordPress database
$destdb = "WORDPRESS-DATABASE"; // WordPress database
$wp_prefix = "wp_"; // WordPress table prefix
```

First you set your database connection info. You also set the table names for the source of the content you plan on importing. This example assumes both the source tables and WordPress tables exist in the same database server. Then you set your WordPress tables and table prefix.

Next you need to initialize your database connections. You will have to modify this depending on the MySQL connection libraries available in your PHP. Preferably, you should be using PHP's PDO library, but for compatibility, a straight up MySQL connection library is shown here:

```
//database connection
$db_connect = @mysql_connect($hostname, $username, $password)
    or die("Fatal Error: ".mysql_error());

mysql_select_db($sourcedb, $db_connect);


$srcresult = mysql_query("select * from $sourcetable", $db_connect)
    or die("Fatal Error: ".mysql_error());
```

After setting your database connections, you execute a query to select the data from your source table. This is the data you are going to import into WordPress as posts. Next, you create your `sanitize` function for creating permalinks. This function removes and replaces any characters that are not legal for URLs and also replaces spaces with dashes to conform to the WordPress permalink structure.

```
// used to generate the dashed titles in the URLs
function sanitize($title) {
  $title = strtolower($title);
  $title = preg_replace('/&.+?;/', '', $title); // kill entities
  $title = preg_replace('/[^a-z0-9 _]/', '', $title);
  $title = preg_replace('/\s+/', ' ', $title);
  $title = str_replace(' ', '-', $title);
  $title = preg_replace('|-+|', '-', $title);
  $title = trim($title, '-');

  return $title;
}
```

After your `sanitize` function is in place, you start your `while` loop to loop through the data you are going to import as posts in WordPress:

```
while ($myrow = mysql_fetch_array($srcresult))
{
```

Next, you set variables for your post title, content, and permalink values:

```
//generate post title
$my_title = mysql_escape_string($myrow['title']);

//generate post content
$my_content = mysql_escape_string($myrow['content']);

//generate post permalink
$myname = mysql_escape_string(sanitize($my_title));
```

Notice that you send the values through the `mysql_escape_string` function. This PHP function escapes a string for use in a MySQL query. Next, you create the query to insert the post data into the WordPress posts table:

```
//generate SQL to insert data into WordPress
$sql = "INSERT INTO '" . $wp_prefix . "posts' (
  'ID' ,
```

```
                    'post_author' ,
                    'post_date' ,
                    'post_date_gmt' ,
                    'post_content' ,
                    'post_title' ,
                    'post_name' ,
                    'post_category' ,
                    'post_excerpt' ,
                    'post_status' ,
                    'comment_status' ,
                    'ping_status' ,
                    'post_password' ,
                    'to_ping' ,
                    'pinged' ,
                    'post_modified' ,
                    'post_modified_gmt' ,
                    'post_content_filtered' ,
                    'post_parent',
                    'post_type' )
                    VALUES (
                    '$myrow[sid]',
                    '1',
                    '$myrow[time]',
                    '0000-00-00 00:00:00',
                    '$my_content',
                    '$my_title',
                    '$myname',
                    '$myrow[category]',
                    '',
                    'publish',
                    'open',
                    'open',
                    '',
                    '',
                    '',
                    '$myrow[time]',
                    '0000-00-00 00:00:00',
                    '',
                    '0',
                    'post' );";
```

As you can see, you set specific values for each row in the `wp_posts` WordPress table. At this point, you will need to match the values you want to import from the source table with the correct table fields in WordPress. The preceding script is just an example showing how that can be accomplished. Next, you execute the generated query:

```
mysql_select_db($destdb, $db_connect);
//execute query
mysql_query($sql, $db_connect);
```

After your query has successfully run, the source data will start to populate in the WordPress `posts` table. Now you need to import the post comments and associate them with the correct posts. The first step to accomplish this is to load the ID of the post you just inserted, as shown here:

```
// load the ID of the post we just inserted
$sql = "select MAX(ID) from " . $wp_prefix . "posts";
$getID = mysql_query($sql, $db_connect);
$currentID = mysql_fetch_array($getID);
$currentID = $currentID['MAX(ID)'];
```

This is the ID used to associate a comment with a post in WordPress. Next you need to execute a query to retrieve all of the comments from the source table:

```
// retrieve all associated post comments
$mysid = $myrow["pn_sid"];
mysql_select_db($sourcedb, $db_connect);
$comments = mysql_query("select * from "
    .$sourcecomments. " where pn_sid = $mysid", $db_connect);
```

Next, you start a loop to loop through all of the comments attached to this post and insert them into the WordPress comments table:

```
//import post comments in WordPress
while ($comrow = mysql_fetch_array($comments))
{
  $myname = mysql_escape_string($comrow['pn_name']);
  $myemail = mysql_escape_string($comrow['pn_email']);
  $myurl = mysql_escape_string($comrow['pn_url']);
  $myIP = mysql_escape_string($comrow['pn_host_name']);
  $mycomment = mysql_escape_string($comrow['pn_comment']);
```

You also set some variables with the comment data you are going to insert into WordPress. Remember that these values will need to be matched to whatever system you are importing from. Next, it is time to build the query and insert the comment data in WordPress:

```
$sql = "INSERT INTO '" . $wp_prefix . "comments'
(
  'comment_ID' ,
  'comment_post_ID' ,
  'comment_author' ,
  'comment_author_email' ,
  'comment_author_url' ,
  'comment_author_IP' ,
  'comment_date' ,
  'comment_date_gmt' ,
  'comment_content' ,
  'comment_karma' ,
  'comment_approved' ,
  'user_id' )
  VALUES
  (
    '' ,
    '$currentID',
    '$myname',
    '$myemail',
    '$myurl',
    '$myIP',
```

```
        '$comrow[date]',
        '0000-00-00 00:00:00',
        '$mycomment',
        '0',
        '1',
        '0'
      );";

  if ($submit)
  {
    mysql_select_db($destdb, $db_connect);
    mysql_query($sql, $db_connect)
      or die("Fatal Error: ".mysql_error());
  }
 }
}
```

As you can see, you match each value to the correct WordPress table field in the INSERT query. After generating your query, you initialize the database connection and execute the query. Remember that this is in a loop, so if ten comments exist on this post, it will execute this INSERT statement for all ten comments.

The final section of code in the importer updates the comment _ count value on your posts. When viewing total comments on a post, WordPress does not dynamically generate that number. Instead, it is stored as an integer value in the post record. The first step is to load a single post to count comments for:

```
//Update comment count
mysql_select_db($destdb, $db_connect);
$tidyresult = mysql_query("select * from $wp_prefix" . "posts", $db_connect)
  or die("Fatal Error: ".mysql_error());

while ($myrow = mysql_fetch_array($tidyresult))
{
```

You also start a while loop to loop through each one of the posts in the WordPress posts table. Next, you run a SELECT COUNT query to count how many comments this single post has:

```
$mypostid=$myrow['ID'];
$countsql="select COUNT(*) from $wp_prefix" . "comments"
  . " WHERE 'comment_post_ID' = " . $mypostid;
$countresult=mysql_query($countsql) or die("Fatal Error: ".mysql_error());
$commentcount=mysql_result($countresult,0,0);
```

Once this code has executed, the variable $commentcount will contain the total number of comments attached to this post. The final part is to update the comment _ count field in the WordPress posts table to match this value:

```
$countsql="UPDATE '" . $wp_prefix . "posts'
  SET 'comment_count' = '" . $commentcount .
  "' WHERE 'ID' = " . $mypostid . " LIMIT 1";

$countresult=mysql_query($countsql) or die("Fatal Error: ".mysql_error());

}
```

The UPDATE query updates the comment count based on the value of $commentcount. This is a loop so it iterates through each post in the WordPress posts table and updates the comment count for each post.

Remember that this is an example of how to create a script to do a direct import from a source database table into the WordPress database tables. The individual values set in this script would need to be matched to the appropriate values in your source database tables to import.

Whichever method you choose to transport your content, the next step is to import into WordPress. We recommend importing into a fresh installation of WordPress. Or make sure that your import plan includes purging existing content in order to avoid duplicate entries. If you are layering your import on top of existing content, you will need to hand-edit your import files or scripts to make sure no conflicts occur.

Next, do a trial import and see where you end up. Even with up-front planning and consideration there is very little chance you can get it all right on the first try. Review the new site and see what needs to be hand-edited in the script. Again, there will be more "grep-fu" and find-and-replace fun.

If you are going the WXR route, you can use the WordPress Import screen to import this file. An important consideration is the maximum file size and execution time for PHP. If your import file is large, you may need to edit your PHP configuration to increase these timeouts.

MEDIA MIGRATION

There are really two sets of media and asset files for your site: graphics that make up the theme and site frame and graphics and documents that are embedded in the content.

We discuss the theme presentation later in this chapter. This section is about moving the media that is embedded in your content portions of the page—for example, linked Word documents, PowerPoint Presentations, and Adobe PDFs. This also includes any images in your content, like screenshots or graphs. In a traditional WordPress installation, these files are uploaded into your uploads folder and, depending on your configuration, are filed by dates.

Odds are that your existing site is not going to have this sort of directory structure. But, as you know, link structures and naming conventions matter, and if you are moving from Windows to Linux, case now matters, too. You have options for moving your content and how to structure it in the new site. Each migration is different, so you will have to evaluate which method is going to work out best for your case.

Many sites have a top-level folder in the webroot for images, often called /img/ or /images/. The simplest method to move this directory over is just to keep it intact and put it in the top level of your WordPress site. This is primarily copying files from one directory tree on the source server to the new server using a file transfer protocol (FTP) utility and a tarball file. Really, we would rather you used a secure file transfer protocol utility (SFTP) to move files, but it all depends on what your server supports. Keeping the original images in the same directory structure on the new server as the old—for example, it might be /pdfs/—is beneficial because you may not have to remap each image in the content. However, you will see in the cleaning-up stage that changing the URLs is not that difficult, or you could edit the WXR import file ahead of time. This technique may be undesirable because it breaks from the WordPress convention of storing your assets in the wp-uploads directory and your media assets will become separated into two different locations when you start using the WordPress Media Manager to upload new images.

The second option is to move all the images into the WordPress uploads folder on the new server. Make sure the target directory choice matches the WordPress configuration; otherwise, you are not really using this method effectively. You can set WordPress to organize uploads by month and year in the Media Screen. This option pretty much guarantees that you will need to remap every image in your content so you will either need to plan ahead for this in your import scripts or handle the image URL changes in the clean-up phase.

MOVING METADATA

If you need to maintain a certain site structure, you should establish that back in the planning phase. If your existing site already has categories and tag information, likely that information will transfer as part of your migration. You will need to pay careful attention that all your information is exact, or the import will make multiple similar categories.

Otherwise, you may just want WordPress to establish new categories for your content during the import. You should review the template files in your theme, and the template file hierarchy discussed in Chapter 9. You may find that some of the structure that you had to manually maintain in the old site is automatically created in WordPress simply through the WordPress site architecture.

Remember to consider your permalink structure and how it relates to your new structured content. Likewise, consider the category base and tag base URL settings in the Administration Screens. Setting all of these properly on your new site can save you a fair amount of time.

Preserving the site structure or at least the URLs is important if you are moving an established site. Search engines have been indexing your previous site and you have probably made some efforts to optimize the site for search engines, so having the search engines' indexed links remain will continue to drive traffic to your site.

Even if the default WordPress URL for content is a different link than your original site, you will want to map the old URLs to the new ones. We cover this step in the section "Cleaning Up," later in this chapter.

MOVING AUTHORS AND USERS

Most brochureware websites are author agnostic. That is, you do not really have content attributed to specific site authors because they are representing a business entity. You can continue with this method, even when using WordPress, which enforces authorship. All you need to do is turn off the author information in your theme.

However, if you are moving from a site that has authorship ingrained, or this is something you want to implement on the new site, you will need to set up your authors in WordPress and attribute the appropriate posts. If you are using the WXR method, your authors can be created for you automatically. If you are using the SQL conversions from another CMS, you will want to carefully build this information into your transformations.

If you are creating a multi-author WordPress site, you may also want to consider the multi-user functionality of WordPress Multisite. WordPress Multisite is covered in depth in Chapter 10.

THEME AND PRESENTATION

The presentation of your new site represents the next set of decisions for your migration. Is your new site going to look exactly like your old site or are you making a design change at the same time?

If you are making a design change, you can use an existing theme or build a new theme and not have to dwell on this step too much. Remember to evaluate whether certain content areas need specific, or unique, design considerations. Otherwise, activate your new theme and work out the kinks.

However, if you intend to keep the look and feel consistent across the migration, you are most likely in for building a new theme. Usually this is not too much of an undertaking because most websites are created with essentially the same building blocks: header, footer, content area, and sidebars. You can pretty easily map these to the proper theme template files.

Nevertheless, you will have to decide if you are going to take your current HTML files and add in the proper WordPress hooks and code, or start with a working WordPress starter theme or theme framework and style it to match. It really is a mixed bag, and you will have to decide the best path for yourself. For practicality, we recommend taking a theme framework and styling it to match your site's look and feel. In the long run, this has worked out better for us.

UNIQUE FUNCTIONALITY

For integration and functionality, there is really nothing to migrate, except for the actual operations—for example, contact forms, event calendars, and polls. Unless you move the existing PHP code to the WordPress site through page templates, your best bet is to find equivalent plugins. There are many plugins for various tasks; you will simply have to pick the one that closely matches your needs, and activate and configure it.

CLEANING UP

Even when you are done moving the bulk of the visible content, there is always the final fit and finish work. You have done the heavy lifting and at least have something to look at on the new site. Now you need to go through and review all the content with spot tests, fix any glaring issues, and then do some cleaning up to put the final polish on the site.

This section also covers some steps of the "go live" process of launching a site. The balance between when you can make these final changes and when you are still testing can often be difficult to gauge. At some point you have to bite the bullet and make the change. Remember that shipping is a feature.

Though this is called the cleaning-up step, you could be making some drastic changes in this phase so we recommend doing your first backup of the new WordPress database. The wp-DBManager plugin by Lester Chan (http://wordpress.org/plugins/wp-dbmanager/) is an excellent plugin for the job. It allows you to make a backup of the database so you will have this point to roll back to. In addition, this plugin allows scheduling of the backups and some other database tools.

Manual Fine-Tuning

An important pre-launch task is to check all the page links, posts, and page names to make sure everything is how you want it. You can tweak all of the relative paths now. You will be changing the fully qualified URL at launch time. This is the time for you to go through the entire site and manually inspect and adjust your imported content. Rarely is a migration import flawless and nearly always your site will require some manual intervention, either because the import was incapable of making the necessary changes or because the effort required to automate, or fix and re-import, requires more than simply making the adjustments by hand.

Import Limitations

Be mindful of the PHP memory limit on your server. Because the entire import script file is loaded into memory and executed, you can easily hit low limits. If you have a large number of posts to import, try breaking the source export file into pieces and run the import in sections.

Also, an import cannot catch everything. You will have to manually review all your content. It is time-consuming and painful, akin to being forced to listen to your own recorded voice, but it is worthwhile to get fully up and running on WordPress as well as to ensure that all of your content appears on the other side of the migration.

Updating URLs

If many of the links in your content contain hard-coded test site URLs, you can set these to site relative links to make the launch easier. By default, WordPress uses fully qualified links to reference assets and other pages. Changing these links to site relative means that when you make the final DNS switch, you will not have to run this process again, unless of course, you have added new content after this step.

To change some of the common absolute paths that you would encounter in your content you can run some simple SQL queries. Use the SQL page of the wp-DBManager plugin, phpmyadmin, or the command-line MySQL to update them.

Change all the in-site links from absolute to site relative. This query assumes you are running your WordPress site on the `test.example.com` domain:

```
UPDATE 'wp_posts' SET post_content=replace(post_content,
'href="http://test.example.com/','href="/');
```

This query changes all your absolute image source links to site relative, again assuming you are running your new site on the `test.example.com` domain:

```
UPDATE 'wp_posts' SET post_content=replace(post_content,
'src="http://test.example.com/','src="/');
```

Now all your internal site links and image sources are root relative, meaning you can check out your site for bad links either manually or with an automated tool and look for missing graphics. It does not matter what your test URL is. This is temporary and allows you to test all your images and graphics on the test site. Again, if you add any new content after this step, WordPress will use fully qualified URLs using the settings in the WordPress Administration Screens. As part of launching, you will want to run what is essentially the reverse of this SQL statement to set all the paths to the live URL. This preserves links in RSS feeds and other syndication systems to link back to your fully qualified domain name path.

Another method for updating hard-coded URLs in your content is the Search Regex plugin (http://wordpress.org/plugins/search-regex/). This plugin adds a powerful set of search-and-replace functionality to WordPress. It also allows you to view the content before and after without making any database changes so you can fully test your methods before pulling the trigger. Regular expression (regex) patterns can also be used for defining search-and-replace rules.

Redirection

This is a very important step. You will want search engines that have previously indexed your site to continue to refer visitors to the same content. You do not want to lose any investment of time and achievement just because you are switching underlying website platforms. The search spiders do not care how you make your website, other than being readable to them, but they do care where your content is located. After all, it is the only way they can find you.

You have a couple of options for maintaining your existing URL structure on your shiny new WordPress site, the most basic being permalinks. Depending on how your site was laid out and how the planning phase went, you may be able to duplicate the site structure by manually editing the permalink structure of your pages and posts.

If you are running on Apache, this is an easy fix. You can use the site map created in the content migration step to build a list of redirects from the old URL to the new WordPress permalink.

A second option is to use an .htaccess redirect to map the old URLs to the new URLs. Generally this option is only for Apache web servers with the mod_rewrite module enabled, but some .htaccess-like modules exist for IIS and nginx web servers. The .htaccess method is an easy fit if you created a site map back in the planning or import file creation phase. You can easily take this import file and with a small script generate the necessary lines for your .htaccess file. Your .htaccess then includes the simple one-to-one matching, one match per line, such as:

```
Redirect /about.php http://example.com/services/
Redirect /portfolio.php http://example.com/category/portfolio/
Redirect /cool-article.php http://example.com/2009/10/09/cool-article/
```

Make sure these redirect pairs are listed first in your .htaccess file, and make sure you include the WordPress redirect stanza at the bottom of the file. Also make note that if you use the built-in WordPress permalink changer, you risk overwriting this file, so make a backup.

Finally, there is a great redirection plugin, aptly called Redirection (http://wordpress.org/plugins/redirection/). This plugin, made by John Godley, incorporates your redirect settings directly in the WordPress Administration Screens. This can make it very easy for you to set up the necessary redirects if you are unfamiliar with editing .htaccess files. The redirection plugin also supports WordPress-based redirects in case your site is not on an Apache host.

This plugin has several other notable features, including support for regular expression redirects, 404 logging to track broken links, and several import and export functions. Monitoring your

404 pages is an excellent way to see what you missed in a migration, but will also help you in the long term when you add new content. It will show if you mislinked something in your own site. Reviewing 404 logs is not a fun task, but something that our developers do daily to ensure sites are running fully functional.

LAUNCHING

At some point you have to bite the bullet and launch your new site. You have done all the manual review and automated updates you can, and for better or for worse you are going to make the move to switch sites.

The actual steps for launching your site vary depending on how you did your import and new site development. You may need to make the actual DNS change. If this is the case, you will also need to change the URLs in the General Settings Screen of WordPress. Change these URLs to the live site URLs. This will intentionally break the website rendering. You can temporarily add `define('RELOCATE',true);` to the `wp-config.php` file to regain access to your site. Remember to pull this setting back out when the DNS finally propagates. If you set your internal links to root relative during the testing phase, you can now set them to use your live URL. This is also a final opportunity to validate that your planning and the migration process worked. You should verify each and every page on your website and double-check all functionality.

Some other things to consider when moving your WordPress site to production include enabling privacy settings to make your site visible. Set the admin e-mail address to the proper value. Often, if you are moving someone else's site, you develop the new site with your own e-mail address so the final user does not get confused. Finalize the database backup plugin to regularly back up the database, or if you have some other backup plan, put it into effect. Likewise, confirm the settings of other plugins that should be active in the live site; caching is a good example. Double-check your 404 handling. Finally, make sure your web traffic statistics, like Google Analytics, are enabled. We usually disable analytics in the development phase.

WP-CLI

The first section of this chapter covered the essentials. These are the building blocks, the nitty-gritty so to speak about the process. As you have seen in this book, we are teaching the fundamentals of being a professional WordPress developer. We feel it is important for you to understand the process of what you are trying to accomplish before you learn the shortcuts. If you are importing content from a non-WordPress source into WordPress, you are going to have to brute-force the migration through trial and error and using the previously mentioned tools will give you a starting point. However, if you are moving from a WordPress site to another WordPress site, such as changing hosting servers or domains names, this section is going to show you an easier way, using a newer tool.

What Is WP-CLI?

WP-CLI is exactly what its name suggests—a command line interface for managing WordPress. It's a PHP application that provides useful tools to control and manipulate WordPress functionality without browser interaction, therefore making it scriptable.

WP-CLI is available online at http://wp-cli.org. Originally created by Andreas Creten and Cristi Burcă, it is now a community project maintained by Daniel Bachhuber.

WP-CLI includes many commands that allow you, the site administrator or developer, to install WordPress and take control of the features, functionality, and content of the site. Furthermore, because it is a community project, many plugin authors have contributed additional commands that extend the capabilities of the application.

Installing WP-CLI

WP-CLI requires a UNIX-like environment to operate. That means you are restricted to using Linux, Mac OS X, or Cygwin on Windows. WP-CLI will not work on Windows without it. WP-CLI also requires PHP 5.3.2 or later, and WordPress 3.5.2 or later. To be clear, WP-CLI is an advanced tool.

Installing is simple, and there are steps on the website. First, download the installer from GitHub. com. Because you are using a UNIX-like environment, you can use wget or curl to download this package, such as:

```
curl -O https://raw.githubusercontent.com/wp-cli/builds/gh-pages/phar/wp-cli.phar
```

Most users want to alias the command wp to use WP-CLI. In order to use wp as the command instead of php wp-cli.phar, you need to make the file executable and relocate it to somewhere in your system path. For example:

```
chmod +x wp-cli.phar
sudo mv wp-cli.phar /usr/local/bin/wp
```

Once you have WP-CLI in your executable path, give it a try to make sure you have everything working correctly. Type **wp --info** on the command line to see some basic information about WP-CLI. For example:

```
vagrant@vvv:/srv/www/wordpress-trunk$ wp --info
PHP binary: /usr/bin/php5
PHP version: 5.5.9-1ubuntu4
php.ini used: /etc/php5/cli/php.ini
WP-CLI root dir: /srv/www/wp-cli
WP-CLI global config:
WP-CLI project config:
WP-CLI version: 0.16.0
```

Depending on your situation, you may need to make configuration changes for finding the correct versions of your LAMP stack or tab completions. See the WP-CLI website for more configuration steps and support.

MIGRATION EXAMPLE

This example is going to focus on taking an existing WordPress site, for example your local development site, and launch it on a production server, such as launching test.example.com to example.com. We are going to assume you have WP-CLI installed on both your development site and also your production servers.

First, we will focus on your local development environment and gather the necessary elements for moving to your production server. Export the database from your development site using WP-CLI.

```
wp db export
```

This will give you an SQL file of your content and configuration from WordPress. When doing this manually, as shown earlier, you would want to hand-edit this file or run it through some regex substitutions to make the necessary URL changes. However, using WP-CLI we will save this step for later.

The other development files you need are your custom theme. You can either zip or tarball your development files, or if you are deploying a theme from source code control, you can skip this step and checkout your theme files into your production location. Copy the SQL export file and your theme to your production server via SFTP or whatever access you have. You can store them in your home directory for now, as we will be moving them into the proper location shortly.

Now, ssh into your production server. Note that you should have already set up your web server to serve your domain name and installed WordPress in the document root. (However, you can also use WP-CLI to install WordPress.)

Change to your WordPress directory and then import your SQL file into WordPress using WP-CLI. Your paths may be different, but the following offers an example

```
cd /var/www/example.com/htdocs
wp import db ~/test_example_com.sql
```

It is very important that you do not copy and leave your SQL file in your webserver document root as it can be accessed via the web and you might leak sensitive information.

At this point, you can install any plugins needed. With WP-CLI, this is as simple as

```
wp plugin install wp-super-cache --activate
```

This command will download and activate the WP Super Cache plugin.

Copy your theme files to the appropriate directory so it is available to your WordPress installation. Using WP-CLI, you can view which themes are available on your site. The command

```
wp theme list
```

will display a table showing all the themes available, which theme is active, and their current versions, like so:

```
vagrant@vvv:/srv/www/wordpress-trunk$ wp theme list
+-------------------------+----------+-----------+---------+
| name                    | status   | update    | version |
+-------------------------+----------+-----------+---------+
| child-of-twentyfourteen | inactive | none      | 1.0     |
| responsive              | inactive | available | 1.9.6.9 |
| thematic                | inactive | none      | 1.0.4   |
| twentyeleven            | inactive | none      | 1.8     |
| twentyfourteen          | active   | none      | 1.1     |
```

```
| twentyten              | inactive | none     | 1.6     |
| twentythirteen         | inactive | none     | 1.2     |
| twentytwelve           | inactive | none     | 1.4     |
+------------------------+----------+----------+---------+
```

Next, activate your custom theme with WP-CLI. In this example, you will activate the Child of Twenty Fourteen theme that you created in Chapter 9:

```
wp theme activate child-of-twentyfourteen
```

You now have all the basics in place with one thing missing. All the content and configuration still has the test domain set. This is where WP-CLI really shines. You can use WP-CLI to change the domain names in the WordPress database. As you will recall from the first part of this chapter, this is a time consuming and error-prone step. With WP-CLI, it becomes super simple. Using the following command, you can run a test to see everywhere the URL information will be changed in the database without making any changes, yet.

```
wp search-replace test.example.com example.com --dry-run
```

This command will display a comprehensive table of all the places this change will be made. To actually run the changes, remove the `--dry-run` flag. As you can see, this method is significantly easier than the manual method.

This example is just the tip of the iceberg of all the commands available in WP-CLI. Furthermore, with the scriptable capabilities, full WordPress migration and management scripts can be developed with minimal effort.

SUMMARY

In conclusion, transitioning a website to WordPress can seem like a daunting task. However, when you break it down into steps and spend a little time planning up front, the process easily falls into place. The real trick is to establish a new development environment with a fresh WordPress installation, and then you can iterate over trial imports until you get an import that is far enough along to finish up with some manual fine-tuning. Remember that a little elbow grease will go a long way and in the end, the long-term reward of using WordPress and all the built-in and plugin functionality will make the endeavor worthwhile. In addition, the ecosystem of managing WordPress is expanding through tools like WP-CLI, which make the administration of WordPress simpler.

Now that you have your site functioning in WordPress, the next chapter will focus on how you can improve the user experience for both human and non-human visitors.

12

Crafting a User Experience

WHAT'S IN THIS CHAPTER?

➤ Understanding the principles of the user experience

➤ Learning the benefits of usability and usability testing

➤ Recognizing how to optimize your site for search engines

➤ Improving the built-in WordPress search

The last few chapters have been about creating and presenting your great content to the user. In truth, those chapters are really about your own goals—how you want the site to look and function and what content you are presenting. But it is not all about you. What about the visitors to your site? This is where the user's experience is a factor.

Up to this point, the focus has been on how to create a site and manage its content. Now the question is whether the site is going to attract and retain viewers (users) with the mechanics and decisions you have put in place. Because you are dealing with people and their unique perceptions, it is an entirely nondeterministic exercise. That is, beauty is in the eye of the beholder.

The user experience really involves more than what an actual person sitting at a browser in Middle America thinks. Indirectly, web spiders, search engines, and service consumers such as RSS readers are also your users. Your site needs to be designed and structured so that all classes of users benefit and have a great experience.

USER EXPERIENCE PRINCIPLES

User experience is a topic that is open to interpretation; everyone sees it a little differently. But some good guidelines are available. Some of these guidelines are common sense, or seem to be. They all strive to establish a balance between what is aesthetically pleasing but also practical.

These are not hard-and-fast decrees that must be followed. Humans are fickle and these guidelines need to be flexible to meet their needs.

Here are some basic questions to ask:

➤ Does my site have a consistent look?

➤ Is the design helpful or hurtful?

➤ Is my content easy to find and access?

➤ Is my content well structured?

➤ Is my site reasonably quick to load?

This list itemizes the pillars of the user experience. How you choose to use them, or in what combination, is really what this chapter is about. The following sections delve into these topics for a little more clarity.

Consistent Navigation

This is almost a no-brainer these days; it is difficult to not have a consistent look and feel with WordPress themes. You want your visitors to be aware that they are consistently using your site, independently of the path taken to get there. That means having a coherent look and feel to your site—such as a masthead and dependable global navigation.

That does not mean that different sections cannot have their own flair, but it needs to be coherent. It will be very disorienting for a visitor to read some of your content on one page and then click through to the next page with a totally different look and feel to it. Visitors will think they have left your site and you will not get credit for the great content you have created.

Likewise, each page in your site should have a dependable global navigation. Dependable means that it does not change and does not move. Visitors should be able to explore your content without fear of getting lost. It may sound silly to a technologist like you, but the average user has a different relationship with technology. This global navigation is a safety line for your visitors to get back to where they came from.

Good global navigation also tells visitors where they are in the site. Specifically, setting an "active" item in the menu and making it clear that it is lit up, or somehow distinguished from the rest of the global navigation. This enables a visitor to glance at the navigation and immediately see where he is in your site with respect to the other sections or pages. The built-in menu system in WordPress does this automatically; you will automatically receive a `current _ menu _ item` or `current _ page _ item` class in your currently active menu items like so (this is the rendered HTML):

```
<li class="page_item page-item-2 current_page_item">
  <a href="http://local.wordpress-trunk.dev/?page_id=2">Sample Page</a>
</li>
```

Alternatively, if you are manually creating navigation in the templates, using WordPress's built-in `is _ page()` function, you can achieve the same result (this is the PHP code in the template file):

```
<li class="benefits
   <?php if(is_page('benefits')){ echo "current_menu_item";}?>">
     <a title="benefits" href="/benefits/">
       Benefits
     </a>
</li>
```

In both cases, some nice CSS on the `current_menu_item` class would differentiate this menu item from the rest. We are firm believers in the user feedback functions of the anchor element. First, mousing over the element should provide some sort of feedback beyond switching the cursor to a hand. Usually, this means a highlight or darkening of the font, background, or border. Second, the currently active navigation section should be similarly delineated, but different. These two tenets, when taken together, create a nice global navigation that visually presents a multitude of information on where the visitor is in relation to the rest of the site and where he can go to read more. The following is sample CSS from the Twenty Fourteen theme:

```
.primary-navigation li:hover > a,
  .primary-navigation li.focus > a {
    background-color: #24890d;
    color: #fff;
  }

  .primary-navigation ul ul a:hover,
  .primary-navigation ul ul li.focus > a {
    background-color: #41a62a;
  }
```

This works in Chrome, Safari, Firefox, and Internet Explorer. In Figure 12-1, you can see how this plays out in the web browser. If you browsed this site in real life, you would see that the global navigation across the top is in the same place on each and every page of this test website. You will also notice that this screenshot is of the Child Page of the Sample Page menu item, and that navigation item is visibly different from the other menu items to indicate that it is the active page, and also the active top-level navigation item.

FIGURE 12-1: Active navigation

Notice that it is referred to as *global* navigation. That does not mean that every page in your site has to be listed in the main menu. It can be, but it does not have to be. Sections can have a local navigation block once you are inside them, but the main sections should be accessible via the main menu. This is what makes navigation dependable. It reinforces what the visitor can expect on your site and the methods used to navigate it.

A consistent style and dependable navigation comfort your visitor and reinforce the validity of your content.

Visual Design Elements

Specifically, are the visual assets of your site helpful or distracting to the user? Does the theme reinforce the persona you are portraying with your content or detract from it? This is another one of those topics that are open to personal interpretation. Photos and colors trigger differing subjective responses from different people, but the overall impression of your site should match the general content.

For example, a business site should not have a bubble-gum pink theme if it wants to be taken seriously—unless, of course, the site is selling toys or bubble gum. At the other extreme, there has recently been a bit of backlash against the use of pink to denote sites or content addressing women's health issues; overuse degrades its impact and importance if blindly applied. Visual design should reflect the brand and brand values you are trying to develop with your WordPress site.

Colors evoke different feelings. Blue instills trust, which is why it is so prevalent in business and financial logos. Orange suggests new technology and is often used in the telecom industry. Color and branding is a whole topic unto itself, but just consider that pink ponies may not be the way to market your bank, and skulls and crossbones may not be the way to market your children's furniture site.

This topic is pretty difficult to gauge. It is a very emotional topic and often marketing takes over rather than common sense. For example, it is likely that many of you have worked for clients who were absolutely certain that each new addition to the index page will be the most important thing on the page. That meant that every design element was oversized and blinking, causing the whole page to become nausea inducing. Sort of along the same lines as laundry detergent: If every brand is ultra-new-super-improved, are they not really all the same again?

One design theory that that works well when working up a new mockup is to toil away at the composition. Build up layers of elements working toward the end goal. Once you are happy with what you think could be the final mockup, remove an element. Kick it back one rung and use that. This is a variation on the less-is-more approach.

Take, for example, the mockup being created in Adobe Photoshop in Figure 12-2. You will notice in the Layers palette on the right side that all the components that make up the mockup are broken into individual layer groups. During the development of this mockup, each graphic element was composed using this method, which means that you can easily move and change them without interfering with other layers. You will also notice that a couple of the layer groups are currently turned off: The little eyeball icon is not there next to them. When creating this mockup, both of the graphic elements in those layers were tried and deemed to be too much. Turning them off, kicking it back a notch, created a stronger layout.

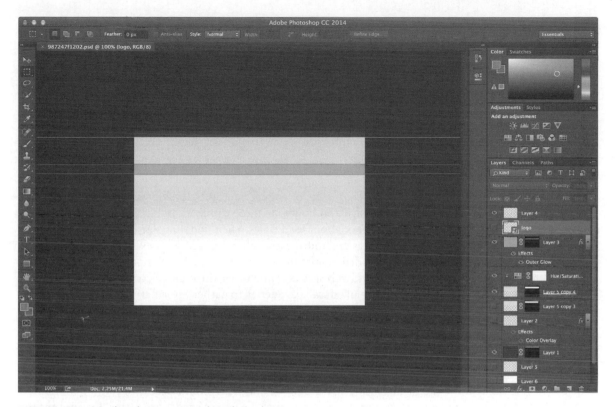

FIGURE 12-2: Mockup being created in Photoshop

Making Content Easy to Find

With a successful site, you will reach a point where you have a substantial body of content. Often, the visitor to your site does not categorize or organize content mentally in exactly the same manner as you do. Therefore, there should be multiple paths to get to all of the content on your site. This increases the likelihood that visitors will be able to find what they are looking for. This is also an excellent reason for having categories, tags, and calendar-based archives templates, as discussed in Chapter 9. Having these templates addresses three popular ways in which people remember where something was. They also serve as a way to drive more content interaction and consumption, exposing your thoughts (as the creator) on content sorting.

WordPress assists in this strategy right out of the box. First and foremost, your site should have a dependable global navigation, as mentioned previously. WordPress encourages this with its native structure, but how you actually build and organize the navigation is up to you.

Second, WordPress does come with a built-in search functionality. Although it can be improved, as discussed later in this chapter, some search is better than no search. Tagging your content helps with search.

Third, WordPress offers many alternative views of the content. Either with special templates or by simply using the default index template file (see Chapter 9 for more information on template files),

WordPress can offer up your content by date, category, title, or author, or through several other variations. Creative use of these templates and other custom loops offers another vector into your content. The catch here is that this method also serves duplicate content, which the search engines discourage, but that is covered later in this chapter.

Fourth, many plugins are available for related posts. Adding a related posts list to the bottom of a post is another method for providing a deeper dive into your content. This is particularly effective if you have already piqued the interest of your reader with one set of content. Offering similar content is a great idea, and it is a way to provide more information on the subject that can be useful to your visitor.

Site Load Times

Back when dial-up was the most prevalent means of connection, web developers were extremely conscientious about the weight of the page and how long it took to load. But as broadband access has increased, developers have become lax about load times when updating existing sites. CSS files have bloomed as new selectors and styles are added rather than merged with existing styles. AJAX and JavaScript libraries have been included, sometimes more than one JavaScript library, just to achieve neat-o gee-whiz effects. iFrames, web services, and other third-party components all add to the bloat of an HTML document. Multiple database queries to gather information slow down the page on the server side.

In addition, elaborate new designs require more CSS and images and other effects, which adds to the bandwidth inflation. This is a problem for both new greenfield development and with the maintenance of legacy designs.

Is the time to load still a factor to consider? It should be and with mobile access becoming more prevalent, it might even be more important. The fact that the access speeds are faster does not mean you should ignore optimizations in the code. However, never optimize too early in the process. Premature optimization slows down the development and deployment of your site. This is a delicate balance between getting things done and out the door and optimizing them so the launch is successful. Page load times should be a consideration when developing your site. A nicely optimized site loads much quicker than one that was put together by someone who does not understand the implications.

This can be a complex issue: Think about all the aspects that affect load times of your website. There are the obvious ones that you should be familiar with, including the quantity and sizes of images, the number of JavaScript libraries being used, and to what effect those JavaScript libraries are being used. Consider also your integrations with third-party sites, such as using a few too many Facebook badges with Status and Like updates, or multiple hotlinked images from image hosting sites. What happens when these remote locations are slow to respond, or worse, do not respond at all? Does your site's response time suffer because of something outside your control? Think about the *tree* of performance dependencies that you create by referencing other sites. That does not mean that you should not use them at all, but that you should recognize how they can affect your own site's performance.

Firebug continues to be an excellent tool for working through optimizations and network bandwidth on your site. Google Chrome's Developer Tools is also a very popular choice. In addition, Yahoo! and Google each have add-ons for Firebug and Chrome Developer tools to help improve your page speed: YSlow (`http://developer.yahoo.com/yslow/`) and Page Speed (`https://developers.google.com/speed/pagespeed/`), respectively.

A caveat with YSlow and Page Speed is that they are provided by Internet power houses. These sites likely see more traffic in an hour than you see all year. The problems and speed issues that they need to address are not the same types of issues that you need to address. YSlow always recommends a Content Delivery Network (CDN). Sure, a CDN distributes your assets across a geographically diverse set of servers to increase reliability and reduce latency, but does your site really need this? Do you really need to incur the costs? It is a developer choice, but in short, just remember that your site is probably not on the same scale as Yahoo! or Google.

You need to pick and choose your battles in the area of site load times. Here is a quick checklist of things to consider, starting with the low-hanging fruit:

➤ Optimize your graphics and pick the right DPI, color depth, and format. Do not forget about higher DPI Apple and other mobile devices.

➤ Standardize your JavaScript library and use only one. Measure the benefits of packing and minifying your JavaScript and CSS. Those efforts may not improve page load times.

➤ Evaluate the number of external references made, whether hotlinking an image or including a Facebook badge with a status update. Consider using transients, as discussed in Chapter 11.

➤ Be sensitive to MySQL database performance on your hosting site. Because every page or post displayed involves database queries, make sure you're not overtaxing the expected performance of your hosting option. Plugins that store content in the database give you flexibility, but also add to the database query burden when you're generating page output. Again, transients may help you here.

➤ Caching your output may be a viable solution; that is covered more in Chapter 15. You will have to weigh the deployment options and come up with a solution to meet your site's scale requirements and deployment obstacles.

Using JavaScript

One more tip when using JavaScript in your web design: You may be tempted at times to base your entire site navigation (or another design element) around a super-cool jQuery plugin. The JavaScript may be a really neat effect, but JavaScript should not be the core of your design. jQuery effects should be the sprinkles you put on top of the frosting on the cake. You need to have a solid foundation so that the site still functions and is aesthetically pleasing, even if the JavaScript sprinkles fail. You should build a site from the bottom up and only add the glitter to a functioning site. Realize that each new JavaScript library and gee-whiz effect you add to your site increases the load time for the end user. Consider if the effect really adds something to your site, or if you are just using it because it looks neat to you.

Furthermore, make sure that your site degrades gracefully if the JavaScript does not work. That is, make your cake still taste good even if a slice does not have any sprinkles on it. If your site relies on JavaScript for some functionality to work, and it is the only way for it to work, your site may not be accessible. You have to consider that some visitors will not have JavaScript enabled, or perhaps not even available to them, and your site should be able to elegantly downgrade to support them.

In every case, there is a level of effort or visual trade-off required to improve page load times, and you will have to measure the work input versus the user experience output improvement.

USABILITY AND USABILITY TESTING

Your client is probably not the end user. Furthermore, your clients do not know what their users really want. For that matter, those in the content creation side of things, be they developers or writers, do not know what the eventual users—the readers—really want, unless there is some sort of feedback mechanism, such as testing. Web design is one of those weird trades where everyone thinks they know what is best. Think back to the marketing person who wanted every element to be the most important element on the page, which in the end created a wash of blinking badges.

Your clients generally think they know what their users want because it is what they would want when visiting a site of this nature—that is, the site you are building. This works sometimes. But often, your clients have an intimate knowledge of the topic that their visitor does not have, making it impossible to be objective. For example, one of the authors did a project where 60 percent of the traffic to the site came directly from the client's own employees. However, the nature of the business meant the client could only enroll 12 new customers a month and based on the business's growth goals these low traffic 12 visitors for the year are the most important visitors to the site.

If you are serious about having a well-crafted user experience, test early and test often. You have to decide what you are going to test and this really depends on what the goals are for your site. For example, an e-commerce site generally wants to sell products.

> **NOTE** *The story at* `http://www.uie.com/articles/three_hund_million_button/` *has been used as the poster child for usability testing for quite a while now; it is older but still appropriate. This story is an interesting anecdote about how changing one button made a $300 million difference during checkout:* `http://www.uie.com/articles/three_hund_million_button/`.

How can you apply this type of thinking to testing your own site? A/B testing is a nice way to test what works in a real-world laboratory. With A/B testing, you have two different versions of an actionable web page. Your site will randomly display one version or the other to each visitor. The process involves some nice code trickery and provides an easy way to do usability testing with the general public so it does require that your site be live. Using the results of the test, you can see which version of your action item performs better. This is, in some ways, also how Google does usability testing—it modifies its services on-the-fly and sees what generates actual traffic. If you are going to try A/B testing on your WordPress site, there are several plugins that simplify this process. Some even work in conjunction with Google Analytics's Content Experiments for tracking.

Some other options are to use your family and friends, or call for help on Twitter or other social networks. This is called *crowdsourcing*.

Any testing is better than no testing. Having a second set of eyes is just a good idea. You do not always have to accept the results and make the changes the users suggest, but you should at least consider them. Again, a fresh set of eyes and a new perspective from someone who is not intimate with the site, as you are, is a good idea.

If your budget does not have room for usability testing, use your family and friends and watch them interact with your site. Observing how they find information enables you to isolate places where your design can be improved, and listening to their comments enables you to see what is good and bad about the overall feel. Generally, your family and friends represent the average user's computer skills and make a nice test audience.

Likewise, you can solicit help from strangers via social networks. However, the results you get back vary greatly. Generally, people will be polite and tell you one or two little things either positive or negative, but rarely will you get a cohesive user test back. It is just too time-intensive for the average Joe.

You may be able to get more focused results by enlisting your local WordPress User Group. These are likely fellow developers and they will have that sensibility in their feedback. Some groups are more heterogeneous with developers and users, especially on show-and-tell nights. This can be a good opportunity to solicit some feedback and testing.

If you do have a budget, many sites are available that provide you access to user testing agents. Generally with these services, you submit your application or site and provide some goals for the user to achieve. You can also select which level of computer literacy you are targeting. The service then contacts its agents, who are average users at home, and using special software, the user records a session while trying to accomplish your goals.

We have used one of these services to test a whole new front-end interface to one of our core web applications (not WordPress-related). The resulting videos allowed us to watch how the user interacted with the site and provided audio commentary from the users. Some comments were quite overt whereas others required us to interpret the emotions of grunts and "OKs." In the end, the user testing showed us some places that required immediate improvement to make the actions more clear and reinforced some changes that were made based on more experienced internal focus groups.

The WordPress team has done some user testing with the Dashboard Screens in the last several releases. It seems that the administration dashboards were receiving complete overhauls every couple of versions. WordPress is, by virtue of being community-developed, a terrific example of crowdsourcing, in both development testing and usability. These user tests focused on what features WordPress users used the most and directly led to the development of the QuickPress and other features. This crowdsource testing has led to the very usable Administration Screens.

Along these same lines, a little user testing goes a long way in improving the layout and design of your site. It is usually overlooked because developers are smart people and often know best, but you are also very intimate with the site and the fresh perspective can make your site better if you listen to some of the advice.

STRUCTURING YOUR INFORMATION

How your site is organized is critical to your visitors and to search engine spiders. In general, WordPress does a good job of keeping your content organized. After all, that should be a core function of a content management system. However, you do have to put a little thought into the overall structure of your site.

One of the first things you want to ask clients who want to redesign their site, or develop a new one, is to create an outline of the pages or content for the new site. This forces the client to think about the structure and organization of the entire site from a 10,000-foot view. Including what type of content each outline item represents also helps in structuring the overall flow of the site. Using this outline, developers are able to stub out an information architecture of post categories, custom post types, pages, and parent pages that will align with the client's outline and make creating the site a smoother operation. This also allows the client to see the layout of the site with dummy copy, such as *lorem ipsum*, early in the process to make any structural changes as needed.

Once upon a time, there was a golden rule for websites that no page in your site should be more than three mouse clicks deep. This was back in the days when dialup connections were the most prevalent form of Internet access. Although we are not fans of deep sites, we are not sure if this rule is still true today. It is not that the attention span of the visitor has increased at all; in fact, it has probably diminished. And certainly broadband is more widespread nowadays, but you also have to consider mobile access. It is not page load times that are affecting our opinion here.

The short answer is: Search has largely replaced top-down navigation. In our opinion, people do not go to a website's index page and run through the global navigation to find the particular topic, article, or product they are looking for. Rather, they go to a search engine. The search engine provides a link to the exact page, or as close as it can get, regardless of how deep in the site it is.

So, although we still favor "everything in three clicks" as a design rule, it is only because it adheres to the K.I.S.S. methodology and makes your site easier to use. But do not think this is a hard-and-fast rule, as sites are far more complex and encompass more content than they did when this rule was in favor. Putting in effort to make your content easier to find through search engines, and then structuring the content itself with the "three clicks rule" will together improve the user experience.

This is also the ideal time to evaluate what the individual pages or sections are titled. Here is a sad truth of web design: No one actually reads your content. In a now classic 2006 study by Jakob Nielson (`http://www.nngroup.com/articles/f-shaped-pattern-reading-web-content/`), the researchers found that visitors scanned the content of a web page in a very fast F-shaped pattern, meaning their eyes scroll down the left-hand side and skim the headers searching for the content they are looking for. The year 2006 seems like a long time ago, and it is in the technology world, but this study has been continually cited since.

Again, this is not a blanket statement. Obviously, people do read the articles and content on websites or there would be no reason to have them. But, when you are still trying to attract visitors and get them to stick around on your site, what should you take away from this study?

Headers matter. Headers should be concise and descriptive. Your content should start with the most important and evocative information and then get more in-depth. They should also be properly formatted to use the different levels of HTML headers (more on this later). Headers should contain action words. They should be interesting and make visitors want to read your content, assuming that is your goal. Given that visitors are scanning your site, having actions and descriptions in your headers will allow the visitor to get the overall gist of your page, help them find what they are looking for, and possibly entice them to read the rest of the section.

For example, which of the following outline structures is more meaningful and interesting? This one:

- How to Use WordPress
  - Overview
  - The Technology
    - Software
    - Hardware
- How to Get Started

Or this one:

- Publishing Your Content on the Internet Using WordPress
  - What Steps Are Involved?
  - What Do I Need?
    - Installing the Applications
    - Configuring the Server
  - Getting Started Publishing

As you can see, with the first outline, you grasp the general idea of the website. But the second outline is much more engaging and draws you in with actionable tasks. You can also see the structure of the site and how it flows.

Remember back in school when you had to write an outline with several levels of headings? This is the same endeavor. Your content should have structure and headings and supporting paragraphs. If a heading intrigues a visitor enough, he will read the supporting paragraphs. If not, he will scan on to the next header. Funny how school actually taught you things you can use in real life, isn't it?

GETTING YOUR SITE FOUND

Search engine optimization (SEO) is how to get your site discovered by the search engines. One of the key ways to do this is to use the permalink structure in WordPress. These search engine–optimized permalinks are one of the key features that actually show up in the results pages of all the search engines. Making them meaningful and descriptive is a must.

Unfortunately, out of the box, the WordPress URL structure uses the query string post identifier format (`http://example.com/?p=100`). For compatibility reasons, this is the default because it works across the board on different platforms and servers.

Given the choice in a search engine results page between this:

```
http://example.com/?p=42
```

or this:

```
http://example.com/this-is-the-information-you-want
```

which would you choose? The choice is pretty obvious. With the second option, the visitor or potential visitor at least has an idea of what he is going to find at the site. This descriptive URL helps with search engines and click-throughs because the savvy web user knows to look in the status bar of his browser to see the target site. Therefore, we heartily recommend that one of the first things you should do when setting up a WordPress site is change the permalink structure, as shown in Figure 12-3. Of course, you have to be on a platform that will support them.

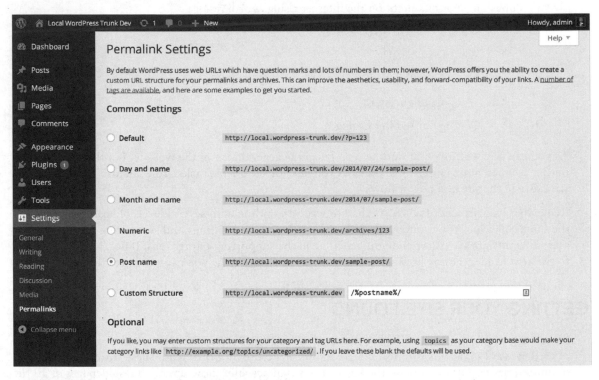

FIGURE 12-3: Setting the permalink structure in the Dashboard

Shorter URLs are generally better because they are easier to type, yet they need to maintain some inherent descriptive nature. Therefore, we recommend the Post name setting, which is the same as a custom permalink structure using /%postname%/. This will use the slug from your post or page and create the nice SEO-friendly URLs referenced in the preceding example.

In previous versions of WordPress, using this setting included a heavy duty parsing penalty during the search. That is, the database query really needed a number to get good performance. However, as of WordPress 3.3, the database query rules have been simplified and improved with the result being a performance boost during parsing.

Additionally, you have two optional fields on this Permalink Screen to rewrite the category and tag base URL elements. For example, when you visit a category page in your WordPress site, the URL usually looks something like `http://example.com/category/cool-stuff/`. You can replace the word "category" with whatever you key into these optional fields. You can just use a letter *c* for category and *t* for tag to make the URLs shorter, but some creative uses of these fields can lead to some interesting and meaningful URL structures.

> **NOTE** *Chris Shiflett has an interesting post on his PHP Security blog (`http://shiflett.org/blog/2008/mar/urls-can-be-beautiful`) that discusses how URLs can be beautiful. At the time, Chris worked for OmniTI, and the URLs for the new site involved action words that conveyed a very clear meaning: for example,* `http://omniti.com/is/hiring` *and* `http://omniti.com/helps/national-qeoqraphic`.

Duplicate Content

When a search engine is spidering your site, if you have duplicate content, or more specifically, multiple paths to the same content, the search engine may divide up your ranking (and SEO equity) across these multiple pages, diluting your overall ranking for any specific content piece. This section addresses how to keep multiple paths to content from appearing as distinct content views.

WordPress practically encourages duplicate content. Your posts are shown on the front page and on the category page for each category the post is in. Each tag creates a tag page for that content; plus your posts are kept in the yearly and monthly archives. So, while this provides you multiple paths to get to your content, which was considered a good thing in a previous section, it also weighs you down with duplicate content issues. Duplicate content on your own site may or may not actually be a bad thing; the jury still seems to be out on it. For example, the Google crawler, which indexes your site, has built-in logic to try and determine the nature and cause of your duplicate content. The crawler knows how to handle different views of the same content, such as for print versions. It also does its best to reinforce the primary source of the content—for example in a WordPress site, the `single.php` view.

In addition, Google provides a Webmaster Tools site that can provide insight into how the Google crawler sees your website. Use the Google XML Sitemaps plugin from Arne Brachhold, available online at `http://wordpress.org/plugins/google-sitemap-generator/`. This creates an XML sitemap for Google to use when indexing your site, which helps the spiders find everything. But Webmaster Tools also has some other interesting tools and investigative features. For example, under Search Appearance ➤ HTML Improvements, you can see duplicate content that the spider saw, as shown in Figure 12-4.

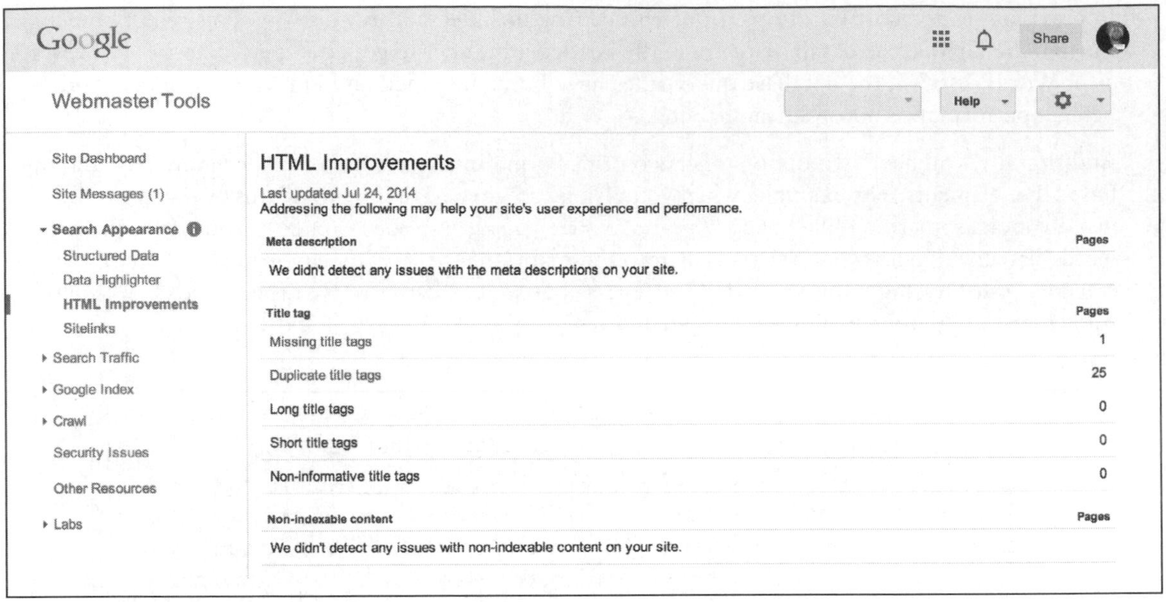

FIGURE 12-4: Google Webmaster Tools

Further clicking into the duplicate content suggestion will indicate exactly which pages are causing you problems. In all fairness, Microsoft's `Bing.com` has a similar set of tools that are just as nice.

Additionally, you should edit your `robots.txt` file. The `robots.txt` file provides some more guidance to the search engine spiders on what should not be indexed. By default, a spider will aggressively index whatever it can find. The `robots.txt` file tells the spider what it is explicitly not allowed to index. Again, you are relying on the spider to play by the rules, but here is a good start for your `robots.txt` file:

```
Sitemap: http://www.example.com/sitemap.xml

# global
User-agent: *
Disallow: /cgi-bin/
Disallow: /wp-admin/
Disallow: /wp-includes/
Disallow: /wp-content/plugins/
Disallow: /wp-content/cache/
Disallow: /wp-content/themes/
Disallow: /trackback/
Disallow: /comments/
Disallow: */trackback/
Disallow: */comments/
Disallow: wp-login.php
Disallow: wp-signup.php
```

If you include your sitemap, do not forget to change the URL in your `robots.txt` file to match your actual site. Pretty much, you are asking the crawlers to look at your actual content pages while ignoring all the other components of your WordPress site—which makes sense because you content is what people are searching for in the search engines.

Trackbacks and Pings

Google increases your page rank by counting links to your site through *trackbacks*. Trackbacks are a validation of your content by other sites. They started as a way for one site to inform its readers that they may be interested in this content from another site and also to let the other site know, "Hey, I talked about your content and here's the link." They can basically be thought of as comments about your content on a remote site.

By default, WordPress groups comments and trackbacks together, further validating that they are remote comments, but this can often look messy to your reader. A common practice is to separate out the trackbacks from the actual comments in the comment loop. The Twenty Twelve theme did this for you in the default templates using the twentytwelve_comment() function found in functions.php:

```
$GLOBALS['comment'] = $comment;
switch ( $comment->comment_type ) :
  case 'pingback' :
  case 'trackback' :
  // Display trackbacks differently than normal comments.
  ?>
    <li <?php comment_class(); ?> id="comment-<?php comment_ID(); ?>">
      <p><?php _e( 'Pingback:', 'twentytwelve' ); ?>
      <?php comment_author_link(); ?>
      <?php edit_comment_link( __( '(Edit)', 'twentytwelve' ),
       '<span class="edit-link">', '</span>' ); ?></p>
      <?php
    break;
  default :
  // Proceed with normal comments.
```

As the comments are walked, this function determines if it is a trackback or an actual comment and displays it accordingly. You can review the Twenty Twelve functions.php template file for more information and to view the remainder of the function. Automattic did not choose to separate comments and trackback into different formatting styles in the Twenty Thirteen or Twenty Fourteen themes.

You can also override this rendering function in a child theme to make the display logic your own. What this gets you is a clear separation between the active discussion on your site, for your visitors to participate in, and a list of related sites that have also mentioned your content. They can be divided logically and visually, making it easier to digest for the visitor.

Pings, on the other hand, notify other sites when new information is published. Generally, your WordPress site would ping an update service, such as Ping-o-Matic, that you have new content on your site. Likewise, if you are writing about content on another WordPress site, your site may ping that other site to let it know about your content. In this respect, pings are similar to trackbacks.

Pinging update services is a good way to drive traffic to your site. Some sites take the information from these update services and create information link sites about them. The theory is that casual surfers of these sites may discover your content related to a topic they are browsing. In this respect, pinging works very much like a push version of RSS or tweeting your new content.

Signing up to use an update service such as Ping-o-Matic is really simple to do. Simply browse to the site at `http://pingomatic.com/`, sign up your site, and it starts working. There is not much to it.

Similar to pings is a newer protocol called PubSubHubBub, which besides being glorious to say out loud, is another way to broadcast that your content has been updated. PubSubHubBub, or PuSH, works by pinging a central hub that your content has been updated and subscribers get notified. Google runs open hubs for anyone to use, or you can run your own hub, making this a decentralized protocol. There are several WordPress plugins that enable this functionality on your website.

In practice, the pinging and PuSH functionality are not used very much. Social media is the new word of mouth and news travels faster when shared via this route. Building a custom application that parses the RSS feeds of your WordPress sites and tweets new posts on Twitter and shares on Facebook as they are posted in near real time may be more effective broadcast marketing. In certain situations, this type of notification works better.

HOW WEB STANDARDS GET YOUR DATA DISCOVERED

HTML is text markup. That is literally what it means. When HTML was first developed, the intention was to take content and mark it up in a consistent and meaningful way. Many different HTML tags accomplish this. It was originally for scientific and academic use and the majority of content fit this nature.

Eventually, the marketers showed up and got their greasy hands involved. They wanted fancy layouts, graphics, sales pitches, and pretty pink ponies. To accomplish this, designers and developers, both good and bad, lost sight of the original markup and used whatever means necessary to create the best-looking site on the web. This included table-based layouts.

In recent years there has been a back-to-basics mentality among the better developers. This likely includes you, because you are reading this book. These developers recognize the power of separating concerns, such as presentation and content, CSS and HTML. They also recognize the advantages of using semantic HTML. The explosion of mobile access has further accelerated and emphasized this push.

Semantic HTML

POSH stands for plain old semantic HTML. This acronym expresses a back-to-basics mentality in the underlying HTML of websites. For all the glittery design and flair, developers can use CSS to make it happen. Look at CSS Zen Garden online at `http://www.csszengarden.com/` for an example.

Why should your site use POSH? There are a few reasons. First, it is the best thing for the future web. Paying it forward, if your site continues to use semantic HTML, browser manufacturers will continue to support it in their browsers.

Second, for the developer, it makes the content easier to validate and maintain. There is much less cruft in a properly semantic HTML document than in one that is coded old style. Consider this,

```
<div style="
  background: #F0CCFA;
```

```
    border: 1px solid # D894EB;
    color: #f00;
    font-size: 2em;
    margin: .25em 0;
    padding: .5em;">
      This is my subheading
  </div>
```

versus this:

```
<h2>This is my subheading</h2>
```

And that is not even really old style. This still uses CSS instead of the multiple nested <font> tags that really clutter up the old HTML documents. Valid, lean HTML is easier to maintain. It is that simple.

Speaking of lean, stripping all the cruft out of your HTML can really make your pages load faster. Think of all the extra markup that is moved out of each page load and into a browser-cached CSS file. This can be a significant weight loss for your pages.

The third reason to use POSH is accessibility. Structuring your HTML semantically increases the likelihood of screen readers figuring out your content and having it make sense to the visitor.

Finally, valid semantic HTML helps with search engine optimization. Search spiders are not very smart. They do not care how pretty the site looks or the cool new graphic treatment you created. They only care about the content. And they cannot think for themselves.

Semantic HTML conveys the meaning of the text you are marking up. That is why it is called semantic, after all. Using the proper HTML tag for the content is the first step. For example, six levels of headers are available to you in HTML. Using them in the correct order is essential for SEO. Similar to using a site outline to map out your site, this is also how the crawler knows the order of your content.

Even if you separate your CSS properly into a style sheet, the spider cannot determine the value of this HTML:

```
<div class="pagetitle">My Site Is About Something Important</div>
```

If you use the <h1> tag, however, the spider knows that this is the header for the entire page and attributes this content with the appropriate weight.

```
<h1 class="pagetitle">My Site Is About Something Important</h1>
```

Scrolling down through your content, you should use the appropriate levels of headers for additional content. The general consensus is that each page on your site should have only one <h1> tag to indicate the top level of each rendered page. Conventional wisdom is that this <h1> is reserved for the name of the site and then there can be multiple instances of the other heading levels as needed. The only flaw in this is that the name of your site does not really change, so it is not the <h1> that matters the most for each page. Using headers in this manner makes the <h1> really irrelevant; the <h2> would be the page title describing the rendered page's content. It is easy to understand both sides of the argument; you will have to make your own decision.

Images should always have `alt` attributes. This informs the spider what the image is rendering because the spider cannot see the graphic itself. This information is also what screen readers use.

The `<div>` tag is for blocks of content and the `<p>` is for paragraphs. Use the more meaningful `<em>` and `<strong>` to emphasize and strongly emphasize your content. Also discussed later in this chapter are HTML5 tags for specific blocks of content, such as `<header>`, `<footer>`, and `<article>`.

Use proper lists to organize your data. Ordered lists (`<ol>`) and unordered lists (`<ul>`) are easy ways to convey information to the spider. A properly formatted list is semantically more information to rate than a paragraph filled with `<br>` tags. There is also the lesser-known definition list (`<dl>`) element, which is very effective in paired information lists, such as Frequently Asked Questions. This list and explanation of HTML attributes can go on and on.

In short, semantic HTML is all about using the proper HTML tag for its intended use. It is worth reading through the W3C specifications and learning the different tags and their purpose. Adding these additional tools to your bag of tricks will make you a better developer, but will also make your pages lighter, more meaningful, and more accessible, all of which are good things for your visitors and your search engine rankings.

Valid HTML

For you, the developer, valid HTML and valid CSS are just plain easier to maintain. It is a simple fact. If your code is structured correctly, you can get in and out and make the changes you want quicker. We still have some ancient table-based layouts lying around from clients that have never wanted to update the look of their site. If you have not had to work on one of these in a while, it is astonishing to remember how hard they were to work on. But at the time, this is what we had.

Valid HTML also helps in solving cross-browser rendering issues. All developers dread the day they have to test their great looking site in one of the older less standards-compliant browsers. You know which one. It is important that the developer has completely consumed the requisite amount of coffee and moved all sharp objects out of arm's reach before opening this browser for testing. Inevitably, something will not be right. Having validated HTML is the first line of attack when dealing with this browser's rendering challenges. Always start from clean code before taking measures to make it look reasonable in these browsers. And have hope, maybe, that someday this browser will not be around anymore. Fortunately, supporting the older browsers is becoming easier as users become more aware of the need to upgrade and try alternate browsers.

In addition, some new tricks in the theme HTML allow you to target specific browsers with conditional comments. Take a look at the source code of your rendered Twenty Fourteen theme. Notice the first few lines of the HTML include conditional comments to set the root `<html>` element to focus on specific browsers and set the root CSS class for further CSS and JavaScript hooks:

```
<!DOCTYPE html>
<!--[if IE 7]>
<html class="ie ie7" lang="en-US">
<![endif]-->
<!--[if IE 8]>
<html class="ie ie8" lang="en-US">
```

```
<![endif]-->
<!--[if !(IE 7) & !(IE 8)]><!-->
<html lang="en-US">
<!--<![endif]-->
<head>
```

The Twenty Fourteen theme is only specifically going after Internet Explorer versions 7 and 8, but your theme could use additional conditional comments to target any number of specific browsers.

For SEO, it is back to a "spiders are not very smart" problem. Valid HTML makes your content easier for the spider to understand and therefore rank. If your HTML is not properly valid, the search engine can lose the content that is not visible to it while it is looking for the closing tag or attribute. This can severely limit the content that is viewable to the spider and hinder your site's ability to rank. Browsers tend to be more forgiving on invalid HTML and do their best to render what they can, but a spider is working on speed and quantity of content to digest. The spider is just going to breeze past anything it does not understand. Again, use a tool like Google Webmaster Tools to see how a spider perceives your site.

Many resources are available to validate your HTML, including the W3C's own Markup Validation Service at `http://validator.w3.org/`. In addition, most browser developer tools have a plugin or extension to use the W3C's validator service.

Microformats

Microformats are the more complicated brother of POSH. The idea is to add simple tags to HTML that convey contextual information for the HTML content. Once you see how they work, some are an almost natural way of dealing with the content, similar to an implementation of XML in HTML. The microformat convention is to format certain information in HTML so that it is reliable and can be discovered by microformat-enabled tools such as smartphones. For example, you will often see contact information and addresses expressed in a microformat syntax. You might even be using microformats already and not even know it.

For example, the Technorati tags mentioned earlier are microformats. The `rel` attribute on an anchor tag linking to `Technorati.com` indicates that the page you are linking from has been tagged for Technorati consumption. This is a microformat:

```
<a href="http://technorati.com/tag/wordpress" rel="tag">WordPress</a>
```

Prior to WordPress 3.5, WordPress used a common microformat built right in called the XFN (XTHML Friends Network). This microformat is simply an attribute you place on links to indicate your relationship with that person. This feature is built-in on the Links screen, also known as your blogroll. While this feature was removed in WordPress 3.5, all of the functionality is still available with the Link Manager plugin (`http://wordpress.org/plugins/link-manager/`) by Andrew Nacin.

Using this handy screen, you can easily add microformat attributes to your link indicating how and where you know the individual you are linking to. For example, consider the settings shown in Figure 12-5.

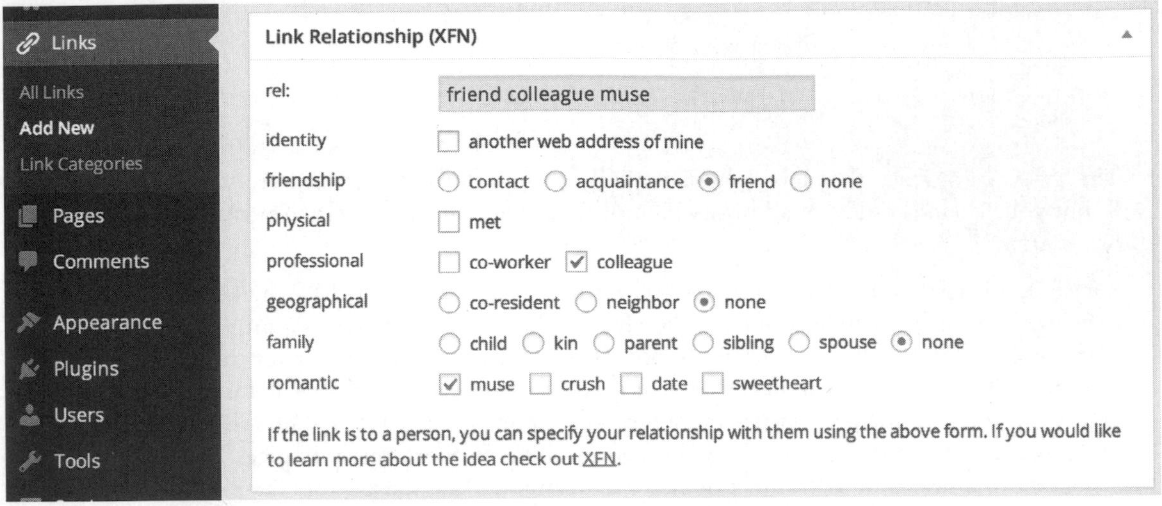

FIGURE 12-5: Editing the XFN of a link

These settings will render the HTML as:

```
<a title="WordPress.org" rel="friend colleague muse"
href="http://WordPress.org">WordPress.org</a>
```

This is a simple yet effective way to create some meaningful information about the link. The key is the simplicity of it. To a web browser, this information does not affect the rendering, unless you are applying CSS or JS specifically to it. In fact, only recently has Internet Explorer even allowed developers to use the `rel` attribute as a CSS selector.

But imagine the power when a search engine spider or other tool can create a social graph out of the information contained in microformats. You can find more information about the XFN at `http://gmpg.org/xfn/`.

Another microformat that is gaining traction is the hCard. The hCard microformat is for displaying contact information for a person or organization. It is the HTML rendering of the common vCard format used in e-mail and e-mail address books such as Microsoft Outlook and Mac OS X Address Book.

Here is a sample hCard:

```
<div id="hcard-David-Damstra" class="vcard">
  <a class="url fn" href="http://mirmillo.com">David Damstra</a>
  <div class="org">Professional WordPress</div>
  <div class="adr">
    <div class="street-address">123 Main Street</div>
    <span class="locality">Grand Rapids</span>,
    <span class="region">MI</span>,
    <span class="postal-code">49525</span>
  </div>
</div>
```

The hCard is one of the most common microformats used. It is very similar to the vCard format used in e-mail and address book software.

Render the preceding hCard on your site and it looks like an innocuous address block. But running this same code through a tool or spider that understands this microformat can lead to much more intelligent use of the information.

Microformats allow external tools to make better use of your site content, ideally driving more viewers to your site. Conversely, they make use of external services using metadata in your microformat tagged posts possible.

Currently, search engine spiders do not weigh microformatted data any differently than the other content on your site. However, microformats are emerging and continue to gain traction, and eventually spiders will recognize them and be able to harvest the semantic data included. The bottom line is that microformats are becoming the de facto convention for marking up this type of information. So although the microformat is spidered the same as traditional content, by using the microformat conventions you are working toward future-proofing your content.

Microformats continue to be an investment in the future. They are relatively simple ways to structure specific content so that at a later time this information can be used to do something informative or cool. Hopefully in the future, you will be able to search for a name and find that person's social graph along with it, search for a business and automatically have the contact information logged to your smartphone, or search for a location and time and have an aggregated list of events that are occurring in the vicinity. The data is starting to emerge, so the tools cannot be far behind.

HTML5

While talking about progressive HTML elements, let's take a quick dive into HTML5. While not WordPress-specific information, this topic is very appropriate for web development in general.

What is HTML5? Basically, it is the next iteration of the HTML standard that web developers have been using for years. But the term itself is a little loaded. It has become a marketing term to encompass many, many aspects of web development above and beyond the basic HTML syntax. It is essentially a buzz term for executives to indicate the latest and greatest web development techniques, sort of like Web 2.0 was in the late 2000s. So when you hear someone mention HTML5, you have to ask yourself whether they mean HTML5 specifically, or the current crop of web development techniques, including HTML5, CSS3, and JavaScript.

Let's focus on actual HTML5. What is included in HTML5? Quite a bit actually—some things that you can use immediately, some that you can use selectively depending on your audience, and many things that you will have to wait for browser adoption to really take up.

The biggest feature of HTML5, and likely the one most web developers think of first, is the new tags. HTML5 introduced many HTML elements that are more descriptive and have a semantic purpose. With a little help, you can actually use these new tags today, but more on that in a minute. If you have been developing websites or WordPress themes for a while, you will recognize the common `<div id="header">` and `<div id="footer">` as pretty pervasive to all websites. With HTML5, these elements are replaced with the new `<header>` and `<footer>` tags. Additional tags have been created that are particularly appropriate to WordPress themes, including `<nav>`, `<article>`, and `<aside>`.

As you can imagine, the `<article>` tag specifically fits right into the pages and posts paradigm of WordPress. In fact, the Twenty Eleven theme started using these tags for that purpose. The Twenty Fourteen theme leverages many of the new HTML5 tags in the theme templates and is a good place to start when exploring how to use these tags in your own custom themes.

Another good resource for seeing the HTML5 tags in action is the HTML5 Boilerplate by Paul Irish, online at `http://html5boilerplate.com/`. This resource is not WordPress-specific but takes all the best practices and recommendations and bundles them together in a HTML5 starter set. Additionally, there are several WordPress themes that have been created using the HTML5 Boilerplate as a source.

A quick cautionary note about HTML5 tag elements: They are not directly supported by all browsers, notably Microsoft browsers prior to Internet Explorer 9. However, all is not lost. There are JavaScript solutions to make these older browsers recognize the new HTML5 tags and let you style them appropriately. The Twenty Fourteen theme uses HTML5Shiv (`http://code.google.com/p/html5shiv/`) to achieve this functionality. Another option, the one used by HTML5 Boilerplate, is the `modernizr.js` from `http://modernizr.com`. Modernizr includes the HTML5Shiv to allow older browsers to recognize the new HTML tags, but also includes additional feature detection to enable you to use additional HTML5 features and CSS3 attributes. Which one you use is dependent on your needs. Depending on your browser support matrix, this may not even be an issue. Unfortunately for those developers among us who have to support an enterprise or corporate network, this remains a fact of developer life.

In our opinion, HTML5, with the appropriate JavaScript, is safe to use in production sites. You can and should be building new themes with the HTML5 tags. The fact that Twenty Fourteen uses these tags is an additional stamp of approval from Automattic, and they even started using these tags more than three years ago. Just make an evaluation of the browsers you need to support and make a decision based on your requirements.

In addition to the new more descriptive HTML tags, HTML5 has a bevy of additional features. As mentioned before, some of them you can use today and some of them you'll need to wait until browser adoption takes off. A convenient website for determining browser support is `http://caniuse.com`.

This website tracks past, current, and development versions of the common web browsers and assesses their support of new features, including HTML5, CSS3, and others. It does not take into account when you apply a JavaScript shim such as HTML5Shiv or Modernizr.js. The site tracks out-of-the-box support. This can be a very convenient resource when you are planning your design and settling on which browser to support and which features you want to include.

Some of the additional features of HTML5 include offline storage, which could be used for mobile device web applications when the mobile device does not have an Internet connection. Media and canvas tags are available for delivering certain media files directly in the browser. An especially exciting feature is the new form validation and helpers. These updated form tags include the actual validation mechanism built right into the browser and include additional features such as placeholder text on the forms and formatting. Basically, the new form features are trying to solve the problems on the web that you currently deal with every day.

As mentioned, HTML5 has many more features; to learn more, check out `http://www.html5rocks.com`.

CSS3

This section is about cascading style sheets, version 3, or CSS3. This is the next iteration of styling websites. Currently, many of the new CSS3 styles are implemented in browsers using browser-specific prefixes. This allows you to try out these new features on specific browsers but also makes maintenance more difficult when you have three to four lines in your CSS file to produce the same effect on different browsers.

Again, `http://caniuse.com` is an invaluable resource for determining which features you can use across browsers using official CSS3 syntax and when you need to implement browser-specific prefixes. Also, the general consensus now is that developers do not need all browser versions to render websites exactly the same. Being reasonably close is usually good enough. Also, adding flourishes and design details to browsers that support them while leaving older browsers to render it without them is also acceptable. This is generally called *progressive enhancement.*

A common example of progressive enhancement is rounded corners. Imagine your design mockup has rounded corners on certain design elements. Prior to CSS3, web developers had several tricks for making rounded corners, including images, both positive and reverse in color, as well as countless JavaScript libraries. With CSS3, rounded corners is a simple CSS3 style using the `border-radius` style.

You can apply this style and check it in your browser, and it works fine. However, if you look up border radius on `www.caniuse.com`, you will notice that Internet Explorer 7 and 8 do not support this style—which is why you had all those tricks in the first place. At this point, you can choose to accept progressive enhancement. The website still renders fine in Internet Explorer, but certain elements have squared off corners. Browsers that support the enhanced effect have the look you intend. The thought here is that eventually (one hopes), all browsers will converge on the standards, and eventually (one hopes), your enhanced design will become the design that everyone sees. The flip side is that you still have to test your design in the older browsers to make sure they do, in fact, render reasonably well, assuming you do need to support these older browsers. We know Internet Explorer 7 and 8 sound like dinosaurs, but if you do not still have to support them from time to time, consider yourself lucky.

One of the biggest, most immediately accessible features of CSS3 is a media query. Media queries enable the designer to tailor a website to specific screen resolutions, prompting a new type of mobile website experience. This topic, called responsive web design, is covered in a little more depth later in this chapter.

HTML5 adds new semantic tags to make your site's content more understandable to devices that are rendering or crawling your data. Couple this with CSS3 styling to add new appearance and design attributes to the look and feel of your content. Together they are making the user experience easier to maintain for both human and nonhuman consumers.

SEARCHING YOUR OWN SITE

So far, you have learned how to make your site visible and effective in the big search engines by structuring, organizing, and coding your site to raise your listings, or at least get the ranking you deserve. What happens when the visitor gets to your site and uses the built-in on-site search? Do the same rules and guidelines apply?

The answer is yes and no. The SEO principles and practices discussed are a solid foundation to build on. They are tried-and-true rules, although the search engines can make up their own rules and change them on a whim—you are in the Wild West Internet. The change lies in the built-in WordPress search.

Weaknesses of the Default Search

Out of the box, the WordPress search is probably good enough for most small sites. After all, this is how WordPress evolved, and good enough was good enough. But as your site grows, or as you build larger, more prominent sites, good enough is no longer good enough. The default WordPress search has some serious deficiencies for larger sites, and there are a couple of important challenges to be addressed here.

Results are sorted by date, not relevance to the search terms. WordPress loves showing content in chronological order. Chronological posts are the heart of the WordPress engine. So the default search will return results of the search term in reverse chronological order. It suffers from a recency effect.

Even if you have a large, excellently written article about a topic, if newer posts about the same topic exist, the newer ones will get top billing in the results pages. Relevance to the search terms does not matter. There is no weighting in the results for search term counts. The search strictly glances through all the post and page content, and if the term appears, it flags it for the results and then spits them out in date order.

This brings you to the next shortcoming. The search only searches some of your site's content. The default search only looks in the post content and page content—not the headlines, not the comments, not the links, not the categories, not the tags, nothing else. You learned earlier that headlines matter, and visitors only read the headlines, so if your catchy article headline sticks in someone's head and they return to your site to search on some variation of your headline, your search may not find it because headlines are not indexed.

Ideally, your content supports the catchy headline you made, so eventually your content will be found with a search. But there is so much more content to your site that could be used to empower the search to make it more effective or even to broaden the search. After all, it could have been one of your comments that really sparked the interest.

Next, there is no logic to the search. That is, you cannot use any sort of Boolean syntax in the query. The search is a straight up "find this word in the posts" kind of search. Search power users use Boolean syntax all the time to create very refined search engine results. WordPress search does some silly things with these keywords.

For example, try searching on your WordPress site using Boolean keywords in your search string, such as searching for *keyword1* AND *keyword2*. In this case, you want to find content that contains both keywords. You will find that WordPress search treats the AND just like any other keywords and will include content that contains all three words, that is, the keywords and the word AND. In all likelihood, you will have no results.

WordPress search handles a Boolean "or" in the same fashion. Try searching for content with either *keyword1* or *keyword2* in it using the search string *keyword1* OR *keyword2*. Again, WordPress search treats the OR just like the actual keywords. Now search for either keyword independently and compare the results. Depending on your site, you will notice that the OR search does not contain the same results as the two independent searches combined. After some simple experimentation, you will see that WordPress search does not know how to handle these generic Boolean queries.

Some people complain that the WordPress search does not highlight the search terms in the results. In some situations highlighting is handy; other times, it does not affect the usefulness of the search results. This definitely seems like a personal developer choice, which makes it ripe for a plugin. On the other hand, this could easily be handled with some creative PHP and CSS also.

The WordPress search has been good enough, but it does not take advantage of some available tools such as MySQL FullText search or other third-party search engines such as Lucene or Sphinx. Understandably, WordPress needs to keep the installation process simple and reduce the dependencies on external software packages. This definitely complicates the whole installation. But if a developer is capable and willing to integrate these other packages, why not let them?

Some of these seem like big deals, and for some developers they certainly are. But search is a pretty personal thing. Different developers want it to have specific functionality or algorithms and because WordPress has a great plugin system, each developer can have what he wants. You can either find an existing plugin or you can write your own to scratch that pesky search engine itch.

Alternatives and Plugins to Help

Obviously, we are not the first to recognize these inadequacies in the default search mechanism. Some very talented developers have set out to create plugins that enhance or replace the built-in search. Many, many plugins are available. Some target specific issues, and others change the whole search process. Following are some of the more popular search engine plugins for WordPress.

Search Everything (`http://wordpress.org/plugins/search-everything/`), now developed by Zemanta, extends the breadth of the WordPress search to include the different content sources in the index, including comments, tags, and categories. Search Everything also has settings for search term highlighting, and all the settings are managed from an Administration Screen.

Relevanssi (`http://wordpress.org/plugins/relevanssi/`) by Mikko Saari is another search replacement plugin. This plugin comes in both a free version and a premium version that includes support and additional features. This plugin includes search term highlighting and also searches additional fields such as comments, tags, and custom fields. But the biggest advantage of this plugin is that it uses syntax that will be familiar to Google users. This plugin supports the Boolean logic operators AND and OR. It supports phrase searches when included in quotes and partial word matches. This is much more of the search experience users are expecting.

Alternatively, you can actually match the experiences users expect by using a Google Custom Search Engine (`http://www.google.com/cse/`). Google Custom Search Engine (CSE) is a service offered by Google to provide your own subset of Google's existing search results. Google offers two programs for your Custom Search Engine. The basic free edition enables you to customize the look and the index but includes Google Ads. The second tier starts at $100 per year to remove the ads and the Google branding, if you desire. Either option integrates into your WordPress site in the same way.

There are several plugins for integrating a Google CSE into your site. Alternatively, you can integrate it manually using page templates and the code provided by Google. Page templates were covered in depth in Chapter 9, but here is a quick example of how you could set this up.

First, sign into the Google Custom Search Engine control panel and create your new custom search engine. After you have set it up, you will want to modify the look and feel. Change the layout to the Two Page option. This enables you to put the search box anywhere on your website and then have a specific page designated for the results. Save this setting and get the code.

Here you need to do a little juggling to create the page you need for the code page of the Google Custom Search Engine. Switching back to your WordPress site, you need a specific page for your search engine results and you want to assign that page a specific template. First, make a new page template for the results. It could be as simple as the following:

```php
<?php
/*
 * Template Name: Google Search Results
 */
get_header(); ?>
<div id="FileName_primary">
  <div id="content" role="main">
    <!-- google search engine results -->
  </div><!-- #content -->
</div><!-- #primary -->
<?php get_footer(); ?>
```

Notice there is a spot in the content area where you will paste in the search results code provided by Google. Save this template file and push to your WordPress theme on the server.

Next, you need to make a page that uses your theme to show the results. Create a new page on your WordPress site. Select the page template you just pushed and publish the page. Because you are using the preceding page template, you do not need anything in the content area of the page; Google will fill it in for you.

Finally, you need to create the search box on your WordPress installation. Probably the simplest method is to use a text widget in one of your widget areas. Simply copy the Search box code provided by Google and save it in a widget.

Now you need to test that it all works together. Depending on when your website went live, you may need to wait for Google to index your pages.

To really leverage the power of a Google Custom Search Engine, make sure you connect it to your Google Analytics and Google Webmaster Tools accounts. In addition, evaluate some of the additional features in the Google Custom Search Engine such as Refinements to modify the indexing, and Promotions to highlight certain search results.

MOBILE ACCESS AND RESPONSIVE WEB DESIGN

Mobile access continues to be a hot topic because of an enormous market increase of smartphones with high-speed data services and stores that proliferate fat client applications for these phones. Forrester, a global research firm, reports that more than half of the world's population has a mobile device (http://blogs.forrester.com/susan_huynh/12-02-21-mobile_internet_users_will_soon_surpass_pc_internet_users_globally). Google reports more of its Google+ users are on mobile devices than desktop devices (http://www.engadget.com/2012/06/27/

google-has-250-million-users-more-mobile-than-desktop/). Morgan Stanley has been saying for years that mobile access will exceed desktop access in the next several years (http://mashable.com/2010/04/13/mobile-web-stats/). In looking to update these statistics and projections for this edition of this book, we realized that these projections continue to hold true with little updates, in our opinion.

Mobile users are clearly an audience you cannot afford to ignore. The question is how much attention you need to give to this set of visitors. Do you customize an experience for each type of device? Can you keep up with device proliferation? Screen sizes and features and the feature API all vary. There are currently a couple of schools of thought on how to handle this.

Leave It Alone

The first paradigm, and obviously simplest, is to leave it alone—that is, show mobile browsers your full website. Give them the whole experience that you are providing to desktop users.

The idea here is that the newer browsers on the smartphones, such as the Apple iPhone and Google Android devices, can render traditional websites acceptably fine. The tech savvy users of these devices know that the browser is limited and the screen is small and they do not expect a stellar user experience. In short, leave it to the user and the device. Tablets and smartphones can zoom and scroll and users are used to these techniques. If you have young children with tablet experience, you probably have fingerprints on your desktop monitor from the child trying to scroll the screen and subsequently complain when it does not work.

In practice, this method generally works well for certain classes of websites but not others. All of the information on the website is still accessible on a mobile device. The visitor continues to use learned website conventions and behaviors from the traditional browsing experience. The challenge is the small text and limited screen real estate.

Lightweight Mobile

Another school of thought is that you have the technology available to create custom themes for these devices, especially with the power of WordPress. Mobile themes hearken back to the lightweight themes of dial-up days to conserve the limited bandwidth available. This makes mobile themes faster to load over the wireless bandwidth. In addition, they should be tailored to fit the small screen real estate and focus on the information that the mobile visitor is really looking for—often locations and contact information.

WPTouch is a plugin that converts your site to look like a native iPhone application. The WPTouch Plugin was created by Dale Mugford and Duane Storey from Brave New Code and is available at http://wordpress.org/plugins/wptouch/.

After installing this plugin, your site will automatically detect mobile browsers and offer them your entire site, but in a specific mobile-enhanced theme. This theme uses AJAX requests and other effects, giving the illusion of a native application. In addition, WPTouch offers an extensive Administration Screen to manage all the settings.

WPTouch also offers the ability to set a custom index page for mobile browsers. This is a fantastic feature and enables the developer to create a custom page for the quick information that the mobile visitor really needs. In addition to the multiple default themes, WPTouch includes the capability to tweak the CSS to create a theme that matches your traditional site theme. WPTouch also offers the capability for the mobile visitor to select to view the traditional desktop theme.

A couple of notes of caution: If you are using a caching plugin, discussed in Chapter 15, you will have to set it to exclude showing cached content to the mobile browser. Otherwise, the caching will supersede the WPTouch browser detection and the traditional theme will be shown. Second, every mobile detection algorithm behaves a little differently. Should the iPad browser be considered mobile, or is the screen large enough to offer the desktop version? What about the Amazon Kindle with a slightly smaller screen? What about those in-between devices popularly called *phablets*? Should it behave differently if the device is on WiFi or a slower cell signal? Compound these automatic software decisions with user preferences.

Responsive Design

A responsive design is the current craze. Responsive web design was first proposed by Ethan Marcotte on A List Apart in 2010 (`http://alistapart.com/article/responsive-web-design`). In essence, responsive web design uses the CSS3 media queries' functionality, mentioned previously, to reformulate the layout and design of your website theme to match the screen size of the device it is being viewed on. The theory here is that you manage the content and theme at once, and then tweak the rendering for different screen resolutions. That is one set of content for every screen size that adapts, or responds to the viewing environment through selective CSS rules. In practice, it is much more complex.

This works because of media queries. Media queries existed prior to CSS3. Print style sheets are a form of media query that web developers have used for a long time. What changed with CSS3 is that the media queries now support screen resolution calculations. These queries now allow you to apply certain CSS styles only if the screen resolution falls in a certain range, as determined by you. Best practices recommend targeting a desktop, full scale version, a mid-scale or tablet version, and then a small screen or smartphone resolution.

The specific intricacies of responsive web design are not WordPress-specific and are outside the scope of this book, but let's take a quick look at how they might work.

A common responsive design change on a WordPress site is dealing with the sidebar. On a desktop browser, you have the screen real estate and generally the sidebar is located on the left or right-hand side. This is a traditional website. However, on a mobile small screen, where space is much more limited, this sidebar information may not be as important as the primary content of the page. For example, when viewed on a handheld device, perhaps the sidebar content gets moved below the primary information. Using a media query block in your style sheet, you can change the flow of your content pieces. This would leave your primary content, generally considered the most important information, front and center on the small screen, and relegate the secondary content to a less prominent position.

Again, the actual implementations of responsive website design could fill an entire book. Many tutorials and how-tos are available online for best practices and recommendations. Furthermore, many responsive WordPress themes are already out there, including Twenty Fourteen, for you to try and explore how they work.

Responsive web design is a popular solution among developers to address the mobile audience right now. It is a solution deployed on many websites. But the more involved the responsive themes get, the more complicated the process becomes. Anyone remember the days when you made separate website themes for Netscape Navigator and Internet Explorer? Some days, responsive themes feel the same way when you are managing multiple versions of your site for different sizes, under the guise that you are not. You end up troubleshooting and debugging the theme multiple times at the different resolutions. And as devices proliferate, this may become more and more convoluted as you try to match designs to resolutions. The flip side is that you are in complete control and responsive web design will only be as complex as you make it.

Mobile themes continue to be an up-and-coming area of web development. As smartphones with reasonably supportable browsers become more and more the default mode of web access, this type of functionality will become a requirement for all sites. You will continue to see mobile optimized themes and responsive themes pop up all over the place. Most theme frameworks and starter themes include responsive elements from the start, making the whole process easier.

SUMMARY

This chapter covered the user experience that makes your site interesting and available to both readers and devices. Techniques included HTML5 and CSS3 as well as general user experience principles. In the next chapter, you learn about securing your site against several types of common threats.

13

Securing WordPress

WHAT'S IN THIS CHAPTER?

➤ Common best practices for securing websites

➤ Keeping your WordPress site healthy and secure

➤ Delegating proper permissions to your users

The past few chapters have covered how to present your fabulous content in effective and beautiful ways, how to increase the likelihood of visitors finding your content, and how to move content from other sources into your WordPress website. What happens when (if?) this all succeeds and your site gets noticed? Well, now you have a live and active site, which opens up a whole range of other challenges you have to think about. In this chapter, you will look at mechanisms to deal with the resultant attention you will get in terms of unwanted content, malicious visitors, and other ne'er-do-wells. This chapter will address conceptual best practices for securing any online web property and also focus on specifics for WordPress.

SECURING YOUR WORDPRESS SITE

Unfortunately, with success and popularity, you also become a target. WordPress is a successful and popular platform for websites and with that brings the attention of the hackers and bad guys. It is simple economics that bad guys looking to build a network of sites will look to the most widespread applications and attack their vulnerabilities. Unfortunately, one of the vulnerabilities with WordPress (similar to PHP) is that, because of the low barrier of entry and ease of use, users who are generally not too tech savvy or security minded can utilize WordPress without recognizing the full security ramifications involved.

This portion of the chapter covers some of the basic security principles you should employ when using WordPress. Some of them seem like common sense, but surprisingly, they are not put into practice on the average site. Many of these options simply use WordPress functionality to change the defaults of your installation to make the job harder for the bad guys. Defaults are known and create an easy attack vector, but complicating the process can make it more work than the attacker would like to invest.

These are all preventative measures that you should put into place before you really need them. As Benjamin Franklin said, "An ounce of prevention is worth a pound of cure." The time you spend protecting yourself will pay off should you have to work on cleaning up an exploited website.

Staying Up-to-Date

Rule number 1 is to always stay updated. WordPress developers are constantly working to make WordPress a better, more secure, and stable platform. This is one of the key advantages to open source software. Many developers, each with different skill sets, are looking over the code every day and performing various audits and updates to improve the overall codebase.

Updates often fix security concerns before there are exploits in the wild. Generally, exploits have been targeting outdated versions of WordPress while consistently updated sites are immune.

Several versions ago, WordPress implemented new notices in the Dashboard letting you know when there is a new version available. Once logged into your WordPress Dashboard, view the Updates Screen to see which components of your WordPress installation might have updates.

Another new feature is the ability to upgrade WordPress directly from the Dashboard. The WordPress team has been working to make upgrading as painless as possible. This new feature lets the site administrator update the WordPress core right from inside the web interface.

If your web server has the ability to write to the files in your WordPress directories, then the automatic upgrade functionality works. If not, WordPress prompts for your FTP credentials to update the files for you. Both of these situations are of concern. In general, your web user should not have write permissions to your entire web root. This is just asking for trouble, especially on a shared hosting platform, except, of course, certain directories such as the uploads folder that must be writable by the web user in order to function.

Second, it is not clear how this FTP credential information is stored or used. Although it is unlikely anything nefarious is happening, users are not encouraged to key in FTP (an unsecured protocol at that) credentials into any form that asks for it. However, if you do decide to go this route, you can set some WordPress configuration variables in your `wp-config` file that will further automate the FTP process.

There is definitely a balance here between the simplicity of keeping the WordPress core updated, which is of the utmost importance, and with keeping the web root security intact. As with all things security related, ease of use for the user is in direct opposition to security practices and to the goal of making it difficult for the bad guys.

Finally, another feature is the update notices in the Dashboard and changelogs. The notices alert you to pending updates to WordPress core, themes, and plugins that you have installed. Many of these updates include changelogs that let you keep tabs on what is actually changing in the new version. This can help you make a decision as to whether the update is critical and needs to be performed immediately, or whether it can wait until a scheduled maintenance window. It is up to the developer to keep the changelog information current.

Hiding WordPress Version Information

This section is about concealing which specific version of WordPress you are running from the public eye. Honestly, there are mixed opinions on this. WordPress evangelists would say leave it in there. Say it loud and say it proud. On the other hand, security-conscious users would say to take it out. It is a way for the bad guys to easily find vulnerable sites, so why give it up?

Then again, the WordPress developers have a good point. For a botnet scanning for vulnerable sites, it does not make sense to waste time looking for specific WordPress versions when a botnet can just run the attack against the site. It will take the same amount of time, so why take twice as long? If you are going to get hacked because of your old version of WordPress, hiding the version number is not going to stop it. You should have been upgrading anyway.

In a standard WordPress installation, the version number is shown in the HTML source code as a meta tag for anyone to view the source and see. However, if you want to remove this meta tag, there are several plugins that can do it for you. Or you can edit your functions.php file and at the bottom add the following:

```
Remove_action('wp_head', 'wp_generator');
```

Also, be on the lookout for certain themes and plugins that also include version information in your header.

Never Use the Admin Username

WordPress used to always create a default administrative user with the username Admin. This is no longer the case, but older installations may have this username still in the system, or naïve users could create this username. Never use "admin" as a username. The bad guys attempt to brute force attack this username all the time. If you have this username in your WordPress Users Screen, remove it. Plain and simple.

Limit Login Attempts

Further precautions include limiting the number of login attempts on your WordPress Dashboard. This can prevent or discourage bad guys from brute-force attacking your site. By default, WordPress will allow unlimited invalid login attempts, meaning that an automated script could be, and probably is, whacking away at your site all day long.

There are several ways to accomplish limiting login attempts; most of the WordPress Security plugins mentioned later in this chapter have this feature. Slowing down the number of login attempts before an IP address is blocked reduces the attractiveness of your site to an automatic attack script. Note that generally these offer temporary IP address blocking, so that valid users who accidentally fat finger their password have an opportunity to log in after the ban has expired.

Using Good Passwords

Furthermore, use good passwords for your account—not just your WordPress accounts, all of your online accounts. Yes, we all have hundreds of passwords to remember, but there are tricks to using good passwords, including mnemonics and password safes. WordPress has a nice JavaScript indicator when you are setting your password to let you know the quality of the password you have chosen. Remember that you can pick a strong password that is something you remember or use a secure password-safe application to store it. Your password is your key to your kingdom, so make it a good key. You can always use a reputable online password generator to help create a strong password, for example `https://identitysafe.norton.com/password-generator` or `https://lastpass.com/generatepassword.php`.

Changing Your Table Prefix

This is another method to obscure a default attack vector. By default, new WordPress installations have a table prefix of `wp_`. That means every table in your WordPress database has a very predictable name, making it easier for attackers to form an assault on your site. If you are deploying a new site, set something unique for this prefix. This means that if a bad guy does manage to infiltrate your database, the normal attack vectors on predictable database tables are not available, and he will have to determine your custom schema.

If you are already on an existing site, plugins are available that can handle renaming your tables for you. The WP-Security Scan by Acunetix, which is covered later in this chapter, offers the functionality to change your table prefixes for you. Make sure you make a database backup before performing this task because the implications if it does not work are quite severe.

Moving Your Configuration File

By default, the WordPress configuration file is located in the root of your website. In the event that PHP stops functioning on your web server for any reason, you run the risk of this file being displayed in plaintext, which will give up your passwords and database information to visitors.

You can safely move the `wp-config` directory up out of the root directory. This will stop it from ever being accidentally served. WordPress has built-in functionality that will automatically check the parent directory if it cannot find a configuration file.

In some situations on certain hosts, this is not an option. An alternative on Apache web servers is to set your `.htaccess` to not serve up the `wp-config` file. Add the following line to your `.htaccess` file in the root directory:

```
<FilesMatch ^wp-config.php$>deny from all</FilesMatch>
```

Moving Your Content Directory

Since WordPress 2.6, you can move your `wp-content` directory. This way, you can take a large portion of your WordPress installation and move it to a non-default location. Again, this makes hoops for the bad guys to jump through, hopefully discouraging them.

Make two additions to your `wp-config` file:

```
define('WP_CONTENT_DIR',
    $_SERVER['DOCUMENT_ROOT'].'/mysite/wp-content');
```

```
define('WP_CONTENT_URL',
    'http://example.com/mysite/wp-content');
```

Some plugins may have difficulty dealing with a nonstandard directory structure. If you are experiencing problems with certain plugins, you can add the following lines to your wp-config file for compatibility:

```
define('WP_PLUGIN_DIR',
    $_SERVER['DOCUMENT_ROOT']. '/mysite/wp-content/plugins');
define( 'WP_PLUGIN_URL',
    'http://example.com/mysite/wp-content/plugins');
```

Moving your content directory does not in and of itself make your site more secure. What it does is prevent the automated tools used by attackers from working on your site. These automated tools are looking for the least common denominator of sites; so essentially, they are looking for stock WordPress configurations with default settings because that will give them the most bang for the buck. Security through obscurity is not security, but it does make your site a less attractive target.

Using the Security Key Feature

In your WordPress config file are secret key values for encrypting user cookies. There are four keys (since WordPress 2.6) to establish the secret, or private, key used by WordPress to protect session information stored in user cookies. Each key also has a "salt value," which is used by the cryptography functions to reduce the likelihood that a directory based attack will discover a password through brute-force. A potential attack would have to start with both the guessed password and the salt value. If you do not specify salt values, WordPress generates them.

You should set both the secret keys and salt values to make the encryption of user session data for your site stronger. Either make them up or visit https://api.wordpress.org/secret-key/1.1/salt and get randomly generated ones. If you make them up, make sure they are long and complicated.

You can change these keys at any time, but it will force anyone who is logged in to log in again.

```
define('AUTH_KEY',
    '+Ic#]DCGrn<}=Vg]0n0;|C{mc7-G$g[VEc`ix(VhRLMvR]55`xmh+7l)gd;z3$KR');
define('SECURE_AUTH_KEY',
    'BnArFk)y<*d?nd}_Nuvv5{a_q[0[FPC*-^mG: x{>WjKS._fY<B[pe0pN#@5#d>v');
define('LOGGED_IN_KEY',
    '92CxK-u:Xj)x,{rQ)HXmx1Oi{zY$L;H}ueT|+ZC@rmrN(!R>g/iJw[ ^`n3`}bGO');
define('NONCE_KEY',
    ',#$@.%Ea9JTrF1jRGKP?aZ_!diTLo|dCf37Wz{7wioFnvwZIx{|dN+Ic[x%(Bql}');
define('AUTH_SALT',
    'R@Y@:&jU1xnE4Oo0<@9n%XkHZ72Cv``<K$M53((~U3Dk43}[=Y~mRu$]H$Fy6KS^');
define('SECURE_AUTH_SALT',
    'W-=-s}8E8-b{QBw*O=H,1H+)UxO@5[+FE$@dN}`8+G:^5yvab+YFj1h.z>MU_{(R');
define('LOGGED_IN_SALT',
    '^ZTm{^1Mz!UpYF|U1qWv-OTUQv#F:Y|)hq5X$[mIUc@B6oJ}`_]w<B)/;6EK$iDz');
define('NONCE_SALT',
    '%au=<O=V!:+ni/!c^_l`+&H|KapN>#cxL24w<KE^3C9x,F]i4bHwuw(0P9|O|.N+');
```

Do not use these values; set up your own. The easiest way is to use the provided generator and cut and paste into your `wp-config.php` file.

Forcing SSL on Login and Admin

You can force your visitors and administrators to log in via an SSL-encrypted page, assuming you have that set up already. Edit your WordPress `config` file and add the following flag:

```
define('FORCE_SSL_LOGIN', true);
```

You can also force the entire WordPress Dashboard to be served over HTTPS. Again, edit your `config` file and add the following line:

```
define('FORCE_SSL_ADMIN', true);
```

Please do not just blindly enable these features. This can be problematic if you are using a self-signed certificate on your site. Note that WordPress likes to build internal post links using the URL that you are accessing the Dashboard with. So if you forced SSL on the Dashboard and are using a server self-signed certificate, the internal post URLs will do the same and your visitor will be have to accept the certificate also. Generally, this is not a good practice. Work with your hosting provider to obtain a certificate from a respected certificate provider. SSL certificates have come down substantially in price and may be worth investigating.

Apache Permissions

Permissions will vary depending on your configuration, but a good rule of thumb is to set files to 644 and folders to 755. If you cannot upload to the uploads folder, adjust those privileges alone. Never assign a folder with 777 privileges. This opens this folder up as a massive attack target because anyone can now read and write to that directory. Generally, the files are set to be in the same group as the web server and owned by the local user. For example:

```
drwxr-xr-x   24 ddamstra   staff     816 Sep 10 10:10 .
drwxr-xr-x   11 ddamstra   staff     374 Jun 21 14:22 ..
-rw-r--r--    1 ddamstra   staff     418 Jun 13 21:06 index.php
-rwxrwxr--    1 ddamstra   staff   19930 Jun 13 21:06 license.txt
-rwxrwxr--    1 ddamstra   staff    7192 Sep  8 22:32 readme.html
-rw-r--r--    1 ddamstra   staff    4951 Aug 20 20:22 wp-activate.php
drwxr-xr-x   88 ddamstra   staff    2992 Sep 10 09:21 wp-admin
-rw-r--r--    1 ddamstra   staff     271 Jun 13 21:06 wp-blog-header.php
-rw-r--r--    1 ddamstra   staff    4946 Jun 13 21:06 wp-comments-post.php
-rw-r--r--    1 ddamstra   staff    2726 Sep  8 22:32 wp-config-sample.php
-rw-r--r--    1 ddamstra   staff    1588 Jun 13 21:06 wp-config.php
drwxr-xr-x    8 ddamstra   staff     272 Aug 21 11:19 wp-content
-rw-r--r--    1 ddamstra   staff    2956 Jun 13 21:06 wp-cron.php
drwxr-xr-x  125 ddamstra   staff    4250 Sep 10 09:21 wp-includes
-rw-r--r--    1 ddamstra   staff    2380 Jun 13 21:06 wp-links-opml.php
-rw-r--r--    1 ddamstra   staff    2714 Jul  9 15:19 wp-load.php
-rw-r--r--    1 ddamstra   staff   33043 Sep  8 22:32 wp-login.php
-rw-r--r--    1 ddamstra   staff    8252 Jul 22 17:51 wp-mail.php
```

```
-rw-r--r--   1 ddamstra  staff  11115 Jul 22 17:51 wp-settings.php
-rw-r--r--   1 ddamstra  staff  26256 Jul 22 17:51 wp-signup.php
-rw-r--r--   1 ddamstra  staff   4026 Jun 13 21:06 wp-trackback.php
-rw-r--r--   1 ddamstra  staff   3032 Jun 13 21:06 xmlrpc.php
```

Note that this will most likely break some of the cool functionality such as one-click upgrades and theme and plugin installations from the control panel. In this case, you may have to provide WordPress with the FTP credentials to your site for this functionality to return. See the section "Staying Up-to-Date" in this chapter for more on why this is a concern.

MySQL Credentials

Set your MySQL login and permissions correctly. For the love of all things open source, do not connect your WordPress site to your database with the MySQL root user. Set up a special user for each WordPress site. Make sure it has access only to the database it needs, and make sure it has only the privileges it needs. For example, your WordPress database user never needs to grant access to another user. This helps contain any breach that might occur by limiting access through the principle of least privilege. Provide the least amount of access that you can for everything to work. In the next section, you will apply this same principle to user roles.

USING WORDPRESS ROLES

The WordPress role system allows you to assign different privileges to different user accounts. WordPress's default roles cover the basics and start to establish a publishing workflow through the fundamental capabilities of each role. These can be further extended through various plugins to create new roles with additional capabilities for specific tasks.

In a security context, this is making sure that a particular user has only the access that he needs to complete his job. Whether that user goes rogue on you or the access is compromised, this contains the amount of damage that can be done. User Roles can also be useful for managing publishing workflows, as discussed in Chapter 15.

If you are the only person managing your site, you probably do not need roles. It boils down to you, the site administrator, and them, the unregistered masses. This setup, with no ability for a new user to register, is a secure way to operate your site. But it also discourages participation. Eventually, you may want to open it up to allow regular visitors to log in and reap some additional ease-of-use benefits.

You assign roles to users in the User Screen of the Dashboard. Each user must be assigned to a role, and your site will have a default role for registered users. Setting each of these appropriately in the Dashboard depends on your actual needs and the security permissions you need to delegate. To reduce your security footprint, you want to lower user permissions to the minimum level you can.

Subscriber Role

The Subscriber role is essentially the same as a non–logged in visitor. So why do you need it if this person can read posts and post comments the same as a guest visitor?

You may need the Subscriber role for a couple of reasons. First, you may want to allow this role for regularly returning visitors. If they are registered, they get some advantages such as not having to fill out all the fields to post a comment each time. Second, as a spam control measure, you may allow only registered Subscribers to post comments. This will weed out many of the automated spambots. Finally, certain plugins require this base level for functionality.

Contributor Role

The next step up is the Contributor role. The Contributor role is the first step in delegating responsibilities to your site users. The key privilege for Contributors is they can create new posts, but they cannot publish them to the site. That requires a higher role. This allows users to contribute information to your site, but you still maintain control over what is actually published.

In addition to creating draft posts, Contributors can also edit their own posts at any time and delete their own unpublished posts. Contributors cannot upload files and images to be used in their own draft posts.

Author Role

Authors are the next level up the hierarchy. Authors are more trusted individuals than Contributors in that they can upload files to be used in their posts and can publish their posts without approval. Likewise, Authors can edit and delete their own published posts.

Authors are restricted to working with their own posts. They can read and comment on any post just like any other user, but they can only modify their own content.

Editor Role

The Editor role introduces two new capabilities. Up until this role in the hierarchy, you have been restricted to posts, but the Editor role can also work with pages. In addition, the Editor is privileged enough to modify any content on the site.

This role cannot manage users or site settings such as themes and plugins, but the actual content is wide open. In practice, this is the role you assign to the client for a managed WordPress install. It provides enough capabilities that the client can manage the day-to-day content of the site, but not so much that he can muck around with the overall site settings and mess things up.

Note, however, that Editors cannot manage menus or widget areas, which thus limits the extent of the content they can manage.

Administrator Role

This is the root level role. Everything in the WordPress Dashboard is open to an Administrator so you want to assign this role carefully. This role can modify users, themes, plugins, and all of the content.

Make sure your Administrator users are security conscious and using good passwords. Should bad guys get access to your Administrator account, they will have full access to your site.

Super Admin Role

This role is only used on Multisite Networks. Essentially, the primary purpose of this role is to manage the different WordPress sites in the network and manage the network overall. WordPress Multisite is covered in Chapter 10.

Role Overview

Table 13-1 shows a simplified overview of the capabilities assigned to each role. For more exact information about the capabilities of each role, visit the WordPress Codex at `http://codex.wordpress.org/Roles_and_Capabilities`.

TABLE 13-1: Capabilities of Each WordPress Role

CAPABILITY	SUPER ADMIN	ADMINISTRATOR	EDITOR	AUTHOR	CONTRIBUTOR	SUBSCRIBER
Manage network	X					
Manage themes	X	X				
Manage plugins	X	X				
Manage users	X	X				
Manage site options	X	X				
Moderate comments	X	X	X			
Manage categories	X	X	X			
Manage links	X	X	X			
Manage all posts	X	X	X			
Manage all pages	X	X	X			
Manage others' posts	X	X	X			
Read and manage private posts	X	X	X			
Read and manage private pages	X	X	X			
Upload files	X	X	X	X		
Publish posts	X	X	X	X		
Delete own published posts	X	X	X	X		
Edit own posts	X	X	X	X	X	
Delete own unpublished posts	X	X	X	X	X	
Read	X	X	X	X	X	X

Extending Roles

In most cases, the default roles will be enough. However, in certain circumstances you may need to extend roles to include more permissions or fine-grained control over content-editing capabilities.

The Role Scoper plugin by Kevin Behrens (`http://wordpress.org/extend/plugins/role-scoper/`) is a very powerful tool to manage these access control situations. With this plugin, user access is augmented beyond the default permissions covered previously, with specific access controls related to content-specific settings.

That is, any level of user can have escalated permissions to edit and manage content based on specific categories, pages, or posts. This access permission can go both ways to either enable content modification, or the reverse, to remove the ability for a role to read content.

For example, you created a multi–product line site. Each product line had a product manager responsible for its content. In this case, each product line became a WordPress category. With this plugin, you were able to restrict product managers to be able to post only new content within their respective categories.

Role Scoper is a very powerful plugin that allows you to build fine-grained controls. However, it may be more than you need for your particular situation. Many other plugins are available that allow you to supplement the built-in WordPress roles in other ways.

RECOMMENDED SECURITY PLUGINS

Being vigilant is an important step in security. You cannot expect what you do not inspect. That is, you cannot expect things to be working, if you do not check in on them periodically. Some plugins help with security maintenance and configuration on your WordPress installation. Just like antivirus and malware detection on workstations, these tools are here to assist in strengthening your security posture. The following are a few examples of WordPress security plugins that address many of the previously mentioned best practices. This is a burgeoning area for development so make sure to check out other plugins in the plugin repository.

BulletProof Security

BulletProof Security by Ed Alexander is an all-in-one security plugin for your WordPress installation. It incorporates intrusion detection scans and multiple types of logging to help in forensic analysis and discovery of attack attempts. This plugin will also assist in configuring your web server through `.htaccess` and PHP configurations.

You can find more information on BulletProof Security at `http://wordpress.org/plugins/bulletproof-security/`.

WP-Security Scan

WP-Security Scan by Acunetix provides an overall security scan of your WordPress installation. It checks many of the items listed previously, including WordPress version, table prefix, and absence of the admin account. It also includes a filesystem scanner to verify that the permissions are set to the recommended settings and includes some files to protect against directory browsing. WP-Security Scan provides a nice mechanism to make sure the base settings are in line with a good security posture as well, as this plugin has a tool for changing your database table prefix. We look forward to new features in future releases.

You can find more information on WP-Security Scan at `http://wordpress.org/plugins/wp-security-scan/`.

WordFence Security

WordFence Security by Mark Maunder is a comprehensive security plugin. This plugin checks your installed core files against the current revision in the WordPress repository. It checks both your core WordPress files as well as plugin files. WordFence Security is evaluating your core and plugin files for changes or variations from the source code, which can indicate a compromised site.

WordFence also scans your actual content for malware and phishing signatures looking for types of content injection. WordFence has a limit-login-attempt functionality to prevent brute force attacks as well as the capability to send notifications on logins so you can see who is and is not logging into your WordPress Dashboard. WordFence has many other security features covering a large spectrum of potential threats or attack vectors.

One of the more interesting features of WordFence is the live traffic information that ties into a software-level firewall. Using the live traffic and firewall features, you can block specific IP addresses or countries from accessing your site. This can help when an attacker is attempting to compromise your site. Furthermore, you can configure WordFence to automatically block or throttle access for IP addresses when usage from those traffic sources exceeds limits that you set. WordFence is also introducing a new caching mechanism to improve the speed of your site.

You can find more information about WordFence Security at `http://wordpress.org/plugins/wordfence/`.

SUMMARY

This chapter covered some of the challenges that can occur when your WordPress site begins to get noticed on the web. Popularity attracts attention so securing your WordPress installation is a fact of life for being on the web today. Security is an ongoing cat and mouse game between site administrators and the bad guys, and keeping on top of best practices and latest advancements is an important job skill for the professional developer. Choosing a security plugin and keeping your WordPress updated are now regularly occurring maintenance tasks for your site development and management process.

Finally, role definition is key in controlling the scope of permissions for your users. Contain when you can, and use the principle of least privilege to the fullest extent. Security is a fundamental component of using WordPress in the real world either as a website foundation or an application framework. You will tackle those topics in the next two chapters.

14

Application Framework

WHAT'S IN THIS CHAPTER?

➤ Understanding an application framework

➤ Reviewing application framework features

➤ Using WordPress as an application framework

➤ Common WordPress framework features

Over the years WordPress has grown from a simple blogging platform to a full-fledged content management system. In the past few years, a new trend has emerged—using WordPress as an application framework. Matt Mullenweg, the co-founding developer of WordPress, has often referred to WordPress as a web operating system. With that in mind, it's important we stop thinking of WordPress as a specific type of platform, but rather a framework that can be used to build any type of web application imaginable.

This chapter reviews what an application framework is and how you can leverage WordPress to create amazing web applications.

WHAT IS AN APPLICATION FRAMEWORK?

An application framework consists of a software framework used by software developers to implement the standard structure of an application. More simply, a framework consists of a set of conventions used to easily build applications for the web.

For example, let's assume you are going to build a customer relationship management (CRM) application. Your application would require a database abstraction layer for storing and retrieving the data from your CRM. Your application would also require an application layer with flexibility to extend the framework to fit your CRM application's requirements. The final piece would be the presentation layer, which would handle the display of your CRM. Does this sound familiar? It should, because it sounds just like WordPress!

WordPress as an Application Framework

Now that you understand what an application framework is, let's examine how WordPress can be used as a framework for your web applications.

Let's review some standard application framework features:

➤ User management

➤ Template engine

➤ Error logging

➤ Localization

➤ Form and data validation

➤ Uploads and media management

➤ Image manipulation

➤ Scheduled tasks

➤ Friendly URLs

➤ External APIs

➤ Caching

➤ Flexible

This is not an exhaustive list, but some of the more popular framework features offered by most application frameworks. This list of features should look very familiar because this is also a list of WordPress features available for use in your applications.

Now let's dig into a few of the more popular framework features and how they relate in WordPress.

User Management

If you have ever logged in to a WordPress website, you have interacted with the WordPress user management system. WordPress, by default, creates five user roles:

➤ Subscriber

➤ Contributor

➤ Author

➤ Editor

➤ Administrator

As discussed in Chapters 12 and 13, user roles in WordPress can be easily extended to include custom roles and capabilities. In the case of your CRM application example, you may want to define a custom user role that can only view customer information. You may also want to define a role for a user so he or she can view and modify customer information.

User capabilities are also a very important part of user management in WordPress. A capability gives the user role a very specific action the user can perform. For example, there is a capability for publishing a new post. User roles and capabilities are not only used for granting permissions, but can also be used to restrict access to various parts of your application.

Let's register a user role for customers in your CRM. This role will be assigned to any customers that are allowed to log in to your CRM application.

```php
<?php
register_activation_hook( __FILE__, 'prowp_create_role_on_activation' );

function prowp_create_role_on_activation() {

    //register new customer role
    add_role(
        'customer',
        'Customer',
        array(
            'read' => true,
            'edit_posts' => true,
            'delete_posts' => false,
        )
    );

}
?>
```

When registering a new role, the new role is stored in the WordPress options table. Because of this, there's no reason to run your code on every page load. Instead, you'll use the `register_activation_hook()` function to register the customer user role when your plugin is activated.

Next, you'll use the `add_role()` function to define your new customer role. The first parameter is the user role name. The second parameter is the user role display name. The final parameters are the capabilities for the user role, which accepts an array of capability names. In this example, you are assigning your customer user role with permissions to read and edit posts, but not to delete posts. If you wanted even more granular user control, you could register custom capabilities that only customer user roles would use.

Now that you have a customer user role, let's look at creating a new user with that role. If you are building a web application, you will probably want to provide the user the ability to create a new user account in your application. Let's assume you have a registration form that accepts an email address.

```php
<?php
if ( null == username_exists( $email_address ) ) {

    // generate a password and create the user
    $password = wp_generate_password( 12, false );
    $user_id = wp_create_user( $email_address, $password, $email_address );

    // set the user role to customer
    $user = new WP_User( $user_id );
```

```
        $user->set_role( 'customer' );

    } else {
        // user already exists
    }
    ?>
```

The preceding example accepts an `$email_address` variable containing the new user's email when registering. First, you'll use the `username_exists()` function to verify that the email address is not already in use by another user. Next, you'll generate a random password using `wp_generate_password()`. Now that you have the user's email and a random password, it's time to create the user with the `wp_create_user()` function.

The final step is to set the user's role. First, you'll create a new instance of `WP_User` from the `$user_id` variable that was set when the new user was created. To set the role, you'll call the `set_role()` function and set the role to `customer`. You now have a new user created, with their user role set to `customer`, who can log into your web application in WordPress.

User accounts are a main component for most web applications and WordPress makes working with users incredibly flexible. Because of this flexibility, you can easily customize your setup to fit any application you are creating using WordPress.

Template Engine

The WordPress template engine will power the presentation layer of your application. In Chapter 9, you learned how to create custom theme templates for WordPress. As discussed, WordPress has a very flexible template engine, allowing you to create any number of customized templates for your applications.

Using the CRM example, you may need public facing templates to accept new customer leads, register user accounts, allow customers to manage their accounts, and more. For your applications, anything that deals with the public facing display will use WordPress theme templates.

WordPress themes can also be used for administrative interfaces. Rather than trying to customize the default WordPress admin dashboard, it can be a much easier approach to create a custom admin only theme. This theme could give your users all of the admin features they need and nothing more. You won't need to worry about hiding default WordPress admin features you don't want your users having access to because the admin theme will only have the features you introduce in it.

For more information on templates in WordPress, visit the Codex at `http://codex.wordpress.org/Templates`.

CRUD

CRUD, or "Create, Read, Update, and Delete," is a basic function of persistent storage in programming. A web application framework will include help for performing these basic operations, and WordPress is no different.

WordPress not only provides CRUD out of the box, but automatically handles the CRUD operations for all of your custom post types. Let's look at an example registering a custom post type for the customers in your CRM:

```php
<?php
add_action( 'init', 'prowp_create_post_type' );

function prowp_create_post_type() {

    register_post_type( 'customer',
        array(
            'labels'    => array(
                'name'          => 'Customers',
                'singular_name' => 'Customer'
            ),
            'public'      => true,
            'has_archive' => true,
        )
    );
}
?>
```

Now that your post type is registered, you have full CRUD integration automatically in WordPress. You can easily create customer entries (C), read entries (R), update existing entries (U), and delete entries (D). This is a very simple example that demos some very powerful tools at your disposal with a few lines of code.

WordPress includes a set of functions for CRUD operations related to settings, post content, users, metadata, and more. Let's review the CRUD functions for these operations:

Settings

CRUD operation functions for Settings in WordPress are:

➤ `add_option()`—Create a new option (C).

➤ `get_option()`—Retrieve an options value (R).

➤ `update_option()`—Update an existing option (U).

➤ `delete_option()`—Delete an option (D).

Posts

CRUD operation functions for Posts in WordPress are:

➤ `wp_insert_post()`—Create a new post (C).

➤ `get_post()` – Retrieve a post (R).

➤ `wp_update_post()`—Update an existing post (U).

➤ `wp_delete_post()`—Delete a post (D).

Post Metadata

CRUD operation functions for Post metadata in WordPress are:

➤ `add_post_meta()`—Create new post metadata (C).

➤ `get_post_meta()`—Retrieve post metadata (R).

➤ `update_post_meta()`—Update existing post metadata (U).

➤ `delete_post_meta()`—Delete post metadata (D).

Users

CRUD operation functions for Users in WordPress are:

➤ `wp_create_user()`—Create a new user (C).

➤ `get_userdata()`—Retrieve a user's data (R).

➤ `wp_update_user()`—Update an existing user (U).

➤ `wp_delete_user()`—Delete a user (D).

Any web application that you create will have some type of CRUD operations. WordPress includes the functions needed to make storing, retrieving, updating, and deleting data in your web applications a breeze.

Caching

WordPress features a simple-to-use cache layer for your applications. Not all applications require data caching, but caching should always be used to cache data that may be computationally expensive to regenerate. For example, a complex database's query results should be cached on initial load and only refreshed if parameters require it. There are two APIs available in WordPress for caching: Cache API and Transient API.

The Cache API allows you to store data in a cache that resides in memory only for the duration of the request. That means, cached data is not stored persistently across page loads with the use of a persistent caching plugin. The Cache API features a few different functions:

➤ `wp_cache_add()`—Adds data to the cache key if it doesn't already exist. If data already exists for the key, the data will not be added and the function will return `false`.

➤ `wp_cache_set()`—Adds data to the cache key. If the key already exists, the data will be overwritten; if not, the cache will be created.

➤ `wp_cache_get()`—Returns the value of the cached object.

➤ `wp_cache_delete()`—Clears data from the cache for the given key.

➤ `wp_cache_replace()`—Replaces the cache for a given key if it exists; returns `false` otherwise.

➤ `wp_cache_flush()`—Clears all cached data.

Let's review a simple example of working with cached data:

```php
<?php
//load the cache value if it exists
$result = wp_cache_get( 'prowp_cached_data' );

if ( false === $result ) {
    $result = $wpdb->get_results( $query );
    wp_cache_set( 'prowp_cached_data', $result );
```

```
}
// do something with $result
?>
```

In the preceding example, you're using the `wp_cache_get()` function to retrieve the cached data to the `$result` variable. If `$result` is empty, meaning there is no cached data, you generate the data for the cache. Once the `$result` variable has a value, you'll use the `wp_cache_set()` function to save the cached data. After the code has been executed, the `$result` variable will contain the cached data from your custom `$wpdb` query.

For more information on the WordPress Cache API visit the Codex at `http://codex.wordpress.org/Class_Reference/WP_Object_Cache`.

The Transient API allows you to cache data in the database and expire that data at a specific date and time. Because the data stored via the Transient API is saved in the database, it is available across your entire application. The Transient API functions are very similar to the Cache API, with the addition of an `$expiration` parameter:

```php
<?php
//load the transient value if it exists
$result = get_transient( 'prowp_cached_data' );

if ( false === $result ) {
        $result = $wpdb->get_results( $query );
        set_transient( 'prowp_cached_data', $result, 12 * HOUR_IN_SECONDS );
}

// do something with $result
?>
```

As you can see, the preceding example is very similar to the Cache API example. The only difference is you are using the `get_transient()` and `set_transient()` functions and setting an expiration time for the cached data. The expiration time is using a WordPress constant that returns the number of seconds in an hour, so in this example the expiration time is set to 1 year.

For more information on the Transient API, visit the Codex at `http://codex.wordpress.org/Transients_API`.

Friendly URLs

A web application's URL structure can be a very important feature of your application. Keyword injected URLs, or permalinks as they are known in WordPress, are a common feature on the Internet today. Rather than having URLs that contain confusing query strings (`http://example.com/?ID=54`), friendly URLs contain meaningful terms in the URL structure (`http://example.com/join`).

It's important to understand how the Rewrite API works in WordPress. It breaks down to a four-step process:

1. A URL is requested from the web server.

2. If a physical file exists, it will be returned (images, fonts, and so on).

3.   If a physical file does not exist, the request will be directed to `index.php`.

4.   The content will be returned from WordPress.

When visiting `http://example.com/join`, WordPress will take the `join` slug, query the database for the content, and return the join page content to the visitor.

The default WordPress permalink feature is a very powerful and easy-to-configure option for defining your permalink settings. You can adjust the default permalink settings in the Permalink Screen of the WordPress dashboard.

WordPress features a Rewrite API that enables you to customize your URL structure to fit your application requirements exactly. This API will help you go beyond the permalink settings in WordPress and programmatically build custom rewrite rules for your URLs. The Rewrite API is one of the more advanced WordPress APIs available, so it's important to always test your rewrite code logic in a development or staging environment prior to deploying to a live website.

For more information on the Rewrite API, visit the Codex at `http://codex.wordpress.org/Rewrite_API`.

External APIs

WordPress features two primary external APIs: XML-RPC and the REST API. These APIs can be used to interact with your web application externally. For example, you could create a native iOS application to view and update entries in your CRM application using one of these APIs.

The WordPress XML-RPC is the older of the two APIs and has been in WordPress core for a long time. Currently, all of the WordPress mobile apps utilize the XML-RPC API to post and pull content from WordPress remotely. This API also handles authentication when logging into your WordPress site through the API.

The REST API is the newest WordPress API on the block. You can install the JSON REST API plugin located at `https://wordpress.org/plugins/json-rest-api/`. The REST API is a powerful tool that allows you to get your site's data in simple JSON format, including posts, taxonomies, and more. Retrieving and updating data via this API is as simple as sending an HTTP request. There are plans for the REST API to be included in the core of WordPress, but for now it lives in a plugin.

The WordPress REST API has an extensive documentation website for learning how to interact with the API. You can view the documentation at `http://wp-api.org/`.

Uploads and Media Management

Requirements for any web application are file upload and media management capabilities. These could be as simple as uploading a custom user avatar or as complex as a document file management system.

When discussing media management in WordPress, we're not just talking about images and videos. Media can include any type of file, including documents, spreadsheets, PDFs, executables, or any other type of file you'd like to use. WordPress features a robust media management system that will work with any files your application requires.

WordPress also features some advanced image operations for cropping, flipping, and resizing uploaded images. Image gallery support is a default feature in WordPress, making it very easy for uploaded images to be displayed in a gallery layout.

All of these media tools are available for use in your web applications.

Scheduled Tasks

As you work to build more complex web applications, you will no doubt need the ability to run tasks on a schedule. For example, your CRM application may send a weekly digest email of all newly registered users in your app.

WordPress features a cron system for executing tasks on a schedule. You can easily schedule a function to execute at a specific recurring interval or to only run once and never again. Let's look at an example using the WordPress Cron API to send an hourly email reminding us to stay awake:

```php
<?php
register_activation_hook( __FILE__, 'prowp_cron_schedule' );

function prowp_cron_schedule() {

    //verify event has not been scheduled
    if ( ! wp_next_scheduled( 'prowp_cron_hook' ) ) {
        //schedule the event to run hourly
        wp_schedule_event( time(), 'hourly', 'prowp_cron_hook' );
    }
}

add_action( 'prowp_cron_hook', 'prowp_cron_email_reminder' );

function prowp_cron_email_reminder() {

    //send scheduled email
    wp_mail( 'brad@webdevstudios.com', 'Elm St. Reminder', 'Don\'t fall asleep!' );
}
?>
```

You'll use the `register_activation_hook()` to register your cron task. In this example, the cron schedule will be set when the plugin is activated. The first thing to do is verify the cron task is not already scheduled, which you'll check using the `wp_next_scheduled()` function.

After you verify the cron task has not been scheduled, it's time to schedule the task using the `wp_schedule_event()` function. The first parameter is the time you want the cron task to run initially. Setting that parameter to `time()` will set it to the current local time configured in WordPress. Next you'll set the recurrence, or how often the event should reoccur. In this example, you want the email to send every hour, so you'll set that value to `hourly`. The final parameter is the hook you want to trigger when the cron schedule runs.

Now that the cron job is scheduled, you need to actually tell cron what you are wanting to do. To start, you'll register a new action hook called `prowp_cron_hook`, which is the hook parameter you passed when scheduling the cron job. This hook will execute your `prowp_cron_email_reminder()`

function, which uses `wp_mail()` to send out your email reminder. That's it! You have now scheduled an hourly email to remind you to stay awake.

This is a pretty basic example of scheduled cron jobs in WordPress, but it does highlight how powerful this feature can be. You can schedule custom cron jobs for any number of tasks including different recurrence settings, whether it be monthly, weekly, daily, hourly, or even by the minute.

Flexibility

As you've learned throughout this book, WordPress is an endlessly flexible platform that can be customized to build any website imaginable. The extensibility within WordPress is one of the major reasons that WordPress has become so popular over the years. WordPress core includes over 2,000 hooks available to modify every component and feature within WordPress.

Beyond the WordPress core, over 34,000 plugins are freely available in the WordPress.org Plugin Directory. The saying "There's a plugin for that" rings very true when searching through the Plugin Directory. When you need the ability to introduce a new feature for your web app, chances are there is a plugin for that, which will ultimately save you time and money.

There are also nearly 3,000 free themes available in the WordPress.org Themes Directory. Aside from designing and building a custom theme, there's no need to start your web apps design from scratch. There are thousands of free options that can serve as a starting point for your web application.

Beyond WordPress.org, thousands of resources are available online including shared code on Github and Bitbucket, tutorials and demos, documentation, and more to help you extend WordPress when developing your web applications.

SUMMARY

The primary reason to use an application framework is to make the project quicker to complete and maintenance easier. As a WordPress developer, you are already working with WordPress regularly, which gives you the added bonus of working with a framework you already understand.

It's clear that WordPress is perfectly capable of being an application framework for your web apps. With its robust APIs, large featureset, extensibility, and ongoing active development, WordPress can rival some of the best frameworks out there.

WordPress in the Real World

WHAT'S IN THIS CHAPTER?

➤ Examining content management system tasks that are easily performed with WordPress

➤ Configuring WordPress to handle more complex content organization and display

➤ Integrating interaction vehicles such as forms, e-mail, and shopping carts

➤ Considering real-world challenges and how to address them with WordPress

In the real world, WordPress is generally used as the base for websites because of its extensive CMS capabilities. However, as you saw in the last chapter, WordPress can be so much more. Using WordPress as a content management system (CMS) seems to come up every month on the web. Run that phrase through a search engine and you will see countless results on the whys, why nots, and hows. It seems that WordPress is trapped with the stigma of being "only" a blogging engine when, as you have discovered by now, it is so much more. Since the first edition of this book, this topic and discussion around it have grown. WordPress is no longer pigeonholed in the "blog engine" space as it once was.

This chapter focuses on traditional content management from the perspective of a WordPress system, looks at the major functional areas associated with a CMS, shows you how to implement them via WordPress, and finally points out some areas where WordPress, despite its flexibility and simplicity, is potentially not the best tool for the task.

IS WORDPRESS THE RIGHT TOOL?

When is WordPress the right tool for the job? Making this determination can be challenging. Clearly, WordPress works for certain businesses and will most likely work for yours. Following are some reasons why.

Many of these reasons are well-known reasons to use WordPress, or reasons to use WordPress as a CMS, which are essentially one and the same. Look at all the functionality you receive out of the box when you use WordPress. WordPress, by its very nature, is easy to set up and use, and is search engine–optimized, security-aware, and well maintained, and countless other features have made it as popular as it is today.

This base functionality is what allows you to create fully functional, professional websites quickly, whether they are for one of your marketing initiatives, a new brand, or for a department or a client. This standardization, coupled with theme development consistency covered previously, ensures that your website infrastructure is predictable and manageable, thus making the development process more efficient and cost effective, all of which are enterprise-worthy goals.

WordPress could be the right solution for other reasons. The primary benefit is the capability to delegate content creation to subject matter experts. There is no way the development team can know the happenings and updates of every department company wide. Furthermore, even if these other teams provided content and relied on the web developers to perform the updates to the sites, the developers could be endlessly occupied with maintenance work. By using WordPress and some select plugins you are able to hand the updates back to the respective content owners to manage their own content creation, control, editing, and maintenance cycles.

WordPress is extensible. This has been covered throughout this entire book. You can extend WordPress in countless different ways by using plugins, and if the plugin that you need does not exist, you can use the plugin API to make your own. This allows you to integrate WordPress into your existing IT infrastructure.

The simplest form of integration is using RSS (really simple syndication), which does not require a plugin. We use RSS throughout our company as a way to organize content coming from different locations and reuse that content in new places. For example, press releases are syndicated from one central site, and by using tags and post categories, these content pieces are broadcast to the individual department sites as needed. This permits our content creators to post once and publish across a wide array of websites.

Furthermore, using RSS you are able to publish alerts and other timely news pieces from a central site to various locations around the country for use in their intranets and portals. This provides you with a one-stop location to publish from, and presents the consumers with a one-stop location from which to review the information.

Other integration pieces could include authorization with an existing identity provider, which is covered later in this chapter, calendaring applications, project management, or system status indicators. Because of the open API, you could integrate anything that you put your time and talents to.

In terms of cost, you cannot beat the price of WordPress. Given that the monetary outlay to try WordPress is so insignificant, your company can afford to give it a try and see if a proof of concept works (assuming, of course that you follow good security practices).

WordPress is open source software. That means that when you download it, you have everything. There are no magic compiled libraries of which you cannot see the direct functionality. Being open source and completely transparent prevents vendor lock in. Should you decide in the future that WordPress is not the right fit, all of your content is extractable. Sure, Automattic is a driving force behind WordPress, but with access to all the source code you can always maintain the code should Automattic go away. Or you could fork the codebase and make your own changes if you do not like the direction Automattic is taking, although other risks are involved here, such as disenfranchising the WordPress community by not respecting the spirit of the licensing. In other words, changes and improvements should be contributed to the greater community. Generally, a better approach would be to get involved with the development and direction of WordPress, which is covered in Chapter 16.

WHEN WORDPRESS IS NOT THE RIGHT TOOL

Depending on your circumstances, WordPress can be a good fit for your needs. But also consider the flip side. There are times when it does not match up with your goals, virtues, or culture, or the functionality does not match up with your needs or requirements. Here are some examples of when WordPress may not be the right fit.

WordPress may not have the exact functionality you require. It is not a panacea and cannot be all things to all people. For example, editorial workflows and default permissions are two places that may not line up directly. Plugins exist or are being developed that address these deficiencies, such as the Flow plugin (`http://editflow.org`) and the Members plugin covered later in the chapter. Should you find a requirement that a plugin does not address, perhaps you have actually stumbled across an opportunity to develop one yourself.

This next challenge is not WordPress-specific, but a common concern about free/open source software (FOSS) is that there is no single entity to hold accountable. Sadly, this is a reality for some developers. They want someone to hold accountable should something go wrong. In the worst circumstances, this could be you. At the same time, misconceptions about licensing, copyright, copyleft, and layering of software still persist in the business and technology communities. Some of these were touched on in Chapter 1. Likewise, there is no "go to" for support situations. But if you look around, you can find copious amounts of information on the Internet, both good and bad, and there are tons of consultants (possibly including you, after reading this book). Automattic also offers paid support through its WordPress VIP Program (`http://vip.wordpress.com/our-services/#self-hosted`) for clients that truly want to pay for accountability.

Because it is open source software, anyone and everyone can develop for it. When picking plugins, you are at the mercy of the developer. Short of doing it yourself, you do not know the quality of the plugin or the developer's credentials and security awareness. So prepare to get your hands dirty and actually evaluate the code you are going to use on your site. Be sure you know what you are getting into with a plugin.

The last challenge is the development progression, which begins with local development, then moves to a staging or quality assurance server, and then finally deploys to a live production server. In most cases, this progression is not a big deal. Themes and plugins developed locally can easily be deployed through these stages. The challenge really comes into play when you are making drastic content changes on a production site, such as massive copy revisions to a set of product line pages. Aside from multiple imports and exports of the data or database syncing, a viable, low-maintenance solution for this challenge is still needed. As touched on in Chapter 3, however, there are smart people working on this, such as Crowd Favorite's RAMP: `https://crowdfavorite.com/ramp/`.

DEFINING CONTENT MANAGEMENT

"Content management" has become hard to precisely define because it has been applied to a wide array of software tools and systems. On one end of the spectrum you have wikis, with explicit, multi-author editing and version control, but almost no page organization, navigation, or display mechanics. At the other extreme are commercial software packages aimed at the enterprise that handle access control, audit performance, repository functions, and community sharing of documents. Clearly there is a difference between the "transactional content management" realm of enterprise document control and self-directed publishing, but trying to pin the content management label on just one or the other ignores the richness of the software tools in those spaces. Since the rise of low-cost, easily used Internet tools, content management has more typically been applied to the systems used to build a site for Internet commerce, featuring online catalogs and customer interaction.

Where does WordPress fit on this spectrum? In the narrowest definition, blog engines are a form of CMS, handling a minimal number of content types (pages and discussion) in a chronological display order. Although WordPress started out as a blogging system, and some popular opinion still tries to narrowly describe it as such, it has the power, flexibility, and resources to perform most, if not all, of the tasks required of a package more typically marketed as a CMS. The mechanics of managing a site, administering users, and bucketing content for structure and distribution are not specific to blogs or any flavor of content; they require customization, design, and a multi-role delegation system. We hope this has been conveyed so far in this book, where we have liberally referred to the "content management" functions of WordPress, and now we can tie the pieces together in a more general CMS view.

Following are the CMS real-world challenges discussed in this chapter:

➤ **Workflow and delegation**—Often the holy grail of the CMS world is enabling multiple authors with minimal technical expertise to control the editing and publishing process. WordPress makes it simple for nontechnical users to add content and manage its distribution.

➤ **Content organization**—From mimicking a simple network portal to building complex page hierarchies, content organization involves handling multiple, complex types of content and choosing the appropriate display patterns for each.

➤ **Interactivity**—Mailing lists, forms, discussions, and commerce functions are typical CMS functions that require a bit of WordPress extension.

➤ **Site statistics**—Methods for reviewing the engagement of your visitors and the technology platform being used to access your site to determine what is working and where your focus needs to be.

➤ **Scalability**—Successful sites may need additional resources in order to provide acceptable user experience for your visitors.

➤ **Cache management** —Repeated processing either through database access or dynamic script parsing can slow down the responsiveness of your site. Caching at various levels can alleviate some of these bottlenecks.

➤ **Load balancing**—Once your site is scaled out to multiple servers, problem load balancing optimizes the utilization of the resources but also introduces some challenges.

➤ **Dealing with spam**—Unfortunately, spamming is a way of life on the web. However, there are some tools to mitigate the onslaught.

➤ **Other content management systems**—As a pure website management system, WordPress can be a powerful editing and content production platform, feeding other content management systems such as Drupal. This chapter also looks at areas in which WordPress is not the best choice.

At their core, blogging and content management may have come from different starting points and established their own functional lexicon, but the extensibility, design customization, and diverse developer community around WordPress has blurred the lines between what is "only blogging" and the now in-vogue "content management."

The goal in covering WordPress in the real word is to highlight approaches to solving typical content management problems, building on the techniques and examples provided in previous chapters. Of course, no one wants every conversation to start out with a defense of WordPress, either in these pages or by you in a setting where you are choosing tools. Whatever your definition of content management, or your goals for creating a website that goes well beyond a list of blog entries, the content management process starts with simplifying the workflow.

WORKFLOW AND DELEGATION

One of the primary appeals of a classic CMS is that it simplifies content creation and management. Closely tied to that effort is a separation of duties, such that those users and administrators with editorial control over the content are given access, responsibility, and control over what is actually published through the CMS.

User Roles and Delegation

Just like in the real world, user management in a CMS has all of the separation of powers and policy creation complexity of politics, government, or standards bodies. You have to allocate roles based on the types and categorization of content you expect, as well as set boundaries on users' abilities to publish and edit previously published content. In a purely multi-author website environment, the distinction may not appear that important, but if you are using WordPress as the face of an e-commerce site or for a company's product catalog, multiple departments and approvers typically demand involvement.

Justin Tadlock's Members plugin (https://wordpress.org/plugins/members/) was covered in Chapter 13 as part of the security and user management discussion. This plugin allows you to create new roles for your users and assign them very fine-grained permissions. In a CMS environment, this would permit you to delegate content generation to different departments and authorize them to make changes only in their respective areas.

Assignment of authority goes up the hierarchy of users, not down from an editor to an individual author. In a typical publishing environment, an editor will be able to dole out work to writers and composition experts, creating a workflow for the finished product that is organized in a tree structure similar to an organizational chart. WordPress mobilizes the leaves in that tree structure: Every user that has contributor or author privileges can create content (and upload files, in the case of authors) and manage publishing of their own posts. Deciding how and where to divide responsibilities is a key part of establishing a CMS framework with WordPress:

➤ Be diligent about administrator roles. Give them out like `root` or `sudo` passwords. At the same time, do not confuse editors with administrators. Editors may want to change the way a page appears, or aggregate content differently. Administrators are going to fix themes, core files, and plugins, and each has to be clear about the bounds on their domains.

➤ Treat editors as such. They will be given permission to edit pages, modify the content or status of any posts, and change metadata on the WordPress site. They should be using their editorial roles to manage the work of the authors and contributors as well.

➤ If you really want every piece of content reviewed before it hits the public web, separate contributors (who cannot publish) from authors (who can publish their own work but not edit that of others). Establishing a contributor class of users ensures that your editors will be busier, but also fully delegates the publishing decisions to those editors.

➤ Note that roles and delegation cover the creative process, not access control to content once published. As soon as the content is accessible as a published post, it is public until deleted (and even then, it may be cached or replicated elsewhere through a feed mechanism). In contrast to other content management systems, WordPress does not focus on a mechanism to control access to published content; it is not about intellectual property management or control in the same way a corporate document repository might track access, references, and provide auditing mechanisms.

A wrinkle on the multi-role and multi-user WordPress administration framework is WordPress Multisite, discussed in Chapter 10. WordPress Multisite powers `WordPress.com` because it allows multiple independent user trees to run independent but cohosted sites. This may be attractive if you have independent product groups or multiple brands that each want their own WordPress installations but you are limited (or want to be restrictive) in terms of administrator people power.

Workflow

Having established users and their roles, the next step is to clearly establish a workflow for getting content out of people's heads and onto the web. After a simple editorial user structure, workflow is probably the next most matched term when asking what users associate with mainstream CMS. Two major components to workflow within WordPress exist: post revision history and post control.

Revision history is visible within the Post screen of the Dashboard, where entering edit mode on a post shows you the list of revisions. If you are running a system with multiple authors and editors, where the editors may fine-tune the first writing output, ensure that the editorial staff is using the revision feature to track content added, subtracted, or different between post revisions. It is effectively source code control for post content, managed within the MySQL database under WordPress.

Although many people are big fans of the simple Dashboard and find it compact yet powerful, some site administrators may find that the interface is too complicated given the technical background of their editor or administrator delegate. Some people freeze up when they have too many options or choices. You can use the WP-CMS Post Control plugin by Jonathan Allbut (`http://wordpress.org/plugins/wp-cms-post-control/` to turn off unneeded features. This plugin installs a new

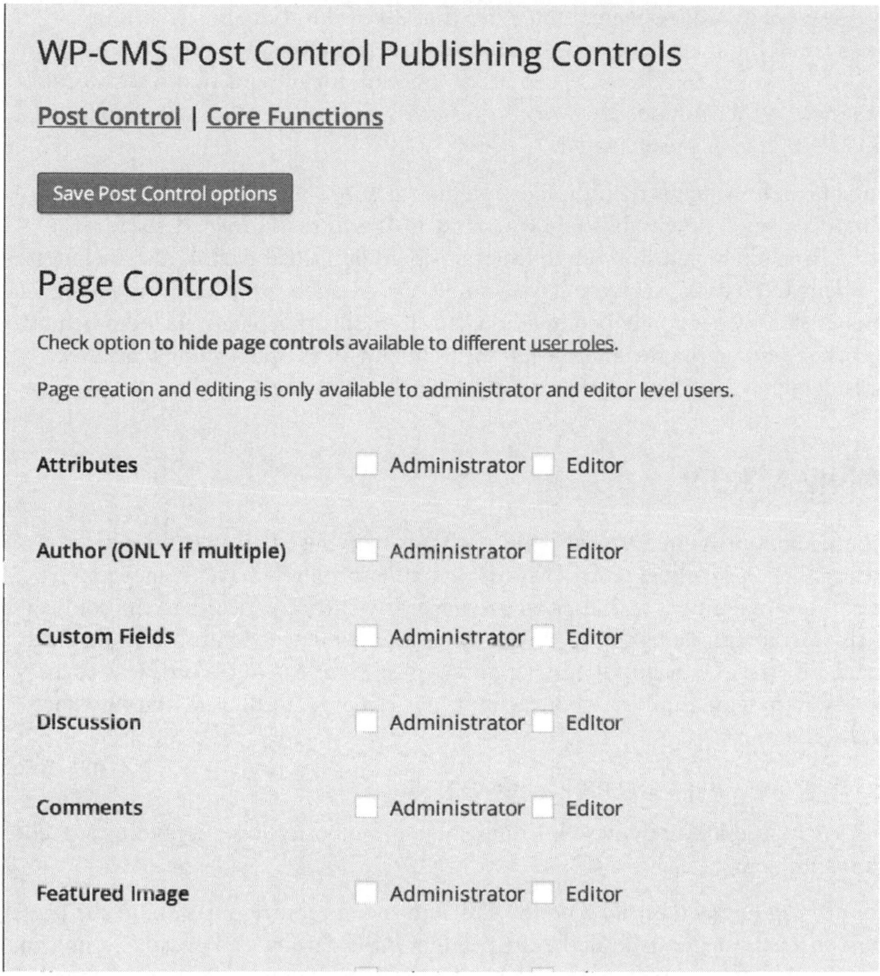

WP-CMS Post Control Publishing Controls

Post Control | Core Functions

Save Post Control options

Page Controls

Check option **to hide page controls** available to different user roles.

Page creation and editing is only available to administrator and editor level users.

Attributes	Administrator	Editor
Author (ONLY if multiple)	Administrator	Editor
Custom Fields	Administrator	Editor
Discussion	Administrator	Editor
Comments	Administrator	Editor
Featured Image	Administrator	Editor

FIGURE 15-1: Using WP-CMS Post Control to set the Dashboard options

control panel that allows you to configure the Write Panel to show only the fields you want them to see, as shown in Figure 15-1.

This plugin offers many options, but it is a simple management control. Using this plugin is the administrative control step that is complementary to creating simpler (or more specific) post editing panels, described later in this chapter.

The second part of content workflow is the process of taking posts from the draft state to published state, with stops at "private," "future," and "pending" along the way if warranted. A post written by a contributor will be held as "pending" until published by someone with that permission. Much of the post workflow happens through the Posts screen on the Dashboard, where the status of each post is clearly labeled, and there are menu items for publishing or making other post status changes such as marking a post as private or setting a future publication time.

If you are running a multi-writer WordPress site, remember that all of the content is stored in the same MySQL database, making it easy for other users to see the current state of the content. WordPress provides the `wp_transition_post_status()` function for plugins that want to catch individual post status changes, either to update a work-in-progress page or to otherwise signal to other users that a workflow change has propagated.

A particularly interesting plugin to watch is the Edit Flow plugin (`http://editflow.org/`). This plugin was designed to model a newspaper publishing workflow in WordPress. It includes several new post statuses, starting from pitching a story up to the traditional published post. It also includes special story budgeting calendars to make sure you have content spread out appropriately and assigned to writers and photographers for proper content completion. Additionally, this plugin includes behind-the-scenes notes between the editor of the site and the author to help with the publishing workflow with remote workers. It is definitely a niche plugin, but if your needs align, check it out.

CONTENT ORGANIZATION

There is an ongoing debate about posts in a WordPress site that is being used as a traditional, static content website. Posts are an indelible part of WordPress and absolutely have a place and use in any website, but the common argument is that posts are naturally chronological and that only time-based content fits this paradigm. Posts can represent any small content block that can be used multiple ways, as evidenced by the expansion of custom post types. Part of using WordPress as a CMS involves changing your strategic thinking about what types of content are used and to what effect they are used on the site.

Here are three simple examples of using posts for a commerce site:

➤ Create a post for each product that you sell. Comments on the post allow users to offer feedback and recommendations.

➤ Create a category or tag for each product on the site, and then organize posts about the product. The first post in each category should be the product information, and possibly a link to a shopping cart through which a user can purchase the product—something covered shortly. Now you can use the posts structure to provide deeper information about each product: Why are you offering it? How is it created, defined, or sourced? What other reviews, feedback, or public commentary exist?

➤ When creating a help section for a product, each help topic could be a post. Each help topic would be one small bite-sized piece of content that addresses a specific task or feature, using the tag and category mechanisms to sort and provide navigational guidance to users looking for self-directed help. Comments on the posts allow for users to describe the relative helpfulness of each post. Similarly, although not e-commerce, the jQuery team is using this method to document its API at `http://api.jquery.com`, creating a help resource and community resource via comments, all in one.

In every one of these simple examples, you want to change the default behavior of WordPress away from showing the most recent posts, and instead create a mix of static and dynamic homepage content reminiscent of a static website. You can see a variety of WordPress CMS application examples at `http://wordpress.org/showcase/tag/cms`.

Theme and Widget Support

Theme support for content management is key. Your goal may not be to make WordPress look decidedly non-blog-like but, rather, to find a theme that gives you the flexibility to display the types of content in the visual style that fits, whether it is a product sales site or an online newsletter. As an extreme case, the P2 theme (`http://p2theme.com`) developed by Automattic puts a posting panel, real-time updates, and inline editing right on the homepage, combining the best of Twitter, a blog, a discussion forum, and a news site. WordPress can be molded through themes to look completely different from any other WordPress site.

If you are going to be using a theme with widget areas and want to expand the content types available in those sidebar areas, you will want to leverage the TinyMCE JavaScript-based editor to turn HTML text areas into something more theme-appropriate. The Black Studio TinyMCE Widget plugin addresses the challenge that default text widgets support only plain old text. When you enable this plugin (`http://wordpress.org/plugins/black-studio-tinymce-widget/`), as shown in Figure 15-2, you have a new widget available in your widget screen. This widget has the built-in TinyMCE editor, so your content creators can put more than text in the sidebar.

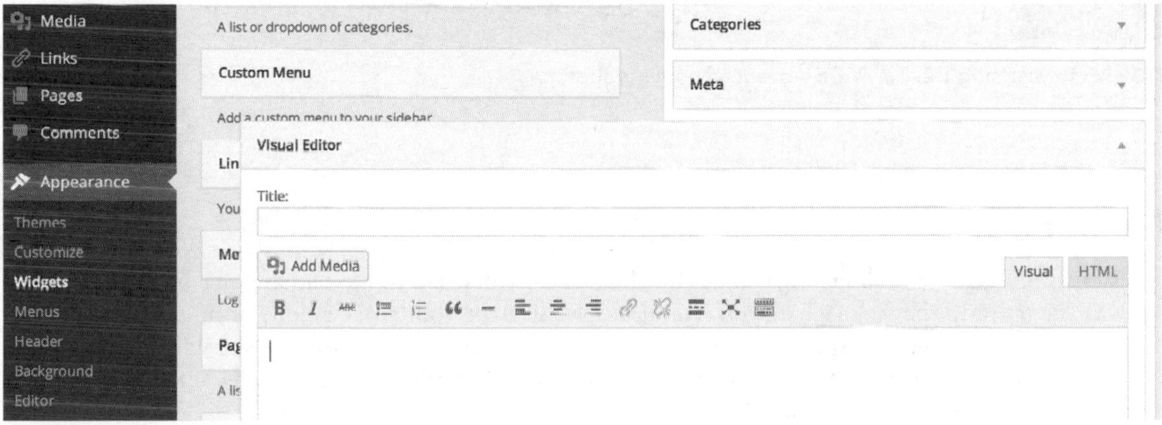

FIGURE 15-2: Editing a rich text widget

You do have to exercise some caution when using this plugin. Usually, your sidebar and other widget-ready areas have fixed widths. With this plugin, your content creator can upload anything into the widget and potentially break the layout of the site. However, this can be remedied with some proper training.

The bundled TinyMCE editor is workable but does not support some frequently used features such as adding tables. The TinyMCE Advanced plugin by Andrew Ozz (`http://wordpress.org/extend/plugins/tinymce-advanced/`) steps in and tries to address these shortcomings; however, be forewarned that the more elaborate your content, the more opportunity you create to break your site (again) with ill-formatted or rendered tables. Figure 15-3 shows the TinyMCE Advanced configuration panel.

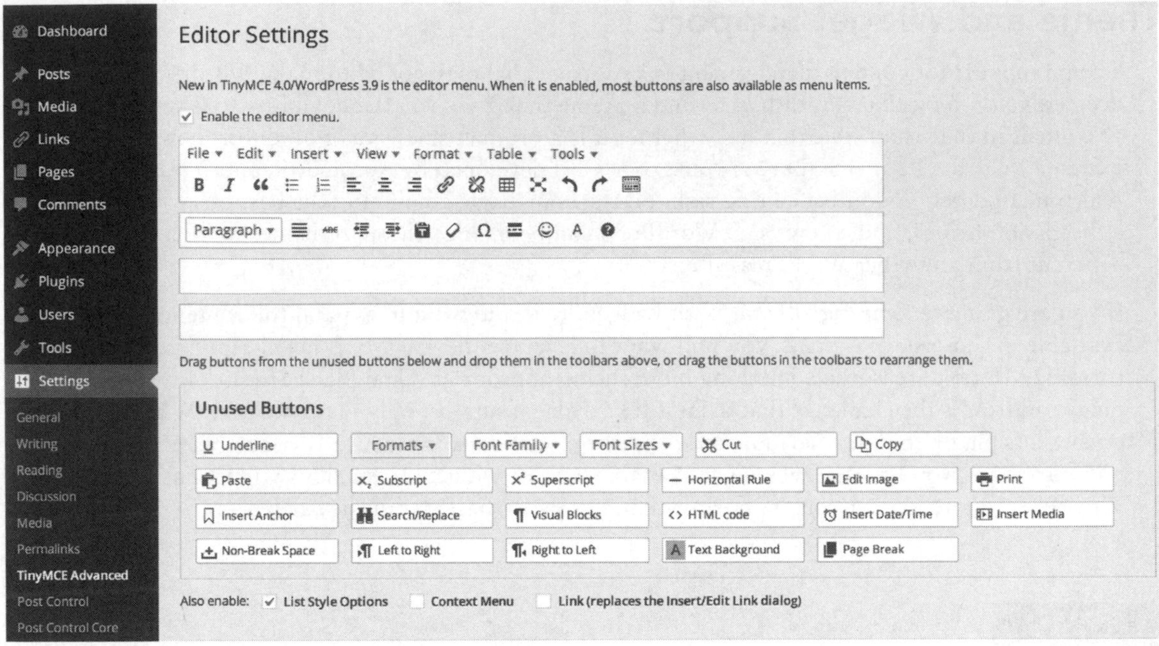

FIGURE 15-3: Using the TinyMCE Advanced configuration panel

Homepages

Remember high-school writing courses in which every story had to have a narrative hook? The hook was the point in the story where you established what made your story unique or interesting and encouraged your reader to keep going. A good narrative hook on a WordPress site will engage the reader and kick off the remainder of your storyline, whether it is product-related content or a mix of static and time-sensitive posts.

The common approach is to set a static front page. As discussed in Chapter 9, you can do this in several different ways. The easiest is to use the WordPress Reading Settings screen to set a static page for your front, or homepage. In addition, this page could use a page template to modify and distinguish the layout from the rest of your site. You will need to create a page (not a post) specifically for this purpose and then use the Dashboard to set it as the front page.

The other option is to use a special WordPress template file to serve as your front page, replacing the default listing of posts. WordPress looks for a template file named front-page.php in your theme, as discussed in Chapter 9. Using a template file will afford you more flexibility in the layout and functionality of your index page because you can edit the PHP code directly, choosing, for example, to list sticky posts or featured products first, and then related content or more recent chronological posts. Using a mix of additional page data fields and the custom loop query mechanisms described in Chapter 5, you can hand-tune the selection of content for your homepage as finely as you want.

Featured Content Pages

A good tool for your narrative hook on your static index page is a featured item. This is very common among the magazine-style themes in particular, as well as many other websites. Often, in the top third of the content area, you will see a large image area with a headline featuring content from elsewhere in the site. This position is sometimes called the "hero spot" and is featured prominently on popular websites. It is a frequently deployed device because it works.

Generally when you deploy a featured item on the index page, it is best to have several different images and use jQuery (or another JavaScript library) to cycle through them. That way, you are not relying on one hero item to save the day, but putting forth a couple of different ideas, and with luck, one will catch the visitor's eye. The goal here is to feature items managed as posts, custom post types, or media by WordPress so that the editorial staff can control them rather than the site administrator.

The first thing to do is set up a system for the featured items. You can use a category named "Features" and use just those posts for the slideshow. But that means that in other parts of the site, if there is a news section that shows all posts, you will want to exclude this category from those Loops, which can be a pain. This is the old school way to manage this type of feature on a WordPress site, and some themes continue to do so.

However, as covered in Chapters 7 and 9, you can use custom post types to achieve this functionality without the extra loop overhead. Again, this is only one way to implement this content management element; there are many others. In this example, you are going to edit the theme template files directly, but this functionality could be built into a plugin also.

The plan is to showcase three random features from the "slides" custom post type for display. First, register a new custom post type, as discussed in Chapter 7. This code goes in your `functions.php` file. For this example, it might be something like this:

```
/*
 * SLIDES FOR FEATURE
 * Register post type for feature
 */
add_action( 'init', 'wppro_create_post_types' );
function wppro_create_post_types() {
  register_post_type( 'slides',
    array(
      'labels' => array(
        'name' => _x( 'Slides', 'post type general name' ),
        'singular_name' => _x( 'Slide', 'post type singular name' ),
        'add_new' => _x( 'Add New', 'Slide' ),
        'add_new_item' => __( 'Add New Slide' ),
        'edit_item' => __( 'Edit Slide' ),
        'new_item' => __( 'New Slide' ),
        'view_item' => __( 'View Slide' ),
        'search_items' => __( 'Search Slides' ),
        'not_found' =>  __( 'No Slides found' ),
        'not_found_in_trash' => __( 'No Slides found in Trash' ),
        'parent_item_colon' => ''
      ),
```

```
        'public' => true,
        'exclude_from_search' => true,
        'supports' => array('title','thumbnail','editor'),
        )
    );
}
```

For the display on your site, you are either going to edit your `front-page.php` template file or make a new page template file for your index page. These code changes will go into that file.

Next, you have to get the slides from the database. You can get these posts with a simple WordPress `WP_Query()` object:

```
$feature_query = new WP_Query('post_type=slides');
```

This query will gather all of the slide custom post types; you could also pass in some limiting parameters to tune the result. Then, in the content area of the template file, you mix a little HTML for the jQuery to hook into and then loop over the result object:

```
<div id= "feature-container-container ">
  <div id= "feature-container ">
    <?php if (is_front_page() && $feature_query->have_posts() )
        : while ($feature_query->have_posts()) : $feature_query->the_post();
    ?>
      <div id= "slide_<?php echo $post->ID; ?> "
        class= "entry-content slide " title= "<?php echo $post->post_title; ?> ">
        <?php the_content();?>
        <?php edit_post_link( 'Edit', '<span class= "edit-link ">', '</span>' ); ?>
      </div>
    <?php endwhile; endif;?>
  </div>
  <ul id= "feature-nav "> </ul>
</div>
```

What you are doing here is creating some wrapping `div`s to contain the slideshow, looping over each custom post type in the query result, and pulling out the content. When you put this to use, the content image should be specifically sized so as not to break your theme layout. This can be extremely convenient because you now have featured slides advertising on your index page that link to individual landing pages, which makes it handy for tracking success rates through your traffic analysis. Furthermore, you are not cluttering up your traditional post and page content with ephemeral advertising posts.

If you view your site now, you may see stacked images or content on top of each other, so the next step is to take these posts and use a little JavaScript magic to turn them into a slideshow or carousel. Many people are big fans of the jQuery Cycle plugin by Mike Alsup (http://malsup.com/jquery/cycle/). Note that this is a plugin for jQuery and not WordPress. This plugin is really easy to use and has several neat transition options. Using this plugin, you can convert the HTML into an autoscrolling slideshow. This JavaScript code goes into the bottom of your page template file or where you would normally place your JavaScript. The jQuery could be something like this:

```
$('#feature-container').cycle({
  fx:    'fade',
```

```
speed:  1000,  //time the transition lasts
timeout: 6000, //time between transitions
pause: 1, //stop the show on mouseover
random: 0, //random order (our mysql does this already)
delay: -1000, //delay before show starts first transition
next:  '#next',
prev:  '#previous',
pager:  "#feature-nav ",
pagerEvent:    'mouseover', // name of event that drives the pager navigation
autostop:       true, // true to end slideshow after X transitions
autostopCount: 100,       // number of transitions

// callback fn that creates a thumbnail to use as pager anchor
pagerAnchorBuilder: function(idx, slide) {
  var thetitle = slide.title;
  var desc = jQuery('#'+slide.id+' img:first').attr("alt");
  var href = jQuery('#'+slide.id+' a:first').attr("href");
   return '<li><a href="'+ href +'" title= "Show: '+ desc +' "></a></li>';
 }
});
```

Experiment with the different effects and timing using the other parameters you can set to create unique results. This same method could be used to showcase some testimonials. Either keep it in a slideshow pattern, as outlined previously, or pull a random post from the testimonial category. Rather than using images as your content, you can have the actual formatted post data. You are only limited by your imagination.

Content Hierarchy

In addition to the featured item concept to draw users' attention, most content management systems will allow you to create a content hierarchy to improve navigation once you have hooked the user. A typical hierarchy for real-world websites contains content of different types in a tree-like structure to impose navigational patterns, and that allows you to mix static content features with more dynamic content.

One obvious path to a content hierarchy is to use categories and tags to sort posts into related groups. This is useful when you are using posts as the primary content type and organize equivalent classes of posts by category or unique tag information. In addition, you saw in the previous section of this chapter how custom post types can be used for featured image content on an index page carousel.

The custom taxonomy features discussed in Chapter 7 provide another way to organize and search posts, giving you even more flexibility when customizing a theme's Loop. This section digs into these custom pages and post hierarchies more, providing examples of plugins that let you craft the content management aspects of WordPress to suit your desired site look and feel.

You can start with a complex navigation challenge: You have a hybrid site that has sections where pages are the obvious content type, but you also have some sections where post categories make more sense, which is often the case in live sites. You do not want to manage a hard-coded navigation tree, and implementing menus is not perfect because the post content is (intentionally) regularly changing.

One solution is the Page Links To plugin by Mark Jaquith (`http://txfx.net/wordpress-plugins/page-links-to/`). This plugin creates a new field on the page Write Panel. Using this field, you can create a page that functions as a redirect to another web page. This enables you to use the menu system as your site's global navigation but still empowers you to create menu items that can redirect to offsite links. Or, more often, you can now create a menu item as a page but have it redirect to a post Loop page.

For example, pretend that under your About Us menu you have the traditional History (of your company) and Contact Us pages, and to further complicate matters, you also have a job posting page. But your company uses a third-party service for job postings, which creates a problem in your navigation. With this plugin, you can create a new page called Careers but have the page link to the third-party job-posting site instead. You can see how this would be set up in Figure 15-4.

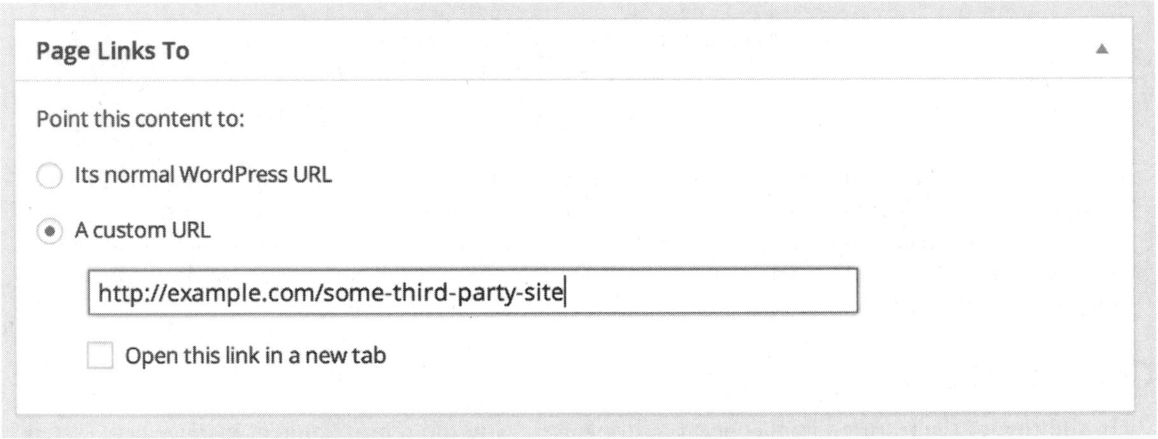

Page Links To   ▲

Point this content to:

◯ Its normal WordPress URL

◉ A custom URL

    http://example.com/some-third-party-site

☐ Open this link in a new tab

FIGURE 15-4: Creating a page that links to a third party with the Page Links To plugin

The next challenge with a large site is managing the pages. After a while, your site grows to have multiple pages, under multiple parent pages. This structure is necessary to make your site coherent, as discussed in Chapter 9. Themes have several ways to handle global navigation, and determining which method your theme uses is important. Most themes are moving toward using the WordPress menu system.

The built in WordPress menu system is nice and flexible, but it is disconnected from your actual content. With the menu system, you can automatically add pages to the navigation, but only at the top level. But when you remove a content page in the Dashboard, it does not affect the menu, leaving you with orphaned navigation links. This disconnect can be very baffling to inexperienced WordPress administrators, and it can be frustrating for experienced administrators that the two systems are not coupled. Make sure this is something you train your client on because it is not intuitive for them to be disconnected.

INTERACTIVITY FEATURES

The most basic interactivity feature is Search, discussed in Chapter 12. The other primary user interaction features found in real-world websites are forums, forms, and basic e-commerce features.

Forums

Comments on posts are the simplest content discussion type. At times, you may want to move from content that you create in an attempt to stimulate conversation into user-led and threaded conversation. A forum is an open discussion, most commonly called a bulletin board in the pre-broadband days of the Internet. The easiest way to add forums to WordPress is through bbPress (http://bbpress.org), a WordPress-related project also delivered by Automattic. bbPress will share user data with WordPress so registered users can participate in forum discussions. It is possible to load them both and have your forums simply appear as a section of your website.

If you want a simple forum feature as a content type, the plugin route is likely to produce an acceptable result. On the other hand, if you want to integrate multiple content management repositories into a single user experience, take a page (literally) from WordPress.org: bbPress powers the WordPress.org user-generated support area.

Forms

The next challenge for a website is creating and managing forms, such as contact forms and other similar web form to e-mail features. Countless plugins are available for contact forms, but for a full-featured site, you will eventually have to move beyond this. For the longest time, the cForms II plugin by Oliver Seidel (http://www.deliciousdays.com/cforms-plugin) has been the regular stand-in. CForms works very well and is extremely powerful. You can customize it to all ends of the Earth, but the user interface is very daunting at first. You cannot really hand off CForms to your content administrator to make new forms as needed.

An alternative to CForms is Gravity Forms by RocketGenius (http://www.gravityforms.com/). This is one of the few plugins mentioned in this book that costs money to use. But to be honest here, Gravity Forms is a very enticing prospect. Ask any WordPress developer what her favorite plugin is, and if she has used Gravity Forms, that is usually the answer. Gravity Forms lets you create any type of form you need with a simple, easy-to-use AJAXy interface. It is so easy to use that many content administrators are shown how to use it. Not to gush too much, but the clean, intuitive interface is truly one of the best among plugins.

In addition to the user interface side, the HTML rendering is top notch. It looks fantastic without any additional styling required. However, should you desire to change the look and feel, the HTML is filled with CSS class and ID hooks for you to use. In addition, this plugin is so popular that many themes include styling for it. A final, powerful feature of Gravity Forms is that, in addition to the traditional "e-mail the form contents to a specified address" functionality, Gravity Forms also adds a Dashboard module that tracks the forms submitted. Although CForms has similar functionality, the usability of Gravity Forms really justifies the cost.

E-Commerce

If you are building a site with featured products and pages, product tags, and categories, ideally you would like to sell something. Shopping cart and payment systems integration fill the last category of user interaction. If you search the plugin directory on WordPress.org, you will see at least a dozen different shopping cart and checkout plugins available. Rather than itemize them all, here is a quick checklist of things to look for:

➤ How hard is it to configure the shopping cart? Are you going to be burdening your administrators with minor details such as updated discounts, or can content managers handle that task?

➤ What kinds of statistics can you get from the cart? Learning how and why users abandon items will help you improve the site, whether through more product information or an easier checkout process.

➤ What payment systems are supported? If you are not looking for anything more complicated than the ability to accept PayPal payments with a specific product or item number filled in, you can use PayPal button templates and hand-edit them into your pages or sidebars.

The WP e-Commerce plugin (http://getshopped.org) combines nearly all of the extension mechanisms covered: It uses custom post types for product pages, organizes them in custom taxonomies, and adds plugin-specific database tables to maintain product attributes. It integrates with a variety of payment mechanisms and clearly demonstrates that you can give WordPress a hand-crafted look and feel.

SCALABILITY

At some point, the question arises—can WordPress scale? And the answer is, of course it can. Just look at WordPress.com statistics (http://en.wordpress.com/stats/traffic/). You can clearly see that it is capable. But the actual task of scaling a WordPress installation involves many layers, including the WordPress code, plugins and themes, the PHP version and settings, the web server software and the underlying operating system, and finally, the actual server hardware. The key to scaling a WordPress installation is to secure and tune each of these layers.

Performance Tuning

Securing and tuning your WordPress installation is covered in Chapter 13. Be sure to review that content. This chapter touches on more enterprise-specific issues, with the assumption that in a larger technology deployment, you will have access to the web, database, and file servers that form the bulk of your WordPress installation. We are big believers in DevOps, and you, as the developer, should have knowledge and access to all these layers to understand how all the moving parts work together. Sadly, in some organizations these levels remain in department silos.

Tuning your theme should be part of any theme development process. That process includes checking the file sizes of all images, making sure the JavaScript and CSS are as small as possible, perhaps even minified, and reducing the total number of HTTP requests a browser has to make. Using a tool such as YSlow! for Firebug, the Firefox add-on or Chrome developer tools (http://developer.yahoo.com/yslow/) can help isolate these problems. Our caution about YSlow! is that although it is a nice tool to assess slowdowns, it was designed by Yahoo! for Yahoo!, and even though this is talking about scalability, Yahoo!'s sense of scale is likely bigger than yours. So, take the results with a grain of salt and use some commonsense in weeding out the low-hanging fruit. Generally, good web development practices will help your theme scale.

For plugins, you have to look at the code. As mentioned previously, it is unlikely that you know the credentials or skill level of the plugin developer or the terms under which it was created. Some plugins are created in a straightforward, get-it-done style and may not be very efficient, even if they are effective. You can often see this style with multiple SQL queries to get the information required at any given time rather than a thought-out data access plan. If you are making improvements to existing code, notify the creator. Put your enhancements back into circulation so the entire community can prosper. Chapter 16 offers additional information on supporting the WordPress community.

Scalability really goes hand in hand with performance. The more efficient your website is, the easier it is to handle more requests and therefore scale. For the PHP layer of the application stack, turn off any PHP functionality you are not using. This is good for performance, security, and scaling. Much of this was covered in Chapter 13 under the subject of security and performance; here, the same rules apply for scalability.

In your `php.ini` file, disable any extensions you are not using, like all those extra database extensions. The default `php.ini` file is designed to work for most people in general circumstances. In other words, it is designed to just work for everyone. Here, we are referring to tuning PHP to meet your specific needs and requirements. The following are pretty safe settings to turn off:

```
;Hide PHP for security
expose_php = Off
;Turn off for performance
register_globals = Off
register_long_arrays = Off
register_argc_argv = Off
magic_quotes_gpc = Off
magic_quotes_runtime = Off
magic_quotes_sybase = Off
```

Set your memory allowances to the correct values for your server environment and needs. Make sure error reporting is configured properly for the environment—do not show errors on the production site.

The next layer up is the web server software. Apache is the most common, but WordPress can run on any number of web server applications, including Microsoft IIS and nginx. In general, do some research on your web server and the functionality it requires in order to tune its operation. Turn off any module or extra features you are not using. Like PHP, the stock Apache configuration file is designed to work for most people in typical usage situations. It is in the developer's best interest to reduce the amount of effort to get something to work from the get-go. This can be a huge barrier to entry if too much tweaking is needed just to get something to work.

Tuning for scalability is the exact opposite of this general use case scenario. You want to disable as much as possible to make the software as lean as can be and still serve your sites properly with only the functionality your sites require. A side effect of slimming down your configurations is that you also increase your security posture by not having as many options to exploit.

Another option for scaling is to consider serving static content from an assets server or Content Delivery Network (CDN). This is a specific variant of throwing more hardware at the problem, which is looked at shortly. In short, using one web server for serving dynamic content and another for serving the static assets, such as images and CSS, can reduce the load across the board. Different web servers have different strengths. Moving your static content to a secondary URL on a web server using lighttpd or nginx, which are better at serving this type of content, may be more efficient because each web server can be tuned for a more specific function. This will also reduce the load on your dynamic content server, giving it more resources to perform its own duties.

A faux method is also available here to accomplish similar results. You can serve static assets from a subdomain, even if it is on the same server. Most web browsers are set to download two to four items in parallel at a time. By moving some of these requests to a subdomain, such as static.example.com, you can trick the browser into effectively doubling the number of items being fetched at a time.

Moving your static assets to a CDN accomplishes the same thing, but on a much larger scale. CDNs distribute your content across their network of servers, so this not only off-loads the transfer from your web server, but it can also make the content geographically closer to your visitor. However, you are also now relying on a third party for portions of your site. Many WordPress-specific hosting providers are incorporating CDN services into their hosting packages.

Database Optimizations

The database level also has several opportunities for optimizations. MySQL has two main storage types for tables: MyISAM and InnoDB. Others are available, but these are the two that MySQL installations have enabled by default.

The ISAM table type was the original storage engine for MySQL. The MySQL team later improved the engine and created MyISAM. MyISAM is a good general-purpose storage engine. It performs better with a table with many reads or many writes, but not both. That is, it is good for storing or retrieving data, but not ideal for a situation that requires frequent switching between the two. This is also the default table type for WordPress.

InnoDB, on the other hand, provides better concurrency through row locking and transactional support. InnoDB can use non-locking reads to maximize efficiency and performance. This makes InnoDB a good storage engine for large volumes of data and datasets that are used in both read and write contexts. If you're going to use WordPress in an enterprise where you have many contributing users, or lively discussion of topics posted by a core group, the write and update load on the database will be significantly higher than that of an individual blogger who posts weekly thoughts on buildings and food or the Talking Heads.

Switching some of your WordPress tables, such as the highly dynamic ones like wp_comments, to the InnoDB storage type can create performance improvements, and therefore scalability benefits. Additionally, MySQL also has a configuration file that can be tuned to match your environment. Again, this is really enterprise-level tuning of your MySQL. The average site probably is not going to dive into the underlying database storage engines, but a high traffic site that has extensive infrastructure on MySQL may have the expertise to make the appropriate adjustments for scaling and performance.

Regular Database Maintenance

Finally, your MySQL database needs to be maintained. From time to time, you should run checks on your database tables and optimize and repair if needed. Maintaining your database is like changing the oil in your car or defragmenting your hard drive—you have to do it regularly to keep everything running smoothly. This can easily be done through PHPMyAdmin or another MySQL interface. Plugins such as WP-DBManager by Lester Chan (`http://wordpress.org /plugins/ wp-dbmanager/`) allow you to schedule these tasks, as well as backups, and not have to worry about it again.

Hardware Scaling

The previous optimizations were all low cost software configurations. This next one is a more expensive option, adding more hardware. A default WordPress installation is all encapsulated on one machine. This machine functions as both the web server and database, as shown in Figure 15-5. This is the simplest and most basic WordPress hardware scenario. Many, if not most, sites run this way.

FIGURE 15-5: WordPress on one server

The next option is to split the database and web server functions into two servers, as shown in Figure 15-6. This allows each server to focus on a specific task and is the next logical step when your hardware starts to get taxed by the workload. At the same time, make sure that you account for the independent database and web hosts when you create your WordPress configuration files; you will need to know the name of the database host because it is no longer the "localhost" with respect to the web server. This is common web application architecture and is very easy to implement with only a few configuration changes. Again, make sure you re-tune your database and web server software to run on their now independent boxes.

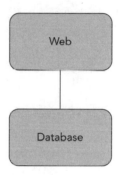

Hardware scaling can quickly get complex, and the possibilities are endless, so you are only going to briefly review some common scenarios. Depending on your existing infrastructure, you may have other options available.

FIGURE 15-6: WordPress on two servers

You may need to do some investigative forensics to determine your next step. That is, really figure out what the bottleneck is. Regrettably, this can be a reactive plan of attack rather than a proactive one. So, while preparing to scale out your site, invest some time in some server monitoring infrastructure. You can also do some load testing using tools such as Apache Benchmark to see how your current infrastructure performs and make some educated guesses on where the problems might develop.

Generally, the next step in scaling is to load-balance your front-end web servers, as shown in Figure 15-7. In this scenario, you deploy two web servers with identical copies of the WordPress installation and use a single database server to store all the data.

There are a couple of challenges with this approach. First, you need a load-balancing mechanism. This can be a hardware appliance or a software solution. There are many different load-balancing mechanisms to choose from, and your infrastructure will dictate which you

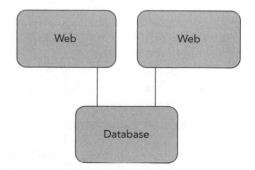

FIGURE 15-7: WordPress with load-balanced web servers

choose. You may be deploying into an enterprise network, which typically will have well-established network infrastructure for virtual IP and load-balancing, and any horizontal scaling topology should fit into that IT approved plan.

The second challenge is that you will need to synchronize your `wp-content/uploads` folder. That is, if a content creator uploads media onto one server, because the front ends are load-balanced, the next request could pull from the other server where the file does not exist. You have the option of moving the uploads folder to a common location, perhaps on the shared database server, or you can set up a scheduled task to copy the files across. The rsync (`http://rsync.samba.org/`) utility is a good solution for this type of synchronization. You will have to accept that the files will not be there until after the copy has occurred. This means that there can be a lag between when new content is published and when it is available on both nodes of the web front-end. Some of this lag can be mitigated through a front-end caching mechanism such as the Super Cache plugin, which will be discussed later in this chapter.

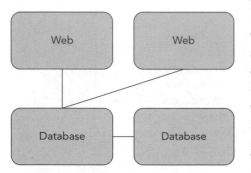

FIGURE 15-8: WordPress with a hot spare database server

The next scenario for scaling means adding a second database server and implementing MySQL replication. You continue to keep the load-balanced web servers, but now you have two database servers, as shown in Figure 15-8.

Technically, this does not offer better performance, but it does offer the ability to failover should the database server have a problem. This standby database server is called a *hot spare*. That means it is on and up-to-date, but not in current use. Part of scalability is availability. Now, you have two web servers and two database servers, which means you can remove one server from each tier and still have a functioning site.

Putting that second database into active work on the website is the next layer up. You still have load-balanced web servers, but now you can distribute the load on the database servers using MySQL replication, as shown in Figure 15-9. In this situation, you want the writes to the database to be written to the master MySQL database, and all the reads to come from the slave MySQL database. This solves the MyISAM challenge, where the storage engine excels at reading or writing but not both.

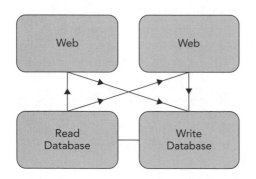

FIGURE 15-9: WordPress with load-balanced web and database servers

Finally, another WordPress-specific option to consider is HyperDB (`http://codex.wordpress.org/HyperDB`). HyperDB was designed by Automattic and is a drop-in replacement for the standard WordPress database access layer. It is, however, more powerful than the standard access objects because it can support sharding, or partitioning of the WordPress database information across multiple databases. This can permit you to move the highly dynamic data to a more robust server, while the content that is less in flux can be used on a database server with more aggressive caching. HyperDB also supports replication and failover functionality. However, the documentation is sparse, so implementing this solution is not for the faint of heart.

In the real world, this is how we run some high-traffic, higher-profile sites for our clients. We combine load-balanced web front-ends with caching plugins, each of which reads the content from its own individual slave database server. All writes to the database are written to the master database server and replicated to the slaves. All uploaded content is duplicated to the other web front-ends through an rsync-like process.

STATISTICS COUNTERS

Viewing traffic statistics allows you to see which content on your site is actually bringing visitors in. This shows you what content is working and what is not. In addition, traffic statistics can show you valuable information about your visitors and their hardware and software setups. This information enables you to tailor your site to accentuate the positive and support your visitors' browsers to create a more pleasant and meaningful experience.

Statistics packages employ a couple of different methods for gathering data, and each has its own advantages and disadvantages. Likewise, each vendor puts its own spin on the traffic statistics.

You can gather traffic statistics in a couple of ways. The grandfather in this realm is to parse your log files. Your web server, if configured properly, will create log files for each and every request and error that it handles. Certain statistics packages can parse these logs and create human-consumable information. Some packages even let you download these logs to your local machine and let it do the busy work offline.

The second method is to put a snippet, nearly always JavaScript, on each page of your site that reports back to a central server, which then accumulates the data and makes it meaningful to you. This method is the current trend.

Each of these packages has an available WordPress plugin. Each package also varies in its specific vernacular. You will have to determine what the truly meaningful metrics are from each package; for example: visitors versus unique visitors, and hits versus page views versus unique page views. Deriving useful real-world information from statistics depends on your goals. If you want more viewers and are trying to attract attention from Google searches, social network recommendations, and other external aggregators, you may be happy with an increasing number of visitors who look at only one page or spend under a minute per visit on your site. A site that aims for more discussion and community feel should have more return visitors, a longer interval between visitor entry and exit, and multiple pages viewed by each visitor.

AWStats

AWStats is the granddaddy of web traffic statistics. Actually, there was a package that predated this but had many security problems, and AWStats took over as the main statistics package.

AWStats is of the log parsing variety of statistics counters. It can be run on the server, or you can download the log files to another machine and run it if you do not have access or permission to change the configuration of the server running your WordPress site. AWStats requires Perl to run, and it has been used successfully on both Apache and Microsoft IIS servers, although it requires a little configuration of the log file formats for IIS. To install and get AWStats up and running automatically for your site, you will need to be familiar with server administration tasks. As a log parsing package, AWStats is designed to run automatically in the background via a `cron` job on Unix systems.

Because AWStats is a server-side log parsing package, it easily tracks the actual request information of your website. You can extend the information gathered by adding in the special JavaScript tag for AWStats to catch browser-side information such as screen size and browser plugin support for various technologies.

One good thing about AWStats is that it is one of the original open source log parser statistics packages. It has survived so long because it is reliable and free and relatively easy to get going. This also includes many contributed scripts and tidbits of help and support from various sources around the web. Numerous hosts rely on AWStats, and like any good open source software package, there is a robust support community around it.

What is not so good about AWStats is that it sometimes loses track of dates, mainly because of an unintentional system admin error. In order to provide certain historical information and to process logs quicker, AWStats maintains cache files. If dates get out of order or other time problems exist, these cache files trump any new logs to be parsed and can provide inconsistent data. Basically, you have to go back and rebuild all the cache files. Fortunately, with some searching you can find some scripts to assist in this. Another complaint with AWStats is that the browser agents were not updated for a long time, but this does not appear to be the case anymore.

AWStats is a tried and true option and is good for those sites that want to remain self-contained. AWStats works in conjunction with your web server application, so WordPress integration is not part of the package or necessary. If you do not want to include statistics tracking JavaScript calls that make references to other sites, for performance or JavaScript avoidance reasons, AWStats is a venerable alternative.

You can find more information online at `http://awstats.sourceforge.net/`.

Google Analytics

Google Analytics is currently the big dog in hosted web traffic statistics. It has a clean and generally intuitive user interface for seeing the reported statistics. It works by injecting a special JavaScript tag into your rendered page, which reports traffic and browser information to Google for parsing.

And therein lies the rub with this free statistics package. You are reporting all of your traffic information to Google. Many people use Google for nearly everything these days—e-mail, calendar, and web traffic statistics included—although some distrust giving all this information to what could become Big Brother. While people have some trust in Google, in reality, the company could use the information they get for any number of purposes. Just think of the wealth of information Google has at its fingertips related to browser and OS share, and then combine this with the AdSense and keyword information from your site. Today, Google allows you to track campaigns and site "reach" by cross-referencing AdWords and AdSense traffic with Google Analytics data. The amount of data related to website use and marketing trends is staggering. The trade-off of data access is a business decision you will have to make.

Google Analytics is definitely marketing-oriented. Many powerful tools are built in and learning how to use them will greatly benefit the quality of the reported data, including advanced segmentation of your traffic and custom reporting data.

Many WordPress plugins are available for Google Analytics, which anecdotally serves as a barometer for the popularity of this service. Each offers slightly different functionality, but all essentially do the same thing, which is to inject the appropriate JavaScript into the page. Some offer additional features to track the extra events via the control panel. You can find more information online at http://google.com/analytics/.

For all practical purposes, Google Analytics is the *de facto* standard in web traffic statistics. Nearly every site uses it to some extent. But there are alternatives if you do not want to put all your eggs in Google's basket. Check out StatCounter (http://statcounter.com/) and Mint (http://haveamint.com/) for other options. Mint is essentially a self-hosted Google Analytics–like system. There are also emergent players such as Woopra (http://woopra.com/), which includes real-time visitor information, that are popping up from time to time.

JetPack by WordPress.com

We would be remiss if we did not mention JetPack by WordPress.com. This is actually a super plugin that bundles several of the WordPress.com hosting features into a single plugin for use on self-hosted WordPress sites. This plugin has many features, including social media integrations, photo gallery enhancements and, obviously, because you are in the traffic statistics section, it has this functionality, too.

JetPack works the same as Google Analytics—by injecting some JavaScript into your rendered HTML template and reporting back to the WordPress.com servers for tracking. JetPack is built by WordPress developers for WordPress so it has some specificity about the way the statistics are presented with regard to posts and pages.

In addition, JetPack stats are presented right in the WordPress dashboard. Although there are plugins to make other statistics packages do this through iFrames, the in-Dashboard view is the default method for JetPack. Basically, JetPack was designed from the ground up to be included in the Dashboard. For some end users, it is nice to have everything to manage the site contained in the Dashboard.

Also, for quick reference, JetPack can enable a quick view of the last 48 hours in the admin toolbar at the top of the screen. You can find more information online at http://jetpack.me/.

If the statistics are giving you good news—your site is gaining in popularity, readers are actively participating in discussions, and search engines are sending new users your way—you will likely want to turn your attention to site scalability. Now you will look at ways to improve the overall performance of the WordPress system components.

CACHE MANAGEMENT

WordPress is a content management system, which by its very definition means it creates a dynamically driven site. In today's technology environment, that essentially translates into managed content and all of its metadata is stored in a database. Every page request has to access the database to determine which content is to be displayed, versus, with a static site, simply fetching HTML files from the web server's local directory. The trade-off in handing over content storage to a database is that you are going to take a speed hit in the individual page access in exchange for more powerful persistence, selection, and organization tools—those features used within the WordPress core. Basic computer science comes into play here: When you introduce a new abstraction layer that is slower than the layer above it, you typically introduce a caching mechanism as well to improve average access times.

It helps to think of caching in a sequence of access methods, starting closest to the user and working back to the MySQL database. Each point in the sequence has some caching and tuning that can be done; however, like all performance tuning work, your mileage varies depending upon the access patterns, content types, and actual workload moving through that point in the system. Here is one view of the WordPress caching hierarchy that the following sections walk you through:

➤ **Browser**—Most of your end users' browser performance is going to come from optimized CSS, graphics, and JavaScript libraries. Because these affect the single-page load times, we covered them in Chapter 12's exploration of user experience.

➤ **Web Server**—WordPress and its plugins are largely written in PHP, an interpreted language that relies on the web server for an execution container. Improving the web server's PHP caching will speed up some portions of the WordPress user-to-database path.

➤ **WordPress Core**—Caching objects used by WordPress effectively build a database results cache, the same approach taken by highly scalable, MySQL-based sites such as Facebook. Changing some dynamic page generation to static HTML rendering speeds up page access at the expense of possible small windows of update inconsistency. In addition, you can use transients to cache external or complex data for quick retrieval.

➤ **MySQL**—Caching objects at the database layer prevents an eventual disk access, turning a query into a memory reference where possible. These options are independent of, and frequently complementary to, enabling a caching plugin within the WordPress core.

Again, the actual benefit provided by each or any of these approaches depends on many factors, including your hosting provider's database layer; whether you can configure web and database servers yourself; the size, frequency, and complexity of database queries; and the overall load on your WordPress installation.

WordPress System Complexity

First and foremost, WordPress is a complex system, and honorably so. WordPress simplifies the process of content management and broadens its core feature set through the plugin system. But providing these various hooks and flexibility comes at the cost of database accesses, PHP processing, handling each plugin's unique requirements, and any special theme prerequisites. Each plugin adds additional overhead to the page rendering, and the quality of code in plugins varies from author to author. Using an execution path analyzer such as WebGrind or KCacheGrind, which profiles your application to determine where bottlenecks in the code may occur, you can create a graphic representation of the complexity of a web application. Take, for instance, a plain vanilla WordPress installation using the default theme. Running a simple page load through this profiler and viewing the resulting execution graph, you will find more than 963 different functions called to render the index page, as shown in Figure 15-10.

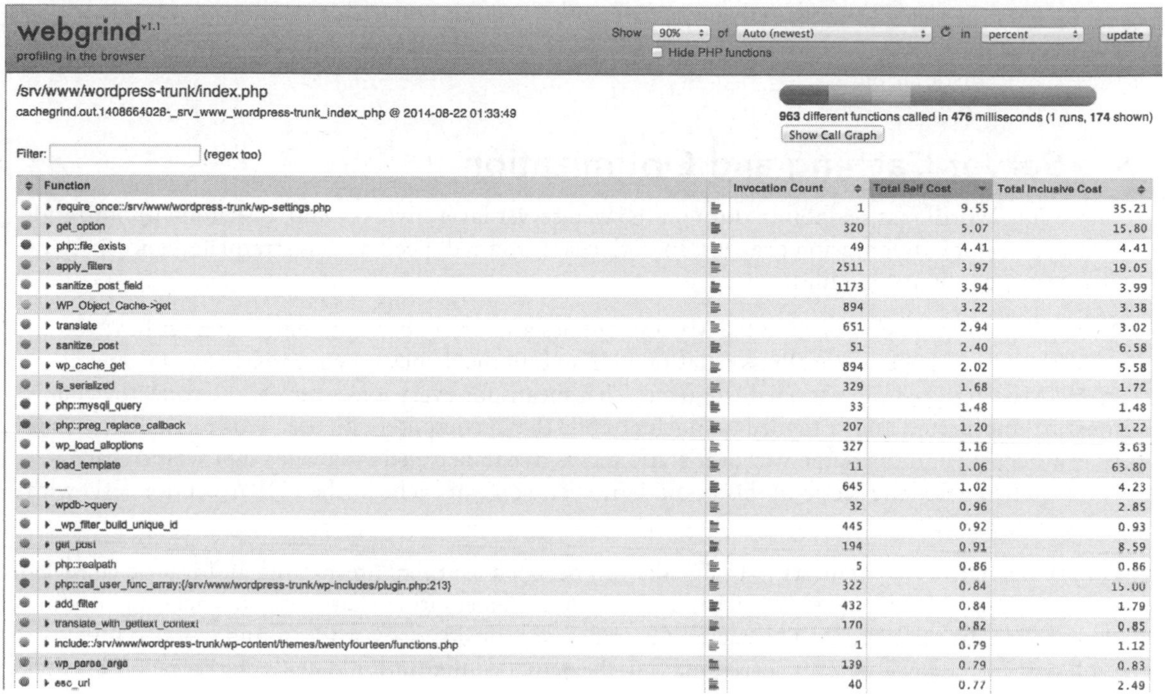
webgrind v1.1
profiling in the browser
Show 90% of Auto (newest) in percent update
Hide PHP functions
/srv/www/wordpress-trunk/index.php
cachegrind.out.1408664028-_srv_www_wordpress-trunk_index_php @ 2014-08-22 01:33:49
963 different functions called in 476 milliseconds (1 runs, 174 shown)
Show Call Graph
Filter: (regex too)

Function	Invocation Count	Total Self Cost	Total Inclusive Cost
require_once::/srv/www/wordpress-trunk/wp-settings.php	1	9.55	35.21
get_option	320	5.07	15.80
php::file_exists	49	4.41	4.41
apply_filters	2511	3.97	19.05
sanitize_post_field	1173	3.94	3.99
WP_Object_Cache->get	894	3.22	3.38
translate	651	2.94	3.02
sanitize_post	51	2.40	6.58
wp_cache_get	894	2.02	5.58
is_serialized	329	1.68	1.72
php::mysql_query	33	1.48	1.48
php::preg_replace_callback	207	1.20	1.22
wp_load_alloptions	327	1.16	3.63
load_template	11	1.06	63.80
__	645	1.02	4.23
wpdb->query	32	0.96	2.85
_wp_filter_build_unique_id	445	0.92	0.93
get_post	194	0.91	8.59
php::realpath	5	0.86	0.86
php::call_user_func_array::{/srv/www/wordpress-trunk/wp-includes/plugin.php:213}	322	0.84	15.00
add_filter	432	0.84	1.79
translate_with_gettext_context	170	0.82	0.85
include::/srv/www/wordpress-trunk/wp-content/themes/twentyfourteen/functions.php	1	0.79	1.12
wp_parse_args	139	0.79	0.83
esc_url	40	0.77	2.49

FIGURE 15-10: WebGrind visualization of WordPress complexity

Even without being able to zoom in and see the details, you can perceive the inherent complexity of WordPress. Each of those functions or actions is the WordPress core gathering the necessary data for your site, including action hooks for linking in plugin and theme functionality.

Each and every thing you add to your site, including that fancy theme control panel that lets you set particular runtime rendering characteristics of your site and plugins that parse your content for related posts, creates overhead and more boxes on the execution graph.

There is no need to be alarmist here and disable plugins and choose overly simple themes. This challenge is not unique to WordPress. The flexibility enabled through WordPress, especially the configurable runtime flexibility of WordPress, which is so powerful, is an expensive operation. The alternative is a statically fixed set of features that require new built-in code to accomplish new features, rather than the versatile plugin architecture of WordPress. Each of those plugins and theme hooks adds functionality and features to your WordPress installation. That is why you enabled them in the first place. Just accept that there are tradeoffs in features versus performance, some negligible and some larger.

In practice, your site does not really change that often. You are probably not running the next Twitter through a WordPress installation (although you can build a reasonable facsimile with the p2 theme) and the content does not change every 30 seconds. Leveraging the ideal situation in which your content is viewed significantly more frequently than it is updated, and allowing for minor windows of inconsistent updates, you will now look at caching layers from the web server back to the MySQL installation.

Web Server Caching and Optimization

Improving WordPress scalability through the web server layer involves PHP execution optimization and web server configuration changes. In both cases, you will need administrator-level access to the web server configuration files.

You will work your way back to the MySQL queries and object caching, but no matter how you end up with a list of pages, WordPress relies on PHP to pull the displayed page together and generate its HTML. PHP is an interpreted language. That means for every execution of the code, the code must be interpreted and compiled to machine code that a computer can use. This methodology has pros and cons, and the flame war over static versus dynamic typed languages that would ensue is completely outside the scope of this book. However, you can cache at the PHP execution level with an *opcode cache*.

A PHP opcode cache attempts to bridge the gap between runtime interpreting and full-on compiled code. APC (or Alternative PHP Cache) is one such implementation that works to cache and optimize the intermediate PHP code. This method is completely outside of WordPress and works on the underlying PHP layer of your server, making the actual configuration outside the scope of this book.

To get APC set up, you will need full access permissions on your server. Once APC is set up, it caches the compiled PHP files that make up the WordPress core. The biggest downside is that you have to restart the server every time you change a PHP page. If you are making theme changes, this means a restart each time you modify a template file. You can find more information about APC at `http://us3.php.net/manual/en/book.apc.php`. Again, the ability to enable APC and start/stop the web server depends on whether you have sufficient administrator privileges.

Caching can be further augmented by using `memcache` and `memcached`, both of which also require server administration level of implementation. `memcache` uses your server's RAM to cache frequently used objects. RAM is significantly faster than file-based operations, and because `memcached` runs as a local daemon, it is also completely outside of your web server. You can find more information about `memcache` at `http://us3.php.net/manual/en/book.memcache.php` and `http://memcached.org/`. The key benefit provided by these in-memory systems is to add another layer of caching between WordPress and the MySQL database. As discussed in Chapter 6, WordPress caches the last results retrieved via SQL queries on its MySQL database, but if your site is consistently loading and then flushing the cache as users navigate between several popular sections of the site, this additional layer of caching will improve performance by keeping the result sets of several recent queries in memory. What is happening under the hood is that the WordPress object cache is mapped to objects managed by `memcached`, allowing repeat queries to be satisfied out of the cache rather than through another SQL query to the database. This level of caching is the PHP code level caching, which allows the PHP runtime to short-circuit previously cached information. As you will see, there are many locations in the execution pipeline where caching can be enabled.

While you are considering the PHP level of the WordPress stack, you should also optimize (and secure) your `php.ini` configuration. PHP has prospered by having so much built-in functionality that it lowers the barriers of entry and empowers developers to just get the task done. This has been the boon and the bane for PHP. Take a look at your php.ini file and disable extensions you are not using. You can always turn them back on if you need them in the future. Also take this opportunity to secure your PHP execution container and help it run faster.

Finally, on the system administration level, optimize your web server. In most cases, the stock configuration for your web server is designed to handle the most common basic use cases. Certainly, it has not been tweaked to match your specific server's capabilities. Apache, for example, comes with tons of extra modules to handle general-case situations. If you do not use those modules, disable them. This will reduce the overall memory footprint of Apache.

In practice, it has been possible to tweak Apache to perform better under restricted resources (such as low-memory virtual private servers) by adjusting the Apache PreFork configuration. The default configuration is pretty generous, and depending on your site's traffic and system configuration, you can usually pare this down. For example, on a low-traffic site hosted on a low-memory shared server, you could edit your Apache2 configuration file to the following, assuming you are using Apache2:

```
<IfModule mpm_prefork_module>
    StartServers          3
    MinSpareServers       3
    MaxSpareServers       3
    ServerLimit          50
    MaxClients           50
    MaxRequestsPerChild 1000
</IfModule>
```

These settings are for a relatively low-traffic site on a low-memory server. Your results will vary, but these changes anecdotally affected the web server's response time for our WordPress installation. Of course, you will have to adjust these settings to meet your own requirements.

Realize that the LAMP stack has become so popular because often it just works when you install it. That is because the default configurations are general-purpose setups designed to work across a broad spectrum of situations. You will need to adjust the configurations to optimize to your specific situation when the time comes.

Tuning the individual components of the LAMP stack warrants a book unto itself. Like WordPress, the LAMP development stack is very popular because of its flexibility and capability to handle a multitude of different tasks. The management and administration of LAMP components are required skills for the full stack solution developer. Invest some time learning your tools and how to deploy them effectively.

WordPress Object Caching

The goal of web server caching is to keep frequently accessed files and popular chunks of code in memory and ready to serve or execute. Within WordPress, caching has to deliver a request for a page without going through additional code or database accesses, which really boils down to short-circuiting the PHP WordPress core and serving up a static representation of your page or parts of your page directly.

Object caching keeps certain frequently used and expensive data sets in memory. This is very similar to the transient cache discussed next, but while transients are set by you, the developer, object cache is set by the WordPress core. The flexibility of object caching means that when certain information does change, that does not affect the entire cache, but only the objects in the cache that actually changed. However, object caching still requires the plugin to execute PHP to determine which aspects of the cache are still valid and also for WordPress to execute the PHP to pull the parts of the page together for rendering. As previously discussed, optimizing your web server's PHP environment and enabling WordPress level object caching are quasi-independent as a consequence.

There may be times when your content is static enough, or being served so frequently, that you need to short-circuit the whole PHP and object cache overhead—for example, when your page is being listed in the top echelons of Reddit and Slashdot. A good way to do this is to have your page rendered to static HTML and served directly by the web server. After all, this is what the web server was designed to do in the first place.

In our opinion, the best plugin for this is WP-Super Cache by Donncha Ó Caoimh. WP-Super Cache is based on and an improvement of the WP-Cache plugin. (See, this one is SUPER!) WP-Super Cache functions in various modes, including writing out static HTML files. However, it does require mod _ rewrite for the static HTML files, so this plugin will only work on Apache servers.

WP-Super Cache has an extensive control panel that allows the site administrator to adjust the settings to meet specific needs. It even includes a full lockdown mode that prepares for a heavy traffic spike.

Other caching plugins such as W3 Total Cache are also viable options. Many caching plugins build on the basic theme of generating HTML for a page and caching it with the URL used to access the page as a key. Each plugin will have variations on cache invalidation and page lifetime policies, and all of them disrupt the general dynamic nature of WordPress page generation, intentionally. If you are going to change your theme, add new plugins, or otherwise alter the flow of data from MySQL to the user's browser, either disable WordPress caching until you are sure all of your changes work, or frequently invalidate and flush the cache so that you can see the freshly generated pages as you test.

Transient Caches

Transient caches are developer-defined caches that you set up in your code. Transients are very similar to the WordPress Options feature discussed with plugins in Chapter 8. The major difference is that transients include an expiration time. By their very nature, they are available only for a defined period of time—you can think of this as though they are self-refreshing or self-updating. This makes them ideal for caching "expensive" data for a defined period of time.

What is expensive? Expensive data is data that takes longer to retrieve or calculate. In the upcoming example, you will look at how accessing a third-party API could be considered expensive, depending on network latency; most importantly, you do not want your site rendering to have to wait for a third-party access. However, it could also be a computationally intense query or calculation—for example, generating a complex menu for your site, or a query that spans a whole network of sites on MultiSite. What you are doing here is caching some data for quick retrieval, which is to say, having the information at WordPress's fingertips.

What is a defined period of time? Here is the rub: You have to balance having data readily available but without it becoming stale. This is always the trade-off with any level of caching. In the real world, you may never know how often the data gets updated or needs to be refreshed. As you have seen, to further complicate this, there could be many levels of caching on your WordPress site.

The source of your data might have caching or be delayed in presenting the internal information to the API for you to consume. Your transient data has a caching expiration on it, and your WordPress HTML rendering might have a caching mechanism. Your visitor has browser caching and possibly even network-level proxy caching. This means that there are many factors that could affect the pipeline of getting data from an offsite source to your visitor's browser. This can be a big, and sometimes frustrating, factor when developing and testing your integration but it also affects the time period you select for storing your transient data.

So what is the defined period of time? It depends. It depends on your data, your tolerance for stale data or requirements for up-to-date information, and the load on your site. As the developer, you have to set the expiration time to balance expectations of current data while reducing the access load. Your goal is to find the longest time period during which old or stale data will not produce an adverse user experience. To borrow from the world of non-SQL databases, you need to determine how you will make the data eventually consistent without introducing errors in user action due to inconsistent, cached data.

Here is an example using transients to locally cache some piece of information. In this case, you are going to access a third-party website that gives you a designated color of the week. In your `functions.php` file, you will modify the function to include the transient storage. The first thing to do is check if you already have any existing, non-expired data. If your transient data does not exist, or is expired, the `get_transient()` function will return `false`.

```
if (($color = get_transient('color_of_the_week')) === false) {
```

If this check returns `false`, that means you need to access the API and get new data. Again, this caching is separate from any HTML- or PHP-level caching your site is performing. This check is directly related to this specific piece of information. The following is the same code that accesses a third-party website to retrieve the color of the week:

```
$feed = file_get_contents('whatever URL');
if ($feed) {
  $xml = simplexml_object($feed);
  $color = $xml->color;
```

Now that you have the updated data, you need to store it in the transient and set the expiration time. This essentially works the same as the WordPress options API with the added expiration parameter.

```
set_transient('color_of_the_week', $color, 60*60*24*7);
```

For readability, you are presenting the expiration time as a calculation. WordPress expects this parameter in seconds. In this example, we want to hold this data for one week, so the calculation is 60 seconds × 60 minutes × 24 hours × 7 days giving us a week's worth of seconds. You could also push 604,800 as the second parameter, but often it is easier to read the intent of the time with the calculation.

If you put this all together, the new function with transient caching might look like this:

```php
function get_color_of_the_week() {
  if (($color = get_transient('color_of_the_week')) === false) {
    $feed = file_get_contents('whatever URL');
    if ($feed) {
      $xml = simplexml_object($feed);
      $color = $xml->color;
    } else {
      $color= "white ";
    }
    set_transient('color_of_the_week', $color, 60*60*24*7);
  }
  echo $color;
}
```

Finally, to use this color in your HTML, you will need to inject its use into your WordPress template files. All of the new caching magic is encapsulated in the function from the previous code snippet. Your `header.php` template changes could look like this:

```php
<body <?php body_class(); ?> style= "background-color: <?php echo
get_color_of_the_week();?> " >
```

As you can see, by adding a few simple lines of code to your custom feature, you have added caching functionality to reduce load time on your site, removed reliance on a third-party connection (during the caching period), and decreased the access load on that third-party server. It is a pretty simple process and can drastically affect your site performance for data that does not have to be immediately current.

Another use for transient caches is to store complex computed data. For example, you might have a function in your `functions.php` template that does a complicated query across your entire WordPress Multisite network to generate a network-wide navigational aid. This data likely does not change very often, but the computation of the query is significant enough that it may slow down page rendering.

You can perform the complicated query and store it in a transient cache so the next visitor does not have to wait for the SQL query to execute. Using a transient in this way improves site performance by reducing the queries to the database.

MySQL Query Cache

While conducting research for this book, we set up a stock WordPress installation using the TwentyFourteen theme and no additional plugins—essentially an out-of-the-box installation. To render the index page, WordPress used more than 31 MySQL queries. Try it yourself by adding these two PHP lines to your `footer.php` template file:

```php
<?php echo get_num_queries(); ?> queries.
<?php timer_stop(1); ?> seconds.
```

Reload your page and you will see the number of queries and the time it took at the bottom of your page (see Figure 15-11).

Proudly powered by WordPress

31 queries. 0.385 seconds.

FIGURE 15-11: Number of queries on initial page load of TwentyFourteen

You have to evaluate your site, but odds are the database-persisted content is not changing quickly enough that you need to make all these database calls for every page load. The translation of a URL into a MySQL query was covered in Chapter 5, and Chapter 6 looked at the underlying data models, so the volume of database traffic required for the basic index page should not be too surprising.

WordPress caching improves access times to content extracted from MySQL. If you want to further improve MySQL performance and make it more responsive to queries from the WordPress core, you will want to explore the MySQL query cache. The MySQL query cache stores the results of `select` statements so that if an identical query is submitted, the already retrieved results can be immediately pulled from the system RAM and returned. This will significantly increase your response time, as long as your data is not changing that much; under higher rates of change you may not see the updates immediately.

To enable the MySQL query cache, you will have to edit your MySQL configuration file on the server, assuming you have adequate permissions at your hosting company to do so. If you edit your MySQL configuration file, you can raise the memory limit. For example:

```
# enable 16 MB cache
query_cache_size   = 16M
```

Be careful not to go overboard here. Allocating too much RAM to MySQL caching will adversely affect other subsystems on your server. It is always a balance. Even just enabling this cache creates a management overhead in MySQL, but generally speaking, this trade-off works in your favor.

LOAD BALANCING YOUR WORDPRESS SITE

At some point, you (let's hope) hit the performance limit of a single software stack on one physical server. That is when you may want to load balance your WordPress site with one or more additional servers. As we discussed earlier in this chapter, you may decide to add servers either for scalability to handle more requests, or as a failover precaution to increase the availability of your site. Whatever the reason, load balancing your site gets you both of these features, but it is a complex issue. Now you will briefly consider some of the challenges you will encounter when attempting to load balance a dynamically generated site in the real world.

First and foremost, you need a means to load balance. The simple approach of using round-robin DNS to bounce successive HTTP requests between your servers as needed will cause problems, especially with session cookies. You will need a legitimate load balancer to handle this. The load balancer could be a software package such as Pound (http://www.apsis.ch/pound/) or a full hardware solution such as an F5 BIG-IP (http://www.f5.com/products/big-ip/). Both will handle the session stickiness and load balancing for you.

The second challenge is keeping your dynamic data in synchronization between your two (or more) web front-ends. Consider that your site administrator could effectively log in to either web front-end, post new content, and upload a graphic asset to the uploads directory. However, the next request could be load balanced to the other server, where this content may not exist.

Look at the uploads directory first. This content is uploaded from the WordPress Dashboard to the uploads directory of that WordPress installation. By default, content is uploaded into /wp-content/uploads/. However, you can change the uploads directory by editing your wp-config.php and defining a new location. Depending on where you set your uploads folder, you could also reap the benefit of having shorter asset URLs.

As we touched on earlier in this chapter, at this point you have options. One option is to have a shared folder that both web servers can access. Most likely this would be an NFS/Samba share on a third server, which could also serve as your MySQL server. A second option is to use rsync or a similar tool to coordinate uploads between the two servers and make sure each has the same assets in place. Using the shared folder makes the assets immediately available but introduces a single point of failure. Alternately, rsync'ing the assets to multiple locations replicates the data, removing a single point of failure, but introduces a time delay on when the asset is available at the remote locations. Pick your poison depending on your needs.

The second challenge is your dynamic data that is stored in the database. Assuming your database is not the bottleneck and the reason for load balancing, you could use a third server as your database server. Both web servers can then read and write from the same source. This can be a more secure deployment architecture when your database server is not directly addressable on the public Internet, but it also creates a potential single point of failure. Technically, you are only load balancing the front-end web servers in this situation.

Adding a second database server increases the redundancy but introduces the problem of keeping two MySQL database tables in synchronization. MySQL servers can be configured for replication in a master-slave setup. Technically, this again is not load balancing because only one server is being accessed at a time, but this type of configuration does provide additional redundancy. Changes to the master MySQL database are replicated to the slave database in near real time via a journaling log. Should the master database fail, the slave has a full set of data for a manual cut over.

Finally, there is also a special WordPress-specific solution for multiple database servers. HyperDB (http://codex.wordpress.org/HyperDB) was created by Automattic to handle the requirements of WordPress.com traffic. HyberDB is a full replacement for the built-in WordPress database access layer and includes functionality for using multiple databases, sharding or partitioning your database across multiple servers, and also replication and tiered failover. Unfortunately, the documentation is far from complete.

As you can see, load balancing for performance and high availability is an extremely complex topic. There are countless variations of systems in place to handle a vast expanse of needs and requirements. This short overview of the topic certainly skirts over many nuances and challenges being faced when deploying WordPress into a high-availability environment. Cloud computing and content delivery networks continue to be hot topics right now, and you should expect to see WordPress utilizing these services for critical aspects and redundancy as those technologies and services mature.

DEALING WITH SPAM

Spamming, unfortunately, is a fact of life. As your WordPress site gets noticed and generates traffic, it becomes a natural target for spammers. Most likely, your posts will accrete a variety of spam comments as a side effect of being popular.

You can recognize spam by a list of links within the comment, or content-free comments saying that the poster enjoyed your writing, with an attached URL or source address that invites you to a less-than-reputable destination. In either case, the goal of comment spam is to generate more web content that points back to the spammer's site, taking advantage of the page popularity ranking algorithms used by Google and others that give weight to incoming links. The best way to deal with spam is to simply get rid of it, denying spammers the opportunity to use your site to boost their own visibility.

There are three basic approaches to dealing with the problem: Make it impossible for anyone to leave comments, increase the difficulty of a spammer sneaking a comment onto your site, and enable auto-detection of common spam patterns. Obviously, disabling comments (through the Dashboard) is a bit harsh and defeats the goals of establishing conversation with your readers. On the other hand, if you decide to take this drastic step, remember that changing the settings for posts on the control panel affects future posts only; anything already on your blog will still have comments enabled unless you go through the Dashboard and turn them off individually. If you do not mind an even greater bit of brute-force effort, you can remove the wp-comments.php file from the WordPress core, which somewhat unceremoniously puts an end to the ability to comment on your posts. We recommend something a bit more subtle.

Comment Moderation and CAPTCHAs

One approach to comment spam is to slow down the spammers; this simple approach, however, slows down valid commenters as well. You can require commenters to register as site users before being allowed to post comments, but that has the downside of preventing passing-by users from adding their thoughts. It also requires that you stay on top of the user registration, as you may see seemingly valid users that are created purely for the purpose of posting spam to your site.

Moderation is another tool in the slow-but-don't-stop vein; you can hold all comments for moderation or require all commenters to have a previously approved comment. In effect, you are putting the burden of spam detection on yourself, looking at each comment as it appears and deciding whether to post it to your site or flush it. Again, an innocuous looking comment may be the approval stepping stone for an avalanche of spam later on from the same user. As with many security mechanisms, the bad guys are continually getting smarter and more automated, and testing the edge protection and response of the systems they want to infiltrate.

A variation of the brute-force and moderation method is to blacklist IP addresses that seem to be the primary sources of spam; the access controls can be put in your `.htaccess` file. Again, this is perhaps a bit like hunting bugs with an elephant gun, as you are likely to block valid IP sources from common carriers who are unfortunately home to some low-limit spammers. Also, spammers jump IP addresses easily using botnets and other resources, so this can be a never-ending war that you cannot keep up with.

Enter CAPTCHA methods—based on a phrase coined at Carnegie Mellon University that ostensibly stands for "Completely Automated Public Turing test for telling Computers and Humans Apart"— which impede spammers' ability to post unwelcome comments by requiring them to enter some additional, dynamic piece of information. There are quite a few CAPTCHA-generating plugins for WordPress, all of which add a displayed word or math problem to the end of the comment posting form, requiring the user to enter the correct information before the form is submitted. The simplest of these displays a two-term addition problem that must be solved by the user. The basic idea is that an automated spamming process will not be able to recognize the distorted words or solve the problems, alleviating the spam at the point of insertion. There is some debate as to the effectiveness of CAPTCHAs, with their failure rates suggested to be as high as 20 percent. You are also adding a step for commenters, albeit a trivial one. If your site attracts a large, non-English speaking audience, CAPTCHAs that depend on wavy English words will be effective, but only in preventing valid comments from frustrated users.

The WP–SpamFree plugin is an inverse CAPTCHA; it tries to ensure that the commenter is using a browser, and not coming in via an automated process. This combination of JavaScript tricks is a variation on the spam impedance theme, and like the others, its effectiveness and user impact will vary depending upon the demographics of your site viewers.

Automating Spam Detection

The first step in automating spam detection is blacklisting certain types of posts or particular words. In the Dashboard, choose Settings ➤ Discussion. In the Comment Moderation box, you will find an option to block any comment that contains more than a particular number of links. Do not set this to zero, or anyone who includes his own site URL in a comment is going to be filtered. This cuts down on the obvious spam messages, however. Similarly, adding words to the blacklist like "Vicodin" will eliminate the faux-pharmacy spam, but if you are perturbed by offers of fake Rolexes, do not add "watches" to the blacklist or you will drop any comment that uses "watches" as a verb as well as a fake product noun. Word blacklists are universally effective in blocking comments with those words, irrespective of context.

Fortunately, WordPress has the Akismet plugin built in for dealing with comment spam, which relies on a crowd-sourced blacklist and is transparent to users. Go to `http://akismet.com/` to register for an API key for the service; when you open up the Dashboard and configure the Akismet plugin, you will need this to make sure your instance of WordPress can connect to the Akismet service. Effectively, Akismet takes each comment as posted, runs it through a database of spam comments hosted by Automattic, and decides whether or not to mark the comment as spam. Statistics on the `akismet.com` site claim that upwards of 80 percent of all comments are spam, and that they have caught and marked more than 150 trillion spam comments.

There are other implementations of the Akismet service besides the built-in plugin, and Akismet works on other content management systems as well. Akismet is priced based on the size and type of your site, ranging from free to $50 per month. While the freely available nature of WordPress and most of its related plugins and themes has been highlighted, paying for Akismet spam protection is also highly recommended. Compared to the cost of a commercial WordPress hosting option, most low-end Akismet plans are minimal in cost. You remove a time-consuming administrative burden from your plate for a few dollars a month.

OTHER CONTENT MANAGEMENT SYSTEMS

You have seen how WordPress is so much more than a blogging platform. It can be used for a wide range of different types of websites, but aside from what a plugin can offer—which can be substantial—the functionality of the WordPress Core is what it is. Sometimes you want to complement your website with additional functionality found in other traditional web-based applications, such as forums like bbPress, social network features like BuddyPress, e-commerce applications, or other CMS solutions.

Given the range of content management systems available, and the fact that most enterprises already have one, if not several, content repositories up and running, it is often useful to integrate WordPress with another CMS. This section takes a brief look at when you should use WordPress as an external content consumer or producer and when you should not use WordPress as the core of a content management system solution.

WordPress Integration

Integrating an application like WordPress with another content-oriented application requires that you align user management, content packaging and, potentially, look-and-feel issues. It is not something easily accomplished with a plugin or theme extension, and typically requires custom bridge code. You will find building blocks in the plugin directory; this section presents a rough outline of the problems to be solved.

How does the external system provide content? Are you getting an RSS feed, in which case you can use an RSS as a starting point, or do you get raw JSON that requires editing and parsing before being turned into a post?

If you have a remote resource URL, can you embed it using an oEmbed (`http://oembed.com`) provider plugin? oEmbed takes a URL and returns a variety of content types that can be integrated into WordPress themes, allowing them to be displayed without WordPress having to parse the content type. WordPress does include several oEmbed renderings, so this could be a viable option.

Do you need to manage user credentials between the sites? Do you have to store user login information for the external site (in the WordPress MySQL database, using a table created by your plugin), and if so, how do you handle error conditions such as password changes or user deletion in the remote system?

It is possible to treat WordPress as a content-only engine, producing posts for consumption by a CMS like Drupal. In this case, WordPress becomes a component of Drupal, managing its content as the source of the posts but ceding presentation control to the Drupal configuration.

Where Not to Use WordPress

Not every content management problem is a nail waiting to be pounded home by the WordPress hammer. Sometimes you will need to pick a different tool, or set of tools, for the job:

➤ **Handling rich media**—Streaming video, audio, and images with copious quantities of metadata can be displayed and included in WordPress posts, but if you want to be able to tag and index video files or search images based on their EXIF (Exchangeable Image File Format) tags, you probably want to use a CMS designed for rich media management.

➤ **Backend for Rich Internet Applications**—The next generation of mobile clients is emerging. They usually expect to talk to a back-end data repository or service, rather than a full-featured website. WordPress eventually emits HTML, not JSON or other data packaging formats most likely consumed by APIs. WordPress can do it, but is it the right tool? It depends on your needs—as you read in Chapter 14, WordPress can be a viable application foundation.

➤ **Simple network storefront**—If you are just building a store, use a storefront builder with shopping cart, payment systems, and product catalog. You will miss the integration of product discussion, feedback, recommendations, and the ability to describe how and why you are carrying (or have built) a particular product, all of which are possible using the approaches described in this chapter, but sometimes you just need users to be able to click and buy.

➤ **Event and calendar focus**—Several types of sites manage calendars, event registrations, event materials, and notifications or reminders about upcoming calendared items. WordPress does not (yet) have a built-in highly functional calendar and event management plugins, making this an area where using Drupal or BuddyPress may be simpler out of the box. BuddyPress, in particular, has a fair number of features for calendar-driven activities and content, but gives you the context of a community management tool, similar to a private social network, rather than a pure content management system.

➤ **Force-fitting a solution**—If you have to make modifications or changes to the WordPress Core, either you are doing something wrong or, more likely, WordPress is not the right solution. When hacking the core WordPress code, you break your upgrade path, such that you overwrite any changes you made to the core package files that enabled your specific functionality to work as soon as a new version of WordPress was released. As stated in Chapter 4, do not hack the core.

➤ **Plugin overload**—Plugins rock, and a large portion of this book has been devoted to identifying appropriate plugins for specific functions or outlining how to create your own for those uses. But you can go overboard. If you are using too many plugins, you may hurt the performance of your site and probably make it more fragile as a result of unknown dependencies between the plugins. Each plugin also increases the resource requirements of your site, specifically, memory and processing power.

SUMMARY

WordPress is a powerful content management system with many of the features found in commercial systems that pre-date the blogging craze of the early 2000s. In equal parts tribute to its open source roots, strong developer community, and simple extensible design, WordPress has established itself as a tool that goes far beyond a simple blog engine. In the real world, WordPress can often be the right tool for the development project, though not every development project. In addition, common challenges experienced by most website operators also have solutions in the WordPress ecosystem. Chapter 16 discusses the WordPress ecosystem—specifically, community resources that are available as well as how to get involved.

16

WordPress Developer Community

WHAT'S IN THIS CHAPTER?

➤   Contributing to the WordPress project

➤   Using the Trac software

➤   Working on the WordPress core using Subversion

➤   Exploring valuable WordPress resources for further learning

The WordPress community is what truly makes WordPress. As an open source project, WordPress is continually developed for and by the community, and without community support, the WordPress project would dry up and eventually development would cease. By getting involved, you can help make WordPress the best open source software package on the market.

This chapter discusses the different methods by which you can contribute to the WordPress project. It also covers some valuable WordPress resources to help expand your knowledge of WordPress and how it works.

CONTRIBUTING TO WORDPRESS

You can contribute to the WordPress project in many different ways. The most obvious way is to help with the source code that powers WordPress. Helping with the code can include finding and testing bugs, creating patches to fix bugs and add functionality, and helping test the patches against the latest WordPress trunk.

Understanding Trac

Trac is the open source bug-tracking and project management software used to develop the WordPress project. You can visit the official WordPress Trac website at https://core.trac. wordpress.org/.

Trac is an easy way to create and discuss tickets regarding WordPress. Whether it is a bug report, feature request, or enhancement, Trac helps in creating these tickets and having discussions around them. Have you ever had a new feature idea that you thought would be perfect for WordPress? The easiest way to start that conversation with the WordPress core Developer team is to create a feature request ticket in Trac. Have you ever found a bug in WordPress that keeps appearing in every new version? Creating a bug report is the quickest way to get the issue resolved in the next version. Even if you aren't a developer, creating tickets and getting involved in the discussions will ultimately help WordPress grow in a positive way!

Bug Reporting

All software has bugs and WordPress is no different. All open source projects such as WordPress need help from the community to identify and fix bugs. Fortunately, by utilizing Trac, WordPress makes it very easy to report any bugs you might come across.

The first step in reporting a bug is to verify that the bug is, in fact, a bug in WordPress and not a plugin or theme issue. The easiest way to accomplish this is to post the bug in the WordPress Support Forums. You can also discuss the bug in the #wordpress or #wordpress-dev IRC channels, or post a question to the Testers and Hackers mailing list. Finally, you can search Trac to confirm that the bug you are reporting doesn't already exist in Trac. After you have confirmed that the bug exists, it's time to create a new ticket in Trac detailing the bug.

To report a new bug in Trac, you first need to log in. The Trac login account is synced with your WordPress.org account so you can use the same account to log in. If you don't have an account, you can create a new one at the WordPress.org Support Forums.

After logging into Trac, click the New Ticket link at the top. You'll be presented with a form to fill out to submit the new bug ticket. Fill in the following fields on the new ticket:

➤ **Summary**—Short but accurate and informative title summarizing your bug ticket.

➤ **Description**—Detailed description of the bug. Include steps to reproduce the bug and add an example URL displaying the bug, if possible. Also include platform versions such as operating system, web server, PHP version, MySQL version, and WordPress version.

➤ **Type**—The type of ticket you are submitting. In this case, use the default of "defect (bug)" but other options are available.

➤ **Version**—The version of WordPress in which the bug was found. This applies to bug tickets only and not new feature requests.

➤ **Component**—The component in WordPress where the bug was found.

After you have filled in all of the new ticket information and previewed the ticket to verify that it's correct, click the Create Ticket button to create a new Trac ticket. If you have any attachments to upload, such as a screenshot of the bug, select the box next to "I have files to attach to this ticket." On the following screen, you will be allowed to upload any files attachments you would like.

Trac Keywords

In Trac, a number of defined keywords are commonly used for WordPress tickets. These keywords are used for reporting to make finding tickets easier. Following is a list of these keywords and their appropriate usage:

➤ **has-patch**—A solution patch file has been attached to the ticket and is ready to be tested before committing to the core of WordPress.

➤ **needs-patch**—The ticket has been confirmed and a patch is needed to fix the problem.

➤ **needs-refresh**—The patch no longer applies; it needs to be merged and resubmitted.

➤ **reporter-feedback**—Additional feedback is needed from the ticket creator.

➤ **dev-feedback**—A response is needed from a developer.

➤ **2nd-opinion**—A request for a second opinion is needed regarding the problem or solution.

➤ **close**—The ticket is a candidate for closure.

➤ **needs-testing**—Someone needs to test the solution.

➤ **ui-feedback**—Response is needed from the WordPress UI Group.

➤ **ux-feedback**—Response is needed from the WordPress UX Group.

➤ **needs-ui**—The ticket requires updates to the visual appearance of one or more items.

➤ **needs-unit-tests**—Unit tests needed to verify and test any patch that may exist.

➤ **needs-docs**—Inline documentation for the code is needed.

➤ **rtl-feedback**—Feedback is needed regarding Right-to-Left language support (RTL).

➤ **needs-codex**—Documentation in the WordPress.org Codex needs to be updated or expanded.

➤ **commit**—Patch has been reviewed and tested by a trust member of the community and is ready to be committed to WordPress core.

➤ **good-first-bug**—Signals a ticket would be a good starting point for a new contributor.

By adding the correct keywords, your ticket will automatically be included in Trac reports created for WordPress. For example, the `has-patch` report shows all tickets with the `has-patch` tag: `https://core.trac.wordpress.org/report/13`. These reports are extremely useful if you want to help contribute to WordPress.

View and Search Tickets

Trac features many different ways to search and filter through the tickets available. To view Trac tickets, click the Tickets link at the top. The next screen displays multiple predefined searches for filtering tickets. To view the most recent tickets in Trac, click the View Tickets link in the Trac menu. The list of all active tickets opened in the last two months can be a bit overwhelming because there are usually hundreds of tickets in Trac.

To make Trac more manageable, some predefined reports have been created to help filter the tickets down. Following is a list of the most commonly used reports in Trac:

➤ **Lastest Tickets**—Displays all tickets in Trac created in the last two months

➤ **Next Minor Release**—Tickets assigned to the next minor release (4.1.*x*)

➤ **Next Major Release**—Tickets assigned to the next major release (4.*x*)

➤ **Patches Needing Testing**—Lists all tickets with a patch that need to be tested and verified to fix the ticket issue

➤ **Tickets Without a Patch**—Lists all tickets needing a patch

➤ **Active Tickets**—All tickets active in the past two weeks

➤ **My Tickets**—All tickets created by you

➤ **My Patches**—All patches submitted by you

You can also create your own custom search queries within Trac. To do so, click the Custom Query link that appears after you click View Tickets.

By default, the Custom Query page displays all open tickets in Trac. To refine this list with your custom query, you are going to add a filter. To the left of the screen is a drop-down select box with different filters. For this example, select Milestone. After you select Milestone, the filter appears under the Filters section across the top of the page. Here you can select the Milestone you want to view tickets for. Select the next version of WordPress to be released to view all tickets assigned to that Milestone, as shown in Figure 16-1.

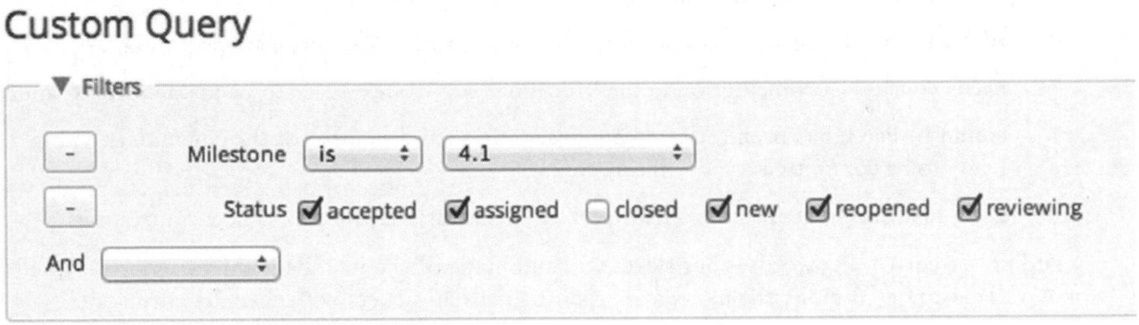

Custom Query

FIGURE 16-1: Custom Query in Trac

The number of open tickets is always a good indication of how close the new version of WordPress is to being released. You can add multiple filters to your custom query. For example, you could add a filter for the needs-testing keyword to filter the tickets to show all tickets that need to be tested for the upcoming version of WordPress.

Trac Timeline

Trac also features a timeline of all recent activity within the system. This is great for a top-level overview of what changes have happened in Trac daily. You can also filter the date range and ticket status. To view the Trac timeline, visit `https://core.trac.wordpress.org/timeline`.

Browsing Source

One of the major advantages of the Trac software is how it integrates with Subversion (SVN). Subversion is the version control software used by WordPress to track code changes and commits. Within Trac, you can view the most current version of the WordPress software, which is sometimes referred to as bleeding-edge. To view the current WordPress source, click the <> icon in the Trac menu. The current bleeding-edge version of WordPress is located in the `trunk/src` folder.

Viewing the WordPress source in Trac is extremely useful for seeing new changes made to WordPress. Next to each file, the Last Change is listed and linked to the Trac ticket that has details about that change. The Age is also listed, showing the date when the file was last edited.

Notice at the very bottom of the page that there is a link: `Download in other formats: Zip Archive`. Just click this link to download the entire bleeding-edge copy of WordPress. After downloading WordPress from Trac, you can install it on your own server just like a normal installation of WordPress. This is great for testing out new features in the upcoming version of WordPress. Keep in mind that this is bleeding-edge software so bugs will most likely exist. You wouldn't want to run this version of WordPress on a production website.

Working on the Core

The WordPress software is built by the community, which means anyone can help contribute to the codebase. When someone says WordPress is built by the community, it doesn't mean that anyone can go edit the WordPress source code. To contribute to the WordPress core, you must create a patch file with your changes and submit that file for review. If accepted, your changes will be incorporated into the WordPress core and will be included in the next version release. Contributing code edits, bug fixes, and additional functionality is done using Subversion.

It was stated rather emphatically throughout this book that you should never hack the core. In this case, you aren't actually hacking the core of a WordPress installation, but rather creating patch files to submit for inclusion into the WordPress software.

Understanding Subversion

Subversion is used to make modifications to the current codebase and generate patch files. A patch file is a text file that contains the changes that were made to a specific file or files. To work on the WordPress core you will need to generate patch files and submit them for review. Once a patch file has been accepted as the best fix for the issue, it will be committed to the WordPress core code.

Hooking into the WordPress Core

The first step in hooking into the WordPress core is to check out (download) the latest codebase using SVN. To do so, you'll need an SVN client on your development machine. For the rest of this chapter, you'll consider examples that use the TortoiseSVN client, which is one of the more popular choices for Windows. The WordPress SVN repository is located at `http://core.svn.wordpress.org/trunk/`. Checking out a repository creates a copy of it on your local machine. This is the copy of WordPress you will modify when fixing bugs and adding new functionality.

Using TortoiseSVN, right-click the folder you want to download the WordPress codebase to and select SVN Checkout. Make sure to fill in the SVN repository URL for WordPress and click OK to download the codebase. For more information on using Subversion with WordPress, check out `http://codex.wordpress.org/Using_Subversion`.

Creating a patch/diff File

Now that you have downloaded the WordPress codebase, it's time to make some changes! Pick any file you want to modify and make the appropriate changes as needed. Make sure to save the file after you are finished making edits. Now you need to create a patch file that details the changes you made. To do so, right-click the file you modified and select TortoiseSVN ➤ Create Patch. A dialog box appears, allowing you to select the modified files; in this case, only one file should appear so click OK to proceed. Next, choose a location to save your patch file to and give it a unique name. It's a good practice to name your patch file the same as the file you edited, so if you modified `wp-config-sample.php`, name your patch file `wp-config-sample.patch`, and click Save. You have just successfully created a working patch file for WordPress! This patch file can be submitted to any Trac ticket as a bug fix or feature recommendation. If the patch is accepted, a core WordPress Committer will commit your patch file to the core of WordPress. After a patch you have submitted has been accepted into the WordPress core, you can officially call yourself a WordPress core Contributor!

Submitting Plugins and Themes

Submitting plugins to the Plugin Directory is the best way to release a plugin to the public. This also holds true for submitting themes to the Theme Directory. Ultimately you want as much exposure as possible for any theme or plugin that you release. Adding your plugin and theme to the appropriate WordPress.org directory is the best way to accomplish this. Remember that both directories are hooked in the admin side of every current installation of WordPress. This means anyone running WordPress can easily install your theme or plugin with just a few clicks.

To submit your theme or plugin, visit the official submission page on WordPress.org:

➤ **Plugin submission**—`https://wordpress.org/plugins/add/`

➤ **Theme submission**—`https://wordpress.org/themes/upload/`

Here you'll find instructions on the proper submission process for both. The submission process is covered in more detail in Chapter 8.

Documentation

Documentation is a thankless job, yet nearly every developer relies on the documentation at some point. A great way to contribute to the WordPress community is to help keep the documentation updated. Assume that every time a new WordPress release comes out, the documentation needs to be updated to reflect the changes, whether new functionality is added, behavior is modified, or certain aspects are scheduled for deprecation.

Keeping the documentation current is a daunting task, and given the volunteer nature of the project, is sometimes neglected. You can often find out-of-date information in the Codex for WordPress releases from long ago that are no longer best practices, applicable, or even supported.

Documentation updating is not glamorous—it is not the shiny new functionality and features that everyone is excited about—but it is one of the best ways to support the community and help new users. Sometimes, solid documentation is what draws new developers in and helps keep them in the community.

If you are interested in helping out with the WordPress documentation, please subscribe to the Documentation Mailing list at `http://codex.wordpress.org/Mailing_Lists#Documentation`.

SISTER PROJECTS

WordPress has a few different sister projects currently available. These software projects are considered sister projects because they are developed in much the same way as WordPress. Many of the developers behind these projects also contribute to the WordPress project. Sister projects are also built as plugins, which makes WordPress integration simple and easy.

BuddyPress

BuddyPress is a plugin that adds a social networking layer to WordPress. BuddyPress can be themed to match your current website design.

Some of the features available include extended profiles, private messaging, friend connections, user groups and activity streams, status updates, forums, and more! All BuddyPress features are independent, meaning you can enable just the features you want and not the entire BuddyPress suite. For more information on BuddyPress, visit `http://buddypress.org`.

bbPress

bbPress is an open source forum software plugin. The goal of bbPress is to be lightweight, powerful, fast, and easy to use. bbPress has many of the features you would expect from message board software, including a simple interface, customizable templates, and spam protection. bbPress can also run plugins to extend its functionality just like WordPress. bbPress was originally offered as a separate installation package, but has since been ported over to a WordPress plugin. You can download bbPress at the official Plugin Directory page, `https://wordpress.org/plugins/bbpress/`, or learn more about bbPress at `http://bbpress.org`.

Future Projects

WordPress is growing at an amazing rate and new projects are always popping up. It's hard to imagine what new projects you'll see in the future, but if WordPress has taught us anything, it's to expect the unexpected.

RESOURCES

Many different resources are available for WordPress. This section provides a list of the most popular resources that you should be aware of to expand your knowledge of WordPress.

Codex

The WordPress Codex is one of the largest and best resources available for WordPress, and is essentially an online manual for WordPress users. Powered by MediaWiki, the Codex is a wiki-style documentation project, meaning anyone can contribute to the articles and content featured. Featuring tutorials, examples, function references, and much more, the Codex takes you through everything from installation to customization. The official site is `http://codex.wordpress.org/ Main_Page`.

Handbooks

Some of the newest resources in this chapter are the WordPress Handbooks. The Handbooks are a community created guide to working with various areas of the WordPress project. These guides are created, edited, and published by the WordPress community, and anyone interested can get involved to help expand these resources.

The following is a list of the available WordPress Handbooks:

➤ **Core Developer Handbook**—Guide to contributing to WordPress core development (`http://make.wordpress.org/core/handbook/`)

➤ **Plugin Developer Handbook**—Guide to proper WordPress plugin development (`http:// make.wordpress.org/docs/plugin-developer-handbook/`)

➤ **Theme Developer Handbook**—Guide to proper WordPress theme development (`http:// make.wordpress.org/docs/theme-developer-handbook/`)

➤ **Support Handbook**—Guide to participating in the WordPress support forums and contributing to the Codex (`http://make.wordpress.org/support/handbook/`)

➤ **Documentation Handbook**—Guide to creating proper documentation for WordPress (`http://make.wordpress.org/docs/handbook/`)

➤ **Mobile Handbook**—Guide to getting involved in the WordPress mobile app development community (`http://make.wordpress.org/mobile/handbook/`)

Support Forums

The WordPress Support Forum is another great resource. You can visit the support forum at the official URL: `http://wordpress.org/support/`. The support forum is powered by bbPress, the forum plugin mentioned in the previous section.

The support forum is separated into multiple sections covering many different topics. The quickest way to locate related threads is to search the forum using the Search box. There is also a tag cloud powered by hot topics in the forum. This can be a quick way to see what the trending topics are in the forum.

Forum threads can also be tagged with keywords about the post. Any post tagged with the name of a plugin is automatically added to the plugin's support forum. The new forum post will be counted under the Support section in the right sidebar on the plugin detail page, as Figure 16-2 shows.

This provides a support forum section for every plugin in the repository. To create a forum post about a plugin, just add the plugin slug as a tag on your post. For example, to create a post about the WordPress Custom Post Type UI plugin, you would tag your forum post with `custom-post-type-ui`, which is the slug from the plugin URL `http://wordpress.org/support/plugin/custom-post-type-ui`.

You'll also notice the Compatibility section shown in Figure 16-2. This allows users of the plugin to verify if the plugin works with their version of WordPress. If enough people report that the plugin is broken, it is probably not a stable enough plugin to use.

Forum posts can also be marked as resolved. If you post a question and someone replies with a response that helps you resolve your problem, you should mark your post as resolved. This will add the text [resolved] to the front of your post topic to let others know the problem has been resolved. This helps other community members find answers to their questions by viewing the resolved threads.

FIGURE 16-2: See what others are saying

WordPress Chat

WordPress has some very active chat rooms on IRC (Internet Relay Chat). To join a WordPress chat room, you will need to install an IRC client on your computer. Once an IRC client is installed, you can connect to the Freenode server at `irc.freenode.net`, and once you have connected, you can join one or more of the chat rooms listed here:

➤ **#wordpress**—The primary WordPress chat room. Great place to get questions about WordPress answered quickly and accurately.

➤ **#wordpress-dev**—Chat room dedicated to WordPress core development. Topics are restricted to working on the WordPress code itself and not for general WordPress inquiries.

➤ **#wordpress-themes**—Chat room for the theme review process.

➤ **#wordpress-ui**—Chat room for the WordPress UI Group.

➤ **#wordpress-core-plugins**—Chat room for WordPress core plugin development to be discussed. This is not a general support channel for plugin development.

➤ **#wordpress-mobile**—Chat room for WordPress mobile app discussions.

➤ **#wordpress-polyglots**—Chat room for WordPress internationalization discussions.

➤ **#buddypress-dev** — Chat room dedicated to all BuddyPress-related conversations.

➤ **#bbpress**—Chat room dedicated to all bbPress-related conversations.

These IRC chat rooms are a great resource for getting real-time help. Many WordPress experts hang out in these rooms regularly and love to help out other WordPress enthusiasts. This is also a great place to expand your knowledge of WordPress.

The WordPress core developers host a weekly development chat in `#wordpress-dev`. This scheduled chat covers a preset agenda of topics regarding the future development of WordPress, and many decisions are made on features and functionality in these weekly chats. The topics typically cover features being developed for the upcoming version of WordPress, but can also cover additional items.

For more information on IRC and WordPress chat rooms, visit the official Codex IRC page at `http://codex.wordpress.org/IRC`. This page details how IRC works, how to download and install an IRC client, how to connect to an IRC server, and also how to join a WordPress chat room.

Mailing Lists

WordPress has multiple mailing lists focused on different topics of the WordPress project. Most mailing lists are two-way conversations, meaning that an e-mail is sent to the list with a problem or question, and another member of the mailing list responds with the answer. Anyone subscribed to that mailing list will be able to track the conversation. To register for any mailing list, just visit the corresponding join link.

Available mailing lists include:

➤ **Announcements**—List for major announcements regarding WordPress. E-mail is very low frequency and one-way, meaning no conversations can take place.

➤ **How to Join**—Edit your WordPress.org profile and select Subscribe to WordPress Announcements under Mailing Lists.

➤ **Accessibility**—List for discussing the accessibility of the WordPress administration interface.

➤ **How to Join**—`http://lists.automattic.com/mailman/listinfo/wp-accessibility/`

➤ **Documentation**—List for coordinating and collaborating on WordPress Codex documentation. If you plan on contributing to the Codex, this list is a must join.

➤ **How to Join**—`http://make.wordpress.org/docs/`

➤ **Hackers**—Primary mailing list for discussions on extending through plugins or core code modifications. Many discussions revolve around core functionality of WordPress.

   ➤ **How to Join**—http://lists.automattic.com/mailman/listinfo/wp-hackers

➤ **Testers**—Discussions regarding the current nightly, alpha, or beta version of WordPress.

   ➤ **How to Join**—http://lists.automattic.com/mailman/listinfo/wp-testers

➤ **User Interface**—Discussions to improve the interface or user experience of WordPress.

   ➤ **How to Join**—http://lists.automattic.com/mailman/listinfo/wp-ui/

➤ **Support Forum Volunteers**—Discussions involving WordPress Forum Support and providing support to users.

   ➤ **How to Join**—http://lists.automattic.com/mailman/listinfo/wp-forums

➤ **SVN Updates**—List for tracking SVN repository updates. E-mail is sent for every update along with information on the changes made. SVN is the version control system WordPress core developers use to track changes in the WordPress core files.

   ➤ **How to Join**—http://lists.automattic.com/mailman/listinfo/wp-svn

➤ **Trac**—List for tracking changes in Trac, the open source bug tracking system WordPress uses for tracking development on the WordPress core. This is a very high-traffic e-mail list.

   ➤ **How to Join**—http://lists.automattic.com/mailman/listinfo/wp-trac

Certain WordPress mailing lists can be high traffic, so it's a good idea to create a rule in your e-mail program to automatically filter WordPress mailing list e-mails to a specific folder. That way, you can review the conversations taking place at your leisure.

To subscribe to any of these mailing lists, or for more information, visit the official Codex mailing list page at http://codex.wordpress.org/Mailing_Lists. To view all available mailing lists, visit the official Automattic mailing list page at http://lists.automattic.com/mailman/listinfo.

External Resources

There are many external resources for WordPress outside of WordPress.org. Following is a list of the most common:

➤ **WordPress Hooks Database** (http://adambrown.info/p/wp_hooks)—Website detailing all hooks (actions and filters) in WordPress by version. Great for referencing latest hook additions when a new version of WordPress is released.

➤ **PHPXref for WordPress** (http://phpxref.ftwr.co.uk/wordpress/)—Features cross-reference code library for WordPress. Use to easily view all variables, functions, classes, and constants used in WordPress. Xref shows where each item is defined as well as where it is referenced through the WordPress code.

➤ **Hookr** (http://hookr.io/)—A dynamic WordPress Hook/API Index that allows you to easily view all WordPress action and filter hooks by version. This website also includes hook lists for some of the most popular WordPress plugins.

WordCamp and Meetups

WordPress is powered by the community behind it and because of that the community loves to get together and talk WordPress! This can happen in a number of different ways but the two most popular events are WordCamps and WordPress Meetups.

WordCamps are conferences focused on anything and everything WordPress. These events usually have hundreds of attendees and multiple tracks for speakers with a wide array of topics. If you are interested in WordPress at all, these are must-attend events. To find a WordCamp in your area, visit the official WordCamp Central website at `http://central.wordcamp.org/`.

WordPress Meetups are smaller, locally based gatherings. These are usually informal get-togethers where attendees talk WordPress and share their experiences and knowledge with others. WordPress Meetups are typically held monthly or quarterly. To find a Meetup in your area, check out the official WordPress Meetup Groups page at `http://wordpress.meetup.com/`.

WordPress.TV

WordPress.TV is a website dedicated to videos about WordPress. The website features tutorials for both WordPress self-installs and WordPress.com. Also featured on WordPress.TV are WordCamp footage and speaker sessions, interviews, and much more. This is a central repository for all videos related to WordPress. WordPress.TV is a great resource for learning more about WordPress through videos. Visit the official site at `http://wordpress.tv/`.

Theme/Plugin Directories

The first places to visit after installing WordPress are the Plugin and Theme directories. In the Plugin directory, you can download thousands of plugins to add all sorts of amazing functionality to your website. The Theme directory features more than a thousand free themes for WordPress that can be used to give your site a new look. Remember that both of these directories can be browsed from within your WordPress installation:

➤ **Plugin directory**—`https://wordpress.org/plugins/`

➤ **Theme directory**—`https://wordpress.org/themes/`

WordPress Ideas

WordPress.org features an Ideas area for gathering ideas for future features in WordPress. Here you can vote on your favorite ideas and view a list of the most popular ideas based on votes. The most popular ideas are usually reviewed before the development of a new version of WordPress and typically a few of them will make it into the new release. You can visit the official Ideas page at `https://wordpress.org/ideas/`.

WordPress Development Updates

Staying informed with the development of WordPress is a great resource for tracking upcoming WordPress changes and features. As new versions of WordPress are developed and released, they come with new features and functionality. Understanding what these new features are can help with planning new projects for WordPress. The easiest way to do this is at the official WordPress Development Updates site at `http://make.wordpress.org/core/`.

The Make WordPress core site uses the popular P2 theme, which is very similar to a Twitter-like theme for WordPress. The site features updates and discussions on the WordPress project. The site is also the location for information regarding the weekly WordPress Developer Chats in the `#wordpress-dev` IRC channel. The date and time for these meetings is featured in the sidebar. There is also a post detailing the topics for the weekly meeting. Anyone can contribute topics for the meeting by responding to this post.

Make WordPress.org

A new resource is `http://make.wordpress.org`. This section of WordPress.org is a central hub for official resources to help people develop for WordPress. Currently, there are eight sections that are specific to different areas of WordPress:

- ➤ `make.wordpress.org/core/`—Blog for the core development team of WordPress.
- ➤ `make.wordpress.org/ui/`—Blog for the WordPress UI design group.
- ➤ `make.wordpress.org/plugins/`—Blog for announcements and resources for plugin developers.
- ➤ `make.wordpress.org/themes/`—Blog for announcements and resources for theme designer and developers.
- ➤ `make.wordpress.org/support/`—Blog for support members. This is not a blog for receiving support. Rather, it's for members who provide support, and it covers how they can improve the process.
- ➤ `make.wordpress.org/polyglots/`—Blog for WordPress translators.
- ➤ `make.wordpress.org/accessibility/`—Blog for the WordPress accessibility group.
- ➤ `make.wordpress.org/docs/`—Blog for the documentation team.
- ➤ `make.wordpress.org/mobile/`—Blog for announcements and resources for WordPress mobile developers.

The sites listed provide an excellent way to get involved in a specific area of WordPress.

WordPress Podcasts

Podcasts are a great way to stay informed on the latest news and information on any topic. There are currently quite a few WordPress-centric podcasts being actively produced with each focusing on different topics around WordPress.

DradCast

The DradCast podcast (`http://dradcast.com`) is a live weekly podcast hosted by Brad Williams (that's me!) and Dre Armeda. Each week, the show features a different guest host, who is generally a prominent member of the WordPress community. The show is created and released on DradCast. com. The podcast also streams live video of the shows being recorded so you watch the hosts and guests of the show as they discuss all things WordPress.

WordPress Weekly

The WordPress Weekly podcast (`http://wptavern.com/wordpress-weekly`) is a live weekly podcast that talks about all things WordPress. The show is hosted by Jeff Chandler of WPTavern. com and generally includes a guest each week.

WP Water Cooler

WPwatercooler (`http://www.wpwatercooler.com/`) is a round-table–style weekly video podcast that features multiple hosts each week from the WordPress community. The podcast is hosted by Jason Tucker and features up to ten guest hosts each week.

Matt Report

The Matt Report (`http://mattreport.com/`) is a business-focused video podcast hosted by Matt Medeiros. Matt interviews different WordPress community members, focusing on entrepreneurs, startups, and freelancers.

Apply Filters

Apply Filters (`http://applyfilters.fm/`) is a podcast dedicated to WordPress development. The podcast is hosted by Pippin Williamson and Brad Touesnard. The show focuses on development topics, including WordPress core, plugins, and themes.

WordPress News Sites

Many different WordPress-related websites exist. This section provides a list of the most popular WordPress-focused sites for news and information regarding anything and everything WordPress-related.

WordPress Tavern

The WordPress Tavern (`http://wptavern.com/`) is one of the oldest active WordPress news–focused websites online today. The WP Tavern has a steady stream of in-depth editorials, detailed tutorials, community member interviews, podcasts, and more. It's easy to see why the WP Tavern is the resource for WordPress-related news.

Postat.us

Post Status (`http://www.poststat.us/`) is dedicated to informing WordPress professionals and enthusiasts about the industry. Post Status specializes in long-form articles and providing in-depth reviews and commentary on various WordPress topics. The website is run by Brian Krogsgard and features a number of new articles each week.

ManageWP.org

ManageWP.org (`http://managewp.org/`) is a different type of WordPress news site. Instead of unique articles, the website features user-submitted content, which can then be voted up or down by the community. ManageWP.org is more akin to Reddit- or Digg-style community curated news and is a great resource to see what topics are buzzing in the community.

Torque Mag

Torque Mag (`http://torquemag.io/`) is described as the WordPress News Core. The goal of Torque Mag is to create a hub for community building and offer a forum for WordPress news. Torque Mag actually goes beyond WordPress news and features news relevant to the WordPress community.

WPEngineer.com

WPEngineer (`http://wpengineer.com/`) features tips and tricks, news, and improvements for WordPress. The site features more in-depth tutorials that dive into the core of WordPress and its functionality. These tutorials are focused on intermediate-level WordPress users and developers.

WordPress Alltop

Alltop (`http://wordpress.alltop.com/`) is basically an RSS aggregator for specific topics. The WordPress Alltop page features news and information from the top WordPress-related websites. It also lists important WordPress Twitter accounts that are worth following for news and information.

WordPress Planet

WordPress Planet (`http://planet.wordpress.org/`) is an aggregation of blogs writing about WordPress. This includes posts from core contributors and very active community members. This is the same news feed featured on the Dashboard of every default installation of WordPress under the Other WordPress News Dashboard widget.

Planet WordPress

Planet WordPress (`http://planetwordpress.planetozh.com/`) is also an RSS aggregator that keeps track of bloggers who contribute to WordPress. This feed differs from WordPress Planet in that it extends the WordPress Planet feed with even more bloggers. These bloggers are mainly plugin developers and core contributors for WordPress. The news feed is maintained by Ozh Richard, a very respected developer in the WordPress community.

SUMMARY

In this chapter, you learned the different ways you can contribute to the WordPress project, including using Trac bug-tracking software, working on the WordPress core using Subversion, and submitting plugins and themes. You also learned about sister projects to WordPress, including BuddyPress and bbPress. Finally, you learned about the diverse resources available as you work with WordPress.

INDEX

X-Y-Z